PRAISE FOR

The Russia Hand

"Talbott's book is a fascinating memoir of a weirdly unpredictable world."
—*The New York Review of Books*

"Strobe Talbott has written a wonderfully rich and revealing account of the turbulent relationship between the U.S. and Russia during the first post–cold war years. Colorful, full of surprises and intimate portraits of the key people involved—by a man who was at the center of it all—this book is and will remain essential for any understanding of this critical and even dangerous period." —ELIZABETH DREW

"A savvy insider's account of the diplomatic twists and turns of U.S.–Russia relations in the '90s, Talbott's anecdote-stuffed book is a treasure trove for Russia specialists. But it will also fascinate anyone with an interest in the personal dynamics of statecraft." —*BusinessWeek*

"*The Russia Hand* is easily one of the best memoirs of presidential diplomacy ever written. With his great command of history, gift of language, sense of detail and eight years at the center of American foreign-policy making, Strobe Talbott has brought us a fascinating, often surprising account of a historic and pivotal period. *The Russia Hand* shows us what a complex and impressive achievement it was for the United States to build a lasting relationship with its old enemy of half a century. When historians begin to assess the presidency of Bill Clinton, this book will be basic and mandatory reading." —MICHAEL BESCHLOSS

"A fascinating portrait of diplomacy as it really works (and sometimes doesn't), written with clarity and grace by a wise man."
—EVAN THOMAS

"Once again Strobe Talbott has written an important and insightful diplomatic history. This richly crafted book, the first authoritative inside account of President Clinton's personal diplomacy with Russian presidents Boris Yeltsin and Vladimir Putin, could have been written only by Talbott, with his reporter's eye for the telling anecdote, his deep knowledge of Russia and his intimate personal involvement in the events he describes."
—Hedrick L. Smith

"I read [*The Russia Hand*] as if it were a detective novel—I was unable to put it down until late in the night, picked it up again first thing in the morning, and didn't stop until I had finished."
—Anne Applebaum, *Slate*

"Readers will . . . relish Talbott's intimate portraits of the two leaders, down to the challenging task of maneuvering around Yeltsin's flagrant alcoholism."
—*Salon*

"Talbott . . . is a keen and insightful observer as well as a key player in the story. Anyone interested in U.S.–Russian relations will find his new book a source of riches."
—*BookPage*

"Talbott brings to the task his abundant reportorial skills, producing voluminous previously undisclosed details on the management of our relations through multiple crises, from NATO expansion to the war with Serbia over Kosovo."
—*San Jose Mercury News*

"This lively memoir, based largely on the author's diaries, gives a vivid picture of the frenetic pace and frequent jet lag of the Clinton administration as officials juggled many competing issues in unexplored policy territory."
—*Library Journal*

"This is not just a contender for being the best recent memoir of a political insider; it is also unique, a book of instant history and analysis that is so close to the action and the key players, and so deeply informed, that only Talbott could have written it. . . . This is as honest as it is useful, a very rare book indeed."
—UPI Newswire

STROBE TALBOTT was the architect of the Clinton administration's policy toward Russia and the other states of the former Soviet Union. He served as deputy secretary of state for seven years. A former *Time* columnist and Washington bureau chief, he is the translator-editor of Nikita Khrushchev's memoirs and the author of six books on U.S.–Soviet relations. Formerly the director of the Yale Center for the Study of Globalization, he is now president of the Brookings Institution. He lives in Washington, D.C.

THE
RUSSIA
HAND

RANDOM HOUSE TRADE PAPERBACKS / NEW YORK

THE RUSSIA HAND

A MEMOIR
OF PRESIDENTIAL
DIPLOMACY

STROBE TALBOTT

Library of Congress Cataloging-in-Publication Data
Talbott, Strobe.
The Russia hand : a memoir of presidential diplomacy / Strobe Talbott.
p.   cm.
Includes index.
ISBN 9780812968460
1. United States—Foreign relations—Russia (Federation). 2. Russia (Federation)—Foreign relations—
United States. 3. United States—Foreign relations—1993–2001. 4. Clinton, Bill, 1946– —Contributions
in diplomacy. 5. Yeltsin, Boris Nikolayevich, 1931– 6. Talbott, Strobe. 7. Diplomats—United States—
Biography. 8. Political consultants—United States—Biography. I. Title.
E183.8.R9 T27 2002
327.73047—dc21   2001048843

Random House website address: www.atrandom.com

Book design by Victoria Wong

147028622

TO BROOKE, DEVIN AND ADRIAN

CONTENTS

THE
RUSSIA
HAND

THE HEDGEHOG AND
THE BEAR

TRINCULO: A howling monster; a drunken monster!
CALIBAN: . . . Freedom, high-day! high-day, freedom! . . .
STEPHANO: O brave monster! Lead the way.

The Tempest

AT NOON ON Monday, June 5, 2000, Bill Clinton and Vladimir Putin emerged from the Czar's Entrance of the Grand Kremlin Palace. While they paused for a moment in the sunshine, I hovered behind them, trying to catch anything of significance that passed between them as they said good-bye. But at this moment, which brought to an end the official portion of Clinton's fifth and final visit to Moscow as president, the nuances were all in the body language: the burly Clinton looming over the welterweight Putin, the ultimate extrovert still trying to connect with the coolest of customers who just wasn't buying.

As they shook hands one last time, I pocketed my notebook and hustled down the steps to take my place on a jump seat in the rear of the armored Cadillac that had been flown in from Washington for the summit. John Podesta, Clinton's chief of staff, and Sandy Berger, his national security adviser, were already on the seat behind me, crammed together to leave plenty of room for the president. Once Clinton had settled into place, he looked out at Putin through the thick bullet-proof window, put on his widest grin and gave a jaunty wave.

As the limousine pulled away from the curb and sped across the cobblestone courtyard, Clinton slumped back and a pensive look came over his face. Usually he found these events, including the ceremonial sendoffs, exhilarating. Not this time. The talks over the past three days had been inconclusive, not so much because the two leaders had been unable to agree as because Putin had not even tried. Clinton had come to Moscow hoping to make progress toward a number of objectives: reconciling a new American missile-defense program with long-standing arms control treaties; coordinating U.S. and Russian diplomacy in the Balkans; ending Russian military assistance to Iran. Clinton had also registered concern over Putin's domestic policies, especially the crackdown he'd launched against the leading independent television network, the deals he was cutting with the communists at the expense of reformist parties and the war he was waging in Chechnya.

On all these issues, Putin had given Clinton what was calculated to seem a respectful hearing, but Clinton knew a brush-off when he saw one. Missile defense was a complex problem, Putin had said with a mildness of tone that belied the firmness of his message: precipitous American deployment would jeopardize Russia's interests and provoke a new round of the arms race. As for the targets of his get-tough policy, they were criminals, not champions of democracy and free speech. And Chechnya was a nest of terrorists; America's own international Public Enemy Number One, Osama bin Laden, had contributed to the infestation there, so the U.S. should be supporting Russia's campaign against a common enemy. On all these subjects, Putin urged Clinton to rethink American policy and the assumptions on which it was based.

Clinton felt patronized. It was no mystery what Putin's game was: he was waiting for Clinton's successor to be elected in five months before deciding how to cope with the United States and all its power, its demands and its reproaches. Putin had, in his own studied, cordial and oblique way, put U.S.-Russian relations on hold until Clinton, like Putin's predecessor, Boris Yeltsin, had passed from the scene. Realizing that, Clinton had even more to think about as he headed toward the western outskirts of Moscow, where Yeltsin was now living in retirement.

The Cadillac barreled out of the Kremlin through the Borovitsky Gate and took a sharp right turn. The rest of the motorcade, including several vans full of press, tried to follow but was stopped by Russian security police and diverted directly to Vnukovo Airport, south of Moscow, where Air Force One was waiting.

With a motorcycle escort, Clinton's limousine hurtled down the center of the eight-lane artery out of the city he'd first visited thirty years before. Clinton remarked on various landmarks as we sped past: the massive Russian State Library, once named after Lenin, where the presiding presence was now a statue of Dostoyevsky; the glitzy nightclubs, casinos and designer boutiques of the New Arbat, Yeltsin's biggest restoration project when he was running the city in the late eighties; the Russian White House, which had been, at different times, the scene of Yeltsin's greatest triumph, the command center of his most implacable enemies and the site of a spasm of bloodletting from which neither he nor his country had recovered nearly seven years later. As we crossed the river and headed out of the city along Kutuzovsky Prospect, Clinton recalled that it had been the route Napoleon used to march into Moscow with the Grande Armée in 1812. That set him to musing in three directions at once: about Russia's vulnerability to invasion, its close but complex ties to the West and its preoccupation with its own history.

I'd heard riffs like this from Clinton over the years, going back to when I'd first known him in the late sixties. Russia had always been a subject that stirred him when, for one reason or another, it came to his attention. But that had happened only episodically. As a governor in the seventies and eighties, he'd had more reason to think about Japan as a source of foreign investment and as a market for Arkansas rice. He'd brought me into his administration to think full-time about Russia and the former Soviet Union while he went about being president, which he expected would mean concentrating on the American economy.

Then, almost immediately, events in Moscow and the importuning of the man shakily in charge there thrust upon Clinton the portfolio he'd hoped I'd handle for him. It became apparent that being president meant, much more than he'd anticipated, doing the heavy lifting in the management of relations with a giant nation that was reinventing itself and, in so doing, reinventing international politics and requiring us to reinvent American foreign policy.

By the spring of his first year in office, Clinton had become the U.S. government's principal Russia hand, and so he remained for the duration of his presidency.

WITHIN TWENTY MINUTES after leaving the Kremlin, we reached the capital's high-rent exurbia, where modern redbrick cottages had sprouted amid leftovers of the old power structure—sprawling VIP dachas, rest homes and clinics behind stucco walls or high green wooden fences. After slowing down to navigate a narrow potholed road, we arrived at Gorky-9, a heavily guarded complex where Yeltsin had been living since his last years in office, largely because it was near the Barvikha sanatorium that cared for him during his numerous and prolonged illnesses.

Yeltsin was waiting at the front door, his wife, Naina, on one side and, on the other, Tatyana Dyachenko, his younger daughter. As the car slowed to a stop, Clinton remarked that Yeltsin's face was puffy, his complexion sallow; he looked stiff and propped up.

Over the eight years they had known each other, Clinton and Yeltsin often bantered about the advantage of both being six foot two: it was easier for them to look each other in the eye. Now, as the limousine rolled to a stop and Clinton scrutinized his host through the window, he noted that Yeltsin seemed to have lost an inch or two since they had last been together, seven months before, when Yeltsin had still been in office.

After Clinton got out of the car, he and Yeltsin embraced silently for a full minute. Yeltsin kept saying, in a low, choked voice, *"moi drug, moi drug"*—my friend, my friend. Then, clasping Clinton's hand, he led the way through a foyer into a living room bright with sunlight pouring through a picture window that looked out on a manicured lawn and a stand of birches. They sat in gilt oval-backed chairs next to a sky blue tile stove while Naina bustled about, serving tea and generous helpings of a rich multi-layered cake that she proudly said she'd been up half the night baking.

Clinton settled in for what he expected would be a relaxed exchange of memories and courtesies, but Yeltsin had work to do first. Turning severe, he announced that he had just had a phone call from Putin, who wanted him to underscore that Russia would pursue its interests by its own lights; it would resist pressure to acquiesce in any American policy that constituted a threat to Russian security. Clinton, after three days of listening to Putin politely fend him off on the U.S. plan to build an anti-missile system, was now getting the blunt-instrument treatment.

Yeltsin's face was stern, his posture tense, both fists clenched, each sentence a proclamation. He seemed to relish the assignment Putin had given him. It allowed him to demonstrate that, far from being a feeble pensioner, he was still plugged in to the power of the Kremlin, still a forceful spokesman for Russian interests and still able to stand up to the U.S. when it was throwing its weight around.

Clinton took the browbeating patiently, even good-naturedly. He had seen Yeltsin in all his roles—snarling bear and papa bear, bully and sentimentalist, spoiler and dealmaker. He knew from experience that a session with Yeltsin almost always involved some roughing up before the two of them could get down to real business.

When the chance came, Clinton steered the discussion toward the subject of where Russia was heading under Putin. But Yeltsin wasn't yet ready to yield the floor. He had more to say about the past.

I was on a couch, across from the two men, listening intently as they talked. Seated next to me was Tatyana, whom I had seen in passing only once in more trips to Moscow than I could count. When Yeltsin launched into a self-congratulatory account of how he had maneuvered Putin from obscurity into the presidency over fierce resistance, Tatyana looked at me and nodded solemnly. She leaned toward me and whispered, "It really was very hard, getting Putin into the job—one of the hardest things we ever pulled off."

I noticed the "we." I was meant to. She wanted me to know it was true what they said: even though she had kept out of the public eye, including during state visits, she really had been one of Yeltsin's most influential confidants. It was as though she had decided to make her first appearance on-stage in a curtain call.

As Naina plied her husband and his guests with more tea and cake, Yeltsin rambled on, but the refrain was simple: Putin was "a young man and a strong man." Yeltsin kept returning to these two attributes—youth and strength—as though they were the essence both of what Russia needed and of what he, by promoting Putin, had hoped to preserve as his own legacy.

When Yeltsin finally wound down, Clinton gently took control. He too had one piece of business to do. He wasn't sure, he said, how "this new guy of yours" defined strength, either for himself or for the nation. Putin seemed to have the *capability* to take Russia in the right direction, but did he have the values, instincts and convictions to make good on that capability? Why, Clinton wondered aloud, was Putin so ready to make common cause with the communists, "those people you, Boris, did so much to beat back and bring down"? Why was Putin putting the squeeze on the free press, "which, as you know, Boris, is the lifeblood of an open and modern society"?

Yeltsin nodded solemnly, but he didn't answer. All the pugnacity, swagger and certainty had gone out of him.

"Boris," Clinton continued, "you've got democracy in your heart. You've got the trust of the people in your bones. You've got the fire in your belly of a real democrat and a real reformer. I'm not sure Putin has that. Maybe he does. I don't know. You'll have to keep an eye on him and use your influence to make sure that he stays on the right path. Putin needs you. Whether he knows it or not, he really needs you, Boris. Russia needs you. You really changed this country, Boris. Not every leader can say that about the country he's led. You changed Russia. Russia was lucky to have you. The world was lucky you were where you were. *I* was lucky to have you. We did a lot of stuff together, you and I. We got through some tough times. We never let it all come apart. We did some good things. They'll last. It took guts on your part. A lot of that stuff was harder for you than it was for me. I know that."

Yeltsin was now clutching Clinton by the hand, leaning into him.

"Thank you, Bill," he said. "I understand."

We were running late. There was a quick group photo on the veranda, some hurried good-byes and another bear hug.

"Bill," said Yeltsin, "I really do understand what you said. I'll think about it."

"I know you will, Boris," said Clinton, "because I know what you have in *here.*" Clinton tapped Yeltsin on his chest, right above his ailing heart.

Back in the car, Clinton was, for several minutes, even more somber than during the ride out. He looked out the window at the birch trees glinting in the sunshine that lined the country road leading back to the highway.

"That may be the last time I see Ol' Boris," he said finally. "I think we're going to miss him."

FOR SEVEN YEARS, from Clinton's inauguration in January 1993 until Yeltsin's resignation on New Year's Day 2000, these two men had been the dominant figures in international politics. During that period, they met eighteen times. That was almost as many meetings as Clinton's nine predecessors combined had held with the seven Communist Party chiefs who ruled the Soviet Union over a period of forty-six years, from Harry Truman's first and only encounter with Joseph Stalin in 1945 to George H.W. Bush's last summit with Mikhail Gorbachev in 1991.

The interaction between Clinton and Yeltsin was as controversial as it was frequent and intense. In 1996, when Clinton ran for reelection and again in 2000 when his vice-president, Al Gore—who was intimately involved in managing relations with Moscow—ran to succeed him, the Republicans denounced the administration for what they called the "personalization" of American foreign policy.

The description was justified but not as an indictment. The personal diplomacy between Clinton and Yeltsin, augmented by the channel that Gore developed with Yeltsin's longest-serving prime minister, Victor Chernomyrdin, yielded half a dozen major understandings that either resolved or alleviated disputes over Russia's role in the post–cold war world. The two presidents were the negotiators in chief of agreements to halt the sale of Russian rocket parts to India; remove Soviet-era nuclear missiles from Ukraine in exchange for Russian assurances of Ukraine's sovereignty and security; withdraw Russian troops from the Baltic states; institutionalize cooperation between Russia and an expanding NATO; lay the ground for the Baltic states to join the alliance; and ensure the participation of the Russian military in Balkan peacekeeping and of Russian diplomacy in the settlement of NATO's air war against Serbia.

None of these breakthroughs came easily. While Clinton and Yeltsin considered each other friends and their work together a partnership, virtually all of their eighteen meetings were contentious. One reason they had to meet so often face-to-face was that so many problems arose, and persisted, between their governments.

To some extent, frictions were inevitable. The U.S. and Russia were still two big countries with different interests. Russia's interests, along with its identity and destiny, were a matter of tumultuous internal struggle, therefore all the more difficult for Russia's president to determine and to present to the world.

Quite a few of Yeltsin's countrymen regretted the dissolution of the Soviet communist system; more lamented the breakup of the USSR itself, and many more were fearful about what would happen next. Yeltsin bore the brunt of those resentments and apprehensions. He was always on the political defensive in his conduct of Russian foreign policy. His domestic opponents charged him with further diminishing Russia's power abroad even as he abused his own powers at home. There was constant muttering about a new *smutnoye vremya,* or "Time of Troubles," a repetition of the disasters that had befallen the country between the Rurik and Romanov dynasties at the beginning of the seventeenth century. Yeltsin was often compared to Boris Godunov, the nobleman who worked his way to prominence in the court of Ivan the Terrible and had himself elected as czar, only to preside over famines, peasant uprisings, foreign interventions and machinations by pretenders to his throne.

Yeltsin fit this role all too well. His flaws were debilitating in their effect on him as a human being, politician and statesman. His erratic tendencies, boozing, vanity, irascibility and bouts of depression and isolation all contributed to Russia's troubles, causing some, aggravating others and further roiling Russia's relations with the outside world. His chronic ill health became, for his numerous critics and his aggrieved constituents, a metaphor for the condition of the state over which he presided.

But this Time of Troubles was different from Russia's entire previous experience of statehood. Russia had, in Yeltsin, its first elected leader. For half the time he and Clinton dealt with each other, Yeltsin was worried about his own reelection, for the other half about who would succeed him when Russians went to the polls in 2000. For long stretches of time, he faced the threat of impeachment by the Russian parliament—not a fate earlier residents of the Kremlin had to think about. The upheavals of the Yeltsin years played out in a free press, in the stump speeches and back-room deals of politicians running for office by the rules of a popularly approved constitution.

For Clinton, all this amounted to a big, messy problem, but it was also a new and better problem than the one that the Soviet system had posed to its own subjects, to the world and to all Clinton's predecessors since Woodrow Wilson. Clinton, himself a highly intuitive politician, believed Yeltsin had the right instincts: when locked in conflict with his domestic opponents, as he so often was, Yeltsin gave the citizenry a voice, through an election or a referendum; when push came to shove with the West, as it so often did, he never permitted an irreparable breach or a return to confrontation and conquest as the basis of Russia's relations with the outside world.

Isaiah Berlin—whose lectures Clinton and I had attended at Oxford when we first knew each other in the late sixties—divided the thinkers, writers and, by extension, actors of history, particularly Russian history, into two categories, which he captured with a line of Greek poetry: "The fox knows many things, but the hedgehog knows one big thing."

Bill Clinton knew one big thing: on the twin issues that had constituted the casus belli of the cold war—democracy versus dictatorship at home and cooperation versus competition abroad—he and his friend Boris Yeltsin were now, in principle, on the same side.

In practice, however, matters were more complicated. The hedgehog was beset by foxes, and for eight years the fur flew.

THE NATURAL

I first met Bill Clinton in Philadelphia in September 1968, the afternoon before he and I, along with the thirty other Rhodes scholars, took a bus to New York and set sail for England aboard the SS *United States*. My first conversation of any substance with him was during the ocean crossing, and the subject was the Soviet Union, the giant, alien, antagonistic country that had preoccupied U.S. foreign policy all our lives. We had been ten when the Warsaw Pact crushed the uprising in Hungary, fifteen when the Berlin wall went up and sixteen when Soviet missiles appeared in Cuba. The leader in the Kremlin during those crises was Nikita Khrushchev, whose career I had made a hobby of studying since I was fifteen. Clinton, too, was intrigued by Khrushchev, mostly as the principal foreign adversary of John F. Kennedy, who was a role model in the profession Clinton had already chosen.

Even then, at twenty-two, Clinton was a natural politician, a prodigious talker but a good listener too, with an easygoing, engaging manner and a capacity to project empathy, not just retail but wholesale, making individuals in a group, even a crowd, feel singled out. His enthusiasm for the process and the substance of governance was infectious and entertaining. On election night in November 1968, I was part of a gaggle of Americans clustered in front of a television at Rhodes House in Oxford. Clinton, who had let his hair go shaggy and was already growing a beard, gave us a running commentary that put the analysts of the BBC to shame. He knew everything, it seemed, about every issue, every state, every senatorial, congressional and gubernatorial race, every twist and turn in what had been a particularly acidic campaign, mostly because of the war in Vietnam. Clinton was wonking out, but in a fashion that brought us along with him. The long night that stretched into dawn was surprisingly good fun, given how virtually all of us, including Clinton, were hoping Hubert Humphrey would pull off a surprise victory over Richard Nixon.

Many of us who knew Clinton in those days were pretty sure why he was so exuberantly knowledgeable about the presidency: he conveyed a sense not just of direction but of destination.

MY OWN AMBITION was considerably more modest but no less clear: I wanted to be a foreign correspondent specializing in the Soviet Union. I'd studied Russian at the Hotchkiss School in Lakeville, Connecticut, majored in Russian literature at Yale, and at Oxford I was writing a thesis on Vladimir Mayakovsky, a poet who put his immense talent at the service of the Bolshevik Revolution, only to be driven to suicide by the onset of Stalinism. My tutor was Max Hayward of St. Antony's College, a renowned translator of Boris Pasternak, Alexander Solzhenitsyn and Nadezhda Mandelstam.

Over the long Christmas holiday, in December 1968 and January 1969, I visited the USSR for the first time, traveling across Germany and Poland by train to Moscow. The city was muffled in snow, the buildings better heated than those in Oxford and foreign visitors in the dead of winter rare enough for me to make friends easily, especially among younger people who were eager for any contact with the West. Thanks to introductions from Hayward, I also made contact with a number of poets, novelists and critics, some of them, including Mandelstam herself, justifiably famous, others unjustifiably obscure, and all of them, to one degree or another, repressed by the powers of the state and bleak about their country's future. On my return to Oxford, I described the adventure to Clinton, who started thinking about making a similar journey at Christmas time a year later.[1]

In the summer of 1969, I landed an internship working for Jerrold Schecter, the chief of the *Time* magazine bureau in Moscow. In the three months I spent there, I made a number of lasting friendships with Russians. The closest was with Slava Luchkov, a psychologist and writer who was in trouble with the authorities for having protested against the Soviet invasion of Czechoslovakia the year before. Slava, his wife, Rita, their daughter, Anya, and their circle of friends occupied a position on the border between the actively dissident intelligentsia and the larger category of people who quietly detested the Soviet system, boycotting its more insidious and corrupting aspects and going about their business of trying to live honest, decent lives. I spent long evenings in the tiny kitchen of the Luchkovs' apartment, drinking tea and sipping wine I'd bought at the hard currency store near my hotel, making a meal out of pickled herring and black bread. On the street outside, a taxicab, its driver a KGB plainclothesman, waited patiently, uninterested in any fare but mine.

WHEN I RETURNED to the university in September 1969, I shared a townhouse on Leckford Road in North Oxford with Bill Clinton and Frank Aller, a cheerfully serious student of Chinese language, history and culture from Spokane, Washington. Frank nicknamed me "Strobovich," and I called him something vaguely Chinese-sounding.

That fall I was pursuing a long-distance courtship of a Stanford undergraduate, Brooke Shearer, the sister of a Yale classmate, Derek Shearer. She visited me in Oxford over the Thanksgiving holiday and organized a feast for our household. She put Clinton and Aller in charge of basting the turkey at half-hour intervals late into the night. I remember falling asleep to the sound of their steady chatter about every conceivable subject but with a lot of American and Chinese politics thrown in. The next day several of the guests at the crowded table were Russians who lived in the neighborhood. I had developed close ties with the local community of Russian émigré intellectuals, who tended to be natural schmoozers and were therefore drawn as much to Clinton and Aller as to me with my interest in their culture.

Throughout that academic year, a number of the Oxford Russians made a habit of coming by our house in the evenings to sit in our tiny, cluttered kitchen, where they stayed for hours, listening to tapes of classical music—Clinton, Aller and I shared a fondness for Shostakovich—and thus re-creating on Leckford Road the combination of relaxation and intensity, with its undertone of melancholy about the fate of Russia, that I'd experienced at the apartments of my friends in Moscow the previous summer.

Clinton was writing an essay on Russian politics under the tutelage of Zbigniew Pelczynski, a don at Pembroke College. The title of the eighteen-page paper sounded like an oxymoron: "Political Pluralism in the USSR." Clinton had sifted through the prognostications of a dozen Kremlinologists and cautiously sided with those who believed that Khrushchev's policy of de-Stalinization had weakened totalitarianism to the point that the USSR might someday become a multi-party parliamentary democracy.[2] Clinton tried out this theory on Yasha Zaguskin, my closest friend among the Oxford Russians. A septuagenarian from Odessa, Yasha had fled the Red Army at the time of the Revolution. He listened with a look of bemusement to Clinton's discourse, then congratulated him on "your charming Yankee optimism about my beloved and hopeless homeland."

ONE EVENING in the late autumn of 1969, Max Hayward invited me to join him for dinner with George Kennan, who had lectured at Oxford in the fifties. I had not previously met Kennan, but his memoirs and books of history had made him as influential a figure in my life as Kennedy was in Clinton's. In both of his careers, as a diplomat and as a scholar, Kennan treated the study of czarist Russia as a prerequisite for understanding Soviet politics and foreign policy, yet he did not make the common mistake of regarding Russian despotism as a permanent condition. Even as far back as 1947, the year after Clinton and I were born, in the bleakest days of Stalinism, Kennan had discerned in the USSR "tendencies [that] must eventually find their outlet in either the break-up or the gradual mellowing of Soviet power."[3] His concept of containment was not meant to consign Russia and the West to endless stalemate; it was to give the Russians time to get over being Soviets.

I joined the two old friends at Max's regular corner table at his favorite restaurant, La Luna Caprese on North Parade Street. The discussion, naturally enough, turned to Russia, its writers and its future. Max tended to a gloomy view, in part because the Kremlin had persecuted the authors whose works he had put into English. It was impossible for Max to forgive, or to have much hope for, a Russia that could so abuse and disdain its greatest treasures. For Kennan, by contrast, it was impossible entirely to hate, fear or give up on a country that could produce such paragons of humanism.

DURING THAT WINTER and through the spring of 1970, an extracurricular project derailed my thesis on Mayakovsky. The memoirs of Nikita Khrushchev, who had been living under house arrest outside Moscow since his overthrow in 1964, had come into the hands of Time-Life, and Jerry Schecter recruited me to do the translation.[4] The venture was all very hush-hush, but since I was doing much of the work just upstairs from Clinton's room on Leckford Road, I took him into my confidence. He savored being in on a secret project. He was a night owl, while I was a morning person. But during that spring, he adjusted his schedule to mine, often getting up early to fry eggs for breakfast. I'd take a break from my work and sit with him in the kitchen, regaling him with tales of Kremlin skullduggery that I'd gleaned from the thick stack of transcripts strewn around my room. It was one of the few times, then or since, when I was the storyteller and Clinton was the audience.

The self-portrait of Khrushchev that emerged was different from the rogues' gallery of cunning misanthropes who had been his comrades and, in the case of Stalin, his master. "Ol' Nikita," as Clinton called him, ulti-mately failed both as a reformer and as a political survivor. But somehow, despite a career in the service of a monstrosity, he retained a degree of hu-manity, and once he clawed his way to the top of the system, he repudi-ated its most monstrous features. The memoirs were the result of one such alteration in the political culture of the Soviet Union: when Khrushchev fell from power, instead of being shot in a prison basement, he was al-lowed to live out his life as a "special pensioner," with access to a tape recorder and, as it turned out, to history.

For the next thirty years, right up to his meeting with Vladimir Putin in June 2000, Clinton liked to retell the story about how his omelets sus-tained me as I slogged away on the Khrushchev memoirs. The episode seemed to serve as a marker for my place in Clinton's ever-expanding uni-verse of associations.

IN THE FALL OF 1970, when Clinton entered Yale Law School, I re-mained at Oxford for a third year to finish my thesis, but with further in-terruptions. I spent much of the winter of early 1971 at Stanford, ostensibly delving into the Russian archives at the Hoover Institution but in fact stepping up my campaign to get Brooke to marry me. She agreed and took a crash course in Russian because she knew she'd be hearing a lot of that language.

Late that spring, my thesis finally finished, I went back to Stanford to be with Brooke while she completed course work for her own degree a year early so that we could get married in the fall before I joined the staff of *Time*. Bill Clinton and Frank Aller, who were footloose for the first part of the summer, spent a few idyllic weeks with us, poking around Palo Alto and exploring the Bay Area and the Monterey peninsula. Frank had been embroiled for years in an anguishing struggle with his conscience, his family and his draft board over his opposition to the war in Vietnam, but he seemed to have worked things out and was preparing to go off to Saigon for the *Los Angeles Times*.

A woman Clinton had met at Yale, Hillary Rodham, who was working at an Oakland law firm that summer, showed up at Brooke's house and joined us—Brooke, Bill, Frank and myself—for a Joan Baez concert at Stanford's amphitheater. The tickets cost $2.50 each; it was one of the first times Baez sang "The Night They Drove Old Dixie Down," which im-mediately became a Clinton anthem; and it was the last reunion of the

Leckford Road gang. About two months later, on September 14, for reasons that neither the note nor the people he left behind could ever explain, Frank shot himself at his home in Spokane. I called Clinton, who was then back at Yale, to break the news, but I couldn't get the words out. Brooke had to take the phone from me and finish the call.[5]

THE ICE AGE

When I went to work for *Time* as a correspondent in the fall of 1971, the editors wanted to groom me for an assignment as the magazine's correspondent in Moscow by sending me first to cover the communist countries of Eastern Europe. Brooke got a job as a stringer for *The Christian Science Monitor* and the *Sunday Times* of London. That November, the day after we were married in her parents' garden in Los Angeles, we set off for Yugoslavia, which was to be our base for the next two years. As we roamed the region, with a telex tape-punching machine in the trunk of our car, we found little good news. Bulgaria, an easy drive from Belgrade, was virtually the sixteenth republic of the USSR. Prague, only three years after the Soviet tanks had rolled in and crushed "socialism with a human face," was one of the most beautiful cities on earth yet also one of the most depressed and depressing. Most of the young friends we made in Hungary were looking for ways to emigrate to Australia or the West. The first time I traveled to Bucharest, a Romanian professor who shared my train cabin asked me in a whisper, as we crossed the border, whether I recalled the inscription at the gates of hell in Dante's *Inferno:* "Abandon all hope, ye who enter here."

Brooke and I felt like explorers trekking across a glacier that showed no sign of receding in our lifetimes.

Moscow itself was the North Pole. On my fleeting visits there, I found my friends—Slava, Rita and the others—hoping and, in the case of those who had embraced religion, praying that their children, or at least their grandchildren, would see the thaw. Brooke and I made a new friend, formerly of Leningrad, the poet Joseph Brodsky. We met him first in Vienna just as he began his lifelong exile, and later we drove from Belgrade to Venice to celebrate New Year's Eve with him in a pension near San Marco's. He toasted the next century, then nearly three decades away, with grappa, not vodka, and with the hope that what he called the Great Sadness would someday end.

—

As our stint in Eastern Europe came to an end in 1973, Brooke and I prepared to move to Moscow for our next assignment. But Nikita Khrushchev came back into our lives, even though he'd died two years before. Jerry Schecter received a second installment of dictated material. A little more than half of it Khrushchev had taped after the first book came out; the rest his family and friends had felt was too sensitive to be published while he was still alive. Once again, I went on a crash schedule to translate and edit the material.

When the second volume of memoirs was published in 1974, the Kremlin was furious. I was denounced in *Izvestia*, the government newspaper, as a "young sprout of the CIA," and the Soviet embassy in Washington told the editors of *Time* that I was an "unacceptable person."

With a posting to Moscow ruled out, *Time* assigned me to its Washington bureau, where I spent most of the next eighteen years as a reporter and columnist on foreign affairs, with a specialty on arms control, a subject that then occupied a position both crucial and anomalous in U.S.-Soviet relations. On almost every front, the superpowers maneuvered for advantage against each other. However, a totally unregulated competition in nuclear weaponry carried with it a danger of miscalculation that might lead to a thermonuclear holocaust. The weapons were so destructive as to be, in a practical and rational sense, useless except for purposes of mutual deterrence. That meant both sides had an interest in maintaining a balance of forces. Starting in the late sixties, the U.S. and the Soviet Union began negotiating agreements to limit the size, number, capability and disposition of their intercontinental-range missiles.

The Strategic Arms Limitation Talks (SALT), as the process was then known, was suspect in the eyes of American conservatives, who tended to believe that the more ruthless and hard-headed Soviets would out-negotiate us. For their part, the Soviets believed that arms control enhanced both their prestige and their security—largely because it was just about the only game they had much hope of not losing over the long run in their global rivalry with the U.S. They saw the SALT II treaty that Jimmy Carter and Leonid Brezhnev signed in 1979 as a codification of "parity," or equality with the U.S. I saw it as a means of slowing the arms race and reducing the danger that the weapons would ever be used.

My writings in defense of SALT II brought me once again to the attention of Soviet officials, this time in a more favorable light. One of these was Georgi Arbatov, the USSR's best known "Americanologist" and the director of the Institute for the Study of the U.S.A. and Canada. In late 1979, he intervened with the KGB to have me removed from the blacklist, so I was able to resume traveling to Moscow.

For the next dozen years, I was a regular guest at Arbatov's institute, which was housed in a converted mansion on a quiet side street in downtown Moscow. Through him I met other academicians with an open-door policy toward outsiders. One whose subsequent career would intersect with mine was Yevgeny Primakov, then the director of the USSR's premier academic institution for specialists on the Middle East. He was a former *Pravda* correspondent in Cairo and a recognized Arabist, reputed to have close ties of his own to the KGB.

Arbatov and Primakov were both protégés of Yuri Andropov, a ruthless believer in discipline as the cure for what ailed the Soviet Union. When Brezhnev finally expired in 1982 and Andropov assumed the top job, I sensed in Arbatov and Primakov a new feistiness and confidence: finally, the USSR had a leader who would make the place work and who would put Soviet power back on a competitive footing with the arrogant and assertive West.

But Andropov disappeared from public view less than a year after his ascendance, and he died of kidney failure six months after that. His politburo comrades closed ranks behind what seemed like a safe choice, Konstantin Chernenko, an aged agitprop hack who had been a yes-man to Brezhnev. For the next thirteen months, Chernenko was constantly reported to be recuperating from "colds." He died in March 1985.

AT FIRST, many expected the next general secretary of the Communist Party of the Soviet Union, Mikhail Gorbachev, then fifty-four, to be a healthy reincarnation of Andropov. That was certainly the prediction, and the hope, of Arbatov and Primakov when I knocked on their doors in the mid-eighties.

But Gorbachev turned out to be more a successor to Khrushchev than to Andropov. Gorbachev introduced the concept of *glasnost,* or openness, which was an explicit repudiation of totalitarianism's claim to a monopoly on the truth and therefore the germ of a free press and a civil society. I took it as an indicator of how profoundly the Soviet Union was changing when my friend Slava Luchkov, who had been alienated and persecuted under Brezhnev, went to work for a government commission assigned to develop a strategy for reforming the country.

In his approach to foreign policy, Gorbachev sought to rely less on brute force and more on voluntary and cooperative arrangements with other countries. He and his foreign minister, Eduard Shevardnadze, the longtime boss of the Soviet republic of Georgia, came up with a new word to describe the ties they wanted to have with the U.S.: partnership. The term was a gesture of accommodation with the West, even of assimilation, since the Russian word, *partnyorstvo,* was borrowed from English (as was the title that Gorbachev had adopted for his own post, *prezident*). As partners, the U.S. and the Soviet Union could move beyond "negative peace"—the avoidance of war—toward joint management of the world's problems. The Soviet leadership was proposing an end of the cold war on essentially Western terms.

To encourage Russia's continued movement in this direction, George Bush, along with Helmut Kohl, the chancellor of Germany, and the other leaders of the Group of Seven major industrialized democracies, or G-7, invited Gorbachev to make a guest appearance at their annual summit in London in 1991.* The prospect of the USSR's admission—or as Bush put it, "integration"—into the company of powerful, prosperous and democratic nations was intended as a further inducement to what George Kennan had predicted in 1947: the "mellowing" of the Soviet system.

THE OTHER PRESIDENT

A hero in the eyes of much of the outside world, Gorbachev was trapped at home between critics on either side. Beneficiaries of the old system attacked him for trying to change the country too fast, while many liberals felt he was moving too slowly. My friends and acquaintances were mostly in the latter category. Slava Luchkov, for example, had become disillusioned with the bureaucratic aimlessness of the commission he had been working for. Gorbachev, said Slava, was a transitional figure; the man to watch, and in whom to invest our hopes, was Boris Yeltsin.

Yeltsin was a product of the Soviet system who had reinvented himself as Russia's premier post-Soviet politician. He had taken full advantage of the liberalization Gorbachev had introduced and positioned himself to replace Gorbachev, who was reaching the limits of his own vision, effectiveness and mandate.

As a young man, Yeltsin had prided himself on being a builder of new structures—a skilled stonemason, carpenter, glazier and plasterer.

---

*The seven are Canada, France, Germany, Italy, Japan, the United Kingdom and the U.S.

He also knew how to give orders, how to make others work hard, and he rose quickly as a foreman on construction projects in his hometown of Sverdlovsk, an industrial city in the Urals known before the Revolution as Yekaterinburg. He entered politics in the late sixties as the chief of the construction department of the local Communist Party.

Yet it was not by virtue of what he built but by what he obliterated that Yeltsin came to the attention of Moscow. In 1977, the Brezhnev politburo, as part of a campaign to erase reminders of the pre-Soviet past, ordered the authorities in Sverdlovsk to destroy the Ipatyev House, where the last czar, Nicholas II, and his family were executed in 1918. Yeltsin completed the job in less than twenty-four hours, earning himself a series of promotions.

Gorbachev brought him to Moscow and put him in charge of the city's party organization, the largest and most important in the country. Yeltsin fit in with the spirit of *glasnost,* quickly establishing himself as a man of the people. He passed up a spacious dacha and lived in a two-bedroom apartment. American diplomats I knew at the time would sometimes encounter him on street corners, waiting for a bus or a tram and chatting with others in the line, eliciting their complaints about the municipal government. He made himself popular with Muscovites by renovating historic areas in the heart of town, like the Arbat, and by giving speeches attacking the complacency and remoteness of the rulers; they should be held accountable to the people, not to the party, he said.

At first, Yeltsin's determination to get things done and his impatience with the sluggishness of the system made him useful to Gorbachev, who wanted to prove that the system, with the right leadership—i.e., his own—could be made to work. Yeltsin was like a pile driver in Gorbachev's great renovation project for the Soviet Union, *perestroika.* The word means "restructuring" or "rebuilding." Its premise was that the system, while broken, could still be fixed.

Yeltsin came to believe that the system was so fundamentally flawed that it had to be replaced, and the man in the Kremlin along with it. Yet even though that conviction put Yeltsin on a collision course with Gorbachev, and their relationship would deteriorate into one of epic animosity, Yeltsin's conversion from a Soviet reformer to revolutionary would have been unimaginable without Gorbachev. It was Gorbachev who had created a political environment tolerant and pluralistic enough for a Yeltsin to be possible.

———

GORBACHEV DID Yeltsin another favor: in 1987, when Yeltsin had become too much of a gadfly, Gorbachev had him fired from the Moscow city party leadership and from the politburo. The shock sent Yeltsin into an emotional and physical collapse, but it also broke forever his ties to the Communist Party. Over the next year, he recovered his health and began a comeback outside the party, winning a seat in the Congress of People's Deputies of the USSR, a parliamentary body made up of elected as well as appointed members. He quickly became a leader of a group of deputies who pushed human rights and democratic reforms.

In that capacity Yeltsin made his first trip to the U.S. in September 1989. It was not a success. Part of the problem was that he had been preceded by his reputation as a hothead with a conspicuous bad habit, which he did nothing to lay to rest. His consumption of whiskey at a reception at Johns Hopkins University earned him an article in the "Style" section of *The Washington Post* under the headline: "Yeltsin's Smashing Day: Boris's Boozy Bear Hug for the Capitalists." President Bush, only to counter the perception that he was too closely tied to Gorbachev, consented to see the bumptious visitor. Afterward Bush pronounced him a "jolly fellow" but not someone he could imagine playing in the same league as Gorbachev.

OVER THE NEXT YEAR, Yeltsin, who had already shifted his power base from the apparatus of the party to that of the state, cut himself loose from the decrepit structure of the Soviet Union and established himself as the leader of the Russian Soviet Federative Socialist Republic. In May 1990, he became the speaker of the republic's legislature, known as the Supreme Soviet. It was housed in a brand-new edifice with a gleaming white marble façade at the western end of the New Arbat near the embankment of the Moscow River. As a piece of late-Soviet architecture, the building had its own political symbolism. Many Muscovites remembered the site from the mid-sixties as a *dolgostroi,* or long-term construction project—an ugly hole in the ground that served as a daily reminder of why they called Brezhnev's long tenure the "era of stagnation." When the project was finally finished and the newly elected Russian parliament set up shop there, Russians started calling it the White House. The nickname was yet another way for them to thumb their noses at the Soviet communists, who had their own headquarters just off Red Square, and at Mikhail Gorbachev in the Kremlin. In June 1991, Yeltsin won 57 percent of the vote to become Russia's first democratically elected president. Nominally, Russia was still a republic of the USSR, but with Yeltsin's election, it was a big step closer to independence.

RUSSIA ALSO NOW HAD, in Andrei Kozyrev, its own foreign minister. I'd known him since the 1980s, when he had been a Soviet diplomat working on arms control and United Nations issues. Even then, he had cultivated a look and a style that were studiedly un-Soviet. He wore a crew cut and tended toward tweed sport coats, thus avoiding both the baggy suits of the old-school Soviet diplomats and the sleek, blow-dried look of the young hot shots. Kozyrev's soft-spokenness would have seemed like diffidence if it were not so unmistakably a deliberate contrast to the bombast and dogmatism then practiced by his government. Even when toeing the party line, he would find ways of signaling—with a knowing smile, a roll of his eyes, a gentle wisecrack—a hint of irony about the absurdities in which he was required to traffic. Kozyrev was a full generation younger than Arbatov and Primakov, encumbered with neither the old guard's mistrust of the West nor its psychic investment in the Soviet system.

The overarching objective of Russian foreign policy under Yeltsin and Kozyrev was to create international conditions conducive to Russia's achievement of independence. Here again, Gorbachev had set the process in motion without meaning to. Starting in the late eighties, he and Shevardnadze had begun releasing the Central European states from the Soviet empire. Czechoslovakia, Hungary and Poland pulled out of the Warsaw Pact in 1990, and the others followed within a year. The next logical step was the disintegration of the USSR itself, since its constituent republics were as much in bondage to Moscow as the satellites.

That realization horrified Soviet conservatives and galvanized their opposition to Gorbachev. He tacked in their direction by threatening military force against would-be secessionists. In December 1990, Shevardnadze, who had until then been a steadying influence on Gorbachev when he wavered under pressure from the hard-liners, resigned in protest, warning that "dictatorship is coming."

Seeing that danger as well, Russian liberals, led by Yeltsin and Kozyrev, stepped up their support for the right of other republics to leave the USSR, thus solidifying the precedent for Russia's doing so.

In January 1991, Gorbachev approved a violent but feckless crackdown against peaceful demonstrators in the three Baltic states, Estonia, Latvia and Lithuania, whose parliaments had declared independence the year before.[6]

It was to Gorbachev's disgrace that the bloodshed occurred, but it was to his credit that it stopped in the Baltics and didn't happen again as the Soviet Union continued to unravel.

GEORGE BUSH AND MOST OTHER Western leaders sympathized with Gorbachev as he tried to cope with the centrifugal forces he had unleashed. They wished that the leaders of the various independence movements around the USSR, including Boris Yeltsin, would ease up, lest they provoke a communist backlash.

In early August 1991, Bush visited Ukraine, which was in the throes of a breakaway movement of its own. He gave an address in Kiev urging the Ukrainians to find a federalist compromise with the beleaguered Soviet leader rather than going their own way. The president's advice bombed locally and back home. William Safire of *The New York Times* excoriated Bush for "the Chicken Kiev speech." The phrase stung, and it stuck, just as Bush was beginning his campaign for reelection.

DOING NO HARM

I'd seen Bill Clinton only sporadically since our paths had parted after Oxford, but we'd never fallen out of touch, since he regularly checked in with phone calls and notes with news of himself and mutual friends. In the late seventies, I made a few trips to Arkansas to tag along as he worked diners, country stores and gas stations, running unsuccessfully for Congress, then successfully for attorney general. After serving one term as the youngest governor in the country, he became the youngest ex-governor and had to fight his way back into office two years later. I visited him and Hillary a few times in Little Rock, and on his trips to Washington, he sometimes stayed with Brooke and me. He made a lasting impression on our sons, Devin and Adrian, as the only houseguest who came with a bodyguard of state troopers, and as the fellow who tended to show up late at night and eat all the ice cream in the refrigerator, then fall asleep on the couch in the living room, often with the television on. When he came in from a meeting or a speech, Brooke and I would stay up to sit with him while he wound down from the day and tried out on us his themes for the campaign he was getting ready to mount.

The one foreign-policy subject that kept coming up during those years was what was happening in the Soviet Union and what it meant for the U.S. Only if the American people saw a receding Soviet threat would they vote against an incumbent who was perceived to be stronger in foreign than domestic policy and elect a new president who concentrated on the nation's economy.

For four days in August 1991, the revolution under way in the Soviet Union seemed to have gone suddenly into reverse. A cabal made up of virtually all Gorbachev's comrades, including Vice-President Gennady Yanayev, staged a coup d'état and placed Gorbachev under house arrest at his summer retreat on the Black Sea. The usurpers were inept, and there was impressive resistance on the streets of Moscow. Boris Yeltsin sent his foreign minister, Andrei Kozyrev, out of the country to prepare for a government-in-exile.

The defining moment and image of the coup came when Yeltsin climbed atop a tank in front of the besieged Russian White House and called on the citizenry to defend their hard-won democracy. His courage and clarity of purpose galvanized domestic and international support for those standing up against the putsch—although not immediately from the U.S. government.

President Bush, who was vacationing in Maine, seemed to be struck mute. He had been Gorbachev's air traffic controller over the previous three years, smooth-talking him toward a soft landing, only to see what suddenly looked like a crash. Another factor in Bush's initial dithering was a desire to preserve his options in case the coup leaders emerged as the new rulers of the USSR.

When the news of the coup broke, Clinton, who was about to announce his candidacy, telephoned me from Seattle, where he was attending a meeting of the National Governors Association. The coup, Clinton feared, could turn out to be "the end of the end of the cold war" and therefore the end of his chances of being the first post–cold war president.

Bush was already under attack, even from within his own party, not so much for failing to speak out against the coup as for having staked too much on his relationship with Gorbachev. On the third day of the crisis, Robert Dole, the minority leader of the Senate and a rival of Bush's for the Republican presidential nomination four years earlier, said that the coup proved "we can't put all our eggs in Gorbachev's basket."

Clinton asked me how I felt about the attack on Bush. I said it was a bum rap: Bush had been right to back Gorbachev in the past and ought to be doing so now, not hunkering down and waiting to see what happened next and who emerged as the winner. Clinton thought for a few seconds, then said, "I guess the beginning of statesmanship, at least for a guy in my position, is to do no harm."7

Other Democrats were less restrained. A pit bull of the party, Congressman Robert Torricelli of New Jersey, tried out a new version of an old battle cry. "Who lost Gorbachev?" he demanded. The line bombed, primarily because it was ridiculous, but also because the coup itself dissolved into farce. The perpetrators, failing to muster the support of the military, lost their nerve. Yeltsin sent out posses to round up the kingpins. They found Yanayev in a drunken stupor, and before they could arrest one of the masterminds, Boris Pugo, he shot his wife and then himself.

When Gorbachev returned to Moscow, he was politically crippled. The conservatives had turned against him, and the liberals had gravitated toward Yeltsin. The other republics began a stampede to the exit, led by the Baltic states, who won diplomatic recognition from the European Community and from the Russian government, even though it was still technically subordinate to the USSR.

Gorbachev resigned as head of the Communist Party, and, at Yeltsin's behest, the Soviet parliament banned all party activities. After seventy-four years in power, the Communist Party of the Soviet Union had collapsed.

In the immediate aftermath of the coup, there was relief in both camps of the American presidential campaign. The president's son George W. Bush was confident that the crisis would remind voters that the world was a dangerous place, requiring a steady and experienced hand on the tiller of U.S. foreign policy. Encountering a reporter in the back of Air Force One as the president and his family returned to Maine to continue their vacation, the junior Bush asked, "Do you think the American people are going to turn to a Democrat now?"

But Clinton was breathing easier too. Shortly after formally announcing his candidacy, he lit into Bush for being "reluctant to offer Boris Yeltsin, Russia's freely elected president, a helping hand" and for putting the U.S. in the position of being "thirty-seventh among the world's nations to extend diplomatic recognition to [the Baltic states]. We should have been the first."

On December 1, the Ukrainians went to the polls and voted themselves out of the USSR. The following week Yeltsin met in Minsk with the Ukrainian president, Leonid Kravchuk, and President Stanislav Shushkevich of Belarus to announce the formation of the Commonwealth of Independent States as the successor to the Soviet Union.

Gorbachev cut an increasingly pathetic figure, shuffling the deck in the leadership and reaching out to familiar and loyal figures associated with his attempt to save the Soviet Union. He had already put Yevgeny Primakov in charge of the foreign intelligence branch of the KGB. At the very end, Gorbachev enticed Eduard Shevardnadze to return as foreign minister, just in time, as it turned out, for Shevardnadze to smooth the way for his native Georgia to join the other Soviet republics in gaining independence.

On December 24, the Soviet Union gave up its seat in the United Nations to a country that now called itself the Russian Federation. The following day, Gorbachev had a final, nostalgic telephone conversation with George Bush, who was with his family for Christmas. Then, in a televised speech, Gorbachev announced his resignation from the presidency. A day later, the Council of the Republics, the upper house of the Supreme Soviet, declared the USSR no longer in existence. Boris Yeltsin moved from the Russian White House to the Kremlin, and the hammer and sickle was lowered for the last time. In its place was raised the tricolor that Peter the Great had introduced three centuries before.

Throughout what the world was suddenly calling the former Soviet Union, fourteen other flags, some old, some new, were going up. Yet even shorn of empire, Russia was still by far the largest country on earth, almost twice the size of the U.S. It sprawled 6,200 miles across Eurasia. Moscow still had an army of 2.8 million and an arsenal of over 20,000 nuclear weapons. No country on earth had as many immediate neighbors, and all thirteen of Russia's were nervous.

Yeltsin went a long way toward calming these fears when he dispatched Andrei Kozyrev to assure the three Baltic states that the new government in Moscow would withdraw within two or three years the 100,000 troops that the Soviet Union had stationed on their territory. In addition to being the first democratically elected leader in Russian history, Yeltsin looked as though he would also be the first nonimperialistic one.

BORIS AND GEORGE

During the opening months of the 1992 presidential campaign in the U.S., President Bush tended to downplay foreign policy so that he could burnish his credentials as a domestic president. When he held a summit with Yeltsin in early February, it was a relatively low-key event at Camp David, the presidential retreat in the Catoctin Mountains of Maryland. The meeting was significant, however, because Bush and his secretary of state, James Baker, came away newly impressed by their Russian guest. They saw none of the buffoonery that had marred Yeltsin's American debut over two years before. Yeltsin was relaxed, confident and well prepared. Without notes, he ranged over subjects from economic reform to strategic arms control to the situation in the Middle East in the aftermath of the Gulf War. As a memento of what Bush hoped would be the beginning of a personal and working relationship as long and fruitful as the one he had had with Gorbachev, he presented Yeltsin with a pair of hand-tooled cowboy boots. By the end of the meeting, they were calling each other Boris and George.[8]

Clinton had little comment on the summit and no criticism. Now that Bush and Yeltsin were putting their heads together on the great issues of the day, calling attention to U.S.-Russian relations would only reinforce whatever advantage Bush derived from being a foreign-policy president.

That changed in the spring, when American and Russian domestic politics began to interact to Clinton's benefit.

AFTER THE BRIEFEST and most illusory of honeymoons, Yeltsin had entered the early stages of what would become a mortal struggle with the parliament. At the core of the problem was an economic disaster exacerbated by political gridlock.

Russia's new leaders inherited a miserable state of affairs from their Soviet predecessors. Under the Soviet system, prices had been low, but there were few goods available; citizens stood in line in the snow for hours to buy stale bread and rotten sausages; the rubles in people's pockets were all but worthless; the system of manufacturing, supply and distribution never worked efficiently and had long since broken down; the Central Bank's reserves were virtually exhausted.

Yeltsin surrounded himself with young, pro-Western technocrats led by Yegor Gaidar, a scholar and economist in his mid-thirties from a distinguished family of the Moscow intelligentsia. For a suddenly powerful figure in the rough-and-tumble of his country's politics, Gaidar was almost comically contrary to type—diminutive, cherub-faced, refined in his manners—but he was also smart, tough, determined and straight-talking, especially with Yeltsin.

Through a program known as shock therapy, Gaidar and his team tried to bring under control a deficit that had ballooned to about 20 percent of gross domestic product. They slashed credits and subsidies to massively inefficient state-run factories. They cut the budget for the armed forces and reduced government support for the military-industrial complex. They believed, with the wholehearted support of most Western experts, that these stringent measures were essential for two reasons: first, to create the conditions for the eventual solvency of the Russian state, and second, to break the back of the Soviet leviathan.

In order for a market to come into being, individuals and enterprises had to be able to buy and sell as they wished, at home and abroad, and prices were allowed to run free. But these measures unleashed inflation, which reached the level of over 2,500 percent a year. The effect on consumers and pensioners was devastating. The average monthly wage was not enough to purchase a grocery basket of necessities.

Meanwhile, the unloading of state property at kopek-on-the-ruble prices, combined with the sudden introduction of market incentives and the almost total absence of property or tax laws, enriched a new class of robber barons, who in many cases were the old robber barons—Soviet-era factory managers and local party big shots who took advantage of political connections to cash in on inside deals. Crime and corruption, which had been deeply embedded in the Soviet system, were, like everything else, privatized.

The euphoria that had been so apparent in the immediate aftermath of the August 1991 coup gave way to widespread pessimism. As Slava Luchkov told me, "We have only two words in our language—*Hurrah!* and *alas!* After seventy-five years of being forced to chant *hurrah!* in unison, we're now free, so we are all chanting *alas!*"

Much of the disillusionment was focused on Yeltsin himself. Even if memories were short and scapegoating rampant, the hardships were real. The Soviet Union had been a condemned structure, like the Ipatyev House in Sverdlovsk: a wrecking ball and a few bulldozers could knock it down in a single night, particularly with Boris Yeltsin in charge of the job.

Yeltsin was part of the solution in that he was a master demolitionist of great determination and conviction, but he was also part of the problem in that he was not much of an architect. He knew what he hated about the Soviet Union far better than what he wanted to put in its place. All Russia now seemed like a massive *dolgostroi,* a political and economic hole in the ground. Many of its citizens felt they were being forced to live and work amid the rubble, listening to bossy but incompetent foremen who seemed to do nothing but bicker over the blueprints.

If there was an incapacitating if not fatal flaw in Russian reform at its birth, it was the absence of a collaborative relationship between Yeltsin's government and the parliament. One reason for this polarization was that the third Russian Revolution of the twentieth century was peaceful. This time the old regime, instead of being purged, simply went into opposition in the parliament, still known as the Supreme Soviet. Even retention of the word "soviet" was a sign that conservative forces in that body were looking for ways to rein in and, if possible, reverse the dismantlement of the old system.*

Yeltsin might have been able to recast the structure of political power in favor of reform if he had moved quickly and decisively in the immediate aftermath of the August 1991 coup, when the communists were most disheartened and discredited. Gaidar and Yeltsin's other youthful advisers pleaded with him to seize the opportunity to dissolve (and rename) the Supreme Soviet, call new parliamentary elections, form his own party, establish alliances with the liberal reformers and replace a constitution that dated back to the Brezhnev era. Instead, Yeltsin preferred to remain above the fray of partisan politics and rely on his personal prestige and the traditional power that came with residence in the Kremlin.

Those turned out to be waning assets. Within months, his opponents in the Supreme Soviet were able to exploit growing popular discontent with the economy. Their obstructionism and nostalgia for the past were now institutionalized and, because the institution was electoral, they could claim a legitimacy that they had never had in Soviet times.

By early 1992, only about three hundred out of the approximately one thousand deputies in the parliament were self-avowed democrats. They were pitted against those who still identified themselves as communists, the "reds," and a small but raucous group of "browns," or ultranationalists

---

*The Russian word *soviet* means, literally, "council." Workers' soviets, revolutionary soviets and communist soviets were originally supposed to be the building blocks of what became the USSR.

(so called because of their similarity, in the eyes of their critics, to the brownshirts of the early Nazi period in Germany).

Both groups had a would-be standard-bearer in Yeltsin's own vice-president, Alexander Rutskoi. A year earlier, Rutskoi, as the head of the Communists for Democracy faction in the old Soviet parliament, had seemed like a good running mate for Yeltsin, since he would attract the support of communists, nationalists and the professional military. But he soon threw in his lot with conservative elements, opposing cuts in defense spending and grumbling over the loss of empire. Rutskoi had a large map of the USSR on the wall of his office near the Kremlin. "That's the past," he liked to tell visitors, "but it's also the future."

Yeltsin's other principal antagonist was his former deputy and successor as speaker of the Supreme Soviet, Ruslan Khasbulatov, a politically active professor of economics and a Chechen, a member of a Muslim nationality in southwestern Russia. Khasbulatov had wanted to be prime minister, but Yeltsin was grooming Gaidar for that job.

During the first of several reporting trips I made to Moscow in 1992, I paid a call on Khasbulatov in the office at the Russian White House that he had inherited from Yeltsin. There, at his side, was Georgi Arbatov, spewing accusations about how the government was bankrupting the state and beggaring the people. Gaidar, he added, was a "stooge of the West." The scene saddened me. Arbatov had helped open the system to outside influences, making possible the rise of people like Gaidar—and, for that matter, the whole Yeltsin phenomenon. Yet here he was, personally embittered and siding with the forces of reaction.

I noted, however, that my other host of years past, Yevgeny Primakov, had made the transition to the post-Soviet era seamlessly: Yeltsin had retained him as head of what now became the Foreign Intelligence Service of the Russian Federation.

BY THE SPRING OF 1992, American support for Russian democracy and economic reform became an issue in the American presidential campaign, and it was Richard Nixon, as much as anyone, who put the Bush administration on the defensive. For a little over a decade, Nixon had been on a campaign to consign the Watergate scandal to the footnotes of history by establishing himself as a sage on foreign policy and, in particular, a purveyor of advice on U.S.-Russian relations.

In early March, Nixon sent President Bush a memo calling Yeltsin "the most pro-Western leader of Russia in history . . . whatever his flaws, the alternative of a new despotism would be infinitely worse." Yeltsin had appealed to the G-7 for an emergency infusion of loans. Nixon warned Bush that unless there was a Western response comparable to the Marshall Plan for Europe after World War II, the United States and the West would "risk snatching defeat in the cold war from the jaws of victory." He made the case on political as well as strategic grounds: "The hot-button issue in the 1950s was 'Who lost China?' If Yeltsin goes down, the question of 'who lost Russia?' will be an infinitely more devastating issue in the 1990s."

Bush assured Nixon that there was major G-7 assistance in the works, then directed Baker to make it so.[9]

On April 1, Clinton gave a speech before the Foreign Policy Association at the Waldorf-Astoria Hotel in New York chiding Bush for being "overly cautious on the issue of aid to Russia." The White House, having gotten wind of what Clinton planned to do, tried to preempt but ended up looking reactive. Twenty minutes before Clinton started speaking in New York, Bush rushed to the podium in the White House press room and announced that the G-7 would make $24 billion available to support Russia.[10]

THE TWO CANDIDATES' EFFORTS to outbid each other gave aid to Russia a bipartisan cast and served for the duration of the campaign to close any meaningful gap between Bush and Clinton on the substance and strategy of Russia policy. Bush worked during the spring and summer of 1992 with the G-7, and especially with Helmut Kohl, to bring the resources and expertise of the World Bank and International Monetary Fund to bear on Russia's staggering economic problems.

As a result, when Yeltsin returned to the U.S. in June 1992, he regarded Bush as a supportive friend. Unlike the February meeting at Camp David, this was a state visit, intended to highlight Bush's standing as a statesman. Yeltsin had just announced that he would not run for a second term in 1996, citing the physical strain of the job, but he wanted to help Bush get reelected, since that would assure him an American counterpart whom he knew, liked and trusted.

Over the years, Kremlin leaders had tended to root for Republicans over Democrats. They blamed Harry Truman for starting the cold war, John Kennedy for going to the brink over Berlin and Cuba, Lyndon Johnson for escalating Kennedy's anti-communist crusade in Southeast Asia and Jimmy Carter for haranguing them on human rights. By contrast, they respected Nixon for initiating détente and Gerald Ford for trying to keep that policy going. Even Ronald Reagan, for all his fire-breathing about the evil empire, had established an amicable relationship with Gorbachev, which Bush had consolidated and then, in their first summit at Camp David, transferred to Yeltsin.

But Bill Clinton wanted to get a boost out of Yeltsin's visit as well, and it was traditional in an election year for visiting heads of state to accept a courtesy call from the challenger. One of Clinton's foreign-policy advisers, Toby Gati, drawing on a long-standing friendship with Andrei Kozyrev, arranged a meeting. Yeltsin was at first reluctant, especially since his embassy in Washington told him that if anyone was going to beat Bush in the fall, it was the independent candidate, Ross Perot. The Bush administration tried to prevent the Clinton-Yeltsin meeting, then, when that proved impossible, to keep it from occurring in a "presidential" setting. But on Kozyrev's advice, Yeltsin received Clinton for half an hour on the morning of June 18 at Blair House, the official visitor's residence across Pennsylvania Avenue from the White House.

When Clinton arrived, he tried to break the ice by complimenting Yeltsin on the address he had given the day before to a joint session of the U.S. Congress, saying it would generate support for economic assistance to Russia and adding that he had been a supporter of aid to Russia ever since he'd watched the television footage of Yeltsin standing on the tank during the attempted coup the year before.

This opening attempt at flattery backfired, largely because of Clinton's use of one word: "assistance." Yeltsin interrupted to point out that he had not said anything about wanting help during his two and a half days in Washington. "We're not asking for handouts," he said. "Russia is a great power. What we want from the U.S. is a model of leadership for others to emulate. If the U.S. leads, then Japan, Great Britain, Germany will follow." It was in the interest of the whole world for Russian reform to succeed, he continued. He was proud of his appointment of Gaidar and dismissive of the flak he was taking from the Supreme Soviet. "In this country, you have two big parties," he said. "We have over twenty small ones, and the president isn't part of any of them. He goes directly to the people. He has a majority of the support of the people."

Clinton tried another line of praise. "You represent something profoundly different from what we have ever seen come out of Russia," he said. "Something all these politicians [in the U.S.] can appreciate is the astonishing degree to which you can give bad news to the people and still stay with reform. I think they believe you'll stay with reform to the very end."

This time the massaging worked. "Thank you," said Yeltsin, beaming. "I see that you appreciate the essence of our situation. My announcement that I won't run in 1996 has had an important psychological impact. The Russian people appreciate that I'm not fighting to stay in office but to ensure that the reforms become irreversible. I know they are working hard, that a lot of what I'm doing is unpopular, that it has a lot of people depressed. But they can see that I'm not looking over my shoulder to see if I'm popular . . . There's no choice but to administer these bitter pills. We have to find a cure."

Clinton remarked that he knew a little about persistence himself. "You know," he said, "they've written my obituary ten or fifteen times."

Yeltsin gave a hearty laugh. "However the situation turns out this fall," he said, "you've got a lot of time ahead of you. You'll have your chance."[11] He was still betting on Bush.

BY LATE SUMMER, as the polls turned increasingly against Bush, he began to play the Russia card more aggressively. He peppered his stump speeches with an appeal that voters remember that he had personally "won the cold war."

It was a softball for Clinton. "The notion that the Republicans won the cold war," Clinton said in a speech in Los Angeles on August 13, "reminds me of the rooster who took credit for the dawn." He attributed "America's victory in the cold war" to the bipartisan procession of presidents, but noted that it all started with a Democrat, Harry Truman.

I was sorry to hear Clinton use this line. I knew that American triumphalism—whether in the form of Bush's boasting or Clinton's talk of an American victory—set teeth on edge in Moscow, particularly among the reformers who needed our help. They felt that they were the ones who had brought down the Soviet system, and that Soviet leaders who attempted reform, from Khrushchev to Gorbachev, were responding more to internal pressures than external ones.[12]

But I kept my reaction to myself. Only one member of our family was involved in the Clinton campaign, and that was Brooke, who had left her job in Washington to crisscross the country with Hillary. When Brooke called in from whistle stops, she would sometimes put Clinton on the phone for a quick exchange of jokes or good wishes. We steered away from substance, and I also avoided writing about him in my column for *Time*.[13]

Clinton sought my advice only once during the campaign—in early October 1992, the month when front-runners most worry about their opponents pulling off a surprise that turns the tide. While barnstorming through the Midwest, Clinton called to ask about a rumor that the Russians were about to make a dramatic concession to Bush in the negotiations over START II, a successor to SALT, that would give Bush a last-minute, high-visibility diplomatic achievement and remind the electorate that he was a skillful and seasoned custodian of the nation's security interests.

I knew from my own reporting that the negotiations were stalled and not likely to produce a breakthrough before the election. While the White House was eager for a deal before the election, the Joint Chiefs of Staff were digging in their heels against compromising on a technical detail that mattered greatly to the Russians.[14] I told Clinton that I doubted that the chiefs would relent until they saw who their commander in chief was going to be after election day.

Clinton was relieved. He asked what his message should be to calm the Russians down about a change in administration. The one-word answer, I said, was continuity: just as he didn't want an October surprise, the Russians didn't want a Clinton surprise—a new administration that either put the relationship with Russia on hold while it decided what it was going to do or, worse, that changed course radically.

The Russians shouldn't worry, Clinton replied. He was running against George Bush's overall conduct of the presidency, especially his management of the American economy, not his handling of Russia. He sent word through various advisers and Democratic Party elders who were in touch with the Russians that there would be a smooth hand-off; Clinton would build on what he regarded as Bush's good work, not just in arms control but across the board in helping Yeltsin toward his stated goal of building "a modern, democratic, civilized state."

Late in the afternoon on November 3, 1992, a taxi pulled up in front of our house, bringing Brooke home after nearly ten months on the campaign trail. She unpacked just in time to join me in front of the television and watch the first reports of exit polls showing that Bill Clinton had won the presidency.

THE
FIRST
TERM

CHAPTER 2

THE MAIN CHANCE

*Unless the reformer can invent something which substitutes
attractive virtues for attractive vices, he will fail.*

Walter Lippmann

W HEN BILL AND HILLARY CLINTON made their first
post-election visit to Washington the week before Thanksgiving in 1992, Brooke took me to a crowded event in their
honor.[1] Security was tight, but she persuaded a Secret Service agent she
had befriended during the campaign to loan me a lapel pin so that I could
accompany her to the holding room where the president-elect came to
relax after working the crowd. As he entered, he was bear-hugging and
chatting up everyone in sight. When he reached me, he threw his arm
around my shoulder and thanked me effusively for putting up with
Brooke's long absences from home. Lowering his voice, he said he'd just
gotten a message from Yeltsin that he wanted to talk about privately.

The next morning, when I arrived at his suite in the Hay-Adams Hotel,
across Lafayette Park from the White House, Clinton told me that Yeltsin
had phoned him two days after the election, ostensibly to offer congratu-
lations but really to plead that he come to Moscow as soon as possible.
The weight of opinion among Clinton's advisers was that he should not
accept. Tony Lake, an experienced, energetic and imaginative thinker,
writer and practitioner in the field of foreign policy who was about to become the president's national security adviser, believed that dashing off to
Moscow would be exactly the wrong way to begin the first post–cold war
presidency. George Stephanopoulos, one of Clinton's key campaign and

domestic aides, wanted the new president to hit the ground running at home, not on the diplomatic high road. So far, Clinton was following their advice, but he wasn't happy about it. He didn't want to "keep stiffing" Yeltsin, he said. He'd been getting intelligence briefings in Little Rock on the mounting parliamentary opposition to the economic reforms of Yeltsin's government, and he didn't want to "appear to be letting Yeltsin hang out there, naked before his enemies." Now a letter had arrived from Yeltsin urgently renewing his request for the earliest possible meeting; Yeltsin was prepared to meet Clinton in a third country, presumably since that would make it easier for Clinton to agree.

"His letter reads like a cry of pain," said Clinton. "You can just feel the guy reaching out to us, and asking us to reach out to him. I'd really, *really* like to help him. I get the feeling he's up to his ass in alligators. He especially needs friends abroad because he's got so many enemies at home. We've got to try to keep Yeltsin going."

Out of the blue, Clinton asked me if I was available to go to Moscow as his ambassador. In many ways, it would have been a dream job, but I'd thought about it and knew I couldn't accept: our sons, Devin and Adrian, then sixteen and twelve, were thriving in their school, their friendships and their soccer leagues. Clinton said he understood and let the matter drop.

About three weeks later, I got a call from the secretary of state–designate, Warren Christopher, who told me that Clinton wanted to find a way of bringing me into the State Department to help with policy toward the former Soviet Union.

I had known Chris, as he preferred to be called, since the late seventies, when I was covering the foreign-policy beat for *Time* and he was deputy secretary of state. I knew him to be courtly and shy to a degree that masked a steeliness that was easy, but unwise, to underestimate. I remembered in particular how he had spearheaded, quietly but effectively, the Carter administration's effort to focus American foreign policy on the promotion of democracy and human rights.

I accepted the offer with enthusiasm, since it allowed me to stay in Washington and be part of the policymaking process. I worked out the terms of a new position at the State Department with Peter Tarnoff, who had served with Chris in the Carter administration and who was slated to be the under secretary for political affairs, the number three position in the department. I also sought the advice of a friend and soon-to-be colleague, Richard Holbrooke. I'd known him for more than twenty years, first when he had been the managing editor of *Foreign Policy* magazine in the 1970s, then when he'd been responsible for policy toward Asia in the Carter administration. In the late eighties, when I was a journalist and he was an investment banker waiting for a Democratic restoration, he and I had traveled together in the Soviet Union, including to the Baltic states. On those travels, he was boundless in his curiosity about the events then unfolding in Europe and forceful in his view that the U.S. should be playing more of a role in shaping them. Dick understood how government worked and what it took to make it work well. While waiting with some uncertainty to see if he'd be offered a job himself, he threw himself into helping me design my own.

Previously, the Soviet Union had been under the purview of the regional assistant secretary responsible for Europe. That barely made sense when it was one giant country, in which virtually all decisions of any importance to the U.S. emanated from one man in Moscow. It made no sense at all now that the USSR had split into fifteen countries and communism had given way to a messy but genuine pluralism. My title was to be one of the longest in the federal government: ambassador-at-large and special adviser to the secretary of state on the new independent states of the former Soviet Union. In the jargon of Foggy Bottom, the bureau was designated S/NIS, the prefix "S/" signifying that the office reported directly to the secretary.*

Chris proposed to Tony Lake and his deputy on the National Security Council staff, Sandy Berger, that I chair a new interagency committee to coordinate the activities of all departments of the U.S. government with respect to the former Soviet Union.

For the ambassadorship to Moscow, Clinton considered a range of candidates, including prominent academics and members of Congress. My candidate for the job was Condoleezza Rice, who had been Bush's senior expert on the former Soviet Union at the NSC and instrumental in his handling of Gorbachev during the suspenseful but relatively peaceful breakup of the empire. In addition to her expertise and experience, Rice would have brought to our administration's policy toward that region two other valuable attributes—continuity and bipartisanship. In the end, the president-elect decided, on Chris's advice, that what the Moscow post

---

* Of the fifteen former republics, twelve were covered by S/NIS; the three Baltic states remained in the European bureau, since the U.S. had never recognized as legitimate their annexation by the USSR.

really needed was a seasoned professional diplomat. They zeroed in on the one with the most distinguished and diversified record in the foreign service: Tom Pickering, who had served as ambassador to the United Nations, Israel, El Salvador, Nigeria and Jordan, as well as an assistant secretary of state and executive secretary of the department, and who was, in early 1993, ambassador to India.[2]

Dick Holbrooke was named to be ambassador to Germany.

WHILE THE NEW ADMINISTRATION was preparing to take over in Washington, the Yeltsin government was reeling from one setback after another in Moscow. At the end of November 1992, the constitutional court eased the ban that Yeltsin had imposed on the Communist Party after the August 1991 coup: the communists now had the right to organize and thus to reconstitute themselves as a force in future elections.[3]

Sensing the pendulum swinging in their direction, Yeltsin's opponents pressed for the dismissal of Yegor Gaidar, who had been serving as prime minister since June 1992, and for veto power over Yeltsin's nominees for the four "power ministries"—defense, security, internal affairs and foreign affairs. Yeltsin attempted a compromise that would have allowed him to keep Gaidar, but the opposition merely pocketed his concessions without making any of their own. Feeling betrayed, Yeltsin went before the parliament on December 10, 1992, delivered a fiery and defiant speech, then called on his supporters to stage a walkout with him. Most stayed in their seats while he stomped out of the hall. His confidence shaken, Yeltsin concluded that he had no choice but to promote to the premiership Victor Chernomyrdin, the deputy prime minister in charge of the energy sector, and fire Gaidar. As the former head of the state-owned gas consortium, Gazprom, Chernomyrdin was an archetypal "red manager," a potentate of Soviet industry who had profitably made the transition to what now passed for capitalism.

Gaidar and the other young reformers were dismayed by Chernomyrdin's appointment, both because it symbolized compromise with, if not capitulation to, the conservative opposition and because they suspected Chernomyrdin's economic instincts were essentially retrograde. So, they feared, were his political instincts.

One of Russia's most pro-Western figures, Foreign Minister Andrei Kozyrev, decided to give the world a preview of the ugly scenario he saw unfolding. On December 14, he was in Stockholm for a meeting of foreign ministers and other high officials from fifty-two countries.[4] When it came time for Kozyrev to address the conference, he delivered a speech that sounded like a declaration of a new cold war. Instead of pursuing "freedom and democracy," he said, Russia would now give priority to defending its interests against the West. He called on the former Soviet republics, whose foreign ministers were arrayed in front of him listening agape, to band together under the leadership of a Russia that was fully "capable of looking after itself and its friends."

For half an hour, there was near pandemonium. Some reporters dashed to the phones, while others held off filing the story because they found the speech so provocative that they thought the speaker was an imposter.

Lawrence Eagleburger, James Baker's deputy who had taken over as secretary of state at the end of the Bush administration, pulled Kozyrev aside and demanded to know what was going on.[5] Somewhat sheepishly, Kozyrev explained that the speech had been an "oratorical device" intended to focus the world's attention on what might happen if hard-liners in Russia gained the upper hand. He later told Dennis Ross, one of James Baker's closest aides who was in charge of the Russia account for the State Department, that the warning was really directed at the incoming American administration. Clinton's refusal to accept Yeltsin's invitation to an early summit led Kozyrev to fear that Russian reformers were going to have to fend for themselves, without active, high-level American engagement and encouragement. If that happened, he said, "we're finished."

Ross was sufficiently concerned that when he returned to Washington, he called me to urge that I make contact as soon as I could with Georgi Mamedov, Kozyrev's deputy in charge of U.S.-Russian relations and arms control. Dennis regarded Mamedov as the ablest, shrewdest and most creative diplomat on the Russian side. "You folks are going to inherit a lot of problems with the Russians," Dennis said, "and you'll probably get into a few of your own. Mamedov is the one guy over there you can work with. He's in the solution business."

Dennis also recommended that I get word to Clinton to pay attention to the deteriorating political situation in Russia.

I didn't need to. Clinton phoned me on December 17 from Little Rock. He had taken a break from planning the inauguration to work out at the YMCA and, while running on a treadmill, found himself worrying about "this whole unbelievable mess in Russia." If the situation got completely out of hand, he said, we'd see hundreds of thousands, maybe millions of refugees streaming west. He could also imagine Yeltsin being swept aside and Russia "going bad on us," returning to a policy of confrontation with the outside world. During his presidency, he said, he wanted to do "good stuff with Russia and really take advantage of what's new in a positive sense over there." But it looked as though first we had to concentrate on "averting disaster."

I NEXT SAW the president-elect over the New Year holiday. Brooke and I took our son Adrian to Hilton Head, South Carolina, for Renaissance Weekend, an annual retreat that the Clintons had been attending for years.[6] Since we were both entering the administration—Brooke was about to become the director of the White House Fellows program—we decided to participate in a gathering that had, with Clinton's election, turned into a celebratory reunion of Friends of Bill, a phrase now capitalized in the press.

On Saturday morning, January 2, Brooke and I went jogging on the beach with Clinton, who was outfitted in a red University of Arkansas track suit. Edwin Moses, the Olympic hurdler, was setting a brisk pace, making it difficult for anyone, even Clinton, to talk. Trailing us were two trucks, one with reporters and cameramen, the other with heavily armed Secret Service agents. After several miles, we came on Hillary power-walking alone. Clinton and I slowed to chat with her for a while, then she and Brooke set off back to the hotel. Clinton asked his Secret Service detail to hold the rest of the entourage at a distance so that he and I could talk alone.

What was happening in Russia, he said, was "the biggest and toughest thing out there. It's not just the end of communism, the end of the cold war. That's what's over and done with. There's also stuff *starting*—stuff that's *new*. Figuring out what it is, how we work with it, how we keep it moving in the right direction: that's what we've got to do."

Russia was on Clinton's mind that day in part because George Bush was in Moscow. The headline event of that final Bush-Yeltsin summit was yet another landmark in the history of arms control, the signing of the START II treaty. American and Russian negotiators had finally broken the impasse that prevented its completion before the election.

As we walked on the beach in South Carolina that bright, chilly morning, Clinton was thinking hard about Russia, but not much about arms control. That was partly because he knew that START II, which required ratification by the Supreme Soviet, faced stubborn opposition from Yeltsin's opponents. They were not about to acquiesce in anything he proposed, especially if it entailed further accommodation with the U.S. on the size and composition of the arsenal that Russia had inherited from the USSR, which constituted one of the last vestiges of Russia's status as a superpower.

In addition to recognizing that political obstacle on the Russian side, Clinton saw strategic arms control as old business—unfinished, worthwhile and necessary, to be sure, but nonetheless not high on his agenda. He liked to refer to himself as "a tomorrow guy," and where Russia was concerned, that meant letting others (like me) think about how many warheads the Russian Strategic Rocket Forces had aimed at the U.S. Unlike his predecessors from Truman to Reagan, Clinton didn't have to get up every morning and worry about whether the leaders in Moscow were going to go to war against the West. His concern was whether, as he put it, Russia was going to "blow up in our faces."

Both near term and long term, the core problem was the Russian economy. While continuing the emergency aid programs that the Bush administration had launched—medicine for a country where the pharmaceutical industry had, like everything else, collapsed; food for vast regions that were on the brink of starvation—we had to put in place a strategy that would increase the chances of Russia's becoming "a going concern within ten years"—just beyond the horizon of what Clinton hoped would be his own tenure in office. Making that happen, he said, was "the main chance." It would take a combination of internal reform and external assistance on a scale far beyond what the U.S. could provide on its own. Clinton was relying particularly on Helmut Kohl of Germany, then a dominant figure in the G-7 and Yeltsin's closest friend in the West now that Bush was leaving office. He imagined Kohl and himself double-teaming Yeltsin so that he got "the right message in full stereo" on the reforms he had to undertake if Western assistance was going to do any good.

Yeltsin, said Clinton, had already demonstrated that "he's got guts and he's got his heart in the right place." But he hadn't shown himself to be deft or farsighted as a politician. His looming impasse with the parliament over START II was only the latest in a seemingly endless set of examples. Why, Clinton wondered, wasn't Yeltsin engaging more in basic coalition-building? Why wasn't he reaching out more aggressively to the reformist splinter parties, or laying the ground for a party of his own?

I pointed out that these were almost exactly the steps that Yeltsin's own liberal advisers like Gaidar had been urging him to take for a year and a half.

Clinton had his own guess about the nature of the problem: Yeltsin was "psychologically straddling a divide between the old and the new, and he doesn't know which way to jump." He embodied the conflict that was under way in Russia itself.

Clinton had been talking to Robert Strauss, the Washington power broker who had been Bush's ambassador to Moscow in the immediate aftermath of the August 1991 coup. Strauss predicted that Clinton would find Yeltsin "educable" in the craft of politics. Clinton was clearly intrigued by Strauss's advice and eager to put it to the test by "getting together with Ol' Boris." In his own mind, he was already on a first-name basis with the president of Russia.

With that, he loped off down the beach, now lined with autograph-seekers in bathing suits. I hadn't said much. When Clinton was in transmit mode—conducting a kind of Socratic dialogue with himself, ruminations and instructions flowing out of him in a coherent but high-speed sort of stream of consciousness—having a conversation with him was a bit like going for a run with Edwin Moses: he set the pace and you did the best you could just to keep up. But that was all right: what he'd transmitted was a more articulate version of much of my own thinking. Besides, he was now my boss. I might qualify as an FOB, but I'd called him Bill for the last time. From now on, I would refer to him when we were alone together as "Chief" and on all other occasions as "Mr. President."

YELTSIN, TOO, was in transmit mode when Clinton telephoned him the Saturday after his inauguration—but for a different reason: the president of Russia was drunk. The words were slurred, and he seemed barely listening to what Clinton had to say, which was all intended as good news: he was going to give the highest priority to relations with Russia and to developing a solid partnership—he used the word repeatedly—with Yeltsin himself. When Clinton mentioned that I would be his point man for dealing with Russia, Yeltsin burbled with delight at the news, but only because he somehow misheard my name as "Bob Strauss," whom he remembered favorably as Bush's ambassador at the time of the coup. Clinton made a couple of stabs at correcting the misunderstanding, but gave up. All

Yeltsin wanted to hear was that Clinton was going to meet with him, and the sooner the better.

When Clinton called me later to report on the conversation, he was more bemused than shocked by Yeltsin's condition.

"A candidate for tough love, if ever I heard one," he said, chuckling.

THE FOLLOWING MONDAY, I reported for duty. Like other officials who were awaiting confirmation by the Senate, I set up shop in a small temporary office on the ground floor of the State Department. Several times a day I would ascend to the seventh floor to consult with Secretary Christopher in his spacious office. In one of our first meetings, Chris sent me a twenty-two-page paper with parting thoughts that Larry Eagleburger had left for him. Chris had underlined this passage: "If reform succeeds in Russia, it may not assure the success of reform in the other states of the FSU; but if reform fails in Russia, it most assuredly will mean the failure of reform throughout the former Soviet empire." The new administration, concluded Eagleburger, must "stay engaged with the Russians and help Yeltsin, or his successors, find ways to keep conflicts on the periphery from boiling over."[7]

I had just finished reading the memo when I received a pair of visitors from Georgia, Tedo Japaridze and Gela Charkviani. I was supposed to avoid contact with foreign officials until I was confirmed, but I felt I could make an exception for Tedo and Gela because I knew them from my days wandering around the Soviet Union as a journalist. Tedo had been on the staff at the Arbatov institute, and I'd met Gela in Tbilisi, where he was the host of a highbrow talk show as well as an accomplished pianist and a translator of *King Lear.* Both were confidants of Eduard Shevardnadze, the last Soviet foreign minister, who had returned to his native Georgia and was now its president.

In the eyes of much of the world, Shevardnadze was a hero for his part in dismantling the Soviet empire, but many nationalistic Russians regarded him as a traitor. Tedo and Gela suspected the Russian military and intelligence services of stirring up trouble in Georgia. They doubted Yeltsin was personally to blame and even believed he might be trying to rein in "dark forces" within his government. Yeltsin might be irascible, unpredictable and, as they delicately put it, "undisciplined in his personal habits," but he was better than any other Russian political figure who was likely to come to the fore anytime soon.

If the Clinton administration wanted to support "Shevy," as they both called their own president, then it must also support Yeltsin against his domestic enemies. "Remember," said Tedo, "as our big neighbor goes, so goes the neighborhood."

ON FEBRUARY 4, I got the same advice from Richard Nixon. He was passing through Washington on his way to Moscow and asked me to come talk to him at his hotel. Toby Gati, the Clinton campaign adviser who was now the senior official at the National Security Council working on the former Soviet Union, accompanied me. I had interviewed Nixon a number of times in the eighties, so I knew what to expect: an encounter that was awkward bordering on weird. Nixon opened with five minutes of stilted bonhomie laced with phony compliments and strained jokes, followed by a thirty-minute lecture that was carefully prepared, artfully crafted, substantively dense and delivered as though Toby and I were an auditorium full of people whose hostility Nixon took for granted but whose views he was sure he could influence by the sheer force of his experience, intelligence and—his favorite word—hard-headedness.

Nixon believed that the criticism of Bush for "sticking too long with Gorbachev" was justified since the alternative to Gorbachev had been Yeltsin, who was an improvement insofar as he had turned against communism and wanted to dismantle the Soviet Union. But now Yeltsin had supplanted Gorbachev and the alternative was "those crazy communists and fascists." Therefore Clinton should throw the weight of American power behind "this new and very different sort of guy in the Kremlin. He may be a drunk, but he's also the best we're likely to get in that screwed-up country over there. The main thing is, Yeltsin doesn't want to be our enemy. We've got to keep him from becoming our enemy, or from being replaced by someone who wants to be our enemy."

WHEN I RETURNED to my office, Brooke phoned to say that she had just had a call from the White House asking if the president could stop by our house that evening. The visit caused a stir in our neighborhood. The police towed several cars that were legally parked in front of our house. When I got home, the Secret Service stopped me from coming up the driveway. Brooke, who knew the agent in charge, had to vouch for me.

For an hour or so after the president arrived, he just wanted to kick back from work. Devin assured him that we had plenty of ice cream in the refrigerator; and Adrian brought out his saxophone, played a few show tunes and then turned the instrument over to Clinton for some jazz. The president was obviously in no hurry to leave, so Brooke invited him to stay for lamb chops.

After dinner, I told him about Nixon's advice.

"He's preaching to the converted," said Clinton. "In fact, he's preaching to the preacher." He said he was deeply worried by the strength of the Russian opposition: "If Yeltsin is going to stand up to all his enemies in the parliament, he's got to be able to show progress on the economy, and he can't do that unless we help him big-time." He was already preparing to submit his first budget to the Congress and wanted to "set something aside for Yeltsin."

As he'd told me on the beach at Hilton Head, Clinton wanted a fresh infusion of American assistance as a way of priming the pump for a massive international support by the G-7, which was due to hold its annual summit in Tokyo in July. The G-7 exercised considerable influence over the policies and programs of the International Monetary Fund and the World Bank, which had the deep pockets Clinton was looking for. He recalled his own role in pushing Bush to assemble a package of $24 billion in aid to the former Soviet Union in 1992—a dollar figure that made a splash when it was announced but a program that hadn't had much impact on the Russian economy because not much of the money could be delivered unless Russia restructured its economy.

Clinton wanted to do better in Tokyo, not necessarily by slapping a bigger price tag on the package but by designing contents that would reach "real Russians" and improve their lives.

THE IMF WAS the purview of the Treasury Department, so the next morning I arranged to get together with Larry Summers, the under secretary of Treasury for international affairs. In earlier administrations, Treasury had maintained a mistrustful and haughty distance from the State Department. Its officials did their best to shield international economic policy from the meddling of diplomats. That changed with the Clinton administration largely because of the powerful influence of Summers. He had confidence in his ability to protect Treasury's equities, and he was eager to participate as actively as possible in the formulation of policy toward the former Soviet Union.

At thirty-nine, Larry still qualified as a wunderkind. He had already been one of the youngest tenured professors in the history of Harvard, chief economist at the World Bank and a recipient of a prestigious award to the outstanding American economist under forty. Larry's brain was like a tank powered by a Lotus engine: it purred as it rolled over anything in its way. Over the next eight years, I was flattened more than once, but I usually found the experience educational.

As Larry and I learned our way around the bureaucracy at the beginning of the administration, we concluded that we were natural allies, and Larry quickly established himself as the intellectual and bureaucratic driving force behind the economic component of our policy toward the former Soviet Union. There, too, as Russia went, so went the neighborhood.

Larry's principal deputy for dealing with Russia was David Lipton, an economist with experience at the IMF who had been an adviser to Gaidar and other liberal Russians during the post-Soviet transition of 1991–92. Larry and David worked out a broad understanding with the Russian reformers, led by Gaidar, who were still in the government in early 1993: the U.S. and the other G-7 countries would, through the IMF and other international bodies, loan Russia the funds it needed to bolster the ruble, help pay foreign debts and buy food supplies, all with less stringent conditions than the IMF usually imposed on its debtors; for its part of the bargain, Russia would bring inflation under control, create incentives for domestic savings and investment, ensure the equitable collection of taxes and attract foreign capital.

To take these steps, the Russian government didn't just need funding from the West—it needed a governing consensus with the legislative branch; it needed the parliament to pass laws on property, contracts and taxation. In the spring of 1993, however, the Supreme Soviet had no interest in creating the legal and regulatory structures necessary for a modern economy. Instead, it was busy blocking the executive branch on every issue, from the ratification of START II to social and economic policy. The parliamentary opposition drew strength from an increasingly disgruntled public. Protestors in the streets regularly carried hammer-and-sickle flags, portraits of Lenin and Stalin and posters with the slogan "Down with capitalist ministers!"

THE MOST VULNERABLE of Yeltsin's ministers was Andrei Kozyrev, since he was the face and voice of Russian aspirations to be part of the West. In late February, he held his first meeting with Secretary Christopher in Geneva. In order to accompany Chris, I had to get a dispensation from the Senate, which had yet to confirm me in my post as ambassador-at-large. While it was my first trip abroad as a government official, it was not by any means my first ride on the ageing Boeing 707 that the U.S. Air Force made available to the secretary of state. As a reporter assigned to the State Department in the seventies and eighties, I'd logged hundreds of thousands of miles, including quite a few on this same aircraft when its principal passenger had been Henry Kissinger. But back then I'd been in steerage with the rest of the press, and now I was in what I thought of as business class—the flying staff office, equipped with computers, printers, copiers and secure telephones, immediately behind the secretary's private cabin. With the upgrade came a lot of work, mostly revising background papers to prepare for the secretary's use once we hit the ground.

As soon as we arrived at the Russian diplomatic mission in Geneva, Kozyrev told Chris he wanted to meet privately. Once they were alone, Kozyrev warned that he might be sacked at any time if the U.S. pressed its many advantages too hard; the new American administration must show "sensitivity" to Kozyrev's position, otherwise this lonely and beleaguered proponent of partnership would be replaced by a foreign minister less to our liking.

Chris found this approach off-putting in the extreme. It was an early glimpse of a danger that came with personal diplomacy: Russian liberals' penchant for a not-so-subtle kind of pressure tactic—"do what we say or you'll get somebody worse."[8]

WHILE KOZYREV was throwing himself on Chris's mercy, Dennis Ross, the former Baker aide whom Chris had asked to stay in the State Department to help him with the Middle East peace process, introduced me to Georgi Mamedov, the deputy foreign minister whom Dennis had urged me to regard as my principal point of contact the previous December. While Dennis went back to join Christopher, Mamedov and I peeled off for a walk through the nearby Botanical Gardens.

Most of Mamedov's American contacts called him "George," which he rather liked because it certified his status as an "Americanist." But the Slavist in me preferred to call him Yuri, his nickname among Russians, and he didn't object. His father, Enver Mamedov—a senior propagandist and expert on the U.S. for the Soviet Communist Party during the Brezhnev period—was an Azeri by nationality, hence his Muslim name (Mamedov was a Russianized version of Mohammed). Yuri's mother, Tamara Solovyova, had been active on the Moscow cultural scene. As a boy,

Mamedov had lived with his parents when they were posted to the U.S. Like Tedo Japaridze and many other Russian officials I had known over the years, Yuri had been a protégé of Georgi Arbatov's, having spent nearly eight years at the Institute for the Study of the U.S.A. and Canada in the seventies before joining the Soviet diplomatic corps.

Yuri had a gift for gab and a razzle-dazzle style that he could turn to any purpose—old-fashioned polemics, head-butting negotiation, insight into the roughhouse politics of his country or, for that matter, of mine. He had a wit that could be either lighthearted or mordant, and he peppered his banter with American colloquialisms, especially ones he'd picked up from gangster movies (he knew whole swatches of dialogue from *The Godfather* saga). Sometimes he would get the idioms slightly wrong, and sometimes stubbornly so, but even those quirks gave a customized vividness to his self-expression and added to the entertainment value of our conversations.

Yuri was very serious indeed about his own work on behalf of the new direction of Russian foreign policy, and about the work he and I would do together. He believed that Russia was undergoing a change for the better and that with the end of the cold war came an opportunity for genuine co-operation with the U.S. For him, "partnership" was not a vapid or cynical cliché, like "peace and friendship" in Soviet times—it was a noble project to which he wanted to devote the rest of his career.

His capacity for straight talk made him all the more effective in arguing his side's case and in probing for give on the American side. While he was always prepared, if the moment required, to engage in slash-and-burn debating tactics, his preferred activity was what he called joint brainstorming. Just as Dennis Ross had told me, I quickly found that once Yuri identified the nub of a problem, he threw himself with tenacity and ingenuity into solving it.

THE PRINCIPAL PROBLEM on Mamedov's mind that day, as we strolled among the tame peacocks and the exotic flora on the shore of Lake Geneva, was where to hold the first Clinton-Yeltsin summit. The Russians were no longer asking Clinton to come to Moscow: they'd settle for a third country. The U.S. had proposed Vancouver, Canada, in early April, since Clinton had other plans that would take him to Seattle and Portland at that time. Mamedov wanted to talk us out of Vancouver: the venue might be convenient for Clinton, but it would be awkward for Yeltsin to meet the American president "on the doorstep of the United States, not to mention on the territory of a NATO ally . . . Yeltsin's got enough problems without appearing to be in the U.S.'s hip pocket." Couldn't we hold the summit in Helsinki or Stockholm, since they were neutral capitals closer to Russia?

I checked with Chris, and the answer was no. Even though Vancouver was less than twenty miles from the U.S. border, Chris felt that was as much of a gesture as Clinton should make to a Russian leader who might be on his last legs.

"THINK BIGGER!"

Richard Nixon passed through Washington again on March 8, on his way home from Russia. This time he called on Clinton in the family quarters at the White House. Nixon urged Clinton to "pull out the stops" in backing Yeltsin and his government. Afterward, Nixon asked me to come by his hotel so that he could reinforce what he had told the president. He said he'd picked up hints at the White House that Clinton was under pressure from his political advisers to "tend to his knitting here in this country." Nixon was contemptuous of that line of thinking: "All that domestic stuff doesn't matter very much. Either the American economy will improve or it won't. If it does, Clinton will get credit, and if it doesn't, he'll get blamed. There's not much he can do about it. What Clinton will be remembered for is how he deals with Russia. And that means leading the rest of the world, especially those G-7 assholes, in support for what we're in favor of in Russia."

Late that night, the phone rang and I snapped out of a deep sleep when the White House operator said the president was calling. Clinton liked to wind down at the end of his working day, well into the night, by working the phones. He wanted to talk about his session with Nixon. He said Nixon was right in stressing the importance of Russia even if he was wrong in dismissing the domestic agenda. The Vancouver summit with Yeltsin, now set for April 4, should be "seen as something new," and there had to be "high-impact, high-visibility follow-up" at the G-7 meeting in Tokyo in July.

I'd gathered my thoughts enough to summarize the conversations I'd been having with Larry Summers about ways that the G-7 could help Russia put in place a social safety net to ameliorate the hardship that came with the privatization of state enterprises.

"That's exactly what we've got to help them do," said Clinton. "What Russia needs is a huge public works project . . . They're in a depression and Yeltsin has got to be their FDR. But he can't do that without our help. And that means us and the G-7."

THE NEXT DAY, I told Chris about the midnight phone call. Chris suggested I set down on paper what he called a "theory of the case" synthesizing what I understood to be Clinton's instincts and instructions with my own thinking and recommendations. The result was my first memorandum to the president, which I showed first to Chris. He sent it along to the White House on March 15 under the heading "A Strategic Alliance with Russian Reform":

> The prospect of your summit with Boris Yeltsin has concentrated all our minds on the challenge of dealing with a muscle-bound, palsied and demoralized giant. Russia has preoccupied your predecessors for nearly half a century because of its presumed strength. It threatens to complicate your presidency because of its evident weakness. . . . Until now most Americans have understood their government's policy toward the former Soviet Union primarily in terms of what we do *not* want to happen there. We don't want the economic distress and political turmoil to trigger a civil war. . . . We don't want a nuclear Yugoslavia in the heart of Eurasia. Nor do we want to see the rise of a new dictatorship that represses its own subjects, threatens its neighbors and requires the United States and its allies to return to a cold war footing. . . .
>
> Our objective and our policy can—and should—be put more positively. . . . Russia is on the path toward becoming a modern state, at peace with itself and the world, productively and prosperously integrated into the international economy, a source for raw materials and manufactured products, a market for American goods and services, and a partner for American diplomacy. It should be U.S. policy not just to prevent the worst but also to nurture the best that might happen in the former Soviet Union.

I urged that we not give in to pressures to change American policy in response to every shift, or even upheaval, of Russian politics. We shouldn't impose sanctions or suspend assistance every time the Russian government did something we didn't like:

> We need to make sure that we don't react spasmodically in a way that's intended to punish the bad guys who seem to have come out on top in

the latest twist of the plot but has the effect of punishing the good guys who will still be protagonists in the on-going drama. . . .

The most recent Russian Revolution, I wrote, was actually three in one: the Russians were trying to transform their country from a totalitarian system to a democracy; from a command economy to a market one; and from a multinational empire to a nation-state. On each score, they had already had some success—tentative, to be sure, but significant and encouraging nonetheless. They had reduced and nearly eliminated terror as the central organizing principle of political life. They were inching toward the adoption of institutions, laws and constitutional and parliamentary procedures to replace the tradition of absolute Kremlin rule. There were the first, unpretty but vigorous, even robust stirrings of private enterprise:

> Think of the [former Soviet Union] as a case of 280 million people emigrating—in many cases involuntarily—to a new country, or even to a new planet. We're trying to help them get where they're going. . . . We, and the Russians themselves, must keep in mind that the first two world-transforming events of this century, World War I and World War II, resulted in the loss of approximately 60 million lives. The meltdown of the Soviet Communist system has so far been relatively bloodless. That in itself is nothing less than a miracle—the greatest political miracle of our era. Doing what we can from the outside, marginal and modest as it may be, to keep that miracle going constitutes the greatest single task facing American foreign policy in the years to come.

ON MARCH 18, Clinton convened his advisers to review preparations for Vancouver. He was coming down with the flu and was listless and impatient as we gave him a lengthy recitation of Russia's deepening problems. But when we got around to what the U.S. could do to help, he perked up. Every time we mentioned an area for possible assistance—humanitarian relief, energy, housing, agriculture, stabilization of the currency—he asked why we couldn't do more. "Go back and think bigger!" he ordered.

Before long, he was giving us, the hard core of his Russia team, a pep talk, to the obvious consternation of his domestic advisers who were sitting in. I could hear them behind me fretting among themselves about how all these grandiose schemes for helping Russia would keep the administration from meeting its priority goals of reducing the budget deficit and stimulating the domestic economy.

George Stephanopoulos got up from his chair by the window, came over to me and whispered in my ear, "No new money! No new legislation!"

I found George's agitation out of place. I didn't owe him a private hearing in the middle of a briefing for the president. Besides, his argument was more with Clinton than with me, and I'd already heard enough from Clinton, going back to the transition, to know that George didn't stand a chance in winning that argument.

Clinton noticed the byplay. As we were breaking up, he caught my eye and said, "I'll worry about George and our Congress—you worry about Yeltsin and his."

THERE WAS PLENTY to worry about. The second week in March the parliament reduced Yeltsin's presidential powers, proclaimed itself the supreme authority of the land and endorsed the perilously inflationary policies of the Central Bank.

The Kremlin announced that Yeltsin would strike back with a televised address on Saturday, March 20. Tony Lake called early that morning and asked me to come to the White House to help gauge the implications of Yeltsin's speech for the Vancouver summit, then about two weeks off. I drove past the State Department and picked up Victoria Nuland, a foreign service officer who had joined my staff after several years covering the Russian parliament for our embassy in Moscow. She'd been on the phone with her colleagues there, who had just learned that Yeltsin was going to throw down the gauntlet to the parliament and would need an instant outpouring of international support.

When I arrived at the White House, I found the president in his private study off the Oval Office. He had two television sets turned on—one tuned to CNN so that he could watch the broadcast of Yeltsin's speech, the other to the NCAA East Regional basketball tournament between the Arkansas Razorbacks and the St. John's Redmen.

"You know who I'm rooting for in both cases," he said.

WHEN YELTSIN APPEARED on the screen, he was in full man-on-the-tank form. He announced that there would be a referendum on April 25 to decide once and for all who ran the country, the executive or the legislative branch. Until then, a "special rule of governing" would be in effect. That did not mean the dissolution of the parliament, but it did mean that all presidential decrees would remain in force, regardless of legislative action to suspend or revoke them.

For us watching from Washington, the question posed by the speech was whether Yeltsin's brinkmanship was sufficiently within the bounds of democratic and constitutional rule to justify our continued support. His reliance on the referendum had the virtue of taking the issue to the people, but his invocation of "special rule" had the look of martial law. Clinton's senior advisers who had assembled at the White House that day—Vice-President Gore, Secretary Christopher, Tony Lake, Sandy Berger and Madeleine Albright, the ambassador to the UN—were all worried that Clinton would stand by Yeltsin no matter what, even if he went off the rails of democracy. I had that concern myself. Chris spoke for the rest of us in warning the president not to let himself get drawn into "color commentary and judgment calls" on the legality or constitutionality of Yeltsin's position; we should limit ourselves to support for "principles and process," not Yeltsin himself.

"I agree with that," said the president, "but principles and process don't exist in a vacuum. What's going on over there is about people, in this case, some people versus other people. This is a zero-sum thing. They're not splitting the difference. That's why we've got to take sides. We can't dance around for too long. Let's get our minds into more than just what we're going to say to the press today. We've got to start thinking about what we're going to do when we meet with Yeltsin, and how we can use that meeting to keep his spirits up and keep him moving in the right direction."

Gore went back to his own office down the corridor from the president's to take a previously scheduled phone call from President Shevardnadze of Georgia. Russian-backed separatists had been shelling the Georgian Black Sea port of Sukhumi, and Gore was calling Shevardnadze to buck him up.

"Ask him what he thinks about Yeltsin's situation," said Clinton as Gore was leaving.

Gore didn't have to ask. It was the main subject on Shevardnadze's mind. Angry and frightened as he was about his own troubles, he, too, was riveted to the television, watching Yeltsin's speech. He asked Gore to pass along to Clinton an updated version of the advice I had heard from his envoys Tedo Japaridze and Gela Charkviani in January: the U.S. must support Yeltsin against communists who wanted to turn back the clock and re-create the Soviet Union. Yeltsin's victory, said Shevardnadze, was "the only hope" for Georgia.

Gore's report on his conversation with Shevardnadze reinforced Clinton's view. "Yeltsin's at an impasse with those characters in the parliament," he said, "and he's got to see it through and come out on top. He's not suspending civil liberties, right? He's taking his case to the people, right? And that's a time-honored tradition." He paused to scan the furrowed brows around him. "Look," he continued, "I know you're worried that I might end up backing a loser, but I'm not worried about that as long as he's the right loser. I've lost plenty of times myself. And besides, maybe he's just a little bit less likely to lose if we're there for him."

We went to Tony's office to craft a press statement that endorsed democracy rather than Yeltsin's move per se. When we took it back to the president, he did some editing to make it less equivocal and more encouraging than admonishing in its message to Yeltsin.[9] Once he was satisfied, he dismissed us again, more cheerfully than before: "Go with it! And don't worry, guys. Yeltsin may be down, but he's not out—just like my team!"

Arkansas had come back from a ten-point deficit at halftime to win 80–74.

Still, there was considerable unease among Clinton's advisers—again, myself included—that unlike the basketball game, the contest in Moscow was far from over and might end badly. Stephanopoulos worried that we were letting ourselves in for a replay of the "Who lost Russia?" that had flared briefly during the coup in 1991. Worse, he feared, we might be giving our seal of approval to a Russian leader who had just shown his true colors as a tyrant.[10]

In the public statements we put out during the course of the weekend, we did our best to depersonalize our support: the U.S. was backing the process of post-communist transition in Russia, not Yeltsin as an individual.

WE WERE PROTECTING the president but we weren't really speaking for him. Clinton had no interest in hedging his bet on Yeltsin. "I think he's the duly elected president of Russia," he said to a group of reporters the next day after attending church, "and he's a genuine democrat—small 'd'—and he is leading a country that is trying bravely to do two things: one, escape from communism into market economics, a world they never lived in before, and second, to preserve real democracy. That's a pretty tough job . . . I intend to do what I can to be supportive of that process, and to be supportive of him while he serves as president of Russia."

THAT EVENING, Larry Summers came over to my house to talk about how we could send an immediate signal of international support to Yeltsin. Larry had heard from Boris Fyodorov, the minister of finance, that Yeltsin intended to follow up on his speech by seizing control of the Central Bank and slowing down the reckless printing of rubles. Larry recommended that we be prepared to respond quickly by helping the Russian government pay pensions, stabilize prices and provide emergency food aid to stricken regions. Since these steps would address the needs of Russian citizens, they might help validate Yeltsin's determination to stick with anti-inflationary policies.

In the midst of my conversation with Larry, Clinton called from Arkansas, where he and Hillary had gone to visit her father, who was in the final stages of a terminal illness. Even in the midst of a family crisis, Clinton had been thinking about Yeltsin, whose situation seemed to be growing more dire by the hour. The opposition deputies had declared Yeltsin's decrees unconstitutional and were now threatening to remove him from office and replace him with Vice-President Alexander Rutskoi, who was already cutting deals with prominent hard-liners, promising to appoint them to the power ministries. A new word—like *partnyorstvo* and *prezident,* borrowed from English—reverberated in Russian politics: "impeachment."

"This thing is getting serious," said Clinton. "We've got no time to lose."

I summarized Larry's latest plan, based on his conversation with Fyodorov.

"Good," said the president, "keep at it. We're a big, rich country with deep pockets. We need big, bold ideas. We're not worth shit if we can't put together a bigger package than the one we've been talking about. We've got to remember that we really do have a dog in this fight."[11]

OVER THE NEXT FEW WEEKS, Larry worked with the Canadians, West Europeans and Japanese on a program to be unveiled at the G-7 summit in Tokyo in July aimed at supporting stabilization of the Russian economy and the privatization of state assets. I concentrated on what the U.S. could do on its own to provide emergency food, fuel and medicine and to begin helping the reformers stitch together the fabric of democracy and capitalism.

By then it was well known throughout the U.S. government that the president wanted an increase in the size and an acceleration in the delivery of American assistance to the former Soviet Union. That made it relatively easy to assemble a proposal for $1 billion—about $600 million more than the Bush administration had allocated and nearly a 50 percent increase in our own initial request for fiscal year 1994. We presented the $1 billion package to Clinton on March 18, telling him we thought it was as much as the traffic would bear on the Hill.

"Not bold enough," he said. "You guys tell me what you think needs to be done on the merits. Don't worry about how Congress will react. I'll deal with those guys. That's my job, to sell it to the Hill."

Only when we came back to the president on March 23 with a package worth $1.6 billion was he satisfied. Larry reviewed the latest version of the G-7 program, including a currency stabilization fund, World Bank loans, and investments by the European Bank for Reconstruction and Development. Especially with the devaluation of the ruble, said Summers, $100 million in pension support would give us "big bang for the buck."

The president nodded enthusiastically. "That could be the best $100 million we ever spent."

His domestic advisers tried, as they had before, to warn him off any measures that might strain or break the budget, and Clinton, once again, blew them off. "If it's worth doing, it's worth doing right," he said, ending the debate. Turning back to Larry and me, he pushed us to do more in every area, especially those that would make it easier for Russia to demilitarize its economy: housing for decommissioned military officers, work programs for nuclear scientists and assistance in dismantling weaponry. "I don't care what it costs," he said, "it'll be a bargain. If Russia goes bad—if those guys trying to impeach Yeltsin win—we'll be back here talking about reversing our defense cuts and spending really big money to wage a new cold war."[12]

That afternoon I had an appointment with the Senate Foreign Relations Committee to testify in connection with my nomination to be ambassador-at-large and the head of the new office for the former Soviet Union. With Brooke and my father seated behind me, I made the case for backing the Russian government with increased financial assistance. There was no opposition to speak of. Senator Joseph Biden, the presiding Democrat, seemed to be speaking for the whole committee when he urged continuing support for Yeltsin as "the only horse to ride."

WHILE I WAS ON CAPITOL HILL, Andrei Kozyrev was at the State Department predicting that Yeltsin might not last a week. In the privacy of Chris's back office, Kozyrev said that Yeltsin faced a "quasi-constitutional coup." The moment of truth would be the coming weekend, March 27–28, when the parliament voted on a resolution of impeachment. If the measure passed, said Kozyrev, Vice-President Rutskoi, whom he called "a dangerous psychotic surrounded by fanatics," would take power.

Later that day, when I met with Kozyrev privately, he told me he was feeling lonely in the Russian government as an advocate of cooperation with the U.S. We needed, somehow, to "institutionalize" the concept of partnership. One possibility, he said, would be to set up a commission cochaired by Vice-President Gore and Prime Minister Chernomyrdin. That way, Chernomyrdin, who still had fairly broad support in the parliament, would have more of a personal stake in the American connection. Also, foreign economic assistance would be politically more palatable in Russia—less like "patronizing charity"—if it were put in the framework of U.S.-Russian cooperation. However, Kozyrev did not dare officially propose the idea himself, and he wasn't sure he could sell it to Yeltsin as something to suggest to Clinton in Vancouver. Better for Clinton to raise it.

The proposal appealed to me immediately. Among other things, it would help on our side to have the vice-president personally engaged in Russia policy. Given Yeltsin's erratic streak, the presidential connection was an uncertain flywheel in the machinery of U.S.-Russian relations. It would help to have another channel at the second-to-highest level. I told Kozyrev I'd take soundings within my own government and see if we could get Clinton to float the idea in Vancouver.

The next day, I went to see Leon Fuerth, the vice-president's national security adviser. A former foreign service officer who had gone to work as a congressional staff member in the seventies, Leon had been working for Al Gore for a dozen years. I'd rarely known two people more closely wired into each other's brains than the vice-president and his principal aide. They had many of the same mannerisms of speech, including a fondness for metaphors drawn from science, mathematics, cybernetics and high technology. For both of them, problems existed to be solved by deduction, by careful weighing of alternatives and by dogged advocacy.

While I summarized Kozyrev's idea, Leon half closed his eyes and looked off into space, thinking hard. After I'd finished, he remained silent, still thinking.

"I like it," he finally said. "I think the vice-president will like it." He promised to work on his boss while I looked for an opportunity to speak to Clinton.

ON SUNDAY, MARCH 28, as the deputies of the People's Congress gathered in Saint George's Hall of the Kremlin, tens of thousands of pro-Yeltsin demonstrators—including Gaidar and Elena Bonner, the widow of the late dissident physicist and Nobel Peace Prize winner Andrei Sakharov—gathered on one side of Red Square carrying Yeltsin's portrait and the Russian tricolor, while on the other side, a much smaller crowd waved the hammer-and-sickle flag and chanted their support for impeachment. The measure required a two-thirds majority, or 689 votes. It failed by 72. At least for now, Yeltsin would survive. He emerged from the hall, looked around for a vehicle to mount, found a truck and from there thanked the cheering crowd in terms intended to recapture his moment of greatest glory in August 1991: "The communists failed to mount a coup. They were defeated by the people, by reform, by democracy, by the young Russia."

I put in a call to the president to give him the news. He phoned me back that evening, reaching me at Pizzeria Uno on Connecticut Avenue where I had taken my family and a group of friends. Clinton was in Arkansas at his father-in-law's bedside. He sounded exhausted. After describing the sadness in his family, he told me he was also having to "fight the blues" about the trouble he faced from Congress in getting approval of a hefty aid package for Russia. Just before leaving Washington, he'd had a rough session with congressional leaders who put him on notice—just as Stephanopoulos had done repeatedly in White House meetings—that any major foreign-policy project with a big price tag would jeopardize the administration's goal of quick and impressive progress toward a balanced budget. Clinton said he had no second thoughts about the $1.6 billion he'd be asking the Congress for in U.S. aid, but he saw more clearly than before the need to back it up with a G-7 package that not only had a big price tag but that had a major impact on the Russian citizenry, in contrast to his predecessor's: "I want what we do in the G-7 to be real, and I want it to have support here at home. In other words, I don't want to be George Bush Junior."

It seemed to brighten his spirits somewhat when I told him about Kozyrev's suggestion of a U.S.-Russian intergovernmental commission to be co-chaired by Gore and Chernomyrdin. Clinton accepted the plan instantly, saying he liked the idea of involving Gore in a "central, highly operational role on the biggest foreign-policy issue we'll have in this administration." Gore's engagement would help generate public and congressional support for Russia, and it would also give us additional leverage with the Russians themselves.

AFTER CLINTON RETURNED TO Washington, he and Gore summoned the top congressional leaders to the Oval Office for another go at them about the need to "think big and act big." Clinton concentrated his blandishments on Bob Dole, the minority leader of the Senate, who was one of the leading skeptics.

"Bob," said the president, "you could summon the lessons of history better than me. You had to go off to World War II and put your life at risk because the countries then in the saddle screwed up the aftermath of World War I."

Dole's resistance seemed to melt. He promised to help when the bill came before the Congress.

In a separate meeting with members of the House of Representatives, Clinton let himself be upstaged by Newt Gingrich, the House minority whip, who gave a stem-winding speech on the overriding importance of helping Russia at "one of the great defining moments of our time." This most partisan of Republicans was also a former professor of history and a self-styled internationalist.

Clinton thanked Gingrich profusely, then whispered to me as the meeting was breaking up, "Ol' Newt's trying to do to me exactly what I did to Bush a year ago—out-Russia me. That's fine, as long as I can keep him with me."

FIRST IMPRESSIONS

My confirmation passed the Senate the day before the opening of the Vancouver summit, just in time for me to catch a flight to Portland, Oregon, where Clinton and Gore were participating in an environmental conference. That night, in the Benson Hotel, Clinton administered the oath of office. Secretary of Labor Bob Reich, a friend of Clinton's and mine from Oxford, held the Gideon Bible from my hotel room, while Gore, John

Podesta, the president's staff secretary, and Toria Nuland, my assistant in the State Department, looked on.

After a quick toast with beer from the mini-bar, Clinton told me he'd been thinking back over seminal meetings his predecessors had held with Kremlin leaders, particularly the 1961 summit in Vienna at which John F. Kennedy allowed Nikita Khrushchev to get the upper hand in a debate over ideology. The encounter left Khrushchev confident he could push Kennedy around over Berlin and Cuba.

When he dredged up this bit of history, I first thought Clinton was confiding in me his anxiety about what Yeltsin might try to do to him in Vancouver. But as he spun out his thinking, it turned out he was saying just the opposite: he was confident that Yeltsin would not "pull a Khrushchev since he needs us a hell of a lot more than we need him. We're into a whole new deal here. This isn't about which of us is going to beat the other guy in some great global contest. It's about whether we can help him beat the odds of what he's up against at home."

Maybe, I said, but Yeltsin would still be out to test Clinton's mettle, to extract as many concessions and high-visibility favors as possible and to show off in front of the Russian officials he was bringing with him to Vancouver, a number of whom were poised to abandon Yeltsin and join the opposition if the April 25 referendum went badly. I urged Clinton not to appear too eager to accommodate Yeltsin; he should make Yeltsin work for a good meeting.

Clinton was impatient with this advice. "Look," he said, "Yeltsin's already working plenty hard at home. I'll get further with him if I don't add too much to his troubles."

THE SUMMIT BEGAN on Saturday, April 3, with a meeting between the presidents in a so-called restricted format—that is, with just a few aides and interpreters present. The purpose was to break the ice, begin to establish a personal bond and give the two leaders a chance to sound each other out on the agenda before a more formal encounter between the delegations over dinner that evening and a full plenary session the next day.

Much as he'd done in their first meeting during the presidential campaign the previous summer, Clinton tried to win Yeltsin over at the outset by proclaiming his admiration for what Yeltsin was trying to accomplish against heavy odds. "I know this is not an easy time in your country," Clinton began. He said he wanted to concentrate at the summit on "what I can do that would most help you between now and April 25."

Yeltsin listened with obvious impatience as Clinton began to unwrap the contents of the assistance package, then interrupted. Once again, like the summer before, Yeltsin didn't like the implication that the U.S. was coming to his rescue. Yes, he needed outside help, but not too much, since a "dramatic increase" in American aid would bring him "under fire from the opposition: they will say Russia is under the U.S.'s thumb." He was looking for a "modest" boost in U.S. assistance as a demonstration that the outside world stood ready to help Russia in its transition.

There was one area, however, where Yeltsin said he needed as much help as possible and as soon as possible, and that was in emergency funds to build housing for the Russian officers whom Yeltsin had promised to withdraw from the Baltic states in 1994. In our own program, we had set aside $6 million for this purpose. When Clinton mentioned that figure, Yeltsin said he needed much more, adding that he could raise this request only in private, since it was embarrassing for him to talk about the wretched conditions in which the once-proud Russian army was living.

"Tents, Bill!" he said. "Can you imagine? They're living in tents!" He had to do something to "keep the military calm" when, in addition to pulling out of the Baltics, he was cutting Russia's overall troop levels approximately by half.

Clinton immediately promised to beef up support for officer housing.

"Good!" said Yeltsin. With that piece of business requiring American magnanimity out of the way, Yeltsin went on the attack, complaining about various pieces of cold war legislation still on the books in the U.S. that had the effect, in Yeltsin's view, of "treating Russia as a communist country, which is offensive to me as a democrat." First on his list of examples was an American law, the Jackson-Vanik amendment, that Congress had passed in 1974 linking free trade with the U.S. to freedom of emigration from the former Soviet Union. Many activists in the American Jewish community wanted to retain Jackson-Vanik for the leverage they felt it gave the U.S. over the Russian government's treatment of Jews, but it had virtually no impact on the Russian economy or on U.S.-Russian trade. Yeltsin had a similar objection to Captive Nations Week, an annual observance established in 1959 to draw attention to the plight of nations like Poland and Hungary when they were part of the Soviet empire. No one in Congress wanted to expend the energy or take the political risk of rescinding this anachronism, nor did anyone in the administration want to see Clinton waste his political capital on third-rate, mostly symbolic issues. Yet Yeltsin stayed on the offensive—jabbing, wheedling, even trying to mousetrap Clinton into approving public statements that would be interpreted as American concessions.

None of this seemed to bother Clinton. When the time came to thank Yeltsin for a good first meeting, he seemed to mean it.

I was puzzled, especially given Clinton's recollection on the eve of the summit of the cautionary tale about Kennedy and Khrushchev in Vienna. When I had a chance to speak to him alone, I asked him why he was letting Yeltsin off so easy. Wasn't there a danger that, given the importance of first impressions, Yeltsin would conclude that Clinton was a pushover?

"Nope," he said emphatically, "he's not so much trying to make me look bad as trying to make himself look good with his real enemies back home. Vienna was about Khrushchev versus Kennedy—what's going on here is Yeltsin versus those guys who are trying to do him in."

He instructed George Stephanopoulos to tell the press that he'd found Yeltsin "full of piss and vinegar, a real fighter," and then added—not for use with the press—"I do my best when I'm under the gun, and so does this guy. He's not deterred by long odds, and now he's at the top of his form."

THAT COULD HARDLY BE SAID when the two delegations embarked on a boat ride around Vancouver Island that afternoon. We were barely away from the dock before Yeltsin had downed three scotches. At dinner that evening, he knocked back four glasses of wine and ate barely a bite. Chris passed George Stephanopoulos a note: "No food, bad sign. Boat ride was liquid." Keeping count of Yeltsin's intake was to become a standard feature of summitry.

Yeltsin's speech grew sloshy, his message sappy ("Beeell, we're not rivals—we're *friends!*"). His aides eyed him ever more nervously as the evening went on. They tried to shoo off waiters with drinks, only to be countermanded by their president.

Our own president was unfazed. He seemed rather to enjoy Yeltsin's antics. Besides, Yeltsin was in an obliging mood, so it seemed to Clinton like a good time to try out the idea of the commission that Kozyrev had suggested we propose. It would be headed, Clinton explained, by the vice-president.

A cloud passed over Yeltsin's face and the word *"Nyyyetttt!"* rolled like thunder.

Kozyrev, sitting next to Yeltsin, went pale. Clinton realized what was wrong. "Wait, Boris!" he said, laughing. "Let me finish! I'm talking about *my* vice-president, Al Gore, not yours! On the Russian side the chairman will be your prime minister, Chernomyrdin."

It took Yeltsin a moment to absorb this clarification. Once reassured that Alexander Rutskoi had no place in the plan, he brightened: "Great idea, Bill! Let's do it!"

That evening, back in the presidential hotel suite, Chris, Tony and I lamented the prospect of having to conduct high-stakes diplomacy under the conditions we'd witnessed during the day. Clinton told us to relax. "I've seen a little of this problem in my time," he said, referring to his experience growing up with an alcoholic stepfather. "At least Yeltsin's not a mean drunk."

IT WAS A COMMON PRACTICE at summits for experts on the two delegations to pair off and try to solve, or at least manage, problems that might otherwise dominate and sour the leaders' sessions. That happened the first day and well into the night in Vancouver.

At issue was nonproliferation—the effort by responsible governments, working in concert, to prevent lethal technology from falling into the hands of irresponsible ones. Russia already posed a serious problem in this regard. The most flagrant case of Russian proliferation was a contract Moscow had with Iran to build a nuclear reactor. If completed, the project would contribute to the covert nuclear-weapons program of a regime that supported international terrorism and violently opposed the Middle East peace process. The Bush administration had tried, without success, to persuade the Russians to restrict the deal and therefore balked at easing American restrictions on Russian high-technology sales in the West.

During the first presidential meeting in Vancouver on Saturday, Yeltsin had cited the U.S. position as yet another discriminatory throwback to the cold war.[13] He and Clinton instructed two members of their delegations who were knowledgeable on the subject to thrash it out and report back to them the next day. That night, Lynn Davis, the undersecretary of state for arms control and nonproliferation, squared off against Victor Mikhailov, Russia's minister of atomic energy. Lynn had worked on the arcane substance of nonproliferation for many years and was experienced in the diplomacy of the subject as well, having served at a high level in the Pentagon during the Carter administration. Mikhailov's domain was more than a mere ministry—it was a rich, powerful remnant of the Soviet military-industrial complex that was alive and well in its post-Soviet incarnation.

Lynn patiently explained to Mikhailov the logic of the U.S. position. Russia's transformation into a modern state would depend in large measure on whether it could convert its vast natural resources, technical expertise and production capacity from military to civilian purposes. We could help by underwriting the conversion of defense industries and enabling U.S. aerospace companies to launch commercial satellites into space aboard Russian rockets that had originally been developed to hurl thermonuclear warheads at the U.S. But for us to justify the necessary changes in American law, Russia had to adopt and enforce export controls that met international standards. In exchange for the long-term benefits of access to Western markets that the U.S. was prepared to support, it was reasonable to expect Russia to resist the temptation to make a fast buck off the likes of the Iranians. The restraint we were asking the Russians to show in their dealings with Iran was compatible with Russia's own security interests, since it was hard to imagine why Russia would want to hasten the day when Iran had a nuclear-weapons capability.

For three hours, the chain-smoking Mikhailov harangued Lynn on how outrageous it was that the U.S., under the self-righteous guise of concern for nonproliferation, was trying to keep Russia out of a legitimate market for its nuclear technology.

It was the testiest high-level exchange between the two governments since the Clinton administration came into office, and it augured years of trouble ahead—starting the next morning when Clinton and Yeltsin reconvened with their technical experts and other advisers.

WHEN THE TWO DELEGATIONS met on Sunday, April 4, they squared off across a long table, the presidents in the center, flanked by their ministers and assistants. From the outset, it was clear that Yeltsin was, if anything, even feistier than he'd been during the private session the day before. Now he had an audience to impress, particularly on his side of the table. He wanted word to get back to Moscow, including to his political enemies there, that he had put the new American president on notice that Russia wasn't going to let itself be pushed around.

He called on Mikhailov to report on his discussions with Lynn. It was the only point during the summit when Yeltsin turned to a member of his team on a major subject. Oozing sarcasm, Mikhailov commented that he had found that "Dr. Davis is a very tough lady" who was not sufficiently respectful of Russia's legitimate commercial and security interests—or, for that matter, of its sovereignty: what Russia sold, and to whom, was none of the U.S.'s business.

ON THE OTHER SECURITY ISSUES, Yeltsin alone spoke for the Russian side, but he galloped through the agenda in a way that suggested he was interested more in creating the overall effect of being in charge than he was in achieving concrete results. His technique was to pretend to have an inspired idea on the spur of the moment about how to achieve a breakthrough on a highly technical arms-control issue that had been in dispute for years, then try to browbeat a concession out of Clinton on the spot.

"Let's you and me decide this right now, Bill!" he would say, banging the table with the flat of his hand. "You're a statesman, I can see it! You're a man of vision! We must seize the moment!"

In fact, his proposals were not off the cuff at all—they were thinly disguised versions of familiar Russian positions that earlier U.S. administrations had been fending off over the years. When Tony Lake, Lynn Davis or I objected, Yeltsin would look daggers at us and curl his hand into a fist, all the more menacing and clublike because of the missing thumb from a boyhood accident.

"Bill," he intoned with mock solemnity, "your bureaucrats are trying to stop us from making decisions that only presidents can make!"

"That's an interesting idea, Boris," Clinton kept saying mildly. "Let's have our people look into it." Thus ever so gently rebuffed, Yeltsin would shrug and move on to the next item on a wish list that his own bureaucrats had drawn up for him.

As with the private session the day before, I worried that Clinton was allowing Yeltsin to dominate the meeting, so I passed him a note: "You're getting the post–cold war version of the Khrushchev Vienna treatment."

He wrote back, "Yes, but he knows it's different and so do I. This is all show. He needs us."

FINALLY, AND MERCIFULLY, the time set aside for discussion of security issues expired, with nothing of substance agreed and plenty to worry about for the future. The next item on the agenda was economics. The demeanor of both presidents changed markedly. Now Clinton was in charge while Yeltsin, for all his earlier disclaimers, was a supplicant. Clinton briefly summarized the contents of the $1.6 billion U.S. package, taking care to describe its purpose as cooperation rather than assistance, then gave the floor to Lloyd Bentsen, the former Texas senator and 1988 vice-presidential candidate who was secretary of the Treasury. Working from a paper that Larry Summers had prepared for him, Bentsen gave a preview of the resources that the G-7, at the Tokyo summit in July, might make available to bolster Russian reform.

Yeltsin furrowed his brow, first in concentration, then in impatience, then in what looked like desperation. I guessed what was bothering him. July was too late to do him any good in the referendum, now only three weeks off. He began to scribble furiously on a piece of notepaper, then passed it across the table to Bentsen, who was still talking. Bentsen, taken aback, paused and showed me the note. Yeltsin locked his eyes on Bentsen and nodded meaningfully while I whispered a translation in the secretary's ear. "It would be good," Yeltsin had written in block letters, "if we could receive $500 million before April 25."

Bentsen, recovering, ignored the interruption and continued his presentation. While he was talking, I wrote out a translation of Yeltsin's note and showed it to Clinton, who gave me a quick I-told-you-so wink. As far as he was concerned, all the other issues that had come up at the summit—arms control, security and nonproliferation—were matters to be delegated to Chris, Lynn and myself, along with the newly constituted match-up of Gore and Chernomyrdin. Clinton's own job, as he saw it, was to give Yeltsin a political boost. He couldn't quite accommodate Yeltsin's request for a Treasury check for half a billion dollars on the spot. The money would have to wait until the G-7 met in July and Congress voted on the U.S. aid bill in the fall. In the meantime, rhetoric would have to do.

In preparing for a joint press conference with Yeltsin that would bring the curtain down on the summit, Chris, Tony and I urged the president to cast what he said as much as possible in terms of Russian reform as a process and Russian reformers as a plural noun, rather than focus on our support of Yeltsin. Clinton understood the point and followed our advice, up to a point. "We know where we stand," he said to the press. "We are with Russian democracy. We are with Russian reforms." Then, as the mantra built to its climax, Clinton slipped in the telltale pronoun: "We actively support reform and reformers and you and Russia."

And you, he had said, meaning the man at his side, his new friend Boris, who was heading back to Moscow to resume the fight of his life, with Clinton backing him all the way.

WHILE THE TWO PRESIDENTS were saying their good-byes, I met briefly with Mamedov. He seemed upbeat to an extent that I found odd, given how shaky Yeltsin's performance had been and how many issues, particularly in the area of Russia's nuclear cooperation with Iran, seemed to loom larger now than before the summit.

"Our presidents seemed to get along all right," I said, "but they left plenty for us to do."

"Don't underestimate the importance of their chemistry," said Yuri. "If they set the tone and direction, we can solve the problems."

He and I agreed that we should formalize the channel between us. We would meet several times a year, alternating between capitals, for a day or two of consultations that included key colleagues from around our governments. Yuri proposed that we call ourselves the Strategic Stability Group. That phrase implied the essence of what mattered most to the Russian side: predictability and a semblance of parity in relations with the United States.

We originally conceived of the group as a kind of early-warning mechanism for scanning the horizon and thinking about the big picture, but it quickly became a device for crisis management as well. The requirements of preparing for regular meetings with an American interagency group helped Yuri form alliances within the Russian bureaucracy and work out common positions with the Defense Ministry, the intelligence services and the Kremlin. Our get-togethers gave Yuri and me more opportunities than would otherwise have been the case to try our hand at unsnarling problems that had developed between our governments.

ON THE WAY BACK to Washington from Vancouver, Clinton gathered his advisers in the conference room aboard Air Force One. He told us he was prepared to go to Congress for funds beyond those that he had already asked for. Several of us spent the five-hour flight preparing an expanded request and sketching out a structure, agenda and timetable for what we were already starting to call the Gore-Chernomyrdin commission. Two days later, on April 6, we gave the president a new proposal for $2.5 billion in assistance to the nations of the former Soviet Union. Of that about two-thirds would go to Russia on the theory that success there would help lift the other former republics out of their own troubles.

Direct U.S. assistance was fundamentally different from the G-7 package. Rather than going into the Russian Treasury to help finance projects, pay bills and restructure the economy as a whole, the American program would reach recipients outside the government and to a large extent outside Moscow. It was targeted on those parts of the population that had been particularly hard hit by food and medicine shortages; on the private sector, especially small businesses; on independent media outlets; on nongovernmental organizations promoting civil society and rule of law; on public-interest advocacy groups, stock markets, start-up political parties and labor unions. Most of the help was in the form of technical assistance—i.e., know-how provided by American experts under contract to the U.S. government—so there was little cash to be siphoned off by corrupt local officials. We would also ask Congress to provide Russia with specialized equipment to help dismantle strategic missiles and bombers under the terms of past arms control agreements and safely dispose of the nuclear material from warheads. Another centerpiece was an exchange program that would bring tens of thousands of students and young professionals from Russia and other new independent states to the U.S. for two weeks to two years. Most Russians had never been out of their country, and very few had been to the U.S.[14]

A LITTLE MORE THAN TWO WEEKS after his return from Vancouver, Yeltsin tried to land a knockout blow against his opponents. On Saturday, April 24, he published the outlines of a new constitution that would strengthen the presidency and replace the Supreme Soviet with a new parliament that jettisoned the word "soviet"; it was to be called the Federal Assembly and would consist of a lower house, the State Duma, and an upper house, the Federation Council.[15]

The next day, the Russian people voted in a referendum that the pro-Yeltsin newspaper *Izvestia* said gave the citizens of Russia a chance to choose between liberty and a form of communism that was "mutating into fascism." The referendum was framed in the form of four questions that the parliamentary deputies hoped would elicit a response that could be construed as a repudiation of the president: (1) Do you have confidence in Yeltsin? (2) Do you approve of his policies? (3) Should there be early elections for the presidency? (4) Should there be early elections for a new parliament?

Clinton followed the referendum as though it were an American election. He called me a number of times during the day and into the evening to see what was happening. Not until the next day did we know the results: a healthy margin of victory for Yeltsin on the key questions of confidence in his leadership, approval of his policies and, crucially, the need for a new parliament.

Clinton called Yeltsin to congratulate him and released a statement hailing the outcome as good news "not only for the people of Russia, but for the people of the United States and all the people of the world. . . . This is a victory that belongs to the Russian people and to the courage of Boris Yeltsin, but I am very glad that the United States supported steadfastly the process of democracy in Russia."

Yeltsin's win, however partial and tentative, gave us a boost with our own Congress. It was now easier to make the case that the forces of reform stood a chance against those of reaction and that Yeltsin himself was likely to be around for a while, and it was harder for opponents of our policy to accuse us of backing a loser.[16]

On May 3, Clinton made his first appearance as president at the annual White House Correspondents' Dinner, where tradition required him to roast himself. "When I first took this job," he said, "I dreamed that in a hundred days, I'd pick up the newspaper and read about a popular president who had broken the gridlock and gotten popular approval for a dramatic economic program and enjoyed the support of his people; and I did, and I resent the hell out of Boris Yeltsin." The line drew laughter and applause.

For a brief moment, Clinton was pleased to be riding Yeltsin's coattails.

CHAPTER 3

THE SPINACH TREATMENT

Honesty is the best policy, and spinach is the best vegetable.

Popeye

CCORDING TO THE PLAN we had mapped out for the second quarter of 1993, the path from Vancouver was supposed to lead straight to Tokyo. That was where the Group of Seven major democracies would open their arms and checkbooks to Boris Yeltsin. The back-to-back summits, in April and July, were supposed to dramatize the priority that the G-7, following the U.S.'s lead, was giving to the Russian economy.

But the map was not the territory. The U.S. and Russia spent most of the three months between the Vancouver and Tokyo summits managing disagreements over other issues.

The most severe and chronic source of tension was the conflict in Bosnia. The violent dissolution of Yugoslavia had started in the summer of 1991. In rapid succession, the former Yugoslav republics headed for the exit, spilling blood on the way: first Slovenia, then Croatia. Bosnia was the most complex in its ethnic and religious composition. Its population was divided into three groups: Orthodox Serbs, Catholic Croats and Slavs whose ancestors had converted to Islam under Ottoman rule. Serbia's leader, Slobodan Milošević—a communist hack turned businessman turned Serb jingoist—wanted to annex those parts of Bosnia that had Serb majorities. Fearing precisely that sort of partition, the Bosnian Muslims demanded independence for the republic as a whole. With Milošević's political and military backing, the Bosnian Serbs attacked the capital, Sara-jevo, and other predominantly Muslim areas. They turned city streets into snipers' alleys, lobbed mortars into village squares, committed mass mur-der and mass rape and set up concentration camps. By the time the Clin-ton administration came into office, Bosnia had already experienced the worst outbreak of political violence in Europe since World War II.

The horror in the former Yugoslavia put in perspective what was, and wasn't, happening in the former Soviet Union. Like Yugoslavia, the USSR was coming apart at the seams, but unlike Yugoslavia, it was doing so peacefully. It could have been otherwise. If a post-Soviet Russian leader had tried to create a Greater Russia that incorporated Belarus and those parts of Ukraine, northern Kazakhstan and the Baltic states that were populated by Russian speakers, there could have been conflict across eleven time zones with tens of thousands of nuclear weapons in the mix. Yeltsin deserved—and received—credit for insisting on the conversion of the old republic boundaries into new international ones, and for keeping in check the forces of revanchism among communist and nationalist deputies in the Supreme Soviet.

But Yeltsin's government and the U.S. differed over what to do about Milošević and the warlords he was abetting in Bosnia. Already in the last year of the Bush administration, it was apparent that nothing was going to stop the Serb rampage unless the United Nations stepped in and used force, presumably supported by the airpower of the North Atlantic Treaty Organization, since there was no other international body with the mili-tary wherewithal or political will. That prospect was repugnant to many in Russia. Among intellectuals, there had long been sympathy for the Serbs, who were, like most Russians, Orthodox Slavs. With Marxist-Leninist in-ternationalism now in tatters, pan-Slavism was making a comeback in Russia. So was a fear of "the green menace"—the Islamic threat to Chris-tendom. For the U.S. and other Western nations to be taking the Bosnian Muslims' side against the Serbs was just one more reason for Yeltsin's ene-mies to denounce him for his delusional notion that Russia and the West could be partners.

For their part, Russian liberals knew that Milošević was a scoundrel and that to defend him was disgraceful, but they feared that Western military action would set off a new cold war in the Balkans and, closer to home, stir up a xenophobic backlash in Russian politics.

Andrei Kozyrev was obsessed with this danger. It overrode all other considerations in his mind. In the spring of 1993, he was desperate to head off even the threat of force against the Serbs.

With the Russians running interference for them in the UN, the Serbs felt they had a free hand to commit massive and systematic violence, bombing Muslim villages in eastern Bosnia in flagrant violation of a so-called no-fly zone that the UN had proclaimed over the area. The U.S. pressed for a resolution in the Security Council to warn that NATO would shoot down Serb aircraft if they continued to flout the no-fly zone. Kozyrev came to Washington in late March in a panic. If Russia allowed the resolution to pass, he said, it could cost Yeltsin the votes he needed to avoid impeachment and we'd end up with "a Russian Milošević in the Kremlin."

Secretary Christopher replied that we couldn't let Russian domestic politics provide the Serbs with international cover for a rampage that imperiled the peace of Europe.

A few weeks later, during the Vancouver summit, Clinton urged Yeltsin to support a tightening of UN sanctions against Serbia. Yeltsin refused. For him to go along with such a measure, he said, could tip the April 25 referendum against him. "The Serbs are communists," he said, "and they're working with our communists who are at my throat!"

In the end, the UN Security Council voted to stiffen sanctions, but with Russia abstaining. The Serbs were unimpressed. Within days they attacked the town of Srebrenica, sending thousands of Muslim refugees into the mountains. The United Nations responded by creating six "safe areas." The term immediately became a cruel joke both for the Muslims who sought refuge and for the foreign troops, who were too lightly armed to defend themselves, much less the Bosnian civilians in their charge.

Yet Kozyrev still tried to keep toothless diplomacy alive. After Vancouver, he was pinning his hopes on a UN peace plan that would divide Bosnia into ten ethnically defined enclaves, all ostensibly under a central government in Sarajevo but each with a high degree of autonomy. Clinton and Christopher believed that the scheme, particularly in its power-sharing arrangement, was too complicated to work and too lenient in its treatment of the Serbs.

In order to put more muscle into the UN's response to the almost daily atrocities that the Serbs were committing, the president dispatched Chris to Europe in early May with a proposal for "lift-and-strike": the UN Security Council would lift its arms embargo on Bosnia, so that the Muslims would better be able to defend themselves, and authorize air strikes against the Serbs if they persisted in their attacks.

As soon as it was known that Christopher was coming to Europe, Radovan Karadžić, the Bosnian Serb leader, announced with fanfare that he accepted the UN peace plan, but with the proviso that the Bosnian Serb parliament would have to give its own approval.

In London, Paris, Rome and Bonn, Chris found the Europeans unwilling to support lift-and-strike, especially in the wake of Karadžić's apparent concession. In Moscow, Yeltsin told Chris that "all this war talk" was pointless now that the Serb parliament was about to endorse Karadžić's acceptance of the UN plan. He turned for confirmation to Vitaly Churkin, a smooth operator who was the Russians' point man for the Balkans.

"Absolutely!" said Churkin. "Mark my word: the parliament will obey Karadžić."

Two days later, the Serb parliament rejected the UN plan by a vote of 51–2. We'd fallen for a bait-and-switch scam. It was a low point for American diplomacy and for Chris personally.[1] He dispatched me to Moscow— my first trip there since joining the government—to see if the Russians, having been made to look at best like dupes of the Serbs and at worst like their accomplices, might now be willing to support the use of force.

The answer I got was no, most resoundingly from Pavel Grachev, the Russian defense minister, a bluff, burly paratrooper who had supported Yeltsin during the August 1991 coup. Grachev had arrayed in front of him what he said were the latest intelligence reports, no doubt straight from Belgrade. He depicted the Serbs as holding back the tide of "Muslim extremists and terrorists," a species of international villain Grachev said he knew well from his service in Afghanistan during the Soviet occupation in the eighties. Should the Bosnian Muslims succeed in establishing their own state, he warned, the Turks and Iranians would gain a foothold on the continent.

Grachev spoke with the confidence of a man who not only knew he was right but also knew he had popular and parliamentary opinion behind him.

Kozyrev, by contrast, seemed to be in almost as much anguish over the Russian attempt to defend Milošević as he was over the American desire to bomb him. Kozyrev, flanked by half a dozen dour aides, received me in a conference room on the seventh floor of the Stalin-Gothic skyscraper that housed the Foreign Ministry. Behind him, in front of the dirty-paned window, was a black marble replica of a statue of Laocoön in the coils of a sea serpent. Laocoön was a priest in Troy who warned his fellow citizens to beware of a giant wooden horse that had shown up overnight at the gates of the city. His advice was scorned, he was killed by the gods and Troy fell to the Greeks. Laocoön's fate seemed suited to Kozyrev's mood that day. He made a brief, halfhearted, barely coherent plea for the U.S. to "exercise restraint" and to give the UN plan one more chance.

I had prepared for the encounter by writing out in advance a detailed argument on how it was in Russia's own interest to join us in threatening military retribution against the Serbs since that was the only way to stop their onslaught and prevent a full-scale war in the region. Halfway through my presentation, Kozyrev, with a look of exasperation, cut me off.

"You know," he said, "it's bad enough having you people tell us what you're going to do whether we like it or not. Don't add insult to injury by also telling us that it's *in our interests* to obey your orders."

Afterward, in the car riding back to the U.S. embassy, my assistant Toria Nuland could tell I was rattled. "That's what happens when you try to get the Russians to eat their spinach," she said. "The more you tell them it's good for them, the more they gag."

Among those of us working on Russia policy, "administering the spinach treatment" became shorthand for one of our principal activities in the years that followed.

MY SUBSEQUENT DEALINGS with Kozyrev went better, in part because we avoided formal meetings in which he was surrounded by subordinates, a number of whom he neither liked nor trusted. In private, I saw more of the irony, openness and basic good sense that had made him such a refreshing exception among Soviet diplomats when I'd first known him a decade earlier. When I returned to Moscow later in May, Kozyrev invited me to a production of Prokofiev's ballet *Romeo and Juliet.* During the intermission he remarked that the story had set him musing about the "tragic, murderous idiocy of all this feuding going on in the Balkans." He truly hated making excuses for the Serbs, he said, but the domestic politics of Russian foreign policy made it simply impossible for him to support air strikes. If, in a moment of weakness, he gave in to my arguments in favor of lift-and-strike, "I might as well just fly home with you and defect."

IN THE WEEKS that followed, the Serbs kept on slaughtering and evicting Muslims in their path while the Security Council dithered and the UN peace plan fell of its own weight. By the time Christopher and Kozyrev next met, in early June in Athens, the Serbs had overrun Goražde, another of the communities that the United Nations had designated a safe area. They shelled a soccer stadium in Sarajevo, killing more than a dozen and wounding over a hundred people. Both Serbs and Croats stepped up their attacks on UN humanitarian relief convoys.

Faced with this mounting carnage, the Russians reluctantly conceded that force might indeed be necessary, and on June 4 they agreed to a UN resolution authorizing the deployment of peacekeepers to protect the safe areas and the use of NATO airpower to support them.

AND SO IT CONTINUED: week in and week out, the Serbs brutalized the Muslims in Bosnia while the West issued warnings and Russia did everything it could to make sure that nothing came of our threats. It was an ignominious pattern that would prevail for the next two years, taking its daily toll of lives in Bosnia, casting shame on the international community and discrediting the notion of U.S.-Russian partnership.

Part of the problem on the Russian side was the suspicion that the Balkans was not just a gateway for Islamic inroads into Europe but a staging area for the expansion of American power right up to the border of Russia itself. I heard this view several times during the spring of 1993 from the Russian ambassador in Washington, Vladimir Lukin, whom I'd known for years. He was at the liberal end of the spectrum at home—as a young man he had protested against the Soviet invasion of Czechoslovakia in 1968, taken refuge in Arbatov's institute and gone on to help found a political party that championed democracy—but as the mouthpiece of Russian foreign policy in Washington at the beginning of the Clinton administration, he was truculent toward us and openly contemptuous of Kozyrev.

Not only was the U.S. conducting an "anti-Serb vendetta" in the Balkans, said Lukin, but we were clearly preparing for future encroachments into "the near abroad." This term, with its connotation of a Russian sphere of influence throughout the old USSR, was a repudiation of a key tenet of American policy toward the former Soviet Union. In the first days after the dissolution of the USSR, George Bush and James Baker had moved quickly to open embassies in all the fifteen former republics as symbols of their entitlement to direct relations with Washington. Even before Clinton assumed office, he set as a guideline for his administration's policy toward the former Soviet Union that we must convince everyone in the region that "Russia's not the only game in town" and that the U.S. was committed to helping what we called the new independent states survive to become old independent states.

One of my jobs was to deliver to leaders of all the new independent states messages of American support for their sovereignty and willingness to help them resolve their disputes with each other and with Moscow. Accompanied by a team of colleagues from the State Department as well as representatives from the National Security Council, Treasury, Defense and CIA, I took a series of whistle-stop trips to all fifteen former republics. We called these the *zdravstvidaniya*, or "hello–good-bye," tours. As a rule, we would rendezvous, usually on a Sunday evening, at Dulles Airport to board a United Airlines red-eye to Frankfurt. There we would pick up an Air Force executive jet and hopscotch around Eurasia for a week or so, usually spending no more than a day and sometimes only a few hours in each capital. We packed a lot of business into that short time: meetings with the head of state or government, the defense and foreign ministers, parliamentarians, local journalists and human rights activists.

Invariably, we encountered evidence that Russia's neighbors in the near abroad wished that they were a little less near and a little more abroad. They understood the lesson of the Balkans too, and the ominous implications for them of Russia's support for Milošević's attempt to incorporate adjacent lands into Serbia. They wanted us to put their problems with Moscow on our agenda. Whenever possible, we did so, feeding the Russians' darker misgivings about what we were up to.[2]

THE ORPHAN MISSILES

The first of the *zdravstvidaniya* tours, in early May 1993, began with a visit to Kiev, the capital of an unhappy and nervous country that had been free for less than eighteen months and wasn't at all sure that it would last much longer. Ukraine had only episodically experienced freedom from Russia over the past two centuries, most recently in the turbulent period at the end of World War I and after the Bolshevik Revolution. The euphoria of Ukrainian independence that so unsettled George Bush in 1991 had long since given way to insecurity, instability, pessimism and, most ominously, a polarization between the country's two principal groups, Ukrainians and ethnic Russians. Many of those Russians had voted for secession in 1991, thinking that they'd live better lives if governed from Kiev rather than Moscow. But now they were having second thoughts.

The essential cause of their disillusionment, as in Russia, was economic —only the problem was far worse in Ukraine. While it had shucked off Soviet rule, Ukraine retained an essentially Soviet economy along with many of the systemic weaknesses that had been the undoing of the Soviet state. In Russia, post-communist reform was proving not up to the task; in Ukraine, reform was virtually nonexistent.

In the spring of 1993, many experts in the West, along with many Ukrainians, feared that the country was spiraling into chaos. The situation was all the more complex and dangerous because of the presence on Ukrainian territory of nearly 170 intercontinental ballistic missiles. They were orphans of the Soviet arsenal. Moscow wanted Ukraine to send the warheads to Russia immediately and unconditionally, while nationalists in Ukraine wanted to keep them as a deterrent against Russian intimidation or aggression. The Ukranians were paranoids with real enemies, especially in the Russian parliament, where reds and browns were pressing historical Russian claims against Ukrainian territory. Yeltsin was prompt and categorical in quashing any thought of such land grabs, but Ukrainian nationalists attached more attention to the Russian parliament's provocation than to the Kremlin's repudiation of them.[3] The resulting distrust between Kiev and Moscow made resolution of the dispute over the nuclear warheads hard to imagine without the U.S. brokering a compromise.

When I met with Leonid Kravchuk, the Ukrainian president, in Kiev on May 10, he set an astronomical price for giving up the weapons: billions of dollars in "compensation" and an American promise that we would treat an attack on Ukraine as though it were an attack on the U.S.—virtually the same security guarantee that we gave our closest allies; it would have obligated us to take Ukraine's side if it found itself in a crisis with Russia over the nuclear weapons or any other issue. I told Kravchuk that the best we could do was help finance the return of the warheads to Russia, where they would be dismantled with American economic and technical assistance, in exchange for Moscow's assurance, underwritten by the U.S., that Russia would respect Ukraine's independence.

I also proposed a process: Ukraine's deputy foreign minister, Boris

Tarasyuk, would join Yuri Mamedov and me in a three-way negotiation to hammer out the details of the deal the U.S. had in mind. Without having checked with him in advance, I was volunteering Yuri's services on the basis of only two fairly brief meetings with him, but I had a hunch the challenge would appeal to his notion of diplomacy as problem-solving. It did, but he warned that the U.S. should expect thanks from neither Ukraine nor Russia if we succeeded. "Those people you're dealing with in Kiev will resent your taking away the strongest card in their hand," he said, "and many on our side will resent your meddling in something that they believe is none of your business. Remember, anything between us and the Ukrainians is a family affair, and any disagreement we have is a family feud."

Ambassador Lukin was even blunter. Russia's relations with Ukraine, he told me reprovingly, were "identical to those between New York and New Jersey"; the U.S. should treat what happened within the former USSR as the contents of a "black box."

Yevgeny Primakov, the head of the Russian Foreign Intelligence Service, compared the Ukrainians to children who had gotten their hands on their father's loaded hunting rifle and had the reckless delusion that they could use it to get their own way. Primakov's patronizing attitude toward the Ukrainians was matched by his mistrust of the U.S.: perhaps the real motive for America's "generous offer of assistance" was to lure Ukraine into a U.S.-led camp that would "encircle Russia with our former fraternal republics and allies."[4]

Whether that view would prevail depended on Yeltsin. The initial signs were not encouraging. When Yeltsin accepted Tom Pickering's credentials as American ambassador to Russia on May 22, he grumbled that the U.S. was "coddling" the Ukrainians, encouraging their hostility toward Russia and creating a major domestic headache for himself. His opponents in the parliament already blamed him for the demise of the USSR and for Ukraine's status as an independent country; now they were accusing him of creating the conditions for Ukraine to become a nuclear-armed enemy of Russia.

The first half of that complaint against Yeltsin was true: he had indeed been the moving force behind the peaceful dissolution of the USSR; he had indeed demonstrated that he was prepared to accept Ukrainian sovereignty. But the second half was patently untrue: he wanted the warheads in Ukraine safely returned to Russia. So did we. The trick was to persuade him that the U.S. could help him achieve that goal, and that we had no ulterior motive hostile to Russia's interest.

IN EARLY JULY, I received, via Yuri Mamedov, what amounted to an urgent summons to the Kremlin. I'd come to respect Yuri's ingenuity in kneading solutions out of problems and his instincts about when, and at what level, our governments should connect. Yeltsin apparently wanted to talk to someone close to Clinton before their upcoming meeting in Tokyo. He was worried that the U.S. and Russia were so at odds on a variety of issues that it was going to spoil the summit. The latest irritant was Russia's desire to sell rocket engine parts to India, a deal that would have fanned the arms race between India and Pakistan, triggered American sanctions against Russia and prevented U.S.-Russian cooperation in space.[5]

When I saw Yeltsin on July 3, it was only my second time in his presence and my first as the American seated directly across from him at the negotiating table. Yeltsin seemed to enjoy making the experience as unnerving as possible. At several points, I thought if we were very lucky, he was merely going to throw me out of his office. U.S.-Russian relations were off to a terrible start, he said, and it was all the U.S.'s fault—not his friend Bill's, but that of bureaucrats like myself.

However, at one point in the course of this otherwise rough session, Yeltsin suggested that he might, under certain circumstances, accept a compromise on the Indian rocket deal. At another point, he mentioned, almost in passing, that he and President Kravchuk had agreed on an idea for how to solve the problem of the Soviet-era weapons in Ukraine. Then he went back to working me over mercilessly.

I had come to Moscow for this memorable experience on the advice of my new friend Yuri Mamedov, who so far was nowhere to be seen. On my way out of the Kremlin, battered from the presidential mugging, I inquired with some annoyance where Yuri was. I was told that he was off on a trip to Cuba (his portfolio included Latin America). Yuri returned that evening and came straight from the airport to the U.S. embassy compound where I was staying. He and I took off our coats and ties and dug into takeout from a nearby Pizza Hut. While I described the impasse our negotiators had reached over India and how it was indeed likely to spoil the presidential meeting in Tokyo, Yuri adopted the manner of a parent who has left the children home alone and come back late at night to find the house a mess. Now it was cleanup time. In the hours that followed, the outlines emerged of a Russian counterproposal that might put an agreement in reach.

As I staggered off to bed, I had the sneaking suspicion that Yuri had been working within his government for weeks on a solution along these lines, and that the session with Yeltsin had been a bit of theater in which my assignment was to play the representative of American intransigence so that Clinton could be spared that role in his own meeting with Yeltsin six days later.

EARLY THE NEXT MORNING, Sunday, July 4, I flew halfway around the world to San Francisco to meet Clinton for the flight to Tokyo. The president and I went on an early-morning jog in a park overlooking the Golden Gate Bridge. As we huffed and puffed up one of the many hills, he told me he had a mirror image of Yeltsin's concern: "I've got a lot to do with that guy, and I don't want to have to spend all my time beating up on him. He's a good ol' boy, but I don't think he takes kindly to my playing his Dutch uncle."

Judging from my own encounter with Yeltsin, I said, I believed that in addition to scrubbing my head, he was cracking heads within his own government so that their meeting would yield progress, not hit a brick wall.

"Good," said Clinton. "Then I'll let you have some water when we get back to the car."

THE TOKYO SUMMIT got off to a good start, largely because Yeltsin was on his best behavior and at his most impressive. At a round-table meeting with the G-7 leaders on July 9, Yeltsin radiated confidence and displayed a mastery of his various briefs, discoursing comfortably on the Russian economy, its great promise as well as its many problems and needs.

Clinton sat back beaming like an impresario whose star was doing well. He whispered to me at one point that he was "proud as hell of Yeltsin." But he was still fretting about whether those pesky other problems—India and Ukraine—would get in the way of what was shaping up to be a successful summit.

The next morning, as Yeltsin emerged from his limousine and approached Clinton, he spotted me off to one side, stopped in his tracks, gave me a big smile and blurted, "Aha! You!" He told me he had decided to fire his chief negotiator, Alexander Shokhin, who had been stonewalling us over the Indian rocket sale, and replace him with Yuri Koptev, who was the head of the Russian space program and who therefore had an interest in removing any obstacles to U.S.-Russian space cooperation. Koptev, said Yeltsin, would have instructions to come to agreement expeditiously, before American sanctions went into effect.

Clinton, who was waiting with his hand outstretched, looked at me with a puzzled expression. I flashed an okay sign to him.

During the meeting, Yeltsin unveiled a concept for solving the Ukraine problem as well: he and Kravchuk had agreed to join Clinton in signing a "trilateral accord" that would resolve once and for all and "as a package" the problems of the warheads and Ukraine's territorial integrity.

Clinton agreed on the spot. He knew that the chances of our three-way diplomacy succeeding went way up if Yeltsin had a personal stake in the outcome.

Three days later, Koptev came to Washington and closed a deal on the rocket sale that obviated the need for American sanctions.[6] This development was welcome in its own right and, we hoped, augured well for progress on nonproliferation more generally, including with respect to Iran.

Koptev was followed a week later by Yuri Mamedov, who brought with him several key officials from the Defense Ministry and intelligence services. I matched them up with my own colleagues from the Pentagon and the CIA under the aegis of the Strategic Stability Group, the joint interagency body that Yuri and I had set up in the spring. Over the course of two days, we began fleshing out the contents of a U.S.-Russian-Ukrainian accord that the three presidents would sign. We agreed that as an interim measure, the U.S. would try to induce Ukraine to "deactivate" the missiles on their territory—that is, by disarming the mechanisms that detonated the warheads—as a prelude to their return to Russia as part of the package deal that would include U.S. financial help for both parties and Russian assurances to respect Ukraine's sovereignty and security.

The brainstorming within our government and the hard slogging with the Russians and Ukrainians fell to a small team of diplomats and technical experts drawn from around the government, notably Rose Gottemoeller of the National Security Council, a frequent companion on our *zdravstvidaniya* tours. Within my own office, I relied on one of my deputies, Steve Pifer, a foreign service officer with years of experience in arms control and just the right combination of doggedness, patience and ingenuity (he would later serve as our administration's ambassador to Kiev).

In early August, Yeltsin told Tom Pickering that he could assure President Clinton that no one in the Russian government would be allowed to stand in the way of American mediation. The suddenly improved prospect of a trilateral accord increased Ukraine's chances of survival and meant that there would be only one nuclear-armed state on what had been Soviet territory.[7]

These two breakthroughs occurred largely because of Yeltsin's eagerness to have an upbeat meeting with Clinton and the G-7 in Tokyo. This, too, was a pattern we would see for the next seven years: Yeltsin's desire for the spotlight at high-prestige international gatherings gave us leverage over him on issues where we had run into an impasse with his government.

YELTSIN HAD COME TO TOKYO wanting, in addition to a warm welcome, money—lots of it, and Clinton had worked for three months with his G-7 counterparts to make sure he got it. With its price tag of $28.4 billion, the package of support to help Russia and the other former Soviet states fight inflation and restructure their economies was only somewhat bigger than the one that George Bush, goaded by Clinton (and Richard Nixon), had helped assemble with the G-7 the year before in Munich. But the Tokyo package included features—such as a new $3 billion fund designed to help companies provide social services to employees as they made the transition from state-owned to private enterprises—intended to have near-term, high-impact benefit on the lives of citizens.

For the Tokyo package to meet the goals of its sponsors and the needs of its intended recipients, the Russian government had to meet a series of conditions: reduce inflation by cutting government spending and controlling the money supply, establish a rational and equitable tax system, pass laws governing private property and curb corruption. Otherwise the Western money would do no good.

"Conditionality" in IMF lending was the economic equivalent of the spinach treatment, and the master chef was Larry Summers. He believed that Russia's ability to make proper use of the G-7 money depended on the outcome of a struggle within the Russian government. On one side were the pro-Western economic reformers like Yegor Gaidar, who in September had assumed the post of first deputy prime minister for economics, and Boris Fyodorov, the finance minister who was at Yeltsin's side through most of the meetings in Tokyo. On the other were those who believed in maintaining employment through subsidies to inefficient enterprises and churning out rubles, propelling Russia back toward the brink of hyperinflation.

Larry saw Prime Minister Chernomyrdin as at best schizophrenic and at worst in the camp of the obscurantists. Unless Chernomyrdin threw his political weight behind the reformers, Larry warned, the big bucks unveiled in Tokyo would either never materialize because the Russians would fail to qualify for disbursement, or, worse, the money would disappear into the maw of a leaky, inefficient and corrupt system.

Vice-President Gore gave Larry a chance to deliver this message in person when Chernomyrdin arrived in Washington on September 1, 1993, for the inaugural session of the commission that Clinton and Yeltsin had agreed to establish in Vancouver. Over a small dinner at Blair House, Larry walked Chernomyrdin through the logic of conditionality. Chernomyrdin bristled. He was used to giving orders and not to having interlocutors talk back, especially ones below his rank. He told Larry that his government had to conduct economic policy within the bounds of what was tolerable to the parliament and the electorate. Besides, he added, however well motivated in their advice, Russia's foreign partners must respect the pride and sovereignty of a great power.

Larry persisted. The rules that governed IMF lending weren't arbitrary or intrusive—they were a reflection of the immutable principles of economics, which operated in a way similar to the rules of physics. Of course it was Russia's business how it chose to restructure its economy. But it was the right of the U.S. and its G-7 partners to choose whether to spend their money in support of what the Russian government decided.

Gore seemed to enjoy refereeing this exchange and told Leon Fuerth and me afterward that he judged it to be roughly a draw. Larry's arguments were right on the merits, he said, but they needed to be balanced against the imperatives of Russian democracy, since they, too, exerted "a force as powerful as gravity or thermodynamics." Our policy, said Gore, ought to be a "synthesis between the iron laws of economics and the hard realities of Russian politics."

The personal chemistry between Gore and Chernomyrdin was good, just as Kozyrev had predicted when suggesting the commission. They set up working groups covering over a dozen areas of potential government-to-government cooperation. These included the development of energy from the Caspian basin and the Russian Far East, the joint exploration of space and steps that would make it easier for American companies to launch commercial satellites on Russian rockets. In exchange, the Russian government promised, in a memorandum of understanding, to adhere to internationally established guidelines in its sale of high-technology goods and services to other countries. That understanding, we hoped, would help us come to grips with the problem of dangerous Russian exports and, in particular, Russia's nuclear cooperation with Iran.

BLOODY SUNDAY

We were especially glad to have established the Gore-Chernomyrdin connection that September, since it looked as though Boris Yeltsin was descending into a new personal and political crisis. There were fresh reports that he was engaging in heavy drinking and suffering from bouts of depression and a range of physical ailments, from heart trouble to high blood pressure. Sensing the physical weakness of the president, the more obstreperous deputies of the Supreme Soviet returned from their August holidays on the offensive, with Ruslan Khasbulatov, the speaker of the parliament, leading the charge in a public war of words and in various legislative maneuvers aimed at thwarting government policy.

In the face of what was shaping up to be a new outbreak of instability in Russia, there was some skepticism in the U.S. Congress about whether to support the administration's request for what now amounted to $2.5 billion in American aid to the former Soviet Union. On the morning of September 21, I was testifying in support of our program before the House Foreign Affairs Committee when Toria Nuland, who was sitting behind me, passed me a note: Yeltsin had just announced that he was suspending the parliament and calling elections for December 12; I was expected to help the president prepare for a phone call with Yeltsin in twenty minutes.

By the time I got to the White House, the situation in Moscow was even more tense. Khasbulatov had called his fellow deputies into extraordinary session and rammed through a vote removing Yeltsin from office. The radio was reporting that Alexander Rutskoi was to be sworn in as acting president of Russia by midnight Moscow time. Recalling the last parliamentary crisis in March, Tony Lake remarked that it was "*Groundhog Day,* only worse."

When Clinton arrived at his study in the residence on the second floor of the White House, he had been immersed in other issues and was not yet focused on what was happening in Moscow, so I gave him the most head-snapping summary I could think of: "If this turns out badly, you'll have a new Russian counterpart tomorrow, and it'll be a whole new ballgame. No more win/win—it's back to win/lose. Think August '91. Yeltsin's going for broke."

"Got it," Clinton said. "If Yeltsin's really playing this close to the edge, then I've got to go for broke too."

"Not quite," I said, realizing that I'd tipped him too far in the direction of unqualified support for Yeltsin. "You'd better lean into him on how he's got to play by the rules he's put in place. That means the constitution. We don't want to treat the old Soviet constitution as the Ten Commandments, but it's the only one Russia's got until it adopts a new one, and constitutional rule is essential to what we're supporting there. There are constitutional ways for a parliament to fire a president, but not the other way around. See if you can find a way to tell him he can't destroy democracy in order to save it."

"I know that and I bet he knows that," said Clinton, "but we've got to remember that he knows what he's up against better than we do." As in March, Clinton was not going to let himself be talked into anything that looked like equivocation.

When the call came through, Clinton adopted a relaxed, friendly, I'm-here-for-you-Boris tone. His only admonition was that Yeltsin had to keep the political process open—he shouldn't restrict his enemies' access to the press, since free media was at the core of the democracy Yeltsin was defending. For most of the call, however, it was Yeltsin doing the talking. He sounded pumped and combative: he became almost euphoric when he was on the barricades or in a showdown with his enemies. Perhaps for that reason he tended not only to relish crises but to provoke them.

He told Clinton that the parliament was "totally out of control . . . it no longer supports the reform process. Those people have become communist. We can't put up with that." He said that the military and internal security services were with him and that he neither wanted nor expected violence. He lavished gratitude on Clinton for his support and professed absolute confidence that he would prevail. In response to Clinton's emphasis on the importance of preserving democracy, Yeltsin promised that elections would go forward and would be free and fair.

"That guy's in the fight of his life," said Clinton when the call ended, "and he thinks he's going to win!"

He instructed me to go work on a public statement emphasizing his personal backing for Yeltsin.[8] He wanted, he said, to use the crisis in Moscow to shore up support in Congress for our aid package.

Opposition to the bill all but evaporated, and it moved quickly, passing in the House 321–108 on September 29 and in the Senate 87–11 on September 30, the last day of the fiscal year. The president signed it into law that evening.

MEANWHILE, THE FIRST BLOOD was spilled in Moscow. On September 23, a detachment of armed men linked to the defiant parliamentarians raided a military facility and killed several militiamen. In response, the mayor of Moscow, Yuri Luzhkov, demanded the surrender of all weapons in the hands of the deputies. On September 25, Interior Ministry troops surrounded the White House, allowing people to leave but none to enter. Khasbulatov issued a call for the Russian armed forces to come over to his side, and Yeltsin appealed to the patriarch of the Russian Orthodox Church to mediate.

Once again the Russian White House was besieged, but this time with Yeltsin in the Kremlin and about two hundred hard-line deputies and several hundred heavily armed men holed up inside. On Saturday, October 2, Khasbulatov and Rutskoi sent detachments of fighters out into the streets to hurl Molotov cocktails and attack police officers with metal rods sharpened into spears. The insurgents briefly occupied Smolensk Square in front of the Foreign Ministry, shaking their fists at the windows above and noisily vowing to hang Kozyrev.

The next day, the police cleared the square, only to have another wave of rioters sweep back in, chanting, "President Rutskoi! All power to the Soviets!" Meanwhile, a much larger and better armed group of protestors, carrying hammer-and-sickle flags and portraits of Stalin, marched on the mayor's office, just opposite the White House, then on Ostankino Television Center, Moscow's main studio that housed a number of national stations. They set the building ablaze by firing rocket-propelled grenades into the lobby. Special forces troops inside returned fire. That evening, Russia's First Channel, which was broadcast from Ostankino and which had provided live coverage of the attack as it took place, finally went off the air. Defense Minister Grachev promised Yeltsin that army units were on their way into the center of the city to restore order, but there were none in evidence. Yeltsin, fearing that the military was hedging its bets, went to the

Ministry of Defense and gave an impassioned speech to shake the generals into action.

Yegor Gaidar issued an appeal to the Russian people from a makeshift television studio, calling the crisis "a battle for the future of Russia."

Leaders of other former Soviet republics, including Eduard Shevardnadze of Georgia and the presidents of all three Baltic states, issued statements in support of Yeltsin. Vaclav Havel, the president of the Czech Republic, said that what was happening in Moscow was not a "power struggle but a fight between democracy and totalitarianism."

I HAD STARTED that Sunday in my study at home, preparing for another round of congressional testimony. Toria called me and said I'd better turn on CNN, which had its cameras trained on demonstrators chanting, "Beat the yids, save Russia!"—a refrain from the pogroms of czarist times—and "All yids out of the Kremlin!"

As the crisis deepened that Sunday, I stayed in touch by phone with Secretary Christopher, who was already having a bad day dealing with confusing but disturbing reports from Mogadishu, Somalia. U.S. forces there, originally sent by the Bush administration to help distribute food aid, had just tried to capture the warlord Mohamed Farah Aideed. Something had gone horribly wrong, though no one seemed able to tell Chris exactly what. He asked me to monitor the situation in Moscow while he concentrated on Mogadishu.

I went to my office and spent the day working the phones, primarily to Tom Pickering in Moscow, as well as returning calls from concerned members of Congress. Clinton called just before he was due to meet with reporters on the South Lawn. "I guess we've just got to pull up our socks and back Ol' Boris again," he told me, then went out and said essentially the same thing in public: "It's clear that the violence was perpetrated by the Rutskoi-Khasbulatov forces. It's also clear that President Yeltsin bent over backward to avoid the use of force, to avoid excessive force from the beginning of this. I'm still convinced that the United States must support President Yeltsin and the process of bringing about free and fair elections. We cannot afford to be in the position of wavering at this moment or of backing off or giving any encouragement to people who clearly want to derail the election process and are not committed to reform in Russia."

Shortly afterward, I talked to Clinton again. He sounded weary and grim—but not because of what was happening in Russia. "Bad as that

Moscow deal is," he said, "believe me, it's worse in Mogadishu." It now appeared that two American Blackhawk helicopters had been shot down and five Americans were dead. In the hours that followed the toll would rise to eighteen Americans killed and seventy-four wounded.

Of the two stories competing for the attention of the world that Sunday, the pitched battle in the heart of Moscow dominated the news.

SHORTLY BEFORE MIDNIGHT, I went to sleep on the couch in my office. At 3 a.m., I popped awake. A mental alarm clock told me it was now around noon in Moscow. I went down the corridor to the department's operations center, our communications hub, where we had established a round-the-clock task force to monitor the crisis. Using one of the phone banks, I called Mamedov, who was in his own office, less than a mile from the embattled Russian White House, and asked him for an update. Russian soldiers, he said, had already forced their way into the White House and taken control of the first two floors. Chernomyrdin had issued a demand to the forces inside to come out under a white flag. There had been a cease-fire, but the latest word was that Rutskoi, while prepared to negotiate, refused to surrender.

Suddenly, in the midst of our conversation, Mamedov and I both fell silent. After a long moment, Yuri asked: "Are you watching what I'm watching?" I was. We had our television sets tuned to CNN, which had begun a live broadcast from the scene as Russian armored personnel carriers moved into position and commandos prepared to storm the White House. For the next half hour Yuri and I stared at the screens in our offices, exchanging occasional impressions. A column of tanks opened fire on the White House, setting the top floors of the building ablaze. Not long afterward three bedraggled rebels appeared waving a white flag, followed by Rutskoi, Khasbulatov and the others, who were carted off in buses and put in detention.

Shortly afterward Kozyrev spoke with Chris by phone and assured him that Yeltsin planned to go ahead with the election in December. Clinton departed for the West Coast and phoned Yeltsin from Air Force One with a message of support. In Russia, news of the call was broadcast over and over throughout the day—a sign of how desperate Yeltsin and his backers were for validation. In a televised speech to the Russian people, Yeltsin struck a note of anguish tinged with contrition.

"The nightmare of those dark days is now behind us," he said. "Nobody has won, nobody has scored a victory. We have all been scorched by the lethal breath of fratricidal war. Our people, our fellow countrymen, have perished. No matter what differences existed among us in our political views, they are all Russia's children. This is our common tragedy. This is our huge grief. Let us remember this insanity so that it will never happen again, as long as we shall live."

Clinton, too, was shaken by the latest turn of events in Russia. He could see that even though Yeltsin had, for the moment, prevailed over his most extreme and conspicuous enemies, the shelling of the White House was a political setback of considerable proportions and potentially lasting consequences for a leader who had claimed, with good reason, to have introduced "civilized" politics to Russia.

Meanwhile, the full magnitude of what had happened in Somalia was also sinking in on Clinton. He had hoped to prove that he could use American military power to meet the challenges of the new era: peacekeeping, humanitarian intervention, standing up to warlords like Aideed and Milošević, who had replaced the Soviets and their minions as the principal threats to peace. The debacle in Somalia would make it even harder for Clinton to win the confidence of the public, the Congress and the U.S. military when it came time to back diplomacy with force in the Balkans.

On October 6, I saw the president in Tony Lake's outer office, and he gave me a rueful look. "Boy, do I ever miss the cold war!"

CHAPTER 4

KICK THE CAN

Needed: a large playing area and a large group, e.g., a whole class.
Skills: running, hiding, listening.

Handbook of rules of recess games

I N MID-OCTOBER 1993, just as Russia was recovering from its brief
bout of civil war, the Clinton administration was coming to grips
with whether to enlarge the North Atlantic Treaty Organization. The
decision to do so would put further strain on Russian politics and on Russia's relations with the West, especially with the U.S. Nonetheless, it was
the right thing to do. The challenge was how to do it right.

NATO had been founded in 1949 for the sole purpose of deterring, and
if necessary repulsing, an attack on Western Europe by the Soviet Union
and its satellites in the Warsaw Pact. With the dissolution first of the pact,
then of the USSR, many in Russia—and indeed, quite a few in the
West—wondered why NATO shouldn't be disbanded rather than expanded. One answer was that there were new threats to the peace of Europe and dealing with them required military muscle of a kind that only
the alliance possessed. The most obvious example was in the Balkans. In
1993, there was not much doubt that sooner or later it would be necessary
take military action against the Serbs, and NATO was the only available
means for doing so. That argument in favor of NATO's continued existence did nothing to allay the misgivings of the Russians, given the sympathy many of them felt for the Serbs and the distaste with which they
regarded the specter of NATO airpower being unleashed in Bosnia.

Another reason for NATO to stay in business was its political function.

From its inception and throughout the cold war, the alliance had induced better relations among its own members by making them feel safe enough to rebuild their economies ravaged by World War II, strengthen their democratic institutions and get on with the task of European integration. In the early 1950s, several allies, especially France, were reluctant to bring West Germany into NATO, but the U.S. argued that doing so would reward the Bonn government for turning away from its totalitarian past and bind it more firmly to the West. Had West Germany not entered NATO in 1955, the European Union would probably never have come into being. Spain's admission to the alliance in 1982 helped ensure civilian control of the military and protect Spain's transition to democracy.

NATO had already expanded once since the end of the cold war. In the course of ten dizzying months in 1990, East Germany had pulled out of the Warsaw Pact, abandoned communism, ceased to exist as a separate country and merged with West Germany. The Bush administration gave the Soviet leadership assurances that NATO would stop there.[1] The Poles, Czechs, Hungarians and other Central Europeans protested vehemently. After all, they had suffered as much as the East Germans under Soviet domination. To exclude them from NATO on the grounds that Moscow would object to their entry would be a grotesque double jeopardy.

In April 1993, Presidents Lech Walesa of Poland, Vaclav Havel of the Czech Republic and Arpad Goncz of Hungary made the case for their countries' admission to NATO directly to Clinton when they visited Washington for the opening of the Holocaust Museum. Their appeal did not generate much publicity, in part because another guest, Elie Wiesel, made headlines by calling on the U.S. to lead the West in ending genocide in Bosnia.

Three weeks later, when I held one of my first meetings with Yuri Mamedov in Moscow, he remarked—in an offhand fashion that suggested he didn't want to stir a pot that wasn't boiling—that it would be "discriminatory to Russia's interests" if NATO admitted into its own ranks former Soviet allies, to say nothing of former Soviet republics.

Yet the Baltic states already had hopes of their own for membership in NATO, as I discovered a few days later when I stopped in Tallinn, the capital of Estonia. I was received by President Lennart Meri, one of the seminal figures in the Baltic independence movement and someone I'd known since the eighties. His family had been deported to Siberia when the Red Army occupied Estonia in 1941. He survived for decades by writing books and making films on ethnography and culture that were acclaimed in the West and banned in the USSR. After becoming president of Estonia, Meri elicited from Yeltsin—an early proponent of Baltic independence—a promise that all Russian troops would be out of his country by August 1994. When I called on Meri in May 1993, I assured him that the Clinton administration fully supported him on that score. That was all well and good, he replied, but the only way to keep Russian troops from reoccupying his country when Yeltsin gave way to a more traditional Russian leader was for Estonia to be in NATO and protected by the American nuclear umbrella. Meri couldn't have been more forthright: Russia was a malignancy in remission; the Yeltsin era was at best a fleeting opportunity to be seized before Russia relapsed into authoritarianism at home and expansionism abroad.

Meri's explicitly anti-Russian motive for knocking on NATO's door was understandable after what he and his nation had been through. But pessimism like his could be self-fulfilling. If NATO adopted an anti-Russian rationale for taking in new members, it could tip the balance of forces in Russian politics in exactly the direction that we—along with Meri, Walesa and Havel, not to mention many Russians—most feared.

Over the long term, pan-European integration depended both on the Central Europeans joining the major structures of the West, including NATO, and on Russia's remaining on a reformist track internally and a cooperative track in its foreign and defense policies. These goals were in tension but not necessarily irreconcilable. Because of Russia's mistrust of NATO and the Central Europeans' mistrust of Russia, we needed to find ways of breaking down the suspicions and stereotypes of the cold war and building cooperation between NATO and all the former Warsaw Pact countries, including Russia.

With that strategy in mind, the Bush administration had helped set up a NATO-sponsored body called the North Atlantic Cooperation Council in 1991. In early June 1993, I joined Secretary Christopher for the annual meeting of the council in Athens. As a photo op and an exercise in high political symbolism, it was inspiring: here were the foreign ministers of thirty-eight countries that used to be squared off against each other on either side of the Iron Curtain now gathered around a huge U-shaped table in alphabetical order, from Albania and Armenia at one end to the United States, Ukraine and Uzbekistan at the other. But for purposes of dealing with problems like ethnic cleansing in the Balkans and Russian-Ukrainian squabbling over the residue of the Soviet armed forces, the council was of little utility.

Secretary Christopher found the Athens meeting cumbersome in procedure and vaporous in substance. Worse, it put him on the spot. While sitting through two days of tedium as his fellow foreign ministers waited their turn to speak, Chris was accosted by Polish, Czech, Hungarian and other colleagues from Central Europe wanting to know when they could get into NATO; the British and German foreign ministers, meanwhile, wanted to know what American intentions were with regard to the future of the alliance, since that would influence their own governments' thinking; and Andrei Kozyrev—who was under attack at home for even showing up at a meeting that was so obviously an American-run show— pleaded for assurances that the U.S. was *not* contemplating enlargement.

In response, Chris could say nothing more than that the matter was under study.

One way to force the U.S. government to face up to a tough issue is to schedule a highly visible presidential event at which to announce a decision. Chris contacted Tony Lake from Athens and asked him to set aside time on Clinton's calendar in early 1994 for a summit meeting of the leaders of the sixteen member-states of NATO to make decisions about the future of the alliance.[2]

HAVING PROMISED Yuri Mamedov that one of the working principles of our relationship would be no surprises, I told him during a meeting in London on August 25, 1993, that the issue of NATO expansion was going to be front and center early in 1994, which would also be around the time of President Clinton's first trip to Moscow.

Mamedov grimaced. "Only our worst enemies would wish that topic on us," he said with a mirthless smile. "NATO is a four-letter word in Russian. Let's concentrate merely on the difficult jobs—like Bosnia and Ukraine—and not assign ourselves Mission Impossible."

We moved on to other topics. An hour later we were interrupted by a news bulletin: Boris Yeltsin had just announced at a press conference in Warsaw that Russia had no objection to Poland's joining NATO.

"In the new Russian-Polish relationship," Yeltsin proclaimed, "there is no place for hegemony and one state dictating to another, nor for the psychology of the 'big brother' and the 'little brother.'" He and Walesa signed a joint declaration affirming that Poland had the sovereign right to provide for its own security and that if Poland chose to join NATO, it would not conflict with Russia's interests.

In the eight years I dealt with Yuri, I rarely found him at a loss for words, but at this moment he was thunderstruck. He said he'd have to get back to me with clarification once he determined what had really transpired in Warsaw, and what it meant.

Some midlevel Russian officials and commentators, appalled at what Yeltsin had said, subsequently claimed that their president had been expressing his "private opinion," not government policy. Other Russians even put out the story that Walesa had gotten Yeltsin to endorse Poland's desire to be in NATO by plying him with vodka.

The Poles, with whom we consulted closely, insisted that that was not the case: Yeltsin was sober when Walesa raised with him the matter of Poland's aspiration to join NATO during a long private walk in the gardens of the presidential palace. According to the argument that Walesa used, Poland faced a stark choice: either it could form an alliance with Ukraine, which as Yeltsin knew was seething with fear and resentment of Moscow, or Poland could seek to join NATO and the European Union, both of which were committed to cooperating with Russia. Walesa's preference, he said, was to go west, but that depended in part on whether Russia tried to stop him from doing so. He also implied that by taking a permissive and forward-looking view, Yeltsin could demonstrate that his Russia really was different from Stalin's and Brezhnev's.

Since the question of NATO enlargement had yet to stir much attention, either in the West or in Russia, Yeltsin hadn't been subjected to much domestic political passion on the subject. Walesa's appeal made sense to him: Poland was indeed a free country now—it had broken out of the Soviet empire, just as Russia itself had done. Yes, NATO was anti-Soviet in its origin, but Yeltsin was anti-Soviet himself. He and Walesa shook hands and announced their agreement to the world.

Foreign Minister Kozyrev and Defense Minister Grachev did their best to persuade Yeltsin to backtrack. He would be committing political suicide at home, they said, if he didn't amend his position. They succeeded in getting him to sign a letter, drafted by the Foreign Ministry and sent to the leaders of NATO member-states, suggesting that, as an alternative to enlargement, NATO and Russia should offer joint security guarantees to the Central Europeans, an idea guaranteed to offend the Poles and others since it sounded like a replay of the deal that Franklin Roosevelt, Winston

Churchill and Joseph Stalin had made when they carved up Europe at Yalta in 1945. Yeltsin did not, however, reverse the essence of what he had agreed with Walesa; in fact, his letter reaffirmed the right of any state to choose its own methods and associations for guaranteeing its security.[3]

CONFRONTED WITH WALESA'S pitch and in the absence of contrary advice from his own staff, Yeltsin relied on his liberal instinct, much as he had in 1991 when he had been in the forefront of those advocating independence for the Baltic states and when he had promised Lennart Meri to withdraw Russian troops from the region.[4]

But in the context of events as they unfolded in the late summer and fall of 1993, Yeltsin's statement in Warsaw was a quickly fading blip on the screen, in part because NATO enlargement itself was not yet the stuff of headlines, in part because the press conference occurred in the dog days of August, and also because Yeltsin's own ministers threw up so much chaff of their own.

When Mamedov got back to me with the clarification he'd promised in London, it was simple: *Don't do this!* Pressing ahead with NATO enlargement, especially in early 1994, would, as Yuri put it, "blow up the circuits" of U.S.-Russian relations.

IN WASHINGTON, we were less focused on trying to anticipate what the attitude of Russia would be to enlargement than on figuring out what American policy should be. As Chris had intended, the January 1994 NATO summit in Brussels—to be followed by the Clinton-Yeltsin summit in Moscow—was what in the bureaucracy is known as an action-forcing event. By mid-October, with only three months to go, various key individuals and agencies had staked out their positions.

Tony Lake and several of Secretary Christopher's advisers, particularly Lynn Davis, the under secretary of state for international security, favored using the NATO summit to designate the Czech Republic, Hungary, Poland and Slovakia as "associate members" and thus put them on what they sometimes called a "fast track" toward full membership. Only by extending NATO into that part of Europe could the West combat new threats like those that had already erupted in the former Yugoslavia.[5]

The Pentagon was overwhelmingly opposed to enlargement. Les Aspin, the secretary of defense, felt that the end of the cold war gave us a chance to cut back on the U.S. military commitment to Europe; bringing new members into NATO would push us in the other direction. Aspin's deputy, Bill Perry, believed that expansion would impede and perhaps ruin the chances of making progress on what he saw as our two principal objectives in the former Soviet Union: the demilitarization of the Russian economy and the denuclearization of Ukraine. NATO enlargement, he believed, would make the Russians less likely to cut back on their levels of armaments; and the Ukrainians, fearful of ending up in a security limbo between an expanding NATO and an angry Russia, would be less likely to give up the nuclear warheads on their territory.

Most senior officers in the American military were also unenthusiastic about enlargement. The Central European armed forces were burdened with old equipment as well as doctrines and command structures incompatible with the West's, hence nowhere near ready to mesh with those of NATO. The uniformed military also worried that extending American security guarantees into Central Europe would require the U.S. to intervene in more conflicts like the one that had already broken out in the Balkans. During our travels together in the spring and summer of 1993, the military adviser to the State Department, Lieutenant General Barry McCaffrey, more than once told me that if we weren't careful, we would "get ourselves sucked into some godforsaken Eurasian quagmire," which carried with it the risk of stumbling into a shooting war with Russia.

Still, there was a recognition in the Pentagon that we needed to promote practical cooperation between the military establishments of NATO and its former adversaries of the Warsaw Pact as well as nonaligned European countries like Austria, Sweden and Finland that were prepared to help in trouble spots like Bosnia. Like Secretary Christopher, officials of the Defense Department saw the inadequacies of the North Atlantic Cooperation Council, which was little more than a talk shop. Therefore during the summer of 1993, the Pentagon developed the idea for a new institution, to be known as the Partnership for Peace, or PFP, that would bring officers and units from NATO, the former Warsaw Pact and the ranks of the neutrals together for joint planning, exercises and peacekeeping missions.

PFP's highest-ranking and most visionary proponent was General John Shalikashvili, who preferred to be known as Shali. He had been the Supreme Allied Commander in Europe until he succeeded Colin Powell as chairman of the Joint Chiefs of Staff just as the issue of what to do about NATO was coming to a head. Shali's biography was itself an advertisement for the potential of East/West integration. Born in Poland in 1936 to a Georgian father and Russian mother, he came to the U.S. as a teenager already speaking three languages and learned English by watching John Wayne movies.

By October, the civilian and uniformed leaders of the Pentagon had closed ranks behind PFP as something we could—and should—do in the short run while the U.S. and its allies figured out whether they should expand NATO over the long run.

MY OWN VIEW was somewhere between the Pentagon's and that of Tony Lake and Lynn Davis. I didn't agree with Les Aspin and Bill Perry that enlargement was a bad idea in itself, but I felt timing was everything, and that moving ahead at the pace Tony and Lynn were urging was a mistake. I certainly shared Perry's concern that announcing expansion in January could sink whatever chance we stood of brokering the trilateral accord with Russia and Ukraine. I also believed that opening the doors of NATO in January 1994 would give Russian hard-liners an excuse to renege on Yeltsin's commitment to withdraw troops from the Baltics, since Lennart Meri and the other leaders in that region were making no secret of their desire to move quickly toward membership.

I saw NATO enlargement as an objective that not only made sense in theory but might work in practice—as long as we could avoid causing a train wreck (a phrase common in the predictions of the policy's opponents) in our relations with Russia. But if the Russians knew that the prospect of a collision would cause us to hit the brakes on enlargement, they'd have no incentive to acquiesce in our going forward. Whatever the solution to that dilemma, I knew it would take time.

I WOKE UP EARLY on Sunday morning, October 17, and set forth my views in a six-page memo to Chris. Our strategic goal, I wrote, was to integrate both Central Europe and the former Soviet Union into the major institutions of the Euro-Atlantic community. We were more likely to succeed in the long run if, in the early stages, we emphasized an inclusive body, Partnership for Peace, rather than an exclusive one, NATO. Cooperation between NATO and the Russians on practical projects, such as peacekeeping in Bosnia, might help them adjust to the idea that neither the alliance nor its expansion was contrary to their interests.

In our ten months of working together, even though we saw each other several times a day when we were in the same city, Chris and I developed the habit of communicating on paper. My background as a reporter had proved, in some useful respects, transferable to my new line of work. Reporting is largely a matter of figuring out what questions to ask, and I quickly discovered that asking questions wasn't a bad place to start in policymaking. In thinking my way through a gnarly issue, I found it helpful to sit down and attack it on a computer screen. A good policy should make a good story. I would lay out the problem as clearly as I could, as though I were writing a piece of news analysis, then give my view on the solution, as though I were a columnist or an editorial writer. Chris, too, was a scribbler at heart (he had edited his high school newspaper and the *Stanford Law Review,* and been a speechwriter for Governor Pat Brown of California). He read my memos carefully, penning comments and instructions in the margins.

My October 17 memo concluded by suggesting that instead of designating who the first new members would be, the Brussels summit in January should commit the alliance to "an evolutionary process" in which the creation of Partnership for Peace would be "an important first stage," leading to the admission of new members in the future.

Chris agreed with this approach, and since it fit with Aspin and Shali's desire to stress PFP in Brussels, it carried the day at a cabinet-level meeting the next day, October 18.

IMMEDIATELY AFTERWARD, Chris flew to Europe to explain our position to the interested parties, and I joined him. We stopped first in Budapest to meet with the foreign ministers of the Central European countries. They reacted with undisguised disappointment. In Moscow, I found Mamedov, who met me at the airport, relieved—excessively so, I felt.

"This takes care of the matter for the moment, Yuri," I told him, "but it's coming back at us."

"So what you're telling me is that you've really just kicked the bucket?" he asked.

"It's 'kick the can,' Yuri. Kicking the bucket comes later and it's more personal. But, yes, that's what we've done," I replied. "It just buys us a little bit of time to work on the cooperative side so that we're in better shape in that regard when enlargement actually goes forward."

"Time is what we need," he said. "A decision to go ahead with enlargement now would have been a disaster between us but an even bigger disaster here, in its impact on our politics."

Kozyrev, too, was interested only in Chris's assurance that NATO wasn't going to announce that it was taking in new members right away. Once he had established that there would be no formal designation of new members in January, he took us by helicopter to a presidential dacha in Zavidovo, deep in the forest outside Moscow, that had once been Joseph Stalin's hunting lodge. We were ushered into an overheated solarium filled with stuffed game and potted plants.

Boris Yeltsin welcomed us looking like a stunned bull. When Chris conveyed "greetings from your friend in the White House," Yeltsin seemed to think he was talking about the Russian White House, where he had no friends. He launched into a long, barely coherent boast about how he had crushed the communists: "The only thing left is to rebury Lenin!"

Finally Chris laid out our decision on NATO: we would not proceed immediately with enlargement but concentrate instead on developing the Partnership for Peace . . .

Without letting Chris finish, Yeltsin spread his arms and intoned, drawing out the words, *"Genialno! Zdorovo!"* (Brilliant! Terrific!). "Tell Bill this is a wonderful decision!"

After a brief review of other issues, Kozyrev and Yeltsin's other aides virtually shooed us out the door. They had a happy president, and they didn't want any further discussion. As we were saying good-bye, Yeltsin gave me a military salute and, dropping his voice to a stage whisper, thanked me personally for the good news.

Kozyrev did much the same on the chopper ride back to Moscow. Mamedov had obviously told him that I'd thrown my body in front of a freight train full of American officials who wanted to bring new allies on board right away. I started to explain to Kozyrev that the issue was still very much alive; the message he and his president should be getting from us was: PFP today, enlargement tomorrow. He waved me off, pretending not to be able to hear over the noise of the engines, and ostentatiously closed his eyes as though to take a nap. If he had really gone to sleep, which I doubted, I could imagine that his nightmare would have featured an expanding NATO bombing Serbs.

THE ANATHEMA COMETH

Andrei Kozyrev had always been preoccupied by the troublesome interaction between Russian foreign policy and Russian domestic politics, but that fall he had a new, more personal reason for looking over his shoulder. Taking advantage of a provision in the Russian constitution that allowed ministers in the government to hold seats in the new Duma, Kozyrev had decided to run as a candidate in Murmansk, a naval port near the Arctic Circle. His party was Russia's Choice, formed and led by Yegor Gaidar, the principal architect of economic reform and the first deputy prime minister under Victor Chernomyrdin.

Kozyrev, like all Russian liberals, faced an uphill battle in the parliamentary election scheduled for December 12, 1993. Anti-Yeltsin forces seemed to be growing stronger by the day, largely because they were successfully capitalizing on widespread discontent with the economic stringencies imposed by Gaidar and Boris Fyodorov, the minister of finance. Seeing his old enemies regrouping and believing he was the only leader who could stand up to them, Yeltsin backed away from the pledge he had made only six weeks before to hold presidential elections in June 1994. Instead, he announced, he would remain in office until 1996, serving out the full five-year term provided for in his recently proposed but as yet unapproved constitution.

Yeltsin's move, which he announced on November 6, sent another shudder of concern through the White House, primarily among the president's political and media advisers. Clinton was due to appear on NBC's *Meet the Press* the next day, and he was sure to get the old question: Was Yeltsin really a democrat? Were we, by supporting him, really supporting democracy? George Stephanopoulos urged Clinton to "put distance" between himself and a Russian president "who may be going fascist on us."

"Come on," Clinton snapped, "knock it off. We're in this thing for keeps. Yeltsin's hanging in there, and we've got to stick with him."

On the air, Clinton said, "As long as [Yeltsin] is promoting democracy, as long as he is promoting human rights, as long as he is promoting reform, I think the United States should support him. He has been brave and consistent." Clinton went on to say that Yeltsin was taking a chance by holding the election, but it was the right thing to do because, first, it gave the people a voice in the process of governance and, second, it would lead to a system of checks and balances. "One of the things that Boris

Yeltsin has really understood is that it's not good if he's the only source of legitimate democratic power in Russia. He's been elected twice by the Russian people in the last couple of years. After the elections, we'll have another major player, sort of like the president and the Congress here; there will be a different source of legitimate democratic power."

A LITTLE MORE than two weeks later, over the long Thanksgiving weekend, Brooke and our sons and I visited the Clintons at Camp David. The president was unwinding after a bruising but victorious battle with Congress over the North American Free Trade Agreement, and he was interested primarily in relaxing. He spent hours with his new Big Bertha golf club on the driving range. After dinner, the families gathered in the bowling alley, where the president competed ferociously with those who were competent in the sport (Devin and Adrian) and gave detailed instruction to the rest of us.

On Friday afternoon, he invited me to join him as he tooled around the fenced perimeter of the compound in a golf cart. He wanted my read on the welter of disturbing developments inside Russia and also on "the mood" in the ranks of our own government—a reference, I suspected, to what I knew was Stephanopoulos's view that Clinton had tied himself too closely to Yeltsin.

We had to be careful, I said, not to let ourselves be spooked into accepting the verdict that Yeltsin was a dictator or an imperialist—especially when he was locked in combat with forces that were unambiguously antidemocratic and aggressively nationalistic. The confusion and murkiness in Russia argued all the more for steadiness and clarity in American policy. We should use our public statements and the president's upcoming summit to reiterate long-term goals and to encourage overall trends in Russia. The key fact about Russia in the fall of 1993 was that the citizens would be going to the polls to elect the new parliament and approve the new constitution. Russia was still a long way from being a stable, mature democracy, but it was also a long way from being a police state, and Yeltsin had been instrumental in moving his country in the right direction.

"That's why I want to stay close to him," said Clinton, pounding his palm on the steering wheel of the golf cart. He wanted to use his upcoming summit "to really bond with the guy. When he's got hard calls to make, he's more likely to make the right ones with the knowledge that I'm there for him."

The next morning, after breakfast, Clinton took me aside again, this time with Hillary joining us—the first time that had happened and one of the few that it would over the course of the administration. She had already become prominent and controversial over the issue of health care but kept very much in the background on foreign policy.

Clinton said he'd been thinking more overnight about what he saw as the implication of criticism we were getting both from Congress and from some of his own advisers.

"You listen to those folks, and what they're saying comes down to: Write that place off. It's going down. Step back so we don't get sucked in."

"Before we give up on Russia," interjected Hillary, "we should look at Taiwan, or South Korea," which had undergone their own long transitions to democracy. "Democracy comes by fits and starts after all those years of dictatorship. Russia's not doing that badly when you compare it to Asia. We've got to give them time."[6]

"That's right," said Clinton. "This business of helping Yeltsin overcome the worst of the past—including his own past—isn't for the faint of heart. It's going to be a two-steps-forward, one-step-backward deal."

I asked him if he knew he was quoting Lenin. He gave me a chiding look: "There's nothing you can out-wonk me on, Strobe, not even on Russia wonkery."

By then the sun was out, so the president went back to whacking golf balls, while I gathered up my family and drove down the mountain toward home, more confident in the long-range soundness of our policy than in the immediate prospects for Russian politics. Public opinion–polling—a new phenomenon in Russia—predicted that the new parliament, while genuinely post-Soviet, would be every bit as anti-Yeltsin and anti-reform as the old Supreme Soviet that had gone up in smoke in October.

WHEN RUSSIAN VOTERS went to the polls on December 12, I was with Vice-President Gore while he toured Central Asia as a demonstration of American support for the other new independent states of the former USSR. From there he was flying to Moscow for his second commission meeting with Chernomyrdin. Gore was still in Kazakhstan when the results started coming in from the Russian voting, and they were even worse than expected. Russia's Choice, the party of Gaidar, Kozyrev and other reformers, had been expected to get at least a third of the vote but it looked as though they were going to get only about half that.

Andrei Kozyrev won a Duma seat from Murmansk, but the big winner in that region and elsewhere around Russia appeared to be the grotesquely misnamed Liberal Democratic Party, led by Vladimir Zhirinovsky, the most theatrically outrageous of Russia's ultranationalists. Zhirinovsky, who had placed third behind Yeltsin in the 1991 election for the Russian presidency, campaigned in the 1993 parliamentary race on a platform of lowering the price of vodka, "defending the rights" of ethnic Russians against various alien elements, including Jews, and claiming to speak for the twenty-five million ethnic Russians whom the breakup of the USSR had stranded outside the borders of Russia proper; Russia, he vowed, would regain its lost lands in Turkey, Finland and Alaska.

As Air Force Two headed toward Moscow, Gore told Leon Fuerth and me that he had decided to suspend the usual practice of not commenting on other countries' domestic politics and declare Zhirinovsky the person-ification of much that the U.S. was sworn to oppose. As soon as he arrived at his hotel, the vice-president phoned Clinton, who had been closely fol-lowing the early returns from Russia. Clinton knew that Zhirinovsky was thoroughly bad news and agreed that Gore should say so, but the presi-dent was more relaxed about what the elections meant than we were in the Gore traveling team. Clinton sensed that Zhirinovsky was a powerful magnet for political disaffection but not, in his own right, a factor of last-ing importance. (Another indication that the surge for Zhirinovsky was more of a protest against Yeltsin than an embrace of belligerent national-ism and racism was the surprisingly weak showing of the communists.)[7]

What mattered, Clinton said, was that the election was a "wake-up call . . . If you're going to let folks vote, you've got to look at the conditions in which they live." And it wasn't just the Kremlin and the Moscow min-istries that needed to smell the coffee, but ourselves as well and our part-ners in the G-7 and the international financial institutions: "The IMF and the outside world had better get the message."

Listening to this, Gore nodded vigorously. Going back to the debate he'd moderated between Chernomyrdin and Larry Summers over dinner at Blair House in early September, the vice-president had been concerned that the strict conditions the International Monetary Fund attached to its loans to Russia put economic reform on a collision course with the po-litical realities of a fledgling democracy. The results of the parliamentary election seemed to bear out that concern.

When Gore met with Chernomyrdin shortly after our arrival in Mos-cow, the prime minister gave him a bleak assessment of the consequences we could expect from the parliamentary election: even though the Duma had less power under the new constitution than the Supreme Soviet had had under the old one, the government's political opponents could claim they had a popular mandate. As a result, everything that the U.S. and Russia were trying to do together—closing the gap between us over the Balkans, brokering a deal with Ukraine, cooperating on weapons proliferation more generally—would be harder. Worse, the election augured badly for what Russia was trying to do on its own, which was to transform itself into a modern country. But the battle wasn't over, he said. Much would depend on whether the U.S. and the West remained stalwart and generous in their support. Generous, he added, had to mean lenient IMF conditionality.

Gore, who already had some sympathy for that appeal, decided to go public with his endorsement of it. Standing next to Chernomyrdin at a press conference, he denounced Zhirinovsky for propounding views that were "reprehensible and anathema to all freedom-loving people in Russia, the United States and everywhere in the world," but he also criticized the IMF for contributing to the conditions that had caused the Zhirinovsky backlash. The fund, he said, had been "slow to recognize some of the hardships that are caused by some of the conditions that have been overly insisted upon in the past. . . . The world has to recognize the gravity of this situation and the enormity of the opportunity for the world to integrate this magnificent nation into the common effort of humankind to build a better way of life for the peoples of our world."

With the vice-president's comments obviously in mind, Michel Camdessus, the managing director of the IMF, complained that his organization was being made a "scapegoat." But he seemed to get the message: over the next few months, Larry Summers and his colleagues at Treasury worked with Camdessus to push through a $1.5 billion IMF loan to help stabilize Russia's economy.

I MADE MY OWN contribution to the debate on this issue shortly after our return from Moscow in a briefing on the election for the State Department press corps. Within the administration, I said, we had begun "intensive deliberations" on "refining, focusing and intensifying our reform support efforts" with the goal of promoting "less shock and more therapy" for the Russian people.

The reporters arrayed in front of me began to take notes furiously and a few headed for the exits to file a bulletin. I knew I was in trouble. In substance, the catchy phrase was self-evidently true: the hardships accompanying reform were backfiring against the reformers; the Russian electorate was demanding regular paychecks, decent medical care and reliable pensions. My mistake was to let my mind slip back into journalistic gear. "Less shock and more therapy" would have been a good headline for a column in *Time,* but as a pronouncement from the podium of the State Department press room, it eclipsed everything else I said and invited oversimplification both of developments in Russia and of our policy.

With five words, I managed to infuriate both Russian liberals and my colleagues at Treasury. They were already smarting over what Gore had said publicly in Moscow. Now it sounded to both groups that I too was blaming Gaidar and Fyodorov for the rise of Zhirinovsky and undercutting our own government's insistence on rapid, disciplined structural reform and strict conditionality for IMF lending.

I spent much of the Christmas holidays in one of Washington's most melancholy and futile exercises: clarifying what I had *meant* to say. The "therapy" I had in mind included the sort of social-safety-net programs Larry Summers and David Lipton were trying to encourage the IMF to fund. As almost always happens in such cases, my explanations never caught up with the original sound bite and the furor it caused.

Being good friends and forbearing colleagues who had weathered their own storms, Larry and David forgave me. Fyodorov, however, did not. A month later, he gave a press conference of his own denouncing me for having stabbed him and his fellow reformers in the back.

I knew I could count on some solace from Leon Fuerth, not least because I knew his boss entertained some doubts of his own about the ratio of shock to therapy in the Russian economy. The lesson of the whole flap, said Leon, was, "Loose quips sink dips."

A QUICK TRIP TO KIEV

In the immediate aftermath of the December parliamentary election, there was reason to fear that yet another casualty of Russian domestic politics would be the trilateral accord that Yeltsin, Clinton and President Kravchuk of Ukraine had agreed they would sign when Clinton came to Europe in January 1994. Through the fall, the U.S. had conducted quiet but arduous shuttle diplomacy between the two sides. For me, the short hop between Moscow and Kiev was like passing through the looking glass. From the Russian perspective, everything the Ukrainians did was stupid, childish, reckless, ungrateful and proof that their country had no business being independent. As the Ukrainians saw it, everything Russia did was malevolent, menacing and unfair, and validated hanging on to "their" missiles. From our own standpoint as the go-betweens, both sides were doing just about everything they could to make a reasonable compromise impossible. Finally, in early December, after Gore wrote several letters and made phone calls to Kravchuk, the Ukrainians indicated that they would give up the nuclear weapons on their territory in exchange for U.S.-brokered assurances from Moscow on Ukrainian sovereignty.

Then came the victory of a noisy nationalist in Russia, which hardened the position of the Ukrainians and seemed to cause the Russians to back-pedal as well, no doubt because they feared that the new Duma would be hostile to a deal.

When Gore called on Yeltsin during his visit to Moscow after the election, Yeltsin used the occasion to deliver a tirade on Ukrainian perfidy and American naïveté while the press was still in the room. "Ukraine is deceiving us all," he said. "It's deceiving the United States, Russia, Europe, the whole world and we're so helpless that we can't deal with this evil!" Gore started to respond, saying that we shouldn't give up, but Yeltsin interrupted him and told the press to leave.

In a working lunch with Gore devoted mostly to the Ukraine problem, Chernomyrdin echoed Yeltsin's charge that the Ukrainians were playing us off against each other, saying one thing to us and something quite different to the Russians. That gave me an idea, which I proposed on the spot: as a way of making sure that we were both hearing the same thing from the Ukrainians, why not have Yuri Mamedov and me go together to Kiev the next day? Gore said he thought it was the way to "cut the Gordian knot," and Chernomyrdin, after only a moment's hesitation, agreed.

I glanced down the table at Kozyrev and Mamedov, who both looked as though they were going to lose their lunch. They spent ten minutes trying to talk Chernomyrdin out of what he had agreed to, but he wouldn't budge.

Mamedov laid into me as soon as we were alone. I had made a big mistake, he said; moreover, I'd gotten him in deep trouble with his boss, Kozyrev.

"But not with your prime minister," I said. "And he's your boss's boss.

And *his* boss, your ultimate boss, wants a deal too. So does mine. This is the only way to get one."

The vice-president asked Bill Perry, the deputy secretary of defense who was in Moscow as part of the commission, to join the mission to Kiev. Bill had been the most forceful backer of Ukrainian denuclearization within the U.S. government and would bring the weight of the Pentagon to the talks, along with his own mastery of the subject. He readily agreed, although he was, at that moment, reeling from the sudden news out of Washington that his friend Les Aspin had just resigned as secretary of defense. In a matter of hours, we notified the Ukrainians we were coming— and that this time, we were bringing a friend from Moscow.

The Air Force was not used to having Russian diplomats aboard its VIP flights, so Mamedov was assigned a seat in the rear cabin of Perry's DC-9, amid the security personnel and communications specialists. Yuri looked a bit like a bedraggled tourist who had gotten on the wrong flight, so I went back to sit with him for a while and thank him for being a good sport. He had gotten over his annoyance and was into the mission. In a trademark mamedovism that I'd already given up on trying to correct, he told me I didn't need to "butter" him—he knew that sometimes diplomacy called for improvisation and risk-taking, and he'd make the most of the opportunity.

We arrived in Kiev late at night and went straight into the first of a series of meetings. Yuri's participation caused consternation among the Ukrainians. Like the Air Force, they weren't sure where to seat him— certainly not on their side of the table—so they put a single chair for him at the far end and did everything they could to make him feel like the odd man out.

With Bill Perry leading our delegation, we quickly reached broad agreement on a complex deal that would result in Russia getting the warheads along with American money to help with their dismantlement and Ukraine getting various forms of assistance from the U.S. as well as debt relief from Russia and international assurances on its sovereignty. Yuri's ability to vouch for the Russian end of the bargain proved decisive.

On our way home, we dropped Yuri off in Moscow. As he was making his way out of the plane, he shook my hand and said he exonerated me for kidnapping him. Then, with his briefcase in one hand and a shopping bag with a few overnight supplies in the other, he wandered off into the winter night.

THE MOSCOW SUMMIT

As the administration came to the end of its first year in office, Warren Christopher asked me to become deputy secretary, replacing Clifton Wharton, who resigned in November. The debate in the Senate over my confirmation began in earnest after the Christmas/New Year's recess, just as President Clinton was preparing to attend the NATO summit the second week in January. That timing, coming right after what was being depicted as the Zhirinovsky landslide, made my nomination a lightning rod for criticism of our foreign policy in general and our Russia policy in particular.

When I appeared before the Senate Foreign Relations Committee, it was bound to be a much tougher session than it had been a year earlier, so this time my whole family, including my parents, showed up for moral support. Jesse Helms, the North Carolina conservative who was the ranking Republican on the committee, welcomed Brooke and my mother to the proceedings with an elaborate display of Southern courtesy, then spent the rest of the day skewering me for virtually every view I'd ever expressed as a journalist and every position I'd taken in the year I'd been in government. Among the numerous charges he leveled at me was the insinuation that I had been, at a minimum, a dupe of Soviet intelligence when I worked on the Khrushchev memoirs in the 1970s.[8]

Other Republicans focused on my role in what they saw as the administration's cop-out or sellout in giving Partnership for Peace priority over NATO enlargement in the year ahead.[9] They were encouraged in this line of attack by powerful forces in the Polish-American community, particularly Jan Nowak, a uniquely influential figure of the Polish diaspora, who said our emphasis on PFP amounted to a "green light" to Moscow's "ambitions to restore the Russian empire."[10] Henry Kissinger, whose stentorian voice often scolded us from the op-ed pages, was vehemently opposed to PFP, which he warned would "dilute what is left of the Atlantic alliance into a vague multilateralism." What bothered Kissinger most about PFP was its inclusiveness, and the place it held open for Russia itself.[11]

Senator Richard Lugar, an Indiana Republican who had been a champion of bipartisan support for assistance to Russia, publicly chastised our administration for pursuing a "Russia-first" policy, calling PFP "a Band-Aid offered in place of corrective surgery." Privately, he admonished me that NATO enlargement was necessary "to contain the problem of Russia redux." I found it ominous that an influential and moderate member of the Senate would reintroduce the concept of containment.

General Shalikashvili, the principal author of Partnership for Peace, spoke out in defense of the program. Making the most out of it would give us a way of simultaneously coaching aspirants for membership as they overhauled their military establishments and coaxing Russia toward a less hostile view of NATO. On the other hand, Shali warned, a rush to enlarge NATO would create "a new line of division" in Europe.

The president himself struck much the same theme on the eve of his trip: "We don't want to give the impression that we're creating another dividing line in Europe after we've worked for decades to get rid of the one that existed before." PFP, he predicted, would "permit the expansion of NATO, and I fully expect that it will lead to that at some point."[12]

CLINTON LEFT FOR EUROPE ON January 8, immediately after attending the funeral of his mother, Virginia Kelley, in Arkansas. He was subdued and exhausted when he boarded Air Force One. Normally those of us charged with preparing him for his meetings would have fought with his schedulers for "briefing time" during the long first leg of the trip, but on this occasion, we left the president to himself. He napped for a while, then summoned Secretary Christopher, Tony Lake and me to his cabin in the nose of the plane. He was thinking through how to deal with the volatile mix of hopes and fears awaiting him on the other side of the Atlantic. He would create a whole new problem if he either overencouraged the Central Europeans or excessively reassured the Russians about the pace of enlargement. Tony was more concerned about the former danger— we had to be careful not to make the process sound like "a treadmill" for the would-be allies—while Chris stressed the latter: "It can't be a moving sidewalk that just keeps moving at the same speed no matter what. The direction is not in question, but we've got to be able to control the pace."

In Brussels, Clinton tried to thread the needle by saying that creation of PFP "sets in motion a process that leads to the enlargement of NATO."

Two days later, in a joint press conference in Prague with Central European leaders at his side, Clinton said that the question before the alliance was "no longer whether NATO will take on new members but when and how." It was a catchy phrase uttered by the president in a dramatic setting, so proponents within the administration of moving faster played it as a watershed. In substance, however, it was a reiteration of the decision Clinton had made the previous October.

———

AIR FORCE ONE took off from Prague and headed toward Kiev for
what was probably the most exhaustively negotiated refueling stop in history. President Kravchuk had been agitating for a year to have Clinton
come to Kiev, since it would be the first presidential visit to an independent Ukraine and a boost to Kravchuk's flagging popularity. We had used
Kravchuk's desire as leverage with the Ukrainians in the negotiations over
the trilateral accord. We had seen evidence that Kravchuk wanted a deal
but was being held back by his closest aides. When Secretary Christopher
had a working dinner in Kiev in October, the foreign minister, Anatoly
Zlenko, and the national security adviser, Anton Buteiko, all but stuck a
napkin in their president's mouth during the borscht course and from
then on did all the talking for the Ukrainian side, referring to Kravchuk
in the third person as though he was not at the table. Even after the
impromptu trip that Bill Perry, Yuri Mamedov and I made to Kiev in
mid-December, the Ukrainians haggled over technical details that unless resolved would have scuttled the agreement. We refused to confirm
that President Clinton would stop in Kiev unless every word and punctuation mark in the trilateral deal was agreed in advance. The final pieces
fell into place when Clinton was already in Europe, and only then did
we consent to a presidential "visit" to Ukraine. It lasted two hours and
was confined to the tarmac and the VIP departure lounge at Borispol
Airport.

Once we were on the ground, it looked as though we'd been snookered.
Zlenko and Buteiko tried once again to muzzle their president and reopen
issues that we had already spilt blood to close. Clinton and Christopher,
neither of whom was in the habit of roughing up a head of state, decided
to make an exception. They told Kravchuk in the bluntest of terms that if
he backed out of the deal that had already been made it would be a major
setback for Ukraine's relations with both Russia and the U.S.

While Zlenko and Buteiko sulked, a visibly shaken Kravchuk promised
Clinton he would stick with the agreements in hand and not pull any last-
minute tricks when he came to Moscow two days later to sign the trilateral accord.

I had half a mind to stay behind to keep the pressure on but decided
instead to go on to Moscow in case there were last-minute problems to
attend to there.

CLINTON SPENT MOST of his first day in Moscow seeing the sights.
Tom Pickering, our ambassador, arranged for Clinton to visit Our Lady of

Kazan Cathedral so that he could light a candle for his mother. That evening, Tom hosted a large reception at Spaso House to give Clinton the flavor of Russian politics in nearly all of its rambunctious diversity. Of all the major figures in Russian politics, only Zhirinovsky was not invited.

As Clinton worked the crowd, he found that attitudes toward Yeltsin ranged from veiled criticism on the part of reformers, who felt demoralized, to venomous denunciation from communists.

The center of attention among the guests was Alexander Lebed, a general who had risen to prominence as the commander of the Russian army in Moldova, a small former Soviet republic wedged between Ukraine and Romania. Lebed was right out of a recruiting poster: barrel-chested and steely-eyed, he had a basso profundo voice and spoke in clipped sentences that sounded like orders. If there was a man on a white horse in Russia's future, Lebed was already saddling up.

WHILE CLINTON AND LEBED were talking, Yuri Mamedov, looking grim, beckoned me over to a couch in the corner of Spaso House's cavernous reception hall.

"We've got the makings of a disaster," he said. Victor Mikhailov, the minister of atomic energy who had made such an impression on all of us as Lynn Davis's nemesis at Vancouver, was trying to derail the trilateral accord with Ukraine.[13] I told Yuri about the similar problem we had on the Ukrainian side and how Clinton had braced Kravchuk personally. Now he'd have to do the same with Yeltsin—quickly and privately, when the presidents met for the first time at dinner that evening.

When we arrived at a dacha southeast of Moscow, a string quartet was playing Chopin in the foyer. At the threshold stood a beaming Yeltsin, his hand extended. Clinton got out of his limousine, grabbed Yeltsin by the shoulders, leaned close to his face and said the two of them needed to talk alone right away. Yeltsin, taken aback, let his guest steer him off to an anteroom. Once they were alone, Clinton indirectly attacked the problem at hand. He wanted to notify Yeltsin about a disturbing incident in Kiev the night before, he said in a can-you-believe-this tone; Kravchuk had people around him who were trying to reopen the deal. Clinton then recounted his scolding of Kravchuk in detail, explaining how Kravchuk, duly shamed, now understood that he owed it to both Clinton and Yeltsin to resist the troublemakers in his government. The U.S., Clinton continued, would remain deeply and conscientiously involved in the follow-up, making sure that both of its partners' interests were protected.[14]

Clinton emerged and gave Chris, Tony and me a report: "I laid it on pretty thick. Yeltsin's eyes were locked on mine. He was listening closely. All he said when I finished was, 'I understand.' We'll have to see if we're okay or not. I think we are."

We sat down for a twenty-four-course dinner, including a mystery dish that was identified on the menu as duck in wine sauce but turned out to be sautéed moose lips. Yeltsin led us through several vodka toasts and had five glasses of wine (Chris and I were both counting). Yeltsin presented a blue porcelain figurine of Clinton waving with one hand and holding a saxophone with the other, then called for a real saxophone and asked Clinton to play.

Yeltsin teased Andrei Kozyrev unmercifully for being a ladies' man—an issue that had not so far figured on our agenda with the foreign minister. Suddenly, apparently remembering the importance of equality in all things Russian-American, Yeltsin started ribbing Chris along the same lines.

Amidst the toasts, roasts and musical interludes, the subject of the trilateral accord with Ukraine came up only once, in the form of a proclamation by Yeltsin: "Tomorrow we will talk about foreign-policy issues, but not Ukraine. On Ukraine, we'll meet with Kravchuk *briefly;* we'll discuss a *few* things, but not much. Then we'll go sign the documents. After that, we'll have nothing more to do with him or that issue!"

Clinton caught my eye and winked.

THE NEXT DAY, Yeltsin and Kravchuk both kept their word, and the trilateral meeting came off without a hitch. Yeltsin, as the host of the meeting, was curt but businesslike. Kravchuk was stoical but unhappy, and seemed in a big hurry to get it over with. Only Clinton seemed to enjoy the occasion. He was wearing a tie emblazoned with the words *Carpe diem* and congratulated the two other presidents at some length for following that motto.

ONCE KRAVCHUK hastily departed, Clinton went to work trying to whittle away Yeltsin's resistance to NATO enlargement. Now that the two of them had worked so diligently and successfully to deal with the urgent matter of nuclear weapons in Ukraine, he said, they needed to apply themselves in the same spirit to another big challenge: the architecture of European security. He was committed to building structures that took account of Russia's legitimate interests and aspirations. But Yeltsin had to be similarly sensitive to the hopes and fears of the Central Europeans.

Yeltsin saved his substantive response for the press conference afterward. The integration of former communist countries into the structures of the West was a fine objective, he said, and Russia looked forward to being part of that process. But all those countries must be "integrated together, in just one package. This will make everyone more secure. If, however, you try to dismember us, accepting us and admitting us one by one—that will be no good. I'm against that; I'm absolutely opposed to it. That's why I support the president's initiative for Partnership for Peace."

It was a sober, public reprise of what Yeltsin had done, drunkenly and privately, with Secretary Christopher in October: he was stipulating that Russia would participate in PFP only if it was an alternative to NATO enlargement, or a precursor to the day—very far off indeed—when all former Soviet republics and Soviet satellites would enter NATO together.

Clinton demurred, but only gently: The Brussels summit had made clear, he said, that NATO "plainly contemplated an expansion." That, he quickly added, was for the future, while PFP was "the real thing now."

The president had just given the can another kick.

THE NEXT SUMMIT EVENT—a nationally televised town meeting with an audience primarily of students, and with large-screen hookups to similar groups in St. Petersburg and Nizhny-Novgorod—was Clinton's chance to talk to the Russian people, especially the younger generation. The site, an auditorium at Ostankino television station, was selected at Tom Pickering's suggestion because it had been the scene of the bloodiest fighting in early October and was a reminder of the ongoing struggle in which we had such a profound stake.

Witnessing Clinton prepare for and deliver this speech was both frightening and inspiring, in that it captured both his indiscipline and his genius. He hadn't even looked at the draft prepared by his staff until he was in his armored limousine for the short ride to the TV station. He took me with him in the car, but I had little to contribute as he flipped through the pages, scribbling like crazy and muttering complaints about his speechwriters.

He relaxed the moment he arrived at the studio, which was arranged like the set of a talk show. Clinton was at ease standing in the center, microphone in hand, surrounded by over three hundred young people. As he began to speak, he used the prepared text as a rhetorical home base. He would read a few paragraphs, then arc off into ideas as they occurred to him, return for a brief touchdown to reconnect with the structure of the written version, then take off again into the blue sky of his vision for a Russia that was strong enough and brave enough first to imagine, then to achieve, a better future for itself. The core theme was in the original draft: the redefinition of greatness from terms of the nineteenth and twentieth centuries, when brute force had been the currency of Russian power in the world, to those appropriate to the twenty-first. But as he spoke, the best lines—about Russia's potential to be a contributor to and beneficiary of the emergence of a new global system—were those that he ad-libbed. He also wove into the speech numerous extemporaneous advertisements, some quite explicit, others subliminal, for the virtues of Russian cooperation with an expanding NATO:

> I believe the measure of your greatness in the future will be whether Russia, the big neighbor, can be the good neighbor. That is why it's so important that as your forces operate beyond your borders, they do so according to international law; why it's important that you continue your planned withdrawal from all the Baltic states; why it's important that your nation work with the United States and the rest of Europe to build the Partnership for Peace called for at the NATO conference this year.

Clinton ended on a note that was aimed at the youthful audience, at citizens of a non-evil non-empire that deserved to be integrated rather than contained:

> I believe there are signs you can make a future that is different from the past. Yours is a history of heroism and of persistent hope. . . . This is a crossroad, and a difficult one. Younger generations of Russians will look back on this time with either gratitude or regret, depending on how those questions are answered—the economic, the political, the military questions. . . . I believe you will choose the right future. After all, Russia did not get to this point by making all that many wrong decisions in the past. And every nation makes a few mistakes. There are few people anywhere that have more knowledge of history, both positive and negative, that have more reason to hope for the future than you do. I know the present is difficult, but if you make the right decisions, if you choose hope over fear, then the future will reward your courage and your vision.

The shortcoming of the speech reflected the shortcoming of our policy—and of Russian reform itself: we, like the reformers, had a far clearer notion of where we wanted to see Russia go than how it could get there, how long it would take, and what we could do to help.

IF THE TOWN MEETING had provided the moment of greatest uplift during the summit, the official dinner that Yeltsin hosted that evening at the Kremlin brought us back to earth with a thump. Ever since the shock of the parliamentary election a month earlier, there had been rumors that Yeltsin would have to assuage public discontent with economic reform by dumping the most prominent of the reformers, starting with Gaidar himself. That shake-up was under way literally before our eyes as we, the American visitors, formed a receiving line with scores of Russian political, academic and cultural celebrities in the foyer outside the resplendently renovated Hall of Facets, once the czars' ceremonial throne room.

Yeltsin had privately alerted Clinton the night before to what he was about to do, although he had made it sound like a reshuffling of the deck to strengthen his hand rather than a discarding of the reformers: Gaidar would assume full-time leadership of Russia's Choice so that it could serve as the standard-bearer for Yeltsin's—and the West's—preferred policies in the new Duma.

That wasn't how Gaidar explained what was happening when he saw Larry Summers just before the Kremlin dinner: he and Fyodorov were being fired, pure and simple.

Larry came to me in high dudgeon. Yeltsin, he said, was inflicting a major blow on Russia's chances of developing as a stable economy and thereby forfeiting his claim on Western economic support. Larry asked me to get word to Clinton that he should intercede with Yeltsin immediately to keep Gaidar and Fyodorov in their jobs. We agreed that Clinton couldn't be in the position of explicitly second-guessing a personnel decision Yeltsin had already made, but he could impress on Yeltsin the consequences with the IMF and G-7 if he fired the two people in his government most identified with sound fiscal and monetary policies.

I sent a note to the president at the head table that I needed to see him urgently. After dinner, as the guests adjourned to a nearby hall for a concert, a Secret Service agent collared me.

"The boss wants to see you. He's in the john."

I headed to the men's room, where another Secret Service agent was preventing some rather unhappy-looking Russian guests from entering.

Inside, I summarized what had happened and what Larry felt the president had to do with Yeltsin.

"I'll do it," said Clinton, "but it's a tough one. Their political requirements are at cross-purposes with good economics." He went off to talk to Yeltsin, while I went looking for Mamedov so that I could double-track the message. I found Yuri and took him into an alcove of the concert hall to let him know of our concern over the impending departure of Gaidar. His advice was, as it had been before and would often be in the future, "Don't get excited; don't overdramatize." Gaidar might be a fine fellow, a true democrat, an excellent economist, but many Russians blamed him and Fyodorov for the miserable conditions in which they lived. "You want us to be a democracy," he said, "so don't be surprised when a president and a prime minister have to sacrifice a minister or two who are tarred with the brush of what are seen as failed policies. This is real politics. At least we don't shoot people."

Clinton found two occasions to raise Gaidar's future privately with Yeltsin, first during the dinner that night and again during a farewell conversation at the Kremlin the next day.

"I gave it my best shot," said Clinton afterward, "but it was different from when I pushed him on the Ukraine deal at the dacha. This time I had the feeling his mind was made up and we're just going to have to live with whatever he feels his political situation requires."

GAIDAR'S RESIGNATION came the day after Clinton left Moscow, and Fyodorov's followed ten days later. Gaidar warned that his country faced the danger of a form of fascism "beside which everything else Russia has experienced will pale in significance," and Fyodorov warned that the new government's "red managers"—the most prominent of whom was Prime Minister Chernomyrdin—were carrying out an "economic coup."

I used some time on the margins of the summit to take soundings of my own about what was happening. Almost everyone I talked to was apocalyptic: Zhirinovsky was poised to sweep into the presidency, and it was all the fault of Yeltsin and Gaidar—and the West for supporting them. I heard that view from, among many others, Vladimir Lukin, who had left his post as ambassador to Washington to pursue his parliamentary career full-time and who had been trounced earlier that day in an election for the position of speaker of the Duma.

During the state dinner, Georgi Arbatov buttonholed me like the An-

Brooke, then a sophomore at Stanford, was visiting over Thanksgiving in 1969 when she snapped this picture in front of the townhouse at 46 Leckford Road in North Oxford that I shared with Bill Clinton and Frank Aller, a sinologist of great charm and promise who later took his own life. (Copyright Brooke Shearer)

The closest I ever came to Nikita Khrushchev, other than listening to his voice on tape for hundreds of hours, was a visit to his grave at Novodevichy Monastery on the banks of the Moscow River in 1973. Twenty-five years later I took President Clinton on a tour of that same cemetery, showing him (below) the monument to Andrei Gromyko, the longtime Soviet foreign minister, as well as those to Stalin's second wife, Nadezhda Alliluyeva, and, of course, Khrushchev himself, whose grave was now marked by a headstone half in white, half in black to symbolize the contradictions of his career and legacy. At my side is Dimitry Zarechnak, a veteran State Department interpreter. (Left: John Shaw; below: The White House)

During a walk on the beach in South Carolina at a Renaissance Weekend retreat in January 1993, Clinton laid out in detail his strategy for dealing with Russia. (Author's collection)

On March 18, 1993, Clinton, Vice-President Gore and Secretary of State Warren Christopher convened their advisers to discuss economic assistance to Russia. After listening somewhat impatiently to our plans, Clinton told us to "go back and think bigger!" On my left is Toby Gati, the senior Russia expert on the National Security Council staff, and on my right are Tony Lake, the head of the NSC; Peter Tarnoff, the under secretary of state; Larry Summers, then the under secretary of the treasury; and Nancy Soderberg and Sandy Berger of the NSC. (The White House)

An on-the-road swearing-in in early April 1993, on the eve of the first summit with Boris Yeltsin in Vancouver. We were in a hotel room in Portland, Oregon. Secretary of Labor Bob Reich, who'd been at Oxford with Clinton and me, held the Gideon Bible. (The White House)

In Vancouver, Clinton introduced me for the first time to Yeltsin. In preparation for the summit, Clinton had studied John F. Kennedy's disastrous meeting with Khrushchev in 1961, in which the seasoned Soviet leader seemed to best the young, newly elected American president. Yeltsin came to Vancouver in a demanding and combative mood, but Clinton quickly concluded he wasn't "pulling a Khrushchev"; instead, the embattled Russian leader was trying to protect himself back home by looking tough at the summit. (The White House)

The two presidents held their first joint press conference in Vancouver. These were always suspenseful events, since Yeltsin sometimes used them to announce breakthroughs that hadn't actually occurred, to posture for his domestic audience and to lash out at the press itself. (The White House)

The core team in 1993 for what we called the *zdravstvidaniya* ("hello–good-bye") tours, which took us hopscotching through Eurasia: Eric Edelman, Toria Nuland and Larry Napper of the State Department (top); John Gordon of the Pentagon; David Lipton of Treasury; Toby Gati of the NSC; and John McLaughlin of the CIA. We were solidifying relations with all fifteen former Soviet republics. (Author's collection)

To support the independence of the smaller countries of the former USSR, Clinton invited a number of leaders to Washington. Eduard Shevardnadze, the president of Georgia, had unique standing, given his heroic role in the peaceful dismantling of the USSR. But for just that reason he was detested by many in the political, military and intelligence establishments in Russia, and he was under constant pressure and sometimes physical danger from his enemies domestic and foreign. In this meeting in the Oval Office, "Shevy," as even his own loyalists called him (though never to his face), was accompanied by his personal foreign-policy adviser, Gela Charkviani, who served as interpreter, and, to Gela's right, on the couch, the Georgian ambassador to Washington, Tedo Japaridze. They had been the first two officials from the former Soviet Union to call on me at State at the beginning of the administration in January 1993. (The White House)

Warren Christopher and his first Russian counterpart, Andrei Kozyrev, after signing joint statements at the first Clinton-Yeltsin summit in Moscow in January 1994. Kozyrev's pro-Western leanings made him vulnerable to conservative forces in the Russian parliament; that political liability at home left him little room for compromise with the U.S. (The White House)

Clinton, who was frequently on the phone with Yeltsin, consulted with him during yet another showdown with the Soviet-era parliament, this time in September 1993. Russian radio had just reported that Yeltsin would be ousted by midnight. The situation, Yeltsin told Clinton, was "totally out of control," and he had decided to suspend the parliament and call new elections. (The White House)

Early in the administration, Chelsea Clinton gave Brooke's and my sons, Devin and Adrian, a tour of the White House. The three had known each other since they were children and remained close in the years that followed. (Devin Talbott collection)

Aboard Air Force Two en route to Moscow for a Gore-Chernomyrdin commission meeting. Sitting next to me was Steve Pifer, a State Department expert on arms control, and looking on were Leon Fuerth, Gore's adviser on foreign policy, and Jonathan Spalter, another Gore aide. (Phil Humnicky/The White House)

Brooke and I led the reception committee for Yeltsin when he arrived at Andrews Air Force Base in Maryland in September 1994 to begin his first official visit to the U.S. during the Clinton administration. He had drunk heavily on the long flight over the Atlantic, and it showed. His aides and security team had to work hard to sober him up at Blair House that night for what turned out to be an important meeting with Clinton on the future of NATO the next day. (State Department)

Secretary Christopher and I consulted with Clinton in Halifax in June 1995 just before he met with Yeltsin. Chechen guerrillas had conducted a raid into a neighboring republic and seized hostages, and we had to be ready for a public outburst from Yeltsin. We got it—Yeltsin threw a tantrum with the press that dominated the headlines. (The White House)

Horsing around with Richard Holbrooke after we'd given a briefing for the White House press corps in the fall of 1995 (I was armed with a cane because I'd torn a muscle in a family touch-football game). Holbrooke was in the midst of negotiating the Dayton peace accord for Bosnia. My principal task was to keep the Russians on board an effort that they found distasteful, since it gave diplomatic predominance to the U.S. and the whip hand to NATO. (*The Washington Times*)

Last-minute strategizing before a round of hard slogging with Yeltsin at Hyde Park in October 1995. The meeting produced breakthroughs on a mutually acceptable role for Russia in the Bosnian peacekeeping mission and a reduction in Russia's armaments along its borders. (The White House)

Time out from diplomacy: on a trip to Moscow I broke away for dinner with my two oldest Russian friends, Volodya Rokityansky (left) and Slava Luchkov (right). "What's happened to our culture?" asked Slava. "What's happened to our state? We've dumped the bad, but haven't figured out what the good is, much less found it." (Rita Luchkov)

During a crucial period in 1995, Secretary of Defense Bill Perry (left) established a rapport with his Russian counterpart, Pavel Grachev (right). While their backgrounds and personal styles could not have been more different—Perry was a soft-spoken defense intellectual and Grachev was a bluff, battle-hardened paratrooper—the "Bill-and-Pasha" channel paid off in Bosnia and arms control. Here they are triggering the demolition of a U.S. Minuteman missile silo at Whiteman Air Force Base, Missouri. (Courtesy of William J. Perry)

In April 1996, Yeltsin, who was in the midst of an uphill battle against the communist leader Gennady Zyuganov, summoned me to Moscow. He wanted assurance that Clinton would not have a separate, private meeting with Zyuganov during his visit to Moscow a few days later. (I was joined by Thomas Pickering, our ambassador to Moscow, and Toria Nuland; Yeltsin was joined by his recently appointed foreign minister, Yevgeny Primakov, and Dimitri Ryurikov, the Kremlin foreign-policy adviser.)

En route to Moscow, Clinton passed through St. Petersburg. This picture, taken during a sight-seeing tour with our consul general, John Evans (right), captures a distinctive—and, for Clinton, galling—aspect of the stopover: he was kept away from ordinary citizens. Evans learned that the man responsible for the tight security was the deputy mayor of St. Petersburg, Vladimir Putin.

In Moscow, before a long day of meetings with Yeltsin and others, Clinton and I stretched before a run through Sparrow Hills, near Moscow State University. Clinton used the getaway to vent about being prevented from meeting "real people" the day before in St. Petersburg.

Later in the day, Clinton held a lengthy and lively discussion with a full array of Russian politicians (Zyuganov was opposite the president, Anatoly Chubais was on Clinton's right, Grigory Yavlinsky was second on the left). Only the ultranationalist Vladimir Zhirinovsky was excluded from the event. (Top: The Kremlin; all others: The White House)

In July 1996, while waiting for Yeltsin to come on the line, Clinton reviewed the latest political news from Russia. Defying earlier pessimism, Yeltsin had come in first in the opening round of the presidential election, but he still faced a runoff against his communist opponent. Waiting with us were (right to left) Brooke, Steve Pifer, Tony Lake and Andy Sens of the NSC staff. (The White House)

At a conference sponsored by Columbia University in November 1996, I chatted with George Kennan (left), the distinguished diplomat and historian, whom I'd regarded as a mentor since the sixties, and Anatoly Dobrynin (right), who had been the Soviet ambassador to Washington for twenty years. I'd spent much of the afternoon and evening defending the expansion of NATO—a policy that both elder statesmen, along with much of the U.S. foreign-policy establishment, vigorously opposed. (Lynn Saville)

cient Mariner and told me that the only way to stop the browns from taking over was to shift our support to the reds. "Stop thinking in stereotypes! Work with the communists!" he said. "They're more pragmatic and reasonable than the reformers. Abandon Yeltsin! He's dragging us down. If you cling to him, we will all blame you for the disaster that is about to engulf us."

The only Russian I found who had anything good to say about Yeltsin or our support for him was another figure out of the recent past, Alexander Yakovlev, who had been a member of Gorbachev's politburo and a moving force behind *glasnost*. Yakovlev's counsel was not to worry too much about Zhirinovsky; he was basically a nut case; the Russian people "wouldn't follow him to the bathroom." The communists were the ones we should worry about; it was they, not the fascists, who had given Russia such a miserable century. We should focus on them as the danger for the next round of parliamentary elections, two years in the future. "The communists," he said, "are as committed as ever to violence, to doing whatever is necessary to preserve their own power. They're playing the democracy game cleverly. They're using Zhirinovsky, the extremist, to make themselves look moderate, including in the eyes of the West. They're staking out the center for themselves. You must support the reformers. What they need, above all, is time. That's because what they're up against still has deep roots in the soil of Russian politics—particularly in my generation. Your whole strategy ought to be to buy Russia time so that it can see my generation into the grave where it belongs."

Then he added, "And whatever one might say about Boris Yeltsin, he understands that truth deep, deep in his gut."

Back in Washington, I passed along what Yakovlev had said to Clinton, knowing it would reinforce his view just as it had done my own.

"Yeah," he said, "these things are real hard. We've just got to stick with them and ride it out, including all the second-guessing. We're doing all we can do. We don't have another option. The last thing we should do is get into a deep funk and start sucking lemons."

He also remarked on the firestorm of opposition to me for the post of deputy secretary of state. "Don't let this fuss they're making about you give you a swelled head," he said. "Remember, it's me they're really going after. You're just a convenient target."

When my nomination finally went to the floor of the Senate on February 22, 1994, nearly a third of the body—all Republicans—voted against me. Secretary Christopher, who'd taken his share of criticism during the first year of the administration, made light of what was obviously a shot across his bow as much as mine. "Look at it this way," he said. "Two thirds voted for you, so if you'd been a treaty, at least you would have been ratified."

CHAPTER 5

THE BIG *NYET*

One says a lot in vain, refusing;
The other mainly hears the "No."

Goethe

I N T H E F I R S T H A L F of 1994, Bosnia gave us a good look at what Boris Yeltsin was up against in the new Russian Duma—and what the West would be up against if Vladimir Zhirinovsky or anyone like him ever made it to the Kremlin.

Zhirinovsky was a leader of the opposition bloc that had nearly twice as many seats as the pro-Yeltsin forces. On a visit to Belgrade in late January, he warned that he and his parliamentary allies would consider NATO action in Bosnia a declaration of war on Russia. He traveled across the border into the Serb-dominated part of Bosnia itself and pledged Russian support for the locals as well as for their protector Milošević. During a quick trip to the Serbian-occupied region of eastern Croatia, he vowed to authorize use against the Bosnian Muslims of a Russian secret weapon, called the "Elipton," which emitted lethal bursts of sound. Western military experts whose job it was to stay up to date on Russian weaponry had no idea what he was talking about. Leon Fuerth speculated that the device might be nothing more than Zhirinovsky himself armed with a megaphone.

On Saturday, February 5, 1994, the Serbs fired a mortar into the central market in Sarajevo, killing 69 people and wounding 197 others. This particular act of butchery, even though similar to many that had preceded it, had a catalytic effect on public opinion in the West and therefore on political will. The North Atlantic Council, the permanent body of member-states' ambassadors at NATO headquarters in Brussels, issued the alliance's first real ultimatum: the Serbs had ten days to withdraw their artillery from around Sarajevo; any heavy weapons found within a twelve-mile exclusion zone would be subject to attack.

Russian fears of Western intervention spiked. In a phone call to President Clinton on February 11, Yeltsin said menacingly that the two of them had better stay in close touch on urgent matters that might even involve nuclear weapons. Instead of asking what that was supposed to mean, Clinton adopted his most soothing manner, and by the end of the call he had Yeltsin agreeing that it would probably be necessary for NATO to enforce the impoundment of the Serb artillery. But Yeltsin still would not concede the need for air strikes.

Several weeks later, Clinton asked Richard Nixon, who was on his way to Moscow, to impress upon Yeltsin that to have any chance of success in achieving a diplomatic settlement, the UN had to be prepared to hit Milošević hard. Nixon promised to do so, but Yeltsin canceled their meeting in a fit of pique when Nixon was granted appointments with Zhirinovsky and Alexander Rutskoi, who had just been amnestied by the new Duma, as well as the Communist Party chief, Gennady Zyuganov. On Nixon's return to the U.S., the Clintons were embroiled in the Whitewater controversy, and the press was drawing comparisons to the Watergate scandal. For both their sakes, Nixon decided to put some distance between himself and Clinton. Instead of reporting to the president in person, he dictated a lengthy letter conveying what turned out to be his parting advice to a successor with whom he had developed an odd but very real affinity: the U.S. should continue to support Yeltsin as the best guarantor of Russian democracy and stability. Within a month Nixon suffered a stroke and died.[1]

IN EARLY APRIL, the Serbs turned another obscure Balkan place name into a household word synonymous with ethnic cleansing. After a siege that lasted for weeks, Serb paramilitary forces were poised to overrun the mostly Muslim town of Goražde. The UN Security Council had already passed a resolution threatening to punish the Serbs if they attacked a safe area, so this time the Russians couldn't stop NATO from carrying out air strikes on a Serb artillery command bunker.

It was the first time NATO pulled the trigger against an enemy in its forty-five-year history —and it had done so as a result of a UN action in which Russia had acquiesced. But the importance of this watershed was almost instantly obscured, since the air strikes were ineffectual. "Pinprick" became the latest addition to the vocabulary of the Bosnian conflict. The Russians went into a frenzy to turn off even this level of bombing since, Moscow insisted, the Serbs had finally seen the light and would stop in their tracks.

Once again making fools of their would-be protectors in Moscow, the Serbs conducted a gruesome mopping-up operation in the area around Goražde. Feeling yet again betrayed, the Russians went along with a Security Council resolution demanding the pullback of Serb forces from Goražde. That set the scene for NATO to issue another ultimatum at the end of April: either the Serbs withdrew from the town or they faced more air strikes. Finally, the combination of UN and NATO actions had some effect. The Serbs stopped shelling Goražde and pulled back. A contingent of UN troops and observers, mostly Ukrainians, moved into the town.

SECRETARY CHRISTOPHER met with Andrei Kozyrev and the foreign ministers of the United Kingdom and France in London and established what they called the Contact Group on Bosnia. Subsequently, Germany and Italy would join as well. The Contact Group existed for the sole purpose of including Russia in a kind of steering committee otherwise made up of key NATO allies. Its stated objective was to revive the peace process in Bosnia, but its real purpose, in the minds of the allied foreign ministers, was to keep Russia, as they variously put it, inside the tent, on the reservation or, in Chris's phrase, sullen but not obstructionist.

Kozyrev saw that purpose too. He went along with the Contact Group because he knew that sooner or later diplomacy would have to be coupled with serious military action to have any effect, and when that time came, he didn't want Russia to be left stamping its feet impotently on the sidelines.

The reds and browns in the Duma also saw where the logic of the Contact Group was leading, and since they had written Kozyrev off as little better than a traitor, they turned their pressure on Defense Minister Grachev, chiding him for standing idly by while Kozyrev let himself be used by the Contact Group. Thus provoked, Grachev flailed around for some way of demonstrating that his ministry, at last, was prepared to stand up to the West. He vowed that the Russian military would have nothing to do with the Partnership for Peace as long as NATO was threatening the Serbs.

Outflanked within his own goverment, Kozyrev felt that he, too, now had to play coy on PFP. For months, he put on what Sandy Berger called a Lucy-and-the-football act: figuratively and sometimes literally walking up to a document that would formally associate Russia with PFP but not ever actually signing it. At a ceremony in Brussels the third week in June, he did put his name on a statement of intent to join PFP, but at some un-specified future date—and with a quirky but telling flourish: "It is one thing if a small poodle tries to walk through these gates"—that is, join PFP—"but quite another matter when an elephant like Russia tries to do the same thing." He seemed to be expressing a Westernized Russian's sense of his own country as an exotic, bulky, untamed Eurasian beast not com-fortable in its own skin, unsure whether it was welcome in Europe or, for that matter, in the West, or even whether it really belonged there.

"RUSSIANS GO HOME!"

Boris Yeltsin harbored no such doubt or discomfiture about Russia's size or its place in the world. He wanted Russia to be part of every international organization of any standing, especially organizations that brought to-gether the heads of state from the most powerful democracies, since those were the ranks where he felt the new Russia, and he as its founding father, deserved to be accepted.

During the spring of 1994, PFP was not much on Yeltsin's mind; that was a ministerial problem, for people like Kozyrev to deal with. Yeltsin was focused instead on the annual G-7 summit, to be held in Naples in July. He wanted to know why it wasn't the G-8—or, as he kept calling it dur-ing phone calls to Clinton, "the Big Eight."

Clinton was prepared to oblige Yeltsin by inviting him to Naples as a full participant rather than a guest. He felt it would be a relatively low-cost, high-impact way of anchoring Yeltsin, and therefore Russia, in the West. The G-8 would be the ultimate club, and Russia's clubbability might help serve as an antidote to its pariah complex—at least in the mind, and behavior, of its president.

The Treasury Department, however, was adamant on holding the line against a G-8. For one thing, the G-7 still had important work to do in steering international monetary and financial policy. Russia, as one of the largest debtors to the individual G-7 countries and to the IMF, had no place at the table when those matters came up. Moreover, nerves were still raw at Treasury about the purge of the reformers from Prime Minister Chernomyrdin's government in January. Vice-President Gore's public chastisement of the IMF for contributing to Russia's political problems by imposing overly tough conditions on its lending still rankled. That was worse than unfair, in Larry Summers's view—it was unwise, since it helped take the pressure off the Russian government to institute genuine reforms. Letting Yeltsin into a G-8 would only reward the backsliding already under way in the form of inflationary fiscal and monetary policies and failure to reform the tax and banking systems.

In the face of Larry's strong view, Clinton settled for an arrangement whereby the G-7 leaders would treat Yeltsin as a full participant in their discussion of political issues but not of the economic ones.[2] However, Clinton left no doubt that he regarded this outcome as barely adequate and entirely temporary: sooner or later there was going to be a G-8 at the leaders' level, and he was going to use the Naples meeting to lay the ground. For him, the evolution of the G-7 into a G-8 was a way of fostering Russia's integration into the post–cold war international system. That was a goal worthy of presidents, chancellors and prime ministers; finance ministers could "do their G-7 thing," coordinating fiscal and monetary policies, on the side.

Clinton encouraged Yeltsin's aspiration to be in a G-8 partly because of the experience he'd had the year before in Tokyo. Yeltsin had put on a bravura performance during the round-table discussion with the other leaders and then, in his private session with Clinton, made decisive compromises on the problems of Soviet-era missiles in Ukraine and the Russian sale of rocket parts to India. If Naples represented another step toward the G-8, Clinton was more likely to cajole Yeltsin into breakthroughs on the shape of post–cold war Europe.

Clinton, like Yeltsin, did not have principally in mind the question of PFP, since that was being handled between Secretary Christopher and Kozyrev. What Clinton most wanted to extract from Yeltsin in Naples was a formal, categorical announcement that there was progress in the negotiations that the Russian government was conducting with the Baltic states on the removal of the seven thousand Russian troops stationed there. The Balts and Russians had already agreed on an August 31 deadline for the completion of the withdrawals, and that was less than two months after the Naples summit.

"It's a pretty simple deal," said the president in a meeting to prepare for

Naples shortly before leaving Washington. "We get the Russians into the G-7 and they get out of the Baltics. If they're part of the big boys' club, they've got less reason to beat up on the little guys."

PART OF CLINTON'S STRATEGY was to give Yeltsin a big round of international applause to make it easier for him to cope with the catcalls he would get at home. Powerful figures in the Duma and the military wanted to slow down, halt and even reverse the withdrawals from the Baltics in order to counter the impression that Russian power was in free fall. Throughout the spring of 1994, there were snags in the talks between the Russian and Baltic negotiators. On several occasions the U.S. had helped unsnarl these by mediating among the parties and offering money to help defray some of the costs of withdrawal.³

As the Naples summit drew near, it looked as though the Russians would pull out of Lithuania and Latvia by the August 31 deadline, but the talks with Estonia were hung up over whether approximately ten thousand retired Soviet military personnel residing there would be allowed to stay as civilians. En route to Naples, Clinton was due to stop in Riga, the capital of Latvia, where he would be meeting with all three Baltic presidents. The day before Clinton's departure for Europe, Yeltsin called to ask him to put pressure on Lennart Meri, the Estonian president, to settle on Moscow's terms. We weren't going to take the Russians' side in the dispute, but we'd been monitoring their talks with the Estonians and quietly kibitzing, and we could see a way of breaking the deadlock by allowing the Russian military retirees to apply for Estonian residency. Clinton promised Yeltsin he would work the problem directly with Meri but also told him it was important that the withdrawal go forward on schedule.

It looked as though we were heading into a rerun of what had happened in January between Russia and Ukraine: as a matter of personal pride and national prerogative, Yeltsin didn't relish having to ask the U.S. to mediate with one of Russia's neighbors, but he realized that he needed Clinton's help in getting the problem solved.

I watched the ensuing drama unfold from afar. I had to stay in Washington to work on a crisis in Haiti, where a military dictatorship was brutalizing the population and driving thousands of people to flee to the Florida coast in rickety boats.

CLINTON SPENT only seven hours in Riga, but it was an important first: no U.S. president had ever before visited the Baltic states. About forty thousand people turned out in the sunshine to hear him speak. Around Freedom Square (which I remembered as Lenin Square from my visits there in the 1980s) there were placards and graffiti with variations on the theme "Russians go home!"[4] That afternoon, when Clinton met with the three Baltic presidents, Lennart Meri gave him a letter to pass along to Yeltsin, and Clinton tried out on him our proposal for a compromise.

Three days later, when Clinton met privately with Yeltsin in Naples, he said, "Boris, don't screw this up. You've got to get out of Estonia. Everyone is watching. You either confirm the worst that a lot of people think about Russia or you'll confirm the best that I've been saying about you." Yeltsin indicated he was prepared to come to an agreement if Meri would come to Moscow and meet with him face-to-face. Clinton promised to urge Meri to do that. The meeting ended with Clinton feeling confident that the problem was solved.

At the press conference afterward, Clinton spoke first and played up the significance of Yeltsin's new, upgraded participation in the G-7 for all it was worth—and more, going well beyond what the Italian hosts and the other leaders were saying about Russia's role.

"As you know," said Clinton, "this was a very important day in which President Yeltsin joined us as a full partner in the G-8 for political discussions."

Yeltsin beamed; Larry Summers looked less happy.

Hoping that he had put Yeltsin in the best possible mood, Clinton turned to the subject of the negotiations between Russia and the Baltic states. There had been "a promising development," he said, that might "break the impasse between the two nations over troop deployments." He predicted that the remaining differences could be solved by Yeltsin and Meri "in the near future" and, in a final grace note, added that a Russian withdrawal from the Baltics would have been inconceivable without a democratic Russia—"and I thank President Yeltsin for that."

Yeltsin came to the microphone with all the puffed-up pride and magnanimity of an actor who had just won an Oscar. He pronounced himself "satisfied by the summit of the Political Eight," which, he added, was "just the beginning . . . The Russian bear is not going to try to break his way through an open door. We're not going to force ourselves into the full G-8 until we deserve it . . . We're not asking for any preferential conditions, we're not asking for any special circumstances for us alone. No, we're saying, 'Let's have equal rights; let's once and for all get rid of this red jacket. Take that red jacket off the President of Russia! I haven't worn it for years. I discarded my own red-stained jacket long ago!' You understand what I'm talking about?"

The press corps rewarded Yeltsin with a round of appreciative laughter. The American officials began to relax: it looked as if they were going to get the upbeat story they'd hoped for.

Then came the press's opportunity to ask questions. Yeltsin called on Helen Thomas, the veteran UPI correspondent and the dean of the White House press corps, who had the privilege of leading off.

"You're not going to like my first question," she said. "Will you have all the Russian troops out of the Baltics by August 31?"

"Nyyyyeeeettt!," answered Yeltsin. "Actually, I like your question just fine, because it gives me a chance to say it again: *nyyyyeeeettt!"*

He went on to say that he'd told Clinton he would meet with Meri and "try to find a solution," but the audience barely noticed. The reporters on deadline had already leapt from their seats to file a dramatic piece of breaking news.

I had stepped out of a meeting on Haiti in the basement of the White House to watch the press conference on CNN. When I heard Yeltsin's answer to Thomas's question, I closed my eyes and allowed myself a long sigh. Yeltsin had given our critics in the U.S. Congress red meat. Within days, the Senate passed legislation to suspend all U.S. assistance to Russia other than humanitarian aid if Moscow failed to meet the August 31 deadline. The Republicans were positioning themselves so that when the deadline passed and Russian troops were still in the Baltics, they could declare the beginning of Russia's return to an imperialistic footing and the failure of the Clinton administration's policy.

IN LATE JULY, as Lennart Meri was about to arrive in Moscow for his talks with Yeltsin, I made a quick trip to Bangkok to fill in for Secretary Christopher at an international meeting that Kozyrev was also attending.[5] I requested an urgent meeting with him as soon as I arrived.

"Andrei," I said, "you've got to go home and work your magic on your boss so that he and Meri get this problem solved, once and for all."

An expression of despair came over Kozyrev's face. He looked away from me and stared out the window of the hotel. Finally he spoke: "I'm afraid I've lost my magician's powers." He moped his way through the rest of his meetings in Bangkok and left the conference early to return to Moscow for Yeltsin's meeting with Meri.

On Tuesday, July 26, just before I headed to the airport in Bangkok to fly home, the news came that after five hours of negotiation, Yeltsin and Meri had struck a deal. As I later heard from the Estonians, it was a classic Yeltsin performance. He started where he'd left off in Naples, uncompromising and bombastic. Meri responded emotionally, saying that while the people of Estonia would rather live almost anywhere on earth than next to Russia, the two countries were stuck with a common border, a common history and a common destiny. Yeltsin had heroically broken Russia free from its own history and given it hope of a better future. He'd also been a defender of Estonia's freedom going back to the last days of the Soviet Union. But now he seemed to be behaving like Stalin.

Stung, Yeltsin tried to counter that if Meri had only been willing to talk to him directly, they could have solved the problem. Why, he asked almost plaintively, had Meri turned his friends in the West against him, particularly Bill Clinton? Then, suddenly, as though they'd cleared the air, he announced that he was ready to pull all remaining active-duty forces out of Estonia on schedule if the Russian military pensioners were allowed to stay—essentially the compromise we'd proposed before Naples. Meri agreed, and the two went off to lunch while Kozyrev went to work with the Estonians drawing up a final agreement. After lunch, Yeltsin was so eager to conclude the deal that he didn't even wait for a retyped document—he signed a copy with handwritten changes on it.

AFTER I GOT BACK to Washington, I talked to Clinton about the whole episode. I already knew from Nick Burns of the NSC staff that Clinton had reacted calmly to Yeltsin's unpleasant surprise in Naples. In the immediate aftermath of the disastrous press conference, while the rest of the White House traveling team was fuming about how Yeltsin had lured our president into an ambush, Clinton himself had taken Burns aside and said we'd just have to do a better job of factoring Yeltsin's domestic predicament into the way we planned our own next steps.[6]

"Yeltsin's a good politician," said Clinton. "He's tough and he's brave, and he knows what he's got to do. I knew he'd do the right thing in the end."

Later he amplified: "I knew Yeltsin was going to pull out of the Baltics on time when he answered '*nyet*' to that question in Naples. He was getting it established that he wasn't going to do his thing because of pressure from us—he'd do it for his own reasons."[7]

Still, I couldn't help feeling that I had dropped the ball in the preparations for Naples. I should have taken time out from Caribbean crisis management, gone to Moscow a day or two before the Clinton-Yeltsin meeting and worked out, presumably with Yuri Mamedov, an agreement on how the two leaders would handle the inevitable questions they'd get in public. Maybe that way we could have gotten through the denouement of the Baltic drama with a little less suspense and without the backlash from our Congress. Since there had been a happy ending, I didn't dwell on the lesson. That meant I'd have to learn it again later in the year.

IN SEARCH OF A SLOGAN

President Clinton had soft-pedaled the issue of NATO enlargement during the Naples summit. That was primarily because he didn't want to let it get in the way of his overriding goal at the time, which was Russia's withdrawal from the Baltics. (Yeltsin's opponents had explicitly urged keeping military units in the Baltics as chips to play in the bargaining ahead over whether former Soviet allies would be joining NATO.)

By midsummer, the advocates of moving fairly quickly on enlargement were reinforced by the return to Washington of Dick Holbrooke, our ambassador to Germany, who was about to become assistant secretary of state for European affairs. Dick had served at the same level of the State Department nearly two decades earlier, when he had been Jimmy Carter's assistant secretary for Asia. I joined Peter Tarnoff, the under secretary of state for political affairs, and two other members of Chris's inner circle, Tom Donilon and Jim Steinberg, in urging that Chris bring Dick back to Washington, primarily to spearhead—or, more to the point, help salvage—our foundering Bosnia policy. I had another reason for wanting Dick in the home office: I knew, from my frequent conversations with him when I'd passed through Bonn, that he was not just a vigorous advocate of NATO enlargement but a compelling and thoughtful one. I felt that we were more likely to get the best outcome in our policymaking and diplomacy if Dick was at the center of both processes, subjecting me and my assumptions to constant prodding and letting me do the same with his.

BY LATE AUGUST, just as the Russians were completing their pullout from the Baltics, rumors began circulating in Moscow—based partly on local suspicion and partly on wishful thinking in Central Europe—that the Czech Republic, Hungary and Poland would be formally designated as candidates for membership at the annual meeting of the NATO foreign ministers in December 1994 and admitted as allies before the end of Clinton's first term.[8]

From Yeltsin's standpoint, that would be the worst imaginable timing, given the Russian presidential election that would be taking place in 1996. Yeltsin had told Clinton during their first meeting, in the summer of 1992, that he would serve only one term, but he changed his mind shortly afterward and it was now widely assumed that he would be running for re-election. If NATO brought in new members that year, it would greatly strengthen his communist and nationalist opponents.

For that reason and others—the alliance was already under severe strain over what to do in Bosnia and didn't need an additional internal debate—Clinton decided to use the NATO meetings in December 1994 to begin "discussions" of enlargement rather than to designate new members. Thus, in 1995, we would be talking about enlargement rather than actually doing it. While those talks were going on, we'd make another push to bring the Russians into the Partnership for Peace and also to engage them in negotiations on a charter of cooperation that would come into effect around the time that NATO actually took in new members.

A crucial corollary of this plan was an explicit affirmation that someday in the future—well after most or all of the Central European states had joined—Russia itself might apply for membership in NATO. Its eligibility should not be ruled out in advance, since that would be a gratuitous insult to Russia and would belie our claim that NATO enlargement served the larger cause of inclusive integration. Especially after the changes that had already swept through Eurasia over the past two decades, many of them emanating from Russia itself, treating Russia as an outcast would be foolish.

Yet as hypothetical as the idea of Russia's eligibility was, it was also exceedingly controversial. To traditionalists, bringing an incontinent camel into the tent of the Partnership for Peace was one thing, but bringing an unhousebroken bear into the North Atlantic Alliance was another. They believed a NATO that included Russia was destined to be, at best, just another talk shop like the North Atlantic Cooperation Council, and even considering such a possibility in the abstract would damage the alliance's effectiveness in the here and now.

I mentioned to Clinton that every time we said anything reiterating Russian eligibility, we could expect Henry Kissinger in particular to blast us for what he regarded as pernicious heresy.

Clinton laughed, saying he'd expect nothing less from "Ol' Henry—he's thinking in yesterday terms. We've got to put this NATO thing in tomorrow terms. The Russians' getting in someday may or may not happen, but keeping it out there as something we're not against is a no-brainer."

Clinton's concept of NATO enlargement always included—for reasons that were strategic, not cosmetic or palliative—the idea of Russia's eventual eligibility and indeed its entry. He knew that the idea was, as he sometimes said, "blue-sky stuff." If the day ever came when Russia entered NATO, it would obviously be a different Russia, a different NATO and a different Europe. But anticipating—and, better yet, inducing—transformation was what strategic policymaking was supposed to be all about. Besides, the alteration of national and international politics that would enable Russia to enter NATO was no more unimaginable than the changes that had occurred in the last decade would have seemed if anyone had been so brave or foolish as to predict them a decade before that. Clinton believed it was permissible, when looking at the horizon, to see glimpses of blue.

CLINTON AND YELTSIN were next due to meet in Washington at the end of September. Ten days before that summit, Clinton held a meeting in the Cabinet Room to review a range of foreign-policy and defense issues, including steps that would make NATO enlargement more palatable to Russia and more consistent with the notion that the cold war really was over. Vice-President Gore and Bill Perry, who had succeeded Les Aspin as secretary of defense, raised the idea of reducing levels of American nuclear weaponry in Europe. Listening to this discussion, Clinton grew edgy. He said he wanted to go further than just fine-tuning nuclear deterrence. That was still part of NATO's business, he acknowledged, but it was old business. He exhorted us to think bigger thoughts about "giving people reason to believe there's something really *new* going on over there. We can't just look like we're on autopilot, truckin' forward using the same old maps."

A week later, with Yeltsin's arrival only a few days away, Clinton brought us together again and elaborated on his dissatisfaction: we were dealing with European security as a technical problem, whereas he saw it as a conceptual one. He had joked from time to time about missing the cold war, but there was a serious point he wanted us to think about: the cold war had been an age of certainty in American foreign policy—even the designation of that period implied clarity about the challenge. He was tired of talking about the "post–cold war" era. The phrase itself was agnostic, provisional, backward-looking; it was an admission that while everyone knew what was finished, no one knew what had taken its place, to say nothing of what would or should come next. He didn't want his presidency to coincide with an age of uncertainty.

Clinton had another gripe as well. Part of the administration's frequently stated rationale for NATO enlargement was that the new generation of NATO leaders—that is, Clinton's own generation—had an obligation to consolidate the gains of its predecessors. Clinton hated that line, he said, and he never wanted to see it in a speech draft again. We shouldn't be "telling people who are already bored that their mission is to put icing on the cake that someone else had baked," he said.

That thought set him off in a new direction. He admired Franklin Roosevelt and Harry Truman for intuitively understanding what their world required of them, but they got more credit than they deserved for knowing what they were doing when they were doing it. Clinton had been reading biographies of Roosevelt and Truman that convinced him that neither had grand strategies for how to exert American leadership against the global threats posed by Hitler and Stalin.9 Rather, they had "powerful instincts about what had to be done, and they just made it up as they went along."

Strategic coherence, he said, was largely imposed after the fact by scholars, memoirists and "the chattering classes." It was "a huge myth that we always knew what we were doing during the cold war," he said. "The alleged certainty of that period led us to make massive mistakes," such as letting ourselves be drawn into Vietnam. "Sure, the cold war was helpful as an organizing principle, but it had its dangers because every welt on your skin became cancer."

I made the mistake of trying to insert my own view into Clinton's stream of consciousness. I suggested he had just made a pretty good argument for not being too nostalgic for the stark simplicity of American internationalism during the previous half century. Wasn't it progress when we recognized we couldn't, and shouldn't, describe the world in a single phrase?

The president gave me a look that combined amusement and impatience. I'd just reminded him, he said, of why I was a journalist and not a politician. "You've still got to be able to crystallize complexity in a way people get right away," he said. "The operative problem of the moment is that a bunch of smart people haven't been able to come up with a new slogan, and saying that there aren't any good slogans isn't a slogan either."

At the core of his discontent, he said, was "the big mess in Russia, which has got everyone afraid that things are going to fall apart. We can litanize and analyze all we want, but until people can say it in a few words we're sunk."

NOT LONG AFTERWARD, Secretary Christopher and I had a chance to put the president's question to George Kennan, then ninety. I had made it a practice to invite Kennan to Washington from his home in Princeton once a year or so to discuss policy toward Russia with my colleagues on the Russia team.[10] During a dinner for Kennan in the Madison Room on the eighth floor of the State Department, Chris mentioned that the president had assigned us the job of replicating what Kennan had done with "containment"—reducing a big, complicated task to a single word.

Kennan replied with some passion that we shouldn't try. He was sorry he had tried to pack so much diagnosis and prescription into three syllables. He certainly regretted the consequences, since containment had led to "great and misleading oversimplification of analysis and policy." We would be better off, he said, if we did not follow his example and, instead, contented ourselves with a "thoughtful paragraph or more, rather than trying to come up with a bumper sticker."

I told Clinton about this exchange later. "Well," he said, laughing, "that's why Kennan's a great diplomat and scholar and not a politician."

In the six years that followed, Clinton returned occasionally to chastising his advisers and speechwriters for failing to come up with a catchphrase for the era. It didn't help when Boris Yeltsin generated a bracing headline of his own—and it was exactly the one that Clinton didn't want.

COLD PEACE

The White House protocol office asked Brooke and me to greet Yeltsin when he arrived at Andrews Air Force Base on September 26. According to custom, I was then to accompany Yeltsin in his limousine to Blair House while Brooke rode in a separate car with his wife, Naina. When we pulled up on the tarmac, Yuli Vorontsov, who had replaced Vladimir Lukin as ambassador to Washington, came bustling over and told me curtly that "the president is tired from his trip and would prefer to ride with Mrs. Yeltsin."

My guess about the reason was quickly confirmed. As Yeltsin emerged from the plane and made his way down the mobile stairs, he was gripping the railing and concentrating on each step. His handlers did their best to block the view of the cameras recording his descent. He slipped on the last step and had to grab Naina's arm. That night at Blair House, Yeltsin was roaring drunk, lurching from room to room in his undershorts. At one point, he stumbled downstairs and accosted a Secret Service agent, who managed to persuade him to go back upstairs and return to the care of his own bodyguard. Yeltsin reappeared briefly on the landing, demanding, "Pizza! Pizza!" Finally, his security agents took him firmly by the arms and marched him briskly around in an effort to calm him down.

IN THE FIRST formal meeting at the White House the next day, with both delegations facing each other across a long table, Yeltsin was sober but supercharged. Much as he had during the Vancouver summit, he galloped through a list of half-baked or overcooked proposals. "Come on, Bill, let's just agree!" he kept saying, barely waiting for a reply, which was just as well since the reply was always the same: "We'll have our people talk about that, Boris."

It was only when the two presidents met alone that Yeltsin dispensed with the posturing and Clinton could go to work on him. That chance came over a private lunch in the Family Dining Room in the East Wing on September 27. Clinton asked me to sit in on the lunch, in part because I could listen to Yeltsin's answers twice, in Russian and then as interpreted.

We expected Yeltsin to raise the future of NATO, but he didn't do so. Perhaps that was because he found the subject so painful. Perhaps he simply didn't share other Russians' visceral opposition to the idea of the Central Europeans joining the alliance. That possibility was consistent with his acceptance of Poland's right to join during his meeting with Lech Walesa in August 1993. As the lunch progressed, the two presidents covered what seemed to me every issue on the face of the earth except the future of NATO. I began to wonder whether Clinton, too, wanted to avoid the subject.

Finally, as coffee was served, Clinton put his hand on Yeltsin's arm, leaned toward him and said, "Boris, on NATO, I want to make sure you've noted that I've never said we shouldn't consider Russia for membership or a special relationship with NATO. So when we talk about NATO expanding, we're emphasizing inclusion, not exclusion. My objective is to work with you and others to maximize the chances of a truly united, undivided, integrated Europe. There will be an expansion of NATO, but there's no timetable yet. If we started tomorrow to include the countries that want to come in, it would still take several years until they qualified and others said 'yes.' The issue is about psychological security and a sense of importance to these countries. They're afraid of being left in a gray area or a purgatory. So we're going to move forward on this. But I'd never spring it on you. I want to work closely with you so we get through it together. This relates to everything else. When you withdrew your troops from the Baltics, it strengthened your credibility. As I see it, NATO expansion is not anti-Russian; it's not intended to be exclusive of Russia, and there is no imminent timetable. And we'll work together. I don't want you to believe that I wake up every morning thinking only about how to make the Warsaw Pact countries a part of NATO—that's not the way I look at it. What I do think about is how to use NATO expansion to advance the broader, higher goal of European security, unity and integration—a goal I know you share."

The main points that we'd rehearsed in advance were there—principally, NATO *was* going to expand—but the tone and context were part of an approach Clinton had worked out in his head during the lunch: every time he'd said that expansion was going forward, he'd added that it was part of a larger process including Russia.

Yeltsin was listening intently. "I understand," he said when Clinton was done. "I thank you for what you've said. If you're asked about this at the press conference, I'd suggest you say while the U.S. is for the expansion of NATO, the process will be gradual and lengthy. If you're asked if you'd exclude Russia from NATO, your answer should be 'no.' That's all."

Clinton promised that U.S. policy would be guided by "three no's": no surprises, no rush and no exclusion.

THAT AFTERNOON, Yeltsin and Clinton gave a joint press conference in the East Room of the White House. Yeltsin was in a state that Sandy Berger described as "high jabberwocky"—joking, jabbing the air with his fist, hamming it up, talking a mile a minute, ticking off all the good things that he and his friend Bill were going to do together. The State Department interpreter, Peter Afanasenko, was not just translating but impersonating with great flair. Clinton was doubled over with laughter. He wanted to make sure that the audience took it all in a generous spirit. Several colleagues who knew about Yeltsin's wild first night at Blair House gave me inquiring looks. I knew what they suspected. I gave a slight shake of my head: I'd monitored Yeltsin's alcohol intake at lunch and it hadn't been enough to explain this manic exuberance.

A pattern was developing in Yeltsin's handling of these meetings: in the plenary sessions, with a large audience on both sides of the table, he played the decisive, even peremptory leader who knew what he wanted and insisted on getting it; in the private meetings, he switched from assertive to receptive, becoming susceptible to Clinton's blandishments and suasion; then, in the wrap-up press conference, he went over the top in a way designed, in his own mind, to project self-confidence and to disguise how pliant he had been behind closed doors.

THAT EVENING, during a reception and dinner at the Russian embassy, Yeltsin pronounced himself delighted with the working lunch and asked Clinton, as a personal favor, to attend the annual summit of the Conference on Security and Cooperation in Europe (CSCE), which was to be held on December 4 in Budapest. CSCE had been in existence since the seventies; the USSR had been a founding member; it didn't have the taint of NATO sponsorship.

Clinton had not planned to go to Budapest but promised he would do so "if it matters to you, Boris," and "if there's important business to do."

The timing of the Budapest meeting was potentially advantageous: it came two days after a meeting of NATO foreign ministers in Brussels at which Kozyrev would, we hoped, finally sign the documents that nailed down Russia's participation in the Partnership for Peace and formally launch a NATO-Russia dialogue aimed at producing a charter of cooperation. To have Yeltsin and Clinton meet immediately afterward in Budapest, surrounded by all the other leaders of Europe—NATO allies, neutrals and former Warsaw Pact members—would be a way of dramatizing Clinton's concept of enlargement and PFP as part of the larger process of European integration.

FOR WEEKS, Secretary Christopher and I worked with the European and Canadian foreign ministers to put that choreography in place. I also tried to keep Mamedov abreast of these consultations with our allies. I wanted Yuri to have as much advance notice as possible about what to expect from NATO, along with repeated assurances that all actions and statements coming out of Brussels and Budapest in December would be sufficiently in keeping with Clinton's three no's in September to elicit a yes to Partnership for Peace from Kozyrev and Yeltsin.

In mid-October, I made a trip to Africa and stopped off in London en route for a quick huddle with Yuri. Brooke was with me for that leg of the journey since she had business in London and Oxford in connection with the White House Fellows program. I met with Yuri on October 19 and that evening arranged for him to be invited to a party in a London restaurant in honor of David Cornwell, known to the world as John le Carré, on his sixty-third birthday. My path had first crossed with David's in Israel in the early eighties when he was gathering material for *The Little Drummer Girl.* In 1987, after his first visit to Moscow, he consulted me as he sketched out the plot for what became *The Russia House.*

The birthday party was a kick for Yuri, who was a le Carré fan. David picked up on the camaraderie between Yuri and me and, during the course of his toast, cited it as a reminder of why he'd had to move beyond the cold war in prospecting for the raw material of his novels.

WHILE I WAS IN AFRICA, the White House domestic and political advisers were doing everything they could to keep Clinton from going to Budapest. George Stephanopoulos complained that the president was spending too much time on "foreign stuff" and that he'd been hijacked by "the Russia people" (an epithet that, to me, had a le Carré–esque ring to it).

Leon Panetta, the chief of staff, used an administrative ploy to try to keep the president at home: he had the White House schedulers commit the president to events in Washington both the night before the Budapest summit and on the evening of the summit itself. That meant that the only way the president could go to Budapest was to fly all night, spend five hours on the ground and fly right home.

Opponents of the trip received powerful though unwelcome reinforcement for their arguments on Tuesday, November 8. In the midterm congressional elections, the Democrats lost control of both houses—a blow to the administration on every front, including foreign policy.

Panetta and Stephanopoulos argued that the electoral catastrophe was all the more reason why the president couldn't be off at a fifty-three-nation jamboree on the banks of the Danube. Secretary Christopher, Tony Lake, Dick Holbrooke and I all objected, reminding Clinton he'd promised Yeltsin he would go. Besides, the CSCE summit was key to our strategy for keeping Russia on board our NATO policy, which in turn was important for keeping the allies on board enlargement.

A FEW DAYS LATER, Mamedov told me that the rout of the Democrats had prompted new fears in Moscow that Clinton would lose control of the pace of NATO enlargement. Bob Dole—soon to be the majority leader of the Senate as well as the GOP presidential candidate–presumptive in 1996—had been attacking the administration for not moving faster to open the doors of the alliance. Enlargement in early 1995 was one of the few foreign-policy commitments in the Republicans' party program, the Contract with America. Against that backdrop, said Mamedov, it was all the more important that Clinton meet with Yeltsin face-to-face in Budapest; only the president himself could put the decision that the NATO foreign ministers would have announced two days earlier into proper context for Yeltsin and reassure him of Clinton's ability to manage the new pressures on the American home front. I passed Yuri's view along to Clinton with the strongest endorsement.

Shortly afterward, Clinton decided to go to Budapest. The White House opponents of the trip, in conniving to deprive him of the option of going, had inadvertently outsmarted themselves and, worse, subjected the president to what would still be, even if the diplomacy went well, an insane and punishing schedule.

WHEN CHRIS FLEW to Brussels for the NATO ministerial meeting, I stayed home. Once again, as during the Naples meeting in July, the reason was Haiti. The U.S. had led a force comprised of troops from twenty-eight nations in a UN-authorized invasion of the island in September. My fellow deputies, Sandy Berger at the NSC and John Deutch at the Defense Department, and I were about to fly to Port-au-Prince to deal with various problems that had arisen in the aftermath of the invasion.

IN BRUSSELS, Chris and the other allied foreign ministers followed the plan we'd been discussing with the Russians for weeks. They released a communiqué saying that the alliance would spend 1995 "examining" membership criteria and other procedural matters. The resulting study would not identify favored applicants, nor would it set a timetable for the first round of enlargement. Nothing was said about what would happen in 1996—the year of the Russian presidential election—but the NATO ministers believed the bland and convoluted language in the communiqué served both to dampen the hopes of the Central Europeans and to allay the fears of the Russians that the alliance would rush ahead with enlargement over the next two years. It was, in short, intended as another kick of the famous can.

But that's not how it was received in Moscow. A Russian news agency played up the communiqué as a surprise and as a slap in the face to Russia. When Kozyrev, who was already in Brussels, spoke with Yeltsin by phone, Yeltsin had already seen the wire-service story and was fuming. Rather than trying to extinguish the flames, Kozyrev stoked them. He told Yeltsin he, too, had been misled about what to expect. "I've been invited here for breakfast," said Kozyrev, "but I got served a dinner instead. Maybe it was a fine meal, but it was different from the one I'd been invited for. Now partnership is subsidiary to enlargement." Kozyrev also told Yeltsin that the European allies were all pointing their fingers at Washington as the source of pressure to enlarge quickly.

"What happened with my friend Bill?" demanded Yeltsin. "How could he do this to me?"

Kozyrev tried to persuade Yeltsin to play it cool. "I've made a scandal in Brussels so you can be presidential in Budapest," he said. But Yeltsin said he felt trapped and deceived.[11]

I WAS AT HOME packing to leave for Haiti when Tom Donilon, one of Chris's closest aides, called me from Brussels with the news that Kozyrev had refused to sign the PFP documents. The reason, said Kozyrev, was that the NATO communiqué suggested that the alliance was about to embark on "hasty" expansion—in violation, presumably, of Clinton's promise of "no rush" to Yeltsin in September.

I immediately called Sandy Berger to warn him: "Kozyrev's just done his Lucy-with-the-football fake again, only this time he's setting up the president to be Charlie Brown."

It was too late for the president to cancel his trip to Budapest: he knew, as he put it, that he had to "guts it out." He flew through the night and arrived exhausted. His compressed schedule prevented a private meeting with Yeltsin before the two of them appeared in public. Hence there was no opportunity to calm Yeltsin down and limit the damage of what

Kozyrev had done in Brussels. Moreover, Clinton, who was speaking first, had a text for his remarks that had been prepared by the NSC. It was all yin and no yang—sure to please the Central Europeans and enthusiasts for enlargement, but equally sure to drive the Russians nuts, one Russian in particular: "We must not allow the Iron Curtain to be replaced by a veil of indifference . . . We must not consign new democracies to a gray zone . . . NATO will not automatically exclude any nation from joining. At the same time, no country outside will be allowed to veto expansion."

When Yeltsin's turn came immediately after Clinton's, he started on a note that sounded eerily like what Clinton himself had said on other occasions—and should have said on this one. "It's too early to bury democracy in Russia," said Yeltsin. "The year 1995 will be the year of the fiftieth anniversary of the end of World War II. Today, half a century on, we come to realize the true meaning of the great victory—and the need for historic reconciliation in Europe. There should no longer be enemies, winners or losers, in that Europe. For the first time in history, our continent has a real opportunity to achieve unity."

Then, glowering, he shifted into a minor key: "To miss that opportunity means to forget the lessons of the past and to jeopardize our future. . . . Europe, even before it has managed to shrug off the legacy of the cold war, is at risk of plunging into a cold peace."

There it was—a label for the new era. In and of itself, that phrase might not have been a show-stopper. Yeltsin had not, after all, proclaimed a new cold war.[12] But cold peace was clearly not the slogan Clinton had been looking for during the meeting in the Cabinet Room in September.

To the reporters covering the event, Yeltsin's line sounded like the equivalent of the Big *Nyet* in Naples. Once again, they dashed to the phones to file a story on a major setback for American diplomacy.

FOR CLINTON and his bedraggled entourage, it was a long and unpleasant flight back to Washington. The president was furious at his foreign-policy team for dragging him across the Atlantic to serve as a punching bag for Yeltsin. To much of the world, it looked as though Budapest was the end of the road for Clinton's declared policy of reconciling NATO enlargement with NATO-Russia cooperation. Nick Burns, the senior NSC official on the former Soviet Union and the only member of the administration's Russia team on board Air Force One, bore the brunt of presidential wrath.

Early the next morning, having just gotten back from Haiti, I went to work writing a postmortem for Chris. The bottom line was clear: once again, we had taken too much for granted and left too much to chance. We should have spent much more time making sure that the Russians knew exactly what the communiqué would say, what it would mean and how we should handle our differences in public. I delivered the report to Chris in person. He knew I required no help in appreciating the magnitude of the calamity or the extent of my responsibility for it. The only thing for us to do, he said, was to "pick ourselves up, dust ourselves off, review our game plan and get back onto the field."

For me, that meant never again letting an assignment in some other part of the world, no matter how pressing, take me out of the center of the bureaucratic and diplomatic action of U.S.-Russian relations. I had no illusion that I could prevent more Budapests—the name of that city had, literally overnight, become a synonym for diplomatic disaster—but at least next time, I wouldn't learn about the crash by watching on television or getting the word by phone.

IN KEEPING WITH that resolution, I was on board Air Force Two when it took off for Moscow for the next round of the Gore-Chernomyrdin commission in mid-December. We were now referring to these sessions as though they were Super Bowls: this one was to be GCC IV. While a tad corny, this gimmick captured the sense of enthusiasm and optimism that all of us, starting with the vice-president, brought to an enterprise that was building momentum and producing results. GCC II, in Moscow a year earlier, had produced twenty-two agreements aimed at promoting government-to-government cooperation and foreign investment in Russia. At GCC III, which had taken place in June 1994 in Washington, a consortium of U.S. and other Western oil companies had signed a $10 billion agreement with the Russians to begin development of the oil fields off Sakhalin Island in the North Pacific. Russia's vast energy wealth was seen as key to its economic development and to opportunities for Western investment. There were six cabinet-level subcommissions, including one chaired on our side by Bill Perry that was helping the Russians convert their defense industries to civilian purposes.

Until it was overshadowed by Budapest, GCC IV had promised to be the most productive one to date. The two governments had been working for months to prepare fifteen agreements and six joint statements for signature by the vice-president and prime minister. Among the accords were ones that would strengthen commercial ties, particularly between the

American West Coast and Russia's Far East; promote energy cooperation on fossil fuels; reduce pollution in the Arctic Ocean; and create a new, seventh subcommission on public health that would concentrate initially on women's health and pharmaceuticals. The committee on business development was to begin work on reducing Russian commercial taxes in order to enhance U.S. investment in the private sector.

The headline item at GCC IV was to be the announcement of two new joint projects in space: the flight of a U.S. astronaut on the Russians' *Mir* space station the following March and the first docking between *Mir* and the U.S. space shuttle *Atlantis* in June. This highly visible project was intended, among other things, as an inducement for the Russians to curb their sales and technical assistance programs to Iran, the problem that had bedeviled the relationship since Vancouver.

The Gore-Chernomyrdin commission seemed well on its way to fulfilling the hopes we'd had for it as a means of institutionalizing both partnership and high-level personal diplomacy. Now we needed to use the connection to repair the damage that U.S.-Russian relations had sustained in Budapest.

That chance came when Chernomyrdin took Gore to the hospital where Yeltsin was recovering from an operation for a deviated septum. Yeltsin, his nose faintly bruised and swollen, was propped up in the sitting room of his suite; he had put on a suit and tie for the occasion. A Kremlin camera crew and a still photographer recorded the opening pleasantries in order to squelch the persistent rumor in Moscow that the president of Russia was incapacitated and perhaps dying.

Yeltsin seemed eager to do some repair work of his own.

"Despite all the talk, the reports in newspapers and the gossip," he began, "Russia and America remain partners. Bill Clinton and I remain partners. It will take more than we've been through to ruin that."

He talked candidly about his fear that with the Republicans about to assume control of both houses of Congress, there would be a "toughening of [American] positions on a series of issues," including an acceleration of enlargement. He said he had noticed a difference between the assurances he had gotten from Clinton in September and both the North Atlantic Council communiqué and Clinton's comments in Budapest—which he'd found insensitively triumphalist, even gloating. Worse, it sounded as though the alliance would begin bringing in new members in 1995, just as the Russian presidential campaign was getting under way.

Gore replied emphatically that Clinton's September commitment stood and there had been no change of policy. "In 1995," he said, "no negotiations about accepting new states into NATO are foreseen. Only study of the question is intended. I repeat, it is our position that the process will be slow, gradual, open and with constant and full consultations with Russia."

Yeltsin wanted to hear it again. "Can you now affirm to me that in 1995 it will be solely a matter of working out the concept?"

"Yes, I can," said Gore.

"Then I'll let the matter drop," said Yeltsin.

But he didn't; a few minutes later, circling back to NATO, Yeltsin told Gore that he worried words like "slow" and "gradual" were imprecise; they left room for Poland to ramp up its campaign for membership in 1995.

"Once again," said Gore, "I repeat our absolute assurances that in 1995 there will be only a study of the conception of a possible expansion of NATO."

Well then, suggested Yeltsin, pressing what he saw as an advantage, perhaps they could agree that "gradual" might even mean ten to fifteen years.

No, said Gore: he wasn't going to speculate or make any commitments beyond 1995. But he stressed that in parallel with enlargement, NATO and Russia would be solidifying their own cooperative arrangements. He used the phrase "in parallel" several times, since he knew that would be reassuring to Yeltsin. To make sure that Yeltsin got the point, Gore, who had a fondness for metaphors drawn from the world of high technology and who had the prospect of the linkup between *Mir* and *Atlantis* in mind, compared the U.S.-Russian and NATO-Russian relationships to a docking maneuver between two massive spacecraft, each under steady and autonomous control, coming slowly and carefully together. He hammered it up, using his outspread hands to depict two giant craft maneuvering toward each other.

Yeltsin loved it. *"Da, da!"* he said, nodding and smiling. He then started doing a hand-puppet routine of his own. "Simultaneous! That's good! Simultaneous!"

"Right!" said Gore. "We need a process that brings three things together: our bilateral partnership, Russia's relationship with NATO and NATO expansion. It must be gradual."

"Yes," said Yeltsin, nodding vigorously. "In parallel! Simultaneous, simultaneous! But . . ."—a thundercloud returned to his face—". . . not like *this* . . ." His hands mimicked the movement of one spacecraft moving toward the other but the second veering off in another direction.

As this weird but effective bit of diplomatic pantomime came to an end, Yeltsin remarked, "We [it was the czarist 'we'] are being advised to step up the pressure on Clinton. Please convey to him that we will never do that, that Russia will remain the U.S.'s partner to the end."

Gore reminded Yeltsin, as Clinton had stressed in September, that the American concept of NATO's evolution and expansion included, in theory, a place for Russia.

"*Nyet, nyet,*" said Yeltsin, interrupting, "that doesn't make sense. Russia is very, very *big*"—he stretched his arms wide—"and NATO is quite *small.*"

Yeltsin had suddenly aligned himself, on this question at least, with self-styled realists like Henry Kissinger who had lambasted us for the dangerous delusion that Russia could someday join NATO. In so doing, Yeltsin put Gore in the bizarre position of trying to persuade him that Russia might actually someday qualify.

When Gore reported on this part of the conversation shortly afterward, after we were back aboard Air Force Two, I commented that Yeltsin was reflecting a perverse variant of a principle made famous by Groucho Marx: the Russians weren't sure they qualified for any club that was worth belonging to.

"I guess," said Leon Fuerth, "that means Yeltsin's still a Marxist after all."

As Air Force Two headed home, there seemed to be reason to hope that, for the second time that year, the Big *Nyet* would prove not to be Yeltsin's last word. But getting him actually to accept NATO enlargement when it occurred was still certain to be a harrowing task—and a time-consuming one.

Gore returned to Washington convinced, on the basis of his bedside conversation with Yeltsin, that we had to go beyond ruling out enlargement in 1995 and decide, unambiguously, to hold off until after 1996, presumably until the beginning of a second Clinton term.

Bill Perry thought even that was too soon. He would have preferred to postpone enlargement for a decade, or perhaps forever. Now he had extra ammunition. Before coming to Moscow for the commission meeting, he had been at NATO headquarters in Brussels, where he had found the allies not just traumatized by Budapest but inclined to blame the U.S. for the apparent crisis with Russia. During the commission meetings, Bill's

closest contact in the Russian government, Deputy Defense Minister Andrei Kokoshin, warned that if NATO enlargement went ahead in the next
year or so—that is, before the 1996 elections—"rolling over Russian objections like a tank," the two of them need not waste their time on defense
conversion: Russia would throw itself into the task of turning plowshares
back into swords.

Shortly after our return to Washington, Perry requested a meeting with
the president in which he expressed concern that enlargement had taken
on a life of its own and needed to be brought back under control. He argued strenuously for giving Partnership for Peace at least a year before
making a final decision on when and how to proceed with enlargement.
General Shalikashvili, the chairman of the Joint Chiefs of Staff, con-
curred. So did Gore, not least because what he was hearing was consistent
with the assurance he'd just given Yeltsin.

The president needed no persuading. Opponents of NATO enlargement had been predicting for a year that if we persisted on that track,
there would be the much-feared, confidently predicted train wreck in our
Russia policy.

Clinton didn't believe that was necessarily true, but what he'd experienced in Budapest had come too close for comfort to proving the skeptics
right. He was glad that the weight of the advice he was getting from the
vice-president and the Pentagon meant he wouldn't have to force the issue
again with Yeltsin until both of them were safely into their second terms.[13]

"The policy is right," the president concluded, "but we need to work
with the Russians."

Working with the Russians meant finding a way to coax them into
being part of an outcome that they would regard as something other than
a strategic defeat. Clinton still felt that that was possible, but not until
Yeltsin had gained confidence in his ability to prevail over his domestic
enemies. In the wake of the Democrats' crushing defeat in the congressional elections, Yeltsin would need to be convinced of Clinton's own staying power as well.

CHAPTER 6

THE HIGH WIRE

*Other nations and states gaze askance as
they step aside and give her the right of way.*

Gogol (on Russia's progress through history)

WHILE VICE-PRESIDENT GORE was in Moscow in late December 1994, Russia was going to war against itself in Chechnya. A so-called autonomous republic of the Russian Federation, Chechnya was one of the poorest of the country's eighty-nine administrative regions. Approximately the size of Connecticut, it occupied less than one-tenth of one percent of Russian territory. Chechnya figured in Russian memory and imagination as a distant and hostile frontier of the empire, a place where young men went, often involuntarily, for adventure and war. Before I joined the U.S. government, the little knowledge I had of that remote and exotic land came from nineteenth-century Russian literature and history. Tolstoy wrote stories, based on his posting there as a soldier, about the often brutal and consistently unsuccessful attempt to convert the warlike Chechens into loyal subjects of the czar. Rattling around in my head was a stanza from Mikhail Lermontov's "Cossack Lullaby" about the "evil Chechen," creeping along a riverbank, dagger in hand, looking for a Russian throat to slit.

During the Russian Revolution of 1917, the Chechens fought with great ferocity against the Bolsheviks and succeeded in kicking them out of the region in 1919. But two years later, the Red Army swept in and crushed the Chechens' self-proclaimed Mountain Republic. In World War II, Hitler's forces occupied the North Caucasus, leading Stalin to declare the

Chechens collaborators, to be designated a "punished people" and deported to Central Asia. As many as 200,000 died along the way. The survivors returned in 1957, as part of Khrushchev's de-Stalinization campaign, with a jaundiced view of any further rule from Moscow.

During the Russian Revolution in 1991, Chechnya declared itself a separate country. Had Chechnya actually attained the independence it claimed, it would have qualified instantly as a failed if not a rogue state. Kidnapping, drug trafficking, money laundering, gunrunning, counterfeiting, and trafficking in women and children were rampant. It was an anarchist's utopia and any government's nightmare.

At the top of the bloody mess that constituted politics in Chechnya was Dzhokhar Dudayev, a former Soviet air force general who had served as the commander of a garrison outside the Estonian university town of Tartu in the dying days of the USSR. His loyalties to Moscow disintegrated at least as fast as the Soviet state, and he earned the lasting gratitude of the Estonians by disobeying orders from Moscow to suppress their independence movement in 1991. (When Brooke and I visited Tartu in 2000, our hosts made a point of showing us a plaque—in Estonian, English and Chechen—in commemoration of Dudayev's role in their own liberation from the USSR.)

Dudayev went home to Chechnya to assume the title of president but to behave more like a khan, slaughtering demonstrators and using his bodyguards to assassinate his political adversaries.

The world and most of the rest of Russia barely noticed. The Russian government, then under the premiership of Yegor Gaidar, left Chechnya largely to its own devices. At first, the Chechen leaders reciprocated Moscow's benign neglect and concentrated their troublemaking on their neighbor to the south, Georgia. They gave political and material backing in 1992 to forces seeking the overthrow of Eduard Shevardnadze. Since the Russian military and intelligence services had their own grudge against Shevardnadze, they egged the Chechens on. But before long, Chechen guerrillas fighting in Georgia took their weapons and newly honed skills home to use against the Russian "occupiers." A hit-and-run guerrilla war sputtered on until the spring and summer of 1994, when Chechen rebels threw down a gauntlet to Moscow by carrying out a series of bold bus hijackings.[1]

Defense Minister Pavel Grachev and Sergei Stepashin, the head of Russia's domestic intelligence service, warned Boris Yeltsin that if the republic broke free, there would be a domino effect in neighboring Muslim-dominated areas: Russia, like the Soviet Union before it, would unravel. The solution, said Grachev, was simple: it would take one airborne regiment two hours to capture the Chechen capital of Grozny and eradicate the breakaway regime.

Yeltsin, whose health had taken a turn for the worse, felt he needed to demonstrate that he hadn't lost his grip on the country. He authorized Grachev and Stepashin to crack down.

At first, the Russians tried to subdue the Chechens with what amounted to punitive raids by ground forces. One of the more ignominious engagements resulted in the death of a dozen Russian troops and the capture of nineteen more who were paraded before television cameras and threatened with execution. Moscow issued a series of ultimatums, and in early December the Russians started conducting air raids against Grozny.

Never far below the surface were hints of Russian envy and resentment at the U.S.'s muscle-flexing around the world—in the Balkans, the Gulf and the Caribbean. As Oleg Lobov, the head of the Russian Security Council, put it, "Our president needs a small victorious war, like the one the U.S. has had in Haiti," where fifteen thousand American troops had, with a minimum of fuss, packed the military dictatorship off into exile and established a firm foothold.

On December 11, 1994, four days before Vice-President Gore arrived in Moscow, Russian forces launched an all-out invasion. During Gore's visit, Russian forces began shelling Grozny. The war quickly escalated, taking a staggering toll in civilian casualties, including tens of thousands of local ethnic Russians.

WE HAD KNOWN for months that there was trouble brewing in the Russian hinterland, but at the time of the Gore trip, our minds were on other things—the debacle we'd just suffered in Budapest and Brussels, the ongoing trouble we were having with the Russians over Bosnia, the medical and political condition of the president of Russia. What little we did know about Chechnya and Dudayev inclined us to accept Moscow's version that it was dealing with an ugly mixture of secessionism and criminality.[2] Besides, the independence that the Chechens were fighting for was against American policy. As a global principle, we were for federalist solutions that preserved existing international boundaries and against the fractionation of large, heterogeneous countries into ethnically based microstates. Hence

Gore's terse public comment in Moscow: "We are following [the situation] closely. We hope very much it can be solved by negotiations. We believe it is an internal matter."

The statement was ill advised, and I was one of the advisers responsible for it. What we failed to see, and therefore to say, was that the latest eruption of violence had brought to the surface of Russian politics the single worst and most characteristic feature of the old regime and the single most dangerous temptation for the new regime: a reliance on raw force as the solution to all problems.

The war, in its origins, consequences and reverberations within the Russian heartland, also had a distinctly racist tinge. The Chechens were of a different nationality than the Russians, with darker complexions, a non-Slavic language and an Islamic heritage. Official depictions of them as terrorists fed a resurgence of bigotry and xenophobia that had never been far beneath the surface of much of Russian political culture. It was no accident that Vladimir Zhirinovsky was the loudest and most gleeful of those fulminating against the Chechens and cheering on the Russian military as it pummeled Grozny and outlying villages with bombs and artillery. Thus, in addition to the other dangers it posed, the conflict jeopardized Russia's chances of becoming a tolerant, inclusive, pluralistic democracy just as that idea was beginning to take root.

Largely for that reason, Yeltsin's reformist constituency turned against him almost en masse. Liberals were appalled by the carnage and by Yeltsin's apparent isolation and susceptibility to hard-line advisers.[3] One of the fiercest critics was Elena Bonner, the widow of Andrei Sakharov, who quit Yeltsin's human rights commission in protest over his policy in Chechnya. When she called on me in January, she warned that the war could lead to a return to totalitarianism in Russia.

Our public comments continued to be cautious and minimalist, never going much beyond what Gore had said in Moscow. We compounded the error of not being more critical of the war by coming up with a faulty justification for Russian policy that would haunt us for years afterward.

In at least one meeting on Chechnya in late December, I drew a parallel between Russia's emergence as a newly independent democratic state and America's experience in the eighteenth century. We, too, had undergone a revolution to free ourselves from an imperial tyranny; it had taken us thirteen years before we framed a constitution; seventy-two years after that we plunged into a civil war that pitted a union against a secessionist confederacy. Russia was cramming similar traumas into a single decade.

In general, analysis by analogy is a dubious practice, and this particular comparison carried with it the added peril of sticking in the minds of colleagues who had the daily duty of explaining our policy to reporters who were legitimately critical of us for looking the other way while the Russians marauded through Chechnya. Mike McCurry, the State Department press spokesman, said on January 3, "We have a long history as a democracy that includes an episode . . . where we dealt with a secessionist movement through armed conflict called the Civil War. So we need to be conscious of those types of issues when we look at a new democracy in the former Soviet Union . . ."

One of the reporters shouted a question: "You aren't calling Yeltsin the Russian Abraham Lincoln, are you, Mike?"

"By no means," said McCurry, laughing at the absurdity of the notion and back-pedaling furiously. But—like my "less shock, more therapy" line of a year before—the sound bite was already out there in the ether, and it would soon be in the transcript of the department's daily briefing, available for exploitation, minus the disclaimer, forever after. Our critics had a field day.

I should have resolved then and there to expunge the Civil War comparison from every brain in the U.S. government, starting with my own but quickly working my way up to the president's to ensure that he never used the Lincoln line himself. I failed to do so, and would be sorry later.[4]

AN INVITATION TO MOSCOW

NATO, not Chechnya, was at the top of our agenda when Yuri Mamedov and I met in Brussels in early January. Yuri was as relieved as I was that Gore's meeting with Yeltsin in the hospital just before Christmas had gone well. The experience was a reminder that Yeltsin, despite his temper tantrum in Budapest and his infirmity, was still one of the few figures in the Russian power structure who wanted to proceed with a NATO-Russia partnership in parallel with enlargement—and the only one who could make it happen. The immediate task was to bring Russia to take in 1995 the step it had refused to take in 1994: join Partnership for Peace. The only way to do that was to reactivate the face-to-face Clinton-Yeltsin connection. Clinton, said Yuri, should accept Yeltsin's invitation to come to Moscow on May 9 for the Russian observance of V-E Day.[5]

I, too, had been thinking about a presidential meeting as the only way to put Budapest behind us, but the date I had in mind was June, when

Clinton and Yeltsin would both be attending the next G-7 (and "Political Eight") summit, in Halifax, Nova Scotia.

That was not soon enough, said Yuri. Besides, the V-E Day event in Moscow was of immense political and psychological importance to Yeltsin. He would be in a magnanimous mood if Clinton lent his prestige to the commemoration of a great Russian victory.

Seeing the frown on my face, he said, "I know you've taken your bumps for Budapest . . ."

"*Lumps,* Yuri—it's *lumps.*"

"Okay, okay . . . I know you've taken your lumps for Budapest, but I took a few of my own. You've got to get your president to Moscow in May."

I asked if he was trying to get me fired. He took the question only half jokingly: "Look, Strobe, I'm not asking you to take much of a risk compared to the ones people like Andrei [Kozyrev] take every day. The people who are calling for his head aren't being metaphorical."

I had come to trust Yuri's instincts about what it would take to move his government and decided to support the idea of a May meeting in Moscow, but with the caveat that my credibility as a presidential travel agent had already suffered badly and I wasn't at all sure I could deliver.

I MADE THE CASE to Clinton in the Oval Office on January 20. Going to Moscow would give him an opportunity to "stay in Yeltsin's face on both the good stuff and the bad," Chechnya being the worst of the bad. I repeated Mamedov's argument that the time and setting would predispose Yeltsin to be accommodating on NATO.

"You really are a glutton for punishment, aren't you, Strobe?" said Clinton.

"My gluttony could be your punishment, Mr. President, if we subject you to another Budapest. There's that risk, but I don't think he'll do that again. After all, this time he's the host, and he doesn't want to spoil his own party."

Gore spoke up forcefully in favor of Clinton's going. He believed, on the basis of his own experience in December, that Yeltsin was "persuadable," but only by Clinton himself. Gore believed that a celebration of the last great venture in history when American and Russian soldiers had been on the same side was the most propitious setting for Yeltsin to overcome resistance in Russia to joining Partnership for Peace; and conversely, he was convinced that if Clinton didn't go to Moscow, Yeltsin would come to Halifax in a foul mood and that meeting would be, if not another Budapest, then a "repair-the-damage thing."

Leon Panetta, the White House chief of staff, listened to this exchange with a look of incredulity and dismay. The president's role in foreign policy, he said, was already "Russia-top-heavy" and his going to Moscow would only make it more so. Domestic politics argued against the trip, Panetta said, reminding Clinton that George Bush, toward the end of his presidency, paid a price for being "Gorbo-centric." Now Bob Dole was attacking Clinton for a "Yeltsin first" policy, and others in Congress were—with some justification—increasingly critical of us for giving Moscow a pass on the military's continuing rampage in Chechnya.

"I'm leaving the option of going open," said Clinton after listening to this debate. "We should not be tone-deaf to the human destruction, but we've also got to be careful not to appear to be joining the pile-on against Yeltsin. We should give him a chance to dig himself out of this thing, and I should be there for him if he can do it."

Never before or after was Clinton so conflicted over whether to engage directly with Yeltsin. For two months, he let Panetta and Stephanopoulos pummel him with warnings that there would be political hell to pay if he went while Yeltsin pelted him with importuning letters and phone calls.

In Oval Office meetings, Gore continued to give Clinton pep talks on why he should go. When there were warning signs that the Russians were trying to play us and our European allies off against each other on various issues, including NATO enlargement, the vice-president asserted confidently that Yeltsin and Chernomyrdin cared "a whole lot more about the health and traction of their American connection than whatever they've got going with the Europeans. For them, *not* splitting the U.S. and Russia is a higher good than splitting us from our allies." Clinton, he said, would have "immense psychological leverage" with Yeltsin if he went to Moscow for V-E Day: "Remember, the Russians lost a hundred times as many people as we did in World War II. Yeltsin will be primed to think in terms of the grand sweep of history if you can engage him and help him to be getting the most out of the event with his own people."

Throughout this period, Clinton contacted me more often than at any other time. He would pull me aside when I came to the White House on other business, such as Haiti and Bosnia, phone me late at night (by my standards) and even call me in my office during the day, which was hardly standard practice. These interruptions made quite an impression on whoever was in my office at the time. When I asked my guests to step outside so that I could talk in private, they respectfully scurried out, assuming that the president was seeking my advice.

He wasn't. Clinton knew exactly where I stood and could argue my side of the case for his going better than I could. He had no doubt that the danger of appearing to "stiff" Yeltsin, given "everything we're trying to do with the guy," outweighed the risk of being perceived to "kowtow" to him. Clinton had come to believe that "the only way to get beyond Budapest and not have another one in Halifax is to give Ol' Boris another chance."

What worried him was whether Yeltsin would see it the same way. Budapest had been "the diplomatic equivalent of a near-death experience," said Clinton. It had rattled his confidence in Yeltsin's emotional, physical and political stability, which were closely related.

Even after Clinton had made up his mind to go—a decision that was announced in late March—he continued to use me as a sounding board for his fretting about the trip. If the stars were not in the right alignment in early May, the V-E Day event would turn out to be "a bad scene that will make that one in Budapest look like comic relief by comparison."

As Clinton nurtured this fear, he kept coming back to a low point in U.S.-Russian summitry thirty-four years before—the one that he and I had talked about during our first serious conversation, on the deck of the S.S. *United States* en route to England in 1968, and that had preyed on his mind just before his first presidential meeting with Yeltsin in Vancouver in April 1993: "If Ol' Boris does the Kennedy-Khrushchev thing—if he cuts a shine on me—I'm not going to play Kennedy. I'm not going to let myself be taken to the cleaners and shown who's who the way Kennedy was. That guy owes me. I've shown him a lot of restraint and given him a lot of respect. I stood by him when he was high and dry in 1993. Then he went and pulled that thing on me in Budapest. He really got my attention with that. It wasn't right. Now I'm taking a chance on him again, but he'd better not try high theater at my expense again. He'd better not try to score cheap points at my expense while I'm a guest in his country."

Five months earlier, in the immediate aftermath of Budapest, Clinton had quickly gotten over his anger both at Yeltsin and at his own aides, myself included. But now it was all coming back to him as he anticipated the possibility of a repetition. Since I'd missed his blowup on Air Force One on the way home from Budapest, I was getting for the first time a taste of what Tony Lake and Nick Burns had experienced. It was the only time in eight years I ever heard Clinton really furious at Yeltsin. But even this outburst I heard from him only once, and he let himself vent only when it was just the two of us talking.

Moreover, his anger didn't last. As the late-night phone calls continued, I could hear Clinton talking himself down from blaming Yeltsin and into sympathizing with him. Yes, Yeltsin owed him, but "gratitude's not what makes the world go 'round. I know I've got to find a way of bringing him along with this NATO deal in a way that doesn't make him feel like he's been dragged kicking and screaming." The trick, he said, was to find a way of "capturing Yeltsin's ability to imagine the best and fight against the people around him who are trafficking in all the bad stuff that can happen."

Clinton hadn't given up the search for a slogan, one that would work with Yeltsin. He still couldn't get it down to a single phrase, but he was thinking now not in long paragraphs but in relatively short sentences (by his standards): "In the aftermath of the cold war, every good thing has an explosive underbelly . . . We're fighting a constant rearguard action between the forces of integration and the forces of disintegration . . . The new NATO, with new members and with a new relationship with the new Russia, can be part of that fight."

EVERY NOW AND THEN, however, the old fear would nag at him. I caught glimpses of it in the unprecedented interest he took in the work I was doing with Yuri Mamedov to prepare for the Moscow meeting. Several times, Clinton held me back in the Oval Office after other participants in the meeting had left and asked me how the talks were going.

"Strobe," he said after one such strategy session in mid-April, grabbing my shoulder hard, "I hope you and your pal Mamedov are busting your asses to make sure this thing comes out all right."

Of that, at least, I could assure him. Yuri and I were meeting with great regularity and intensity—in Moscow, Washington and several other capitals where we contrived to cross paths.

Yuri had his own nervous president. While Clinton was worried about a replay of the unpleasant surprise Yeltsin had pulled on him in Budapest, Yeltsin was terrified of another "betrayal" of the kind that he felt had occurred with the NATO communiqué released when Kozyrev came to

Brussels in December. The NATO foreign ministers were getting ready to meet again—this time in Noordwijk, in the Netherlands—at the end of May. That would be less than three weeks after the V-E Day event in Moscow. Yeltsin feared he would have a conciliatory and productive meeting with Clinton in Moscow, only to have NATO then announce what would appear to be another surge toward enlargement. Yeltsin's opponents would accuse him, yet again, of having let himself be sweet-talked into compliance by his friend Bill, with dreadful consequences in the parliamentary election at the end of 1995 and in the presidential one in 1996.[6]

Yuri and I came up with a plan whereby Clinton and Yeltsin would agree in Moscow on general guidelines for the development of a NATO-Russia cooperative relationship that would come to fruition sometime in 1997. When the NATO foreign ministers held their meeting in Noordwijk, they would reemphasize Partnership for Peace and, with Kozyrev in attendance, formally include Russia in PFP and inaugurate a NATO-Russia dialogue. At the end of 1995, a follow-up meeting of NATO foreign ministers in Brussels would announce another round of consultation with partners that would stretch well into 1996. The U.S. and its allies would stick with the mantra that enlargement was coming in due course but not immediately. The U.S. would avoid any suggestion that it was threatening to speed up enlargement, and in exchange Moscow would avoid claiming to have slowed it down.

The Russians could, and we hoped would, infer from the proposed timetable that we were holding off enlargement until after the Russian presidential election in mid-1996, and by implication until after the American election in the fall of that year, but they should not expect us to say so in so many words. The twin processes of NATO enlargement and NATO-Russia cooperation were unavoidably hostages to domestic politics in both countries, but we didn't want to expose ourselves to extra flak in the U.S. from advocates of enlargement, who would accuse us yet again of being Yeltsin-firsters.

THE CHANNEL between Mamedov and me was especially useful during this period because Kozyrev was nearly catatonic with anxiety over his vulnerability at home. More than ever, he portrayed himself as the little Dutch boy with his finger in the dike, holding back the fascist flood, and warning that he and like-minded Russians would be swept away if we kept talking about NATO enlargement.

When Kozyrev came to New York for a meeting in late April at the United Nations, Chris invited him to come to Washington for talks on the Moscow summit. Kozyrev initially refused to make the trip unless he was guaranteed in advance a photo op with Clinton in the Oval Office. At Chris's behest, I flew to New York to try to convince Kozyrev that he was being just plain silly. I found him both stubborn and desperate.

"Personally," he said, "I can live without seeing Bill Clinton. It's not my vanity at stake here. I can go off somewhere tomorrow and become a professor or something. But the press headlines will signal the end. Our opponents will say, 'See, those pro-Western democrats like Kozyrev can be bought so cheaply! Russia has been downgraded from a great power to a status lower than Chad's.' Zhirinovsky will say, 'Elect me president and I'll retarget my missiles on Washington so my foreign minister will get to see the president.' "

He recalled that even during the period when the USSR was the evil empire, the longtime Soviet foreign minister, Andrei Gromyko, never came to Washington without seeing the president: "I know Gromyko's nickname in the U.S. was 'Mr. *Nyet.*' Mine back home is 'Mr. *Da.*' "

I told him he'd see the president if and only if he reaffirmed to Chris the plan we'd worked out for a diplomatic two-step in May: a good Clinton-Yeltsin meeting at the beginning of the month in Moscow, a good Kozyrev meeting with the NATO foreign ministers at the end of the month in Brussels. In other words, the opposite of what had happened in December.

He agreed, came to Washington, said all the right things to Chris and earned a short limousine ride over to 1600 Pennsylvania Avenue for a meeting with Clinton.

As insurance, we arranged for Clinton to phone Yeltsin and summarize the plan. "I'm not asking you to make a public endorsement [of NATO enlargement]," Clinton stressed when Yeltsin came on the line. "I realize you can't do that. What I am asking is that you not let concern over the future process of NATO expansion stop us from building a strong NATO-Russia relationship now."

Just as the interpreter was beginning to translate Clinton's fairly long opening statement into Russian, there was a click at the other end. Yeltsin had hung up. There were obviously other Russians still on the line, probably as nonplussed as we were. After considerable confusion, the Kremlin switchboard got Yeltsin back on the line. He made a vague comment about agreeing with "what Kozyrev described" but said that there were some points he'd want to clarify when he and Clinton saw each other.

I didn't like the sound of that. I jumped in my car and roared over to the Russian embassy and told Kozyrev what had happened. He was strangely nonchalant. He told me he'd checked with his own home office after the presidential call. A "technical" problem had occurred. Yeltsin hadn't hung up on Clinton, but he hadn't heard any of his message either.

Was that supposed to make me feel better? I asked. What was going on? Kozyrev shrugged, gave me a knowing look and used a Russian phrase (*by-vayet*) that roughly translates as "these things happen." I understood, since I knew what so often happened with Yeltsin, especially toward the end of the day.

The incident shook my confidence in the plan Mamedov and I had worked out, and I felt I owed it to the president to warn him that while I still didn't think Yeltsin was going to pull a Khrushchev on him, I feared he might pull another Yeltsin.

To my surprise, Clinton not only took the news calmly—he told me he could understand why Yeltsin didn't want to be locked into a deal before they actually saw each other.

"We've got to play this thing out," he said. "I can't just go there and tell him, 'Go back to the script, Boris, and be a good boy.' Among other things, this guy is just incapable of letting things go exactly the way his aides want it to go." He paused, and added with a smile, "I can kind of re-late to that."

SHORTLY BEFORE he left for Moscow, we broke the news to President Clinton that he had some additional heavy lifting to do with Yeltsin: the perennial problem of Russia's sale of nuclear technology to Iran had got-ten worse and once again required presidential attention.

For two years, Victor Mikhailov, the Russian minister of atomic energy, had been bypassing his own government's export controls, blocking adop-tion of new and better ones and cutting deals with Iran that would accel-erate its development of a nuclear weapon. His latest move in that direction was to offer the Iranians gas centrifuges, which they would un-questionably use to produce weapons-grade uranium, as well as a $1 bil-lion contract for Russia to build as many as four nuclear reactors. When Chris tried to get Kozyrev to persuade Yeltsin to rein in Mikhailov, Kozyrev replied that Mikhailov was "out of control," that he was exploiting lingering resentment in the Russian military-industrial complex and political elite over Russia's capitulation to the U.S. on the Indian rocket sale in 1993 and that Yeltsin was unaware of what Mikhailov was up to.

Whether that was true or not, the whole world soon knew about Mikhailov's latest activities because officials in the U.S. government, motivated no doubt by the conviction that the administration was being too soft on Russia, leaked to the press intelligence reports on the centrifuge and reactor transactions. The articles provided ammunition for our critics on Capitol Hill. Appearing on *Meet the Press,* Newt Gingrich, the new Speaker of the House, presumed to give the president his marching orders for the forthcoming summit: "Your job isn't to go to Russia to make Yeltsin happy—your job is to go to Russia to stop Iran from getting nuclear weapons."

In a meeting with Clinton a few days before the summit, Vice-President Gore suggested that the two of them "double-team this problem—you work Yeltsin, I'll work Chernomyrdin, and maybe we can crack it."

"I'll do it, I'll do it," said Clinton, looking acutely unhappy that he'd just been given yet another assignment for what was already shaping up to be one of his most difficult meetings with a foreign leader.

HOURS BEFORE he left for Moscow, Clinton gave a speech at a V-E Day ceremony at Arlington Cemetery. By the time he boarded Air Force One, he was exhausted, his allergies were acting up and his aides wanted him to go straight to bed. But Clinton was feeling apprehensive again about what lay ahead, and he wanted to talk. He gathered several of us in his airborne office to tell us what had happened at Arlington: "A couple grizzled old vets came up to me and whacked me pretty good. 'Why are you going to Russia?' they wanted to know, and it wasn't a friendly question, but at least it was one I'd heard before. But then they said, 'Well, at least if you're going over there, don't let those bastards do that reactor deal with Iran! Good luck, but don't let those guys get away with anything.' "

It had been, he said, a jolt of reality therapy about the awareness of Russia's nefarious dealings with Iran on the home front.

"I'm tomorrow's boy, and I don't like yesterday's criticism. I know we've got to keep our eyes on the prize, which is everything we're trying to do with Russia, but I've got to get Yeltsin to acknowledge that Iran is a serious problem, otherwise we're not going to get anywhere on the other stuff. He keeps telling me about his political problems, and they're a lot bigger than mine. But I've got a few of my own. I'm going to Russia because of the dogs we have in this hunt, but we've got to do something on Iran. Joe Lunchbucket out there in Ames, Iowa, doesn't care about NATO enlargement. He cares about whether this ol' boy is going over there to Russia and let those people give the new ayatollah an A-bomb."

Ever so briefly, the familiar shades of Kennedy and Khrushchev passed through the fuselage of the presidential 747 as it headed across the Atlantic. "If Yeltsin's determined to look strong at my expense," said Clinton, "then I'll have no choice but say no to him."

But then, just as suddenly, the ghosts were gone, and Clinton recovered his confidence, both in himself and in Yeltsin: "My experience has been that, except for Budapest, Ol' Boris always comes into these meetings with me wanting to do some sort of initiative or deal that will make us both come out okay. I think I should be ready for that this time. He looks for win/win things. I know I'm bragging on him, but he may come up with something that makes him look strong but doesn't make me look weak."

With that, his aides, who had been looking daggers at the president's fellow Russia wonks throughout this monologue, succeeded in coaxing him to his cabin in the nose of the plane so that he could get some sleep.

NAILING IT

While the president and Secretary Christopher were participating in the V-E Day celebrations, I went to the Foreign Ministry to review with Mamedov our plan for the summit and its aftermath in Brussels at the end of the month. I mentioned that we'd found Kozyrev increasingly preoccupied with his political liabilities and asked Yuri if we should be preparing for a change at the top of his ministry. He was careful not to undercut Kozyrev but said that we should probably take seriously the rumors that were circulating about Yevgeny Primakov's succeeding him.

I didn't relish that thought. Kozyrev, for all the annoyance he caused us, really was, just as he said, a personification of Russia's radical break with its past. Primakov, by contrast, at sixty-six, personified continuity between the USSR and the Russian Federation. He had presided over the transformation of the foreign branch of the KGB into the SVR, which sometimes appeared to be little more than a change in initials. Kozyrev's replacement by Primakov would be almost universally seen as a portent that Yeltsin was tacking in the direction of a more competitive approach to the U.S.

Yuri noticed my reaction. "Don't overdramatize," he said. "Yevgeny

Maximovich [Primakov's patronymic] is a real professional. He's got a lot of confidence, and he has the confidence of others. That would have its own advantages not just for us, but for you in dealing with us."

THE NEXT MORNING, Clinton and Yeltsin met in Saint Catherine's Hall of the Kremlin. Clinton decided to deal with the Iran problem at the outset so that they could concentrate on NATO for the rest of the meeting. He introduced the subject by reminding Yeltsin of the good work they had done in arranging for the safe transfer of nuclear weapons to Russia from Ukraine and the other former republics—an accomplishment that wouldn't have been possible without their personal attention, joint effort and mutual trust. Now they had to apply those same ingredients to stemming the tide of dangerous technology to states that could threaten the interests of both countries.

No doubt knowing that Clinton would raise the matter, Yeltsin announced that he had just imposed new controls on Russia's nuclear cooperation with Iran, including a ban on centrifuges. The issue, therefore, was now thereby disposed of, and the two of them should "stop torturing each other" about Iran and leave the matter to Gore and Chernomyrdin to work on.

Clinton replied that he was prepared to turn the problem back over to Gore and Chernomyrdin as long as it was privately understood that the U.S. opposed nuclear cooperation of any kind with Iran and that the two of them would publicly announce that Russia would give Iran no militarily useful nuclear technology, with the Gore-Chernomyrdin commission to work on the details.

"Okay," Yeltsin said, "agreed." He offered his hand and they shook.[7]

TURNING TO NATO, Yeltsin made a long and passionate appeal for Clinton to accept a "pause" in enlargement, to last at least until the year 2000—that is, until both of them would be leaving office. That, he said, would "calm the whole situation down."

Clinton replied that the best he could do was offer assurances that NATO would stick to the decision it had made in December: "no speed-up, no slowdown—we're going to proceed at a steady, measured pace." He explained the timetable for NATO's various studies and consultations in a way calculated to assure Yeltsin that the process of preparing for enlargement would run through 1996.

That was what Yeltsin most wanted to hear: "If you can't postpone until

2000, then at least until we get through our elections so that, between now and then, there's only a theoretical discussion about enlargement. I've got to tell you, my position heading into 1996 is not exactly brilliant. I have to look for positive developments and do anything I can to head off negative ones."

Clinton bore down hard on the importance of Russia's finally signing the Partnership for Peace documents. He had come to Moscow, he said, "despite criticism and advice not to come," in order to be part of a ceremony that reminded the world that Russia had joined in the fight against Hitler. Now that the cold war was over, the U.S. and Russia had a chance to make common cause again—but only if Russia participated fully in post–cold war security structures. That meant joining PFP.

"Do it now!" he said.

Yeltsin, looking pensive and conflicted, suggested a break, no doubt wanting to consult with colleagues.

"I think I'm making some progress," Clinton told me when we were alone. "I really just want to get this thing done, not leave it up in the air so others can shoot it down after I leave."

WHEN THE MEETING RESUMED, Yeltsin said he wanted to depart from their agenda long enough for General Dimitri Volkogonov to make a brief progress report on the work of a joint Russian-American inquiry into the fate of Americans missing in action or presumed to be prisoners of war who might have ended up in Soviet hands during the Korean War. Yeltsin had arranged the interlude as a courtesy to Volkogonov, an officer with a distinguished war record who was devoting the last years of his life to chronicling the horrors of Stalinism and championing democracy. Yeltsin saw Volkogonov as a military version of himself—a product and a servant of the old system who had seen the light and was now combating the dark forces of the past.

Volkogonov was in the final stages of a long battle with cancer. Frail, breathing with difficulty and in obvious pain, he still managed to stand erect and speak crisply, very much the soldier reporting to his commander in chief. Listening to him, Yeltsin's face took on a look I'd never seen there before: one of unadulterated compassion, affection, admiration and sorrow.

After finishing his report, Volkogonov saluted, turned on his heel and left the room.

Seeing that Yeltsin needed a moment to suppress his emotions and put himself back in a frame of mind to resume their talks, Clinton started to pour himself a glass of water. Yeltsin asked if he would prefer something stronger. Clinton glanced at me for the pure pleasure of catching what he knew would be a look of horror on my face, then declined, saying it was too early in the day. To my relief, Yeltsin settled for water as well.

"I accept your plan," Yeltsin announced abruptly but clearly in reference to Clinton's overall approach to NATO enlargement. "But this is something we should not tell the press. Let's tell them that we discussed the issue—not conclusively, but we understood each other. As for the political fallout, we can both absorb the punches we'll take."

"Good," said Clinton. "So join PFP too."

"Okay," said Yeltsin, "we'll sign both documents."

I scribbled "WHEW!" in block letters in my notebook and flashed it to Clinton.

Clinton wanted to insert mention of NATO enlargement in the joint statement the two of them would be releasing at the end of their meeting. Yeltsin was just about to agree when his foreign-policy adviser Dimitri Ryurikov, who was my counterpart in the meeting, suggested that Russian experts look at the language before Yeltsin made any commitments. I assumed Ryurikov was acting on behalf of other officials who were worried about Yeltsin giving away too much. His intervention seemed to work, causing Yeltsin to draw back from the agreement he'd been about to make on the communiqué.

"You know," Yeltsin said reprovingly, "partnership is not just a matter of calling each other Bill and Boris. It's a matter of give-and-take."

Clinton pressed ahead, handing to Yeltsin a Russian-language draft of a public statement that we'd prepared on our side. Ryurikov intercepted it, pursed his lips as he glanced at the text and whispered something to Yeltsin, who then proposed a noncommittal alternative, to the effect that the two presidents would keep discussing European security when they saw each other next at the G-7 in Halifax.

Sensing a serious snag, Clinton immediately offered a fallback: Instead of referring to enlargement per se, the joint statement would reiterate the right of all sovereign states to join alliances. But in exchange for agreeing to that watered-down version of what they would say in public, he asked Yeltsin to agree on the spot, without letting Ryurikov or anyone else second-guess them.

"Fine," said Yeltsin. "We understand each other."

But Clinton wasn't sure. The press was waiting to hear from the two leaders in a giant hall nearby. Just before they went onstage together, Clinton took Yeltsin by the elbow, steered him into a corner, put both hands on his shoulders and looked him straight in the eye. He emphasized again how important it was for Russia to proceed with the PFP documents before the NATO foreign ministers meeting at the end of the month. Yeltsin again said he understood.

During the press conference, Clinton said several times that "Russia has agreed to enter the Partnership for Peace" and that the U.S. had committed "at the end of this month to encourage the beginning of the NATO-Russia dialogue."

In his own remarks, Yeltsin dodged the issue, saying only that they had had a full discussion and would continue their talks in Halifax.

I figured that by Yeltsin standards, that was about as much as we could hope for. He'd publicly equivocated, but at least he hadn't pulled the rug out from under Clinton.

CLINTON STILL wasn't satisfied. He told me he wasn't sure he'd "nailed it with Ol' Boris," and that he was going to take another run at him during the state dinner that evening in the Kremlin Hall of Facets. Once they were seated and finished with the preliminaries, Clinton started talking dates with Yeltsin on when Russia would formally join PFP.

"Would May 25 be all right?" Clinton asked. "I need this to do all I promised."

Yeltsin said he personally would sign the necessary documents the day after the foreign ministers meeting. While confused about the procedure, he was clearly trying to protect his own Lucy-and-the-football option.

"No, Boris," said Clinton, "you don't understand. You don't have to sign anything yourself. It's Kozyrev who has to take the necessary step, and he has to do so no later than the day the ministers meet."

"Okay," Yeltsin said, "I'll have him do it the day before."

"We're completely agreed on this, Boris? Completely?"

"Yes."

Knowing what was going on between them, I was hovering nearby, and Clinton waved me over and reviewed the conversation.

"I think we got the Big *Da*," he said. "You can go have a drink. I assure you *he's* had a few."

BEFORE CELEBRATING, I took Mamedov off into a corner to make sure that the magic words—Yeltsin's commitment to have Kozyrev sign the PFP papers the day before the NATO meeting—were identically consecrated in the official record on both sides of what the presidents had said to each other over dinner.

Kozyrev subsequently used the memorandum of that conversation to beat back an attempt led by Primakov and Oleg Lobov, the chairman of Yeltsin's Security Council and one of the driving forces behind the war in Chechnya, to renege on the Clinton-Yeltsin understanding.

Just before the Noordwijk meeting, I flew to Toronto for a quick review of the plan with Mamedov, who had been in Ottawa for consultations with the Canadian government.[8] I brought with me a letter from Clinton to Yeltsin broadly hinting that the quality of their next meeting—at the G-7 in Halifax five weeks later—would depend in no small measure on whether Kozyrev signed the documents in Noordwijk on schedule and without any diversionary rhetorical tactics.

Yuri warned me that Kozyrev might feel compelled to restate Russia's opposition to enlargement.

If that happened, I said, Kozyrev would be eclipsing the good news of Russia's finally coming on board PFP. We agreed on a compromise: Kozyrev would come out against the "hasty" enlargement of NATO, which we could live with since we weren't advocating haste ourselves.

When Secretary Christopher set off for Noordwijk, I stayed home and waited. Kozyrev came, signed and spoke according to script, including using the word "hasty" as a qualification of what Russia opposed.[9]

Tom Donilon, who had given me the bad news from Brussels the previous December, called me to let me know that this time, "our boy did all right in the end."

FIFTEEN MINUTES OF FAME

President Clinton had every hope of making the Halifax G-7 on June 17 a reward for Yeltsin's fulfillment of his own promise on PFP, but the war in Chechnya kept that from happening.

The fighting had dragged on for six months since Russian forces had taken Grozny, further undermining Yeltsin's popularity and boosting that of his rivals, especially General Alexander Lebed. As a result, while the rest of the world was focused on the challenge that Gennady Zyuganov, the Russian communist leader, was expected to pose in 1996, Lebed was the rival Yeltsin was increasingly worried about. Some of Yeltsin's advisers were urging him to use Chechnya as an excuse to impose a state of emergency and postpone the presidential election scheduled for 1996. The most influential advocate of this course was General Alexander Korzhakov, Yeltsin's bodyguard turned crony who was notorious among Kremlin insiders for pouring Yeltsin drinks and stoking his suspicions about his enemies, foreign and domestic.[10]

By May, Russian forces had captured most of the towns in Chechnya, but at huge cost to the civilian population and in repeated violation of cease-fires that Yeltsin announced in Moscow. In early June, just before Halifax, the Russians pulled off one of their few successful offensives against the rebels, capturing two towns that had been in Chechen hands.

The guerrillas struck back, not frontally but deep inside territory that the Russians thought they fully controlled. One of the Chechen chieftains, Shamil Basayev, led a daring raid into the neighboring Russian territory of Stavropol. With less than a hundred men, Basayev bribed and bluffed his way through Russian checkpoints until the local police put up a fight outside the town of Budyonnovsk. Basayev's band stormed the police station and town hall and holed up in the local hospital, taking several thousand patients as hostages. They executed several wounded Russian soldiers and threatened to kill the rest of the patients unless the Russian authorities entered negotiations over a truce in Chechnya and guaranteed the rebels safe passage home. The Russian forces made two abortive attempts to storm the hospital, killing dozens of hostages and shelling a maternity ward in the process.

This crisis was in full swing as Yeltsin left Moscow for the G-7. He was pilloried for hobnobbing with foreign leaders in far-off Canada while wounded Russian soldiers were being shot in their hospital beds. Worse for him, when he got to Halifax he was politely taken to task by his host, Canadian Prime Minister Jean Chrétien, in front of the assembled G-7 leaders. While deploring what was unquestionably an act of terrorism on the part of the Chechens, Chrétien exhorted Yeltsin to call off the military onslaught and find a political solution. Yeltsin sat through this remonstration impassively, staring into the distance, fiddling with the volume button of his headset. He was biding his time until he had a chance to speak out publicly. He figured he would get maximum attention when the press covered his meeting with Clinton.

WHEN YELTSIN ARRIVED for an early-afternoon meeting, I could tell the minute I saw him that he had been drinking. I later learned he had downed half a bottle of scotch since lunch. Once the reporters and camera crews were in position, a Russian journalist asked a question about the standoff under way in Budyonnovsk, and Yeltsin let fly. His face red with rage and his speech badly slurred, he denounced the Chechen guerrillas as "horrible criminals with black bands on their foreheads . . . Chechnya today is the center of world terrorism, of bribery and corruption and mafia. We couldn't act otherwise. We had to destroy those terrorists and bandits." He claimed that he had explained the situation to an understanding, sympathetic and supportive group of G-7 leaders, particularly "my friend Bill." Reverting to the third person, he said that Clinton "has always supported Russia and President Yeltsin and is doing so now."

Listening to this outburst, Mike McCurry, who had become the White House press secretary, whispered to Sandy Berger, "Well, Bobo just got his fifteen minutes of fame for the day." Yet again, Yeltsin had provided just the headline we didn't want—this time, unlike in Naples and Budapest, even before the meeting started.

As soon as he finished speaking, he asked the press to leave, without giving Clinton a chance to speak.

"Hold it, you guys," said Clinton, "I've got something to say on all this too." His statement was brief and temperate, especially compared to Yeltsin's. He said he shared the view of the other G-7 leaders "that sooner or later, and better sooner than later, the cycle of violence has to be broken and ultimately in any democracy there has to be a political solution to people's differences."

Yeltsin pouted for a moment, but as soon as the press was gone, he calmed down, perhaps because he was confident that his own tirade, and not Clinton's mild rebuke, would make the headlines. Gradually, Clinton coaxed Yeltsin into a discussion of other issues that broke no new ground—which was just as well, given Yeltsin's mood and condition.

As the meeting came to a close, Clinton returned to Chechnya, but in the gentlest fashion possible. He said he knew that Yeltsin was being savaged at home for having come to Halifax despite the crisis in Budyonnovsk. "It took a lot of political courage for you to come," he said, then added that it would take even more political courage to end the military campaign and look for a negotiated settlement.

On their way out the door, they bantered about a performance of the

Cirque du Soleil, Canada's famous circus, that they had watched with the other leaders the night before. Clinton said he'd especially enjoyed the high-wire act of a pair of acrobatic twins: "It kind of reminded me of us, Boris."

"Exactly!" said Yeltsin with a belly laugh, "And no safety net!"

MEANWHILE, back in Moscow, Prime Minister Chernomyrdin ended the Budyonnovsk hostage crisis by negotiating a cease-fire and giving the rebel leader Basayev and his band safe passage back to separatist-held areas of Chechnya. Chernomyrdin also fired Sergei Stepashin as the head of the internal security service for his role in the debacle. Chernomyrdin's standing in public opinion polls was rising as a result. The lesson, which Chernomyrdin impressed on Yeltsin once he returned from Halifax, was clear: The war was militarily unwinnable and politically disastrous for pro-Kremlin politicians in the parliamentary elections coming up at the end of 1995 and for whichever of the two of them ended up running in the presidential election in 1996. They needed to find a compromise with Dzhokhar Dudayev that would give the Chechens a high degree of autonomy in exchange for retaining some sort of federative ties to Russia.

The Chechens, however, were in no mood to compromise. For them, the lesson of Budyonnovsk was that they could take Chechnya out of Russia entirely—and that they could strike Russian targets in the neighboring republics as well.

CHAPTER 7

CHAINS OF COMMAND

*I am not sure your people have quite realized
all that is going on in the Balkans and the hopes
and horrors centered there.*

Churchill to Roosevelt at Hyde Park, August 1943

I N   T H E I R   O T H E R W I S E rocky encounter in Halifax, Clinton and
Yeltsin agreed on a procedural point about U.S.-Russian military cooperation that paid off almost immediately. Now that Russia had
joined the Partnership for Peace, the two presidents would instruct Secretary of Defense Bill Perry and Defense Minister Pavel Grachev to intensify
their discussion of practical ways for the soldiers under their command to
work together. Of all the match-ups between U.S. and Russian officials,
"Bill and Pasha," as we quickly nicknamed them within the Russia team,
were the oddest couple of all. Perry, a scientist and opera buff, was soft-
spoken, patient, confident, systematic and cerebral, while Grachev was
gruff, histrionic and primitive. But within weeks the channel between
them proved instrumental in managing the Russians at a turning point in
Bosnia.

The two Muslim-majority towns that had been the focus of so much
Serb cruelty and international dithering in 1993—Srebrenica and
Goražde—were back in the news in the summer of 1995. In early July, the
Serb armed forces under General Ratko Mladić overran Srebrenica, took
the Dutch peacekeepers there hostage, expelled over 20,000 women and
children, rounded up thousands of men, crowded them into a soccer stadium and a car battery factory and systematically executed thousands of
unarmed captives. It was the worst case of mass murder in Europe since
World War II and the postwar Stalinist terror in the USSR.

Initially, Srebrenica had a divisive effect in the debate over NATO. Many in the West, myself included, felt that the incident clinched the argument for having a robust alliance with a capacity to deter, punish or defeat rampant barbarism.[1] In Central Europe, recoiling at what had happened in Srebrenica and appalled at the absence of an effective international response, some Czechs, Hungarians and Poles began expressing second thoughts about whether they should even want to be in a Western alliance that had shown itself to be so easily cowed. That disillusionment engendered renewed hope in Moscow that maybe enlargement could be stopped after all. The Kremlin and the Foreign Ministry toughened up their rhetoric on NATO-Russia relations, dropping the qualifier "hasty" in their statements about what they opposed and thus backtracking on the formulation Yeltsin and Kozyrev had agreed to in the spring.[2]

Prime Minister John Major of the United Kingdom called for an emergency meeting of foreign and defense ministers from Europe and North America in London the third week in July to discuss how to prevent the Serbs from doing to Goražde, the next Muslim "safe area" in eastern Bosnia on their hit list, what they had just done to Srebrenica. The highly visible, crowded event carried with it the risk of degenerating into yet another display of hand-wringing and chest-thumping, especially with the Russians participating. Yet to everyone's surprise, the meeting produced a breakthrough. Grachev emerged from many hours of private talks with Perry and agreed to a U.S. proposal that gave NATO authority to carry out air strikes against the Serbs if they attacked Goražde. Key to Perry's argument was a promise that Russia would have a "dignified and meaningful" role in the peacekeeping operation that would take over once NATO had forced the Serbs into negotiations.

Back in Washington, President Clinton, Secretary Christopher and Tony Lake decided on a new American-led push to persuade the warring parties to agree to a cease-fire and to attend an international conference that would yield a settlement. To lead that effort, they selected Dick Holbrooke, the assistant secretary of state for European affairs. Determined, resilient and strong-willed, he had already applied his prodigious energy and ingenuity to a wide array of targets, including the transformation of NATO, during the year and a half he'd already been in government, but it was in the wake of Srebrenica and the London meeting in July 1995 that Dick came fully into his own.

On Saturday, August 19, he and his small band of diplomats and soldiers were making their way to Sarajevo in a caravan of two French armored personnel carriers and a U.S. Army Humvee on a narrow road. One of the APCs got too close to the edge, went over the side and plummeted down the mountain. The French driver and three Americans, Bob Frasure of the State Department, Joe Kruzel of the Defense Department and Nelson Drew of the National Security Council, died in the accident. Bob had been our ambassador to Estonia and was my host during the first *zdravstvidaniya* tour in May 1993. Joe was an academic who had mastered the bureaucracy, elevating the sights of his colleagues there from parochial issues to ones of grand strategy. He was one of Shali's principal co-authors of PFP and of our strategy for NATO-Russia cooperation more generally. Nelson was an Air Force colonel who had just joined the NSC to work arduously and imaginatively on Balkans issues.

In the numbing hours that followed, I participated in a conference call that linked President Clinton, who was on vacation in Jackson Hole, Wyoming, and Chris, who was at his home in Santa Barbara, California, with Dick Holbrooke and Lieutenant General Wesley Clark, who represented the Joint Chiefs of Staff on Dick's team. Brooke and I then drove to the home of Katharina Frasure, Bob's widow, and their teenage daughters, Sarah and Virginia. Katharina took us into Bob's study, showed us his favorite chair where he liked to read, next to his ambassadorial flag from his tour of duty in Estonia. Two days later, Brooke, Madeleine Albright, our ambassador to the UN, and I drove out to Andrews Air Force Base to meet the giant C-141 transport that brought home Dick and his team, three of them now in coffins.

Within days, Dick set off again for Europe with renewed resolve to complete the peace mission. Just as he was arriving in Paris on August 28 on his way to the Balkans, a mortar shell fired from a Bosnian Serb position in the hills above Sarajevo exploded in a downtown market, killing at least thirty-five people. I took a call from Muhamed Sacirbey, the scrappy, thoroughly Americanized foreign minister of Bosnia, who demanded that we treat this latest outrage as the last straw.

"No more fucking around with the UN!" Mo shouted at me over the phone. "You people have to bring in NATO air strikes *now!*"

Those were my sentiments exactly—and Dick Holbrooke's too. I talked to him just after he landed in Paris, then called Sandy Berger, who told me that the president wanted to hit the Serbs hard.

TWO DAYS LATER, we were ready to pull the trigger. By then we were heading into the Labor Day weekend, and literally all the principals—the president and his cabinet—were on vacation. I was acting secretary of state, Sandy was acting national security adviser, John White was acting secretary of defense, Admiral William Owens was acting chairman of the Joint Chiefs of Staff and George Tenet was acting director of Central Intelligence.[3] We called ourselves the deputy dogs and joked that the scene of us sitting around the table in the Situation Room, which by the end of the weekend was strewn with stale, half-eaten bagels and pizzas, looked like a sequel to *Home Alone.* Fortunately, the UN, too, was under the leadership of a deputy, Kofi Annan, the assistant secretary-general in charge of peacekeeping operations, who had already earned our respect for being more hard-headed and decisive than the secretary-general himself, Boutros Boutros-Ghali. Madeleine worked closely with Kofi to ensure that NATO could launch air strikes without being second-guessed by other UN officials. The Russians had in effect signed away their rights to prevent the strikes at the London conference in July.

On August 30, war planes based in Italy and aboard the aircraft carrier *Theodore Roosevelt* in the Adriatic began Operation Deliberate Force, pounding Serb artillery positions and ammunition depots for two days. Strikes were then suspended in order to give the UN commander in Bosnia, a French general, Bernard Janvier, a chance to negotiate with Mladić a lifting of the siege of Sarajevo. Mladić responded with a combination of defiance and diplomatic feints.

With the Serbs stalling at the table while rampaging around the Bosnian countryside, the Russians did everything they could to make the pause permanent while the U.S. went back on an all-out diplomatic offensive to get the bombing restarted. The Situation Room was now literally a war room. Sandy Berger and I escaped briefly to attend a wedding reception for Madeleine Albright's daughter Katie. We had to get back to our post before dinner was served, so we took a huge doggie bag of hors d'oeuvres with us to share with our colleagues who were working the phones to NATO headquarters, the UN, allied capitals and Dick Holbrooke, who was moving around Europe agitating for air strikes.

On September 5, we succeeded in getting the operation resumed. Once again, we rolled over Moscow's objections by insisting on "London rules." The Russians erupted with the harshest rhetoric we'd heard in years. The worst of it came from Boris Yeltsin himself. He had suffered a heart attack in early July and had just returned to work. Yeltsin's latest incapacity had further damaged his already flagging political fortunes. Rumors were flying about an imminent resignation. The NATO bombing gave him a chance to prove that he was back on the job and capable of standing up to the trigger-happy, bloodthirsty Americans.

Yeltsin fired off a letter to Clinton branding the air campaign "unacceptable" and calling it an "execution of the Bosnian Serbs." In a press conference he warned of "a conflagration of war throughout Europe." Just for good measure, he let it be known that he was "not satisfied with the work of the Foreign Ministry." To improve his chances for reelection in 1996, Yeltsin was playing off Kozyrev's unpopularity. The immediate and obvious effect was to undermine Kozyrev even further. More worrisome, Yeltsin's comments also indirectly called into question whether Russia was going to keep exerting diplomatic pressure on the Serbs. Clinton wrote him a letter urging that he back Kozyrev's active participation in the Contact Group—the de facto steering committee made up of representatives from Russia and the key allied countries.

To reinforce this message, Christopher sent me to Moscow in mid-September. I arrived just as Dick Holbrooke, in marathon negotiations in Belgrade, wrung out of the Serbs an agreement for a cease-fire and an end to the siege of Sarajevo.

I found Kozyrev in the best mood I'd ever seen—which, while explicable given the good news from Belgrade, was strange, coming after the public rebuke he had just received from Yeltsin. I said as much, and Kozyrev jauntily told me there was no problem: he'd just returned from visiting his president, who was vacationing in Sochi, and he regaled me with stories about learning to windsurf off a beach on the Black Sea. Yeltsin's angry press conference the week before had been merely a warning about what might happen in the future. Now that the bombing had stopped, he was sure Yeltsin would "turn the page" to a discussion of Russia's role in the implementation of a peace.

I was so in the habit of dealing with Kozyrev in panic or depression that it took me a few minutes to realize that this time my job was to shake him up. I stressed that the bombing would resume if the Serbs didn't comply within seventy-two hours.

Even if the peace held, there were some facts of life Kozyrev needed to understand about the peacekeeping operation that would follow. Given the dreadful experience we'd had with the so-called UN "protective" force, known as UNPROFOR, its replacement, to be called the Implementation Force, or IFOR, would have to be NATO-led. American troops would not wear the blue helmets of the UN, and non-American units would be under NATO command. That left us diametrically at odds with the Russian military, who were prepared to operate under a UN flag but not under NATO. The Russians also wanted their own geographical sector in Bosnia, along the lines of what the Soviet authorities carved out for themselves in occupied Germany after World War II. That precedent was the best argument I could think of *against* what the Russians were asking for: a Russian sector in Bosnia would inevitably become a haven for the worst elements on the Serb side, a flashpoint for more fighting and the basis for the partitioning of the country—all the outcomes we were trying to avoid.

The only chance of resolving this dispute, said Kozyrev, was to turn the matter over to Perry and Grachev. They'd done good work in London in reconciling U.S. and Russian policy to the point that we were able to bomb Milošević to the negotiating table, and they now needed to put their heads together again on how the U.S. and Russia could join in implementing whatever peace came out of those negotiations.

The foreign minister of Russia was in effect turning the Bosnia portfolio over to the defense minister—a constructive move, as it turned out, but further evidence that Kozyrev himself was finished.

MISSION POSSIBLE

On his frequent trips abroad, Bill Perry had a preference for using one of the Air Force's four Doomsday planes. These were Boeing 747s that had originally been intended to serve as airborne national command centers during a thermonuclear war. They could be refueled in midair and therefore make long hauls without having to land. They were noisy, windowless, claustrophobic and crammed with communications gear that appeared to be of the vacuum-tube era. The result was a long-in-the-tooth, rough-and-ready ambiance redolent of the *Millennium Falcon* in the *Star Wars* saga, with a bit of Dr. Strangelove thrown in. Secretary Perry had a comfortable cabin in the nose, which he invited me to share, but most of the passengers had to work in nonreclining seats in front of eerie and rather low-tech–looking instrument panels.

As we headed out over the Atlantic toward Geneva for a meeting with Defense Minister Grachev at the end of the first week of October, I took a seat in the plane's conference room surrounded by Perry's traveling team, all wearing earphones in order to hear one another over the drone of the engines.

"Welcome aboard Mission Impossible," said Bill, opening the meeting. Our goal was to coax the Russians into being part of a NATO-led operation with "unity of command." That meant that every officer at every level must report to only one superior, so that there would be no danger of competing or conflicting orders in a fast-breaking combat situation. Compromise or confusion on this point could lead to the sort of debacle that had befallen our military operation in Somalia in October 1993, costing the lives of eighteen American soldiers.

Knowing how strongly the U.S. felt on this point, Grachev and his delegation arrived in Geneva in a foul mood. Any Russian who agreed to put his troops under NATO, Grachev said, would be strangled back home. "So here's what you're doing to me, Dr. Perry!" He gripped himself by the throat, rolled his eyes upward and let his tongue hang out.

Bill looked mildly amused and suggested they get down to work. He started by proposing that the Russian contribution be limited to demining or construction, that is, a noncombat function that wouldn't require putting the Russian troops involved directly under NATO—an idea that Kozyrev had quietly suggested to me during a visit to Washington ten days earlier. Grachev treated the notion as an insult: Russia was a major power with a world-class military made up of warriors, not carpenters; it was entitled to a more "dignified and serious" role. The only solution, he insisted, was that Russian peacekeepers be in their own sector and under their own general. The only international body they would take "political guidance" from would be the UN, not NATO.

Perry reminded Grachev of the disastrous experience of UNPROFOR, which had forever discredited the idea that the UN could run an effective military operation in the Balkans. The North Atlantic Council—NATO's governing body—must retain ultimate responsibility for decisions on the conduct of the military operation.

As the discussion progressed, it became apparent that Grachev was less concerned about who would be giving orders to IFOR as a whole than about who would be giving orders to the Russian contingent. The issue wasn't so much military as political, he implied. If the Yeltsin government agreed to subordinate Russian forces to NATO in Bosnia, the consequence would be a communist victory in the parliamentary elections in

December and Yeltsin's defeat by Zyuganov in 1996—an outcome that would "set Russia back seventy years, and we'll be back in a cold war."

Then came a glimpse at Grachev's own bottom line: Russia had no objection in principle to putting its forces under an American general, as long as there was no direct link between the Russians and the NATO chain of command. Specifically, he was prepared to have a Russian general serve as a deputy to the senior American military officer in Europe, General George Joulwan. Perry instantly recognized in this suggestion the basis for a deal. Joulwan held two positions: commander in chief of American forces in Europe and Supreme Allied Commander (i.e., the top NATO officer). It was in his U.S. capacity that the Russians might agree to assign him one of their own officers as a deputy—an arrangement that would make it possible, after all, for the Russian military to participate, under American command and in cooperation with NATO, as a partner in Bosnian peacekeeping.

BUT FIRST WE NEEDED a peace to keep. In mid-October, after a quick trip home, I flew to Moscow to link up with Dick Holbrooke, who had let Kozyrev chair a Contact Group meeting largely in order to buck him up and to keep Russia involved in the process.

Dick met me at the airport to catch me up on his own next steps. He was in final, though still secret, preparations for a peace conference to be held at Wright-Patterson Air Force Base in Dayton, Ohio. In addition to the Balkan parties, each member of the Contact Group would have a representative at Dayton. Dick had not yet told Kozyrev about the arrangements, but he assumed that the Russian would be Kozyrev's number two, First Deputy Foreign Minister Igor Ivanov, a solid, even-tempered professional diplomat. Ivanov, who had served as Eduard Shevardnadze's executive assistant in the Soviet Foreign Ministry, was, by rank, my Russian counterpart (Mamedov was the next level down in the hierarchy).

When I met with Kozyrev, he seemed almost as laid-back as during my previous visit. Once again, he was in no hurry to get past the small talk. He told me his technique for sleeping on long airplane flights: sip cognac, put on an eyeshade and not think about Bosnia. When I told him about the venue of the forthcoming peace talks, he reacted with little surprise— I suspect he'd already gotten the word from Russian intelligence—and with a mild bit of sarcasm about how the choice of a U.S. Air Force base was no doubt intended to send a threatening signal to the Serbs about what would happen to them if they didn't make peace.

As I was leaving Kozyrev's office, I mentioned that I was scheduled to stop by the Kremlin for a talk with Dimitri Ryurikov, Yeltsin's foreign-policy adviser. I asked Kozyrev if he had any advice for me on what points to stress with Ryurikov.

"Yes," he said, "Tell him that Kozyrev was tough—much tougher than Grachev!"

He said this with a big grin.

It was the last time I saw Kozyrev smile. The next day, October 19, Yeltsin gave a press conference and repeated, in even more scathing terms than he'd used the month before, his dissatisfaction with the conduct of Russian foreign policy. He was asked the obvious question: Did that mean he was looking for a replacement for Kozyrev? For once it was with a booming *"Da!"* that Yeltsin shocked his audience and sent the reporters scurrying to file a news flash.

As though realizing that he had just stuck a knife into a longtime pro-tégé and loyal lieutenant, Yeltsin tried to pull it out, but in doing so, he gave it another twist. Kozyrev had "tried hard," he said, "so let's not squash him. Let him keep working. But my decision will stand."

Two days later, Yeltsin flew to New York for an appearance before the General Assembly of the UN. The presidential Ilyushin-96 with the twin-headed eagle crest on its tail rolled to a stop, and Yeltsin descended rather unsteadily with his wife, Naina, and his principal advisers who were still in favor, including his vizier and sidekick Alexander Korzhakov. Korzhakov made Kozyrev disembark from the rear of the plane, assigned him a car at the tail of the motorcade and, once they reached Manhattan, prevented him from accompanying Yeltsin into the Russian mission to the UN. After arguing and cooling his heels on the sidewalk for almost two hours, Kozyrev went forlornly off to his hotel.

Kozyrev said nothing about these multiple putdowns when he met Secretary Christopher and me for dinner that evening at an Italian restaurant, but he did say that he needed a double scotch "for psychic medicinal purposes." Remembering our conversation in Moscow about techniques for airborne napping, I presented him with an eyeshade, which he immediately tried out. He tilted his head back and let out a long, restful-sounding sigh, drawing some curious stares from customers at nearby tables. Then he asked with a wan smile, "Is this some hint that I should close my eyes for a while?"

Chris expressed sympathy for what Kozyrev had been through at the hands of his boss and admiration for his stamina. "I've always thought of you as having nine lives," he said, "but it now appears maybe you're on your eleventh. I was offended on your behalf, and I admire your forbearance."

Kozyrev shrugged, then tried to put the best face on Yeltsin's denunciation. "He's a very special personality," he said. "In revolutionary situations, you need a leader who is blunt, not necessarily subtle or sophisticated in his techniques. He's under a lot of pressure. Sometimes he deals with them in ways that are difficult for me." Still, he said, the press conference had come as a shock; it was different from other presidential criticisms.

"I won't last long," he said. "I'm tired of being the lonely voice, tired of being the only one in the president's entourage who advocates the kind of positions you Americans would find acceptable." Yeltsin was now under the sway of people whose thinking and orientation were "decades, if not centuries in the past," who saw American and Western policy as motivated by "forces of darkness."

THE NEXT DAY, Yeltsin gave a fire-and-brimstone speech at the UN excoriating NATO for the bombing of Serb targets in Bosnia and warning that NATO enlargement would mean a "new era of confrontation."

That evening, Clinton hosted a giant reception at the New York Public Library in honor of the heads of state and government who had assembled for the General Assembly. Yeltsin arrived florid and weaving. He spotted Secretary Christopher and Madeleine Albright just as a waiter was bringing them champagne. Yeltsin reached for one of the two goblets on the tray.

"Mr. President," said Chris, "that one already has fingerprints on it."

Yeltsin huffed and demanded a glass of his own. He polished it off in a single gulp and turned back to Chris.

"I haven't seen you for a while," he said with an expression of menace so exaggerated that it was comic. "You and Kozyrev are both failures! Total failures! Bill and I are going to fix all these problems that you and Kozyrev have not been able to handle."

Having all but fired his own foreign minister, he apparently felt that he had to do the same to Clinton's.

Yeltsin then galumphed across the room to accost General Shalikashvili with a proposal that American and Russian submarines jointly patrol the world's oceans. He would put this idea to Clinton the next day, he promised.

"Mr. President," said Shali, "please make sure my president understands that I did not agree to this."

By then, Yeltsin had polished off two more glasses of champagne and ordered a third, but his wife, Naina, and his long-suffering, permanently grim-faced chief of protocol, Vladimir Shevchenko, intercepted it. Yeltsin was just starting to protest this impertinence when he spotted Hazel O'Leary, the secretary of energy and an occasional visitor to Moscow in connection with the Gore-Chernomyrdin commission. Hazel, thinking she could do a little business, mentioned that she and her Russian counterpart, Victor Mikhailov, had not been able to come to closure on several issues, principally the festering problem of Russian reactor sales to Iran.

"Then I'll fire Mikhailov immediately!" Yeltsin said gallantly.

"Oh, no, Mr. President, I wouldn't want you to do that!" said Hazel, thus missing one of the better opportunities we'd ever have to eliminate a major obstacle to progress on nonproliferation.

It was hardly an auspicious prelude to the meeting the two presidents were about to have on the grounds of Franklin Roosevelt's former estate at Hyde Park, New York. When Secretary Christopher had a moment alone with Clinton, he warned him, "You'll probably not find Yeltsin in a subtle mood."

RUSSIAN RIVER ON THE HUDSON

The idea of holding the summit at a site associated with Roosevelt had come from Jim Collins, the most knowledgeable and experienced specialist on the former Soviet Union in the foreign service. He had served as Ambassador Robert Strauss's deputy in the Bush administration and run the embassy in the months before Tom Pickering arrived in 1993. Jim had taken my place as ambassador-at-large and head of the office responsible for the former Soviet Union when I became deputy secretary of state in early 1994. Knowing that Yeltsin, like many Russians, revered Roosevelt as a wartime ally and the last American president before the onset of the cold war, Jim believed Hyde Park would be a propitious setting for what was shaping up to be a high-stakes and high-tension meeting.

It was warm and sunny, a perfect Indian summer day, when the two leaders arrived in separate helicopters on the spacious lawn overlooking the Hudson. For the obligatory photo op, they posed in the same rustic bentwood chairs in which FDR and Churchill had relaxed at Hyde Park during World War II. While Yeltsin's mood was still far from subtle, it was much improved from the day before. "In such a place," he said, "there won't be any problems that we won't be able to solve!"

Once inside for their private meeting, Clinton suggested they take their jackets off, and a waiter brought a tray of cold drinks. Yeltsin downed a large tumbler of soda water in a single gulp. Clinton opened with a friendly, conspiratorial challenge: their objective in the meeting and in what the world learned about it in the press conference, he said, should be to "prove the pundits wrong. They want to write about a big blowup. Let's disappoint them."

Yeltsin said he was prepared to deal, but only if Clinton took personal charge on the American side and forced his subordinates, principally Christopher and Perry, to show more flexibility.

"I come here with a sense of opportunity," said Yeltsin, "but also with a lot of anxiety. Everything will depend on what you and I agree to. We can't let our partnership be shattered by a failure to agree. We have to find some sort of compromise—a little from your side, a little from mine—and then we can shake on it, right here. We need to end the discussion today with an agreement. If we don't agree, it'll be a scandal." In the past several months, he continued, "we've gotten off track. It's not a problem between the two of us personally. There are no personal grudges between us, no personal mistrust. But our countries, our governments have started to work on opposite sides of too many issues. We've been pulling against each other rather than pulling together. Somehow we have to restore our personal rapport as the driving force in the relationship."

His tone was more pleading than hectoring or threatening. I glanced at the only other Russian official in the room, Dimitri Ryurikov, who was normally poker-faced but who looked worried, as though Yeltsin was already departing from whatever game plan his advisers had urged him to follow.

Yeltsin said the U.S.'s refusal to let Russia have its own sector in Bosnia was putting him in an impossible position at home. "Extremists" in the Duma were saying, "Yeltsin has sold out to the U.S. and to Clinton! Yeltsin and his government are pandering to the West and forgetting about the East!" As he impersonated his enemies at home, Yeltsin raised his voice, shook his fist and put on a wild look.

The Russian people, he said, were susceptible to these charges because "they have an allergy to NATO." Unless the U.S. found a way of letting

Russia into Bosnia without putting it under NATO, said Yeltsin, "I'll lose, personally, in the election next year. I'll be finished!"

Clinton said he sympathized; the last thing he wanted was for Russia—or Yeltsin—to feel humiliated or defeated. As a way out, he floated the face-saving formula that Perry had tried with Grachev of giving the Russian units in Bosnia responsibility for noncombat functions and establishing a separate "liaison" relationship with NATO.

Yeltsin at first resisted, on the same grounds as Grachev: Russia should be a full-fledged participant, not in a support role. But Clinton persisted.

"Let's not give up, Boris," said Clinton soothingly. "Let's work on this. We can do it." In a slight variant of Perry's proposal calculated to make it more palatable, he urged that Yeltsin consent as a minimal first step—with the understanding that something more satisfactory might be possible later—to send two battalions to Bosnia to do reconstruction, airlift and mine clearing.

"Yes, Bill," said Yeltsin, "I agree. I'll order Grachev to do that."

"ONE DOWN, one to go," Clinton remarked to me under his breath as we gathered up our papers, adjourning to a nearby cabin for lunch with the full delegations. He was referring to another order we wanted Yeltsin to give Grachev: to accept the American position on an issue where we'd hit a snag in regular diplomatic and military channels. This was the future of the Treaty on Conventional Forces in Europe, known as CFE—a piece of unfinished business from the final days of the cold war that was fraught with both symbolic and practical significance for many of its thirty signatories, especially Russia.

CFE had been painstakingly negotiated over two decades and signed a little over a year before the collapse of the USSR. It regulated the number and kinds of armaments that Russia could station on its own territory in Europe (that is, west of the Ural Mountains).[4] Russian nationalists and communists saw the treaty as another of Gorbachev's capitulations to the West, while the Russian military felt a provision of CFE that limited equipment in the North Caucasus was an obstacle to the effective prosecution of the war in Chechnya. After consultations with our European allies and several former Soviet republics on Russia's borders, the U.S. had offered to adjust these geographical limits to give the Russians some additional flexibility, but our proposed changes were not good enough for the Russians, who were threatening to pull out of the treaty altogether. That would have been a major setback to our larger agenda of promoting co-operation with the Russian military, including in the Balkans, so Clinton had come to Hyde Park hoping, yet again, to use the Yeltsin connection to break Russian resistance.

The president had decided to concentrate on Bosnia in the first session and save CFE for lunch in part because Bill Perry's expert on the subject, Ash Carter, would be present. Carter had spent much of the morning with Yuri Mamedov, poring over a map that set forth the adjustments the U.S. was prepared to make. The two of them showed up for lunch sharing Clinton's hope that Yeltsin would agree to the proposed changes.

Conducting serious business of any kind, however, turned out to be difficult for the usual reason. Yeltsin quickly downed three glasses of California wine—Russian River, no less. Clinton regretted having not thought to issue instructions that iced tea be served. Nonetheless, he'd had some success with a tipsy Yeltsin in the past so he decided to see if the two of them could solve the CFE problem on the spot, building on the work that Mamedov and Carter had already done to close the gap. Clinton raised the subject and Mamedov, taking that as his cue, pulled the map out of his briefcase and started to explain a possible solution. Yeltsin scowled at Clinton, then turned gruffly to Mamedov and ruled him out of order. Yuri fell silent and hurriedly put the map away. The rest of the lunch was without substance but full of fellow feeling, lubricated on Yeltsin's part by several more glasses of Russian River.

WHEN THE TWO LEADERS resumed in private after lunch, Yeltsin was flying high. Now that the two of them were away from their delegations, he was more than ready to get into the details of CFE that had hung up our negotiators for months. Yeltsin had indeed come to Hyde Park to cut a deal, but not in front of subordinates. He sent Ryurikov to fetch the map from Mamedov. While Ryurikov dutifully headed out of the room, Clinton reached over and grabbed Yeltsin's arm.

"Look, Boris," he said, "it's not the details that matter—it's the main idea. That's what you and I should concern ourselves with. You and I aren't going to get into the weeds of this thing."

Yeltsin frowned and looked uncertainly at the door through which Ryurikov had just exited.

Clinton leaned even closer and squeezed his arm. "Boris, look at me! Do you understand what I'm saying? Never mind your guy. This is just between the two of us. I believe you should have some relief on the map, and I've worked to get it for you. But we need to get this done quickly. We don't need more haggling. Agreed? Okay?"

"Yes," said Yeltsin, suddenly deflated, "okay."

The waiter appeared again, this time with glasses of dessert wine. Yeltsin tasted it, rejected it as too sweet and asked for a cognac. Clinton, as the host, felt he had to oblige. It therefore fell to me to see if there was any brandy on the premises. I didn't try very hard. I returned empty-handed just as Ryurikov was scurrying back into the room with a load of papers, including, I'm sure, a Russian counterproposal of some kind. However, by then, the conversation between the two leaders had moved on to other subjects. Since I didn't want Ryurikov sabotaging what had been accomplished, I passed a note to him saying that while he'd been out of the room, his president had assented to the proposed American solution and that the U.S. side was proceeding accordingly. He looked unhappy but resigned to the outcome.

Clinton's two objectives for the meeting—on Russia's military role in Bosnia and CFE—were accomplished.

Yeltsin wanted to talk for a minute about their public line with the press. He reprised his opening appeal for closer and more regular constant contact, only with a new burst of maudlin zeal: "Bill, I want to say that our partnership remains strong and reliable. Even on tough problems, like Bosnia, we'll find solutions. Our partnership is the most valuable thing to us. Not only do we need it, but the whole world needs it. You and I might leave the scene, but what we have accomplished together will survive as our legacy. This is the main theme that we must develop between us. It's you and me, Bill and Boris."

Yeltsin recalled Clinton's suggestion at the outset that they set as a goal for the meeting proving the doomsayers wrong. "You were right, Bill. Contrary to the pessimistic forecasts, both in your country and mine, it's been a very good meeting. It's preserved the partnership, for the good of our children and our grandchildren."

As they stood up to go out and face the press, Clinton presented Yeltsin with a pair of hand-tooled cowboy boots that would fit him better than the ones George Bush had given him at Camp David in January 1992. Clinton asked Yeltsin to take off one of his shoes so that they could compare sizes. The two exchanged right shoes, and the fit was fairly close—allowing Clinton to remark, as he almost always did, how similar they were in build. This was a point that always seemed to please Yeltsin. Yeltsin said perhaps they should wear each other's shoes to the press conference, but his protocol chief, Vladimir Shevchenko, now on the edge of panic, persuaded Yeltsin not to do it. "Boris Nikolayevich," he whispered, "the media will make something unflattering of this!"

YELTSIN WORE HIS OWN SHOES to the news conference but still gave the reporters just the sort of Boris Show they were counting on. He mocked the press for having predicted that U.S. and Russian differences over Bosnia would turn the summit into a disaster. Pointing directly at the cameras, Yeltsin bellowed, "Now, for the first time, I can tell you that *you're* a disaster!"

Yeltsin always practiced diplomacy as performance art, and when he was drunk, the performance was burlesque. This was the worst incident so far. Clinton, however, doubled over in laughter, slapped Boris on the back and had to wipe tears from his eyes. When he came to the microphone, he said, "Just make sure you get the attribution right!," then continued to laugh—a little too hard to be convincing.

I sensed that Clinton was trying to cover for Yeltsin. Perhaps, he figured, if both presidents seemed to be clowning around, there would be less of a focus in the news stories on Yeltsin's inebriation. Clinton may also have calculated that if he stoked Yeltsin's merriment, Yeltsin would be less likely, before the press conference ended, to drop a bombshell of the kind that had nearly ruined the Naples summit in 1994 and that had totally ruined the Budapest one.

Whatever Clinton's motive, the whole scene sent a familiar shudder through the American entourage. Going back to their first summit in Vancouver, Clinton's lenience toward Yeltsin was sometimes a consternation for those of us who worked for him. What we found appalling in Yeltsin's conduct Clinton found amusing.

Shortly afterward, as I took a seat next to him aboard the helicopter for the ride back to New York, Clinton, still chuckling, remarked, "That was quite a show down there, wasn't it?" He was, I suspected, looking for praise of his handling of a perilous moment.

I couldn't bring myself to applaud, but I didn't have the heart, or the guts, to criticize him either. So I simply said, "Well, what went on between the two of you in private was all very positive and helpful. You really brought him along on the substance. I just hope the press conference doesn't do any damage."

Clinton got it, and gave me a long look. Then he said, "You know, we've got to remember that Yeltsin's got his problems, but he's a good man. He's trying to do his best in the face of a lot of problems back home. I think we're going to get this Bosnia deal done, and it's harder for him than it is for me. I've got problems, but nothing like his. We can't ever forget that Yeltsin drunk is better than most of the alternatives sober."

I'd heard that refrain before, but this time it had an edge to it. Clinton felt I was not only being too tough on Yeltsin—I should ease up a bit on Clinton himself.

He turned to rewriting a speech he would be giving in New York that evening, and I shifted in my seat to look out the window at the Hudson River valley rolling past below us. I was beginning to figure out something about my boss and his seemingly infinite capacity to put up with, and laugh off, Yeltsin's antics. Part of it wasn't even personal to Yeltsin—it was a function of our support for the general direction in which Russia was moving. The country, like Yeltsin, was a bit of a mess. Its behavior, like his, was erratic. We couldn't go into a self-righteous or censorious snit every time Russia grumbled or bellowed or lurched around. Clinton was a great believer in the importance of staying "on message" in politics. Counting to ten when Yeltsin embarrassed himself was part of staying on message with our Russia policy.

Another factor was Clinton's overall approach to diplomacy. Altercation and remonstration were forms of discourse that did not come naturally to him. His preference was to conciliate in other people's squabbles and to boost leaders whom he liked. A signature of his political technique was to begin his reply to almost any proposition by saying, "I agree with that," even when he didn't. This default to agreeableness was not just a reflection of his desire to be liked—it was also a means, both calculated and intuitive, of disarming those he was trying to persuade, of pretending to begin a conversation on common ground in order to get there before it was over.

But Clinton's indulgence of Yeltsin's misbehavior seemed to go deeper still. I suspected there was more to his affinity with Yeltsin than being approximately the same height and shape and shoe size, or being the leaders of two countries that could blow up the world, or being fellow politicians who had to contend with obstreperous legislatures and hostile media. The key, as I saw it, might be that Yeltsin combined prodigious determination and fortitude with grotesque indiscipline and a kind of genius for self-abasement. He was both a very big man and a very bad boy, a natural leader and an incurable screw-up. All this Clinton recognized, found easy to forgive and wanted others to join him in forgiving. I was only beginning to put this puzzle together. Other pieces would fall into place later.

THE FOLLOW-UP TO HYDE PARK was prompt, positive and another reason for being glad that we now had the Bill-and-Pasha channel. At the end of October, Bill Perry and Pavel Grachev reached agreement on an adjusted map for CFE and a command structure for the Bosnia Implementation Force. Russian troops would perform "special operations" consisting of engineering, transport and construction tasks. Their commander would be designated as a deputy to General Joulwan in his American rather than his NATO capacity. It was the minimum that Clinton had gotten Yeltsin to agree to at Hyde Park. In follow-up talks, U.S. and Russian military negotiators devised a complex but ingenious wiring diagram that preserved NATO's unity of command for the overall operation while allowing the Russians to say that they were "with," but not "under," NATO, and therefore provide combat forces for IFOR. Even if only the professional military understood the scheme, that was all that mattered, since they were the ones who had to make it work.[5]

IT WAS ESPECIALLY useful to have an effective channel between the Pentagon and the Russian Ministry of Defense since the more traditional civilian mechanisms of diplomacy soon stalled, notably at the highest level. Yeltsin suffered another heart attack during his flight home from the Hyde Park summit and had a more serious one shortly afterward. Once again, he was hospitalized at the Barvikha sanatorium. There was a surge of speculation that Chernomyrdin might assume power while Yeltsin was incapacitated, but there was no official procedure to transfer power.[6]

Kozyrev was still hanging on as foreign minister, but there were rumors that he would be replaced any day and he was keeping his head down on controversial issues. His deputy, Igor Ivanov, was carrying the burden of Russia's role in the Balkans, which, in the wake of the Hyde Park agreement and with the opening of the Dayton peace talks, became even more of a domestic political vulnerability than before.

On matters of peacekeeping and virtually everything else, Russia wanted inclusion but not subordination. The Clinton-Yeltsin agreement at Hyde Park, as fleshed out by Perry and Grachev, provided for the Russians' military inclusion while sugarcoating their subordination. Dick

Holbrooke did much the same thing on the diplomatic front. He arranged for Igor Ivanov not just to participate in the Dayton process but to serve as one of its co-chairmen. But titles notwithstanding, there was no doubt that Dayton was an American enterprise, with Dick himself the driving force, calling on Secretary Christopher, Bill Perry, Tony Lake and President Clinton himself to bring their weight to bear at crucial moments.

In early November, Dick asked me to drop in on the talks, primarily to reinforce the message that the U.S. and Russia were working more closely than ever and thus intensify the pressure on the Serbs. Brooke accompanied me for a quick trip. The highlight was a surreal gathering at the Dayton Racquet Club. Peacemakers, war criminals (as yet unindicted) and their victims mixed uneasily over cocktails in a restaurant on the top floor of a skyscraper overlooking the city, which happens to be my birthplace.[7]

Knowing that Brooke and I had lived in Belgrade for two years in the early seventies, Dick seated her next to Milošević at dinner. The Serbian strongman turned on the charm, chatting to Brooke in idiomatic English about everyday life in Belgrade and ruminating airily about how he'd applied the management techniques he'd learned as a banker and businessman to his subsequent career as a politician and president. He was doing his best, he added, to satisfy the basic needs of his citizens while he "looked out for the interests" of their ethnic brethren in Bosnia. Listening to him, Brooke found herself recalling Hannah Arendt's phrase about Adolf Eichmann: the banality of evil.

In addition to giving Brooke and me a chance to see Milošević up close, the visit allowed me to do a piece of useful business, employing the Gore-Chernomyrdin connection to resume Russian energy deliveries to Sarajevo. During a tour of the negotiation site at Wright-Patterson Air Force Base, I called on Igor Ivanov just long enough to thank him for his contribution and to see that he had little to do but keep a stiff upper lip while Dick ran the show.

ON NOVEMBER 21, the Dayton talks produced an agreement that ended the Bosnian war. When I saw Kozyrev in Budapest shortly afterward, he acknowledged the accomplishment and expressed appreciation that Ivanov had been "allowed to appear in the photographs" at the signing ceremony. But, he said, he was going to remain nearly invisible in the period ahead. He didn't want to be blamed when, as he believed was inevitable, violence broke out in Bosnia and the peacekeepers had to start shooting at Serbs. When that happened, it would confirm the view in Moscow that by participating in Dayton, Russia had betrayed the Serbs. (In this prediction, Kozyrev turned out to be flat wrong. For the six years following the Dayton agreement, the war in Bosnia did not resume, and neither NATO nor Russian troops sustained casualties from hostile action.)

There was, Kozyrev told me, already a move afoot, led by Yevgeny Primakov, to oust him and Grachev for making "dishonorable concessions" to the West over Bosnia and CFE.

Kozyrev was no more cheerful about his prospects as a politician. He was spending a lot of time campaigning in Murmansk to keep his Duma seat in the forthcoming parliamentary election. He faced twelve opponents, including Zhirinovsky's sister.

WHEN THE ELECTION took place, on December 17, Kozyrev won his race, although more narrowly than two years before. Across the country, voter turnout was up from 1993, from 55 to 65 percent. The Russian people were now in the habit of voting and they took the obligation seriously. The bad news was that many pro-reform candidates were trounced by communists and Zhirinovskites. Victor Chernomyrdin's party, called Our Home Is Russia, came in third behind the reds and browns, largely because it had Kremlin backing and was seen as a stalking horse for Yeltsin's own reelection campaign in 1996. Yegor Gaidar's pro-reform Russia's Choice fared even worse—it did not cross the 5 percent threshold required to enter the parliament—and Gaidar lost his own seat in the Duma.

When Brooke and I saw the Clintons on Christmas Eve, the president took me aside to express his worry about the Russian election. "How many more of these things is it going to take before they stop electing fascists and communists?"

"Lots," I said, clinging to the only good news there was. "The main thing is that they keep having elections. Eventually they'll get it right."

"Yeah, I guess that's part of the deal, isn't it? Well, let's hope they're a little smarter in the presidential election next year."

CHAPTER 8

RUSSIA'S CHOICE

*The disadvantage of free elections is that you can never
be sure who is going to win them.*

Vyacheslav Molotov, Soviet foreign minister, 1946

W
ASHINGTON WAS staggering under the worst blizzard of
the season on January 9, 1996, and the government was
largely shut down. Secretary Christopher and I were alone in
his office and felt as though we were almost alone in the State Department. We were discussing a trip he was about to make to the Middle
East—if the weather allowed his plane to take off from Andrews Air Force
Base. An assistant rushed in with a wire-service report that Boris Yeltsin
had just fired Andrei Kozyrev and made Yevgeny Primakov foreign minister.

We'd known something like this was coming, not least because Kozyrev
himself had all but told us so. His last year on the job had been a protracted and often humiliating stay of execution. Still, while anticlimactic
and even merciful, the dismissal caused Chris and me to reflect for a few
moments that one of the qualities that had brought Kozyrev down was
that he had a vision for his country that was consonant with our own.

WHEN YELTSIN SUMMONED the senior officials of the Foreign Ministry to the Kremlin to explain his decision and introduce them to their
new minister, he began with an encomium to Kozyrev, who was not present.

"I command you," Yeltsin said, using one of his trademark verbs, "never
to say that our foreign policy under Kozyrev was a failure and that the

change of minister was due to a failure." Kozyrev had worked hard and loyally; he had shown courage and vision during a difficult period when Russia was coming of age as a state; he deserved credit for lasting achievements, including the "virtual liquidation" of the threat of military confrontation with the West, and for his determination to solve problems by political means.

Yeltsin's script, which had been prepared by the Kremlin staff with input from Primakov, would have been much harder on Kozyrev. It included a passage that explicitly criticized Kozyrev for paying too much attention to the U.S. and the West at the expense of the rest of the world. But Yeltsin omitted those passages, saying only that he had instructed Primakov to pursue a "diversified" foreign policy that put new emphasis on relations with Russia's neighbors, Central Europe, the Middle East, South Asia and the Far East.

Yeltsin probably chose not to use the tougher language because his reason for dumping Kozyrev and picking Primakov was not that he'd changed his view of the world, or of relations with the U.S. Rather, his motives were pure politics. For three years everyone had assumed he would run for reelection in 1996, but he had yet to announce his intentions. For a while, he'd entertained the idea of passing his mantle to Victor Chernomyrdin. But the December 1995 parliamentary elections and public opinion polls had demonstrated that neither Chernomyrdin nor the liberals were generating support. Yeltsin was convinced that if he didn't run, Russia would face a choice between the ultranationalist Vladimir Zhirinovsky and the communist Gennady Zyuganov. Now that Yeltsin had made up his mind to run, he was making the change in the Foreign Ministry to increase his appeal to those who might otherwise vote for one of his rivals.[1]

Yeltsin told the Foreign Ministry high command he wanted as foreign minister a recognized and experienced statesman who would guarantee that Russia had a forceful and active foreign policy, since that would be a positive factor in the forthcoming elections. Primakov picked up on that hint when he rose to respond, saying he personally hoped Yeltsin would indeed run for a second term and promising that foreign policy would be a plus for his candidacy.

PRESIDENT CLINTON FOLLOWED Yeltsin's opening moves of the 1996 campaign with a fascination that all of us shared but with an optimism about the outcome that none of us did.

The medical and political prospects could hardly have been bleaker. Yeltsin seemed to have recovered from the heart attacks that had felled him after Hyde Park, but the likelihood of another one within a year was rated at 25 percent, and the chance that it would be a fatal attack was estimated at twenty-five times the average for a man of his age. There were rumors of liver cancer that had metastasized to the brain—false, as it turned out, but consistent with the gloomy conventional wisdom of the time.

When Clinton got a report on Yeltsin's health that was just short of an obituary, he would shake his head with weary patience and say something like, "Yeah, that ol' boy really ought to take better care of himself."

It was the same with the political prognosis. The first round of the presidential election was only five months away, on June 16. If no candidate garnered more than 50 percent of the vote, there would be a runoff July 18 between the first two past the post. Poll after poll projected Yeltsin at about 10 percent—half Zyuganov's and barely even with Zhirinovsky's and General Lebed's. Chernomyrdin was even further back in the field. That meant Yeltsin would probably not even make it into the second round.

Grigory Yavlinsky, the leader of the liberal Yabloko Party, visited the U.S. at the end of January and told me flatly that Yeltsin didn't stand a chance; we needed to get ready for the post-Yeltsin era. When I mentioned this exchange to Clinton, he shrugged it off: "Yeah, they've got their chattering classes too, I guess. It's a rough business he's in—not for the faint of heart, that's for sure."

The president's political aides warned him that he should put as much space as possible between himself and Yeltsin. Otherwise, he would either get blamed or look as if he'd backed a loser when Yeltsin's candidacy crashed and burned. Clinton gave that advice the back of his hand. "This thing's not over," he said. "Let's see how it turns out. That ol' boy's got a lot of fight in him."

In several skull sessions in late January and early February, Clinton gamed out how he was going to handle his public comments on the Russian election. He recognized that outright backing for Yeltsin's reelection would be both inappropriate and counterproductive—"a kiss of death," he said, given how unpopular many American policies were in Russia. On the other hand, as he put it, "we could really do him in if it looked like we were writing him off or hedging our bets." From the way he talked about the dilemma, it was clear that he was more worried about the latter danger and therefore more likely to err on the side of the former.

ON FEBRUARY 15, in a bit of political theater borrowed straight from American politics, Yeltsin traveled to his hometown of Yekaterinburg to make a formal declaration of his candidacy. His complexion was ashen and he coughed frequently, but he rose to the occasion and gave a forceful speech posing the one question that Russian voters might answer in his favor: Did they want to go back to the system that they'd had in the past? Had he asked if they were happy with the state of this country and its present leadership, he would have gotten the answer he didn't want.

Clinton called Yeltsin afterward to cheer him on, playing on the coincidence that both of them were running for reelection that year.

"You're going to be in for a wide-open, rough-and-tumble campaign, Boris—just like me. You have a chance of making a comeback."

The president had confined himself to a prediction that stopped just short of an endorsement. The Kremlin, in playing up the call, stayed on the right side of the same thin line: Clinton had expressed his support for Yeltsin's policies and his hope that the Russian people would again choose reform.

PRINCE GORCHAKOV'S BUST

Meanwhile, Yevgeny Primakov wasted no time in putting his own stamp on Russian foreign policy and trying to set new rules for the conduct of U.S.-Russian relations. Secretary Christopher's first dealing with Primakov concerned the Middle East, the region of the world Yevgeny Primakov knew best and where he had given the U.S. the most trouble in the past, especially when he had been Gorbachev's special envoy during the Gulf crisis in the early nineties.

In early March 1996, in the wake of four suicide bombings in Israel that killed sixty-one people, the U.S., Egypt and Israel convened a twenty-six-nation conference on terrorism to be held in the Egyptian resort Sharm el-Sheikh, on the Red Sea. Chris called Primakov five days in advance to convey Clinton's hope that Yeltsin would attend.

Primakov was miffed at being given so little notice and insisted that Russia should co-sponsor the conference. When Chris refused, Primakov hinted that Yeltsin might boycott the event, but settled for a compromise that put Yeltsin at the head of the table.

When they met at Sharm el-Sheikh, Clinton and Yeltsin had only a brief and rather disagreeable private meeting. Yeltsin grumbled, much as he had in Halifax and Hyde Park the year before, that they weren't communicating often enough. They needed "a better, more direct channel"— a dig at Secretary Christopher. I was sure it had been instigated by Primakov.[2]

MY OWN FIRST ENCOUNTER with Primakov as foreign minister came a few days later in Moscow. The principal topic was the U.S.'s episodic and star-crossed attempt to help mediate ethnic and religious conflicts in the former Soviet Union, particularly in the Transcaucasus. Armenia, Azerbaijan and Georgia wanted active American involvement in the search for some resolution to the region's welter of civil wars and cross-border disputes.[3]

There was nothing new in Russian wariness about what we were up to in their "near abroad." Many Russians suspected that our diplomatic activity there was part of a long-term strategy to replace their influence and exploit the vast oil and gas resources of the Caspian Sea basin, but Primakov's method for fending us off was entirely different from Kozyrev's. Whenever the subject of American intrusions in Russia's backyard had come up with Kozyrev, he tended to go into either his Eeyore act—wringing his hands over how our diplomacy would play in Russian politics—or his Rodney Dangerfield act (why couldn't Russia get any respect for its own rights and activities in its own neighborhood?).

Primakov, by contrast, put on a jaunty display of cynicism and self-confidence. He was relaxed, jovial and absolutely dismissive of any chance that our diplomatic initiatives would be successful. Russia didn't have to thwart us, he implied: the conflicting parties would do that all by themselves. Having spent his boyhood in Georgia, he knew "those people" in the Caucasus, and we, like him, would find them impossible to deal with.

We had a long conversation about his view of the world and the roles of our two countries. He was aware, he said, that he had a reputation in the U.S. for being a hard-liner. That didn't bother him, since it helped him at home, where that was exactly the way he wanted to be seen. I should know, however—and he kept saying I should pass this on directly to President Clinton—that we were lucky to have him to deal with, given the alternative of crazies in the Duma on one side and feckless liberals like his predecessor. Recalling our own long association, he said he was sure I appreciated that he had spent his career working to improve relations between our countries. It was, I felt, a telling advertisement for himself. He was emphasizing the continuity between the role he'd played at the right hand of Andropov and Gorbachev and the one he was playing now for Yeltsin.

We should think of him, he said, as a pragmatist. That struck me as the right label, but he would define pragmatism in ways that had little to do with our concept of partnership. That word might come naturally to his former president, Gorbachev (who had introduced it), and to his current one, Yeltsin, but not to Primakov himself. For him, the underlying dynamic of relations between states was competitive, and the bigger the states the more competitive. The principal requirement for peace and stability was a balance of power. That word—which did come naturally to him—meant nothing as fuzzy-headed as "the power of ideas," whether Marxism-Leninism or Western liberalism. It meant the power of the state as manifest in military, political and economic leverage over others. The world according to Primakov was unstable because the U.S. had too much power and Russia had too little—for the time being. The U.S. was a meddlesome, self-righteous giant, with more aircraft carriers and money than it knew what to do with. We Americans were a problem to be managed as necessary, humored whenever it suited Russia's needs but, above all, outfoxed.

Primakov kept by his desk a small bust of a nineteenth-century predecessor whom he venerated, Prince Alexander Gorchakov. Known for his wit, oratorical skills and all-around craftiness, Gorchakov served as foreign minister to Czar Alexander II. His great accomplishment was masterminding Russia's recovery from its defeat in the Crimean War. That meant nullifying the Treaty of Paris, which had thwarted Russia's expansion into southeastern Europe and imposed limitations on Russia's Black Sea fleet, and forming alliances against Austria and England, the main powers that were trying to hem Russia in.

I took Gorchakov's bust as a totem of Primakov's strategy, which was to play a weak hand well, and a repudiation of the image of Laocoön, the prophet without honor in his own country, that I associated with Kozyrev.

As I thought about the conversation afterward, I remembered that when Yuri Mamedov had first alerted me to the likelihood of the change some ten months before it happened, he had predicted we might actually get more business done with Primakov. I could now imagine that that might be true. With his broad political backing, Primakov could do deals with the West that Kozyrev was too weak to do. Specifically, Primakov might be able to come to terms on a NATO-Russia charter even as the alliance brought in new members.

A FEW DAYS AFTER I saw Primakov, on March 15, the Duma let the world know its own view on Russian foreign policy: the deputies voted to renounce the 1991 agreement that had officially liquidated the USSR.

Yeltsin, who regarded the peaceful dissolution of the Soviet Union as one of his proudest accomplishments, reacted with fury and, at the urging of General Korzhakov, seriously considered postponing the presidential election for two years in order to do battle with the Duma.

Yegor Gaidar alerted Tom Pickering to the danger and appealed for a personal message from President Clinton to Yeltsin expressing the hope that the election would go forward on schedule. Clinton wrote a letter along those lines, and Gaidar later said it helped him and several of his allies in the presidential entourage, including Yeltsin's daughter Tatyana Dyachenko, talk Yeltsin out of postponement.[4]

WHEN SECRETARY CHRISTOPHER visited the Kremlin on March 22, all Yeltsin wanted to hear was that Bill Clinton hadn't given up on him.[5] Chris could, in good conscience, assure Yeltsin of that, since Clinton continued to be far more optimistic than anyone else in the U.S. government about Yeltsin's chances.

When we met with Clinton on March 29, the latest polls showed Yeltsin still trailing Zyuganov, although the gap was narrowing. When several of us, myself included, repeated earlier warnings that the president had to be careful—for his own sake, as well as Yeltsin's—not to slip into boosterism, he thanked us for our counsel and concern but let us know that he didn't want to be lectured further on the subject.

"I know the Russian people have to pick a president," he said, "and I know that means we've got to stop short of giving a nominating speech for the guy. But we've got to go all the way in helping in every other respect. I appreciate that some of you are worried about avoiding any embarrassment for me if Zyuganov ends up winning. Don't worry about that. I'll handle that part of it."[6]

"RUSSIA WILL RISE AGAIN!"

Clinton was next due to see Yeltsin in April, when "the Political Eight"—the leaders of the G-7 plus Russia—would gather in Moscow. The ostensible purpose was to discuss issues of nuclear safety, but the event was—in Yeltsin's eyes and those of his guests—a thinly disguised attempt on the part of the major Western leaders to give Yeltsin some help in his campaign.[7]

As that summit grew closer, Yeltsin began to fret about how his friend Bill would handle his enemies, especially Zyuganov. On April 8, Yuri Mamedov telephoned me to say that Yeltsin wanted to see me three days later to talk about Clinton's program in Moscow.

Why wasn't Primakov calling Secretary Christopher and inviting him to Moscow for a meeting with Yeltsin? The answer, I suspected, was that the Russians had decided to build me up at Chris's expense. That was Chris's reaction, too. He recalled Yeltsin's muttering in Sharm el-Sheikh about the need for a better channel. Chris wasted no time speculating further on the Russians' motivations or worrying about his own prerogatives. We knew from experience that summits went better if they were carefully prepared, so he told me I should definitely go.

On entering Yeltsin's vast office in the Kremlin, I noticed immediately that it had been lavishly redecorated with statues of Peter the Great, Catherine the Great and Alexander II. It occurred to me that this pantheon of predecessors not only served as a reminder of the scope and complexity of Russia's past but also as a hint of the wide range of options for its future: there was Peter the Original Westernizer, Alexander the Liberator of the Serfs (and the Seller of Alaska to the U.S.) and Catherine the Conqueror of the Near Abroad.

Yeltsin was, certainly by his standards, in good form. Nothing seemed to revive him like a rematch in his struggle with the communists. His color was healthy, his gaze steady, his gestures firm and in synch with his speech. When he stepped forward to greet me, he moved slowly and deliberately, but without the robotlike creakiness he'd sometimes displayed in the past.

He started talking and didn't stop for nearly an hour, occasionally glancing at typed four- by six-inch note cards but for the most part off the cuff and with growing animation and energy. He began, as he had in my first meeting with him in 1993, by beating up on me—and through me everyone in the U.S. government aside from Bill Clinton—for the troubles besetting the relationship. It was a diagnosis that sounded quite familiar to me after my session with Primakov a month before, with the difference that Yeltsin invoked partnership repeatedly:

"My impression is that the U.S. doesn't quite know what to do with Russia now—whether to develop a partnership as we have been doing for the last few years, or whether to try to compete with Russia from your current position of superiority. But Russia isn't Haiti, and we won't be treated as though we were. That won't be sustainable and it won't be acceptable. Just forget it! What we insist on is equality. What I began with Bush and have developed with Clinton—an equal partnership—is in the interests of both our people. . . .

"I don't like it when the U.S. flaunts its superiority. Russia's difficulties are only temporary, and not only because we have nuclear weapons, but also because of our economy, our culture, our spiritual strength. All that amounts to a legitimate, undeniable basis for equal treatment. Russia will rise again! I repeat: Russia will rise again! And when we do, even then I don't intend to try to compete with the U.S. but to pursue an equal partnership. We've got to maintain this basis for our relations. We need to be close to the U.S., but not on the basis of your monopoly in the world—rather, on the basis of equality.

"So I'd say that things are going all right in principle, but not in practice. I want the Moscow meeting to reaffirm the principles of our partnership—that we're not competitors, that we're not talking about a relationship between superiors and inferiors, but between equals." As he belabored the importance of the U.S. showing Russia more respect—a word he used as often as partnership and often in the same breath—I thought to myself: Kozyrev might be gone, but not Rodney Dangerfield.

Eventually, Yeltsin got to his real reason for summoning me.

"Normally," he said, turning from an expansive and imperious tone to a confiding one, "I wouldn't make the following request except to Bill Clinton himself, but it's a request I make very bluntly, very honestly, very sincerely to you for you to pass on to him personally. It's the question of how he conducts himself during the Moscow summit, particularly how he conducts himself outside of our own meetings. Our electorate will be watching this very closely. It's important that he not come off like the older brother. He shouldn't seem to be issuing any orders. His conduct, his style should reflect respect for the Russian president and respect for Russia. That will help me greatly in my campaign.

"I'm sure you see how pluralistic Russia has become—too pluralistic, perhaps. We have so many parties that maybe you are afraid the communists will win. Let me tell you: If they win, it will be bad for us and for the whole world. Russia will turn back completely. There will be no more reform.

"Now, when Clinton is here, he'll give a reception at the embassy as usual, but we don't want any separate meeting with Zyuganov."

For the first time, I was able to respond, albeit briefly. Clinton would meet Zyuganov at the reception that was a regular feature in all his visits, but I could assure Yeltsin that there would be no separate meeting with Zyuganov. For emphasis and clarity, I said this in both Russian and English.

But Yeltsin, unsatisfied, pressed on.

"A meeting with Yavlinsky, with Gaidar—that would be okay," said Yeltsin, "but not with Zyuganov because he is my real rival for electoral victory. I don't mean your president can't shake hands with him at the embassy or talk for a few minutes, but no separate meeting in a separate room! I understand you're under pressure from Congress and others who will be watching closely and will be upset if Clinton doesn't meet with a whole range of opponents. But he mustn't have any separate meetings. A photo op is okay, but that's it." As we balanced various considerations in how we handled the Russian elections, he said, we should remember that he was more than just the first president of a democratic Russia.

"I was also," he said, slamming his fist on the table, "instrumental in destroying the Soviet Union and the Communist Party!"

As in his meeting with Secretary Christopher three weeks before, Yeltsin wanted me to assure Clinton that he would win—and he wanted me to assure him that Clinton believed that too. At one point, he said that by June, "my own election will already be behind me."

Primakov leaned over and whispered in Yeltsin's ear that there was sure to be a second round in July.

Yeltsin, hamming it up, gave Primakov a look of wide-eyed incredulity. "What are you talking about! There will only be one round!"

Turning back to me, he shook his head in mock disgust. "Can you believe these ministers of mine? They think it will take more than one round to get me reelected! I don't know what this minister is talking about."

For the first and last time in my acquaintance with Primakov, he looked totally flummoxed and even a bit scared.

Finally, to the evident relief of his staff, Yeltsin brought the meeting to a close. He pronounced himself satisfied with what he said had been "like a good family chat" that had lifted his spirits.

He went off to campaign for reelection in the village of Khimki outside Moscow, and I went back to Primakov's office to nail down our understanding on how we'd handle Zyuganov at the summit: There would be the usual reception and round-table discussion at Spaso House, with nearly all the major figures in Russian politics invited except for Zhirinovsky. Primakov urged that we invite Zhirinovsky as well, saying, "He's like a cat—you stroke him once and he turns all sweet."

Sorry, I said, but we'd be leaving that particular cat outside.

THAT EVENING I HAD DINNER with a small group of my oldest Russian friends, including Slava and Rita Luchkov. It would have been a happier occasion, perhaps, and more in the spirit of our reunion, if I'd gone to one of their apartments, as I'd done so often in the past. But my schedule, as always, was crammed, so they came to the garish restaurant in the Radisson Hotel, where they had to press their way past the hookers, hoods and high rollers who were lining up at the metal detector to get into the hotel casino. Perhaps in part because of the setting, with its obtrusive reminders of the uglier side of their country's transformation, our conversation that evening was dispiriting. Russia, said Slava, had cut itself loose from the "dead weight of that awful system" but was now lurching about like the Flying Dutchman. "What's happened to our culture?" he asked. "What's happened to our state? We've dumped the bad, but haven't figured out what the good is, much less found it."

It was the last time I saw Slava. During my subsequent trips, I was too busy to connect with him or my other friends. He died of a stroke in October 1997, at the age of fifty-seven, approximately the median age of male mortality in Russia.

THE VIEW FROM THE LIMO

President Clinton left Washington in mid-April for a week of summiteering in Asia. I met up with the presidential party in Tokyo and joined Air Force One for the long flight over the North Pole to St. Petersburg. We arrived just after 10 p.m. and were met at planeside by Anatoly Sobchak, a well-known reformer who was the mayor of the city. Sobchak had been one of the bright lights of Russia's incipient democracy during the years of Gorbachev's *perestroika* and an early Yeltsin ally.

I accompanied Clinton and Sobchak for the drive to the Czar's Village, a nearly 2,000-acre imperial summer home. During the ride, Clinton pumped Sobchak for information and analysis about the Russian presidential race. Sobchak predicted that Yeltsin would make it into the second round and go on to win, but that it would be extremely close.

After a tour of the Czar's Village, Clinton and I drove to the Grand Europa Hotel in St. Petersburg. It was now well past midnight, but the president was still alert and expansive. He mused a bit about Yeltsin. "I really like the guy," he said, "but boy, is he ever a chore." Then he turned to his own reelection campaign, rattling off permutations and combinations that he and Al Gore might face in the fall—Ross Perot in or out of the race as an independent, Colin Powell on or off the Republican ticket . . . I fell into a deep and dreamless sleep. When the motorcade arrived at the hotel, Clinton elbowed me in the ribs.

"You ready for an oral exam on all that great stuff I gave you?"

"Does my job depend on it?" I asked.

"No," he said, "your job depends on what's going to happen here—I'll take care of what's going to happen back home."

DURING HIS DAY in St. Petersburg, Clinton attended a memorial at a cemetery where nearly half a million victims of the Nazi siege were buried, then visited the Hermitage. For security reasons, a chance to meet with a group of students at the museum was canceled, much to Clinton's annoyance. He was taken to lunch in the basement of a restaurant deliberately chosen so that there would be no danger of a bomb or an assassin's bullet coming through a window. His motorcade whisked from point to point with sirens blaring. Every time he asked to pull over so that he could shake hands with people lining the street, he was told either that the schedule didn't permit it or "our Russian security friends" had asked that there be no stops.

The senior local official responsible for the trip going smoothly and safely was the first deputy mayor, Vladimir Putin. Putin had risen through the ranks of the KGB, mainly as a Soviet agent in East Germany. In 1990, he returned to St. Petersburg to write a dissertation on international law but switched to politics as an aide to Sobchak, then the chairman of the city council.

Putin was known in Petersburg for his absolute loyalty to Sobchak, for his efficiency in getting things done and for helping representatives of Western companies operate in a murky and treacherous business environment. He did not have a high-profile role in the presidential summit, but the U.S. consul general in St. Petersburg, John Evans, saw considerable evidence that Putin was active behind the scenes, particularly in supervising the security for the visiting dignitary. Putin had a reputation for running a much tighter ship in that regard than his counterparts in Moscow.

After we boarded Air Force One for the short flight to Moscow, Clinton stewed about how he'd been "kept in a goddamn cocoon" the whole time he'd been on the ground in St. Petersburg. He was angry at the Secret Service, but was told that "the Russian side" had been calling the shots. No names were mentioned, since that of the deputy mayor would have meant nothing to any of us.

AT 6 A.M. THE NEXT MORNING, I joined Clinton for a jog along the birch-lined paths in Sparrow Hills, near Moscow State University. At first, he was still in a swivet over how he'd been kept from mixing with the crowds in St. Petersburg. "I could tell looking out the window that there was a lot of alienation, a lot of anti-American feeling there. A lot of those people were giving me the finger. I might as well have been a visiting king or something. It's what they used to get from their czars and their communist big shots. I really hate not being able to get out and move around."

It was as good an opportunity as I was likely to get to tell him about the dinner I'd had with my Russian friends the week before. Over the years, I'd told Clinton about Slava as the sort of Russian who justified hope in, and help for, his country, but I'd rarely talked to Clinton about my personal contacts in Russia since he'd become president. He listened to me summarize the melancholy conversation in the restaurant at the Radisson, then gave me his own take on it.

"I think I know what you mean and what's going on," he said. "We haven't played everything brilliantly with these people; we haven't figured out how to say yes to them in a way that balances off how much and how often we want them to say yes to us. We keep telling Ol' Boris, 'Okay, now here's what you've got to do next—here's some more shit for your face.' And that makes it real hard for him, given what he's up against and who he's dealing with.

"But beyond all that, there's a lot of good old-fashioned transference going on here. There's only so much blame they can dump on their leaders. That leaves a lot left over to dump on us. It's a big problem for us. We've got to remember that Yeltsin can't do more with us than his own traffic will bear." Then came the refrain I'd heard so often: "I've got some domestic politics of my own—stuff I can't do that I'd like to do, stuff I've got to do that I'd like not to. But he's got a much harder deal than I do."

BRIMMING AS HE WAS with sympathy for Yeltsin, Clinton was unprepared for what happened when he got to the Kremlin. With cameras rolling and reporters scribbling, Yeltsin subjected Clinton to a tongue-lashing for violating the spirit of partnership. The offense was Secretary Christopher's latest peace mission to the Middle East. Chris had gone to the area to quell a new outbreak of fighting between Israel and Lebanon. As a rule, the U.S. consulted with the Russians on the Middle East and tried, when possible, to involve them in the diplomacy. But if his particular shuttle stood any chance of success, Chris had to keep Primakov, whom the Israelis deeply distrusted, at arm's length.

As Yeltsin told it, Chris was "going it alone" and "sidelining" Russia. Listening to his rant, I could imagine Primakov having fanned Yeltsin's fury at the arrogant superpower for hogging the diplomatic limelight ("no more Holbrookian master strokes" like the Dayton peace accord, he'd admonished me when I'd seen him the week before).

As soon as Yeltsin had finished what he had to say, his minions ushered the press out of the room, leaving Clinton in the position of having had to sit silently through a public reprimand. Clinton was used to Yeltsin scoring cheap points with the press at the outset of meetings, but this was an egregious case, especially since Clinton had come to Moscow for no other purpose than to give Yeltsin a pre-election boost. Normally, he suppressed his annoyance, but on this occasion, for the first time in their nine meetings, Clinton was angry and for once decided to let it show.

"What you just said is not correct, Boris," said Clinton, his face red and his lips pursed. "No one's sidelining anybody, and I don't think you should be saying that!"

Yeltsin started to explain, rather defensively citing Primakov as the source of his understanding about what Chris was up to in the Middle East. Clinton cut him off. Then, suddenly, as though sensing that this could be the start of a truly awful meeting, Clinton shifted his anger to Primakov as the troublemaker: "I'm not denying that Primakov can be a strong force, but you and I can't let anyone come between us."

As he cooled down further, Clinton slipped into a conciliatory variation on the theme Yeltsin himself had so often struck. "Every time you and I are together, something good happens, Boris," said Clinton. "The world has changed for the better as a result of our work together . . . We've done a remarkable job in getting a lot done while also being honest about our differences. My objectives are, first, an integrated, undivided Europe; and second, a cooperative, equal partnership with a democratic, economically successful Russia which is influential in the world. . . . I want historians fifty years from now to look back on this period and say you and I took full advantage of the opportunity we had. We made maximum use of the extraordinary moment that came with the end of the cold war."

When Yeltsin voiced the suspicion that the U.S. was competing for influence with Russia's neighbors and trying to prevent Russia from promoting integration within the Commonwealth of Independent States, Clinton told him that the U.S. wasn't against the CIS as such. It all depended on whether Russia respected the independence of the other members. "A history of negative leadership in the past doesn't necessarily mean there can't be positive leadership in the future," he said. "But Russia has a choice here."

Russia had another opportunity to reassure its neighbors, said Clinton, segueing into a piece of unfinished business from their previous meeting in Hyde Park. Clinton asked Yeltsin to agree on the spot to an American proposal that the Russian military withdraw 212 armored vehicles from a military base in Novorossisk, a Russian port city on the Black Sea. The withdrawal was required under the terms of the Conventional Forces in Europe Treaty and was important to a number of neighboring states, especially Turkey. Defense Minister Grachev had been dragging his feet on the matter in negotiations with Bill Perry. Clinton presented the American position as a compromise that, if Yeltsin would accept, the U.S. would work hard to sell to our reluctant allies.

As in Hyde Park, Yeltsin folded without putting up much of a fight. "Okay," he said, "thanks for your efforts. We agree to your proposal." Turning to Dimitri Ryurikov, he said, "Send Grachev an order to get those vehicles out of Novorossisk!"[8]

As the meeting broke up, Clinton said to me, "That sure ended better than it started. I think that bad stuff at the beginning just shows this guy's feeling the heat."

OVER LUNCH Yeltsin raised his concern about whether his communist challenger would get a burst of reflected legitimacy at the Spaso House event later that day. He brought the matter up in a joking tone.

"It's okay to shake hands with Zyuganov, Bill, but don't kiss him."

"Don't worry," said Clinton, also lightheartedly. "We've spent fifty years rooting for a different result than that guy represents."

Yeltsin turned suddenly grim: "I'm warning you: If the communists win, they'll go after Crimea and Alaska. We won't permit that."

It wasn't clear whether what Yeltsin was determined to prevent was a communist reacquisition of lost lands or a communist victory at the polls, in which case he might have been threatening to cancel or steal the election.

Without pressing for clarification, Clinton repeated what he'd said in his letter the month before—he was counting on Yeltsin to preserve his single greatest achievement, which was turning Russia into a constitutional democracy—but he coupled this with a fresh assurance that Zyuganov would get no special treatment at Spaso House.

When the round-table discussion took place, Zyuganov was just one politician among a dozen who made presentations. When his turn came, he gave an impassioned soliloquy on democracy as the only future for Russia. Clinton listened politely and had no questions.

IMMEDIATELY AFTERWARD, Clinton huddled briefly with his advisers to prepare for the always-dangerous press conference. One subject sure to come up was Chechnya. For nearly a year, Yeltsin had been trying to end the war so that he could go into the election as a peacemaker—but one who had kept Russia together. The two goals were proving incompatible. A unilateral cease-fire Yeltsin had declared at the end of March had fallen apart, and Russian troops were once again trying to drive rebel forces out of mountain strongholds. Earlier in the week, Chechen forces had ambushed and killed nearly a hundred Russian troops; and while we were in Moscow, a full-scale battle was under way in Grozny.

During the brief preparatory session, Clinton tried out the old comparison of Yeltsin to Abraham Lincoln as a president who had to go to war to keep his country together. I should have pounced on the line the minute it came out of Clinton's mouth and recommended that he never use it again. Instead, I let it pass, and he used it publicly minutes later: "I would remind you that we once had a civil war in our country . . . over the proposition that Abraham Lincoln gave his life for: that no state had a right to withdraw from our Union."

It was instantly clear from the reaction of the traveling White House press corps that this time it was Clinton who had produced the headline we didn't want out of the summit and, in so doing, given his political opponents at home an easy shot at him. He realized it—"I guess I really painted a bull's-eye on my butt with that Lincoln line"—but he was unrepentant about defending Yeltsin. The criticism that he was "shilling for Yeltsin is just chicken shit," he said. "If Yeltsin wins, then nobody will remember that the Republicans kept telling me to back off from supporting him. But if he loses, you just watch: they'll blame me."

LATER THAT AFTERNOON, Clinton went on a walking tour around the VIP cemetery at the sixteenth-century Novodevichy Monastery on the banks of the Moscow River, where I showed him the graves of Vladimir Mayakovsky, whose poetry I had studied at Oxford; Stalin's wife, Nadezhda Alliluyeva; Andrei Gromyko, the dour and long-serving Soviet foreign minister; and Nikita Khrushchev, where we lingered for a moment.

"I wonder how that old fella would feel about what's going on here now," Clinton mused. "I'll bet given the choice, he'd be for Yeltsin too." He paused, then added, "I want this guy to win so bad it hurts. I guess that shows."

LATE THAT NIGHT, the Russians had one of their few successes in Chechnya: They killed Dzhokhar Dudayev. The press later reported that a Russian aircraft flying over the village where the rebel president was holed up launched a missile that homed in on the satellite telephone he was using. But the conflict raged on.

DOWN TO THE WIRE

With the summit behind us, there was little more we could—or should—do but wait. There were continuing rumors that Yeltsin was going to call off the election. In their phone calls through this period, Clinton always found a way to flick into his encouragement a subtle exhortation to resist any advice or temptation in that direction. Yeltsin was usually evasive, although on May 7, he said, "Some are expressing their personal opinion, and maybe they should be fired."[9]

Yeltsin's willingness to go through with the election was a credit to the vigilance and persistence of Anatoly Chubais, Yegor Gaidar and Tatyana Dyachenko in combating the influence of General Korzhakov, but it probably helped that by mid-May the polls showed Yeltsin closing in on Zyuganov. One reason for his improving fortunes was the overwhelming support he had from Russian youth, who saw the choice starkly, in precisely the terms that Clinton had captured in his Ostankino speech in January 1994 and that Yeltsin himself had sounded in his kickoff speech in Yekaterinburg: tomorrow versus yesterday.[10]

A much less savory and far weightier factor in Yeltsin's recovery was the role of Russia's so-called oligarchs—the tycoons who had been the big winners in the privatization of state assets. Privatization had been a watchword of Russian economic reform since the earliest days of the Yeltsin presidency. Gaidar and his deputy in charge of the program, Chubais, believed that rapid transfer of the assets of the Soviet state into private hands was the only way to break the old power structure's grip on the economy and deprive the communists of the basis for a comeback. Through a combination of legislative initiatives and presidential decrees, the government had given local authorities the right to sell off shops and small businesses and, in the case of medium and large state-owned industrial firms, instituted a voucher program that transferred ownership to more than forty million citizens.

In reality, though, a small group of individuals—some of them "red managers," like Chernomyrdin, and other robber barons of more recent vintage—were able to corner the market on shares and buy up companies at bargain-basement prices.[11] As the principal beneficiaries of Russia's rough, primitive, largely lawless brand of capitalism, they had every reason not to want to see Zyuganov win the election. In 1995, Yeltsin's prospects were so dismal that he and his advisers, including Chubais, concluded they needed to siphon as much of the oligarchs' wealth as possible into their campaign war chest and turn the media outlets that the oligarchs controlled into a public relations machine. In return, the Kremlin paid the oligarchs back with vast opportunities for insider trading.

Yeltsin signed a decree implementing a scheme called loans for shares. Assets still owned by the state were sold off not to average "citizen investors" through more vouchers of the sort that Chubais had instituted in 1992, but through an auction rigged in favor of large banks that then made massive loans to the government. As a result, a handful of financial-industrial groups ended up with some of the largest energy and metals companies in the world at liquidation-sale prices.

———

LOANS FOR SHARES introduced a new and distorting factor in Russia's evolution, since it substantially increased the power of the oligarchs as a force in Russian economic and political life, making a mockery of Russia's incipient regulatory structures, like its new Securities and Exchange Commission.

For years afterward, critics of Russian and Western policy treated the episode as a Faustian bargain in which Yeltsin sold the soul of reform. There was also a lingering—and unanswerable—question about whether Yeltsin could perhaps have gotten sufficient support from the oligarchs without having to buy them off with loans for shares.[12]

The poster boy for the oligarchs' long moment in the sun was Boris Berezovsky, a wheeler-dealer who had begun amassing wealth in the late 1980s with an automobile dealership that quickly became the biggest in Russia. Largely as a result of loans for shares, and through a combination of cunning, brazenness and sheer luck, Berezovsky ended up in control of Russia's major airline, Aeroflot, *Nezavisimaya Gazeta* (Independent Newspaper) and Russian Public Television, which, contrary to its name, was one of Russia's most powerful private networks. Thus the bad news that accompanied the good news about the news itself: Russia's media had been liberated from the state, but much of it was now under the thumb of people like Berezovsky.

Berezovsky was also rewarded for his contributions to the Yeltsin reelection campaign with several official appointments that put him at the center of power in the Kremlin and gave him access to heads of state throughout the former Soviet empire. For years afterward, he seemed to figure in every conspiracy theory, every palace intrigue, every shady business deal.

Berezovsky's close ties to Yeltsin's daughter Tatyana earned him a reputation as a modern-day Rasputin. He was believed to have purchased the services of freelancers in Russia's various intelligence services who helped him advance his personal, business and political interests by waging campaigns to discredit and intimidate his rivals. It was assumed he had the ability to wiretap phones, bug offices and gather compromising material on his enemies or on targets of influence. At the height of Berezovsky's influence, when his name came up in people's offices in Moscow—including offices in or near the Kremlin—my hosts would sometimes point to the walls and start whispering or even, in a couple of cases, scribble notes to me, a practice I hadn't seen since the Brezhnev era in furtive encounters with dissident intellectuals.

Berezovsky was always jetting around the world, popping in at the World Economic Forum in Davos, on the Riviera and occasionally in the State Department. I saw him several times when he served as deputy head of the Kremlin Security Council and secretary-general of the Commonwealth of Independent States. I stopped doing so after a while since I found him a poor source of information and an unreliable channel through which to accomplish any business. He would ask to see me privately, then talk to me at great length in soft, ingratiating tones, switching back and forth between Russian and English. I had trouble following what he was trying to say in either language, and when I could figure out the words, more often than not they turned out to be blarney, intended to make him look savvy and connected.

At the time of the loans-for-shares scheme, my principal colleagues in the Treasury Department, Larry Summers and David Lipton, had deep qualms about its consequences, not least because it was sure to make instant billionaires out of the likes of Berezovsky and cast discredit on the very idea of market democracy. They told their contacts among the Russian reformers, who were part of Yeltsin's inner circle, that the scheme was bad economics, bad civics and bad politics.

The Russians replied that the favor they were doing the oligarchs was nowhere near as bad as the communist victory it helped them avert. As they saw it, unlike Dr. Faust, who made a pact with the Devil that guaranteed his damnation, Yeltsin had made an accommodation with what he was convinced was the lesser of two evils—a deal that would help Russia avoid the real damnation of a return to power by the communists. Gaidar and Chubais believed that the oligarchs, over time, would, like America's own robber barons of the nineteenth century, evolve into respectable captains of industry and philanthropists, while the communists—despite Zyuganov's protestations to the contrary at the Spaso round table—would, if given a chance, show their true nature as totalitarians.

That calculation, along with the judgment that the purchased support of the oligarchs would make a difference between victory and defeat in the election, was debatable; and we, as the reformers' constant backers and occasional advisers, should have debated it more with them. We would have done so if we'd had more time, more foresight and more influence over decisions that Russian government officials were making about their own country. In the event, however, one consideration prevailed in our thinking: our agreement with the reformers on the importance of a Yeltsin victory outweighed our disagreement with them over some of the methods they were using to ensure that victory, principally the enrichment and empowerment of the oligarchs.

ON THE DAY of the first round of the Russian election, Sunday, June 16, Clinton kept asking for reports late into the evening. Yeltsin had been running slightly ahead in recent weeks but the final polls had shown Zyuganov closing the gap. Clinton phoned me about 11 p.m. As usual at that hour, I was asleep.

"I've never been as much into one of these things unless I was running myself," he said. "I've got to tell you, I feel in my gut he's going to win, in part because he really wants to. This guy is all-out; he's determined."

He was already thinking ahead to the next challenge: "If Yeltsin wins, we've got to keep him from going into the tank and having a nonstop celebration. We've got to keep him upright."

Other than occasional comments about how Yeltsin ought to take better care of himself, this was the first time in four years that I'd heard Clinton express real concern about his drinking.

I went back to sleep for a few hours, then got on the phone to Tom Pickering in Moscow for the initial tally. Yeltsin was leading with 35 percent to Zyuganov's 32 percent. Lebed was running a strong third with 15 percent, then it dropped off to Yavlinsky—the only young reformer in the pack—at 7 percent, and just behind him, at 6 percent, his antipode (and our anathema) Zhirinovsky.

Because no candidate had broken the 50 percent barrier, a second round was necessary. Yeltsin moved quickly to co-opt Lebed by making him chairman of the Kremlin Security Council.

In an unambiguously favorable development, Yeltsin dismissed Korzhakov, apparently following through on the hint he'd given Clinton over the telephone a month earlier.[13]

Then the news turned bad. Tom Pickering called early in the morning of June 21 to relate that Yeltsin had failed to show up at several public events and there were indications he might have fallen ill, apparently with a combination of chest pains and a sudden bout of depression. After initially wavering and then concluding that an ailing Yeltsin was better for Russia than a robust Zyuganov, Lebed stepped into the breach, appearing on Russian television and publicly urging the Russian people to reelect their president.[14]

On July 3, Yeltsin won the runoff with an impressive margin of nearly 15 percent.

The first person I called with the news was Secretary Christopher, who was, as always, gracious in his understated way. We'd been right, he said, "to hang in there with someone who didn't always appear to be a surefire winner."

I told Chris I just wished we could have transferred a few of Yeltsin's unneeded percentage points to Shimon Peres, who had lost the prime ministership of Israel to Benjamin Netanyahu by less than a 1 percent margin a little more than a month before, an outcome that cast a long-lasting pall over the Middle East peace process in which Chris and Dennis Ross were so deeply engaged.

THAT EVENING, the exhaustion of relief hit me like a wave I hadn't seen coming. My son Devin and I went for a long run through Rock Creek Park with our border collie, Kate. On our way back to the house, we jogged past our local video store and rented a movie of maximum distraction value—a mafia saga that Yuri Mamedov had recommended, *Carlito's Way*. I was fast asleep before the end of the opening credits and, for once, did not wake up until late the next morning.

When President Clinton called Yeltsin to congratulate him, the voice on the other end of the phone was listless, the words came out as though strung together artificially. It wasn't the now-familiar thick-tongued quality we associated with drink—it was the sound of sickness.

TEN DAYS LATER, when I accompanied the vice-president to Moscow for the next round of the Gore-Chernomyrdin commission, the political atmosphere of the city reminded me of visits I'd made there in the eighties, in the era of serial funerals, when Soviet radio didn't dare play sad music for fear it would touch off rumors that yet another sober announcement was imminent.

All eyes, including Chernomyrdin's, were on General Lebed. If Yeltsin died or was incapacitated, Chernomyrdin would become acting president for six months, and then there would be a new election. Now that Lebed had a respectable electoral showing of his own and a reputation unsullied by close association with Yeltsin, he was well positioned for another run at the presidency.

The evening after the Gore delegation arrived, Chernomyrdin and his wife took the vice-president and his wife, Tipper, to an official dacha out-side the city for an al fresco dinner in a sylvan grove. A string quartet and a jazz band alternately played amidst the birch trees. Chernomyrdin took Gore for a walk along the shore of a pond where two swans were paddling about peacefully. The Russian word for swan is *lebed,* so Chernomyrdin and Gore quickly fell into a patter of puns: Was it open season for swan-hunting? If you catch a swan, do you wring its neck? How do you cook a swan? Wasn't the dying swan scene at the end of Tchaikovsky's most fa-mous ballet especially pleasing?

"When you see President Yeltsin," said Chernomyrdin, "tell him you don't like swans. He'll love hearing that."

GORE NEVER GOT a chance to use the line. His meeting with Yeltsin was canceled on the grounds that the president had a "cold"—the same explanation that had preceded Konstantin Chernenko's death in 1985.

Lebed himself showed up at a reception that Tom Pickering hosted for Gore on the evening of July 16. He was immediately mobbed by the other guests. Gore asked me to help him engage the general in conversation, but Lebed dodged Gore's questions with words of one syllable. At first, it seemed that he was being hostile, then that he was merely trying to make a stylistic virtue out of the absence of much to say. As we gave up on the encounter, Gore commented to me, "That guy is either frightening or frightened."

I spotted Grigory Yavlinsky, one of Russia's leading democrats, in a cor-ner of the room. He had come in a weak fourth, with only half as many votes as Lebed. No one was waiting to shake his hand. He was sitting mo-rosely next to Elena Bonner, Andrei Sakharov's widow, who was looking daggers at the entire company, including me. I decided to go over and take my medicine. Bonner ripped into me for the U.S.'s failure to take a tougher line on the wholesale slaughter in Chechnya. She was right, and I told her so: we should have focused earlier, more critically and more con-sistently on the damage that the Russian rampage was inflicting on inno-cent civilians, and on the damage Russia was doing to its chances of democratization and development as a civil society.

Once Bonner had finished with me, Yavlinsky took over. He was disgusted by our "fawning" over Yeltsin and Chernomyrdin. Russia was on its way to becoming a "criminal oligarchy," he said, and the U.S. was largely to blame. This was a criticism I had less time for. I doubted that withholding support from Yeltsin and Chernomyrdin would have strengthened Yavlinsky's party in the December parliamentary elections or his personal showing in the presidential race. More likely, it would have played to the advantage of Zyuganov and the communists in both elections.

I asked Yavlinsky who, other than himself, he thought we should be backing for president.

"That guy," he said, gesturing toward Lebed.

I was surprised that this most pro-Western of the major Russian politicians would be looking to a general with little experience other than as Moscow's military proconsul in Moldova.

There was a one-word explanation: Chechnya. For months, Yeltsin and Chernomyrdin had tried to come to a settlement with the Chechens, but one deal after another had come unglued. In desperation, they had turned to Lebed, an early critic of the war who had presented himself in the presidential campaign as a tough, honest soldier with no tolerance for military bungling and the waste of lives. That made him a credible interlocutor with the Chechens and, in the eyes of many Russians who were fed up with the war, a plausible alternative to Chernomyrdin as a successor to Yeltsin.

Lebed's new post as head of the Security Council included a mandate to end the war in Chechnya. As a condition for accepting, Lebed insisted that Yeltsin fire Grachev as defense minister—a reasonable demand, given Grachev's responsibility for the war in the first place. Grachev's political demise would not have been mourned in Washington except that it meant we'd have to start from scratch with a new defense minister to re-create, if possible, the Perry-Grachev channel that had served us so well over the previous two years.

Lebed succeeded as a peacemaker. At the end of August, he and the chief of staff of the Chechen rebel forces, Aslan Maskhadov, signed a peace agreement that granted the republic "political autonomy." Russian troops pulled out, and the Chechens agreed to suspend their demand for independence for five years.

BY THEN, Yeltsin had gone into almost total eclipse. He reappeared briefly and pathetically at his own inauguration on August 9. He was barely able to walk, and he slurred his way through a shortened version of the oath of office. He then dropped from view for weeks. He gave a televised interview in early September to reveal that he would undergo open heart surgery, then went back to the Barvikha sanatorium.

On September 15, Clinton called Yeltsin to wish him well in the operation. Yeltsin asked if U.S. experts could consult with his own doctors on the procedure. Clinton said he would do whatever he could. "The world needs a healthy Boris Yeltsin," said Clinton publicly. With the help of the White House medical staff, Clinton put Yeltsin in touch with Dr. Michael DeBakey of Baylor University Medical Center in Houston, who examined Yeltsin and recommended a delay in the surgery until early November.

At the end of September, Primakov met with President Clinton at the United Nations and privately assured him that while Yeltsin was undergoing treatment, the Russian leadership could be counted on to ensure continuity. The wording—with its stress on the "leadership" rather than the leader himself, and on institutional continuity rather than on personal recovery—sounded like a prelude to another requiem over Radio Moscow. Clinton visibly recoiled against that implication.

"Well," he said to Primakov, with a note of reproof, "I want your president to get better for two reasons: first, because he still has a lot of important work to do, and we have a lot of work to do together; and second"—he put his hand over his heart—"because I really like the guy and feel for him, so in human terms too, I want him to be okay."

When I saw him later that day, Clinton was still steamed over the tête-à-tête with Primakov.

"That guy reminded me of an undertaker back home"—he meant in Little Rock, Arkansas—"he's in the bad-news business by choice, and he seemed to enjoy telling me that stuff a little too much."

On November 5, Yeltsin was transferred from Barvikha to the Moscow Cardiological Center where he underwent a seven-hour quintuple bypass. While Yeltsin was under anesthesia, Victor Chernomyrdin had responsibility for the briefcase containing nuclear-weapon codes.

Chernomyrdin later called Clinton in Little Rock to tell him that Yeltsin had made it through his surgery and to thank Clinton for sending Dr. DeBakey. Turning to the presidential election taking place that day in the U.S., Chernomyrdin added, "The whole of Russia is in your corner."

By then, Clinton already knew from exit polling that he had won reelection by a comfortable margin. After the call, he remarked that one of his wishes for his second term was that he have "Ol' Boris around for the tough stuff ahead."

THE
SECOND
TERM

CHAPTER 9

SLEEPING WITH
THE PORCUPINE

I have with me two gods,
Persuasion and Compulsion.

Themistocles

As President Clinton prepared for the beginning of his second term, he knew that the toughest stuff that lay ahead in relations with Russia was NATO enlargement. He had promised Boris Yeltsin that the alliance would wait to admit new members until both presidents had been reelected. This schedule was intended to diminish both the impact of enlargement on Russian domestic politics and the perception that it was driven by American domestic politics. The additional time also made it easier to reach agreement with Russia on its membership in the Partnership for Peace, its participation in the NATO-led peacekeeping force in Bosnia and a compromise on adjustments to the treaty regulating conventional forces in Europe. Meanwhile, the process of preparing applicants for membership went forward at a measured pace. As Clinton sometimes put it, his goal was to get Yeltsin to "absorb" or "internalize" enlargement as "one of those things in life that you can't avoid—you just have to get used to and learn to live with."

As early as February 1996, nearly a year before his second inauguration, Clinton reviewed this strategy with Javier Solana, a Spaniard who was making his first visit to the Oval Office as the new secretary-general of NATO. "We need to walk a tightrope," said Clinton. "We should be methodical, even bureaucratic, almost boring. We need as much as possible to take the emotional energy out of this whole thing. We should just smile and plod ahead."

Solana was instrumental in making that strategy work. He was an affable, bearded physicist-turned-politician who, as Spanish foreign minister before taking on the NATO job, had developed a solid working relationship with Yevgeny Primakov. He knew Primakov's deputy, Igor Ivanov, even better, since Ivanov had been the Russian ambassador to Spain from 1991 to 1994. Solana was confident that it was possible to reach an agreement with Moscow. The biggest obstacle, as he saw it, would not be resistance on Russia's part but procrastination or vacillation on ours.

In September 1996, prodded by Solana and Secretary Christopher, the allied foreign ministers decided that NATO would formally identify new members in Madrid in the summer of 1997, when the leaders of the alliance would meet for their first summit since the one in Brussels in January 1994 at which they had announced enlargement as a goal.

Throughout 1996, the Russians continued to object to enlargement as a throwback to the cold war and an obstacle to cooperation in other areas, but Primakov, true to his reputation as a pragmatist, began laying the ground for a deal if enlargement went forward anyway. Adjusting to that unhappy prospect, Primakov said, was like "sleeping with a porcupine— the best we can do is reduce its size and keep its quills from making us too miserable."

As early as the spring of 1996, Primakov began dropping hints about three conditions that, if accepted by NATO, might make enlargement palatable to Russia: a prohibition against stationing nuclear weaponry on the territory of new member-states; a requirement for "co-decision-making" between Russia and NATO on any issue of European security, particularly where use of military force was involved; and codification of these and other restrictions on NATO and rights for Russia in a legally binding treaty.

In those terms, the Russian wish list was unacceptable. NATO wasn't going to consign new members to second-class status by promising never, under any circumstances, to put nuclear weapons on their territory. Nor was it going to give Russia a veto over alliance decisions. And finally, NATO wasn't going to lock itself into a formal treaty with Russia that would be subject to a prolonged, contentious and unpredictable process of ratification by more than twenty parliaments, including the Duma.

However, if Russia was willing to scale back its demands, there were variants of all three items on Primakov's list that would be acceptable to NATO. Instead of signing away forever its right to put nuclear weapons on the territory of new member-states, the alliance could assert that it had no need or plan for such deployments as long as Russia refrained from threatening its neighbors.[1] Instead of "co-decision-making," Solana developed the idea of forming with Russia a "consultative mechanism," a formal NATO-Russia body, based in Brussels, that would give Russia "a voice, not a veto" on joint projects where its interests coincided with those of the allies. Instead of a binding treaty, the alliance would negotiate a formal set of principles to guide NATO-Russia cooperation—what we were prepared to call a political commitment or charter—that Yeltsin and the leaders of NATO could sign in advance of the Madrid summit.

Thus, the shape of a possible compromise was already apparent in 1996. But the gap between what the Russians were still demanding and what NATO could accept was vast. The Russians hoped they could wear down the alliance and play on divisions in its ranks, in which case perhaps they would not have to compromise. Hence, we spent the summer and fall of 1996 in the diplomatic version of skirmishing, staking out high ground and probing for give in each other's positions.

As part of this process, Yuri Mamedov and I met half a dozen times on both sides of the Atlantic, starting with a trip he made to Washington right after the Russian election in July. Of the many issues with which we grappled one of the most troublesome was the U.S.'s insistence on the eligibility of former Soviet republics, especially the Baltic states, which were making the most progress in readapting themselves to the West. Yuri said it helped make that element of our policy "merely unacceptable rather than insulting" that the U.S. was also holding open, in theory at least, the possibility of Russia itself someday being eligible.

After a day and a half of slogging away in my office and a brief courtesy call that I arranged for Yuri to make on Clinton—his first in his own right—I decided we both deserved a break. Brooke, Devin, Adrian and I took him with us to the Uptown Theater on Connecticut Avenue to see that summer's science fiction blockbuster, *Independence Day*. Yuri, who was a big fan of American movies in general, loved this one. Over a pasta dinner afterward, we vigorously debated whether the aliens in the film, who looked like a cross between octopus and pterodactyl, should be eligible only for Partnership for Peace or whether they should be considered for eventual membership in the alliance itself.

WHEN I WASN'T wrangling with Yuri and other Russians about NATO, I was often defending our policy against American critics. It seemed that virtually everyone I knew from the world of academe, journalism and the foreign-policy think tanks was against enlargement.[2] It was discomfiting and sometimes painful to be so continually at odds with friends as well as former (and future) colleagues.

One such cold shower came a week before the U.S. election, when Dick Holbrooke arranged for me to address the Harriman Institute at Columbia University. My speech was mostly a review of our overall policy toward Russia, touching on NATO enlargement in only three short, rather bland sentences recapitulating our policy.[3] That was enough. At an elegant dinner afterward, despite the complexity of events in Russia and the multifarious agenda of U.S.-Russian relations, enlargement was the only topic. One eminent guest after another rose to register his distaste for the policy. Several expressed disappointment in me for defending it.

George Kennan spoke first and set the tone. He called enlargement a "strategic blunder of potentially epic proportions." That opinion was endorsed and amplified by a number of old friends and mentors.[4] Almost all their arguments marshaled against enlargement boiled down to one: *the Russians hated it.* The one prominent Russian present heartily agreed. Anatoly Dobrynin, who had been Soviet ambassador in Washington for nearly a quarter century during the cold war, rose to claim, absurdly, that if it weren't for the "madness" of NATO enlargement, everything would be "beautiful" between Washington and Moscow.

Only one participant spoke in favor of NATO enlargement, and it was, significantly, the only one whose field was Central Europe rather than the former Soviet Union. It was Fritz Stern, an eminent German-born professor of history. Much had been said about the new, democratic Russia's entitlement to security and respect for its historical and geopolitical sensitivities. Why, he asked, did not the Poles, Czechs and Hungarians deserve security and consideration every bit as much as Russia, especially since they had far more reason to worry about being attacked by Russia than the other way around? What did it say about the options that the Russians might want to keep open tomorrow if they opposed Western security guarantees for the Central Europeans today?

WHILE DEEPLY FELT, opposition to enlargement was not broad-based. Public opinion polls showed that it was confined largely to the foreign-policy elite. I believed something similar to be true on the Russian side. Average Russians did not get up in the morning worrying about whether Poland was in NATO. They were far more concerned with the cost of living, the shoddy state of public services, crime and corruption and the generally baleful state of their country.

I was confirmed in this view by a conversation with the most popular politician in Russia, Alexander Lebed, when he made his first trip to the U.S. in November 1996, shortly after President Clinton's reelection. Lebed had recently been fired from his post as head of the Kremlin Security Council. The dismissal had the look of a good career move, since it freed him of any ties to Yeltsin and allowed him to capitalize on his success in having negotiated a peace settlement in Chechnya.

When I met with Lebed at the State Department on November 21, he was more talkative than Al Gore had found him before in July. His purpose in coming, he said, was to see real democracy firsthand, since Russia's was a "sham, a mock-up." He delivered a long and quite astute critique of the Russian economy that wasn't too different from our own: Russia was a country well endowed by nature but hindered in its chances of ever becoming a modern state because it had a crazy tax policy and a rampant, officially sanctioned kleptocracy. Democracy itself, he said, was in ill repute among average Russians because it was identified with crime, chaos and poverty, and because it was seen as an alien ideology imposed on Russia by the West, particularly by the U.S. In order to take hold, Russian democracy would have to be made in Russia, not an import like Coke or Big Macs. Nonetheless, he professed to believe that the U.S. was "Russia's most reliable long-term partner."

If he were in charge, he said, he would continue dismantling state structures and decentralizing state power as quickly as possible, putting executive authority in the hands of the regional governments. Only a few institutions—notably, the armed forces—should remain in Moscow's hands. Paradoxical as it might sound, he said, decentralization was actually the best antidote to the breakup of Russia. The iron hand of Moscow only encouraged secessionists. That, he believed, was the lesson of Chechnya.[5]

After an hour, noticing that Lebed hadn't said a single word about NATO, I asked what he thought about enlargement. Russians, he scoffed, had "real problems—they don't need phantom ones."[6]

THE NEXT DAY, a more familiar visitor to Washington, Yegor Gaidar, then a politically influential private citizen, acknowledged that political passion on NATO was restricted to the Duma and a small circle of foreign-policy and military specialists. Nonetheless, a hostile Duma and national security establishment could raise a lot of hell for Yeltsin and block implementation of any deal he made with NATO. We had to find a way, therefore, to blunt the impression that Russia would be suffering a crushing defeat if enlargement went ahead on schedule.

Chernomyrdin made the same point to Gore in Lisbon on December 3.[7] The "political perception" of his government's inability to stop enlargement had to be managed in Russia. With Gore, Chernomyrdin took the straight-from-the-shoulder, matter-of-fact tone of one politician—and one friend—to another. But as the meeting was breaking up and he'd already said good-bye to Gore, Chernomyrdin grabbed me by the arm and whispered, with a note of abject desperation that I'd never heard before from him or from anyone else at his level, "I beg you, please, please make sure that we solve this problem together! Don't just ram something down our throat!"

Primakov was passing by and did a bit of a double take. When he and I saw each other again the next day, in London, he amplified, in his own cool fashion, what lay behind his prime minister's outburst. The problem of NATO enlargement, he said, was "a life-or-death issue on the political Olympus"—including, I inferred, in its implications for Chernomyrdin's chances of succeeding Yeltsin as Zeus. Our objective must be an agreement that could be presented to the Russian political class before Madrid as proof that Russia was "not acquiescing in a fait accompli."

This was a general proposition to which I could subscribe. The question was whether Russia could live with the specific accommodations NATO was prepared to make. For example, NATO was about to announce that it had no plans to deploy nuclear weapons on the territory of new member-states. It was up to Russia's political leaders to present steps like that one, partial and modest though they may be, as responsive to Russia's security requirements. That way, by the time we got to a final NATO-Russia agreement, it would be easier to manage the political fallout in Russia.

FOR THE NINETY MINUTES we talked, Primakov was markedly less combative and sardonic than I'd found him in the past. I had the sense that with the U.S. election now over, he was shifting gears, preparing the ground for a compromise.

At the end of the conversation, he said he was eager to resume a nuts-

and-bolts discussion as soon as possible—"but not, with all due respect, my dear Strobe, with the *deputy* secretary of state." Some weeks before, Warren Christopher had announced that he was retiring in January, but Clinton had yet to name a successor. "I wish your president would hurry up and make up his mind," said Primakov, "so that I can get to work on this accursed problem of ours with your new boss, whoever he is."

"Or whoever *she* is," I corrected, knowing what would soon be announced back in Washington.

Primakov, who had heard the rumors, laughed. "Don't get me off on the wrong foot! I don't want to be accused of being a misogynist!"

THE FOLLOWING MORNING, December 5, President Clinton announced that Madeleine Albright would be secretary of state; William Cohen, a recently retired Republican senator from Maine would be the new secretary of defense; Sandy Berger would replace Tony Lake as national security adviser, and Tony would be nominated as director of Central Intelligence.[8]

Except for Bill Cohen, the new team was made up largely of the old team. That was true at the subcabinet level of the State Department as well. Madeleine asked me to stay on as deputy and brought Tom Pickering in to be under secretary for political affairs, the number three position in the department, and named Jim Collins as ambassador to Moscow. To take Jim's place as head of the office responsible for the former Soviet Union, we recruited Steve Sestanovich, a leading expert on the former Soviet Union at the Carnegie Endowment for International Peace, whose advice I'd often sought since the beginning of the administration.

Madeleine and I had already worked together for four years, primarily on the issue of when and how to back diplomacy with force. We'd been allies in pushing for the invasion of Haiti in September 1994 and for bombing Serb targets in Bosnia a year later. More than any of the rest of us, she was literally a child of the cold war: she had been eleven in 1948, when a Soviet-instigated coup d'état forced her parents to gather up the family and flee their native Czechoslovakia. As she once put it to me, she felt the Central European case for admission to NATO "in my bones and in my genes."[9] But she also believed that if possible, we should work out a deal with the Russians along the lines of the one that Secretary Christopher and I had been discussing with Primakov and Mamedov throughout much of 1996.

As for Sandy Berger, he had long since become my closest confrere at the White House. He had been instrumental in reinforcing Clinton's instinct to support Yeltsin while at the same time imposing discipline as we shaped those instincts into policy. He also subjected the premises of our strategy to questions at least as probing as those coming from our critics.

Early in the first term Sandy and I had established a ritual of getting together for an hour or so on Sunday mornings, usually at his house, over bagels and coffee. Brooke would often come with me and read the newspapers or chat with Sandy's wife, Susan, around the kitchen table while our dogs romped in the backyard. Sandy and I would lounge in front of the television set, tuned either to the news shows or to a Redskins game, and talk shop. Sometimes that meant process: how to build a consensus among State, Pentagon, Treasury, the intelligence community and other agencies so that we could present a joint recommendation to the president. But more often we talked about substance, trading theories, trying out solutions, weighing trade-offs.

For most of the first term, NATO enlargement had been a staple of what Sandy and I called our bagel sessions. We each had our favorite Greek myth for the difficulties we faced on that issue. For him, it was Scylla and Charybdis, while for me it was Sisyphus. Either way, whether the objective was navigating a passage or pushing a boulder up a hill, 1997 was the year when we had to get the job done.

FINESSE VERSUS NERVES OF STEEL

In early January, Boris Yeltsin received Helmut Kohl at the hunting lodge in Zavidovo. Kohl found him looking five to ten years older than when he'd last seen him only four months before. Yeltsin at first seemed depressed and abstracted; he kept staring off into space. But as Kohl massaged Yeltsin's ego and vowed the undying support of the West, Yeltsin came alive, impressing Kohl not just with the multiplicity of his problems but with the hard-headed way he was thinking about them. On virtually all issues, Yeltsin seemed to have two related objectives: keeping his domestic enemies at bay and avoiding a breach with the outside world.

On NATO, Yeltsin openly expressed bitterness toward the U.S. and toward Clinton personally. Why, he kept asking, had "our friend Bill" unleashed "this monster"? NATO's image as an enemy was so deeply etched in Russia's political psyche that it could not be erased overnight. Russians of all political stripes feared they would end up on the wrong side of a new Iron Curtain. Surely, said Yeltsin, Europeans like Kohl realized, even if Americans didn't, that "the security of all European countries depends on Russia feeling secure." (In that one statement, Yeltsin had captured the nub not just of the immediate problem but of much trouble in the century coming to an end: Russia had habitually defined its own security at the expense of others'; many Russians seemed incapable of feeling secure unless others felt insecure.)

But Yeltsin, while angry, was not hopeless. Like Chernomyrdin with Gore in Lisbon and Primakov with me in London, Yeltsin was groping for a solution that would head off a break with the West—and that he could survive politically—if NATO enlargement did proceed. "I have to be able to look my people in the eye and tell them that their interests are being protected," he said. "We can't keep cooperating with the West unless I can assure them of that."

Kohl returned to Bonn convinced that "eighty percent of the work ahead of us is psychological"—by which he meant we must give Yeltsin the basis for seeing a NATO-Russia deal as a personal victory and presenting it to his own people as such.

Kohl sent word to Washington that he wanted me, as the administration's point man on Russia, to come to Bonn in mid-January to plan a common strategy.[10]

Learning of Kohl's invitation, President Jacques Chirac of France asked me to stop in Paris first. The French had been the most reluctant of our allies about proceeding with enlargement, so I was prepared for a rough session.

When I saw Chirac at the Elysée Palace on January 14, he told me that NATO enlargement had been "poorly handled because the process started during the U.S. election campaign" and that the U.S. was not "taking full account of Russian sensitivities," especially "a traditional fear of encirclement as well as a fear of a humiliation. The problem is not what's in the head of Yeltsin or Chernomyrdin—if that were all we had to worry about, it wouldn't be so serious—but what's in the Russian psyche." He had recently spent an hour with forty Russian women ("babushkas," he called them) who were touring France and who gave him an entirely different impression of public opinion than my own.

"None of those ladies spoke about their standard of living, the mafia or crime," said Chirac. "They all told me, 'We voted for Boris Yeltsin, but we will not do so again because he won't defend us against NATO. We're going to be surrounded. What will Yeltsin do when American nuclear weapons start falling on Moscow and St. Petersburg?' "

Chirac's conclusion was that we must make a deal with Russia in advance of enlargement so that the Russians didn't feel they were being dictated to.

I asked whether that meant we should suspend enlargement if we failed to make a deal with the Russians.

"Failure," said Chirac, "is unthinkable as long as we approach the issue with finesse."

I replied that failure was not only thinkable but certain if we signaled to the Russians that all they had to do to stop enlargement was to persist in their objection to it.

This answer confirmed Chirac's view that "France and Germany inspire more confidence in Yeltsin than the United States on this particular subject. That is why the Russians look to us to be the honest broker."

SINCE CHIRAC seemed to be speaking for Kohl as well, I feared the worst as I headed to Bonn. I knew that Kohl had on several occasions expressed to Clinton his own worry that enlargement would torpedo Yeltsin, ruin Russian reform and scuttle Russia's burgeoning relationship with Europe.

When I arrived at the chancellor's office, he had on the coffee table in front of him a full transcript—neatly typed, translated into German and marked up with a yellow highlighter—of my conversation with Chirac the day before. I figured I was about to get pummeled by the second half of a tag team.

In the several hours that followed, Kohl was careful not to utter a single word in explicit rebuttal of anything I had heard in Paris the day before. From his passing references to Chirac, one might have thought that French and German policy were not just coordinated but identical. Yet in substance, Kohl repudiated Chirac's position and endorsed the American one: We had to stick with the Madrid deadline for enlargement regardless of the Russians. Otherwise, enlargement would not happen.

Kohl's own version of the case began with a simple assertion of equity, of what was fair and right, of what the aspirant states deserved—in effect, the argument Fritz Stern had made in November: "We can't tell the Poles and the Czechs that they are not welcome [in the alliance] after what they did to survive communism."

The chancellor moved from there quickly to what enlargement would mean for Germany itself. In Kohl's view, in addition to its internal demons, Germany had been cursed in the twentieth century by political geography. Immediately to the east were Slavic lands, historically regarded more as Eurasian than truly or entirely European. As long as Germany's border with Poland marked the dividing line between East and West, Germany would be vulnerable to the pathologies of racism and the temptations of militarism that can come with living on an embattled frontier. That frontier could disappear, he said, only if Poland entered the European Union. His country's future depended not just on deepening its ties within the EU but on expanding the EU eastward so that Germany would be in the middle of a safe, prosperous, integrated and democratic Europe rather than on its edge.

"That is why Germany is the strongest proponent of enlargement of the EU," he said, "and it's why European integration is of existential importance to us." Kohl believed that the EU was unlikely to expand unless NATO, nudged by the U.S., led the way. "This is not just a moral issue," he said, "it's in our self-interest to have this development now and not in the future."

In Kohl's view, two other factors argued for moving quickly on NATO enlargement: first, the trends in Russian politics were negative, and second, Yeltsin might not be around much longer.

"New waves of nationalism are mounting in Russia," he said. "Seventy years of dictatorship have left the Russians in total ignorance of the world around them. Two generations couldn't get out into the world. Russia has a surprisingly free press, but the people have no experience in forming independent judgments. Pressures are building. The Russians are frightened. This is key to Yeltsin's psychology, and it reflects his people's psychology. You can make bad politics with a people's psychology—just look at twentieth-century Germany."

Yeltsin, he continued, was "the best of the current political figures that might come to power there," and, he added, whatever venting he'd heard of Yeltsin's anger over enlargement in Zavidovo less than two weeks earlier, Yeltsin regarded Clinton as the best imaginable American president from the standpoint of Russia's interest.

Kohl told me that the two German doctors who had participated in Yeltsin's heart surgery were not optimistic that he would last until the next Russian election in 2000. Therefore the question was how to help protect Yeltsin from his domestic enemies and would-be successors as he dealt with NATO in the coming months. The answer, he said, was to give Yeltsin as much attention and inclusion as possible while demonstrating "nerves of steel" on the timetable for enlargement: if Yeltsin knew the process would go forward with or without him, he would "join us rather than turning his back on us or letting himself be left behind."

KOHL'S CLARITY and steadfastness were the best imaginable antidote to Chirac's talk of "finesse." Nonetheless, just as I'd heard different messages in Paris and Bonn, so would the Russians. We had to minimize the problem of conflicting signals from the Europeans. That argued all the more for relying on Javier Solana as the spokesman, and the negotiator, for the alliance.

Solana was in a delicate position. The NATO bureaucracy over which he presided in Brussels was cumbersome, leaky and inclined to produce half-a-loaf compromises designed to please all the allies. He would have to resist pressure from the French to equivocate along the lines of what I'd heard from Chirac. At the same time, in order to preserve his standing with his fellow Europeans and with the Canadians, he had to avoid the impression that he was taking his instructions from Washington rather than representing their views and interests.

Solana's job was made all the more difficult by a Russian campaign to depict him as, in Primakov's phrase, an American "errand boy." With me, Primakov sometimes used the epithet *stukach,* literally a stool pigeon—which had an especially ugly connotation in the land of the gulag.

When not insulting Solana, Primakov tended to ignore him. He insisted alternately on negotiating directly and exclusively with the Americans, which drove the Europeans crazy, or shuttling around Europe looking for nuances of difference among the allies—and no doubt finding them in Paris—which drove us crazy.

Solana overcame all these obstacles, mostly by dint of his personal and diplomatic skills but also with a lot of backing from us. By the beginning of 1997, Primakov had come to accept the reality that if he wanted an agreement with NATO, he had to negotiate it with Solana. Meanwhile, Solana had worked out with us and the key European allies a process designed to protect European sensitivities, ensure American leadership and minimize the opportunity for Primakov to engage in diplomatic arbitrage. Solana stayed in close, continuous collaboration with Madeleine Albright, Sandy Berger and me on the key components of a NATO-Russia deal.

It was my task, guided by those discussions, to come up with formal language for the charter and other documents. I relied on a small team of colleagues led by Eric Edelman, who had been one of my deputies the first year of the administration and had returned to my office after completing a tour of duty as the deputy chief of mission at the U.S. embassy in Prague. (Eric replaced Toria Nuland as my executive assistant when Toria, who'd been with me since the beginning of the administration, went on maternity leave.) The other full-time members of the team were John Bass of my staff, Sandy Vershbow of the National Security Council and Ron Asmus of the State Department's European bureau. John was an accomplished foreign service officer with a flair for clear thinking and writing. Sandy Vershbow provided imaginative solutions to problems as they arose and made sure that key officials in the White House and Pentagon approved steps we were about to take with the allies and the Russians. Ron had been one of the earliest and most forceful supporters of NATO enlargement at the RAND Corporation. His writings had influenced thinking in the administration, including my own, during the first term, and we brought him into government early in the second term. He worked closely with the NSC staff and the Pentagon on bridging subtle differences within the alliance and profound ones between NATO and Russia.[11]

After reviewing and fine-tuning the results of this teamwork in Washington, Solana would make suggestions to our allies on how to proceed. Once he had their approval, he would negotiate a final text with Primakov.

This arrangement was more kabuki than subterfuge since the actors all knew what was going on and played their parts willingly, if not always enthusiastically. Moreover, they were all striving for the same outcome: a NATO-Russia summit before Madrid, probably in Paris, a venue that would help keep Chirac's disgruntlement under control.

As the weeks went on, Primakov started not just behaving civilly toward Solana but negotiating productively with him. Meanwhile, my own close consultation with Solana became a friendship, not just for me but my family. He became a regular and especially welcome guest for meals around our kitchen table. He took time out from shoptalk to coach Devin and Adrian on their Spanish and, on a couple of Sundays when the weather began to improve, joined Brooke and me for bicycle rides along the towpath of the C&O Canal in Georgetown.

I was also constantly shuttling across the Atlantic for quiet discussions with the Russians and with our allies. My principal concern was to ensure that in our collective desire for an agreement, we did not give Russia undue influence over decision-making within the alliance. These trips also allowed me to stay in touch with the Central Europeans, keeping them abreast of what was going on with the Russians and allaying their concern that the West would sell them out to Yeltsin at the end of the cold war the way they felt Roosevelt had betrayed them with Stalin at Yalta at the end of World War II.

Primakov's overarching objective—which he pursued in both his front-channel negotiation with Solana and his back-channel one with us—was to make sure that nothing in the deal could be construed either as constituting a Russian endorsement of enlargement in the near term or as prejudicing Russia's eligibility for membership in the long term. If we could thread that needle, he told me after a long and grueling session, "I think we can do this hard thing."

BORIS YELTSIN, for all intents and purposes, was out of the picture, either recuperating from one medical setback or suffering another. When a letter in his name arrived for Clinton in late January affirming that he did indeed want to reach an agreement between Russia and the alliance, I was skeptical about whether Yeltsin was even well enough to have seen it.[12] I was in Moscow at the time and paid a visit on Anatoly Chubais at the Kremlin, in hopes of learning more.

Chubais, the former privatization czar in the Gaidar government, had run Yeltsin's reelection campaign and was now the chief of presidential administration. He, like Gaidar himself and like my inquisitors at the Columbia University conference, regarded NATO enlargement as an affront to Russian security interests, a vote of no confidence in Russian reform, a millstone around the neck of the Yeltsin administration and incompatible with the very idea of partnership.

However, Chubais said—it was always the *however* I listened for in these conversations—if we insisted on proceeding with our folly, we might be able to limit the damage by admitting Russia to a full G-8 and to existing bodies associated with the "civilized democratic world," namely the World Trade Organization, the so-called Paris Club of major industrialized countries that managed debts to developing countries, and the Organization for Economic Cooperation and Development (OECD), the Paris-based international organization that monitors and analyzes the economic performance of the world's advanced economies. This sort of "compensation," as Chubais called it, would help Yeltsin get over the "insult" of being kept out of NATO.

That said, no one but Yeltsin himself was going to decide what to do about NATO, and he was going to do so on the basis of his personal confidence in Clinton. Much depended on the next chance to nurture the presidential relationship.

The two leaders had agreed during the winter to get together in March in a third country for an interim meeting between formal summits.

That gave me an opening to inquire about Yeltsin's condition. As I'd arrived at Chubais's office, I caught a glimpse of Yeltsin's daughter Tatyana Dyachenko on her way out, so I was sure Chubais would have the latest health report.

Chubais looked out the window silently, then turned back to me and said, choosing his words carefully, that Yeltsin seemed to be "slowly improving." He added that he had seen Yeltsin in his office at the Kremlin a day or so before, making it sound like the sighting of a rare bird. Apparently realizing that he'd raised doubts in my mind about both his president's physical state and his own candor, Chubais knocked on the wooden arm of his chair and added that he *hoped* Yeltsin would be up to meeting with Clinton in March, but he couldn't be sure.

JEKYLL AND HYDE

The chronic uncertainty over who was really running Russia gave additional importance to Chernomyrdin's visit to Washington for a commission meeting the first week in February. He and Gore had already broached the subject of NATO-Russia relations in Lisbon in December, so the matter was sure to come up again. Especially with Yeltsin's apparent incapacity, we were looking to Chernomyrdin to keep Russia moving in the direction of a deal before Madrid.

I was in the midst of preparing for Chernomyrdin's arrival when I received a letter from George Kennan warning me that he was about to go public with his opposition to NATO enlargement. Echoing what he'd said at Columbia, he called it "the greatest mistake of Western policy in the entire post-cold-war era" and predicted that it would "inflame the existing nationalistic, anti-western and militaristic tendencies in Russian opinion, restore the atmosphere of the cold war to East-West relations, and impel

Russian foreign policy in directions decidedly not to our liking." Kennan wished us success in the diplomatic effort to make enlargement "tolerable and palatable to Russia," but he urged that further steps, unspecified, be taken to mitigate "the unhappy effect this expansion is already having on Russian opinion and policy."

Kennan's article appeared on the op-ed page of *The New York Times* on February 5 under the headline "A Fateful Error." A clipping was lying on the president's desk when I joined a meeting to discuss Chernomyrdin's arrival the next day.

"Why isn't Kennan right?" the president asked when I entered the Oval Office. "Isn't he a kind of guru of yours going back to when we were at Oxford?"

It was common enough for Clinton to ask his advisers tough questions about his own policies, sometimes ones that he thought of on his own, sometimes borrowed from our critics. That way he could test if the answers were convincing enough for him to use in public. But in this case, there was a hint of doubt about the policy itself—not the desirability of enlarging NATO, but the feasibility of reconciling it with the integration of Russia. As the engineer in the locomotive, he was troubled by this latest forecast of a train wreck from a revered figure with a reputation for being prophetic about Russia.

Yes, I said, Kennan had been and always would be someone I admired, but not as a source of all wisdom. Kennan had opposed the formation of NATO in the first place, I said, so it was no great surprise that he opposed its enlargement.[13] I then summarized the logic of our position and affirmed my confidence that the Russians were already making the transition from stomping their feet and emitting primal screams to talking seriously with us about a solution. Yeltsin would make a deal, I predicted—neglecting to add: *assuming he's alive and in office.*

Clinton furrowed his brow and thought about my answer, then broke into a smile. "Just checking, Strobe. Just checking."

WHEN CHERNOMYRDIN and his delegation arrived in Washington, Yuri Mamedov got off the plane looking especially merry. The first words out of his mouth when he saw me were, "We just gave our prime minister a copy of George Kennan's brilliant article. Your hero has saved us having to write talking points on your NATO folly."

During the meetings over the next two days, Chernomyrdin put on a

Jekyll and Hyde act. In plenary sessions, with a roomful of American and Russian officials as an audience, he reprised threats and warnings we'd been hearing for several years: there would be dire consequences for Russian reform ("You'll strengthen Zyuganov and Zhirinovsky! You'll elect Lebed!"); there would be military and political countermeasures (no ratification of outstanding arms control treaties, greater Russian reliance on nuclear weapons, stronger ties with Iran and China). He left us in no doubt that Russia would continue relentlessly to exploit any differences between us and our allies. He made contemptuous wisecracks about Solana, whom he depicted as a ventriloquist's dummy on Uncle Sam's lap. In the midst of this rant, Chernomyrdin landed a glancing blow closer to home: the very position of NATO secretary-general was a joke, he said; all decisions were made in Washington, so we might as well give that job to Mikhail Gorbachev, who would no doubt enjoy living in Brussels and who, he implied, was, like Solana, an American lackey.

However, in private with Gore, Chernomyrdin dispensed with the sarcasm and polemics. On February 8, the two flew to Chicago for an event intended to promote U.S. investment in Russia, and they held an intense discussion of NATO aboard Air Force Two. "I understand that the decision [on enlargement] has been made, and we know you can't reverse it," he said. "But we need help on managing our own domestic politics on the issue."

"Victor," said Gore, "we'll do that, as long as you can find a way to declare victory in what we can offer."[14]

BY MID-FEBRUARY, Yeltsin had recovered his health sufficiently to make phone calls again. He renewed his annual appeal to have the G-7 converted into a G-8: since both presidents were now safely reelected and since Clinton was going to be the host of the next G-7, in Denver in June, why couldn't he just force the change through?

Clinton now wanted just to say yes. So did I, having heard from Chubais a few weeks earlier how G-7 enlargement might help offset NATO enlargement.

But Treasury still said no. Russia's economy was comparatively small, while its debt to the G-7 states was huge. Treasury believed Russia had neither the ability nor the right to help steer the global economy. Bob Rubin, the secretary of the treasury, and Larry Summers kept a wary eye on the president's talking points as drafted by the National Security Council staff to make sure they were unyielding. This pair of heavy hitters started showing up at the preparatory sessions in the Oval Office just before a Clinton-Yeltsin phone conversation and Larry would often stay to monitor the call itself, stationing himself near the president's desk, looking vigilant. Clinton held the line, but without enthusiasm, and with bursts of irritation at his advisers after hanging up.

"We're asking the Russians to eat NATO expansion with a smile," he said during a meeting in the Cabinet Room on February 12, "yet we're nitpicking them over the delicacies of who sits where at the G-7, over lapel pins and stationery. We've got to eat something too . . . This [NATO enlargement] is a big load for them to carry, and we've got to help them carry it . . . We've got to design something for Denver that maximizes appearances for Yeltsin without wrecking the core. I accept that we need to preserve the economic integrity of the G-7, but we've got to push as far as we can."

Clinton enjoined us to get our "heads out of the weeds," to step back and ruminate on how extraordinary it was that the biggest problems we faced were "keeping Russia sullen but not mutinous while we take its former allies into NATO" and "getting Russia itself into the club of leading democracies." All in all, he concluded, "this is a high-class problem, especially when you compare it to what we'd be dealing with if Russia had really gone bad and if Russia was really our enemy."

He summarized his desire to bring Russia into a G-8: "We'll get more responsible behavior out of those guys if they're in the tent."

THE BREAKTHROUGH

We agreed with the Russians to hold the Clinton-Yeltsin summit the third week in March in Helsinki. Finland was easy for the ailing Yeltsin to visit and politically convenient as well since it was a nonaligned—that is, non-NATO—state that had maintained its independence through skillful management of its relations with Russia. Finland's president, Martti Ahtisaari, who had formerly been a member of the Finnish diplomatic service and a senior official of the United Nations, had good relationships with both Clinton and Yeltsin. We had confidence that he would not only provide the best possible setting for the summit but would help us in the hard work that would come afterward.[15]

I joined Madeleine Albright when she went to Moscow the third week in February to introduce herself to Yeltsin as secretary of state and to begin preparations for the summit. Her reputation had preceded her. The Russian press had nicknamed her "Madame Steel," which connoted an even harder line in Russian than in English, since "steel" was the basis for the name Joseph Stalin had chosen for himself. In welcoming her to the Kremlin, Yeltsin said pointedly that he had studied her biography in detail, implying that her background as a Czech émigré had probably left her with a cold war view of his country. "A new Russia has been born," he said, rather sternly, "and it has nothing in common with the former Soviet Union, and that goes for Russian foreign policy as well."[16]

Madeleine told Yeltsin with equal firmness that he shouldn't waste time looking for clues in her past. Instead he should think of her as an American version of Primakov—an experienced diplomat with plenty of first-hand experience of the cold war, strong views about how to advance and defend her country's interests now that the cold war was over, all tempered with a high degree of pragmatism and a willingness to be constructive in working with a Russia that was prepared to develop relations in a similar spirit.

"So you're a constructive lady!" said Yeltsin. "That's more like it!"

He wanted it understood, however, that while she and Primakov should pave the way for Helsinki, no one but he and Clinton could make the decisions that awaited them there: "Russia and the United States have problems to discuss which can only be resolved by the presidents. If we are to come to closure on NATO, he and I are the ones who will decide. . . . When Bill and I meet, it's essential that we agree, and when we do agree, there's no question too difficult to solve. We always make decisions that take care of any outstanding problems. We don't put things aside. We seek compromises that suit the interests of the United States and Russia. We both have roles as leaders of two great nations and are responsible to our people."

He added portentously that he had some ideas of his own on a compromise, but he would save those for Helsinki and his friend Bill.

In the days that followed, Secretary Albright, Javier Solana and I probed our Russian contacts for hints about what those ideas of Yeltsin's might be. They either didn't know or weren't saying. They did, however, float a number of proposals, cooked up by the Foreign and Defense Ministries, which they knew were nonstarters and which we were able to bat down without too much difficulty.[17]

The Russians were harder to budge from their insistence on a prohibition against the stationing of foreign, especially American, forces on the territory of the new member-states. Within NATO, we came up with a compromise that was a variation of the one we'd already used with regard to nuclear weapons: a statement, to be released by the alliance, disavowing the need for permanent basing of large numbers of ground troops in the new member-states "in the current and foreseeable security environment."

It wasn't until early March, on one of my almost weekly trips to Moscow, that Primakov gave us a preview of what Yeltsin had been alluding to in his cryptic remark to Madeleine two weeks earlier. At the end of a long conversation, almost as an afterthought, Primakov said, "Another point that our presidents have to discuss: if any countries of the former Soviet Union are admitted to NATO, we will have no relations with NATO whatsoever. I know this can't be in the NATO-Russia document, but it must be a common understanding. Cuba and Vietnam wanted to be in the Warsaw Pact, but we didn't take them in. We understood where it would lead if we did. So you see, there have been elements of self-restraint in our own policy over the years."

It was obvious which countries he had in mind—the three Baltic states—since they were so far the only former Soviet republics that had formally declared a desire to join NATO. In reply, I reminded him that the U.S. had never recognized the Baltics' incorporation in the USSR and that we didn't accept Russia's right to block any of its neighbors from joining any international organization or alliance.

Primakov dismissed what he called "high theory and legalisms." There was a political reality that we must understand: if NATO expanded to include former Soviet republics, the Yeltsin government would have no chance of weathering the ensuing storm in the Duma.

TEN DAYS LATER, on the eve of the summit, Primakov made a visit to Washington. I took it as a good sign that he didn't raise the subject of the Baltics in his meetings with Secretary Albright or with President Clinton. But when I accompanied him to Andrews Air Force Base for his flight home, he told me that Yeltsin would suggest to Clinton in Helsinki an agreement to exclude the Baltic states from NATO. I urged him to dissuade Yeltsin from making a proposal that Clinton could only reject; if Yeltsin persisted, I warned, it had the potential of blowing up the summit.

Primakov said there was no point in talking about this problem further:

"There are some things that can't be fixed at our level. They're in the hands of the gods or at least of presidents."

ON MARCH 19, the day Clinton left for Helsinki, he assembled his advisers for a last-minute skull session. The president, who had seriously injured his knee five days earlier, was on crutches and his leg was in a cast.

"Still," he said, "I'm going into this meeting with a lot more mobility than Ol' Boris. We've got to use this thing to get him comfortable with what he's got to do on NATO."

He wanted us to be on the lookout for new, imaginative and forthcoming ways of giving Yeltsin every possible reinforcement. That meant using Helsinki to produce a target date for Russian accession to the World Trade Organization and making the Denver summit in June "look and feel more like a G-8 than a G-7."

"It's real simple," said Clinton. "As we push Ol' Boris to do the right but hard thing on NATO, I want him to feel the warm, beckoning glow of doors that are opening to other institutions where he's welcome. Got it, people?"

We flew all night and arrived in Helsinki on March 20. Clinton, in a wheelchair, had to be lowered from Air Force One on a service vehicle with an elevated platform. That night, Ahtisaari hosted a dinner for Clinton and Yeltsin at his residence. No real business was transacted, which was just as well, for Yeltsin seemed tired and distracted, his movements stiff and his complexion cadaverous. Ahtisaari deliberately kept the toasting to a minimum. Still, Yeltsin polished off four glasses of wine and a glass of champagne.

In the presidential suite at the hotel afterward, Clinton, who had in the past tended to be tolerant to the point of denial about Yeltsin's drinking, was genuinely worried. "It's no good," he said. "He put down a lot more than a guy in his shape with his background should have had. Every time I see him I get the feeling that it's part of my job to remind him that the world really is counting on him and he can't go into the tank on us."

As usual, our opportunity to prepare the president for his official program was compressed. It was now 11 p.m., and Clinton was jetlagged and in pain because of his injury. Sandy Berger asked me to run through the agenda and the potential pitfalls as briefly as possible. I dispensed with everything except the near certainty that Yeltsin would plead to exclude the Baltic states from NATO. I started to rehearse the best arguments for the president to use, but Clinton cut me off and said he knew exactly how to deal with the problem; he didn't need either a script or a rehearsal.

THE NEXT MORNING, Clinton and Yeltsin met in the spacious sun-lit living room of the Finnish presidential residence, in front of a picture window opening onto a spectacular view with the sea in the distance. Madeleine, Sandy and I were at Clinton's side, Primakov, Ryurikov and Mamedov at Yeltsin's.

Yeltsin, who had regained his color and vigor overnight, seized the initiative. "The Helsinki summit has got strategic significance not only for our two countries but for Europe and the world," he said. "It's important that in the future we won't look back and say we returned to the cold war. Sliding backward is simply not acceptable . . . We were both voted into office for second terms, until the year 2000; neither of us will have a third term. We want to move into the twenty-first century with stability and tranquility . . .

"Our position has not changed. It remains a mistake for NATO to move eastward. But I need to take steps to alleviate the negative consequences of this for Russia. I am prepared to enter into an agreement with NATO, not because I want to but because it's a step I'm compelled to take. There is no other solution for today." The one condition, he said, was that Clinton promise that NATO would not "embrace" the former Soviet republics. He proposed that they reach "an oral agreement—we won't write it down" to that effect. "This would be a gentlemen's agreement that won't be made public," he stressed.

Clinton, looking relaxed, seemed at first to be ignoring Yeltsin's suggestion. He conjured up the image of a grand signing ceremony, somewhere in Europe, before Madrid, at which a NATO-Russia charter, negotiated by Primakov and Solana, would allow Clinton and Yeltsin to "say to the world that there really is a new NATO and there really is a new Russia."

"I agree," said Yeltsin.

"Good," said Clinton. "But I want you to imagine something else. If we were to agree that no members of the former Soviet Union could enter NATO, that would be a bad thing for our attempt to build a new NATO. It would also be a bad thing for your attempt to build a new Russia. I am not naïve. I understand you have an interest in who gets into NATO and when. We need to make sure that all these are subjects that we can consult about as we move forward. 'Consult' means making sure that we're aware of your concerns, and that you understand our decisions and our positions and our thinking. But consider what a terrible message it would send if we were to make the kind of supposedly secret deal you're suggesting. First, there are no secrets in this world. Second, the message would be, 'We're still organized against Russia—but there's a line across which we won't go.' In other words, instead of creating a new NATO that helps move toward an integrated, undivided Europe, we'd have a larger NATO that's just sitting there waiting for Russia to do something bad.

"Here's why what you are proposing is bad for Russia. Russia would be saying, 'We've still got an empire, but it just can't reach as far west as it used to when we had the Warsaw Pact.' Second, it would create exactly the fear among the Baltics and others that you're trying to allay and that you're denying is justified.

"A third point: The deal you're suggesting would totally undermine the Partnership for Peace. It would terrify the smaller countries that are now working well with you and with us in Bosnia and elsewhere. Consider our hosts here in Finland. President Ahtisaari told me last night that we're doing the right thing in the attitude we're taking toward the future of enlargement. He said that Finland hasn't asked to be in NATO, and as long as no one tells Finland it can't join NATO, then Finland will be able to maintain the independence of its position and work with PFP and with the U.S. and with Russia.

"I've been repeating that I'd leave open the possibility of Russia in NATO and in any event of having a steadily improving partnership between NATO and Russia. I think we'll have to continue to work this issue, but we should concentrate on practical matters. However, under no circumstances should we send a signal out of this meeting that it's the same old European politics of the cold war and we're just moving the lines around a bit."

Clinton then explained that if Russia insisted on a legally binding treaty, opponents of the deal in the Senate would refuse to ratify it. Better, he said, was to settle for a political commitment of the kind the U.S. had been proposing as a charter.

"I agree," said Yeltsin. Only the signature of the heads of state and government would be required, not ratification by parliaments. Solana and Primakov would be charged with concluding the accord.

"Good," said Clinton. "We've got the right solution." He then went back onto the attack against Yeltsin's proposed gentlemen's agreement, which he said "would make us both look weaker, not stronger. If we made the agreement you're describing it would be a terrible mistake. It would cause big problems for me and big problems for you. It would accentuate the diminishment of your power from Warsaw Pact times. The charter will be a much more powerful and positive message. It's without precedent, it's comprehensive, and it's forward looking, and it's hopeful. It will move us toward a situation that's good for both of us."

"Bill," said Yeltsin, "I agree with what you've said. But look at it from my standpoint. Whatever you do on your side, we intend to submit this document to the Duma for ratification. But the Duma will take two decisions. First, it will ratify the document, then it will attach a condition that if NATO takes in even one of the former republics of the Soviet Union, Russia will pull out of the agreement and consider it null and void. That will happen unless you tell me today, one-on-one—without even our closest aides present—that you won't take new republics in the near future. I need to hear that. I understand that maybe in ten years or something, the situation might change, but not now. Maybe there will be a later evolution. But I need assurances from you that it won't happen in the nearest future."

"Come on, Boris," said Clinton, "if I went into a closet with you and told you what you wanted to hear, the Congress would find out and pass a resolution invalidating the NATO-Russia charter. Frankly, I'd rather that the Duma pass a resolution conditioning its adherence on this point. I'd hate for the Duma to do that, but it would be better than what you're suggesting. I just can't do it. A private commitment would be the same as a public one. I've told you—and you have talked to Helmut [Kohl] and Jacques [Chirac], you know their thinking—that no one is talking about a massive, all-out, accelerated expansion. We've already demonstrated our ability to move deliberately, openly. But I can't make commitments on behalf of NATO, and I'm not going to be in the position myself of vetoing any country's eligibility for NATO, much less letting you or anyone else do so. I'm prepared to work with you on the consultative mechanism to make sure that we take account of Russia's concerns as we move forward.

"Another reason why I feel so strongly: look at Bosnia. That's the worst conflict in Europe since World War II. The Europeans couldn't solve it. The U.S. was finally able to take an initiative there, and Russia came in and helped. It took me years to build support. What if, sometime in the future, another Bosnia arises? If the NATO-Russia understanding is done right, then Russia would be a key part of the solution, working with the U.S. and Europe. But if we create a smaller version of the larger standoff that existed during the cold war, there won't be the needed trust. This process of integrating Europe is going to take years. We need to build up the OSCE. It's not going to happen overnight. But if we make a statement now that narrows our options in the future, it will be harder to do the other good things we want to do.

"I know what a terrible problem this is for you, but I can't make the specific commitment you are asking for. It would violate the whole spirit of NATO. I've always tried to build you up and never undermine you. I'd feel I had dishonored my commitment to the alliance, to the states that want to join NATO, and to the vision that I think you and I share of an undivided Europe with Russia as a major part of it."

Yeltsin, looking glum, went to his second fallback: "Okay, but let's agree—one-on-one—that the former Soviet republics won't be in the first waves. Bill, please understand what I'm dealing with there: I'm flying back to Russia with a very heavy burden on my shoulders. It will be difficult for me to go home and not seem to have accepted NATO enlargement. Very difficult."

"Look, Boris, you're forcing an issue that doesn't need to drive a wedge between us here. NATO operates by consensus. If you decided to be in NATO, you'd probably want all the other countries to be eligible too. But that issue doesn't arise. We need to find a solution to a short-term problem that doesn't create a long-term problem by keeping alive old stereotypes about you and your intentions. If we do the wrong thing, it will erode our own position about the kind of Europe we want. I hear your message. But your suggestion is not the way to do it. I don't want to do anything that makes it seem like the old Russia and the old NATO."

Yeltsin simply gave up. "Well," he said, "I tried."

THAT AFTERNOON, at Clinton's insistence, he and Yeltsin reviewed how they would handle the press conference—always a matter of high suspense, but especially this time. Clinton urged Yeltsin that they should both "avoid any answers to questions, any backgrounding with the press afterwards, anything in our public statements that uses the word 'concessions.' I don't want people to score this as you versus me; I don't want them to say that Boris won on three issues and Bill won on two."

Sandy Berger pretended to be a journalist hurling tricky and even hostile questions at the two presidents. One was, "Have you made any secret deals here in Helsinki?"

With a rueful smile, Yeltsin said, "My answer will be: 'We wanted one, but we were rejected.' "

"Perhaps we should have one secret deal," suggested the ever-playful Primakov, "and that's to make Madeleine the next secretary-general of NATO."

I piped up with the observation that Chernomyrdin had already nominated Gorbachev for that job. That stumped everyone, especially Yeltsin.

As the two presidents got up to go face the press, Yeltsin grabbed Clinton by the hand, pumped it and said, "Bill, we have done powerful work."

THE PRESS CONFERENCE came off smoothly, with only a few minor erroneous improvisations by Yeltsin that required correction afterward.[18]

Clinton used the opportunity to announce that the U.S. would, as Chubais had suggested in January, "work with Russia to advance its membership in key international economic institutions like the WTO, the Paris Club and the OECD. And I'm pleased to announce, with the approval of the other G-7 nations, that we will substantially increase Russia's role in our annual meeting, now to be called the Summit of the Eight, in Denver this June."

This latest twist of terminology in Russia's favor allowed our Treasury Department and the other six finance ministries to maintain that the G-7 still existed—and would still meet at the leaders' level. Nonetheless, the G-7 was now officially subsumed into what Yeltsin had been calling, for as long as he'd been attending the get-togethers, "the Big Eight."

Clinton and Yeltsin met once more, for a private dinner that night at a restaurant. The presidents were both weary and doted on the ceremonial pleasantries, including the exchange of gifts. Since Clinton was going to be lame for some time to come, Yeltsin gave him an elegant wooden cane that broke down into three pieces like a billiard cue and had a screw-off top with a telescope inside. Clinton presented Yeltsin with a replica of a Frederic Remington statue depicting an Indian chief on horseback riding down a steep grade.

"You'll see that the horse is on very tricky footing here," Clinton said, "but the rider is strong and a good horseman and knows how to stay in the saddle and not be thrown off stride or pitched off the horse into the mud.

I think that's a pretty good metaphor for you, Boris, in the way you've been able to deal with difficult terrain." He then offered a toast: "Here's to you, Boris, for never giving up, never giving in to your opponents and always coming back for more tough work in a good cause."

THE NEXT MORNING, I flew to Brussels to report at NATO headquarters to the allies and the applicants on what had happened in Helsinki. The Central Europeans were relieved, even joyous. They had been deeply worried that Helsinki would be a "new Yalta."

After my presentation, the first speaker was Andrzej Krzeczunowicz, a former émigré who was now the Polish ambassador in Brussels. Brooke and I had known him and his wife, Nika, in the early seventies when we were reporters in Eastern Europe and Andrzej was working at Radio Free Europe in Munich. Andrzej remembered that earlier association too. In his own remarks to the NATO ambassadors whose ranks he would soon be joining, he recalled how I had once called on him in his office at RFE a quarter of a century before to get his view of the shipyard electrician Lech Walesa, who was organizing an anti-communist labor movement called Solidarity.

THE REACTION TO HELSINKI back home was generally favorable, although there was some grousing from Republicans to the effect that we had gone too far to satisfy the Russians. Henry Kissinger was scathing about our disavowals of intent to deploy nuclear weapons and foreign troops eastward: "Whoever heard of a military alliance begging with a weakened adversary? NATO should not be turned into an instrument to conciliate Russia or Russia will undermine it." Nonetheless, he said, "I will hold my nose and support enlargement." We could live with that.[19]

Yeltsin had a harder time. Some Russian liberals hailed him for his statesmanship, but he took heavy flak from the reds. The communist paper *Sovetskaya Rossiya* wrote that the Helsinki summit resulted "in the capitulation of Russian policy before NATO and the U.S. on every single issue," and Gennady Zyuganov scorned Yeltsin for letting "his friend Bill kick him in the rear." Russia, he said, had been humiliated in Helsinki the way Germany had been at Versailles after World War I.

IN THE WEEKS AFTER the summit, the Russians tried to get their way on some of the details that had not been nailed down in Helsinki. They persisted in their effort to build a firewall against the eastward expansion of the alliance's military capability—in effect, to close the loopholes the alliance had left itself in its unilateral statements of restraint—and they sought additional understandings that would make it as hard as possible for the alliance to take in a second wave of new members once the first had been absorbed.[20]

We wouldn't accommodate them on those points, and they knew they were running out of time to haggle. Yeltsin had publicly announced that he was going to Paris to sign the NATO-Russia charter on May 27. That date was being held tentatively on the calendars of the sixteen NATO leaders, but it depended on a charter being complete and ready for signature. The NATO summit on July 8 in Madrid, by contrast, was firm.

When Madeleine and I went to Moscow in late April and early May for a last round of negotiations, Yeltsin telephoned halfway through the meeting to speak to her. He was calling from Barvikha where he had gone for a checkup. He said several times how eager he was to go to Paris and how much he was counting on his friends Bill, Helmut and Jacques to make sure the meeting went well, thereby undercutting Primakov's last attempt to drive a hard bargain on the points that remained.

That evening Primakov invited Madeleine and the rest of our team to dinner at his apartment in downtown Moscow. It was highly unusual for a Russian official to open his home to foreign visitors. Such hospitality went against the grain of the Soviet-era secrecy, suspicion and insecurity that were still common among Russian officials. Primakov seemed to delight in breaking with that stereotype and presided over a freewheeling, lighthearted conversation over dinner. His wife, Irina, a cardiologist, had made Siberian dumplings but refused to serve them to her husband, who was recovering from gall bladder surgery. Madeleine and I, who were sitting next to him, sneaked him a few dumplings off our own plates.

The three of us fell into a discussion about espionage in fact and fiction. Primakov reminisced about his dealings with Donald Maclean, the British diplomat who had been a Soviet agent in Washington and defected to Moscow in the fifties, and a chance meeting he'd once had with John le Carré in London. I quizzed Primakov about which le Carré novels he knew and liked the best. His knowledge of their plots and characters was comprehensive, and he appreciated the way they captured a world and an era he knew well. Madeleine asked if he identified with Karla, the Soviet spymaster.

"No," he said, "I identify with George Smiley." Without elaborating, he excused himself to open another bottle of Georgian wine.

AFTER DINNER we went back to work in Primakov's living room. It was supposed to be our last session. Primakov said that if the U.S. didn't yield on the remaining points in the NATO-Russia deal, he would "become a pessimist" about getting a deal in time for the Paris meeting.

"Me too," said Madeleine, "and in that case, we'll just have to skip Paris and keep negotiating on a charter after Madrid."

His bluff called, Primakov sighed heavily and suggested that they hold one more meeting the next morning, before her departure.

Our experts, led by Lynn Davis on our side and Yuri Mamedov on the Russians', worked through the night, closing the gap between the two positions but leaving a few disputes for Albright and Primakov.

When the formal negotiations resumed the next day, first in the Laocoön Room at the Foreign Ministry and then in Primakov's private office, Primakov had at his side Colonel-General Leonid Ivashov. I'd gotten to know Ivashov during the spring in my own numerous visits to Moscow. A senior officer of the GRU, Russian military intelligence, he held the post in the Ministry of Defense responsible for "international military cooperation," which my colleagues and I had come to regard as something of a joke, since as far as we could tell, he was devoted heart and soul to thwarting any progress in that direction.

In the final, grueling two hours of talks, Albright and Primakov were negotiating hard but driving for closure. Madeleine tried to give wherever she could, in part, as she put it afterward, "so as not to make Yevgeny bleed too much—we've got to be careful not to overwin the endgame." Ivashov, however, seemed to want a stalemate: he objected to any Russian compromise. That left Primakov no choice but to overrule Ivashov on the spot.

The essentials of a NATO-Russia accord were now in hand, although it took two more rounds of front-channel negotiations between Solana and Primakov, with us working closely with both sides, to iron out the language in the final, ten-page document—including what it would be called.[21] What the Russians had wanted to be a treaty and what we had been calling a charter ended up as the NATO-Russia Founding Act. The "consultative mechanism" that Javier Solana had proposed a year before became the NATO-Russia Permanent Joint Council, which would meet monthly at alliance headquarters in Brussels at the ambassadorial level and twice a year at the foreign and defense minister level.

Clinton's relief was immense, but so was his impatience to get back to the original business of helping Russia with its internal transformation.

"Okay," he said, "so it looks like we're going to dodge a bullet. That's always a good thing, compared to the alternative. But now what? How do we broaden this thing out? How do we get back to basics and get back to the big picture, especially on economics?"

Clinton left for the NATO-Russia summit in Paris hoping that the carefully choreographed event would give Yeltsin a boost in the eyes of the U.S. Congress and the G-7, so that there might be a new surge of international financial support.

As it played out, the event in Paris on May 27 went well enough on the surface, but from where I sat, several rows back in the gallery of officials gathered in the grand ballroom of the Elysée Palace, there was an air of artificial triumphalism and even anticlimax, tinged, as so often, with some embarrassment over the performance of the star.

When Yeltsin joined the sixteen allied leaders and Javier Solana at the podium, he behaved as though he were a famous comic actor listening to testimonials before accepting a lifetime achievement award: He knew that the occasion required solemnity, but he couldn't help giving the fans a little of what they'd come to expect from him. Yeltsin's expression kept changing. One minute he was beaming with pleasure as the other dignitaries, one by one, praised his statesmanship as well as his credentials as a reformer and democrat; the next he was screwing up his face in exaggerated concentration on the weightiness of the moment. When it came time for him to sign the Founding Act, he took a huge breath, wrote his name with a flourish, then gave Solana a bear hug and a big kiss on both cheeks.

When he rose to speak, those of us who had sat on the edge of our seats at his press conferences over the years held our breath. Sure enough, he had a surprise for everyone, including his own entourage. "Today," he announced, "after having signed the document, I am going to make the following decision: everything that is aimed at countries present here—all of those weapons—are going to have their warheads removed."

I was sitting with Mamedov behind Albright and Primakov. They began whispering intently, she with questions and he with highly tentative answers: he didn't know what his president was talking about. Predictably,

Yeltsin's mysterious improvisation dominated the next day's news coverage of the event and caused head-scratching for a long time afterward.[22]

When Yeltsin met privately with Clinton, he burbled on about the day as though it had been the consummation of all his dreams for Russia's position at the head table of the new transatlantic order.

For once, however, Clinton's own mind was elsewhere. He had just learned that the Supreme Court had ruled that the Paula Jones sexual harassment case, dating back to his days as governor of Arkansas, could go forward while he was in office.[23] From the moment he got the news, he seemed to be sleepwalking through the summit.

Fortunately, there wasn't much business to transact. Clinton had already done the hard work required of him in Helsinki, clearing the way for a Madrid summit that would begin the process of admitting the Czech Republic, Hungary and Poland to NATO and holding the door open for other Central European applicants, including the Baltic states, in the years to come.

NATO FORMALLY made the decision to bring in new members five weeks later, in early July. Clinton flew into Madrid for the summit at the last minute from a vacation he and Hillary had just taken with Spain's King Juan Carlos and Queen Sophia on Majorca. When Sandy and I arrived at the presidential hotel suite to brief him for the meetings ahead, Clinton was overflowing with fun facts he had scooped up like a vacuum cleaner: Majorca's role in the Punic wars, detailed impressions of the cottage where George Sand and Chopin had lived, what had happened to Robert Graves's house—on and on and on. He was the ultimate tourist.

Sandy grew increasingly impatient. We had serious work to do. Madrid could still go badly. On Primakov's advice, Yeltsin had decided not to attend, sending Deputy Prime Minister Valery Serov instead. We didn't know what to expect from him—or from Yeltsin himself back in Moscow when the deed of enlargement was actually done.

The French were a problem too. Jacques Chirac was determined to admit Romania into the alliance in the first round, a move we felt unwise, given the shakiness of Romania's economic and political reforms. Listening to Sandy explain our tense and sometimes disagreeable dealings with the French, Clinton grew agitated about how we were, yet again, insisting on having everything our own way. "Politics is about perceptions," he said, "and the perception out there is that we're being rude and arrogant and bragging at their expense and pushing them around." He was, therefore, all the more eager to find a way of not humiliating Chirac in Madrid.

Sandy and I said we were all for treating Chirac respectfully, but not to the point of letting him foist on NATO a new ally that was in as uncertain a condition as Romania.

"I agree with that," said Clinton. "I'm just saying that you shouldn't kick a wounded dog because it will get well and bite you. France is wounded."

Just putting the challenge in those terms (which would probably not have greatly mollified the proud and prickly Chirac) caused Clinton to shift abruptly to his far greater concern about Russia. Somehow, he said, we had to find ways in the months and years ahead to make what he called "Yeltsin's leap of faith" in signing the NATO-Russia charter payoff, "or at least not become a leap into the abyss."

Time for the "briefing" was up. We'd barely gotten a word in edgewise. Clinton had an appointment with some members of Congress who had come to Madrid as observers. I watched from the back of the room as he did his riff: NATO enlargement should not be viewed in isolation; it was part of a package with the NATO-Russia Founding Act and the creation of the Permanent Joint Council. "What we're doing here is hoping for the best and creating the conditions for the best but also being prepared for the possibility of Russia's reasserting itself . . . We're walking a tightrope . . . I'm getting flak from people who are arguing on behalf of Romania and Bulgaria but who would abandon the Baltic states in a heartbeat, which I think would be unconscionable."

He wanted to see NATO evolve in a way that would preserve the possibility of historically neutral states like Sweden and Finland, as well as the Baltics, joining in subsequent rounds. As for Russia, there, too, he was being criticized for "trying to make something that's very hard not entirely impossible for Yeltsin" and for "holding open a place for Russia in some future evolved version of NATO." Everyone should remember, he concluded, that "whatever I'm getting on this subject, including from some of you, is nothing compared to what Yeltsin's getting. I've got the easy job here. He's got the hard one."

ON DAY ONE of the summit, NATO invited the three Central European states to join. Chirac was in a funk that the arrogant and obnoxious U.S. was getting its way once again.

On day two, leaders from forty-three countries across Eurasia—including disappointed applicants like Romania, neutrals and all the states of the former Soviet Union—participated in the first meeting of the Euro-Atlantic Partnership Council (EAPC), a forum designed to promote consultation and cooperation between NATO and its non-member partners. The EAPC was a successor to the North Atlantic Cooperation Council that had brought the foreign ministers of NATO and former Warsaw Pact states together annually since 1991.

I remembered how tedious and overpopulated the NACC meeting in Athens had seemed four years earlier. It had been in reaction to the obvious inadequacy of that mechanism that Warren Christopher had put in motion the process that led to NATO enlargement and its accompanying innovations, including the NATO-Russia Founding Act. The inaugural session of the EAPC in Madrid, while no less ritualistic and even more crowded than the NACC, had an air of excitement and historical moment. This was partly because it was the first of its kind and there were heads of state and government present (Clinton was seated next to the president of Uzbekistan and across from the leaders of Albania, Armenia and Azerbaijan).

But the EAPC had more than novelty going for it; it had come into being as part of a larger enterprise that now included the proven ability of the alliance to open its door and to undertake joint missions with armies that only a few years before had been on the other side of the Iron Curtain.

The protocol called for a *tour de table*, with the head of every delegation invited to say something. Sandy and I were sitting behind the president and Madeleine, occasionally passing them notes and engaging in whispered conversation. As our minds wandered from the less scintillating of these speeches to the significance of the overall scene, we found ourselves thinking about paintings and photographs we'd seen of the great international conferences of the nineteenth and twentieth centuries. There was something different here. In the past—the Congresses of Vienna and Versailles came particularly to mind—the Great Powers met to redraw the map and decide the fate of the little guys. Here were the big and little guys together, each with only a few minutes to have his say. We recalled the pleas we'd heard from the Central Europeans, most eloquently and most recently from the Polish foreign minister, Darius Rosati, just before Helsinki: "Don't talk about us without us; we've had enough of that over the centuries."

Yeltsin's stand-in, Serov, gave a brief speech that barely registered with the press—which was the best news we could hope for.

THAT EVENING, while the king and queen took the Clintons to Granada, Madeleine and I went to the Prado. We spent most of our time in the basement, viewing Francisco de Goya's "black paintings." Standing in front of a picture of a giant stalking a ravaged land, she and I had the same thought: here was not just a depiction of the disasters that had befallen Spain during the Napoleonic Wars but a premonition of those that were in store for Europe as a whole in the twentieth century. Our task was to work with the Europeans to consign that specter to history.

Too bad, we agreed, that Yeltsin could not have been in Madrid, since he—virtually alone in his government, it sometimes seemed—had been willing to make Russia part of the pan-European venture that the meeting earlier in the day was meant to launch. At the same time, perhaps it was just as well he did not come, since he had already strained to the limit the tolerances of his own constituencies.

CHAPTER 10

BAD BUSINESS

Avoid as you would the plague a cleric who is also a man of business.
Saint Jerome

B EFORE THE LEADERS of NATO and its new partners from the east gathered in Madrid, the G-7 held a summit of its own in Denver, in mid-June 1997. Boris Yeltsin attended the Denver event since he was not just a face in the crowd but the guest of honor, and since the host, Bill Clinton, was committed to enlarging the G-7 to bring Yeltsin in as a full member.

The night before the summit formally opened, Madeleine Albright invited Yevgeny Primakov to dinner. Yuri Mamedov and I joined them for what was supposed to be a relaxed evening. Denver was Madeleine's hometown—her father had taught international relations there. She booked a private room in the Buckhorn Exchange, a restaurant rich in local color. Teddy Roosevelt's portrait was on one wall, Buffalo Bill's on the other, six-shooters and other cowboy paraphernalia everywhere. Madeleine introduced Primakov to Rocky Mountain oysters, a specialty of the house. Primakov joked about how Madeleine had, the year before, famously used the word *cojones* in an altercation with Fidel Castro.

The merriment didn't survive the appetizer course. There was always at least a side order of spinach on the menu when American officials met with their Russian counterparts. In that respect, the dinner in Denver was nothing out of the ordinary. But Primakov's appetite for the dish was at an all-time low. When Madeleine mentioned casually that she had a bit of business to do, he tensed up. It quickly became apparent that we were in for a whole new rough patch in the relationship even before we had a chance to catch our breath after the imbroglio over NATO.

The process of negotiating the NATO-Russia deal had been so preoccupying that it had elbowed other issues out of the way. Having festered for months, they would now demand high-level, sustained diplomatic attention of their own. Also, the Russians in general and Primakov in particular were aggrieved over having had to settle the NATO question essentially on our terms. Primakov had come to Denver with a chip on his shoulder. He was looking for opportunities to show us that he and his government were tired of being pushed around by the U.S.

Yet we had more pushing to do, partly because we were being pushed by the U.S. Congress.

Domestic political pressure had always been a complicating factor in the conduct of relations with Russia. For the first Clinton term, the administration had maintained just enough bipartisan consensus to pursue its own goals in its own ways. Congress had kibitzed during the long, arduous bargaining over NATO but never posed a major obstacle to the administration's pursuit of its objective, since most members were in favor of enlargement and tolerant of, even if not enthusiastic about, the NATO-Russia Founding Act.

But with that matter behind us, many in Congress, particularly in the Republican majority, felt it was now open season on anything that they construed as unacceptable Russian behavior. At issue was not whether the U.S. should try to alter Russian policy or activities, but how to do so. The administration had used the threat of sanctions in 1993 to persuade the Russians to cancel the sale of rocket parts to India. But imposition of sanctions could backfire, arousing Russian resentment and strengthening hard-liners. Therefore we relied as much as possible on carrots, seeking to induce the Russians to cooperate by stressing the economic and political benefits of their doing so, with the stick in the background.

Congress tended to push us in the direction of imposing sanctions that were available under existing law. If we dragged our feet in doing so, Congress could pass new laws ramming through compulsory sanctions of its own or refuse to fund our assistance programs. In resorting to these tougher measures, our political opponents could make it all but impossible for the administration to pursue a policy that emphasized cooperation with Russia and put pressure on the executive branch to adapt instead to a policy that was coercive in intent, punitive in impact and often counter-productive in consequence.

That danger loomed as Madeleine Albright and Yevgeny Primakov met for what turned out to be a distinctly uncongenial dinner that balmy summer evening in Denver.

THE DAY BEFORE, nationalists in the Duma had passed draft legislation intended to restrict the upsurge in foreign-sponsored religious activity since the collapse of the Soviet system. The bill declared the Russian Orthodox Church, Judaism, Islam and Buddhism to be the nation's "heritage" religions. All other faiths—including those like Roman Catholicism and the Baptist Church that had had adherents for a long time in Russia, as well as relative newcomers like Mormonism—had to get the permission of the authorities to own property, publish literature, establish schools or conduct charitable work.

The measure was hotly debated in Russia, particularly among those who saw it as violating the guarantee of religious freedom in the post-Soviet constitution. Yeltsin had vetoed an earlier version for just that reason. Now that it was back in a new form, the religion law had vigorous backing from the patriarch, who saw "false faiths" as a threat to traditional Russian culture and to the dominance of the Orthodox Church.

In response, a number of powerful Republican congressmen threatened to restrict U.S. aid to Russia on the grounds that we shouldn't be helping a government that engaged in religious discrimination. They believed that the fate of the religion law was a test of whether Russia was indeed reforming. The administration agreed. We did not, however, believe it should become, in effect, the only test. It would certainly be a mistake to penalize the Russians for their shortcomings in guaranteeing freedom of religion by withholding funds for American assistance programs that were helping the Russians make progress in other areas, such as developing a court system, independent media, labor unions and a private sector.

Many Russian liberals shared our distaste for the law that the Duma had passed but believed that our Congress was holding their country to unreasonably high standards of democracy and civil society. Russia, after all, had been part of an atheistic dictatorship only a few years before.

I had some sympathy for this complaint. I remembered that when I'd started going to the USSR in the late sixties, the local equivalent of "when hell freezes over" was "when the Romanovs are restored to the throne and when Judaism becomes the state religion." Well, here it was 1997, and Judaism had become at least *a* state religion.

Nonetheless, we had to maintain the support of our Congress for our Russia policy as a whole, and we said as much to the Russians in urging that Yeltsin veto the religion law. Madeleine had made this point to Primakov when earlier iterations of the law were under consideration, and she did so again over dinner in Denver, warning that the latest Duma action was certain to arouse opposition from "friends of Russian democracy in my country."

"Madeleine, Madeleine," said Primakov, shaking his head with mock weariness, "sometimes I'm not sure how much more of your friendship we can stand."

THE FAR MORE SERIOUS and chronic problem that made for a contentious dinner was Russia's relationship with Iran, which was still very much under the sway of radical Islamic clerics. The Russian Ministry of Atomic Energy had already contributed to Tehran's program to develop the capacity to build nuclear warheads. Now the Russians were contributing to the Iranians' acquisition of their own ballistic missiles as well. Commercial firms, many of them spun off from the old Soviet military-industrial complex, were providing the Iranians with materials that could be used to make rocket engines, fuselages and guidance systems, while Russian universities and institutes were training Iranians in the development, design and manufacture of missiles.

The motives for this Russian activity were varied and largely a matter of conjecture. Many Russians, including corrupt government officials, were no doubt making money from the sales. Some in Moscow had also convinced themselves that Russia could ingratiate itself with the Iranians as a reliable supplier of equipment, material and know-how for their most secret and cherished programs, and thereby maintain influence over Iranian policy in the future.

For months, we had been trying to persuade the Russians that they were hastening the day when Iran possessed a nuclear-armed missile, and when that day came much of Russia would be within its range.

The Russians' first line of defense was denial: it wasn't happening. Confronted with incontrovertible evidence, they retreated to the claim that their government had neither authorized nor been involved in whatever objectionable activity was taking place. Besides, they said, we were exaggerating the problem.

Our reply was that we were, if anything, understating its magnitude, since other illicit and dangerous transactions no doubt went undetected, and the Russian government had a responsibility to put a stop to all of them. Under existing American law, we had the authority to impose sanctions, and we told the Russians that. Moreover, the Congress was likely to press for new sanctions of its own.

Much of the covert and commercial activity to which we objected violated existing Russian regulations. The Russians could avoid American sanctions by enforcing and strengthening their own laws.

Our principal channel for making these arguments in the first term had been the Gore-Chernomyrdin commission, which had produced agreements limiting Russian nuclear cooperation and conventional arms commerce with Iran.[1] At the beginning of the second term, during the commission meeting in February 1997, Gore confronted Chernomyrdin with evidence that Russia was supplying the Iranians with missile technology. Chernomyrdin dodged the charge, denying only that Russia had "authorized" the sale. When Clinton raised the matter a month later in Helsinki, Yeltsin claimed that Russia had not helped Iran acquire nuclear weapons or missile technology—which we knew to be untrue—and promised that it would never happen in the future.

Within weeks the Ministry of Atomic Energy and other elements in the Russian government seemed to be using NATO enlargement as a pretext for stepping up lethal Russian assistance to Iran. I sent a personal message through our ambassador, Jim Collins, to Anatoly Chubais, the chief of Kremlin administration, warning that what we were hearing made more of a mockery than ever out of Yeltsin's protestations of innocence to Clinton in Helsinki, and that the problem had the potential to ruin the Denver summit. On a subsequent visit to Washington, Chubais showed up at my house on a Sunday afternoon and told me that my message on Iran was understood and that any deals in contravention of Yeltsin's assurances to Clinton were "strictly forbidden." But, he added, there was no question that the hard-liners were exploiting resentment over NATO expansion in their advocacy of "a strategic marriage of convenience with Iran."

When Madeleine and I had dinner with Primakov in Denver, she told him that the problem was "about to go critical on us" and would probably replace NATO enlargement as the most divisive issue between the U.S. and Russia.

Primakov, whose back was already up, dispensed with his usual drollery and went on the attack. Coming on top of NATO enlargement, American "pressure tactics" over Iran were simply unacceptable. Russia's laws, its enforcement of those laws and its relations with Iran were all its own business. He was sick and tired of being told by the U.S. what Russia could and could not do.

With that preview from his foreign minister, we expected Yeltsin to be equally combative in his meeting with Clinton the next day.

WHEN YELTSIN arrived at the Brown Palace Hotel, he had with him a larger than usual phalanx of officials, including Primakov and Chubais. This time Yeltsin wanted his colleagues to hear everything he had to say. At first, I took this as a bad sign. The productive moments in U.S.-Russian summitry over the past four years had been the more private ones, while in larger sessions Yeltsin tended to grandstand and bluster.

Clinton, as the host, began on a positive note, lavishing praise on Yeltsin for his political courage in signing the NATO-Russia Founding Act and making much of the decision of the G-7 to become the G-8 when they next met in Birmingham, England, in the spring of 1998.

I was watching Yeltsin's face for some sign of his mood. In the past, he had tended to fidget and interrupt when Clinton did an overture like this one. This time he listened with passive gratitude, letting Clinton's warm words wash over him.

When Clinton came to the troublesome topics, Yeltsin, instead of putting up his usual fight, seemed eager to please. Clinton mentioned, in a gingerly fashion, the Duma's passage of a restrictive religion law, and Yeltsin promised on the spot to veto it.[2]

I glanced at Primakov. He was staring impassively into the distance.

Clinton, somewhat emboldened by how easily he'd gotten through the first difficult item, started to bear down on the danger of Russian technology going to Iran, which, he said, had gotten worse since he and Yeltsin had discussed it in Helsinki.

Before Clinton got far in his brief, Yeltsin interrupted.

"Bill, Bill . . . ," he began. We all braced ourselves. But instead of the objection we expected, out came an extraordinary admission: "Because of our clumsy democracy, we sometimes allow enterprises to have direct contacts with Iran, and they make agreements on their own." He said he'd set up a watchdog commission to look into the matter, but it had "not provided me with adequate information, so I will establish another, more responsible commission to check on the points you've raised, and I'll report back to you."

Yeltsin proposed that the two of them appoint envoys who would "get to the bottom" of the Iran problem under the aegis of the Gore-Chernomyrdin commission.

Primakov was visibly agitated. He tried twice to intervene, either to rebut Clinton or to correct Yeltsin, but Yeltsin shushed him. I glanced at Chubais, who was seated next to Primakov. Now Chubais was the one gazing impassively into the distance.

Having yielded to the U.S. position on NATO, Yeltsin was coming close to accepting the American version of what was going on between Russia and Iran. In so doing, he was repudiating the official Russian government position that we'd been hearing for years, including from Primakov himself the night before.

THE FOLLOWING EVENING, Secretary Albright was giving Primakov a ride in her limousine to a summit banquet when her security detail reported that a burst of radio traffic suggested Yeltsin had been rushed to the hospital. Hearing this, Primakov looked pensively out the window, then turned back to Madeleine and said, "Oh, God, I just hope this isn't true. Everything will go crazy again."

While the rumor proved false, everyone's assumption that it was true was a reminder of how precarious the situation was, both within Russia and between Russia and the U.S. The presidential meeting in the Brown Palace Hotel seemed to have been the high-water mark of Clinton's influence over Yeltsin, but whether that bond translated into American influence over Russia was almost completely dependent on Yeltsin's personal stewardship of the relationship, and therefore on his physical and political survival.

WHACK WHACK

In an effort to capitalize on Yeltsin's eagerness to resolve the Iran issue, President Clinton chose Frank Wisner, an experienced and highly regarded foreign service officer, as his envoy on the issue.[3] We took it as a good sign when the Russians announced that Frank's Russian counterpart would be Yuri Koptev, the head of the Russian Space Agency, who had helped break the stalemate over the India rocket deal in 1993. Koptev had every reason to want to resolve the Iran dispute, since his ability to launch U.S. satellites on Russian rockets and cooperate with NASA on the space station was in jeopardy if the U.S. imposed sanctions.

Wisner and Koptev buckled down to work in August, and in September they presented their initial report at the ninth round of Gore-Chernomyrdin in Moscow. The results, however, were at best modest. Koptev didn't say so, but we could tell that he was being blocked at every turn by the intelligence services and the military-industrial complex.

Occasionally, we'd call the Russians' attention to a company or an institute that was trafficking in dangerous technology, and they'd do something about it for a while. Shortly afterward we'd find another problem elsewhere, and no doubt there were many more we didn't find. Sandy Berger likened our efforts to the children's game of Whac-A-Mole, and we felt we were losing.

The Ministry of Foreign Affairs was no help. Virtually every time Madeleine met with Primakov, she gave him new information about Russian equipment or experts finding their way to Iran. Primakov would parry much as he had in Denver—with alibis, countercharges, obfuscations and pettifogging. There was a basic difference between his approach to this issue and his earlier, ultimately constructive handling of the NATO-Russia negotiations. While in both cases he was under presidential instructions to get the problem fixed, in the earlier one he had been operating against the deadline of the Madrid summit. On Iran, he probably calculated that he could keep putting us off forever.

But in fact there was a reckoning coming. Sooner or later, it would be implausible for us to claim that we were working cooperatively with the Russians on a common problem. When that day came, it would be both logically and politically impossible to resist the case that Congress was already making for sanctions.

Congressional impatience was stoked by the Israelis, who rightly saw the Iranian nuclear and missile programs as a threat to their very existence. Natan Sharansky, a former Soviet dissident and human rights activist who was now the minister of industry and trade in the Likud government led by Prime Minister Benjamin Netanyahu, made curbing the export of Russian technology into a personal crusade. I'd known him over the years, so when he and I ran into each other in a hotel lobby in Moscow in the fall of 1997, he greeted me as an old friend, politely sat me down, offered me a drink and read me the riot act: the U.S. had to get tougher with the Russians and that meant sanctions. I knew Sharansky was also spending a lot of time in Washington talking to members of our Congress, where receptivity to his advice was growing. I couldn't claim that our approach was working. All I could do was urge him to give us more time.

IN EARLY OCTOBER, I went to see Valentin Yumashev, the Kremlin chief of staff and a member of Yeltsin's inner circle. Like Yeltsin himself in Denver, Yumashev admitted there was a problem within the Russian government, and he implied that Primakov was part of it. This wasn't news to us, but it was an early signal that Primakov might be in trouble in the Kremlin.

Somehow, said Yumashev, we had to reengage the two presidents directly.

On my return to Washington, I worked with Sandy on the draft of a letter from Clinton to Yeltsin. It was one of the longest and toughest to any foreign leader during his presidency. Clinton called on Yeltsin to issue a decree prohibiting all exports to Iran's ballistic missile program. When Clinton signed it, he appended a handwritten postscript: "Boris, this is as hard as any issue we have faced together. I'm giving the highest priority to working with you to bring it under control."

He followed up with a phone call on October 30, ostensibly to congratulate Yeltsin on the birth of his third grandson, Vanka (Little Ivan), born to his older daughter, Elena, but also to alert Yeltsin to the letter and the need for the next Wisner-Koptev session to produce results.

Yeltsin turned snappish. "Iran is not getting any missiles from us," he said. "There's no way they can get it."

Clinton replied that the issue wasn't just the missiles themselves but related technology and expertise. He'd laid it all out in the letter, he said.

"Okay, okay," said Yeltsin, sounding annoyed that this pesky subject was still coming up between him and Clinton.

A reply in Yeltsin's name arrived almost immediately—so quickly that it must have been drafted before Clinton and Yeltsin talked. Much of the phraseology in this letter, however, was pure Primakov.

WHEN YELTSIN FLEW to Krasnoyarsk in early November for a meeting with the Japanese prime minister, Ryutaro Hashimoto, he left Primakov behind and took with him instead Boris Nemtsov, a young liberal deputy prime minister and former governor of Nizhny-Novgorod, one of the showcases of economic and political reform. The exclusion of Primakov from the summit sparked rumors in Moscow that his star was falling. When I saw Primakov in Tokyo not long afterward, he alluded to "the unpredictability of politics" and talked openly about feeling beleaguered in his work. Also, for the first time, instead of putting up his usual fight on

Iran, he promised me that efforts were under way back in Moscow to solve the problem once and for all.

BY THE BEGINNING of 1998, there were signs of real movement. Koptev told Frank Wisner the Russian government was going to submit to the Duma a new law that would stop all transfers of missile technology to Iran. We had been urging such a measure, known as a catchall because it was intended to close the loopholes in Russia's nonproliferation laws.

But draft legislation wasn't good enough since it would be subject to delay and to watering down by the Duma. Frank told Koptev that unless the Russian government acted soon, the U.S. Congress would pass a law of its own imposing sanctions on Russia. After another bruising round of deliberations within the Russian government, Koptev told Wisner in mid-January that the new catchall system could be put in place promptly, by decree, while the Duma deliberated on permanent legislation. Koptev pleaded for just a little more time to get the catchall decree negotiated internally and announced.

Late that month Prime Minister Netanyahu came to Washington and joined the chorus in Congress that was accusing the Clinton administration of coddling the Russians. Newt Gingrich, the Speaker of the House, was poised to sponsor anti-Russian sanctions as soon as Netanyahu gave him the nod. If that happened, the Duma would probably retaliate by not passing any legislation to curb technology sales; if anything, it might try even harder to promote sales. Clinton and Gore managed to persuade Netanyahu that we were close to a deal with the Russians.

I met with Primakov in the Swedish city of Lulea and told him he had a choice: he could validate the hypothesis that the U.S. and Russia were dealing with proliferation cooperatively by throwing his weight onto the side of those, like Koptev, who wanted a solution to the problem, or he could sit back and watch the U.S. Congress vote for sanctions by an overwhelming margin.

That would be a catastrophe, he said. The "quiet work" we were doing in the Gore-Chernomyrdin and Wisner-Koptev channels could continue "only if it goes forward in the framework of cooperation—a kind of joint venture in pursuit of mutual interests."

I told him that we'd tried our best to preserve that framework, but the time had run out for quiet diplomacy. We needed a public announcement of catchall measures right away.

Primakov, looking deeply pained, promised that there would be such an announcement shortly.

When I telephoned Sandy Berger from my hotel room to report, he sounded embattled. "Neither you, nor I, nor our boss is ready to shift the paradigm of how we deal with the Russians," he said. "But there are a lot of people on the Hill who are itching to do so. Even if the Russians give us something to work with, it'll be tough back here."[4]

I FOUND THE WHOLE episode dispiriting, even distasteful. Russia's handling of its relations with Iran was venal, devious, dangerous and dumb, and Primakov was undoubtedly part of the problem. But until now the Clinton administration had been able to handle its own relations with Russia by its own lights and devices. I hated having to admit to Primakov that we were losing control of our Russia policy to an assertive and hostile Congress. For five years, we'd listened to Russian officials point over their shoulders at the Duma and say, "Do what we want or you'll have to deal with those crazy people!" Now we were doing much the same thing.

THE NEXT DAY I met in Helsinki with President Martti Ahtisaari of Finland, who had long since established himself in the eyes of our administration as one of the wisest heads in Europe and a useful channel for reinforcing messages to Yeltsin and Chernomyrdin. I asked him to play that role again and get word to the Russians quickly that we needed to have an announcement on catchall right away.

Ahtisaari didn't like what he was hearing. "You mustn't overplay your hand with the Russians," he admonished. "Slowly but surely they're getting over the post-imperial, post-Soviet hang-ups, but it takes time and patience. Your administration has managed to stay steady when others, in Moscow and Washington alike, were panicking. You've got to stay steady now. Don't crowd the Russians. Don't make them feel punished or on probation. Remember that whatever problems you have with Yeltsin and Chernomyrdin and Primakov, you'd have much, much bigger problems with the people they're dealing with in their parliament."

The problem, I said, was that we had forces in our own "parliament" who had long since lost patience with the Russians and might succeed in slapping sanctions on them in the coming days, over the objections of the White House.

Ahtisaari looked aghast. "That would be just about the stupidest thing you could possibly do," he said. "You" was the United States; he didn't distinguish between branches of government; he held the executive responsible.

All I could do was say that we were doing our best to hold back the tide of sanctions, but it would sure help if we could get Moscow to make a move of its own toward solving the Iran problem.

I phoned Sandy again that night to see how he was doing in his efforts with the Congress. Something was clearly wrong: Sandy's voice was choked, and he was barely able to focus on what I was saying. I asked him what was the matter. After a long pause, he said, "You know, we've got a new problem here." His voice trailed off. I told him I didn't know what he was talking about. "It's a piece in the *Post*," he said. "It's trouble for our boss and therefore for us, but I don't want to talk about it on this line. I can't talk now."

He was referring to a news story that was just breaking: President Clinton was under investigation for having an affair with an unnamed White House intern.

The next day my traveling team and I flew home. When our flight got into Dulles Airport on Thursday evening, January 22, Eric Edelman, my executive assistant, and two other members of my staff, Phil Goldberg and Kent Pekel, squeezed with me into a State Department car for the long drive into town. Lee Young—my driver for the seven years I was deputy secretary, who had become a close and lasting friend—had brought extra copies of the day's newspapers for us to read. Lee knew we'd need to catch up quickly on what was now known to the world as the Monica Lewinsky story. Eric, Phil and Kent pored over papers. The silence in the car was broken by occasional murmurs of disbelief.

My three traveling companions were braver than I. I couldn't even look at the headlines, much less read the articles. I stared out the window. More than just hoping the story was false, I found myself trying to will it so.

As we crossed the Potomac over the Theodore Roosevelt Bridge into Washington, a call came through from the State Department Operations Center with a bulletin from Moscow: Prime Minister Chernomyrdin had just released a statement on behalf of the Russian government announcing the new catchall regulation. The decree, which took effect immediately, might enable us to resist the congressional juggernaut. The good news barely registered. I hung up and went back to studying the night.

———

THE NEXT MORNING, I was one of many in the administration who found it hard to get up, get dressed and go to the office. But I was also one of many who did exactly that. Another was Sandy Berger. He chaired a cabinet-level meeting to decide what to do about continuing pressure from Congress to impose sanctions on Russia. Frank Wisner contended that with Chernomyrdin's announcement of a catchall decree, we were finally getting somewhere, but any hope of further progress in the future would go up in smoke if we imposed sanctions. Madeleine and I argued that imposing sanctions would be abandoning the last semblance of cooperation in favor of an explicitly punitive approach, to the detriment of virtually every aspect of the relationship, including what we had accomplished the year before between NATO and Russia.

The catchall announcement gave us just enough evidence of progress to persuade Congress to hold off for a while longer on sanctions, but the pressure was still on to make more progress as quickly as possible. The next opportunity to do so was the Gore-Chernomyrdin meeting, the tenth, in early March. A key item on the agenda was U.S.-Russian cooperation in space, including the use of Russian rockets to launch American-made commercial satellites. Those contracts represented a lifesaver for Russia's space program. There were also billions of dollars to be made in U.S.-Russian high-tech partnerships, but—as Gore stressed to Chernomyrdin during a cross-country flight to visit Silicon Valley—the U.S. would only let those deals go forward if the Russian government delivered on the promises it had made to date and tightened its controls further. Chernomyrdin professed to be convinced. He promised he would use his influence both with the government and with Yeltsin to make sure that, having turned a corner with catchall, Russia kept moving in the right direction.

A SHAKE-UP

All of us working on U.S.-Russian relations regarded the tenth—or as it was called the "jubilee"—commission meeting as the most substantive and promising to date. In addition to providing further proof of the utility of the personal channel between the vice-president and the prime minister, the session dramatized the extent to which many of the wheels of the two governments were beginning to mesh. Many of the joint projects were unglamorous but important to Russia's chances of becoming a successful modern state. American agencies were helping their counterparts in Moscow and in the regions with tasks as varied as the testing and labeling of foods, guarding against lead poisoning in the blood of children, improving the treatment of tuberculosis, writing a tax code, developing a sophisticated air traffic control system, privatizing farmland and mapping the Arctic.

The commission meetings also gave us a look at the younger technocrats who were beginning to replace the red managers like Chernomyrdin himself. At the tenth session, the American participants found the most impressive member of the commission on the Russian side of the table to be Sergei Kiriyenko, the thirty-five-year-old minister of fuel and energy. A protégé of Boris Nemtsov from Nizhny-Novgorod, Kiriyenko had been a leader of the Communist Youth League when the Soviet Union collapsed but had made the transition to Russia's rough version of capitalism easily, first by running a bank profitably and then by rescuing a regional oil refinery from bankruptcy.[5]

WHILE CHERNOMYRDIN was riding high with his friend the vice-president of the U.S., he was in trouble with his boss, the president of Russia. Yeltsin had yet to make up his mind whether he would indeed step down in 2000, not to mention who should succeed him if he did, and he felt Chernomyrdin was behaving as though he was already the heir-designate. The third week in March, during a visit to Berlin, I encountered Grigory Yavlinsky, who had just seen Yeltsin. Yavlinsky reported that Yeltsin was depressed about the state of the country and increasingly inclined to blame Chernomyrdin.

Two days later, on Monday, March 23, I was back in Washington and got one of those early-morning calls from Moscow that kept my job interesting. It was Jim Collins with the news that Yeltsin had just fired Chernomyrdin and declared his intention to replace him with Sergei Kiriyenko.

The shake-up was a typical Yeltsin move, a lightning bolt that singed loyal collaborators even as it shocked his enemies. He had planned it in the greatest secrecy, confiding, as far as anyone could tell, only in his daughter Tatyana and his personal aide Valentin Yumashev. Once again he was demonstrating how he thrived in a crisis, especially—and from his standpoint, preferably—one of his own making. He explained the changing of the guard as necessary for resuscitating reform: a "powerful impulse to the economy" required "dynamism, initiative, new viewpoints, fresh approaches and ideas," all of which, said Yeltsin, had been lacking in the Chernomyrdin government.

By replacing Chernomyrdin with Kiriyenko, Yeltsin seemed to be reminding the world that it had been only under duress from the old Supreme Soviet that he had replaced Gaidar with Chernomyrdin in the first place, back in December 1992: his heart was still with Gaidar's generation—and, more to the point, with Gaidar's reformist agenda. In his predisposition and in his potential, Kiriyenko was far more of a post-Soviet man than Chernomyrdin could ever be.[6]

For just that reason, however, Yeltsin was throwing down a gauntlet to the Duma—in effect daring his opponents there to reject the nomination. To do so, they had to vote against Kiriyenko three times. That would leave Yeltsin with the option of submitting a new candidate or dismissing the Duma and calling new parliamentary elections. Two votes went against Kiriyenko, but after an intense lobbying effort by the Kremlin, he was approved on the third try.

The shake-up cost us both time and a vital channel. The very phrase Gore-Chernomyrdin had become a synonym for our ability to get attention and action from the Russian government on the hard issues. Whether there would be a Gore-Kiriyenko commission, and whether it would serve us as well as its predecessor, were open questions.

ON THE TOUGHEST, most volatile and debilitating issue we faced in mid-1998—"Russia/Iran," as it was by then known in our shorthand—we didn't have time to wait for the answer, not least because the Russians who were abetting and profiting from bad business with Iran still seemed to be riding high. Yevgeny Adamov, the new minister of atomic energy, was proving himself a defiant and aggressive salesman of Russian nuclear technology to the highest bidder. Once he entered office in March 1998, Adamov pressed for the sale of a Russian research reactor as well as cooperation with Iran in the production of nuclear-grade graphite and heavy water, the stuff Iran needed to produce weapons. Providing Iran such materials would violate Chernomyrdin's 1995 agreement with Gore.

Then, only days after Chernomyrdin's ouster, the government of Azerbaijan intercepted a shipment of a special alloy of steel, suitable for rocket fuel tanks and little else, that a Russian front company was trying to smuggle to Iran—a flagrant violation of Russia's catchall decree. When we informed Moscow, the head of the internal security service smugly replied that Russian law-enforcement authorities had arrested a couple of Tajiks in connection with the case. "So it's 'round-up-the-usual-Tajiks' time, eh?" scoffed Sandy Berger.

Word of the Azerbaijani bust and the Russian cover-up leaked into the press and triggered new demands for sanctions from the Congress, where the mood was more poisonous than ever. The new scandal hovering over President Clinton's head in the fall added to the disinclination of Republicans to do the administration any favors on policy toward Russia or anything else, and it left dispirited Democrats who might otherwise have come vigorously to our defense. Chernomyrdin's ouster put another dent in the credibility of our assurances that we were working the problem quietly at a high level, and his replacement by a thirtysomething unknown looked like one more piece of evidence that Russia was in turmoil.

ON APRIL 6, Clinton telephoned Yeltsin, principally to exhort him, yet again, to do something about the Iran situation. The two presidents were due to see each other in five weeks, at the first formally designated G-8 summit in Birmingham, and Clinton wanted to use their meeting to announce progress toward solving the biggest problem between the U.S. and Russia.

The pre-brief for the phone call was more chaotic than usual. Clinton's new chocolate Labrador retriever, Buddy, was barking and bounding around the Oval Office, much to the delight of the president and to the distraction of his advisers. We were having enough trouble fielding Clinton's questions about why Yeltsin had fired Chernomyrdin, what Kiriyenko was like and what the latest reshuffle augured for the Russian presidential election in 2000. Clinton was intrigued when Gore mentioned the role of Yeltsin's daughter as an influential political adviser.

"Mr. President," I said, "I hope that doesn't mean you're thinking about setting up a Chelsea-Tatyana commission."

"That's not the worst idea I've heard from you, Strobe," he said. "Sounds like we need *something*, now that we've lost the Al-Victor thing, and my deal with Yeltsin is a pretty thin reed sometimes."

So we were reminded when the call came through. Yeltsin ponderously read through an extensive set of talking points, slurring his words and ignoring Clinton's occasional interjections. Suddenly Buddy circled round the desk, leapt up to lick Clinton on the ear and sent the telephone clattering to the floor. For an instant, I thought we'd lost the connection and Yeltsin would believe that this time Clinton had hung up on him. Then, as the president barely suppressed his mirth, I hoped the line was dead, since otherwise Yeltsin would think Clinton was laughing at him. We frantically reassembled the apparatus. Yeltsin was still droning on, apparently oblivious of the commotion at the other end.

When Clinton tried again to make his own points on the Iran problem, Yeltsin started going back over his opening spiel, which was mostly an encomium to the brilliance of his new team. Clinton rolled his eyes at Sandy and me, and went back to listening.

I was listening to Yeltsin too and noticed that in addition to heaping praise on Kiriyenko, he singled out Andrei Kokoshin, his new national security adviser. As Bill Perry's counterpart early in the administration, Kokoshin had been one of our better points of contact in the past and was well placed to be useful to us now.

I gave a eureka look to Sandy Berger, then pointed my finger at him in an Uncle-Sam-Wants-You fashion. He looked momentarily puzzled, then nodded: we needed a new channel, and this could be it.

ASSEMBLING A PACKAGE of carrots and sticks for Sandy to take to Moscow took several weeks, since the biggest of the sticks was in the hands of Congress and Sandy had to negotiate with key members an elaborate set of contingencies that he could lay out to Kokoshin. The Senate was scheduled to vote on sanctions the third week in May, a week after the inaugural meeting of the G-8 in Birmingham. If the Russian government put in place a battery of measures to shut down nuclear and missile cooperation with Iran and open up cooperation with the U.S. on nonproliferation, Sandy would pull out the stops in trying to delay the Senate vote or, if necessary, to recommend that the president veto the sanctions bill.7

Sandy, Leon Fuerth, who would represent Gore's interests, and I traveled to Moscow on May 7. As it turned out, Leon and I were largely along for the ride. Sandy and Kokoshin spent most of the two days one-on-one—in Kokoshin's office, in his limousine driving around the city, on a long walk around the grounds of a church in Kokoshin's home neighborhood and in Jim Collins's study at Spaso House.

It seemed at the time to be one of the most productive Russian-American diplomatic encounters in five years. Kokoshin agreed to all the measures Sandy laid out. He and Yumashev canceled their holiday plans for the long upcoming V-E weekend so that they could crack the whip over the bureaucracy.

But Kokoshin believed that the key, as always, was Yeltsin. He had to sign decrees and browbeat or fire recalcitrant ministers. Keeping Yeltsin engaged required constant tending of the relationship by Clinton himself, and that meant in person. Phone calls and letters, as we'd seen all too often, weren't enough; in fact, they could be detrimental if Yeltsin wasn't in what Kokoshin delicately called "the right mood," or if he was under the influence of "people who don't want to see this problem solved." The Birmingham meeting would be helpful, Kokoshin continued, but what was really required was another stand-alone U.S.-Russian summit of the kind the two presidents hadn't had since Helsinki over a year before.

The Russians had been angling for months to get Clinton to come to Moscow in July, but we'd been holding out for Russian ratification of the START II treaty—which had been languishing in the Duma for over six years—as a condition for Clinton's coming to Moscow again. Kokoshin appealed to Sandy for help in getting an acceptance out of the White House. Sandy said we should take presidential meetings one at a time: Birmingham first, then we'd see about a Moscow summit.

CHEMISTRY

Within days after Sandy's return to Washington, we learned that Russian authorities had begun a crackdown on entities doing business with Iran and a campaign to expel various Iranian "businessmen" in Russia. Others in the Yeltsin entourage, however—and Primakov was the leading suspect—tried to goad Yeltsin into going onto the attack in his meeting with Clinton at the Churchill Intercontinental Hotel in Birmingham on Sunday, May 17. They included in his briefing material detailed intelligence reports depicting U.S. initiatives in Central Asia as part of a plan to sow hostility to Russia along its own periphery.

But Yeltsin decided on a soft opening instead. Quite possibly he remembered how angry Clinton had been when Yeltsin sucker-punched him in public over the Middle East in Moscow two years earlier. This time, Yeltsin used the tendentious reports he'd gotten from Primakov and others as examples of the alarming and accusatory things others were saying about American motives, not what he necessarily believed himself.

"You know, Bill, people are starting to criticize us for the weakening of our relationship," Yeltsin said. "I've been under fire for this, and so have you. I don't think you agree with this characterization, and I assure you I don't either. I hope that you're going to join me in pushing back against the idea that there are deep and irreconcilable tensions in our relations."

I'd seen Yeltsin sometimes manic, sometimes maudlin when pleading with Clinton to tend more to their personal relationship. This time he was neither. It was, in both senses of the word, his most sober performance to date.

When Clinton complimented him on putting together a new government of "fine young people," Yeltsin took it as a disguised question about why he'd fired Chernomyrdin. Knowing how much we valued his former prime minister, he seemed a bit defensive. Chernomyrdin "was always good about seeking my advice and he's a decent person," he said, but "it sometimes happens in the history of a society that the people get tired of this or that official, and you've got to change things, start from scratch, in order to restore momentum." Yeltsin boasted that he had "treated Chernomyrdin very well. I've let him keep his salary, his dacha, his car, his bodyguard. All the perks that he had as prime minister he has today as a pensioner. In this respect I've put in place a radical change from the way we used to do things. It used to be when a top-level person resigned, he became a non-person overnight and everyone was kicking him in the shins. I know your own procedure for dealing with former political leaders is more civilized, but in the case of Chernomyrdin, I think we've gone you one better."

Yeltsin added that he'd ordered Kiriyenko "to take the baton in the Gore-Chernomyrdin commission and hold on to it firmly," but he wanted it understood that where the big questions of U.S.-Russian relations were concerned, the only channel that really mattered was the presidential one. The perception of deterioration had come about in part, he said, because it had been a long time since he and Clinton had met for a stand-alone summit: "Sure, we met in Helsinki, in Paris, in Denver last year. But that's not the same thing as a real official visit. We're looking forward to your making a proper visit in July."

Knowing of the condition we'd imposed, he promised that ratification for START II would proceed "full speed ahead," despite lingering parliamentary opposition.

Yeltsin's mention of his problems with the Duma gave Clinton the opening he was looking for to do our principal piece of business. "We're making progress on nonproliferation of weapons of mass destruction and Iran," he said, "but I'm worried about a vote coming up in our Senate. I think we've got some good channels going—the vice-president and Kiriyenko, Madeleine and Primakov, Sandy and Kokoshin. I've got high confidence in these folks, and they're doing a good job. But they've got to know, and we've got to keep reminding them, that you and I are personally committed to this and making it work and not letting it slip backward. There have been some problems with implementation, as you know, so you've got to send a clear signal that implementation has got your total support."

"Absolutely," said Yeltsin. "I'll do that."

"Otherwise," Clinton persisted, "we'll get a bad vote in the Senate that will infuriate your Duma, and we'll have a vicious cycle going."

It was as close as Clinton came to admitting that Congress was within a hair's breadth of mandating sanctions. Knowing what a hot button the threat of sanctions was for Yeltsin, I half expected him to blow up. Instead, he seemed all the more eager to reassure Clinton that the two of them would find a way to reverse the dynamic that was developing between the two parliaments.

"As a friend and as someone who has worked closely with you," Yeltsin replied, "I assure you that I'm absolutely intent on doing everything in my power for full implementation of all the agreements we've made and not to depart from them or slip backward from them. You're right that we've got a lot of problems to grapple with in this area, but we've also made a lot of headway in a short period of time."

"We have, Boris, but we've got to keep it up. The coming week is going to be especially important. So let's have as much positive activity as possible."

"Okay," said Yeltsin.

Yeltsin seemed ready to end the meeting, which was fine with me since I figured we'd gotten as much as we possibly could.

"I've got a lot of other things that my people have prepared me to talk about. Why don't I just give you these?" Yeltsin said, handing over his printed note cards, which Clinton passed to me and I pocketed with pleasure: it would be analytically useful, and perhaps even fun, to compare his talking points as prepared by his staff with what actually came out of his mouth.

"Okay," said Clinton, "here are ours." Mamedov's eyes lit up.

Clinton decided to make the most of this sudden conviviality.

"You know, Boris, we really are working with the stuff of history here. I'm convinced that twenty years from now, when the Russian economy is booming, people will look back and say we were right; we did the right things. I just hope you get all the credit you deserve while you're still around, because you've done a terrific job of leading your country during one of the two or three most important moments in Russian history."

Clinton's effusion evoked one from Yeltsin: "You and I have an excellent relationship, Bill—more than just a friendship. It's what I would call co-leadership. We've had the fundamental convictions, the courage and the stamina to abandon old stereotypes as well as moving forward with big, big agreements." The work they'd started together, he said, was "truly a task for the next millennium! We'll be in retirement when this comes to fruition. Maybe we'll set up a club or a foundation of former heads of state. I don't think either of us wants to spend his retirement planting potatoes in the garden."

Clinton talked about his own plans for life after the presidency and how he hoped the two of them would get in some hunting together. Picking up on this new and happy theme, Yeltsin bragged about his goose hunting ("a real test of skill—getting START II ratified is nothing compared to that!") and put on a one-man skit about a close encounter he'd had with a bear that ended with a bullet through the beast's heart at twenty meters.

Turning serious again, Yeltsin returned to the appeal he'd made at the beginning of the meeting: "You know, Bill, people keep saying that we're losing confidence in each other, that our partnership is running aground. Let's make sure they know we're doing fine. With the policy you've pursued toward Russia these past five years, you really can't lose, and in the time remaining to you in office you can score more points. As for me, I'm criticized for tilting too much toward you. They keep calling me a Westernizer, and they don't mean it as a compliment."

"Time will bear you out," said Clinton.

"Yes, it will! The two of us have set out together to build an alliance based on full confidence in each other. I don't doubt your good faith and you don't doubt mine."

"That kind of mutual trust and confidence makes all the difference. Personal chemistry really matters."

As they were getting up to leave, Yeltsin reached out, pulled Clinton toward him and gave him a long hug.

———

IMMEDIATELY AFTER the summit, I met Mamedov at an Italian restaurant in London to review where we stood and to plan the next steps. He confirmed that Yeltsin had given strict instructions to Kiriyenko, Primakov and the defense minister, Igor Sergeyev, to put on a full-court press with the Duma and get the START II treaty ratified early in June so that planning could go ahead for a Clinton visit in July.[8] But we shouldn't hold our breath: Yeltsin's opponents in the Duma were still smarting over having had Kiriyenko forced on them and were less likely than ever to do Yeltsin's bidding. By linking the summit to START II, Mamedov said, the U.S. was giving the Duma an additional incentive to delay ratification yet again, since by continuing to hold the treaty hostage, they could block the summit. Therefore, he said, "the clever and farsighted thing to do would be to take a deep breath and de-link."

I told Yuri that I would be prepared to argue for a Clinton trip to Moscow, but only if we had a real breakthrough on Iran in the coming days. He thought it could be done. The report he would prepare on the presidential exchange in Birmingham would enable Kokoshin to deliver on the promises he had made to Sandy. However, he added, it would help if Clinton would veto the sanctions bill, since that would demonstrate "symmetry" in the American and Russian presidents' willingness to stand up to hard-liners at home.

WHEN I RETURNED to Washington, I found neither much enthusiasm for Clinton's going to Moscow nor much surprise that I was yet again advocating a trip.

Vetoing the sanctions bill was an easier sell within the administration, since the president himself, on the basis of his conversation with Yeltsin in Birmingham, and Sandy, on the basis of his work with Kokoshin, were convinced that sanctions would ruin whatever chance there was that the Russians would make good on their commitments.

On May 21, Clinton and Gore invited a group of senators to the briefing in the Cabinet Room.[9] Clinton said he'd found Yeltsin in Birmingham "clearer of mind, stronger of body and more resolute than in a long time." Gore added that the new Russian government headed by Kiriyenko was more compatible with our interests than any we'd had since 1992. We'd be putting the reformers in Moscow in jeopardy if we imposed sanctions. Sandy and Madeleine argued that having the legislation pending, as a sword of Damocles over the Russians' heads, was helpful to our policy, but passing it into law would be harmful.

The senators were noncommittal. They were all under pressures of their own. The bill had everything going for it politically: its proponents depicted it as a way of saving Israel from its worst enemy, Iran; of thwarting proliferation and of sending a clear message that the U.S. was no longer going to coddle Russia. It was also an opportunity for the more partisan Republicans to add to Clinton's troubles.

The next day, the Senate passed the bill by a vote of 90–4, and the House quickly followed by a comparably lopsided margin. On June 23, President Clinton cast his veto, and the administration launched a major effort to sustain it. The Russian government moved with impressive if long-overdue alacrity to implement the plan on which Sandy Berger and Andrei Kokoshin had agreed. The Russians had finally put in place new controls, tightened existing ones and, in a dozen or so cases we'd brought to their attention, cracked down on the offenders.

Now, at least, the Russian authorities were whacking away at the moles themselves. But for them, too, the problem persisted. Several Russian companies and institutes, in defiance of the new Kremlin-ordered measures, maintained their contacts with Iran. Therefore we had little choice: either we imposed sanctions of our own or the Senate would override the president's veto and the more draconian sanctions bill would become law.

After a hectic round of horse-trading with the Congress and negotiations with Kokoshin, Sandy came up with a carefully choreographed compromise: the Russian government would announce that it was conducting a special investigation into the activities of the companies believed to have violated Russian export controls, and the U.S. would simultaneously announce that, "consistent with Russian actions and with our own assessment," we were imposing "trade restrictions"—a euphemism for the s-word—on the offending entities. That way we preserved the appearance of cooperative rather than punitive action, and the Senate was sufficiently mollified to hold off on a vote on overriding the veto.

Now that we had a plausible method for solving the Russia/Iran problem, I found it easier to argue for de-linking a Moscow summit from START II ratification. It was too late to schedule a presidential trip in July as the Russians had originally wanted. But just after the Independence Day weekend, the White House announced that Clinton would go to Moscow at the beginning of September.

CHAPTER 11

JUST SHOWING UP

Any idiot can face a crisis; it is this day-to-day living that wears you out.
Anton Chekhov

FOR SIX YEARS, we'd worried that Russia would come a cropper because of some combination of the systemic weaknesses of the political culture and the personal weaknesses of the top man in the Kremlin. But the heaviest blow to Russian reform, when it landed in August 1998, had its origins four thousand miles from Moscow and a year earlier, when the value of the Thai baht tumbled by 50 percent.

Within months of that initial shock, emerging markets around the world were feeling the effects of what quickly became the Asian financial crisis. Russia was especially at risk because of its dependence on energy exports and the fall in the price of oil. The Russian government had been financing its budget deficit with international loans, which began to dry up, and with government-issued securities comparable to U.S. Treasury bills, which plummeted in value. Russian banks, heavily invested in these securities, began selling off their dollars.

When President Clinton was briefed on the looming disaster in June, he was struck by the irony of it all. One of his principal reasons for being an optimist about Russia was that the country had finally thrown in its lot with the rest of the world. During the spring he had heard Larry Summers, who had regarded Victor Chernomyrdin as a hopeless throwback, express guarded optimism about the economic policies of the Kiriyenko government. Boris Nemtsov, Boris Fyodorov and Anatoly Chubais seemed committed to imposing a degree of order and equity on the process of privatization. They had set up a Securities and Exchange Commission and started to revamp the country's banking sector, capital markets and tax code, all with an eye to integrating Russia's economy into the global one.

Yet precisely because it had come out of its Soviet bunker, Russia was now in the path of the storm.

"If this thing gets worse," said Clinton on July 8, "it'll be bad for the world in security terms as well as economic terms. That's why we've got to be ready to put money in there if they take the steps we're telling them to." We were, he said, "at a fulcrum moment."

Two days later, Yeltsin phoned and, in a tone of urgency we'd never heard before, pleaded with the U.S. to intervene with the International Monetary Fund for another transfusion of emergency loans. "Otherwise," he said, "it will mean the end of reform and basically the end of Russia."

In mid-July, Russia agreed to cut its budget deficit in half (from 5.6 percent of gross domestic product to 2.8 percent) in exchange for an IMF loan of $11.2 billion. To meet its end of the bargain, the Russian government had to cut spending, increase taxes and actually collect those taxes. All three measures were hard—the third perhaps the hardest, because there was neither a tradition of paying taxes nor a mechanism for collecting them—but they were essential. The government had to instill a measure of public and international confidence to show it was coming to grips with the crisis. The Asian contagion, while unquestionably a cause of the problem, would be useless as an alibi if the Russian government failed to come up with a solution.

It quickly became apparent that the Kiriyenko government was simply not up to the challenge. Part of the problem was the young prime minister's own lack of seasoning and political heft. He and his ministers fumbled around among themselves and ran into numerous roadblocks in the Duma in their efforts to cut spending and institute a reliable way to collect taxes. With no hope of meeting the IMF targets, Russia was unable to roll over its Treasury bills, and investor confidence continued to plummet.

At the end of July, Vice-President Gore took David Lipton of the Treasury Department to Moscow to warn the Russians that they weren't meeting the conditions for the money they'd already gotten, much less for any new help. Three weeks later, Lipton returned to Moscow with an even bleaker assessment: The well had run dry. It was pointless for the IMF to pour more money into Russia, since it would flow right back out again with the rest of the capital and international reserves that were fleeing an economy in which investors had lost all confidence.

ON FRIDAY, AUGUST 14, there was a run on several banks. Until then, the crisis had been felt mostly by Russia's small financial elite. Now the Russian public was both affected by the problem and contributing to it. Belatedly, the government saw the need for drastic action.

The following Monday, the government devalued the ruble while at the same time holding back on payment of its bonds and freezing transactions between Russian and foreign banks. Devaluation was deemed necessary because the government couldn't sustain the exchange rate, while the other two measures were intended to limit the extent of devaluation and staunch the flow of reserves out of the country. The result, however, was a deepening of the crisis. With the Russian government in effect in default, capital outflow surged, and the bottom fell out of the banking sector virtually overnight.

The president of Russia was nowhere to be seen while his country seemed to be hurtling off the edge of a cliff. His staff acknowledged that he wasn't even in the Kremlin—he was off somewhere, they said, "working with documents." Reports circulated that he had stopped taking his medication for high blood pressure because someone had told him that alcohol was just as effective. Various cabals were rumored to be maneuvering to take power.

THE MELTDOWN of the Russian economy would have been bigger news that Monday if it didn't have to compete with a spectacular and sordid story breaking in Washington. After seven months of denials, Clinton went on television and confessed that he had indeed had a "relationship" with Monica Lewinsky.

I couldn't watch. I went for a long and miserable jog through the sticky dog-days air. When I got back to the house, Brooke gave me a mercifully brief but still almost unbearable summary. It made me heartsick to contemplate the pain and embarrassment Clinton had brought upon himself, his family and the country.

There were immediate calls for his resignation or, if he refused to step down, his impeachment.

The ensuing political mayhem took a heavy toll on the government and the nation. Policymaking suffered as institutions were diverted from nobler or at least more normal business, and officials were distracted and discouraged in the conduct of their duties. Partisanship reached new levels of rancor. Much of what we wanted to do in foreign policy depended on a degree of cooperation from Congress. That had been hard enough to attain since the Republican resurgence after the 1994 elections, and it became harder than ever now that those who opposed the president, his administration and his party had a sensational issue. The media, which had been paying alarmingly little attention to world affairs for years, now had a giant reason to pay even less. That too was bad for foreign policy and for good governance in general.

Still, the scandal and the uproar it caused seemed to have little effect on Clinton's standing abroad. Foreign leaders and publics alike tended to shake their heads at the whole frenzy and hope that it would subside.

SINCE I COULD NEITHER fathom the private behavior of Clinton as my friend nor mitigate the public consequences for him as my boss, I tried my best simply to concentrate on my job.

From what I could see, that seemed to be the president's way of dealing with the scandal as well. The day after his confession, I participated in a meeting in the Oval Office about U.S. retaliation against the Saudi renegade and terrorist Osama bin Laden, who had been behind the bombing of our embassies in Nairobi and Dar es Salaam on August 7. Clinton showed no signs of the distraction, to say nothing of the despair, that most of us in the room were barely suppressing. He was focused on the topic at hand, asking good questions and formulating sharp decisions. Within forty-eight hours, the U.S. launched over eighty cruise missiles at targets we believed to be associated with bin Laden in Afghanistan and Sudan.

There was considerable international criticism of what was widely seen as the latest instance of the American penchant for unilateral action—motivated, it was now widely suspected, by the president's desire to change the subject. One of the loudest and most intemperate voices was Boris Yeltsin's. Emerging from seclusion, he denounced the air strikes as underhanded, dishonest, outrageous and deplorable.

He, too, was widely suspected of wanting to shift attention from his own problems.

WHEN YELTSIN finally did address the crisis racking his country, on Sunday, August 23, it was with an announcement that he was firing Kiriyenko and Nemtsov.

Remaining at their posts were the so-called power ministers: Yevgeny Primakov as foreign minister; Igor Sergeyev as defense minister; Sergei Stepashin, who had staged a comeback since being dismissed over Chechnya in June 1995, as interior minister; and a relatively recent arrival on the Moscow scene, Vladimir Putin, the former deputy mayor of St. Petersburg, as head of the Federal Security Service (FSB), the domestic offshoot of his alma mater, the KGB.

The downfall of the economic reformers, while saddening, was nonetheless politically understandable, especially since their remedy of devaluation and default appeared to have been worse than the disease. What was nearly incomprehensible was Yeltsin's announcement that he was bringing Chernomyrdin back as prime minister. Politically, it made no sense. Yeltsin's opponents in the Duma had just barely confirmed Kiriyenko earlier in the year, and they were unlikely to oblige Yeltsin again with Chernomyrdin, who suffered the double jeopardy of having been both a longtime Yeltsin lieutenant and more recently a Yeltsin discard.

Rumors about why Yeltsin replayed the Chernomyrdin card at this juncture were rampant, contradictory and inconclusive. Many in Moscow, including ousted officials like Nemtsov, believed that the idea came from Russia's notorious and flamboyant oligarch Boris Berezovsky, who wanted Chernomyrdin in place to protect his own commercial interests. Yeltsin himself later attributed the move to Valentin Yumashev and other members of his inner circle.[1]

My own theory was that in grasping for straws, Yeltsin was hoping to re-create the Gore-Chernomyrdin connection as one of his lifelines to the outside world.

A SCOUTING EXPEDITION

Clinton was due in Moscow on September 1, barely two weeks after the Russian economy went into what was universally described as collapse. The Russian government was out on its ear. Yeltsin, having just thrown an anti-American tantrum, might be facing a coup d'état. Never had there been so many reasons to cancel a presidential trip. Nevertheless, at any other point in the administration, Clinton's instinct would have been to take the risks and apply his own political weight to the fulcrum.

But the latest crisis in Russia coincided with the worst moment of Clinton's presidency. His political advisers were unanimous in recommending that he stay home and face the music on the Lewinsky affair. For him to take any foreign trip around Labor Day, just before Congress came back in session, would look as though he had jumped at an excuse to get out of town. To be meeting with Yeltsin was even worse. Editorial cartoonists would have a field day: two mortally wounded presidents, clinging to each other in one last bear hug while two bands of hunters took aim from the Congress and the Duma.

Clinton, who was on Martha's Vineyard for what I'm sure was the least restful vacation of his life, asked Sandy Berger, who was with him, if there was any way he could get out of going to Moscow. Sandy believed the answer was no. For the president to cancel could be the coup de grâce for Yeltsin. The president provisionally accepted the judgment, but asked Sandy to talk to me about how to keep his options open.

I WANTED TO RECONNOITER the scene in Moscow before the president committed himself to going. On Wednesday, August 26, I set off with Phil Goldberg, who had taken Eric Edelman's place as my executive assistant.[2] Phil and I would have normally made the trip alone, but for the first time in my many official trips to Russia the State Department's Bureau of Diplomatic Security judged the situation in Moscow to be sufficiently unsettled for me to require a bodyguard.

We connected in London to British Airways, and the in-flight entertainment on that leg included a BBC interview with Vladimir Lukin, the head of the Duma's Foreign Affairs Committee, who predicted that within two months Russia would be in total bankruptcy, which would trigger a social explosion and a political upheaval.

When we arrived in Moscow, it was unseasonably cold, and angry clouds were spitting rain. During the ride from the airport, Jim Collins filled me in on the latest rumors: Yeltsin was about to resign; Yeltsin had already resigned; there were several coups in the works; a coup had already taken place—it just hadn't been announced yet. Most of these Jim dismissed outright. Jim took me to the bug-proof vault in the embassy, known to the staff as the submarine, to review the latest that we did know about what was going on. As we were leaving to meet Yuri Mamedov at Spaso House for the traditional pizza, Jim and I passed through a checkpoint where a Marine guard was just hanging up the phone.

"Mr. Ambassador," he said, "I don't know if you've heard the news, but President Yeltsin is dead."

"And where is *that* intelligence from, Corporal?" demanded Jim. The guard had gotten it from another Marine who just heard it on the radio.

"Thanks," said Jim, "now please *don't* pass it on."

"WE NEED YOUR president here," said Yuri when we met him at Spaso. "We need him not because everything's normal but precisely because it's not. Emergencies are times for leadership." Any impression that the U.S. was backing off or hedging its bets could doom Yeltsin and open the way to political forces that had never wanted Russia to open up to the outside world and that would use the financial crisis as an excuse to turn back the clock.

The next morning Andrei Kokoshin took me on a forty-minute drive into the countryside to a sanatorium for members of the military elite. Kokoshin, whose father and grandfather had been Soviet officers, occasionally went there for rest cures. For over an hour Andrei and I walked around the grounds in the rain and bitter cold while his bodyguards along with my own trailed twenty or thirty yards behind us. He, like Mamedov, depicted Clinton's coming to Moscow as a make-or-break factor in averting a political catastrophe. Why, I asked skeptically, did he think Clinton could do any good?

Kokoshin stopped in his tracks, grabbed me by the shoulders and pulled himself to within two inches of my face: "Because, Strobe, if he doesn't, it will look to people here that you've given up on us! If your president comes it will reassure the international financial community, and it will energize Yeltsin"—itself an admission that Yeltsin must be in pretty bad shape.

When I got back to my hotel after midnight, I called Sandy, who told me that reports of Yeltsin's death were swirling. They appeared to be exaggerated, I said. In any event, Sandy continued, our president was worried that in the immediate aftermath of his visit Yeltsin would resign or be ousted. We faced a go/no-go decision within the next twenty-four hours. He instructed me to prepare the Russians for the likelihood of a cancellation. I said I'd do so, but with the proviso that I might still recommend that the president come, depending on what I determined the next day.

"Okay," said Sandy, "but you're under instructions to scare the crap out of them."

"You mean I get to administer a little shock therapy?"

"As long as it's more shock than therapy."

ON FRIDAY MORNING, August 28, Jim Collins and I went to see Kokoshin in his office and ruined his day. He welcomed me with the news that he'd seen Chernomyrdin the night before and received a guarantee that Yeltsin was not going to resign. "Everything's okay," he said. "Your president will have a good summit."

Chernomyrdin's assurances weren't good enough, I said. I would probably recommend cancellation. The danger was just too great that Clinton's visit would end up being a farewell call on Yeltsin, who would step down in favor of Chernomyrdin or someone else immediately afterward. That wasn't a role I wanted my president to play in the drama of Russian politics—especially, I felt (though did not say), given what was under way in American politics. I wasn't going to change my mind, I said, unless Yeltsin himself looked me in the eye and convinced me he intended to remain in office.

I went from Kokoshin's office to the Foreign Ministry and was in the middle of making the same pitch to Primakov when a call came through asking me to come to the Kremlin right away.

I FOUND YELTSIN looking surprisingly robust. Even before we'd settled in our seats he said sternly, "You know, it seems to me that our relationship has been stumbling a little bit of late"—as though that was the problem of the hour. His message was simple: if the summit went ahead, the two leaders would be able to steady the relationship; if Clinton canceled, everything they had accomplished was in jeopardy. He went on at great length with a variation on what he had said to Clinton in Birmingham: the two leaders had great work to do, work that would determine the shape of the twenty-first century.

I was more interested in what was going to happen in the coming days, but I felt I should be polite about it. "Very much in that context, Mr. President," I said, "President Clinton has asked me to convey to him your opinion about the political future of your country and about your personal intentions."

Yeltsin apparently thought I was probing for a hint about what he would do if Chernomyrdin's nomination failed with the Duma. He started to filibuster about what a frank and productive conversation he'd have with Clinton. His foreign-policy aide Sergei Yastrzhembsky helped me out: "Strobe's question was delicately put. What he's referring to, I'm sure, is the wave of rumors in the American press . . ."

"And in the Russian press," I interjected.

". . . rumors that you're going to resign in the near future."

Yeltsin leaned forward and slammed his fist on the table. "Look, Mr. Talbott, first of all, I'm absolutely healthy—especially now. Just look at me! Shake my hand again"—he thrust it at me. "My grip is firm in more ways than one. Second, there are always those who try to pour oil onto the fire, both in your country and in ours. Someone sees an opportunity to profit from these rumors. I swear to you, both as a man and as the president of Russia, that, without any doubt or condition, I will persevere and stay in office not just for now but all the way until the next elections. I will continue to work."

That was all I needed to hear to recommend that Clinton come. But it wasn't all Yeltsin wanted to say.

"At the same time," he continued, "I can tell you and I'll tell my friend Bill that I will not run as a candidate for another term, even though many groups and individuals keep asking me to run"—an astonishing statement that bespoke both his own disconnection from reality and the sycophancy of the people he was listening to.

"I'm serving my second term under this constitution, and I will pass Russia into the hands of another president," he went on. "Then Russia will be calm; we'll continue to develop with the United States good relations. Together we will reduce and destroy strategic weapons. I want the next two presidents of our two countries to be friends. I want the peoples of the two countries to be on friendly terms when I leave office. I want them to stand by each other and to struggle jointly against mutual threats. History has never seen such a mature and widely developed spectrum of relations between our two nations." I could assure my president, he said, that the summit would come off "without any rough spots—no disruptions, no rallies, no protests, no placards; it will be an honorable and dignified event for both presidents."

I CALLED Madeleine Albright and Sandy Berger from the U.S. embassy and said we should recommend to the president that he come. They said they would join me, but more because of the damage it would do if he did not make the trip than for any purpose to be served in his coming.

A few hours later, through the wizardry of the White House Situation Room, a secure conference call linked the president in Martha's Vineyard with the vice-president, Sandy, Madeleine, Leon Fuerth, Larry Summers and several others. I was the lone voice from Moscow, although Jim Collins and Phil Goldberg stood next to me in the embassy's vault, listening as best they could to the strange noises coming through my earpiece. Because of the scrambling of the signal to thwart anyone from being able to tap into the call, everyone on the other end sounded like Donald Duck.

I began my presentation with some corrective on-the-scene reporting. The city where I'd spent the last two days bore only slight resemblance to the one they were watching on CNN. Muscovites were not storming banks, ripping out ATM machines, hoarding food and demonstrating against the government. The country was in a crisis, but not a panic—the situation was dangerous but not hopeless. As for Yeltsin, he was down but not out. Having just seen him, I could report he was in relatively good shape, a B+ or even an A− as long we graded on a curve. He had categorically assured me that he was not about to resign.

Larry Summers, who had been making calls to his own contacts in Moscow, reported that the reformers were utterly dejected, not just about the financial crisis but about the prospect of Chernomyrdin or someone from their standpoint even worse becoming prime minister.

Sandy canvassed the group on whether the president should make the trip. I led off with my view that the risks of not coming outweighed those of coming. Gore said that if the president pulled out of the trip, it would be an admission of defeat for our whole Russia policy—"red meat" to those who were chanting the accusing question "Who lost Russia?"

"I don't think it's close," said Clinton, "I think I've got to go."

A SOUNDING BOARD

After boarding Air Force One the afternoon of Monday, August 31, I took my seat next to Larry Summers. He seemed glum, but he was also feeling compassionate. He put his hand on my arm and said he genuinely felt sorry for me. I must be "fighting back despair," he said. "All of us have invested a lot in this country and this policy, but what's happening must be especially hard on you, Strobe."

The moment was both moving and revealing. Larry and I were committed to the same objective: helping Russia stay on course toward becoming a modern, prosperous, democratic state integrated into the global economy. Since we'd started working together in the preparations for the Vancouver and Tokyo summits in 1993, there had been a division of labor between us but no division over goals. I concentrated on diplomacy and security issues, while Larry and David Lipton tried to bring American resources, advice and influence to bear on the development of the Russian economy. They had a harder job than I did. Theirs concerned Russia's internal evolution. Mine dealt more with its external behavior. It was much more difficult to get the Russians to adopt the legal and regulatory structures necessary to attract and retain investment than it was to get Russia to stop selling rocket engine parts to India or even to cooperate with an expanding NATO. In the final analysis, Russia didn't ultimately have a say over whether Poland joined NATO. Conversely, however, the U.S. didn't have much influence over whether the Duma passed a new property or tax law.

Moreover, I was more fortunate than Larry in my Russian interlocutors, and one in particular. As we—and virtually all of our predecessors—had seen, government-to-government relations often succeeded or failed on the basis of personal relations at the presidential and cabinet level, and also at the so-called working level that Larry and I inhabited. The interaction between Clinton and Yeltsin made it possible to reconcile NATO enlargement with NATO-Russian partnership in 1997; the one between Gore and Chernomyrdin allowed us to achieve a breakthrough in January 1998 on catchall export controls. One thing that kept me going through serial crises and setbacks was Yuri Mamedov's willingness and ability to work even the toughest problem through to a solution, to instill with practical meaning the word "partnership" even when it fell out of fashion as a slogan. His role had been a constant in the equations of U.S.-Russian diplomacy going back to his relationship with Dennis Ross in the Bush administration.

There was, quite simply, no economic equivalent of Mamedov in the Russian government. Larry had his own contacts among the Russian reformers—Gaidar, Nemtsov, Chubais, Fyodorov—but they were variables, since Yeltsin or his prime minister kept firing them. Larry had been at his most optimistic when Gaidar and Fyodorov were riding high in 1993. His discouragement reflected theirs when Chernomyrdin tacked toward statist policies after the December 1993 elections. The reformers' comeback under Kiriyenko in early 1998 had given Larry fresh reason to think that Russia might climb back on the wagon of fiscal and monetary discipline. That's why he regarded the crash of the Kiriyenko government and the prospective return of Chernomyrdin as the death knell of Russian economic reform, while I regarded it as another bump in a long road that stretched as far as the eye could see.

ONCE WE WERE AIRBORNE, Larry and I joined Sandy Berger to brief Clinton in the presidential cabin. There was no hint of any lingering doubt on the president's part about whether he should be making the trip. He was applying himself as much as I'd ever seen to the task of understanding what Yeltsin was thinking and dealing with. His starting point was that Yeltsin was still Russia's best hope, and ours, too, because he was the only figure on the scene who combined real power with a "gut conviction that democracy and freedom are the way to go."

More than ever, and for obvious reasons, Clinton identified with Yeltsin's stubbornness, resilience and defiance in the face of adversity and antagonism. He admired Yeltsin, he said, for his ability to "stand up to the bastards who are trying to bring him down."

"The thing about Yeltsin I really like," said Clinton, "is that he's not a Russian bureaucrat. He's an Irish poet. He sees politics as a novel he's writing or a symphony he's composing. That's one of the things that draws me to him. It's why he's better than the others. But it's also his shortcoming. I've got to convince him that for the next two years, he's got to come to work every day and be a bureaucrat and make the government work."

Here, too, in one of his few criticisms of Yeltsin, I heard an echo of the advice that Clinton must have been giving himself about how to handle the mess he'd made of his own public and private life: I've got to get up every day, go to work, just keep working away, doing the people's business, and maybe they'll let me stay in office.

Clinton recognized, as he often said, that Yeltsin had a harder job than he did—and for a reason related to why Larry Summers had a harder job than mine. Making the Russian government work meant, above all, bringing the economy under control in a way that permitted international help, in the form of both assistance and investment.

We spent about an hour and a half talking about the economic agenda of the talks in Moscow. Larry was concerned that the president, in his eagerness to help Yeltsin, would respond favorably to Russian appeals for more IMF help. Without sweeping structural reforms, he warned, we'd be throwing money away and doing neither Russia nor ourselves any favors.

Clinton told Larry not to worry. He knew from American experience, he said, how important it was to keep inflation and government spending

down despite the political temptation to print money and subsidize factories and mines. That, said Clinton, was the "tough-love stuff," and he assured Larry he would administer it to Yeltsin.

But he still wanted to give the Russians some hope that "if they bite all
these bullets we keep telling them to chew," there would be vast amounts
of international support. Six years earlier, he'd criticized George Bush for
not putting enough "real money" into Russia, and now he was critical of
what had happened during his own administration. What the IMF had
done to date was, he said, "a 40-watt bulb in a damned big darkness. We're
giving them a big, tough reform message, but there ain't no dessert on the
menu we're showing them—hell, I'm not sure they can even see the main
course. They've got to know that there's something worth waiting for after
all this hardship. If they don't, they'll do what people do when they've got
the vote: they'll throw the bums out. That's just Politics 101.

"If we lose Russia," he added—it was the first time I'd ever heard him
use that construct even in the conditional mode—"it will be because we've
neglected the politics of it. And if we do that, we'll be doing ourselves terrible, terrible damage as well. You just can't underestimate the impact on
our own economy and national security and on the global economy if
Russia goes south."

That danger was much on the president's mind that day, since the U.S.
stock market had just plummeted 500 points, in part, according to the instant analysis, because of the Russian crash.

I mentioned that I had been reading James Chace's recently published
biography of Dean Acheson, which Clinton (naturally) had already read.
That got us talking about the Marshall Plan as a model for what the West
might do for Russia.[3]

Larry didn't dispute that our stake in Russia's eventual success over the
long run justified a vast investment in the near term, and Clinton didn't
dispute that Russia needed to reform its economy to attract Western investment and make use of Western largesse. "I'm all for a Marshall Plan for
the Russians," said Clinton, "but not unless they take the steps Larry is
talking about to allow the money to help."

In the final analysis, it wasn't up to us to reconcile the tensions between
these two sets of considerations—it was up to Russia itself. That meant
there had to be a functioning Russian government, and, as we were about
to see firsthand, there was none.

———

WHEN AIR FORCE ONE landed at Vnukovo Airport, Victor Chernomyrdin was at the bottom of the stairs to greet the president and drive him into town. It was a bizarre bit of protocol. Chernomyrdin was, at that point, just a member of the Duma. His nomination for the prime ministership had already been rejected once and faced a second vote in several days. Three strikes and he would be out.

I wedged myself onto the jump seat in the limousine and listened, fascinated but slightly appalled, as Chernomyrdin used the half-hour ride to lobby the president to support his nomination with Yeltsin, who was rumored to be giving up on him.

Clinton was fascinated, period. Here was Russian politics in the raw, the sort of rough-and-tumble that had captured his imagination and sparked his attraction to Yeltsin back in December 1992, when he was following Yeltsin's first showdown with the Soviet-era parliament.

While Chernomyrdin was drawing a breath, Clinton made a stab at delivering the stern economic message. Larry, who was riding several cars behind us, would have been not just relieved but pleased at how hard the president hammered the need for reform. Chernomyrdin's response was perfunctory and predictable: He pleaded for leniency from the IMF. Otherwise, the communists would ride popular discontent back into power. Chernomyrdin had been negotiating with the communists for their support, but they had just come out against his nomination. Nonetheless, he was convinced that he could be confirmed if Yeltsin would just stick with him—and that's what he wanted to talk to Clinton about for the remainder of the ride.

WHEN CLINTON MET with Yeltsin at the Kremlin, he was careful to stay in a sympathetic listening mode and to avoid anything that could be construed as political advice. What he heard made it seem that Chernomyrdin was a goner. Yeltsin confided that he was thinking about two other "serious personalities," whom he left unnamed. Members of Yeltsin's entourage told us the choice was down to General Lebed, now the governor of Krasnoyarsk Province in Siberia, and Mayor Yuri Luzhkov of Moscow.

Neither option looked good from our vantage. While I'd found Lebed sensible and farsighted in the one conversation I'd had with him in which he'd actually had something to say—during his visit to Washington during the fall of 1996—the fact remained that he was a general who had come into the political spotlight as the commander of the Russian forces who had stayed on in Moldova after the dissolution of the USSR. His appointment as prime minister would terrify Russia's neighbors. Luzhkov was the Russian version of a Boss Tweed–type pol. More than any other prominent figure he had cultivated close personal and business connections with kingpins in Russian crime syndicates. Also, in a bid for the support of the ultranationalists, he had made provocative statements about Russian rights and claims in the Baltics and the Crimea.

There had been rumors earlier about Primakov being a candidate too, but his name seemed now to have fallen off the list—to Primakov's own apparent relief. When Madeleine took him aside, Primakov said he was weary in his present job as foreign minister, and the prospect of a "truly impossible" one was not in the least appealing. His wife, who was his "best doctor," felt it would be terrible for his health. He seemed to mean it.

As this strangest of all summits continued, there were signs that Yeltsin was a long way from making up his mind. When he sat next to Hillary Clinton during the state dinner in Saint Catherine's Hall at the Kremlin, he mused about his dilemma in a way that suggested to her that he might stick with Chernomyrdin after all.

The next day, when Yeltsin met privately again with Clinton, he seemed to be leaning in that direction. If the Duma refused to confirm the nomination, Yeltsin would have the constitutional prerogative of disbanding the parliament and calling for new elections. That would plunge Russia into a political crisis on top of the economic one it already faced. Yeltsin seemed ready for that, even to welcome it. He could use his presidential powers, he said, to "wreck the Communist Party once and for all." The communists "have committed plenty of sins in the past. I could make a list of those sins and take it to the Ministry of Justice and prosecute them." Clasping his hands and gritting his teeth, he added, "I could really put the squeeze on them."

Clinton headed home unsure about what Yeltsin would do—and suspecting that Yeltsin had still not made up his own mind.

"I get the feeling the guy is trying out different scenarios from one hour to the next," he told Sandy Berger and me, "and I'm just his latest sounding board."

Clinton was content to have played that role. "Maybe I did some good by just showing up. At least I didn't do any harm—which with these ol' boys can sometimes be a trick all by itself."

DIALOGUE OF THE DEAF

On September 7, the Duma rejected Chernomyrdin for a second time. Yeltsin wrestled with his dilemma for three days, then announced that he had chosen Yevgeny Primakov as his new prime minister. The selection was immediately hailed in the Duma as a conciliatory gesture. Confirmation would be almost immediate and overwhelming. Only at the fringes were there predictably dissonant voices. (Zhirinovsky blasted Primakov as "the pro-American candidate, nominated by Clinton.")

When Yeltsin talked to Clinton on the phone after the announcement, he sounded exhausted and depressed. Instead of the bravado we'd heard in the past after he'd surprised the world with a government shake-up, this time it was he who sounded shaken. Primakov was a compromise with the communists whom Yeltsin had told Clinton nine days before he wanted to crush. Musing on the call afterward, Clinton said that Yeltsin's subliminal message seemed to be, "Primakov's in charge—and I sure hope I did the right thing."

WHEN LARRY SUMMERS and I flew to London on September 13 for a long-scheduled meeting of G-8 officials, we heard Larry's Russian counterpart, Deputy Finance Minister Mikhail Kasyanov, refer several times to the "Yeltsin-Primakov team"—a hyphenated formulation that we'd never heard used to promote any of Primakov's predecessors.

For Larry, the rise of Primakov was thoroughly bad news. "You watch," he said. "He'll be Chernomyrdin minus the good relationship with Al Gore. He's just another unreconstructed Soviet. He won't even talk the talk, much less walk the walk of reform."

Actually, Primakov made an attempt at the talk, although in a way that confirmed Larry's point. When Madeleine Albright called to wish him well in his new job, Primakov said that he was going to do nothing more than what Franklin Roosevelt had done to lift the U.S. out of the Depression—provide jobs for the unemployed, ensure social welfare and promote public works through deficit spending: "We're not going to let the forces of capitalism run wild." His objective was to ensure a "calm, normal transition to the market" that preserved state controls on prices, state subsidies to industries and a state-financed safety net. He undertook virtually no reform of the banking or tax systems. He gave the crucial job of first deputy prime minister for the economy to Yuri Maslyukov, a former head of the Soviet central planning agency and a senior figure in the Russian Communist Party. He kept Boris Fyodorov on for a while as the chief tax collector, then fired him in late September.

In frequent, often gladiatorial encounters with Larry Summers and other visitors from Washington, Primakov blamed many of Russia's problems on his predecessors ("your darlings, the young reformers"), on our administration for backing them and on experts from the IMF ("your university boys who come here to teach us as though we were dunces"). Kasyanov was just as blunt: "We're not here to take exams or listen to lectures from your professors. If our Western partners had had all the solutions to all our problems, we wouldn't be in this mess now, given how hard earlier Russian governments worked to do what you people told us we should do."4 It was one more repudiation of the Westernizing theme that Andrei Kozyrev had represented in Russian foreign policy and that Gaidar and Fyodorov had stood for in economic policy. In its place was economic nationalism: Russia would find its own way to a market economy.

But while Primakov didn't want the West's advice on how to restructure the Russian economy, he still wanted the West's money to help cover the massive budget deficit. We spent much of the fall and winter in a dialogue of the deaf: one American delegation after another urged monetary and fiscal discipline, and the Russians would come back at us about the need to meet payrolls; we would defend the principle of conditionality in IMF lending, and they would complain about our pressure and meddling; we would talk about economics and the laws of arithmetic ("the numbers in your budget plans need to add up!" Larry kept telling them), and they would talk accusingly about our insensitivity to their politics—and hint darkly about what we might be up to in the realm of geopolitics.

"Are you trying to isolate us?" Primakov challenged when we explained why there couldn't be another dose of IMF assistance. "Are you trying to back us into a corner? Why else would you be treating us worse than you treat Brazil or Bulgaria? Do we need to get onto our knees? No way!"

In January 1999, Primakov sent his communist deputy Maslyukov to Washington to plead for IMF help. When I made the case to Maslyukov that reform was a precondition for support, he interrupted me. "You keep talking about 'support.' Well, you know," he continued, assuming the contorted expression of a hanged man, "a noose offers support too! That's the way you're supporting us!"

The Clinton administration spent much of the fall and winter trying to avoid pulling the plug on international aid. Bob Rubin and Larry Summers concluded that the best we could do was a small IMF loan to cover much of what Russia owed the fund. They considered it a virtual welfare payment. It gave the Russians some debt relief while avoiding the dangers of financing profligacy and endorsing a government that was engaged in little reform.

BY EARLY 1999, the Russian economy was making a comeback from the crash of the previous summer. Industrial output was up, inflation and the deficit down. With Asia pulling out of its own slump, Russia's oil revenues were on the rise, and the lower level of the ruble, which had now stabilized, meant domestic production increased in response to the higher cost of imports. By the spring, the IMF pronounced the Russian economy on its way to a recovery, in part because it was now the beneficiary of favorable global trends.

The atmosphere of political crisis in Moscow had also lifted. I found during my visits in the fall and winter that there was no more talk of coups or chaos in Moscow. Vladimir Lukin, who had been apocalyptic in August, summarized the situation in December as "serious but not catastrophic" and the mood as "nervous but not suicidal—or homicidal."

Vladimir Ryzhkov, the thirty-two-year-old deputy speaker of the Duma, was also relatively upbeat. Russia, he said, was "starting the process of putting its house in order rather than setting the house on fire, which is what some of us were worried about in August."

Almost everyone I saw was deep into a guessing game about Russia's next presidential campaign, even though the election was scheduled more than a year and a half in the future, in the summer of 2000. Primakov appeared to be riding high for having brought a measure of stability and normalcy to a country that was, in a phrase then in fashion, suffering from a bad case of crisis fatigue. General Lebed, whose expected march to the Kremlin had so frightened Yavlinsky and other liberals the year before, had run into trouble in Krasnoyarsk, primarily because of a feud with the local aluminum magnate Anatoly Bykov (whose own power was another sign of the rise of the oligarchs as a force in Russian politics).

That left Mayor Luzhkov of Moscow and Primakov himself as the presumed front-runners for 2000, although there was no consensus on how the various rivalries and machinations would shake out. Everyone had his own theory, prediction and preference, and was talking about it freely—which struck me as a good working definition of democracy.

It also seemed that the U.S. and its policy toward Russia were not much on people's minds, even when they were talking to me as an official from Washington. Except for Primakov and his ministers, almost no one asked me what the IMF was going to do. There was an emerging sense that Russia's economic problems were its own responsibility. That too seemed a welcome development.

The only big worry among my Russian acquaintances about the U.S. that winter was how Russia was playing in American domestic politics and whether the president who came after Clinton would give Russia the cold shoulder, or something worse. Lukin and Ryzhkov were both regular surfers of the Internet, and they had come across a report on a recent talk by Condoleezza Rice, the former official in George Bush's National Security Council who had emerged as one of the top foreign-policy advisers to Texas Governor George W. Bush as he prepared to run for president in 2000. "I think really the question," said Rice, "is how close are we now to beginning to think about a policy toward Russia that is really more of containment and quarantine than one of possible cooperation."[5]

Lukin and Ryzhkov expressed the hope that this was just a fleeting burst of partisanship, not a harbinger of policies to come.

"Please keep in mind," said Ryzhkov, "that Russian society is basically healthier than the Russian state. One of the healthy things about us is that we do care how we look to the rest of the world. Only if the world gives up on us will we give up on ourselves."

Boris Nemtsov and Grigory Yavlinsky—two leading liberals who had both, in earlier times, been close associates of Yeltsin's—had picked themselves up off the mat. They too used every chance they got to keep the U.S. from overreacting to the setbacks of 1998. Nemtsov predicted that "the Primakov interlude" would pass quickly and that Russia would work its way—albeit not so quickly—to "something even you Americans with your high standards and short attention spans will recognize as something better." He was contemptuous of the latest round of hand-wringing and finger-pointing going on in the U.S. "You Americans should stop this who-lost-Russia crap," he said. "Marx, Lenin, Stalin, Brezhnev—those guys are to blame. Now let's get on with it. But you've got to hang in there with us."

Yavlinsky urged Westerners to remember the magnitude of what he and other reformers—and, for that matter, Primakov and the Russian government—were up against. "Russia's economy," he said, "wasn't damaged by central planning; it was created by central planning." Creating from scratch a better system required the passing of the people now in charge. Whatever happened in the short run, he said, we had to keep in mind the stakes over the long run. "You people in the West are too much worried about the bad things you see today. They exist, of course. You think I don't know that? But don't lose sight of the good things many tomorrows from now. Russia in twenty-five years can be a European country in NATO."

MUTUAL DISLIKE

I tried to keep the optimism and undaunted pro-Western feelings of Russian liberals in mind as an antidote to the frustrations of dealing with the people in charge of Russian foreign policy during the winter of 1998–99. That period saw another downturn in the relationship and was a prologue for worse yet to come.

When Primakov assumed the prime ministership in September, he had assured Madeleine Albright that there would be plenty of that cherished commodity of continuity in Russian foreign policy. Unfortunately, on the issues of Russia's relations with Iraq and Iran, there was all too much continuity with what we had come to expect from Primakov in the past.

In Iraq, Saddam Hussein had been engaging for years in a cat-and-mouse game with the international community by violating numerous conditions of the cease-fire agreement that had ended the Gulf War in 1991. Of greatest danger was his effort to impede the UN from inspecting facilities where he was conducting programs to develop chemical, biological and nuclear weapons. We had tried unsuccessfully since the spring of 1998 to get the Russians to join us in tightening UN trade restrictions against Iraq as the only way of forcing Saddam back into compliance.

In November 1998, Saddam kicked the UN weapons inspectors out of Iraq. After repeated warnings and on the basis of authorization contained in existing UN Security Council resolutions, the U.S. and Britain carried out air strikes against Iraqi radars and anti-aircraft batteries in mid-December. In a replay of what we'd experienced over Bosnia, the Russians were apoplectic, and Yeltsin led the rhetorical charge, accusing us of having "crudely violated" the UN Charter. Going him one better, the Duma passed a resolution 394–1 denouncing the U.S. and Britain as "international terrorists."

In the aftermath of this flap, on January 8, I gave a farewell lunch for Yuli Vorontsov, a Primakov contemporary and pal, who was completing four years as the Russian ambassador in Washington. He was retiring from a diplomatic service he had entered in 1952, the year before Stalin died. It was a friendly enough conversation until the dessert arrived. I made a passing reference to issues on which we disagreed but had tried to manage our differences, especially Russia's defense of Slobodan Milošević and Saddam Hussein. Out of the blue, Vorontsov unloaded: "You know, Strobe, having worked on U.S.-Russian relations most of my career, including during the Soviet period and the cold war, I must tell you that it is much easier to be your enemy than to be your friend. As your friend, we constantly have to hear you saying to us that we must love all the girls you love and hate all the boys you hate."

Steve Sestanovich, the head of our office responsible for the former Soviet Union, tried to lighten the conversation and shift subjects. He suggested that while, yes, we did have our differences, it always helped when our two presidents got together. Therefore perhaps Yeltsin would join the heads of other former Soviet republics and Warsaw Pact member-states in attending the next NATO summit, scheduled to be held in Washington that April.

"No, he won't," snapped Vorontsov. "I think it's more likely that my president will attend the Senate's trial of your president"—a proceeding that had formally begun the day before.

Vorontsov's eruption captured, in a particularly nasty form, what a lot of Russians had been feeling for a long time: their country's post–cold war settlement with the West was getting harsher as time went on; despite all the rhetoric about win/win, the U.S. was an ungenerous victor.

MEANWHILE, there was at least as much anger in Washington over Russian recidivism with regard to Iran as there was in Moscow over our latest resort to force against Iraq. Since the upheaval in Russian politics during the summer, there had been severe backsliding in Russia's compliance with both its own catchall regulations and its commitments to us on the transfer of dangerous technology. This development was no less disturbing for being predictable. Primakov had always been more part of the problem than the solution on this issue. Most of the progress we'd made had been through Gore's dealings with Chernomyrdin and Berger's with Andrei Kokoshin. Chernomyrdin was now totally sidelined, and Kokoshin had been among the first officials fired during the shake-up in September.[6]

When Igor Ivanov, whom Primakov promoted to take his place as foreign minister, visited Washington in September 1998, he assured Sandy that Yeltsin would appoint a "Kokoshin II" who would carry on the good work that had been accomplished by Kokoshin I. Primakov, said Ivanov, was giving priority to the problem of proliferation because it was "one of the most important aspects of our struggle with corruption, including in the government apparatus."

It was an empty promise. No one in the Kremlin was willing to deal seriously with Sandy or anyone else on the proliferation problem. Primakov himself went back to the dodging and weaving we'd seen throughout 1997. When I raised new evidence that Yevgeny Adamov, the powerful and troublesome minister of atomic energy, was assisting Iran's nuclear program, Primakov told me he had already put Adamov on notice that he was going to "fire his ass" if that were the case. The evidence was indisputable, but Adamov kept his job.

All this came as a blow to Al Gore, who had done so much of the work on Russia/Iran with Chernomyrdin and who was taking increasing partisan flak for his central role in the overall management of our relations with Russia.

On September 11, 1998, the day after Yeltsin announced his new choice for prime minister, I arrived at the White House for a meeting and passed the vice-president in the parking lot next to the West Wing. As he swept past me, surrounded by aides and Secret Service agents, Gore caught my eye and said, through his teeth, "Ah, yes! Russia, the Primakov place! What used to be the market-democracy place; what used to be the non-proliferation place; now the Primakov place. Don't like that guy—suspect it's mutual."

GORE AND PRIMAKOV met briefly and disagreeably in mid-November on the margins of an international meeting in Kuala Lumpur, Malaysia.7 Iran had now tested a new medium-range missile, further threatening its own neighborhood (including Russia) and putting it one step closer to a long-range missile that could reach the U.S. Didn't Primakov understand, Gore asked, that the amount of money Russia was making from Iran was minuscule compared to the billions it could make from commercial space launch and other deals with the West? "You can have a piddling trickle of money from Iran or a bonanza with us," said Gore, "but you can't have both. Why do you keep trying to have it both ways?"

Primakov denied any responsibility. In January 1999, the administration slapped new "administrative actions" on three Russian entities that had been helping the Iranians: we were still using that euphemism for sanctions but the Russians—now that we were in what Leon Fuerth called the "post-Chernomyrdin, post-Kiriyenko, post-Kokoshin era"—were no longer willing to take parallel action of their own against the offenders.

When Gore and Primakov crossed paths a second time, at a World Economic Forum meeting in Davos, Switzerland, at the end of January 1999, it was the single worst high-level U.S.-Russian meeting in the eight years of the Clinton presidency. Both men were tired, in Gore's case because he had been up most of the night working on a speech. They got nowhere on Iran. Gore, his face tight with anger, turned the meeting over to Larry Summers, who gave Primakov a stiff talking-to on economics.

Primakov was still fuming over the Davos encounter when I saw him privately three weeks later in Moscow. After he and I rehashed, without much success, the issues that had proved so intractable, Primakov lapsed into a somber, almost wistful mood. He recalled our first dealings with each other, when he was an *institutchik* and I was a reporter in the early eighties. Yuri Andropov was in the Kremlin and Ronald Reagan in the White House. The relationship had in some ways been simpler back then, he said. The two countries had understood each other better because "we knew what the score was"—a tacit acknowledgment of what I'd always taken to be Primakov's view that U.S.-Russian relations were essentially and eternally a zero-sum game. (It was a more polite version of what Steve Sestanovich and I heard from Vorontsov.)

Not that Primakov was nostalgic for the cold war, he added. It was just that he had devoted so much of his career to the U.S.-Russian relationship, which now seemed to have gone badly off the rails. He missed dealing with Madeleine, he said. She combined "real toughness—good, old-fashioned toughness of the kind I can relate to—with a willingness to listen and to try to understand my problems."[8] Gore, by contrast, was letting himself be driven by domestic politics, said Primakov. Primakov still believed, despite our efforts to persuade him otherwise, that our administration in general and Gore in particular had been "badgering" him over Iran in order to cover our right flank and protect Gore's support from the American Jewish community. Regardless of who won the U.S. presidency in 2000, Primakov predicted, the next American administration would be as basically hostile to Russia as the Clinton administration was basically well disposed.

Realizing that what he'd said was, particularly in context, a pretty harsh commentary on Al Gore, he added that he was not giving up on developing a degree of rapport with the vice-president. He was hoping for a chance to put their personal relationship as well as the U.S.-Russian one on a better track when they saw each other in March, which was when they had agreed to hold the first meeting of the Gore-Primakov commission.

That meeting never happened. The reason was the outbreak of war over Kosovo in the spring of 1999. It was to be the most severe, dangerous and consequential crisis in U.S.-Russian relations of the post–cold war period.

CHAPTER 12

HAMMER AND ANVIL

History is the sum total of things that could have been avoided.
Konrad Adenauer

THE KOSOVO CONFLICT had been brewing for a long time—
more than six centuries, according to the historical mythology
that underlay the politics of the region.[1] The communist regime
of Josip Broz Tito dealt with the multiple ethnic and historical grudges to
be found across Yugoslavia by combining a high degree of federalism with
zero tolerance for aggressive nationalism. Tito made Kosovo a largely self-
governing province of Serbia. When, during our stint as reporters in Belgrade in the early seventies, Brooke and I visited Priština, the capital of
Kosovo, representatives of the Serb minority there told us with bitterness
that they were suffering discrimination at the hands of the ethnic Albanian majority.

In 1989, the Yugoslav president, Slobodan Milošević, stripped Kosovo
of its autonomy. For the next decade, the Albanians in the province chafed
under Belgrade's oppressive rule, while the Serbs of the province looked to
Milošević for protection of their privileges.

In the early and middle nineties, Milošević had his hands full elsewhere, presiding over the breakup of Yugoslavia and the Serb debacles in
Croatia and Bosnia. In 1998, he turned the full force of Serbian vengeance
and repression inward, against Kosovo, and in so doing, transformed a
ragtag band of ethnic Albanian rebels, known as the Kosovo Liberation
Army, into a well-armed and popular independence movement. Serbian

forces slaughtered ethnic Albanian civilians, sometimes in reprisal for guerrilla attacks on policemen but more often as part of a campaign of ethnic cleansing to drive Albanians out of areas where they had lived for generations.

The outside world reacted to these assaults with a combination of rhetorical fulmination and diplomatic gyration similar to its initial dithering over Bosnia. A parade of foreign ministers and special envoys provided Milošević with photo ops that he used to show his own people how he was standing up to foreign pressure. The United Nations Security Council passed resolutions of protest and stipulated conditions for a settlement that Milošević rejected with contempt. He did so largely on the grounds that Kosovo was recognized under international law to be an integral part of Serbia and of the rump state of Yugoslavia (which also included the republic of Montenegro). How the Belgrade regime dealt with separatists and terrorists on its own territory, which was the way it depicted the Kosovars, was its business and no one else's.

For many in the West, including the Clinton administration, Milošević's claim of sovereignty did not trump the right of the international community to stop him from killing and evicting a whole segment of his population. The massive and systematic mistreatment of the Kosovars constituted an ongoing crime against humanity; and the conflagration in Kosovo, if not extinguished, was sure to spread across international boundaries.

As PRESIDENT CLINTON thought about the coming showdown with Milošević, he attached special importance to maintaining some form of partnership with the Russians. For one thing, it would increase the effectiveness of whatever political pressure we applied on Belgrade. For another, it would make Kosovo, like Bosnia in 1995, further proof that not only was the cold war over, but its principal combatants were now on the same side against new threats to international peace.[2]

Clinton tried to raise Kosovo with Yeltsin during both of their meetings in 1998—in Birmingham in mid-May and in Moscow in early September—but he didn't get anywhere. Yeltsin had his mind on his own troubles and treated the conflict in the Balkans as an annoying distraction.

However, once Yevgeny Primakov became prime minister, we started hearing invocations of Yeltsin's name as part of a suddenly vehement Russian diplomatic offensive aimed at heading off NATO bombing.

The third week in September, I took Foreign Minister Igor Ivanov to see President Clinton. In the car on the way to the White House, Ivanov told me that he had been awakened at three that morning to receive a call from Moscow. Yeltsin had personally instructed him to tell Clinton that Russia would "not countenance" air strikes—a phrase that in diplomacy goes beyond disapproval and carries with it at least the option of reprisal. When he saw the president, Ivanov confined himself to warning that the "domino theory" was alive and well in the Balkans, "a region that has been the source of two world wars." Escorting him from the Oval Office back to his car, I asked if he had meant to imply that NATO was in danger of starting a third world war in the Balkans.

"It was as mild a statement as I dared to make and still be faithful to the views of my own president," he replied.

At the time, I suspected that Ivanov was actually speaking more for Primakov, but I was wrong. Not long afterward, on October 5, when Yeltsin spoke directly with Clinton, he was nearly unhinged on the subject of Kosovo. He ranted for twelve minutes, pausing neither for interpretation into English nor for Clinton's reply. Ivanov and Defense Minister Sergeyev had just made an unannounced trip to Belgrade, and, according to Yeltsin, they had saved the day: Milošević had seen the light and would now comply with UN resolutions. Therefore, Yeltsin concluded emphatically, the use of force would be inadmissible and *forbidden*. He repeated several times a Russian word, *nyelzya,* that has the strongest possible prohibitive connotations.

Clinton tried twice to respond, but Yeltsin interrupted him, saying, "Okay, okay, okay, good-bye." The third time Clinton tried to speak, Yeltsin just hung up on him.

"Well," said Clinton, "he hasn't done *that* before. I guess we've got a real problem here."

THE PROBLEM from the Russian standpoint, as we heard repeatedly at every level for months, was that the U.S. was once again acting as though it had the right to impose its will on the world. Once again, the U.S. was throwing its weight around in the UN Security Council, the Contact Group, the OSCE. Once again, as in Bosnia in 1995 and Iraq in December 1998, the U.S. was getting ready to bomb a country where Russia felt it had interests and influence of its own.

The Russians also saw in Kosovo a sinister analogy to Chechnya. Kosovo was a Muslim-majority province on the southern border of a state with a Slavic Orthodox majority. Like Chechnya, Kosovo was boiling with separatist passions.

Ivanov made this point explicitly to Secretary Albright in a phone conversation that winter when he said, "Madeleine, don't you understand we have many Kosovos in Russia?"

As the likelihood of conflict grew, Russian politicians, generals and commentators speculated with mounting alarm that the air campaign the U.S. and its allies were getting ready to unleash against Serbia was a warm-up for a future war with Russia that might begin with the West's claim that it was defending the rights of the Chechens.

Kosovo, in short, was shaping up to be a substantiation of all the Russians' reasons for fearing NATO and opposing its expansion.

While the communists and nationalists shook their fists, the liberals, including many of my contacts who had been relatively sanguine a few months before, wrung their hands. On one of my trips to Moscow, Grigory Yavlinsky sought me out at my hotel and predicted a "hysterical" reaction from the Russian political elite and a big boost for Zyuganov and Zhirinovsky in the 2000 presidential election.

"Your bombs may land on the Serbs," he said, "but there will be a fatal dose of fallout on those in Russian politics who most want Russia to be part of the West. Think about that irony!"

I said I'd thought about it a lot and asked Yavlinsky to think a bit himself about the irony that the Russian government, in its desperation to stop NATO from bombing, was increasing Milošević's confidence that he could get away with murder—and thereby making more likely the NATO intervention that the Russians most feared.

THE U-TURN

Eventually, Russia shifted from blocking NATO intervention in Kosovo to standing aside and letting it happen—a development that reflected Moscow's growing frustration with its client in Belgrade.

Through the summer and into the early fall of 1998, while Milošević's security forces stepped up their rampage against the Kosovars, NATO was paralyzed by the West Europeans' unwillingness to contemplate military action without authorization from the UN Security Council. That gave the Russians (and Chinese) a veto that they repeatedly threatened to cast.

A fresh, particularly gruesome and well-publicized atrocity in September jarred the U.S. government into a new burst of diplomatic activity. Sandy Berger convened a meeting in the Situation Room and, to concentrate our minds, put a copy of *The New York Times* on the table with a large front-page color photograph of the corpse of an elderly Albanian villager whose throat had been slit. The meeting resulted in a decision to redouble our efforts to find a way out of the double bind created by the West Europeans and the Russians. If we could solve that problem, we should be ready, for the first time, to give NATO the authority for immediate action. Armed with that new threat, Dick Holbrooke would return to the region to put pressure on Milošević.

Dick set off on an eleven-day shuttle that took him to Belgrade, Priština, Brussels and London. Both for the administration and for Dick personally, the timing could not have been riskier. Midterm congressional elections were only a few weeks away, and the Republicans had taken a strong position against American military involvement in Kosovo. Dick had been nominated in June to be ambassador to the UN, so by undertaking a high-visibility diplomatic mission, he was making himself—and his nomination, which still required approval by the Senate—a target of partisan attack as well.

After several difficult days in Belgrade, Dick joined Madeleine in the VIP lounge at Heathrow for a meeting with the foreign ministers of the Contact Group, including Igor Ivanov. Ivanov repeated that Russia would never support NATO action in the Security Council. But, in a subtle hint of Russia's changing posture, he made unmistakably clear that Russia would not insist on the matter coming to the council and indicated he was ready to support Dick's ultimatum to Milošević, which, Ivanov understood, would be backed by the NATO threat. After this closed-door meeting, the Contact Group ministers, Ivanov among them, gave Dick a public sendoff for his return to Belgrade.

Finally armed with unified support by NATO and the Contact Group, including Russia, Dick was able to get Milošević to agree to four important and promising measures: NATO's access to the airspace over Kosovo for surveillance of the situation on the ground; the introduction of 2,000 international civilian monitors; the peaceful return of the more than 100,000 Kosovars who had been driven from their homes; and the beginning of a political process.

There were, however, three shortcomings in this package. The international monitors would be unarmed, so there was no means to enforce an agreement; Milošević showed no willingness to make anything like the necessary concessions in the political process; and for their part, the Kosovo Albanians were increasingly in disarray over who spoke for them, a problem that would become critical in the year to come.

In mid-January 1999, a well-publicized Serb massacre of ethnic Albanian civilians in the village of Račak spurred the U.S. and its allies to ratchet up both the diplomatic effort and the threat of force. Working with the British and the French, Madeleine summoned the Serbs and Kosovars to a chateau in Rambouillet, just south of Paris. The aim of the conference was the restoration of Kosovo's autonomy for an interim period until its final status could be determined by a referendum. The settlement would be enforced by a peacekeeping operation backed by the full force of NATO and the U.S. military.

A squad of Russian diplomats hovered around Rambouillet with the aim of protecting the principle of Belgrade's sovereignty over Kosovo, minimizing NATO's role in enforcing the settlement and discrediting the Kosovars as little better than terrorists. While those talks were under way, I was in Moscow, reinforcing Madeleine's message, and keeping in touch with her team through Chris Hill, the U.S. ambassador to Macedonia and the foreign service's most seasoned and skillful Balkan hand. We tried to get the Russians to see that by appearing, yet again, to serve as the Serbs' defense attorneys, they were only encouraging intransigence and thus increasing the likelihood of war.

Milošević's own negotiators in Rambouillet—he never deigned to come himself—played for time but never came close to accepting the terms on which Madeleine insisted. Meanwhile, Serb repression, often accompanied by atrocities, continued in Kosovo.

NATO moved into high gear for a bombing campaign. The prevailing view in the U.S. government was that the operation wouldn't last too long. Bosnia had proved Milošević to be a bully coward: if we hit him hard, he would fold.

THE MAN most responsible for hitting Milošević, Wes Clark, was not so sure. Wes had risen quickly since 1995, when he had been a three-star general representing the Joint Chiefs of Staff on Dick Holbrooke's flying squad and at the Dayton peace talks. Now Wes had four stars on his shoulder and was the senior American and NATO commander in Europe.

When I met with him March 11 at his headquarters in Mons, Belgium, he told me that Milošević was amassing troops to "solve" the Kosovo problem his own way. The Serb forces would surge into the province and through a combination of mass killing and mass eviction, try to break the back of the resistance and the independence movement. Milošević knew he was vastly outgunned by NATO but figured he would be able to withstand the bombing longer than the West would be able to keep it up.

"We can't kid ourselves," said Wes. "If we start this thing, it'll be a long haul."

WHILE WES WAS PUTTING the finishing touches on Operation Allied Force, President Clinton sent Dick Holbrooke to Belgrade with an ultimatum: if Milošević agreed to the immediate cessation of military action in Kosovo, the return to barracks of the Yugoslav forces there and the beginning of serious discussion of deploying in Kosovo an armed international security presence, then diplomacy would continue; otherwise, we would start bombing.

Dick had already arrived in Belgrade on March 22 when the prime minister of Russia took off from Moscow en route to Washington for his long-scheduled commission meeting with Gore. The Russians, having given up on stopping the bombing, had asked us to delay military action until Primakov completed his visit. We couldn't do that, since it would look to Milošević that we'd blinked at the last minute. But Primakov had a dilemma too: he didn't want to be in the U.S. when the bombing started. Therefore Gore called him as his plane was refueling in Ireland and asked him to wait there to let us gauge how Dick fared in his final go at Milošević. Primakov refused and took off for Washington.

I KEPT IN CLOSE TOUCH with Dick in Belgrade. We talked on an open telephone line so that he could, in addition to filling me in on the progress of his talks, send messages to the Serbs and Russians who were no doubt listening.

"I assume you agree, Strobe," said Dick, speaking loudly and in a kind of special English, "we're not going to let ourselves be deterred or delayed" by Primakov's visit.

"Absolutely, Dick," I replied, also with exaggerated enunciation. "That's the way we all see it here."

"Good. And even if Milošević says 'yes' to everything in the Rambouillet agreement, we'll still bomb the shit out of him if he doesn't pull back and cease and desist in Kosovo, since the rolling atrocity he's committing there is trigger enough for bombing."

"Yes, Dick, that's the position of the president and the secretary of state," I said, playing my part.

Milošević remained defiant, and Dick headed for the airport. Once his plane was in the air, I called our chargé d'affaires in Belgrade, Richard Miles, and gave him formal instructions to burn classified material in the embassy, pack up and clear out. Miles and I had first met each other in Belgrade nearly thirty years before, when he had been a junior foreign service officer in the embassy and Brooke and I lived a few blocks away. We talked for a moment about how it was a sad but necessary moment. I asked him to give thanks and good wishes to the Yugoslav staff of the embassy, many of whom had worked there faithfully for decades.

Primakov was also already in the air, heading in our direction. Gore reached him aboard his aircraft and told him that with Dick's departure from Belgrade empty-handed, there was no reason for further delay in military action. NATO had no choice but to strike. Milošević, said Gore, had "blood dripping from his hands"—he was using every passing day to kill innocent men, women and children.

Primakov retorted that it was NATO that would have blood on its hands, and the impact on U.S.-Russian relations would be devastating. He ordered his plane to turn around and head back to Moscow.

On March 24, Clinton called Yeltsin and tried to divert his anger from the U.S. to Milošević as a pygmy who had come between two giants; he was also, said Clinton, a "communist dictator"—a species, regardless of stature, that Yeltsin was known to detest.

It didn't work. In addition to venting his fury and frustration over the failure of Russian diplomacy to stop NATO from bombing, Yeltsin expressed despair at having suffered a defeat in what he was trying to accomplish at home. After all he had done to "turn my people toward the West," it was now going to be practically impossible to keep them headed in that direction. The only way to keep the disaster from being irreversible, he kept saying, was to suspend the bombing immediately. Throughout the call, he never referred to Clinton as Bill or "my friend." Just before he hung up, he refused even to address him in the second person.

"Well," he said, "I've obviously failed to persuade the president of the United States. Good-bye."

Clinton held the phone in his hand for a moment after Yeltsin had hung up. He looked deeply pained. He'd heard Yeltsin rave before, but Clinton usually let it roll off, knowing it would pass. This time, however, as he put it, "something pretty basic is broken and it'll take a lot of fixing."

Within hours, American cruise missiles, launched from warships in the Adriatic, slammed into Serbian air-defense radars and missile sites, clearing the way for NATO bombers to begin the alliance's first sustained combat operation since its founding half a century before.

A COMEBACK

In the immediate aftermath of the first bombs falling on Serbian targets, there were violent street protests in front of the U.S. embassy in Moscow. Many in the Duma wanted Russia to send military assistance to the Serbs, and hard-liners called for the mobilization of "volunteers" to be sent to Yugoslavia. Partly in response to public outrage and political pressures, the Russian government withdrew its military representative from NATO headquarters, reduced the size and level of its liaison staff there, suspended all Partnership for Peace activities and canceled working-level meetings of the NATO-Russian Permanent Joint Council.

However, even in those early days, there were signs that Yeltsin's government didn't want to pull the plug completely on all that had been accomplished in the NATO-Russia Founding Act or sever all ties with the West. Sergei Stepashin, the interior minister, warned publicly against "overreacting." As the days went by, Russian representatives started showing up again at NATO-sponsored meetings in Brussels, though silently and at lower ranks than usual.

"Somehow," Ivanov told Madeleine, "somehow, somehow, we've got to keep diplomacy alive."

MILOŠEVIĆ RESPONDED to the initial air strikes exactly as Wes Clark had predicted. He poured troops into Kosovo and drove tens of thousands of Kosovars over the border into Albania and Macedonia, threatening the stability of those fragile countries, confronting the world with a mammoth refugee crisis and disabusing anyone of the idea that he was going to give up quickly.

Public opinion, especially in Europe, soon began to turn against the bombing, partly because the CNN effect was now working against NATO. Instead of images of Albanian corpses lying in a village square in

Kosovo, the TV news now gave live coverage to ambulances screaming through the streets of Serbian cities while air-raid sirens blared in the background. As Easter approached, there were appeals for a suspension in the bombing, both out of respect for the religious holiday and to see if Milošević might be willing to return to the negotiating table.

At the end of March, I got a call from Yegor Gaidar, then the head of a Moscow think tank, who was in Rome and about to see Pope John Paul II. Could he convey to His Holiness American interest in the idea of a papal mission of peace that would be "facilitated" by a bombing pause?

Absolutely not, I said. A pause would be tantamount to surrender. NATO would observe the suspension of hostilities while Milošević would treat it as a chance to do what he'd done in the past: talk and kill. Given the skittishness within the alliance, turning the air strikes back on would be all but impossible once they were turned off.

"Oh, Strobe," said Gaidar, "if only you knew what a disaster this war is for those of us in Russia who want for our country what you want."

All I could say in reply was that for Milošević to come out on top would be terrible, too—including in its implications for Russia, since Milošević was the antithesis of what Gaidar represented for the post-communist world.

IN MAY, NATO escalated the level of the bombing and began "going downtown," hitting the power grid and targets related to the regime in Belgrade. The alliance also moved additional warplanes, the USS *Roosevelt* carrier group and twenty-four Apache attack helicopters into the theater. The Apaches were intended to signal the allies' willingness if necessary to invade Serbia, an option that President Clinton had come close to ruling out in the early days of the operation.[3]

As the bombing intensified, we worked within the alliance to define what Milošević would have to do for it to stop. The answer we came up with was a more forceful version of the one we'd tried and failed to get Milošević to accept at Rambouillet: Kosovo, while remaining inside Yugoslavia in the eyes of international law, would become, for the foreseeable future, a protectorate of the UN, with NATO enforcing that arrangement. That meant the withdrawal of Serb forces from Kosovo, the deployment of a robust peacekeeping force under NATO command and the return of refugees and displaced persons to their homes.[4]

We used every channel and forum that included the Russians—the

UN, the G-8, the Contact Group—as well as Madeleine's frequent direct dealings with Igor Ivanov, to convince Moscow to endorse our conditions. We argued that the less daylight there was between Russia and the West, the sooner Milošević would give up.

The Russians accused us of deliberately setting the bar too high so that we'd have a pretext for keeping up the war—with the goal, they believed, not just of driving Milošević from Kosovo but of bringing down his regime. If we were really interested in bringing the war to an end, they said, we should make the conditions less onerous, and that meant primarily being more respectful of Serbian sovereignty. The Russians were prepared to join us in demanding a reduction of Serb forces in Kosovo, but only if we would let Milošević keep a hefty, well-armed contingent behind; and their version of an international "presence" would be composed of refugee workers under the command of the UN, not a NATO-led military force.

In pressing us for more leniency for Belgrade, the Russians spread out in all directions, working the allies separately, since they believed that the U.S. was driving a harder bargain than the others and that they could play us off against each other.

THE TEST OF ALLIED UNITY would come at the end of April, when the leaders of NATO met in Washington. The summit had been conceived as a celebration of the alliance's fiftieth anniversary, to be marked with the formal induction of the Czech Republic, Hungary and Poland as new allies. On the second day of the event, much as they had done in Madrid two years before, the allies would meet with many of the member-states of the Partnership for Peace, from Central Europe and the former Soviet Union.

Yeltsin was watching from afar, hoping that the allies would fall out among themselves and either stop the bombing outright or water down the conditions for doing so. But he couldn't be sure of that outcome, and he was already covering his bets. On April 14, Yeltsin announced that Victor Chernomyrdin would be his special envoy for dealing with the Kosovo conflict. The move caught us completely by surprise, but once he'd made it, it seemed entirely explicable. Yeltsin wanted to get the war stopped and to get Russia as much credit as possible. He had never been enthusiastic about Primakov as his prime minister, or even as his foreign minister before that. Now he was taking the Kosovo account away from Primakov and turning it over to someone who he was confident could get the job done.

High on the list of Chernomyrdin's credentials was his proven ability to work with Al Gore. That in itself distinguished him from Primakov. Yeltsin calculated that Chernomyrdin could talk sense to the Americans, perhaps getting them to soften their conditions. But he could also talk tough to Milošević. Serbia was dependent on Russia as a source of energy, and Chernomyrdin, as the former head of Gazprom, the state-owned oil company, had connections that would be useful in applying pressure on Belgrade.

All this was as much as we could guess at the time. Clinton called Yeltsin on April 19 to see if he could learn more about what exactly the Russian president had in mind. Yeltsin played coy, no doubt because he was waiting to make his next move after he saw how the NATO summit played out.

A WEEK LATER, the allied leaders, led primarily by Clinton and the British prime minister, Tony Blair, closed ranks behind a formal reiteration of the three main demands that Milošević must meet for the bombing to stop: Serb forces out, NATO in, refugees back.

Not only did the allies themselves hold firm, but several of the key nonallies who came to Washington for the PFP meeting cheered them on. The most forceful of these was Martti Ahtisaari, the president of Finland. He helped beat back the idea, which the Russians and others were promoting, that the UN should mediate between NATO and Milošević. If we permitted anyone to broker a compromise, Ahtisaari warned, Milošević would end up with enough military force in Kosovo to render the settlement meaningless and guarantee another conflict in the future.

Among the leaders from the former Soviet Union, the most supportive of the NATO operation was Eduard Shevardnadze, the president of Georgia. He believed that the West's show of force in the Balkans would give pause to "Milošević-like figures" in Russia who wanted to suppress non-Russian ethnic groups inside Russia and to reestablish Russian suzerainty over newly independent neighboring states like his own. He did not, he added, put Yeltsin in that category. But there were "people around Yeltsin" vying for his job in the next election who needed to be reminded that the West would come to the defense of "small, beleaguered people who are trying to break free of empire."

Shevardnadze also had some insight into what lay behind the Chernomyrdin appointment. Just before coming to Washington, Shevardnadze had met with Chernomyrdin in Tbilisi. Chernomyrdin had told him that Yeltsin detested Milošević and blamed him more than the U.S. for the crisis that imperiled Russia's relations with the West. Chernomyrdin also confirmed Yeltsin's dissatisfaction with Primakov, in particular for his decision to turn his plane around over the Atlantic the day that Dick Holbrooke's talks with Milošević ended in an impasse.

Shevardnadze's advice was that we do everything we could to help Chernomyrdin succeed in his assignment. Otherwise, the bitter and vengeful forces in Russia that wanted a confrontation with the West in the Balkans would be all the more likely to turn their energies on the Caucasus.[5]

ONCE IT WAS CLEAR that the alliance hadn't cracked as he'd hoped it would, Yeltsin wasted no time in proposing a joint U.S.-Russian initiative to end the war. When Yeltsin called Clinton on Sunday, April 25, the last day of the Washington summit, he began by trying to elicit Clinton's sympathy for what he was up against inside Russia. There were forces in the Duma and the military, he said, that were agitating to send a flotilla into the Mediterranean in a show of support for Serbia, and to provide arms to Belgrade, including anti-aircraft systems that would endanger NATO pilots. Yeltsin told Clinton he had already fired one commander in the Far East who was trying to mount a battalion to go to Serbia.[6] There was even a plan brewing to form a "union" among Yugoslavia, Belarus and Russia.

Yeltsin was determined to hold these forces at bay, he continued, but he needed Clinton to help him by resuscitating U.S.-Russian diplomatic cooperation under the auspices of Gore and Chernomyrdin. For its part, Russia would force Milošević's compliance: "We will not leave any room for maneuver by Belgrade; we'll keep those people in our sights, including their political network"—an apparent hint that Russia would turn the screws on Milošević's political allies, business associates, military commanders and intelligence services. "We'll keep working on Milošević as though we were converting him to another faith."

Clinton agreed to reopen the Gore-Chernomyrdin channel as long as Yeltsin understood at the outset that NATO would have to be in command of the peacekeeping operation that followed a settlement. "The measure of success is bringing the refugees home," he said. "I don't believe anyone but NATO and the U.S. can do this."

Yeltsin wasn't interested in the details of what happened after the war

Informal working dinners were a regular and often productive means of getting diplomatic business done. On the eve of the G-7 summit in June 1997, Madeleine Albright hosted Yevgeny Primakov (reaching across the table) and Yuri Mamedov (across from me), my principal Russian contact, for a meal at a cowboy-theme restaurant in Denver. We were all smiles when she introduced her guests to Rocky Mountain oysters, but by the time the main course arrived we had plunged into one of our toughest sessions, primarily on the subject of Russian assistance to the Iranian nuclear and missile programs.

In early May 1997, as we entered the endgame of negotiations over NATO enlargement and the NATO-Russia relationship, Primakov had several of us to his apartment in downtown Moscow. The featured dish was Siberian dumplings, and before we turned to business the conversation concentrated on the novels of John le Carré, of which Primakov was a big fan. (Top: The State Department; bottom: Eduard Pesov)

Part of our strategy to break through vestiges of the Iron Curtain was to integrate Russia into the community of Baltic and Nordic nations, which included NATO allies like Norway, nonaligned states like Sweden and Finland and applicants for NATO membership like Poland. The annual meetings to advance this goal were always held near the Arctic Circle in the dead of winter. In January 1998, after one such meeting in Lulea, Sweden, my team and I were taken to the airport by a local means of transport. My fellow dogsledders: Ron Asmus, who helped design and manage the linked processes of NATO enlargement and NATO-Russia cooperation; Jim Collins, my successor as ambassador-at-large for the former Soviet Union and Tom Pickering's successor as ambassador to Moscow; and Bill Nitze, a senior official of the Environmental Protection Agency. (Goran Strom)

In early April 1998, Clinton called Yeltsin to exhort him to crack down on Russia's ties to Iran. In the midst of the call, Clinton's Labrador retriever, Buddy, leapt up to lick Clinton on the ear and sent the telephone clattering to the floor. Fortunately, Yeltsin never noticed the commotion and the call yielded agreement on what we hoped would be a promising new channel between Sandy Berger, who was now head of the NSC, and the head of the Kremlin national security council, Andrei Kokoshin. (The White House)

In May 1998, Clinton and Yeltsin met in Birmingham, the first officially designated gathering of the G-8 (previously, Russia had been a guest of the G-7). Yeltsin was joined by Mamedov and Kremlin foreign-policy adviser Sergei Yastrzhembsky, and Sandy Berger was with me at Clinton's side. The American interpreter, Peter Afanasenko (whispering to Yeltsin), had by then become a master at capturing the Russian leader's animated, sometimes bumptious style. (The White House)

My parents, Bud and Jo Talbott, had known Clinton almost as long as I had. In June 1998, along with Brooke's parents, Lloyd and Marva Shearer, they spent a weekend at Camp David. (The White House)

By the late fall of 1998, when Russia was in the midst of political and economic crisis, Larry Summers and I were summoned to testify before a House
of Representatives panel. We didn't know in advance that the Republican
majority had arranged for George Shultz, Ronald Reagan's secretary of state
and a booster of George W. Bush's candidacy, to appear with us by video
hook-up from California. The question of the season was "Who lost Russia?"
and Larry and I figured prominently in the Republicans' answer. (Stephen
Crowley/*The New York Times*)

Javier Solana, then the
secretary-general of
NATO and already, in
American eyes, the in-
dispensable European,
was a frequent visitor to
Washington—and often
to our home. In the fall
of 1998, he spent the
weekend, which gave
Brooke and me a chance
to take him bicycling.
There were not quite
enough bikes for his se-
curity detail, so his
bodyguards waited in
the limousine while
shepherding duties were
assumed by Kate, our
border collie. (Adrian
Talbott)

Solana had an especially friendly relationship with Primakov's successor as foreign minister, Igor Ivanov (center), an able and affable professional diplomat. That tie, however, was strained almost to the breaking point by the onset of NATO's air strikes against Serbia over Kosovo. (Brooke Shearer)

With "Mr. Hammer" (Victor Chernomyrdin, right) and "Mr. Anvil" (Finnish president Martti Ahtisaari, center) after our first round of talks at Ahtisaari's residence in Helsinki in May 1999. We looked more upbeat than we felt. At that point in the war, Slobodan Milošević showed no sign of cracking, and the Russians were still a long way from supporting NATO's terms for peace. (Lehtikuva Oy)

No sooner was Kosovo behind us than U.S.-Russian relations became wrapped around the axle of a dispute over the American anti-missile program. We were also in the early days of what promised to be a bruising and highly partisan presidential election campaign. Russia policy was a prime target for the Republicans, and therefore so was I. Clinton opened a meeting in the Cabinet Room in mid-August 1999 by asking, "Well, Strobe, what have you done today to sell out U.S. national security to the Russians?" This picture was taken at just the moment of my comeback (which is lost to history). On the left are Bob Bell, the National Security Council's leading expert on arms control, and Jim Steinberg, the deputy director of the NSC. At my other side are Secretary Albright; Sandy Berger; Secretary of Defense Bill Cohen; General Joseph Ralston, vice-chairman of the Joint Chiefs of Staff; and Leon Fuerth of the vice-president's staff. The meeting yielded a decision to launch an intensive round of talks with the Russians on amending the Anti-Ballistic Missile Treaty. (The White House)

There were times in our work together when Yuri Mamedov and I felt we were seeing more of each other than of our wives, Katya and Brooke. Only once did we manage to bring the four of us together—in Rome, in March 2000—as Yuri and I were preparing for the first presidential meeting between Bill Clinton and Vladimir Putin. On a Saturday we put the issue of national missile defense aside and traveled to a hill town in the Italian countryside. Driving back into Rome that evening, Yuri and I got back to business. (Author's collection)

Vladimir Putin was all charm and low-key, polite sales resistance when he received Clinton at the Kremlin for a private dinner in June 2000. Clinton was pushing a compromise on anti-missile defenses, but the new Russian president was clearly waiting for a new American president before making any deals. (AFP/Corbis)

Clinton had a final meeting with Yeltsin, now in retirement, at his dacha outside Moscow. Left to right: Vladimir Shevchenko, Yeltsin's longtime—and long-suffering—protocol chief; Jim Collins; Sandy Berger; Tatyana Dyachenko, Yeltsin's daughter and political confidant; Clinton; Yeltsin; Yeltsin's wife, Naina; and John Podesta, the White House chief of staff. (The Kremlin)

In December 2000, I arranged for Yuri Mamedov to pay a farewell call on Clinton. While the outcome of the Florida recount and the battle in the Supreme Court had yet to be decided, Yuri was already wondering how different the policies of a George W. Bush administration would be from those of the past eight years. Clinton predicted that the logic in favor of continuity would prevail over the temptations of a new administration to make a drastic break with its predecessors. (The White House)

ended—he wanted to get on with the job at hand. He pressed Clinton to join him in releasing a statement that day announcing that the Gore-Chernomyrdin commission was back in business. He added, almost as a throwaway line, that of course the bombing pause would begin the moment that Gore and Chernomyrdin began their meeting.

Clinton started to demur, but Yeltsin cut him off, his voice rising. He was "holding himself in check," he said, "suppressing his emotions"; he was trying his best to save face for all sides, to carve out a little space that would permit them to cooperate in the future; they might yet avert disaster if Clinton would just agree to the pause.

Clinton said he couldn't do that. The allies had just set firm conditions for a pause, and until Milošević met those, the bombing would continue.

"Don't push Russia into this war!" said Yeltsin, now practically shouting into the phone. "You know what Russia is! You know what it has at its disposal! Don't push Russia into this!"

When Clinton heard the translation of what Yeltsin had said, he pursed his lips and furrowed his brow. Rather than respond to what had come close to being a warning of the danger of nuclear war between the U.S. and Russia, Clinton chose to reiterate, in as positive a fashion as possible, the conditions for what Yeltsin wanted. The call, he said, had been helpful because it had "clarified" what would have to happen to bring about the pause. Clinton promised that Gore would call Chernomyrdin right away, and he would send me to Moscow to serve as a point of initial contact for the new U.S.-Russian initiative.

Suddenly soothed, Yeltsin pronounced himself satisfied: "I think our discussion was candid, constructive and balanced. We didn't let our emotions get in the way, even if I was a little more talkative than you."

"Good-bye, friend," said Clinton, relieved to be able to end the conversation on that note. "I'll see you."

THE NEXT DAY, while I was en route to Moscow, Gore talked on the phone to Chernomyrdin for over an hour. They agreed that they would have a one-time meeting in Washington seven days later, on May 3, rather than reconstitute the commission. Gore's campaign for the Democratic nomination was off to a rocky start. He faced a challenge from former New Jersey senator Bill Bradley and was having trouble positioning himself against the Republican field. Polls showed him running well behind both the front-runner, George W. Bush, and Elizabeth Dole.

When I saw Chernomyrdin at his Gazprom office on Tuesday, April 27, the first words out of his mouth were: "I really feel for Al Gore. I see what he's going through. I'm a politician, and I know how hard it can be. My heart goes out to him."

"I'm sure the vice-president will appreciate the good wishes," I said, hoping to move us quickly to the matter at hand, "but my impression is that he's doing fine."

Chernomyrdin hadn't finished yet. "I'll tell you frankly that I'm truly worried about Al's participation in problem-solving in the Balkans, because it could either lift him to great heights or bring him down—if not forever, then for a long time to come. For this reason, I want him to make the choice for himself. I haven't insisted on his participation as a condition for my own involvement. However, if this thing works, it could be a plus for Al as a statesman." It pained him, he said, "to see all our previous accomplishments—of which Al Gore and I can be so proud—turning to dust, or to hot ashes. U.S.-Russian relations have been a good part of his life. I want to see the U.S.-Russian relationship continue positively, and I'm glad that President Yeltsin is beginning to be more active on Kosovo. To me, U.S.-Russian relations are sacred, and no one should be able to drive a wedge between our countries. I have heartfelt concerns about the potential negative consequences for Al Gore if our collaboration is fruitless or worse, especially considering that the U.S. presidential election is only a year and a half off."

It was one of the relatively few moments during my time in government when I felt an acute tension between my curiosity and the constraints of my office. I would like to have heard more from Chernomyrdin on this subject, for more insight into him, but I knew that I should be hearing less. Even though we were alone and there would be no formal record of the conversation, I didn't want to encourage him to continue in this vein. All of us on the foreign-policy team were at pains to keep our work at as much of a remove as possible from the campaign.

CHERNOMYRDIN, seeing that I didn't want to continue the conversation about Gore's candidacy, got down to the business at hand, starting with a report on a visit he'd just made to Belgrade. He said he'd told Milošević that Russia was prepared to act "as an intermediary but not as an advocate or a defender. Our goal is to get a peaceful solution—not to do Milošević's bidding."[7]

That said, NATO had "to give Milošević a way out. Right now you're driving him into a corner." If the bombing continued, he said, Milošević would hold out and NATO would have no choice but to invade Serbia. A ground war would give the Serbs "a pretext for a bloodbath, which is a specialty of theirs." It would be "a disaster for everyone if you get into a ground war there, and I mean for *everyone!*" He gave me a long, significant look, to make sure I knew what he meant. After Yeltsin's menacing comment to Clinton two days before, I did indeed.

When I reviewed the conditions for the bombing to stop, Chernomyrdin objected most strenuously to the requirement that Serb forces pull out of Kosovo. We had to "take Milošević's views into account." Unless Serb forces were allowed to remain in Kosovo, the province would, de facto, no longer be part of Serbia. The NATO bombing would have helped the Kosovars achieve independence. That outcome would not only be unacceptable to Milošević, it was impermissible from Russia's standpoint as well, because of the precedent it would create for Chechnya and the disintegration of Russia itself.

Shortly after my meeting with Chernomyrdin, he and Yeltsin complained to Kofi Annan, the secretary-general of the United Nations, about the "crazy" American refusal to permit any Serbian forces to stay behind. To their chagrin, Annan backed the logic of total withdrawal. His hosts, he said, had it exactly backward: as long as there were *any* Serb forces left in Kosovo, the Albanian refugees would not feel they could safely come home, and the peacekeepers would be caught in the crossfire between Albanian guerrillas and Serb forces. There would be no peace to keep, so the bombing would continue.

AT THE BEGINNING OF MAY, Chernomyrdin flew to Washington to see Gore. They met briefly the afternoon of May 3, then resumed their discussion for over three hours that evening in the dining room of the vice-presidential residence on Massachusetts Avenue. Having observed the interaction between the two many times over six years, I found this encounter uncharacteristically stiff, slogging and unproductive. Each of them was reviewing for the record the basics of his own government's opening position. Gore wasn't going to let himself be drawn into give-and-take, and Chernomyrdin, as I'd already heard from him directly, was sensitive to the constraints on Gore. He was in the market for another partner. Near the end of the talks, Chernomyrdin proposed that we find "an international personage" with whom he could work in tandem—

someone, as he put it, "to accept the sword of surrender from Milošević." He couldn't play that role himself, he implied, because he would never survive the political backlash at home. He and his new partner, along with someone representing the U.S., would constitute a "troika" that would drive Milošević into submission.

As we were going to our cars, I suggested to Sandy Berger that there might be a way to make Chernomyrdin's idea work. The trick would be to find a statesman who was not associated with NATO but who agreed with the alliance on the conditions Milošević had to accept. The best candidate was President Ahtisaari of Finland. He was the leader of a nonaligned country and in July would be taking over from Chancellor Gerhard Schroeder of Germany the rotating chairmanship—or presidency, as it was known—of the European Union. Most important, Ahtisaari demonstrated during his visit to Washington just over a week before that he was unswerving on the need for NATO's two key demands: the withdrawal of Serb forces from Kosovo and a NATO-led peacekeeping force, to be known as KFOR.

Sandy liked the plan and gave it a name: Hammer and Anvil. Chernomyrdin would pound away on Milošević; Ahtisaari would provide the backing so that Milošević would be pummeled into acceptance of NATO's conditions. We tried it out on Secretary Albright, and when she joined another round of talks between Gore and Chernomyrdin the next morning, she proposed Ahtisaari. Chernomyrdin agreed instantly. Finland, as he put it, had "always conducted itself respectfully toward Russia" and Ahtisaari had "excellent" relations with Yeltsin.

When I called Ahtisaari with the proposal, he said he was prepared to take on the task as long as he had the backing of the EU.[8] That was quickly arranged with the Germans through the number two in their Foreign Ministry, Wolfgang Ischinger, who had been my principal counterpart in Bonn during the NATO-Russia negotiations.

Before leaving Washington, Chernomyrdin asked me to meet him in Moscow eight days later, on May 12, so that we could "begin this colossal work of ours." For purposes of the project that lay ahead, he now fully understood that his preferred partner, Al Gore, was otherwise engaged— he had seen that during their sessions—and he'd have to accept me as a stand-in. He started addressing me in the familiar form of the second person and calling me by my first name, although it always came out sounding like "Strep."

THE EMPTY CHAIR

At about midnight on May 7, B-2 bombers that had taken off from Whiteman Air Force Base in Missouri and refueled midair over the Atlantic dropped five 2,000-pound bombs on the Chinese embassy in Belgrade, killing three members of the staff and wounding twenty. NATO targeters, operating with an outdated map, thought they were hitting the Yugoslav arms procurement headquarters.

I heard the first reports of the incident on the radio while driving home with Brooke from visiting a friend in the country. I had to pull over to the side of the road and recover from a jolt of abject dismay. There had been other bombing mistakes, with greater loss of life, in the forty-four days of bombing—NATO was flying five hundred sorties a day—but this was far and away the worst politically. My first reaction was that we could say good-bye to any chance for the Chernomyrdin-Ahtisaari initiative, which I was supposed to help launch the following week. Brooke gave me a pep talk: this kind of thing was inevitable in wartime; we had no choice but to acknowledge the mistake and keep bombing.

The Chinese refused to believe the strike had been a mistake and went into a frenzy of protest. Crowds in Beijing tried to storm our embassy, vandalizing the grounds and trapping our ambassador, Jim Sasser, and other employees inside. China, as a member of the UN Security Council, could veto resolutions we would need in the future to establish a NATO-led peacekeeping force in Kosovo. The Russians, I feared, would take heart from the incident and have less incentive to reinforce our hard line with Milošević.

Just before I left for Moscow to see Chernomyrdin, I received word that he was making a quick trip to Beijing but would be back in time for our appointment on May 12. That didn't sound auspicious. When I got to Moscow on Tuesday, I had to run a gauntlet of Serb, Chinese and Russian protestors on the sidewalk outside the U.S. embassy. When I met with Yuri Mamedov at Spaso House that night, he warned me that Yeltsin was close to pulling the plug on Chernomyrdin's mission.

THE NEXT MORNING I awoke to the news that Yeltsin had pulled the plug on Yevgeny Primakov instead, replacing him as prime minister with Sergei Stepashin, the forty-seven-year-old interior minister. Yeltsin had never regarded Primakov either as committed to reform or entirely loyal.

The proximate cause for Primakov's dismissal was his attempt to form alliances in the spring of 1999 with the communists for the purpose of getting legislation passed. But the communists were more interested in impeaching Yeltsin on charges ranging from his mishandling of the war in Chechnya to his responsibility for the dissolution of the Soviet Union.

By shaking up the government, Yeltsin was trying, in a single stroke, to throw his enemies in the Duma off balance and to put at the head of the government someone in whom Yeltsin, his entourage and his "family"—a collective noun that seemed to refer almost exclusively to Tatyana—could be more confident.[9]

Gaidar, Chubais and other reformers were, on the whole, ecstatic about the change, mostly because they, like our Treasury Department, regarded Primakov as hopeless on the economy. Also, they saw Stepashin as a pragmatist of their own generation.

Stepashin's background, however, was heavily in the security field. He bore his own large share of responsibility for Chechnya (and had been fired for his role there in 1995). The Ministry of the Interior didn't seem the ideal incubator for the future leaders of Russian democracy. But security was exactly what Yeltsin—and "the family"—were thinking about: their own. They were already looking ahead to Yeltsin's departure from office and wanted someone in the premiership who could move up to the presidency and, from that post, protect them from the wrath of their opponents in the Duma and elsewhere. They also seriously considered replacing Primakov with Vladimir Putin, the former head of the Federal Security Service who had taken over as head of Yeltsin's Security Council in March.[10] In the end, Yeltsin decided that replacing Primakov with Putin would look bad, since they were both spymasters, and therefore he would hold Putin in reserve for shake-ups still to come.[11]

WHEN I CALLED ON the normally cool and resilient Igor Ivanov at his office in the Foreign Ministry, I found him despondent about the downfall of his friend and mentor Primakov. He had no idea whether Stepashin would keep him on as foreign minister. His only contact with the leadership had been a summons to see Yeltsin, who was "like Zeus hurling thunderbolts," some of which, he implied, were aimed at Ivanov himself for having failed to end the war.

Ivanov had been counting on the Europeans to break ranks with the U.S., especially after the bombing of the Chinese embassy. That bet wasn't paying off. The French, even though they were of all our allies the most openly resentful of American power and resistant to American leadership, remained unshakable on the need to keep bombing.[12]

Chancellor Schroeder sent word to Yeltsin that he, too, wasn't going to be swayed. Even Yeltsin's old friend Helmut Kohl, now in retirement, phoned him to say that the bombing must go on until Milošević gave in to NATO's conditions.

With no sign of letup in the air strikes or give on Milošević's part, Yeltsin faced an unpleasant prospect: in less than six weeks, on June 18, he was scheduled to meet face-to-face with Clinton, Chirac, Schroeder and Blair in Cologne at the next G-8 summit. If the war was still raging by then, Yeltsin would have little choice but to boycott the meeting or stage a Budapest-like blowup there. Neither option appealed to him. The G-8 was a long-sought, hard-won trophy of his presidency. Its annual summit was supposed to be the apotheosis of Russia's new respectability and Yeltsin's personal prestige. He didn't want to be a no-show, the odd man out or a spoiler in Cologne—he wanted to go there as a peer and peace-maker. But that meant there had to be peace—and soon.

WHEN I MET WITH Chernomyrdin at his office, he gave me the full, splenetic flavor of what he'd heard in Beijing about American perfidy. But then abruptly he started probing for some give in the conditions set forth at the NATO summit, particularly in our insistence on the removal of the nearly 50,000-troop Yugoslav army, special forces and police in Kosovo. How many of those might we be prepared to allow to remain as part of a deal? he asked. What about something like 24,000? As I sat there shaking my head at him, he kept jabbing numbers at me: 20,000? 10,000? 5,000?[13]

He was heading in the right direction, I said, but the only answer was zero. Chernomyrdin threw up his hands as though we had reached a dead end, but the exchange actually seemed to clarify for him the way forward: the success of his mission would hinge on a single three-letter word— "all"—and whether it remained in the terms that he got Milošević to accept.

CHERNOMYRDIN, AHTISAARI and I met for the first time together in Helsinki on May 13, just before Chernomyrdin was to make his third trip to Belgrade. Chernomyrdin came to Helsinki hoping that Ahtisaari would side with him against me on the need to leave some Serb forces behind in

Kosovo and to restrict the role of NATO in the Kosovo force. Ahtisaari did just the opposite. As commander in chief of his own country's armed forces, he said, he wasn't going to put a single Finn into Kosovo unless two conditions prevailed: all armed Serbs had to be out, and the Finnish contingent had to be under NATO command. Otherwise the mission was sure to crumble into chaos. That was why the two principles—total Serbian withdrawals and NATO "at the core" of the force—had to be affirmed, in writing, by Milošević before the bombing could stop. (By the end of that round of talks, Ahtisaari had come up with his own shorthand for the two points: "the zero option"—which we regarded as not optional but compulsory—and "hard-core NATO.")

A WEEK LATER Chernomyrdin, Ahtisaari and I reconvened in Moscow so that Chernomyrdin could report on his trip to Belgrade. We met at a government retreat outside Moscow that I knew as Stalin's Nearby Dacha. It was where Chernomyrdin and his wife had entertained the Gores in July 1996. I was glad finally to see the place, since it had figured prominently in Khrushchev's memoirs as the site of boozy all-night politburo dinners.

Chernomyrdin, Ahtisaari and I had a rather lively and lengthy session of our own, although we kept the vodka to a minimum—a few toasts over dinner. Chernomyrdin claimed that with heroic effort during seven hours of brutal talks in Belgrade, he had gotten Milošević to agree that NATO could be "on the ground" in Kosovo.

That was nowhere near good enough, we said. Milošević was obviously reserving the right to choose which NATO countries he allowed into Kosovo, and he would try to exclude all those engaged in the bombing campaign. He had to understand that the major allies would be there in force—and in charge.

If we continued to insist on that condition, said Chernomyrdin, the war would go on indefinitely, turning the entire Balkans into a "sea of blood. Maybe that's what your people in Washington really want!" he said to me.

He was referring particularly to Secretary Albright, whose picture had recently appeared on the cover of *Time* magazine with an article headlined "Madeleine's War." Shortly after this outburst, Madeleine herself called me on my cell phone to check on how the talks were going. Chernomyrdin asked me to put the question bluntly to my *mat-nachalnitsa* (mamma boss): Would she be willing to stop the bombing under any circumstances? I told him he could ask her himself and handed him the phone. He switched into his charming mode and chatted away pleasantly with her in Russian for a few minutes. From that point on in my dealings with Chernomyrdin, Madeleine was always referred to as *mat-nachalnitsa*. When I told her, she didn't mind in the least.

AROUND MIDNIGHT, after almost as many hours with Ahtisaari and me as he'd spent with Milošević, Chernomyrdin gave in to our arguments that NATO had to be in charge of the international military force, and he adopted the magic words "at the core."

Ahtisaari and I both felt we were finally getting somewhere with Chernomyrdin.

But was Chernomyrdin really getting anywhere with Milošević, the past master of the phony concession and the bait-and-switch? To illustrate that point, I got up from the table and brought over an additional chair from the corner to use as a prop. When it became clear that we were closing the gap between us, I would point to the empty chair and ask, "Yes, fine, Victor Stepanovich"—I addressed him, as was the custom in Russian, by his first name and patronymic—"but what about that guy? Will he go along with what we're agreeing?"

"We won't really know," said Chernomyrdin, "until Martti and I go to Belgrade together."

WE SHOULD HAVE PUT a second empty chair at the table representing the Russian Ministry of Foreign Affairs. When I went to see Igor Ivanov the next morning, he repudiated Chernomyrdin's acquiescence to the principle of NATO at the core. What Chernomyrdin had agreed to, he said, was "unacceptable to the Russian government."

When I protested, Ivanov picked up the phone on his desk and called Chernomyrdin at his home, apparently waking him up. I listened while Ivanov politely, patiently explained that Russia might be able to accept the participation of *individual* NATO member-states in KFOR but not "NATO as an organization or as a bloc" being given overall responsibility for the operation.

He was silent for a minute while Chernomyrdin replied. Judging from Ivanov's expression and comeback, I could tell Chernomyrdin was objecting to being second-guessed. Ivanov held his ground. In effect, he dictated new instructions to Chernomyrdin over the phone and told him that he'd be sending me back to see him for a new round of talks.

Normally, I did not include temper tantrums and walkouts in my diplomatic repertoire, but this latest development called for an exception. When Ivanov hung up, I told him that it was up to the Russian side to decide whether he had the authority to overrule Yeltsin's personal representative but he didn't have the authority to send me to go see anyone. I was heading straight for the airport. I would send word ahead to Washington that the U.S. was pulling out of the whole venture.

Ivanov backed down slightly. He asked me if I'd please go see Chernomyrdin again and seek either a clarification or a confirmation of what I'd heard the night before. If Chernomyrdin reaffirmed the notion of NATO at the core, I could take that as an authoritative statement. But, he added, the Foreign Ministry couldn't accept responsibility "for so fundamental a change in Russian policy."

Just then, as I was getting up to go, Ivanov received a phone call from the new prime minister, Sergei Stepashin, notifying Ivanov that he would be retained as foreign minister. Ivanov took the call standing at attention and thanked the prime minister for the chance to serve his country. When I later told some of my colleagues about witnessing this show, they suspected it was precisely that—a show, concocted to impress me with Ivanov's standing and to undermine Chernomyrdin. I don't think so. I think I got a serendipitous glimpse into the workings of a barely functional government that was scrambling to organize itself before my eyes. Ivanov's own performance was more or less what it seemed: he was a foreign minister who didn't know until near the end of our conversation whether he even still had his job and who didn't know who was calling the shots at the top—but who did know that "NATO at the core of KFOR" was poison for the military and the Duma, and therefore for any Russian official who accepted it.

When I saw Chernomyrdin, he was still rattled by the wake-up call he'd gotten from Ivanov—and perhaps from others he'd had as well. He backtracked on our understanding of the night before.

"You've got to find a way out of this for us, Strobe," he pleaded. "If President Yeltsin agrees to subordinate Russian troops to the alliance which has been waging this war, the impeachment process against him will start all over again."

It looked as though the one meaningful bit of progress we'd made at Stalin's dacha the night before had evaporated.

From that day forward, Chernomyrdin was on a shorter leash. It was harder for me to see him alone, and his minders were more intrusive during our meetings. One was a diplomat from the Foreign Ministry, Boris Ivanovsky, who played the role of a grumpy Jiminy Cricket, whispering to Chernomyrdin and passing him notes with reasons he couldn't do whatever we were asking. Foreign Minister Ivanov himself started showing up for some of the negotiating sessions, to the obvious displeasure of Chernomyrdin.

The representative of the Ministry of Defense on Chernomyrdin's delegation was Colonel-General Leonid Ivashov, whom I vividly remembered as the military intelligence officer who had done his best to scuttle agreement in the final round of negotiations over the NATO-Russia Founding Act in 1997. Ivashov threw himself with verve into his new task of driving a spike through a NATO-led international force.

The two Pentagon officers on my team, Lieutenant General Robert "Doc" Foglesong of the Air Force, a fighter pilot who had risen through the ranks, and Brigadier General George Casey of the Army, deserved the diplomatic equivalent of the Purple Heart for the countless hours they spent butting heads with Ivashov and other Russian officers.

Chernomyrdin, who had his eye on the Cologne deadline, chafed at his own military's stalling tactics, and referred several times to Ivashov as "Comrade Commissar."

THE ENDGAME

As we approached the end of May, Chernomyrdin, Ahtisaari and I felt it was time to go for broke. It had become harder by the day for Yeltsin to justify keeping Russia in the diplomatic game while the bombing continued. Ahtisaari was feeling the heat from the Europeans, especially from Schroeder, to deliver a settlement. I faced growing skepticism within my own government about whether the Russians had any clout with Milošević—a point on which I had some doubt myself.

The three of us agreed that it was time for Ahtisaari and Chernomyrdin to double-team Milošević: they would make their long-awaited joint trip to Belgrade the last week in May. We also agreed that the mission was more likely to succeed if the two took with them a single document spelling out the steps that both of them felt were necessary for a halt in the bombing. That would eliminate any difference between what Mr. Hammer and Mr. Anvil would be saying and further reduce Milošević's wiggle room.

We scheduled what we hoped might be our climactic session at Stalin's dacha on Wednesday, May 26, with the principal task of trying to negotiate a joint text.

I arrived in Moscow the afternoon before and was meeting with Mamedov at Spaso House when Sandy Berger called from Washington to alert me that the International War Crimes Tribunal in The Hague was about to indict Milošević for his role as the mastermind of Serbian atrocities against civilians in Kosovo. At about the same time, Ahtisaari, who was just preparing to leave Helsinki and fly to Moscow, received a call from Kofi Annan with the same news.

The indictment was not just warranted, it was imperative if the tribunal was to have any credibility. The timing, however, was not, to put it mildly, ideal from the parochial standpoint of our trilateral diplomacy. When Ahtisaari and I arrived at Stalin's dacha the next morning, Chernomyrdin instructed with great fanfare that the empty chair once again be brought to the table, since dealing with Milošević was now going to be all the harder, thanks to the tribunal.

Nonetheless, Chernomyrdin agreed to make yet another trip to Belgrade alone—his fourth—in order to lay the ground for the one that he and Ahtisaari would make together the following week.

THESE MISSIONS were not just diplomatically arduous and politically punishing for Chernomyrdin, they were physically dangerous as well. Serbian anti-aircraft units were on hair trigger, and there was no telling what Milošević might do if he felt that Russia was indeed about to endorse NATO's demands. As for NATO itself, it had closed the skies over Yugoslavia. I rather enjoyed asking Doc Foglesong to review for General Ivashov and the assembled Russian officers in Stalin's dacha some of the procedures we would put in place to open a corridor for the Russian aircraft, but it gave me no pleasure to see Chernomyrdin's face take on the look of a most unhappy frequent flyer.

Chernomyrdin invoked Yeltsin's name only once during our meeting, after he stepped out to take a call from Prime Minister Stepashin, who was with Yeltsin and calling from the presidential limousine. According to Stepashin, Yeltsin was in high dudgeon over the news out of The Hague, convinced that it was an attempt to sabotage Russian peacemaking and to prevent Yeltsin from having a diplomatic triumph for which he would be applauded in Cologne.

When I heard that Chernomyrdin had talked only to Stepashin, I took it as a bad sign about Yeltsin's condition or Chernomyrdin's access to him, or both.

ON SUNDAY, MAY 30, the Kremlin sent word to the White House that Yeltsin wanted to talk to Clinton the next day, Memorial Day. When the call came through, the Kremlin operator said Yeltsin was "indisposed" and Prime Minister Stepashin was on the line instead. The prime minister was all business. He suggested that Clinton send someone "responsible"—he repeated the word several times with greater emphasis each time—who could, he implied, make the adjustments in the NATO conditions that would be necessary if the Ahtisaari-Chernomyrdin mission was going to succeed. Stepashin left no doubt that he wanted the American representation to be upgraded to the level of vice-president or, failing that, secretary of state.

Listening on an extension phone at the other end of the Oval Office, I gave a start and began to send the president some rather urgent hand signals. He gave me a wink and a not-to-worry gesture. He told Stepashin that I'd be coming with full authority. After hanging up, Clinton was more amused than I was about how close I'd come to getting fired from the most important assignment of my career by the prime minister of Russia.

"I guess you've gotten a reputation with those people for being a real hard-ass," he said. "That's not what they say about you around here."

Then he turned serious: "You know, if I had to guess, I'd bet they think they've got something lined up in Belgrade and they're getting ready to nail it."

THE FINAL MEETING began on June 1 in a German government guest-house on the Petersberg, a mountain overlooking the Rhine outside of Bonn. We chose the site at the request of Chancellor Schroeder so that he could put in an appearance at what he, and we, hoped would be a break-through meeting.

For all of the first day, which continued long into the night, it looked as though the Germans were hosting a fiasco. In addition to refusing to en-dorse total withdrawal of Serb forces, the Russians had refined their de-mand for a geographical division of labor and the command structure for a Kosovo force in a way that made it even less acceptable: the whole operation must be under UN "political" control, and there must be a separate sector for a Russian contingent that would not be subordinated to NATO.

Our position was essentially the same as the one that Bill Perry had gotten the Russians to accept four years earlier in Bosnia: a single, unified NATO command for the whole operation, with the Russian peacekeepers reporting directly to an American officer and thus only indirectly to NATO. We called this arrangement "Dayton rules" or "the Bosnia model."

General Ivashov, who did most of the talking for the Russian side on military questions, replied brusquely that his ministry hadn't liked that model in Bosnia and wasn't going to accept it in Kosovo.

In that case, we told Ivashov, Russia had the option of not participating. Regrettable as that would be, it was better than a separate Russian sector under a separate command, which would be a recipe for the ethnic partition of Kosovo, since the Serbs would gravitate toward the Russian sector.

In *that* case, said Ivashov, there was nothing more to talk about and they might as well go home.

Yet the Russians stayed and argued.

THROUGHOUT THE AFTERNOON, we tried various formats—large groups and small ones, all three delegations together, the Finns and Americans paired off separately with the Russians, double-cutting back and forth, tête-à-têtes between Chernomyrdin and Ahtisaari, between Chernomyrdin and me. Nothing seemed to be working.

Schroeder swooped in by helicopter in the evening, hoping to toast our success and participate in a press conference. We asked him politely to leave us alone, but he insisted on hosting an elaborate and stilted dinner. Chernomyrdin sat through it irritably, picking at his venison and muttering that we had real work to do.

The talks continued into the night around a converted banquet table in a solarium. One of Chernomyrdin's aides set up a laptop computer and began typing a draft of the document spelling out the terms that Ahtisaari and Chernomyrdin would put to Milošević the next day. There were brackets around words in dispute, most notably the word "all" in the passage on withdrawals.

At around 2 a.m., Ahtisaari got up to stretch, lost his footing on a throw rug and took a header. After a brief recess for first aid, he returned to the negotiations with an ice pack on his forehead. An hour later, my executive assistant, Phil Goldberg, was trying to keep himself awake by taking a walk in the lobby and stumbled into a potted plant. So far the only casualties were on our side and the Russians were still going strong, so I decided we'd just have to negotiate through the night.

Then, during a break in the meeting, I overheard Chernomyrdin in the next room screaming at Ivashov: "I'm not anybody's puppet! You assholes can do this thing without me!"

I took this bit of byplay as reason for hope that Chernomyrdin had been letting Ivashov play the heavy and fail, so that Chernomyrdin could then get the political leadership in Moscow—and we didn't know whether that meant Yeltsin or Stepashin—to overrule the military. I decided to suggest an adjournment so that Chernomyrdin could phone home and we could all get some rest. It was 4 a.m.

AT THE STROKE OF SEVEN, the phone next to my bed rang, waking me out of a fitful sleep. It was a CNN reporter calling to get my comment on the news that the Russians had pulled out of the talks and were going home to Moscow. I made a groggy comment to the effect that the story was false, then staggered out of bed, got dressed and went downstairs to see if I was right. I found the Russians clustered by themselves over breakfast, bleary-eyed and ill-tempered but clearly under instructions to keep negotiating. Chernomyrdin told me that he had indeed been on the phone to Moscow almost nonstop and that I was making his life very difficult.

"This can't go on forever," he said. "We must smash all remaining problems this morning!"

I told him I was all for that.

Meanwhile, our aides had gone back to haggling over the joint statement. Draft after draft kept emerging from the printer connected to the Russian laptop. Suddenly, out came a new version in which the brackets had disappeared around the word "all." Without warning or explanation, Chernomyrdin had apparently accepted total withdrawals.

That left only the gnarly problem of command structure and the Russians' insistence on their own sector. After consulting with Washington, I suggested removing that point from the main text and dealing with it in a footnote that stated the NATO and Russian positions without reconciling them. We could, I figured, finesse that issue for the time being, since the military wiring diagram was none of Milošević's business—it was unfinished business between NATO and Russia.

The closer we got to an agreed text, the more obstreperous General

Ivashov became, and the more peremptory Chernomyrdin was in dismissing his objections. At one point, Chernomyrdin turned to Ivashov and said, "If you're going to keep interrupting me, you can go outside and smoke a cigarette."

In order to keep the pressure on, I kept dropping hints that the window for the joint mission to Belgrade was rapidly closing "for technical reasons"—the onset of darkness would make it too dangerous to fly. To improve the atmospherics, I asked Toria Nuland to suggest that the drivers in Ahtisaari's motorcade gun their engines and test their sirens.

Finally, Chernomyrdin leaned across the table and looked me hard in the eye. "If Milošević meets those conditions," he asked, "can you absolutely and immediately guarantee me that the bombing will stop?"

"Yes, Victor Stepanovich," I replied, "once we've verified that he has indeed complied." Having in mind Stepashin's call to Clinton two days before, I added, "And I make this statement *responsibly,* with the full authority of the U.S. government and the president himself."

"Okay, Strep," he said. "I'll hold you to that."

We were just about to get up from the table and shake hands when General Ivashov made a formal statement dissociating himself from the document since the minister of defense had not cleared it. Chernomyrdin pursed his lips and his face turned red at this final display of insubordination, but he said nothing.

For us on the American side of the table, the moment was as disturbing as it was dramatic: Chernomyrdin represented the president of Russia, who was also the commander in chief of the Russian military. Ivashov was committing an act of virtual mutiny. He was certainly flouting the principle of civilian control of the military. Doc Foglesong remarked under his breath as we were getting up from the table, "I can't wait to see what those guys will be like to work with when the orders are coming from NATO rather than from the Kremlin."

AS THE TWO DELEGATIONS hurried to the waiting cars, Jim Swigert, a veteran of Balkan diplomacy on our team, tried to cheer up the lone Russian Foreign Ministry representative, Boris Ivanovsky, who was looking very glum indeed.

"I'll tell you exactly what will happen, Jim," said Ivanovsky. "Milošević will accept this document, and I'll be fired. So see you in Siberia."

Ahtisaari and Chernomyrdin took off from the airport in Bonn within half an hour of each other, between 2:30 and 3 p.m. Ahtisaari had a smoother flight than Chernomyrdin, at least inside the cabin. We later learned that Chernomyrdin and Ivashov had an airborne shouting match. The general returned to his seat muttering about Chernomyrdin, "I'd like to kill that son of a bitch."

WE DIDN'T HAVE TO WAIT long for the first word from Belgrade. I was at dinner with my German friend and counterpart, Wolfgang Ischinger, at a restaurant in the shadow of the Petersberg when a call came through from the Finns reporting that the first round with Milošević had gone "suspiciously well." Milošević seemed ready to come to closure. He tried several times to suggest "improvements" in the hammer and anvil document, but Ahtisaari told him, "Not one comma can be changed."

Milošević said he'd have to consult with his parliament, a pseudo-democratic body that was very much under his thumb.

THE NEXT DAY, Thursday, June 3, just as CNN began reporting that the parliament in Belgrade appeared to be close to approval of the deal, I received a call from Chernomyrdin. He was on a cell phone outside Milošević's office. I could make out voices jabbering in Serbian in the background. "I congratulate you," said Chernomyrdin. Milošević "has taken the decision. I have just one suggestion for you." I feared what was coming next, but it turned out to be good news: Chernomyrdin said we needed to set up a meeting between NATO and the Serbian military as soon as possible to put a cease-fire into effect. Doc Foglesong made arrangements for the NATO commander, Wes Clark, to talk on the phone to General Dragoljub Ojdanić, the chief of staff of the Serbian armed forces.

Early that evening, Ahtisaari flew back to Bonn from Belgrade, and I met him at the airport. The Germans were in a rush to get Ahtisaari into Cologne, where the leaders of the European Union were impatiently waiting for him to present to them the results of his trip. Schroeder, as the host of the event, was afraid that it would offend the *amour-propre* of the EU if Ahtisaari were to "report" to the U.S. before doing so to his fellow Europeans. Ahtisaari, however, refused to be rushed. He invited me to sit with him in the back of his limousine at the end of the runway so that he could fill me in on the essentials of what he'd heard—or, as I saw it, what he'd accomplished.

Even at the hairiest moments of our work together, Ahtisaari had always been blunt and unemotional. He was especially so at this moment—a sure sign, I suspected, that he was both exhausted and exhilarated and therefore all the more determined to keep his feelings under control. He reminded me of a veteran reporter of the hard-boiled school dictating on deadline an eyewitness account of a dramatic breaking story. He started with the facts—there would be plenty of time for the commentary and editorials later—and went straight to the bottom line: Milošević had accepted NATO's ultimatum in its entirety, without qualification. He then gave me the highlights of the meeting.

The first evening in Belgrade, Ahtisaari had read the joint document (minus the footnote) aloud to Milošević and an assemblage of other Serbian leaders. He added four points: Chernomyrdin, who was sitting next to him, agreed to the terms; those terms were non-negotiable; they were the best Milošević could hope for; and if they were rejected, NATO's next offer would be worse from the Serbian standpoint. Milošević put up surprisingly little fight. He seemed interested in getting the deal done as quickly as possible. It was Ahtisaari's impression, from everything he'd heard and sensed in Belgrade, that Chernomyrdin's endorsement of the conditions was a crucial factor in Milošević's decision to throw in the towel.

"Our friend Victor was absolutely magnificent," said Ahtisaari. "He did everything he promised—without equivocation or complaint. The Serbs were clearly counting on him to offer them an out, and he didn't give them one."

Milošević subsequently referred to the document that Ahtisaari read to him as a "joint proposal of Russia and the G-8, that is, the G-7 plus Russia." While an imprecise description of the Ahtisaari-Chernomyrdin mission per se, that was exactly the way we had wanted him to see the ultimatum.[14]

AS AHTISAARI ROARED OFF toward Cologne with a motorcycle escort, I headed across the tarmac in my own car toward our traveling team's plane, which was waiting to take me to Brussels. At planeside, I called the White House and was patched through to the Oval Office. The president was heartened by the news but he was also wary. We had to allow for the possibility that Milošević was yet again trying to fake us out, he said. We had to be sure that we pinned down the Serbs on everything they had to do before the bombing actually stopped. I recommended that we send

Doc Foglesong immediately to the Macedonian-Serbian border to participate in the talks so that we'd be sure there was someone present who knew exactly what had happened in the negotiations with the Russians.

I took off for Brussels to brief the North Atlantic Council, the political directorate of the alliance, on what had happened in Belgrade and how it fit with the agreements we'd made with the Russians.

Sandy Vershbow, formerly of the National Security Council staff and now our ambassador to NATO, met me as I got off the plane. "This is either too good to be true," he said of the news cascading out of Belgrade, "or it's too true to be good." He was referring to the danger, on all of our minds, that Milošević would find a way to stop the bombing without releasing his grip on Kosovo.

When I arrived at NATO headquarters, I went first to Javier Solana's office. He was as Latin in temperament as Ahtisaari was Nordic, and he grabbed me and gave me a long, fierce hug. I suddenly had difficulty keeping my own emotions in check. We said barely a word to each other, but each knew what the other was thinking. For us both, Milošević's surrender was at least as much a relief as it was a victory. Dropping tons of high explosives on Serbia for nearly two and a half months—with all the attendant destruction, all the hardship for Serbia's people and neighbors, all the stress on the alliance and all the strain in relations with Russia—had been necessary but wrenching for everyone who bore responsibility for the policy. Javier would have gladly forgone the distinction of being NATO's first secretary-general to help lead the alliance into a war, just as I would have much preferred to vindicate the principle of diplomacy backed by force without having to make good on the threat. We'd woken up every one of what had already been seventy days of bombing hoping it would be the last. Now the end really was at hand.

Javier and I went to the main NATO conference room where the nineteen representatives of the allied states were waiting expectantly around a giant oval table. There was, I noticed, an empty chair next to Javier's. It was Wes Clark's. He was upstairs talking on the phone to General Ojdanić, arranging for the border talks that would establish the procedures for the Serb withdrawal, the deployment of the international force and the suspension of the bombing. Wes entered the room halfway through my report. All eyes turned to him. I stopped so that he could tell the group how he had stressed to Ojdanić that "every hour we don't have the meeting is another hour I will be destroying your military machine."

The talks would begin thirty-six hours later at a roadside café called Europa 94 just a few yards over the Serb border inside Macedonia.

AFTER MIDNIGHT, my team and I flew from Brussels to Helsinki for what was supposed to be a valedictory session of the troika, but Chernomyrdin called me from Belgrade with his regrets: he had to get back to Moscow, he said, to "deal with certain matters there." Communists and nationalists in the Duma were accusing him of treason, and Ivashov was going public with his denunciation of the Petersberg agreement. Ivanov told Madeleine that Chernomyrdin was "totally, absolutely finished."

Yeltsin had given Chernomyrdin a writ of plenipotentiary powers, but it was contained in a top-secret decree, so it did Chernomyrdin no good in defending himself against charges that he had exceeded his instructions. Chernomyrdin took the heat stoically. Public abuse came with the job that Yeltsin had given him. When Gore called Chernomyrdin to thank him for all he had done, his old friend didn't utter a word of complaint about the political evisceration he was undergoing in Moscow. He promised Gore the deal would stick.

FOR THE NEXT SEVERAL DAYS we weren't so sure. It wasn't clear whether Chernomyrdin's agreement to the Petersberg document was binding on the Russian government. The forces so vociferously represented by Ivashov seemed to get a second wind. Milošević's negotiators in the border talks dug in their heels, in part, it seemed, because the Russians were giving them cover. A number of military officers from Moscow showed up on the Serb side of the table with a pan-Slavic glint in their eyes. The Russian ambassador to the UN, Sergei Lavrov, started haggling over the details of the resolution that was necessary to authorize the international force to enter Kosovo. The Chinese were happy to contribute to the wrangling, since it gave them a chance to show how furious they still were over the bombing of their embassy in Belgrade.

Clinton called Yeltsin on Monday, June 7, to warn him that Lavrov's tactics at the UN were making it harder to get the bombing turned off.

Now that Yeltsin was back in communication, he seemed to be in overdrive. He started replying to Clinton's points before they were even translated into Russian. Insofar as we could make sense of what he was saying, it sounded positive. He was desperate to bring the war to an end, and he promised that Russia would cooperate with us to do so.

Over the next few days, after some additional foot-dragging, the Russians finally closed ranks with us at the UN, and no doubt as a consequence, Milošević instructed his forces—*all* of his forces—to prepare to withdraw. Once again, the Serbs bitterly blamed the Russians for forcing them, however belatedly, to come to heel.[15]

We had, with Russia's help, enforced the only right answer to the question of who should leave Kosovo. Now we had to turn to the question we had deferred: who should enter, and on what terms?

CHAPTER 13

THE JAWS OF VICTORY

I have had a perfectly wonderful evening, but this wasn't it.
Groucho Marx

OUR AIR FORCE GULFSTREAM took off for Moscow in the late afternoon on Wednesday, June 9, 1999. It was our eighth trip to Europe in ten weeks and the last, we hoped, on the subject of Kosovo. An hour into the flight, we got the news that the negotiators at the border had signed an agreement for a NATO-led international force to move into Kosovo. I felt a full-throated whoop was in order. Toria Nuland, who had been accompanying me to Moscow off and on since our first *zdravstvidaniya* tour in May 1993, gave me a comically stern look. In addition to feeling some responsibility for my official dignity, she didn't think I should be engaging in premature displays of relief when there was more work to be done. But within seconds, all hands on board—buttoned-down diplomats and nerves-of-steel military men—were hooting and hollering, and Toria joined in. The co-pilot opened the cockpit door and peered out at us, inquiring whether some new diplomatic catastrophe had struck.

No, I assured him.

The correct answer was: not yet.

OUR FIRST APPOINTMENT after we landed in Moscow on Thursday morning, June 10, was at the Gazprom office. Victor Chernomyrdin cut a lonely figure; most of the officials who had been at his side during our marathon negotiations had turned against him or dived for cover. Our ambassador, Jim Collins, had brought along a bottle of champagne, which Chernomyrdin opened on the spot. We toasted each other with glass tumblers of the sort that Russians usually use to drink tea. In the midst of this impromptu ceremony, word came that the Duma had passed a resolution relieving him of his duties as a presidential special envoy—a gratuitous bit of unconstitutional pedantry, since he served at the pleasure, such as it was, of Boris Yeltsin.

"They're idiots," said Chernomyrdin. "If they'd had their way, we would still be at war. We've been through something very difficult and very dangerous, but we avoided something much, much worse."

Meanwhile, a few blocks away, at the Ministry of Defense, Doc Foglesong and George Casey were having a far less pleasant reunion with General Ivashov. The subject was the terms of Russia's participation in the international peacekeeping force, the one major item we'd left unresolved in the Petersberg document. Doc and George explained that there would be NATO elements—i.e., troops from allied countries—in each of five sectors in Kosovo, and that all non-NATO participants, including Russia's, would serve under the command of NATO. The whole operation would be under General Sir Michael Jackson of the United Kingdom, who in turn would take his instructions from the North Atlantic Council. In order to make this arrangement palatable to the Russians, Doc and George were prepared to let the Russian unit work through an American general in his national capacity rather than his NATO one.

Ivashov reacted to that attempt to save Russian face the same way he had in the Petersberg talks: It was insulting and unacceptable. Russia would not "take orders" from NATO; it would not settle for anything less than its own sector and certainly would not "beg for scraps from NATO's table."

We'd heard it all before, but now there was no Chernomyrdin to overrule him. As Doc reported to me afterward, "That fella Ivashov seems to have a whole new lease on life. When Chernomyrdin was there to tell him to shut up and salute, he was permanently pissed off. Now he's kind of cocky. I don't like the smell of it."

The signs were no better at the Foreign Ministry. Foreign Minister Ivanov was out of town, so I met with his principal deputy, Alexander Avdeyev. He was, in mentality and technique, a diplomat of the Soviet school, only with a taste for Ralph Lauren suits and ascots. I'd crossed paths, and swords, with him before and preferred to steer clear of him as much as possible, especially during the Kosovo crisis, which was difficult enough without oldthink and cheap polemics. But on this occasion, there was no avoiding him, and he radiated the smugness of a poker player who thinks he's finally drawn a winning hand.

Avdeyev told me, almost in so many words, that we were now in the post-Chernomyrdin phase of Russian engagement in Kosovo, and that real defenders of Russia's national interest (like himself, he implied) were now back in charge. There must be no deployment of the international force into Kosovo until the U.S. accepted Russia's terms for its participation— namely, its own sector, independent of NATO command.

"Otherwise," he added, "there could be difficulties ahead."

I didn't like the sound of that; it implied a threat that Russian troops might preempt NATO by establishing a foothold in Kosovo before the forces under General Jackson's command moved in.

Avdeyev's sneak preview of a thoroughly ugly scenario was on my mind when I called later that day on Prime Minister Stepashin in his office at the Russian White House. He opened with a long, portentous statement comparing the Kosovo conflict to the Cuban missile crisis. "We have just avoided an escalation much as we avoided one in the Caribbean long ago," he said. In helping us to force Milošević to accept NATO's conditions, Russia had made significant concessions of its own, and now it was time for the U.S. to reciprocate by giving the Russians what it wanted in Kosovo. At issue was not just that corner of the Balkans but American behavior everywhere in the world: "The majority of the Russian people and our political elite think that the U.S. is trying to dictate to everyone else in the political and military spheres," Stepashin continued. "I would like to recall the situation of Germany after World War I. Several years after the war, following its humiliating defeat and the armistice, Germany was engulfed by hysteria, which led to Hitler coming to power. The analogy with Russia today is obviously not exact. No Hitler will come to power here, but the psychology is similar."

It was a variation of something we'd been hearing from Russians of different stripes for years: you're dealing with a confused, angry, screwed-up country; don't overplay your strong hand with us; give us a break; otherwise we might do something crazy.

I told Stepashin that judging from the testy exchanges we'd had at the Defense and Foreign Ministries, we had a more immediate and practical problem. I wanted to hear from him that the Russian military would make no move into Kosovo unless its entry was coordinated with NATO and its presence integrated into a single operation with a clear chain of command. Otherwise, I said, Russia ran the risk of snatching a defeat for itself from the jaws of the victory that Chernomyrdin had achieved for Russian diplomacy.

Stepashin didn't want to join in an encomium to Chernomyrdin, but he told me not to worry—he was confident that our military experts could work out a mutually acceptable arrangement in the coming hours.

That wasn't the categorical assurance I was looking for, but it apparently went too far for Avdeyev, who was sitting at Stepashin's side. He started to object to what the prime minister had said.

"If we keep talking and talking, NATO will move in and leave us with nothing to talk about . . ."

Stepashin cut him off abruptly, saying, "Mr. Avdeyev doesn't quite understand."

Avdeyev fell silent, a scowl on his face.

I wasn't sure whether, for the second time in three weeks, I had a ringside seat for a squabble among senior officials of the Russian government, or whether I was being subjected to a good cop/bad cop routine.

I was looking for clarification the next day, Friday, June 11, when I went to the Kremlin to see Vladimir Putin, who was now the secretary of the Russian Security Council. He had been keeping his head down, avoiding controversy and publicity, and therefore figured only slightly in our peripheral vision of Russian politics.

Meeting Putin for the first time, I was struck by his ability to convey self-control and confidence in a low-key, soft-spoken manner. He was physically the smallest of the men at the top—short, lean and fit, while all the others were taller and most of them were hefty and overfed. Putin radiated executive competence, an ability to get things done without fuss or friction (which had been his reputation in St. Petersburg when I'd first heard of him). There were no histrionics nor bombast, none of the mixture of bullying, pleading and guilt-tripping that I associated with the Russian hortatory style. If Yeltsin and Chernomyrdin were, in Marshall McLuhan's terms, hot, Putin was just about the coolest Russian I'd ever seen. He listened with an attentiveness that seemed at least as calculating as it was courteous. With me, as with others, he wanted his visitor to know that he'd done his homework for the meeting by reading the dossier prepared by the intelligence services. He made several references to the details of my interest in Russia over the years, mentioning, for example, the poets I'd studied at Yale and Oxford, Fyodor Tyutchev and Vladimir Mayakovsky.

The effect and no doubt the intent of these personal touches were ambiguous. They were both flattering ("I know you") and unnerving ("I know *all about* you"). I could imagine him debriefing the agents he had run in East Germany, or interrogating a captured spy who'd already been softened up by the rougher types.

Near the outset of our meeting, Putin expressed satisfaction with the way the Kosovo war had given way to a peace—a peace, as everyone knew, that Russia had helped to bring about through its combination of forbearance, tenacity and adherence to high principle. He added, almost in passing, that he was glad to have made his own small contribution—a suggestion to Yeltsin that he appoint Chernomyrdin as special envoy. It was the first I ever heard of Putin's having played this role, but I was glad to have him associate himself with our cooperation in the diplomacy to end the war, since that might make him more supportive of cooperation in the peacekeeping operation to come.

About halfway through my meeting with Putin, Toria Nuland passed me a note saying that the military talks had broken down and that Ivashov had issued—not once, but three times—what could only be characterized as a threat: if NATO entered Kosovo from the south, from Macedonia, without a final agreement on Russia's participation, then Russian forces would unilaterally enter Kosovo from the north, through Serbia. I summarized the message to Putin and said it looked as though we now faced the danger of a military confrontation between our countries.

Putin adopted the bedside manner of an experienced physician with a hypochondriac for a patient. Nothing on the Russian side had changed, he said soothingly.

"Who, by the way, is this Ivashov?" he asked. He made it sound not like a rhetorical question but a genuine expression of puzzlement about the identity of the three-star general who had been the Defense Ministry's principal representative on the Chernomyrdin delegation for the past six weeks and who had been constantly in the newspapers and on television, primarily denouncing Chernomyrdin and the agreement. Whoever Ivashov was, Putin continued, the statement that I found so alarming should be taken as an "emotional outburst," not as a reflection of Russian policy or intention. There would be, he promised, "one hundred percent cooperation and coordination" between our militaries while our differ-ences were being worked out. "Nothing improper" would happen; Russia would stick by everything I'd heard from Stepashin the day before, and there would be a formal, public and authoritative statement from the Kremlin "clarifying" Russian policy before I reached the airport for my flight to Brussels.

SINCE WHAT I'D HEARD from Stepashin had been ambiguous and since there was no public statement from the Kremlin by the time I got to the airport, I should not have taken off. But I did, on a wing and a prayer and a ten-dollar bet with Doc Foglesong as we were taxiing that Ivashov would be fired before sundown.

About half an hour later, somewhere over Belarus, a call came to the plane from General Joe Ralston, the vice-chairman of the Joint Chiefs of Staff, and Sandy Berger. Joe reported that the Russian unit that had been based in Bosnia as part of the peacekeeping force there was now on the move, heading through Serbia, presumably toward Kosovo. Sandy in-structed me to have the plane turn around and go back to Moscow and "raise hell." I went to the cockpit to talk to our pilot. We were just enter-ing Latvian airspace when we made a U-turn. Several members of the team had the same thought: we were "pulling a Primakov"—but with the difference, as my assistant John Bass put it, that we were turning around in order not to disengage but to reengage. I sent word ahead that I needed to meet urgently with Foreign Minister Ivanov.

Back on the ground, we cooled our heels for several hours in the U.S. embassy and watched CNN's live coverage of the Russian armored col-umn making its way across southern Serbia. Many of the soldiers were giv-ing the cheering crowds lined up along the road the three-fingered victory salute of the Serbs. When we arrived at the Laocoön Room of the Foreign Ministry, Avdeyev was gloating: his side had finally turned the tables on us. Ivanov, meanwhile, was on the phone with Madeleine Albright, who was in Macedonia visiting the Albanian refugees there. It was a bizarre ex-change: the secretary of state was informing the foreign minister of Russia that his country's forces had already entered Serbia and were approaching Kosovo, and he was telling her that it wasn't true—Ivanov said he'd looked into the matter and been assured that the Russian contingent was merely "in a position of readiness to enter Kosovo as part of a synchronized op-eration."

Madeleine didn't believe what Ivanov was telling her—we had our own information about troop movements in the Balkans, and it came from sources that we trusted better than the Russian Ministry of Defense. She wasn't sure, however, whether Ivanov was lying to her or being lied to by his own military.

Ivanov was in a state of agitation when he took over from Avdeyev in the talks with our team. No matter what, he said, we absolutely must reach an agreement that night, "so that our forces can go in together." Either he knew the Russian units had jumped the gun, just as Madeleine had told him, or he was afraid that they were about to do so unless our diplomacy caught up with the determination of the Russian military not to be left behind.

For the next hours, we pored over maps and organization charts. Our generals, Doc and George, carried the burden of the negotiation on our end, constantly stepping out in the corridor to call Joe Ralston and others in the Pentagon to identify points of flexibility that might save Russian face while preserving NATO's overall command of all sectors. The Russians would either have to adjust to that bottom line or stand aside and let Western troops go in without them.

At one point, a grim-faced aide appeared to tell Ivanov he must take an urgent call. When he returned, he said that he had just been told that American, British and French troops would be moving into Kosovo the next morning, Saturday, June 12. I knew that the plan was to indeed deploy Saturday at dawn, but all I could tell Ivanov was that NATO couldn't let a "security vacuum" arise as the Serbian forces began to withdraw. It was in no one's interest for the Kosovo Liberation Army to take over, wreaking vengeance on Serbian stragglers and civilians who stayed behind. That made it all the more important for us to agree quickly on terms that would allow Russia to join in the operation when it started.

Ivanov took me into his private office, picked up the phone on his desk and called Marshal Igor Sergeyev, the minister of defense. He proposed bringing my team over to the Defense Ministry right away "to solve this problem once and for all." It was apparent from the long silence as Ivanov listened to Sergeyev's reply that the other minister was neither ready for the meeting nor thrilled at the prospect; he would call us back.

While we waited, Ivanov seemed to lapse into a mood of fatalistic nonchalance. Perhaps because the hard work ahead was between his American visitors and the Ministry of Defense, he and his own ministry could consider themselves off the hook. To kill time and avoid talking about command structures, he gave me a tour of his back office, where he had a Stair-Master and massage table, showed me his collection of porcelain turtles and snapshots from his youth. Still, there was no call from Sergeyev's office, so he poured a scotch for himself and a vodka for me, and joked about how we'd both have to remember this whole episode for our memoirs.[1]

When the call came summoning us to see Sergeyev, the rest of our team had to run the gauntlet of the now-vast horde of reporters and television cameras in front of the Foreign Ministry and travel by minivan to the Defense Ministry. Ivanov and I slipped out through the basement in his limousine. We used the ride as we hurtled across Moscow to discuss the best approach to take with Sergeyev. Ivanov suggested I use words like "responsible" and "equitable," and to invoke the two presidents' names at every possible occasion, stressing the importance that they attached to an amicable settlement. We needed somehow to make Sergeyev—unlike Ivashov and the other officers who would be at the table—feel invested in NATO-Russia cooperation. We had to use the meeting to pry the minister of defense out of the clutches of his hard-line advisers and bring him into line with a compromise that Ivanov was recommending.

When we arrived at the Defense Ministry, there was no one to greet us—the whole first floor of the giant building seemed deserted. Toria had been on the phone to Washington from the minivan and learned that CNN was now reporting that the Russian contingent was deep into Serbia.

My colleagues and I waited for half an hour in an immense conference room. When Defense Minister Sergeyev arrived, he looked furious with the world, not just the mad bombers of NATO but his fellow officers as well, particularly Ivashov and General Anatoly Kvashnin, the burly chief of staff of the Russian armed forces. I suspected that Sergeyev had been getting news from them that constituted an unpleasant surprise—either that, or they were giving him a version of events that he didn't believe.

Foreign Minister Ivanov, the lone Russian civilian in the room, began to introduce the issues to be discussed, mentioning that "NATO is getting ready to deploy . . ."

Sergeyev interrupted: "It has already started deploying."

Doc and I corrected him. We didn't tell him when NATO would cross the border, but we asserted that they were still on the Macedonian side.

Ivanov resumed his introduction. He did a good job of describing, though not endorsing, the NATO position as our side had laid it out to him earlier. He was definitely trying to lay the ground for a command arrangement along the lines of what we were insisting on.

Sergeyev subjected me to a twenty-minute inquisition that while hard-edged in tone, also sounded like a possible prologue to a deal. He was not much interested in the military details, he said. Those could be handled by the "experts." What he wanted to know was whether the U.S. and NATO were prepared to accept certain political principles, which he then enumerated in the form of questions, all variations on the same theme: Did the U.S. and its allies *respect* Russia? Were we prepared to treat Russia on the basis of *equality*? It was Rodney Dangerfield in uniform. Sergeyev's questions were either softballs or spitballs, depending on how my affirmative answers were interpreted once we returned to the all-important details. I noted that Sergeyev's inquisition tracked closely with Ivanov's advice in the car coming over—a coincidence that suggested the two of them, at least, were in cahoots.

As quickly as possible, I turned our side of the discussion over to Doc and George, who were then the stars of a show that went on for hours. With the help of maps and organization charts that we'd had translated into Russian, they walked the Russians through our plan. It was in two phases: NATO and Russia would join in a restricted and preliminary deployment under an American commander wearing his U.S. "hat" rather than his NATO one, while the U.S. and Russia worked out a longer-term arrangement.

For all the Russian officers' belligerence and sense of grievance, they were visibly impressed. Doc and George not only had total mastery of the subject, they also backed up their proposal with military common sense; they were firm but respectful in tone, and they were manifestly trying to find some way of reconciling Russian political needs to NATO's military requirements.

Sergeyev seemed inclined to come to closure, but Kvashnin and Ivashov kept pulling him back with objections, accusations and filibusters. It was my first exposure to Kvashnin, who had commanded a tank division during the Afghanistan war and had led Russia's forces in Chechnya in the mid-1990s. He had the deepest voice I'd ever heard except for General Lebed's, and he used it more loudly than either the size of the group or the acoustics of the room warranted.

At a number of points, Ivashov and Kvashnin whispered to Sergeyev or passed him notes suggesting that they go back to his office for another huddle. Even then, they were not entirely out of earshot, and we would be treated to another round of discordant noises-off. Ivanov, who was usually excluded from these sessions, would go off into a corner and talk in hushed tones on a cell phone, presumably to his own colleagues in the Foreign Ministry and the Kremlin. Doc went off into a corner of his own to consult with General Hugh Shelton, the chairman of the Joint Chiefs, and Joe Ralston. I ducked out several times to update Madeleine, who was airborne returning to Washington from Macedonia.

Near midnight, we learned from a Russian aide to Sergeyev that he and Ivanov had gone to the Kremlin to see Yeltsin. When they returned, their own positions seemed to have hardened: They said Yeltsin himself was demanding a Russian sector outside of the NATO chain of command. They also noted reports that the Western forces were about to move into Kosovo (thus acknowledging that they'd been wrong earlier about NATO's *already* being in Kosovo), and would reach Priština Airport the next morning.

"Please inform the president of the United States," said Ivanov, as though he were reading from an official statement, "that we aren't going to introduce any forces into Kosovo first or create additional problems, but if NATO goes in, ours will go in right behind them."

I replied that if that happened without an agreement and without careful coordination, there would be an "unhappy surprise ending to a drama that the whole world thought had already ended well."

"Our deployment will be synchronized with yours," said Sergeyev. "We're prepared to negotiate the boundaries [of the sectors]. There will be no bumping into each other."

JUST BEFORE 2 A.M., we had another CNN moment. The network reported that Russian troops had reached Belgrade and were heading south, and the Serbs in Priština were already out in the streets getting ready to welcome them. When I shared this breaking news with Sergeyev, he looked acutely uncomfortable and said that the Russian unit would stop at the Kosovo border and not enter unilaterally.

"We don't intend to take action without agreeing on an approach," he added.

"Agreeing with whom?" I asked.

"With you. But if you and NATO go in on your own, we reserve the right to go in."

We wrangled for another hour, then Ivanov called for another break. As he and the other Russians were leaving the room, he turned sympathetically to Toria and said, "Why are you torturing yourself like this? You should go get some rest and let the men handle this."

"You're the one who called for a break, Igor Sergeyevich," Toria replied mildly.

IVANOV WAS GONE for a long time—and he wasn't the one I wanted to see anyway. I set off in search of a Russian officer to find out what was going on. I wandered down an empty corridor and finally found a bedraggled-looking two-star general whom I remembered from his service at the embassy in Washington. He reeked of alcohol. I told him I was tired of waiting and wanted to resume my meeting with Minister Sergeyev immediately. He saluted, turned on his heel a little unsteadily and disappeared around a corner.

By now I could hear voices shouting at each other from some distance down the corridor. The drunken general returned, burped and announced with great formality, "The minister has asked me to convey that he has no information on the subject to which you refer."

"Tell the minister that is not an adequate response. I am here at his invitation, and he is, I believe, responsible for the deployment of Russian armed forces. I am here to meet with him."

The two-star toddled off, never to be seen again.

WHEN THE RUSSIANS finally returned, a little after 3 a.m., Ivanov had a look of theatrical severity on his face. "It's not good news," he said. "We have reports that NATO is deploying."

"That's not true," snapped Doc, who had recently been back in touch with the Pentagon and alliance headquarters. Just to be sure, he and George Casey stepped out to call Shelton and Ralston, who confirmed that NATO was holding in place on the Macedonian side of the border.

At about 4 a.m., Phil Goldberg, who had been monitoring CNN from a staff holding room, brought me a note saying that the Russian troops had arrived at Priština Airport. Sergeyev denied it, but his sidekicks whispered something to him, and he called for another break. This time they were gone nearly an hour, and it sounded as though there was a riot under way down the hall. I heard the thump and crash of articles being hurled against the wall.

Finally, Ivanov rejoined us. He was all alone and in what I took to be an advanced state of distress that he tried to disguise with a display of mock casualness. He entered the room humming and snapping his fingers like a lounge singer. He powered past my colleagues, gave me a quick come-along-with-me jerk of his head and led me next door into an even larger room dominated by Soviet-era murals of battlefields after great Russian victories and military parades in Red Square. The room was heavy with the greasy smell of half-eaten pizzas and hotdogs that we'd had delivered hours before.

Once we were alone, Ivanov switched into a different, no less bizarre charade. He struck the pose of a junior military officer reporting to his superior. He snapped to attention, threw his shoulders back and said, "Mr. Secretary"—a form of address he'd never used with me before—"I regret to inform you that a column of Russian soldiers has accidentally crossed the border into Kosovo, and orders have been issued for them to be out within two hours. The minister of defense and I regret this development."

At almost that moment, my cell phone rang. On the line were both Sandy Berger and his deputy, Jim Steinberg, who were watching the Russian march through Kosovo on the television screens in their offices.[2] I told them that I was in the midst of a conversation with Foreign Minister Ivanov, for whom they had a few choice words that I didn't pass along.

I asked Ivanov if he would immediately release a public statement to the effect of what he'd just told me, and he agreed. We went back into the other room with our colleagues. While I got back on the phone to let Jim Steinberg know how we were proceeding, Toria sat down with Ivanov to help him compose the statement in English. It said, in part, "In connection with the information regarding the appearance of Russian military personnel in Priština, unfortunately this did take place. We're in the process of clarifying how this happened. The military will give an order to leave Kosovo immediately." We called the State Department Operations Center and were patched through to CNN headquarters in Atlanta so that Ivanov could read the statement in a live broadcast.

We never saw Sergeyev, Kvashnin or Ivashov again that night. I was later told that Sergeyev was so incensed over having been lied to by his own people—and put in the position of repeatedly lying to us—that he couldn't bring himself to look us in the eye.

Ivanov's position was no less awkward, but he at least led us out of the Defense Ministry to our cars.

It was 5:30 a.m., Saturday, June 12, and the sun was coming up. Within an hour NATO forces would cross the border into Kosovo from Macedonia. By the time they reached Priština in the late afternoon, two hundred Russian troops were ensconced at the airfield and refused to relinquish it.

THAT SATURDAY was Russia's Independence Day, a celebration of the Russian Federation's declaration of its sovereignty from the USSR in 1990. Jim Collins encountered Stepashin and Putin during the ceremonies at the Kremlin. Both claimed total ignorance of the Russian deployment. Stepashin's alibi was that he had been in the North Caucasus dealing with Chechnya, which hardly explained how he could have been unaware that Russia was potentially on a collision course with NATO.

I went to see Putin in his Kremlin office that afternoon. It was as though nothing alarming or surprising had occurred in the twenty-four hours since I'd previously seen him. He set about explaining—slowly, calmly, in a voice that was sometimes barely audible—why what he'd promised wouldn't happen had now happened. It was all politics, he said; we had to bear in mind that even though the next presidential race was a year off, Russia was already in a "pre-election struggle," and that fact had complicated U.S.-Russian relations. There were hawks and doves in both Russia and the U.S., he said, and Russian hawks had been behind the pre-emptive sprint to Priština Airport. There were "people in the Russian government"—including, he implied, himself—who thought that the deployment had been a mistake. But at least it hadn't led to the loss of life. The damage that Russian hawks had inflicted overnight on U.S.-Russian relations was nothing compared to the injury that NATO had caused to President Yeltsin's prestige with its air war against Serbia.

Putin had managed simultaneously to position himself as a dove and to blame the U.S. for the awkward position in which the hawks had put government officials like himself.

Turning to how we could solve the problem, he hinted that we might still agree on the Bosnia-like compromise that Sergeyev and his generals had rejected the night before. What really mattered, said Putin, was that whatever the outcome, "no one in Russia should be able to call President Yeltsin a puppet of NATO." I said that depended as much as anything on how Russia itself characterized the outcome. We needed to try again, this time by getting Sergeyev together with Secretary of Defense Cohen, with each operating under presidential instructions to solve the problem before the G-8 summit in Cologne, now only seven days away.

Putin said he was prepared to recommend proceeding on that basis.[3]

———

BEFORE MAKING my second attempt to leave Moscow, on Sunday, June 13, I stopped by the Foreign Ministry to talk to Ivanov. Dressed in a sport jacket and an open collar ("since it's our day off"), he was as cool as Putin but a lot more revealing about what had really happened. There had been "a misunderstanding" within his government, he said: Russian forces had entered Kosovo at 3:20 a.m. (Moscow time), while NATO had gone in at 7 a.m. It was supposed to have been the other way around.

"This whole episode will actually help us in the long run," he added, "and by helping 'us,' I mean both our side internally and what we're trying to do together."

I took this as a confirmation of our own guess: Kvashnin and Ivashov had concluded that NATO was going into Kosovo without them, and that our talks in Moscow were a stalling device to permit that to happen. Their repeated and fallacious claims that NATO had already deployed were a smokescreen for Russia to preempt. In pulling this stunt, Kvashnin and Ivashov rolled over the objections of the minister of foreign affairs and very likely, judging from the sound of a ruckus coming from Sergeyev's office, the minister of defense as well.

Ivanov was also hinting that the civilian leadership had drawn the appropriate lesson from this experience and would tighten its control over the military.

He said he was still upset, and always would be, about misleading Madeleine in their phone call on Friday. "Big lies, and even little lies," he said, should be "a thing of the past" in Russian diplomacy.

Gore and Stepashin had talked on the phone the day before, and Ivanov had in front of him a transcript of that conversation. The two had agreed on terms of reference for the Cohen-Sergeyev talks to be held in Helsinki four days later. Ivanov told me, in effect, how those talks would end: Russia would agree to participate in KFOR on the basis of the Bosnia model. He also promised that Russia would not reinforce its troops in Kosovo without an agreement with NATO.[4] I was glad to hear all this, but it came from a civilian who had just admitted that civilians were not entirely in control of the Russian military. It was therefore with some apprehension that my colleagues and I got back on our plane for the flight home. Phil Goldberg made a "no U-turn sign" and asked the pilot to tape it to the windshield in the cockpit.

THE FLASHPOINT

Boris Yeltsin had been out of sight and out of contact during the crisis. I'd heard his name invoked during the long night at the Defense Ministry but had no idea whether he was really approving plans and giving orders or even whether he was aware of what was going on. While our plane was heading home, Clinton finally connected with Yeltsin, primarily to ask him to instruct the Russian commander in Kosovo, Colonel-General Victor Zavarzin, to come to terms with General Jackson, the KFOR commander, and end the standoff at the airport.

Yeltsin seemed never to have heard of Zavarzin, even though he had given him a battlefield promotion that very day. Clinton had to spell the Russian general's name for Yeltsin, who said he would write it down. The conversation paused for him to do so. Then he changed his mind and lapsed back into his most familiar mantra: "Never mind those generals, Bill! Only you and I can solve this problem!"

He proposed that the two of them meet right away, if necessary on a ship or even on a submarine.

It was a pathetic and dangerous moment. The importance that Yeltsin attached to his direct relationship with Clinton had been of diplomatic value many times, but this time, in his addled condition, it was worse than useless. Russian officials listening to the call might conclude that their president was incapacitated and might not follow orders from the Kremlin.

WITHIN HOURS, contrary to the last set of assurances I'd gotten from Ivanov, we learned that the Russians were asking Hungary, Romania and Ukraine for use of their airspace to send cargo aircraft loaded with supplies and as many as 10,000 reinforcement troops to Priština. We worked through our embassies in Budapest, Bucharest and Kiev to persuade those governments to deny permission.

At one point during the night, NATO received reports that Russian Ilyushin-76 transports were airborne and heading for Kosovo, despite the denial of permission to overfly third countries. There was no time to convene a meeting at the White House. Sandy Berger ordered the White House Situation Room to patch together a conference call among the key policymakers to review the facts and consider the options. If we let the Russian planes land and reinforce the unit already on the ground at the airport, we'd have the makings of a serious confrontation. Another possibility was to have the NATO troops on the scene overpower the Russians there so that when the transports arrived the troops they were carrying could be prevented from disembarking. We could also blast the planes out of the air if they illegally entered Romanian or Hungarian airspace.

In short, there were no good options. Fortunately, the information on the basis of which we were operating was no good either. It turned out that the Russian planes weren't in the air after all.

In the midst of all this confusion and tension, I called the new Russian ambassador in Washington, Yuri Ushakov, and strongly advised him to wake up Ivanov in the early hours of the morning in Moscow to let him know that the Russian request for use of Romanian and Hungarian airspace had created the "possible preconditions for a genuine confrontation" between the U.S. and Russia.

I'd lost plenty of sleep over Russia during the previous six and a half years, but this was the first time I had real nightmares.[5]

THE NEXT DAY Clinton and Yeltsin had another phone call. This time Yeltsin sounded merely unwell—he coughed and wheezed constantly during the call—but at least he was coherent and there was no more blathering about a rendezvous on a submarine. He was obviously speaking from carefully prepared talking points written, it seemed, by Foreign Minister Ivanov. Yeltsin said the Russian contingent would work under Bosnia rules. He also promised that there would be no reinforcement of the Russian troops in Priština unless it was part of an agreement with NATO and that he would send orders "immediately" to Zavarzin to negotiate arrangements with Jackson. He also agreed that Cohen and Sergeyev would meet in Helsinki for a last-ditch effort to solve the command problem before the G-8 summit in Cologne, then only four days away.

We waited for two days before there was any sign that Zavarzin had gotten new instructions to deal seriously with Jackson. In addition to orders from Moscow, Zavarzin had another incentive for dropping his defiant stance. His men were running out of food and water and were now having to borrow supplies from the British soldiers bivouacked nearby.

Reflecting on the perilous affair after it was over, Clinton said that he had never believed that it had the makings of a full-scale, nuclear showdown. Unlike Khrushchev in 1962, Yeltsin was not testing the will of the

American president. But loose-cannon elements in the Russian military were almost certainly testing the limits of civilian control and exploiting the shaky condition of their own president—and that Clinton considered dangerous enough. If the confrontation had led to bloodshed before it could be defused, the resulting political damage would have made it impossible for NATO and Russia to cooperate in the peacekeeping operation that was to follow.

FOR THE PAST month and a half, I'd been counting on Yeltsin's desire to be well received at the Cologne summit of the G-8 as our trump card in the negotiations with Russia over Kosovo. That deadline had driven Yeltsin to order Chernomyrdin to get the bombing stopped, and it would, I hoped, drive Yeltsin now to order Sergeyev to come to terms with Cohen on the command structure so that Russia could be part of KFOR.

On Wednesday, June 16, I invited Ambassador Ushakov to come to the State Department and join me for a walk. It was a lovely summer day, and I wanted to get him out of the building in hopes that he would be more likely to open up. We strolled first to my favorite memorial in Washington, a statue of a seated Albert Einstein looking relaxed and whimsical in a floppy sweatshirt. Ushakov and I paused for a few minutes and watched as children waited in line for their turn to sit on Einstein's lap. We then walked along the wall of the Vietnam war memorial. Ushakov confirmed that Sergeyev was under instructions to fight for the best deal he could get from Cohen in Helsinki but to make sure he got one before Yeltsin arrived in Cologne.

JUST BEFORE THE SUMMIT, we got word from the Russians that Prime Minister Stepashin would be coming instead of Yeltsin on the first day. Yeltsin would come to Cologne later, we were told. Ostensibly, Stepashin was being given a chance to introduce himself to the other leaders and Yeltsin was being spared the details of the first day's meeting. Our recent experience with Yeltsin, however, left us worried that he might not show up at all—in which case, Sergeyev might be released from his obligation to cut a deal with Cohen.

Madeleine Albright and Igor Ivanov joined the talks in Helsinki and at several crucial points pushed the military negotiators to resolve snags. Knowing that Cohen and Sergeyev would be grappling with a number of issues that had come up during the Chernomyrdin-Ahtisaari negotiations and the weird all-nighter at the Russian Defense Ministry, I sent Toria Nuland to Helsinki so that she could provide continuity and background. On the Russian side, General Ivashov (or "Evil-shoff," as he was now known among the Americans) played his usual role of obstructionist verging on mutineer. By the end, Sergeyev's annoyance with Ivashov rivaled Chernomyrdin's at the Petersberg session. There were also several innocent screw-ups among the Russians. At one point near the end, the Defense and Foreign Ministries produced separate and incompatible drafts of the language to which Sergeyev had agreed. Toria helped them conform the two texts so that the signing ceremony could go forward.

I WAS AT DINNER at Wolfgang Ischinger's home in Bonn Friday evening, June 18, when Toria called to say that Cohen and Sergeyev had come to closure and would shortly be signing the agreement in public. I immediately called Doc Foglesong, who was also in Helsinki, to thank and congratulate him for many things, including putting up with Ivashov.

"Yep," he said in his easygoing drawl, "that guy takes some getting used to. I think now I can stop counting to ten with him."

When Clinton and Stepashin met the next day, they reviewed an agenda that had been neglected for months: trade issues, nonproliferation, strategic arms control, space cooperation. There was barely a mention of Kosovo, except when Stepashin, at the outset, winked at me and then told Clinton that I'd handled the negotiations with Ahtisaari and Chernomyrdin "responsibly."

Mamedov and I spent a few minutes together afterward and agreed that the meeting had been mercifully, even gloriously boring.

When Yeltsin arrived in Cologne the next day, I watched the live television coverage with apprehension. He was unsteady as he descended the stairs from his plane, clutching the rail, his face set in a mask of exaggerated concentration. He made straight for the television cameras, and I held my breath. He got one question from the cluster of reporters: "Are you satisfied with the results in Helsinki?"

"*Da!*"

I was mighty glad to hear him say it. But on the big questions facing the U.S. and Russia, it was the last time that we'd ever hear that word from Boris Yeltsin.

THE BLACK BELT

Talk low, talk slow, and don't say too much.

John Wayne (advice on acting)

As Boris Yeltsin waited for his guest at the entrance of the Renaissance Hotel in Cologne, the headquarters of the Russian delegation to the G-8 summit, he looked like a battered statue that might topple over at any moment. There was something artificial and willful about his immobility. His expression was frozen in what I had come to think of as his power mask—lips pursed in a half scowl, eyebrows knit in a look of Olympian severity—and his skin was the color of plaster.

As President Clinton's limousine slowed to a stop, he studied Yeltsin closely. After sixteen meetings, he knew the signs. "Sober but sick," he said under his breath as a Secret Service agent opened the door.

Once the two delegations settled around the table in the conference room, Yeltsin tried to begin his welcoming remarks but immediately started to cough in dry, hacking bursts that shook his whole body, bringing tears to his eyes. He couldn't stop. His complexion went through a rainbow of transformations—from waxen to florid to ashen. The blood vessels around his temples throbbed as though they would burst.

President Clinton and Madeleine Albright, Sandy Berger and I sat frozen, trying our best to look merely sympathetic and patient, not letting on what we were all thinking: My God, he's going to die right here in front of us!

Foreign Minister Ivanov rushed around looking for one of the doctors who traveled with Yeltsin and returned with two glasses of the foulest-looking green substance I'd ever seen. Yeltsin was coughing so hard that he had trouble swallowing the stuff, but slowly he worked his way through the first glass and halfway through the second, then resumed talking as though nothing had happened.

He had prepared an upbeat opening that would show how all was well again between him and Clinton. Yeltsin announced that the commission that had served the two countries so well in the past could help revive the relationship now that Kosovo was behind them, and it would do so under the joint chairmanship of Vice-President Gore and Prime Minister . . .

He started to use a Russian expression that means what's-his-name, thought better of it and turned to Ivanov, who whispered in his ear, "Stepashin!"

The lapse was all the more striking since Yeltsin obviously wanted to build up Stepashin, who had preceded him to Cologne and had held his own businesslike meeting with Clinton. Instead, he'd put on a display of his own incapacity.

AFTER THE ROCKY START, Yeltsin seemed to settle down and return to some semblance of his old self—coherent and, in his own bumptious fashion, straightforward and affecting.

"Our relationship came to the very brink of collapse," he told Clinton. "If you and I hadn't kept in touch and dealt honestly and openly with each other, it would have gone over the brink. In our phone conversations, while we weren't literally looking each other in the eye, we were doing so with our voices. That's how we kept things from getting out of hand. There were a couple of points when we made pretty clear to each other that our friendship had just about reached its limit. But even at the toughest moment, we asked ourselves, 'Should we keep working together?' And we always answered, 'Yes! We're going to fix this problem this way or that way.' And we'd find a way of agreeing on whatever the question was. Why did we do that? Because everything depends on our two powerful countries, that's why!"

Yeltsin went on in this vein for several minutes. It was a speech we'd heard in some form at virtually every previous meeting. But two familiar ingredients—relief that they'd averted a rupture and reproof of Clinton for having put their relationship to such a test—were more pronounced than ever before. Yeltsin reminded Clinton several times that he'd told him during the bombing campaign that NATO was making a "grievous and dangerous mistake," and he had clearly convinced himself that Russia, by exerting its influence on Slobodan Milošević, had rescued the West, and Clinton personally, from the even greater disaster of a land war.

Clinton wasted no time trying to convince Yeltsin otherwise. He'd said in the limousine on the way over that he wanted to let Yeltsin get "all the credit he deserves and more, and he can rewrite history to his heart's content. We've got to let him be the one to turn the page here so we can move on."

A NORMAL SURPRISE

Just as we'd hoped, Cologne marked a crisp and satisfactory conclusion to the Kosovo crisis. The Helsinki agreement held. NATO and Russian forces settled in for a long, arduous but essentially successful peacekeeping operation that continued well after the restoration of democracy in Serbia in 2000 and after the opening of Milošević's trial before the War Crimes Tribunal in The Hague in 2001.

But Cologne also left little doubt that the Yeltsin era was coming to a rapid and undignified end. The meeting in the Renaissance Hotel, which had begun with a coughing fit, came to a sudden and awkward halt when the Kremlin protocol chief, Vladimir Shevchenko, interrupted Clinton midsentence to say that the Russian delegation had to leave immediately for the airport or they'd lose their departure slot for the return flight to Moscow. Even at the time it seemed like one more omen that Yeltsin was being swept along, and perhaps swept aside, by events back home.

The conventional wisdom of the day focused on Yevgeny Primakov, now the head of the All Russia faction in the Duma, and Yuri Luzhkov, the mayor of Moscow and the leader of the Fatherland movement, as the front-runners for the 2000 election. Speculation was rife that they would cut a deal and run the country in tandem, one from the presidency and the other from the position of the speaker of the parliament. If Primakov and Luzhkov did join forces, promising to end the deadlock between the executive and legislative branches, they would constitute a formidable ticket against the communists, who were seen as a spent force, and against anyone Yeltsin might endorse as his would-be successor.

This scenario was appalling to Yeltsin. He had passed over Luzhkov for the premiership and fired Primakov from that office. He regarded neither as loyalists or reformers. There was widespread speculation that he would shake up his government at least one more time, putting in a prime minister who would be better able than Stepashin to stand up to the tough customers in Moscow and the provincial barons, better able to run a winning campaign and, crucially, better able to look out for the interests of Yeltsin in retirement. Yeltsin's inner circle—principally his daughter Tatyana, his former chief of staff who was still his amanuensis Valentin Yumashev, and the arch-oligarch Boris Berezovsky—were assumed to be pushing this scheme. Berezovsky's reputation as the sinister power behind the throne of a decrepit czar was at its peak. Nikita Khrushchev's son Sergei, who was teaching at Brown University, told me that he regarded Berezovsky as "the Professor Moriarty of Russian politics." In Sergei's book, Primakov was Holmes—a wily, hard-bitten realist who was looking for a uniquely Russian middle course between the dead end of the Soviet system and total capitulation to the West.

IN LATE JULY, a month after the Cologne summit, Sergei Stepashin made a trip to Washington to see Clinton and Gore. I met him at Andrews Air Force Base and accompanied him to Blair House, which gave me a chance to sound him out about what was going on behind the scenes in Moscow. When we settled into the back of his limousine, Stepashin wanted to swap war stories about Kosovo, since, as he put it, we'd been through that ordeal together. Once again he joked about how "responsible" I'd been during the last round of talks with Ahtisaari and Chernomyrdin, then about how interesting it must have been for me to observe Russian decision-making during the long night at the Defense Ministry.

I asked him what I should make of what I'd witnessed and whether he and his colleagues had taken any action as a result.

He hesitated for a moment, then admitted there had been a serious breakdown in "discipline and bureaucratic order." As a result, he had initiated a new practice of convening regular meetings to coordinate foreign and military policy among cabinet-level officials like Ivanov and Sergeyev and the head of the Foreign Intelligence Service, Vyacheslav Trubnikov. In the old days of the Soviet system, the politburo had functioned as a cabinet, and the Central Committee of the Communist Party had served a coordinating function among the "power ministries." It had taken the scare over Priština Airport to shake Russia's leaders into realizing that they needed some equivalent of the National Security Council.

Another factor, Stepashin added, was that "Russia's president has been protective of his own prerogatives" and didn't want too much "bureaucratization" of policymaking at a lower level.

That gave me an opening to observe that Russia's president seemed to have been less than fully engaged during the worst of the crisis. What we'd seen in Cologne raised further concerns about Yeltsin's health. There were now reports that Western doctors were standing by for another emergency visit to Moscow.

Stepashin seemed genuinely surprised by the last bit of news and unsure of Yeltsin's condition. He said that he, like the rest of us, would be watching to see if Yeltsin was well enough to meet with the leader of the ethnic Russian community in Moldova in a few days.

For Stepashin to be relying on old-fashioned Kremlinology for hints about his president's condition didn't suggest he was a member of the inner circle himself. I asked him how secure he felt in his job. He professed to be "relaxed"—which I took to mean more fatalistic than confident. When I dropped Berezovsky's name, his eyes narrowed. "That man," he said, "is not a force for progress or reform or anything else you want to see in our country. He thinks his money and connections make him a political figure, but that's not where political power should come from. He's like one of your robber barons of the last century."

In the day that followed, Clinton and Gore both had what they regarded as promising meetings with Stepashin, whom they found confident, on top of his brief and seemingly earnest about buckling down to all unfinished business that had accumulated during the Kosovo crisis. They concentrated on jump-starting the process of restricting dangerous Russian cooperation and trade with Iran, which had been stalled since the fall of the Kiriyenko government in August 1998.

After the meeting, Clinton remarked of Stepashin, "I sure hope Yeltsin keeps that guy. He's good. Anyway, Ol' Boris can't be changing his government every twenty minutes."

About a week later, Prime Minister Ehud Barak of Israel, who had succeeded Netanyahu in May, visited Moscow, primarily to exert pressure of his own for progress on Russia/Iran. He called Clinton afterward to report on his impressions. He'd found Yeltsin focused, energetic and "radiating power." But he'd later learned that the meeting had exhausted Yeltsin, who had to get emergency medical care. Barak said that he, too, had been impressed by Stepashin, but he'd learned that there would be a new prime minister appointed within a matter of days. "The replacement that was mentioned to me," said Barak, "was some guy whose name is Putin."

—

THE AX FELL on Stepashin August 9, when Yeltsin announced he was nominating Vladimir Putin to be Russia's fifth prime minister in less than a year and a half. Tatyana and Yumashev had convinced him that Putin's combination of executive skill and personal loyalty made him the most reliable successor. "He won't sell us out," said Tatyana.[1] (They believed that Putin would protect Yeltsin and his family against legal actions based on allegations of corruption. Some Duma hard-liners still wanted to try Yeltsin for the treason of dismantling the USSR and turning Russia into little better than a lackey of the West.)

Reading methodically through a prepared statement, Yeltsin said that "next year, for the first time in the country's history, the first president of Russia will hand over power to a newly elected president . . . I have decided to name a man who, in my opinion, is able to consolidate society. Relying on the broadest of political forces, he will ensure the continuation of reforms in Russia."

In addition to myself, the other person in Washington who had dealt with Putin as head of the Kremlin Security Council was Sandy Berger. In an effort to re-create the channel he'd developed a year earlier with Andrei Kokoshin for making progress on Russia/Iran, Sandy had been cultivating a relationship with Putin that seemed to hold some promise. Putin had begun their first conversation by passing along personal greetings from Kokoshin himself, then reaffirmed all previous commitments of the Russian governments, especially those that Chernomyrdin and Kiriyenko had made to Gore, and reported on various executive and legislative initiatives aimed at putting in place tight export controls.

When Putin suddenly became prime minister, Sandy said we should watch him closely but keep an open mind. The first test of what Putin would be like was whether he delivered on his promises of the recent past.

By that standard, I wasn't optimistic. I was still waiting for the public statement Putin had promised me in June repudiating General Ivashov's threat that the Russian military would try to beat NATO to the punch in Kosovo.

THE REACTION IN RUSSIA to Putin's appointment ranged from shoulder-shrugging and head-scratching (just another "normal surprise") to prophecies of doom on the part of many of the young reformers ("a very, very big mistake" that would lead to the disintegration of the country, said Boris Nemtsov).

Yeltsin's announcement that he was not just appointing a prime minister but anointing a successor was taken as further evidence that he had lost his grip on reality.

In Washington, our initial judgment was that the implausibility of Putin's candidacy made some version of the Luzhkov-Primakov scenario all the more likely. In addition to Putin's dearth of relevant experience and connections, he didn't even look the part. Yeltsin, Yavlinsky, Nemtsov, Lebed, Luzhkov, Zhirinovsky, Zyuganov—they were all endomorphs, with some combination of height, bulk and booming voice. Putin was slightly built and had the manner of a disciplined, efficient self-effacing executive assistant.

But Putin also had, on top of the full force of Yeltsin's backing, a gruesome bit of luck. The war in the North Caucasus burst back into flame, this time with a difference that made it as much of a political winner for Putin as it had been a loser for Yeltsin.

At about the time of Putin's appointment, Chechen forces under the militant leader Shamil Basayev crossed the eastern border into Dagestan, driving thousands of people from several villages and killing or wounding scores of Russian troops who were manning outposts in the region. In and of itself, the raid was a bolder version of one that Basayev had conducted in June 1995 when he took hostages during the Halifax summit of the G-7. That earlier episode was one of the few occasions when the secessionist struggle in Chechnya spilled into other parts of southern Russia. Because the Chechen conflict had been mostly contained within the republic's borders, many Russians had come to see, and oppose, the war that Yeltsin waged there in 1994–96 as an attempt to cling to a remote and hostile fragment of the old empire.

However, the Chechens' foray into Dagestan in August 1999 seemed to be explicitly part of an aggressive strategy that would take a new round of warfare into the heartland of Russia. Basayev proclaimed a jihad to liberate the surrounding Muslim-dominated areas from Russian tyranny. That claim seemed all the more credible when it was followed within weeks by a series of bombings against apartment buildings in Volgodansk, Buinaksk and Moscow, killing some three hundred civilians.

The Chechens denied responsibility for the explosions. Some Russians and observers in the outside world suspected a covert provocation by the Russian security services, presumably on orders from their most prominent and powerful alumnus, Putin himself. Berezovsky figured in some of this speculation. In addition to being one of Putin's backers for the presidency, he had extensive ties among the Chechen warlords and therefore might have been able to prod or bribe them into providing the new government of Moscow with a pretext for what might be a popular war.

There was no evidence to support this conspiracy theory, although Russian public opinion did indeed solidify behind Putin in his determination to carry out a swift, decisive counteroffensive. It was organized by General Anatoly Kvashnin, the chief of staff of the armed forces who had played the heavy during the confused drama in June when Russia "accidentally" deployed its troops into Kosovo ahead of NATO.

The Russian armed forces began a massive bombing campaign against Chechnya, killing thousands of civilians and adding to the nearly 200,000 refugees, many of whom fled to the neighboring republic of Ingushetia. Once again, Grozny came under intense bombardment. In early October, thousands of Russian troops invaded Chechnya, secured what they called a buffer zone in the northern third of the republic and launched a pincer movement around Grozny. At the end of October, a rocket attack on a crowded market in Grozny killed dozens of people.

The incident bore an eerie resemblance to the Serb savageries that had galvanized the will of the international community to use force against Milošević. That similarity occurred to some Russian hawks, who had predicted earlier in the year that NATO's war against Belgrade over Kosovo was a warm-up for the one it would someday unleash against Moscow over Chechnya. Now they could imagine their worst fear coming true.

In fact, the West had neither the desire nor the means to engage diplomatically in the Chechen conflict, much less intervene militarily. The U.S. and its allies had no leverage on the rebel leaders, nor did we have sympathy either with their goal of independence or the raids in Dagestan that had precipitated the conflict. They had indisputably—and, it seemed, deliberately—brought down the wrath of the Russian armed forces on their people. That meant there was little we could do but cite Russia's obligations under various international covenants to protect civilian life and call on Moscow to let representatives of the Organization for Security and Cooperation in Europe into Chechnya to help deal with the refugee crisis and monitor the behavior of the Russian troops.

The Russians fended off these appeals on the grounds that they couldn't guarantee the safety of the OSCE mission. That was true enough, since most of the republic was in chaos, but it begged the question of Russia's indiscriminate use of violence against civilians, which was turning the entire population against Moscow and increasing popular support among Chechens for their leaders' demands.

IGOR IVANOV cut a melancholy but stoical and unrelenting figure that fall as he ran the gauntlet of Western criticism. At one international conference after another, his fellow foreign ministers hammered him, ever so politely, on the depredations of the Russian military. Ivanov held his ground, sitting erect, his jaw set, and pushing back hard. While the West was wringing its hands over the plight of Chechen civilians, he said, Russian soldiers were sacrificing their lives to hold back the encroachments of militant Islam. It was another echo out of Moscow's policy in the Balkans: in 1998, Russians had depicted the Serbs as defenders of Christendom against the Muslim hordes in Kosovo; now it was the Russians themselves in that role.

AS THE WAR RAGED, it began to spill over the mountainous and porous border that Chechnya shared with Georgia. Chechen civilians and guerrillas fled into Georgia. Its president, Eduard Shevardnadze, who had his hands full with the ongoing secessionist movement in the western region of Abkhazia (which the Russians had, with the help of Chechens, instigated in the early nineties), had little ability to prevent Chechen civilians and guerrillas from taking refuge in northern Georgia. The Russians conducted several cross-border bombing and strafing runs on Chechen camps and tried to pressure Shevardnadze into letting them base additional Russian units on his territory. Shevardnadze, who was trying to get Moscow to remove the troops it already had in Georgia, refused.[2]

I made two trips to the region that fall and tried to persuade Shevardnadze to tighten control of his border with Chechnya so as not to give the Russians a pretext for incursions; while in Moscow I stressed the importance we attached to Georgian sovereignty. Whenever I raised the subject with Ivanov, his even temper deserted him and he accused me of letting myself be duped by Shevardnadze.

I was taken aback by the venom in his voice. It was a reminder of the raw personal animosities and insecurities that lay just below the surface of post-Soviet politics. Ivanov had worked as an executive assistant to Shevardnadze in the eighties when, as Soviet foreign minister, Shevardnadze sat in the office that Ivanov now occupied. Like many other Russians,

Ivanov seemed to believe that Shevardnadze, on top of his culpability for the rupturing of the Soviet superstate, was now aiding and abetting the Chechens in their attempted dismemberment of Russia itself.

PUTIN'S OWN HANDLING of Chechnya gave us reason to take seriously his well-advertised black belt in judo, the most un-Russian of martial arts. He used his slight stature and soft-spoken manner to his advantage, making himself seem unruffled and reasonable, bowing to the other guy at the outset of the match, pulling him forward, throwing him off balance and *never* calling him an opponent. In response to Madeleine Albright's urging that Russia stop its scorched-earth policy in Chechnya and look for a political solution, Putin replied mildly, "We must respect the opinion of our partners."

Clinton, who was used to Yeltsin's sumolike approach to diplomatic combat, had his first exposure to the Putin technique on September 12, 1999, in Auckland, New Zealand, where they were attending the annual summit of the Asia-Pacific Economic Cooperation forum. Putin thanked Clinton profusely for his support of Russia in the face of mounting criticism in the U.S. and exuded confidence about the future of the relationship now that, together, the U.S. and Russia had weathered the crisis over Kosovo.

Clinton eased into an expression of concern about the bloodshed in Chechnya. Putin nodded, saying he understood the feelings in the West about the human tragedy in Chechnya and welcomed all offers of help. He just hoped we understood that Russia and the West were on the same side in a fight against global terrorism.

When Clinton persisted, urging concrete steps to ameliorate the situation, such as allowing international monitors into Chechnya, Putin's mouth tightened, his posture stiffened and a hard-eyed look came over his face. He had been listening carefully to the "advice" he'd been getting from Russia's friends in the West, he said, and he was taking it. Drawing a map on a napkin, he assured Clinton that the geographical scope of the Russian action was limited: the counteroffensive would stop at the Terek River, which runs east to west across the northern third of the republic. But we had to recognize that what had happened in Dagestan in August was not just a resumption of the war that had gone into suspension three years before—it was the beginning of an invasion of Russia. And an invasion not just by Chechen bandits but by the forces of international Islamic terrorism.[3]

In a meeting afterward in Moscow with our ambassador, Jim Collins, Putin elaborated: the renegade Saudi Osama bin Laden had made several trips to Chechnya in the past year and was helping finance Chechen operations against Russia. This allegation—which our own government found plausible but, as far as I know, never confirmed—was clearly calculated to enlist American sympathy for Moscow. Bin Laden had been behind a series of murderous attacks on U.S. facilities abroad, including the bombing of our embassies in East Africa in August 1998 that led Clinton to order cruise missile strikes on bin Laden's headquarters and training camps in Afghanistan.

CLINTON AND PUTIN met a second time, in Oslo on November 2, and the exchange had a harder edge on both sides. Russian troops had continued to bombard Grozny from the ground and air, and the city had no electricity, gas or water. There was increased speculation that a Russian invasion of the entire republic was imminent. Putin denied it.

Clinton said the Russian strategy could only result in open-ended civilian carnage. He urged Putin to let the refugees return to their villages and seek a political settlement to the conflict through "dialogue" with the Chechen leaders.

Putin retorted that there was no one reliable to negotiate with. The Chechens were committed not just to wresting their own republic out of Russia but to turning the entire region into a hotbed of predatory Islamic radicalism. "You keep telling us to talk to the Chechens," he said, "but what would you have us do if they won't talk and all they want to do is kill Russians?" Seeing that Clinton had no ready answer, Putin repeated the question several times.

Clinton had a question of his own for which Putin did not have a good answer: If talking to the Chechens was pointless and war was the only option, how long would it continue and where would it end? After three months of fighting and with the Russian offensive bogged down on the outskirts of Grozny, he could no longer promise a prompt, decisive victory. Russia was fighting a war of attrition that would go on for many months if not years.

After the meeting, Clinton expressed some frustration. While Putin was obviously demonizing the Chechen leaders, he was correct that they had no interest in compromise. Of course we had to come down on the Russians hard for slaughtering civilians, said Clinton, but he was not comfortable about hectoring them to pursue a political solution when we didn't really know what that meant or whether it was possible.

He judged the debate in Oslo to have been at best a draw.

Aside from the forensics of the encounter, what struck Clinton most about Putin in Auckland and Oslo was his vigor. "I'll say this for that guy," he remarked. "He's tough and he's strong and he's got a lot of energy and determination."

THE REAL SURPRISE

About two weeks later Clinton had a chance to see just how much Yeltsin was losing his grip. On November 18, he and Yeltsin were among the fifty leaders gathered in Istanbul's majestic Ciragan Palace for the annual summit of the OSCE. It began, as Sandy Berger put it, as Budapest on the Bosporus. The difference was that this time Clinton came ready for a public spat of major proportions.

Yeltsin, as often when he expected to be put on the defensive, went pre-emptively on the offensive. What Russia was doing in Chechnya was the only appropriate response to "the bloody wave of terrorist acts that have swept over Moscow and other cities and towns of our country." He was tired of Western "reproaches and sermonizing" about the need for dialogue with the Chechens. "Nobody should be under any illusions on this score. There will be no negotiations with bandits and murderers." Besides, he continued with rising vehemence, the American-led "aggression" against Yugoslavia deprived Clinton of the right to lecture Russia on how it should deal with terrorists within its own borders.

Clinton listened carefully. He had prepared remarks, but in his mind he'd already torn them up and was fashioning a response that would rebut what Yeltsin had said, criticize Russia for what it was doing and, at the same time, reaffirm what the U.S. and the West could admire and support about Yeltsin's leadership. When Clinton took the floor a few moments later, he made no effort to address the assembled leaders. Instead, he looked straight at Yeltsin and, for the next few minutes, spoke to him alone while the rest of the audience sat silent and riveted.

Russia's brute force in Chechnya was unworthy of Yeltsin's own legacy as a champion of democracy, Clinton began. Watching Yeltsin's heroism during the attempted Soviet coup in 1991 had been "one of the most thrilling moments in my life," Clinton said, pointing his finger at Yeltsin.

"Your standing there on that tank said to those people, 'You can do this, but you'll have to kill me first.' " Had Yeltsin ended up in jail instead of the Kremlin, "I would hope that every leader of every country around this table would have stood up for you and for freedom in Russia, and not said, 'Well, that is an internal Russian affair that we cannot be part of.' " The world had moved beyond the era when countries could get away with mass murder within their own boundaries by claiming that it was an "internal affair" and no business of outsiders. That was the real lesson of Bosnia and Kosovo, declared Clinton.

Several minutes into Clinton's speech, Yeltsin decided he'd heard enough. He whipped off his headphones, threw them onto the table in front of him and went into a gargantuan pout. It looked for a moment as though he might stage a walkout. Igor Ivanov started whispering in his ear. Whatever Ivanov said—it was probably a concentrated extract of the sugarcoating in Clinton's speech—seemed to calm Yeltsin down.

When the two presidents met privately a short time later, Yeltsin was in a strange and unstable state, tottering between the anger he still felt over having been contradicted in front of the conference and nostalgia for the old Bill-and-Boris connection. He was breathtakingly abusive to Ivanov, perhaps to demonstrate that, yet again, he and Clinton were being let down by their underlings and would have to step in and set the relationship right.

Yeltsin also chastised Clinton for not being more attentive to their personal ties, a tactic to which he'd often resorted in the past, but this time his tone was more belligerent and accusatory than importuning.

"You owe me a trip to Moscow, Bill!" he said just as the meeting was getting under way. He complained that Clinton had promised him several times he would come but had yet to commit to a date. Neither Clinton nor Sandy Berger, who kept track of presidential commitments, knew what he was talking about.[4]

Picking up where they'd left off publicly on Chechnya, Yeltsin was, if anything, even more defiant and bellicose than he'd been in front of the cameras. He said he had promised Marshal Sergeyev, the defense minister, that this time, unlike in the previous Chechen war, the military would be allowed to finish the job. There would be no political dialogue—it was too late for that.

Then, out of the blue, his face grew red and he almost shouted, "You're the guilty one, Bill! You're the one at fault here!" The U.S. was to blame not just for the overall deterioration in relations with Russia but for Russia's troubles in Chechnya.

It wasn't quite clear what Yeltsin had in mind, although he seemed to be referring to rumors that Turkey, a U.S. ally, was providing covert support to the Chechen rebellion.

Clinton had no chance for rebuttal. Yeltsin had moved on, in his manic, stream-of-consciousness fashion, to a menacing version of an old Soviet theme that Yeltsin had often dredged up before when he was angry at Clinton: The U.S. not only had no business telling Russia what to do in Chechnya—it had no business in *Europe*. He lived in Moscow, Yeltsin reminded Clinton, a European city and the capital of a European country that was perfectly capable of taking care of the continent as a whole. "Leave Europe to us!" he thundered.

This command would have appalled the other leaders assembled in Istanbul and confirmed the darkest fears of the Central Europeans and Russia's immediate neighbors, especially in the south. Moreover, it was ludicrously inconsistent with Yeltsin's stubborn attachment to the idea that he and Clinton were still the Big Two—a refrain to which he returned at the end of the meeting by repeating his opening demand that they next meet in Moscow so that they could get on with the business of solving all problems.

Clinton found the encounter disconcerting. In the past, when Yeltsin had gone on the attack, Clinton had usually managed to disarm him, eliciting his trust and engaging him on the business of the moment. This time Clinton was unable to find a handle, so he just let Yeltsin's tirade run its course.

Steve Sestanovich, the head of the State Department office responsible for the former Soviet Union, believed that Yeltsin's filibuster may have served his purpose. In the past, Yeltsin's bluster in public had almost always given way to submissiveness in private. Not this time: the unhinged quality of his behavior in private kept Clinton from using the meeting to make the case for Russian restraint in Chechnya, which Yeltsin didn't want to hear.

Clinton, as always, had a more sanguine view. On Air Force One heading home, he told Sandy Berger, "That ol' boy was in a different place from where we've seen him before. He was trying awfully hard to prove something, like that he's not finished, that he's still got some fight in him."

In the past Yeltsin's feistiness had been directed against his domestic enemies, while now it was directed at us. Clinton believed the tactics he'd seen on display in Istanbul were the same—to reduce Yeltsin's vulnerability to opponents at home. But whatever the motive, the effect was a new and widely perceived sense that the relationship, in both its personal and state-to-state dimensions, was under unprecedented strain.

Igor Ivanov continued to be the punching bag. During a visit to China in early December, Yeltsin made barbed remarks in front of his hosts about how Ivanov was his "pro-American foreign minister." Then Yeltsin publicly reacted to another burst of American criticism over Chechnya by saying that Clinton might show Russia more respect if he remembered that Russia still had "a full arsenal of nuclear weapons."

The pugnacity backfired, since it contributed to the impression that Yeltsin was fulminating, and it gave Putin a chance to look statesmanlike by making some soothing comments of his own.

As 1999 CAME TO AN END, Putin had established himself as far and away the most popular politician in the country—an amazing development, given his obscurity only a few months earlier and the disadvantage of being Yeltsin's handpicked candidate for president.

Part of the explanation was a public image that could not have been a more dramatic contrast to Yeltsin's. Yeltsin seemed older than his sixty-eight years, Putin younger than his forty-seven. Yeltsin's ill health was a national embarrassment, while Putin was playing up his vigor and his athletic prowess (in addition to judo, he was skilled at sambo, a Russian style of wrestling). He also let it be known that he was abstemious (his wife said that he was "indifferent" to alcohol).[5]

In their style of leadership as well, the two men could hardly have been more different. Yeltsin behaved like a czar, while Putin made a virtue of his background as a manager who could make the system work.

Even the war in Chechnya was playing to Putin's advantage. Russians remembered how Yeltsin had tried and failed to subdue the earlier rebellion in 1994–96. Now, with Putin visibly in charge, Russian forces had captured key towns and pushed many of the militants into the mountains, where they hunkered down for the winter.

ONCE THEY WERE CONFIDENT about Putin's chances of being elected, several of his backers, including Boris Berezovsky, fanned out to talk up their man in the West, no doubt in hopes of generating investment and economic support for Russia. I'd been avoiding Berezovsky for the simple reason that I found him low-value. In earlier encounters, he seemed not just long-winded but stunningly feckless for someone who had amassed such wealth and developed such a mystique of power. But in late November, I agreed to see him, mostly out of curiosity about the new product I knew he was selling.

For half an hour he flitted from one subject to another, dropping hints about how much he knew but wasn't telling me. Finally, as he shifted from an advertisement for himself into one for Putin, the message began to cohere. Putin would be easier for us to deal with, said Berezovsky, because he would not be as "hypersensitive" as Yeltsin had been about Europe. Rather than worrying about NATO, which any "realist" understood constituted no threat to Russia, Putin would concentrate instead on the inroads that radical Islam was making in the Caucasus, largely because of its open border with Georgia. The West should be grateful to him for finally dealing with the problem, since the Caucasus was not just the soft underbelly of Russia but the route by which militants from Afghanistan, Pakistan and Saudi Arabia were mounting an assault on Europe. (Like other Russians, Berezovsky never included Iran on the list of countries exporting terror. Iran, they hoped, was a budding Russian ally.)

As Berezovsky went on in this vein, I realized he was proposing a trade: Russia wouldn't object too strenuously to the next round of NATO enlargement if we would give Moscow a pass to "restore order to Chechnya and the surrounding region," including Georgia.

When I said that the U.S. wasn't going to barter away the Georgians' independence and security for the Central Europeans', he bridled. For an instant, I saw an entirely different and more authentic side of him. He raised his voice and spat out the words, "You talk about the 'rights' of the Georgians! You have no rights of your own in those countries down there—no rights and no interests! They are *our* neighbors, not yours." He said the word "neighbors" as though it were a euphemism for satrapies.

When Valentin Yumashev came calling in early December, he was more skillful than Berezovsky. He said there was no reason to worry that Russia would infringe on Georgia's sovereignty—adding that that would have been a danger under a Primakov presidency, but not a Putin one. On domestic policy, too, Yumashev promoted Putin as a "modern" alternative to Primakov or Luzhkov, whom he depicted as unreconstructed in their Soviet mind-sets and methods. For example, he said, Primakov had shown a tendency when he was prime minister to use the intelligence and security services to intimidate his political opponents, while Putin would rein in the services and supervise their transformation into law-abiding institutions of a democratic state.

I VISITED MOSCOW the third week in December immediately after the parliamentary election. The Putin-backed Unity bloc soundly defeated the Fatherland–All Russia bloc of Primakov and Luzhkov.

There was talk of "the Putin miracle." The prime minister seemed to have been not just the de facto victor in the election but the arbiter in how others did. Yavlinsky had refused, as he told me bitterly, to "kiss Putin's ring" and thus forfeited a Putin endorsement for his party, which came in a disappointing sixth, just behind Zhirinovsky's.

I recalled that Andrei Kozyrev had been fighting to keep his seat in the Duma representing Murmansk. As I made the rounds of various party headquarters, I asked how Kozyrev had fared. No one seemed to know. Finally, a low-level aide in one of the offices I visited went off to find a computer printout with the election results. Only then did I discover that Kozyrev had been trounced. No one's having noticed made it all the sadder an ending to the public career of an architect not only of Russia's independence but of its neighbors' as well.

The reformist party of Sergei Kiriyenko and Yegor Gaidar had gotten a boost in the polls from a blessing from Putin late in the campaign. Kiriyenko, when I saw him, was cautiously optimistic about the direction Putin would take Russia if, as now seemed quite likely, he won the presidency in the election scheduled for the summer of 2000.

Something profound had changed in Russian politics over the past year. It wasn't that Primakov, Luzhkov and Zyuganov, not to mention Yeltsin himself, had the look of men whose time had come and gone—that had been happening for some time. More significant than the passing of the older generation was the shift within the younger one.

I thought back to my visit of the previous winter, when I'd stayed behind after watching Larry Summers try to instruct Primakov in basic economics. On that earlier trip, I'd been heartened to find a surge of optimism on the part of the young democrats whose brief moment in the sun we'd so welcomed in the early nineties. In that earlier winter, of 1998–99, as Russia defied the more alarmist predictions and recovered from the crash of the previous August, Nemtsov, Yavlinsky, Gaidar and Vladimir Ryzhkov sensed a new receptivity to their ideas and, accordingly, a second chance for their political aspirations.

But now, a year later, the "correlation of forces"—a Soviet-era phrase that had been adapted to post-Soviet Russian politics—seemed to have swung away from the unabashedly pro-Western reformers and toward nationalistic bureaucrats who had been waiting in the shadows, many of them, like Putin, from the security services. It was this breed of younger politicians and functionaries, not the ones we'd been rooting for, that seemed to have the institutional base, the organizational and personal discipline and the political appeal to capitalize on the opportunity that came with the coincidence of Russia's political calendar and Boris Yeltsin's decrepitude.

WHEN I MET WITH VLADIMIR PUTIN in his vast office in the Russian White House on December 22, there was an aura of power settling around him. I could see it in the deference of the other Russians in the room, in the frenzied interest of the press and in the cockiness of the man himself. The stratagems I'd noticed before were all the more apparent. He greeted me with a prolonged, firm, two-handed grip. Throughout the meeting that followed, he kept steady eye contact and used my name more often than was common in Russian, particularly given the difference in our rank. Once again, he dropped into the conversation references to my past, just to let me know he'd reviewed my dossier. When an attendant brought him a glass of tea, Putin ostentatiously removed the two sugar cubes from the saucer and put them off to one side, which I took to be a bit of staging to demonstrate his Spartan discipline.

While the television cameras were still present, he put his own spin on our previous meetings in June, at the height of the crisis over Priština Airport. He welcomed me as someone with whom he had personally worked honestly and constructively to "resolve jointly some pointed issues." I recalled that it had taken more than one conversation between us to do so and that it had been necessary for me to turn my plane around and return to Moscow. Putin replied evenly that he remembered "all aspects of the incident" very well and, with an almost imperceptible gesture of his head, dismissed the press from the room.

In the conversation that followed, we concentrated on Chechnya. Putin never raised his voice but didn't give an inch. Russia's conduct of the war was righteous in purpose and restrained in conduct, he said. Russia would "crush" the terrorists, but it would do so with methods that were neither "brutal" nor "uncivilized." Whatever collateral damage the Russian military had caused in the course of its operation had been "insubstantial" and mostly the fault of the Chechen rebels, who were cynically using human shields among the civilians and engaging in genocide against ethnic Russians in the republic, driving 200,000 out of their homes—a figure that bore a suspicious resemblance to estimates of the number of *Chechens* the Russian army had driven from their homes. It was all an unsubtle attempt to counter the impression that the Russian government was behaving in Chechnya the way Belgrade had behaved in Kosovo.

Militarily, said Putin, the war was all but won. There was no organized resistance left. Russian commandos were mopping up the last hotbeds of rebel activity.

When I mentioned Shevardnadze's concern over the possibility of Russian intervention in Georgia, Putin became even more steely-eyed and emphatic. He claimed that Shevardnadze was double-crossing us both—pretending in conversations with Moscow that he wanted Russian help and with Washington that he wanted American protection from Russia, while all the time giving aid and comfort to the Chechen terrorists.

But even on this most contentious of subjects, Putin knew what I most wanted to hear and gave it to me: Despite what he regarded as Shevardnadze's treachery, Russia would respect Georgia's sovereignty. There would be no intervention there.[6]

I hoped so, I said, since this time I was flying home commercially and therefore wouldn't be able to turn the plane around and come back to Moscow if something untoward happened. Putin smiled and said that he was sure the power of the State Department was such that, if necessary, I could order Delta Air Lines to do a U-turn. Even this attempt at humor had an edge, since it left open the possibility that his latest assurances, like those he'd given me in June, were subject to review.

On Russian domestic politics, Putin claimed that he had taken a great risk to help Kiriyenko's party in the election three days before. He was going against the grain of the leftist—i.e., pro-communist—orientation of the Russian public, he said, in order to provide balance in the new Duma. He mentioned several times that he believed Russia "belongs in the West," and that he had no use for those who thought isolation, retrenchment or confrontation was an option. Now that Kosovo was behind us, he wanted to get on with the unfinished business of strategic arms control and nonproliferation, showing "our own people and the world that on the really big issues, we're on the same side." He wanted to be sure that we in Washington had noticed his soothing comments after Yeltsin's outburst about nuclear weapons in Beijing in early December, although he managed to take credit for defusing that tense moment without uttering Yeltsin's name.

In fact, he avoided reference to Yeltsin throughout the conversation. He talked about his own meetings with President Clinton, in Auckland and Oslo, as the beginning of a personal rapport that had already served the overall relationship well and that would, he implied, continue to do so in the future. He was acting as though his assumption of the presidency was not only assured but imminent.

CHAPTER 15

ON DEFENSE

Russia does not sulk. Russia is collecting itself.

Prince Alexander Gorchakov

L IKE ALL OUR ambassadors around the world, Jim Collins was bracing himself for trouble on December 31, 1999. Y2K was at hand, and Russia was considered especially vulnerable to the millennium bug because of the dilapidated state of its infrastructure and the obsolescence of its computers, including those that controlled its nuclear weapons.

Jim and his colleagues were in the midst of reviewing emergency procedures and checking backups for the embassy's equipment when they started picking up rumors of another, less anticipated development that would keep them busy that day. By noon, Jim was sure enough of what he was hearing to call me in Washington, where it was still dark.

"Better get up," he said, in his raspy, matter-of-fact voice. "It looks like this might be Boris Nikolayevich's last day in office."

Shortly afterward, he called back and suggested that I turn on my television set. For the following hour or so, he and I shared another of those CNN moments that had punctuated the seven years we'd worked together. We kept the phone line open between his study in Spaso House and my living room in Washington so that we could compare impressions of Yeltsin's swan song.

"I have made a decision," said Yeltsin, looking grim and pale. "I've thought about it long and hard. Today, on the last day of the waning century, I'm resigning."

Under the provisions of the constitution that Yeltsin had introduced in 1993, Prime Minister Putin immediately became acting president, and the election scheduled for the summer would take place in March instead, leaving Putin's potential rivals—Yevgeny Primakov, Yuri Luzhkov, Gennady Zyuganov—with only three months to campaign.[1] Putin was already well ahead in the polls, largely because of his popular crackdown in Chechnya. Yeltsin's decision to get out of the way, bestow on Putin the advantages of incumbency and advance the election all but clinched it.

There was a flash of the old combativeness as Yeltsin dropped his bombshell. "I've heard many times," he said, "that 'Yeltsin will hang onto power by any means; he won't hand the office over to anyone.' That's a lie!"

Then came a single note of self-congratulation: "We are creating the very important precedent of a civilized, voluntary transfer of power from one elected president to another."

The rest of the speech was melancholy and repentant: "I ask your forgiveness for the dreams we shared that never came true; for the fact that what seemed simple turned out to be torturously difficult. I ask forgiveness for not justifying the hope that we could, in one fell swoop, leap from a gray, stagnant, totalitarian past into a bright, rich, civilized future. It turned out that I was naïve about some things. The problems were more complicated than I realized. We bulled our way forward through mistakes and failures. Many people suffered a terrible shock in these hard times. I just want you to know—and I've never said this before—that the pain you've suffered has been painful for me too, in my own heart."

The farewell performance captured the contradiction between the democrat and the autocrat in Yeltsin. He was acknowledging his accountability as an elected leader for the hardship and disappointment of his constituents. Yet by manipulating the electoral calendar, he was virtually guaranteeing that their next president would be someone more of his choosing than theirs.

While not actually admitting that he was stacking the deck in Putin's favor, Yeltsin explained why he was doing so. "We who have been in power for many years must go," he said, lumping himself together with Primakov, Luzhkov and Zyuganov. "A new generation is relieving me, a generation of those who can do more and better . . . Russia must enter the new millennium with new politicians, with new faces, with new, smart, strong, energetic people." Putin was "a strong man who is worthy of being president."

As Jim Collins and I listened to the speech, we noted the repeated references to strength as the quality Yeltsin believed his listeners wanted their new leader to restore to the Russian state. Strength meant, among other things, standing up to pressure from outsiders.

The world was, we concluded, in for a new phase of Russian foreign policy—less pliant, though not more bellicose. We'd already seen and heard enough of Putin to know that his style was entirely different from Yeltsin's. Yeltsin said "no" when he meant "let's talk." With Putin, it was just the opposite. Instead of slamming his fist or blowing up at a press conference, Putin would say, "You have an interesting point." Or, "We've taken your criticism to heart." Or, as I'd heard in June on the eve of the Russian army's mad dash to Priština, "I'm sure that General Ivashov, whoever he is, doesn't know what he's talking about, and you can be sure nothing improper will happen."

An artful dodge like this was often the equivalent of the Big *Nyet,* and with Putin we figured it was more likely to stick than it had been with Yeltsin.

STAR-CROSSED

The Clinton administration's principal experience with Vladimir Putin as the master of the oblique refusal was on the issue of National Missile Defense.

NMD was yet another in a series of American military programs that the Russians feared and opposed. In some ways, they found it even more objectionable than NATO enlargement or the air campaign against Yugoslavia. It therefore presented a timely and politically useful opportunity for Putin to demonstrate that he would define and defend Russian national interests in contradistinction to American plans and proposals.

For the U.S., NMD was the latest attempt to answer a question that had vexed presidents and their advisers for more than thirty years, since the 1960s, when Bill Clinton, Al Gore and George W. Bush were in college and Vladimir Putin was in junior high school: When is self-defense a threat to the nuclear peace?

For most of the cold war, the U.S. and the Soviet Union were bound by a suicide pact. Safety, such as it was, resided in the knowledge that neither superpower could attack the other without suffering cataclysmic retaliation. This arrangement was known as mutual deterrence, or, sardonically, as MAD, for mutual assured destruction. According to this principle, defense was deemed dangerous. If one side feared its ability to retaliate could be thwarted by the other side's defenses, it could be tempted to strike first with its full force. Such calculations on both sides would lead to a spiraling buildup in offensive capability. There was also an incentive for both to put their missiles on hair trigger, increasing the chance of an accidental Armageddon.

It took awhile for practice to catch up with theory. While some nuclear strategists were making the case for limiting strategic defenses, the U.S. and the USSR began deploying them. In so doing they proved the theoreticians' point. In the sixties, the Kremlin built a system that it claimed was for defense against high-altitude bombers. Suspecting that the facility could be used against American missiles, the U.S. developed offensive countermeasures, primarily multiple independently targetable warheads, known as MIRVs.* In American hands, these devices, with their ability to multiply the number of warheads each missile could hurl at the enemy, restored the U.S.'s confidence that it could penetrate the USSR's defenses and hold Soviet power in check in a crisis.

Eventually, however, the Soviets learned how to MIRV their own missiles. The USSR's MIRVed missiles figured, in American planning, as the principal instrument available to the Kremlin if its leaders ever decided to launch a surprise attack on the U.S. For their part, the Soviets worried that their own rocket force was now an even more attractive target for preemption if the U.S. ever decided to go first. Thus, MIRVing was the single most dangerous innovation since the mating of nuclear weaponry with ballistic rocketry.

In due course, both the U.S. and the USSR accepted the reality of MAD. Through the negotiations known as the Strategic Arms Limitation Talks (SALT), they agreed to codify mutual deterrence, regulate the balance of terror, curb defenses and pave the way for reductions in offensive forces. In 1972, Richard Nixon and Leonid Brezhnev signed the SALT I accords. One of these was the Anti-Ballistic Missile (ABM) treaty. It banned either side from having a "national" defense—that is, a system that protected the entire country—although each could have two ABM sites. Under an amendment in 1974, the superpowers cut back to one ABM site per side. The Russians maintained a system outside of Moscow, while the U.S. briefly kept one at a missile-launch facility in North Dakota.

---

* RV stands for "reentry vehicle," the technical name for the protective container carrying each warhead.

In 1976, in a further acknowledgment of the primacy of deterrence and the futility of defense against an enemy armed with many thousands of warheads, the U.S. shut down its one ABM site. For the remainder of that decade, the principle that nuclear offense trumped defense remained unchallenged.

THEN ALONG CAME Ronald Reagan to challenge it. He was convinced that with enough Yankee know-how and dollars, a high-tech defense against ballistic missile warheads was not just possible but far preferable to MAD. The U.S., he proclaimed in 1983, must undertake a crash program to erect a space-based, impregnable, all-encompassing shield that would render all nuclear weapons, including the Soviet's cherished Strategic Rocket Forces, "impotent and obsolete."

Most American experts considered the Strategic Defense Initiative, as it was officially known, a wildly expensive and dangerous fantasy. Some nicknamed it "Star Wars," in part because Reagan announced the program two weeks after giving a speech to an audience of evangelical Christians in which he'd denounced the USSR as "the evil empire."

The Soviets were less dismissive. Because of their deep-seated sense of vulnerability and their awe of American technology, they could imagine that SDI might just work. If so, it would deprive them of the great equalizer in their otherwise unequal relationship with the U.S. Even if SDI didn't live up to Reagan's high hopes, it would still require massive expenditures for Moscow to offset.

Even after Reagan left office and the program was scaled back, SDI kept its hold on many conservative Republicans. For them, it was more than just a military program of great promise. They believed that the very prospect of SDI had served as a kind of deus ex machina at the end of the cold war: so frightened and demoralized were the rulers of the evil empire by Reagan's vow to turn American technology against them that they had simply thrown in the towel.[2]

THE NEXT AMERICAN PRESIDENT, George H.W. Bush, was as much a traditionalist as Reagan was a revolutionary. Bush believed in maintaining a stable balance of offensive weaponry through the Strategic Arms Reduction Talks (START), the successor to SALT.

But right-wing Republicans who had not given up on Reagan's vision of a perfect defense didn't want Bush to do so either. They pressed the White

House to continue funding development of an ambitious strategic defensive system and to link a START II treaty to a loosening of the restrictions in the ABM treaty.

In 1992, Boris Yeltsin wanted to do his friend George a political favor, and he also wanted to get a START II treaty since that would help him reduce his military budget. Therefore, when he and Bush held their summit in Washington in June of that year, they instructed Dennis Ross, James Baker's right-hand man, and Yuri Mamedov to initiate a "consultation" on a cooperative anti-missile plan to guard against missile attacks from radical regimes or terrorist organizations. As a result, Bush was better able to deflect complaints from pro-SDI Republicans who felt he was giving short shrift to defense.

The START II treaty that Bush and Yeltsin signed in early January 1993 set a ceiling of 3,500 strategic warheads for each side, a two-thirds reduction in the size of the Russian and American arsenals from their cold war highs. The treaty contained another landmark achievement in arms control: "de-MIRVing," a prohibition on land-based missiles with multiple warheads. It was a rare case of the two sides stuffing a genie back into a bottle.[3]

WHEN CLINTON CAME into office, there did not seem to be any reason to continue the dialogue that Ross and Mamedov had begun, since the new president had no enthusiasm for strategic defense. The Russians, too, were more than happy to let the subject drop, since they'd regarded the Ross-Mamedov talks largely as a sop to Bush. Both governments now intended to concentrate on further reductions in offensive weaponry. Each of Clinton's predecessors since Nixon had achieved at least one major agreement limiting or reducing the U.S. and Russian strategic arsenals.[4] Had START II been implemented in 1993, Clinton might have concluded a START III treaty with Yeltsin in his first term and been well into START IV by the second.

But before we could move ahead to START III, START I (which Bush and Gorbachev had signed in 1991) had to go into force, and that required the removal of Soviet-era nuclear weaponry from Ukraine, Belarus and Kazakhstan—one of the Clinton administration's highest priorities in 1993 and 1994. The bigger problem was the Russian parliament's refusal to ratify START II. Yeltsin's political enemies there, who were already defying him at every turn, now had one more chance to do so. As a result of these snags, strategic arms control went into a hiatus that lasted for eight years—and beyond.

Clinton and I talked from time to time about his regret and frustration. He noted the irony that a process that had begun in the depths of the Brezhnev era had gone into suspension largely because Russia was now a democracy. The U.S. was not just negotiating with a potentate in the Kremlin and his minions, but dealing with a pluralistic system that included an obstreperous legislative branch.

It bothered Clinton that because arms control had stopped dead in its tracks, the U.S. and Russia still had some 15,000 long-range nuclear weapons, primarily for use against each other.

"What's going on here?" he demanded in a meeting on defense policy in the Cabinet Room in September 1994. "The cold war's supposed to be over! What do we need this much overkill for? Are we stuck in some sort of time warp, or what?"

Clinton asked on several occasions why we couldn't go further on our own in shrinking the size of our arsenal to take account of the dramatic changes in the former Soviet Union. The Defense Department was reluctant to cut back on the number of strategic weapons available for the conduct of World War III given the danger of what was sometimes called a "recidivist Russia." A bigger obstacle was legislation that Congress had passed prohibiting unilateral cuts below the levels in START I in the absence of START II ratification by the Duma.

WHILE ARMS CONTROL was stalled, the Pentagon continued to experiment with new technologies for defending against ballistic missiles. Clinton's first secretary of defense, Les Aspin, shifted the focus of that program from national missile defense of a scope and capability that could shoot down Russia's intercontinental rockets to "theater missile defense," or TMD, against shorter-range rockets like the ones that Iran, Iraq, Libya and North Korea were beginning to develop.*

There was nothing abstract about the threat posed by these so-called rogue states. The U.S. had lost twenty-eight soldiers in the Gulf War to an attack by an Iraqi SCUD missile. The prospect of nuclear-armed missiles in the hands of Iran's radical Islamic regime had been a preoccupation for the U.S. for years and a major irritant in our relations with Russia,

---

*The term "theater" in this context refers to a regional, or geographically limited, "theater of operation" as opposed to a strategic, or intercontinental, system.

primarily because of the peril it posed to Israel. North Korea, under Kim Jong-il, the son of its founding dictator, was one of the most mysterious and menacing countries on earth. The prospect that it would be armed with both nuclear weapons and ballistic missiles threatened not only South Korea and the 37,000 American troops stationed there but Japan as well.

There was nothing in the ABM treaty that said the U.S. couldn't defend itself or its allies against shorter-range ballistic missiles. At the same time, we didn't want an anti-missile program intended to deal with non-Russian threats to provoke nationalistic fervor in Moscow during a period when the very survival of Russian democracy was in doubt. Therefore in several of his summits with Yeltsin during the first term, Clinton provided formal assurances that the U.S. would keep its testing of TMD systems compliant with the ABM treaty.[5]

Clinton's promise to adhere to the ABM treaty was a red flag to those still-powerful forces in Congress who remained faithful to Reagan's vision of a world in which defense replaced deterrence. In 1994, the Republicans trumpeted that goal in their campaign to take control of both houses of Congress. Once they were in the majority, they began pushing legislation to require deployment of a national anti-missile system and, as a consequence, withdrawal from the ABM treaty.

Leading Democrats urged the White House to come up with an alternative NMD scheme that was compatible with the ABM treaty.

By Clinton's second term, the administration was well on its way to refining a plan to develop a ground-based ABM so fast and accurate that it could home in on an enemy warhead and destroy it in flight. The U.S. cranked up a major program to develop and deploy this technology for TMD purposes and to test its potential against intercontinental-range missiles as well. To facilitate the high-priority TMD program, we initiated discussions with Russia aimed at agreeing on a dividing line, or "demarcation," between TMD, which was permitted by the ABM treaty, and strategic defensive systems, which were sharply constrained by the treaty.

The Russians were wary about giving us any leniency, since they assumed that whatever we were up to was a stalking horse for an anti-missile system that would eventually be able to neutralize their deterrent.

The turning point came at the Helsinki summit between Clinton and Yeltsin in March 1997. The two presidents had an intense but inconclusive go at each other on this subject in the course of a longer conversation about NATO enlargement, then turned the issue over to their aides. For much of the rest of that day, U.S. and Russian officials, who had split into working groups, occupied every room on the first floor of the Finnish presidential residence, including the kitchen, the pantry, the dining room and President Ahtisaari's study. Madeleine Albright and Lynn Davis held three separate and contentious meetings with Yevgeny Primakov, then the foreign minister, and his team.

General Shalikashvili, the chairman of the Joint Chiefs of Staff, and his Russian counterpart, General Victor Samsonov, sat at a coffee table poring over technical documents that the Pentagon hoped would assure the Russians that our TMD program was not an NMD either in disguise or in potential. The senior civilian from the Defense Department present, Jan Lodal, was on the telephone with Secretary of Defense Cohen back in Washington, apprising him of the problems as they arose in the negotiations and coaxing him into agreement with solutions as they emerged.

Yuri Mamedov and I, who had spent much of our careers on nuclear arms control—he as a diplomat, I as a journalist—had been hoping for four years we'd get a chance to sink our teeth into these subjects. We floated among the various working groups primarily to make sure that the right people were talking but also to help with the drafting of compromise language.

After lunch, Clinton and Yeltsin sent Albright, Shali and Lodal off with Primakov, Mamedov and Samsonov with instructions to come up with an agreement based on a draft that Lodal and Mamedov had prepared. In the end, the Russians agreed to a detailed technical demarcation between permissible TMD programs and prohibited ABM ones. The inducement for them to do so was a willingness by the U.S., engineered primarily by Shali, to set a ceiling for offensive systems in START III that would be nearly a third lower than the one in START II, thereby making it easier for Russia to afford a nuclear arsenal roughly equal in size to that of the U.S.[6]

The Helsinki summit had moved the Russians closer to an important threshold: they seemed prepared to consider adjusting the strategic equation, letting the U.S. add defense against certain kinds of threats, while continuing to subtract offense—as long as the smaller arsenal Russia ended up with would still be able to penetrate whatever defenses the U.S. eventually deployed.

We never had a chance to test that proposition because the Duma still refused to ratify START II after Helsinki and our own law continued to prevent unilateral cuts in the U.S. arsenal.

———

MEANWHILE, THE JUGGERNAUT on Capitol Hill in favor of NMD gathered momentum. In mid-July 1998, a congressionally appointed commission chaired by a former (and future) Republican secretary of defense, Donald Rumsfeld, issued a report predicting that rogue states could have ballistic missiles capable of reaching the U.S. sooner than the U.S. intelligence community believed. Six weeks later, on August 31, 1998, the North Koreans tried and failed to launch a small satellite. The shot demonstrated they were well on their way to being able to launch multi-stage rockets.

As much as anything, the North Koreans were probably pursuing the political goal of increasing their leverage over the U.S. and Japan in future negotiations to increase international assistance to their economy, which was in desperate shape. But in the U.S., the launch was seen as presaging a new military threat to the American homeland. The North Korean rocket was believed to be the prototype of a ballistic missile that might, if perfected, be able to hit American territory. In March 1999, the Senate passed, by a margin of 97–3, a bill mandating a U.S. policy to "deploy as soon as technologically possible an effective" anti-missile system capable of "defending the territory of the United States." Therefore NMD was, by definition—by virtue of the "N" for National in its initials—a violation of the ABM treaty's prohibition against a national anti-missile system. The House overwhelmingly approved a similar measure in May.[7]

THE ADMINISTRATION was more in danger than ever of losing control of a key feature of defense and foreign policy. We'd had to deal with demands from Congress in the past, notably over Russia's relations with Iran and the Duma's passage of a restrictive religion law in 1997. But those earlier disputes within the U.S. government were essentially over tactics. The executive branch had as much desire as anyone in Congress to end the leakage of Russian technology to Iran and to promote religious tolerance in Russian society.

We had a deeper disagreement with the more extreme advocates of strategic defense in the Congress. They had already made up their minds that the U.S. would be safer with an unfettered defensive system than it was with existing arms control agreements, while we saw NMD as a research-and-development program that should be continued but that had a long way to go before it was ready for deployment. Even if the technology proved itself, the system should be designed to meet the rogue-state threat but stay within the bounds of the ABM treaty, although those bounds might have to be adjusted through amendment in order to accommodate new threats and new technologies.

There was little room for these considerations in the NMD bill that Congress had passed by a veto-proof margin and that was now heading toward the president's desk. That left us with a dilemma. If we said we were committed to preserving the ABM treaty without regard to its constraints on NMD, we'd spend the rest of the administration in what would very likely be a losing fight with Congress, since the Republicans had the votes to block our policies. If, on the other hand, we acceded to congressional pressure and decided to pursue NMD without regard to its implications for the ABM treaty, we'd have a blowup with the Russians—and very likely a split with our allies, who tended to see NMD as a return to the concept of Fortress America and an abandonment of thirty years of strategic arms control.

THE LONG SHOT

Never did Sandy Berger, the president's national security adviser, have more reason to evoke the myth of Scylla and Charybdis, and never did he do a more masterly job steering between the two. Almost single-handedly, in an intense round of brainstorming and logrolling, he cobbled together a compromise on NMD that balanced military, diplomatic and political considerations.

One challenge was to make sure that when the president signed the bill he wasn't also signing away his prerogatives and responsibilities. Sandy crafted a White House statement stipulating a set of criteria that the president would apply when it came time a year or so later to decide whether to go forward with deployment. The two key variables were whether the technology of the system under development proved itself in tests still to be conducted, and whether proceeding with NMD contributed to the overall security of the U.S., including in its impact on arms control.

This latter criterion, which had the support of key Senate Democrats, allowed the president to evaluate missile defense in a larger context. Even if the bugs could be worked out, American and allied experts were justifiably skeptical about whether NMD would be as effective against enemy warheads as its proponents believed, given the possibility of countermeasures to defeat the defense. Moreover, NMD was useless against suitcases, knapsacks, balloons, oil drums in the holds of tramp steamers and other low-tech "delivery means" for attacking the U.S. with high explosives or weapons of mass destruction (no one, as far as I know, predicted the use of hijacked commercial aircraft for kamikaze attacks on the World Trade Center and Pentagon).

The president also must be able to weigh the benefits of NMD against the negative consequences that going ahead with the program might have for relations with our allies, Russia and other countries as well as the implications for arms control.

Sandy's next task was to get the administration to close ranks behind a version of NMD that had enough political support to keep our congressional opponents at bay, enough military and scientific plausibility to deal with the potential threat we faced from rogue states, and enough compatibility with the ABM treaty to be the basis for a new round of discussions with the Russians.

After weeks of quiet intramural diplomacy with the Pentagon, Sandy presented Clinton with a plan at a meeting on August 18, 1999, in the Cabinet Room. In order to meet the requirement for covering all fifty states, there needed to be two anti-missile sites, one in Alaska and the other probably in North Dakota, with a total of 250 interceptors, as well as a network of highly sophisticated radars on the ground (including outside the U.S.) and sensors in space that would track enemy warheads and help our interceptors home in on them. The full system wouldn't be in place until well into the next decade—sometime between 2005 and 2010. The first step would be a site in Alaska that could have some initial capability by 2005 to counter what was perceived to be the most immediate threat, the one posed by North Korea. To meet that schedule, construction of a radar on Shemya Island off Alaska would have to begin in the spring or summer of 2001. To have the equipment and material in place by then, the president would have to decide on deployment a year beforehand, by the summer of 2000.

That itself was a perverse bit of timing, since the presidential election campaign would be moving into high gear—never a good time for the U.S. government to face politically controversial and strategically important decisions. If the president gave a go-ahead to preparations for the Alaska site, he would in effect be putting Russia and the world on notice that the U.S. was pulling out of the ABM treaty—unless we could persuade the Russians to amend the treaty to permit that first step toward deployment.

Since we had about ten months to negotiate amendments to the ABM treaty, we decided to seek only those changes that were necessary for deployment of the first phase of an NMD system, the Alaska-based part of the system required to deal with the North Korean threat. The second site with additional interceptors and more radars would be the subject of further negotiations a few years down the road. As an inducement to the Russians to go along with this plan, we were prepared to share with them early-warning data and new interceptor technologies, and engage in other measures intended to make anti-missile defense a cooperative venture.

Sandy called the goal a trifecta, since it would allow us to advance—and reconcile—three objectives: first, we would be able to proceed with preparations for a limited NMD appropriate to the new threat we faced from the rogues without violating the ABM treaty; second, by amending the ABM treaty, we would be making it more relevant and durable in a world where the U.S. and Russia were cooperating against proliferation; and third, we would be able to achieve deep cuts in offenses as part of an accompanying START III agreement that would have some prospect of approval by the Senate.

LIKE SANDY, I believed the trifecta was a long shot, probably coming too late in the Clinton presidency to be achievable either diplomatically or politically. It was worth trying for but not betting the ranch on. We should make an all-out effort at getting a deal while leaving the president a range of choices about what to do if the Russians refused.

There was a difference between this challenge and the ones we'd faced over NATO enlargement and Kosovo. In those cases, the U.S. negotiating position had been simple, unbending and, largely for that reason, successful. "Table and stick" we'd called it: Go straight to your bottom line and stick with it; wait until the other side bends. We'd been able to look the Russians in the eye and tell them that we were going forward with or without them.

In the case of NMD, the president *might* decide in mid-2000 that he should go forward with the program in the face of Russian objections, but he might instead decide to defer deployment for reasons unrelated to the Russia factor, such as poor performance of the system in the tests.

Therefore in pressing the Russians to join us in changing the ABM treaty we couldn't credibly adopt the table-and-stick strategy. Instead, we tried to get them to look at the choice they faced in terms of the devil they knew versus the one they didn't. We understood that the Russians didn't want the U.S. to undertake any serious missile defense at all. But that position was unrealistic as well as unreasonable. Sooner or later, the U.S. was going to need some form of missile defense to cope with rogue states. Russia would probably want one too, since it was closer to all three rogues than we were. We were offering Moscow a chance to adjust to that unavoidable reality cooperatively and within the framework of mutually agreed constraints, starting with an understanding in 2000 to amend the ABM treaty enough to permit a limited missile defense against rogue-state threats of the kind we were proposing.

The Russians, we contended, could safely join us in that step, since their Strategic Rocket Forces, even if substantially reduced under a prospective START III, could easily overwhelm a limited American defense that was designed to cope with a very small number of missiles from North Korea or Iran. Therefore NMD was a devil they knew and ought to be able to live with.

The devil they didn't know was the possibility that the next president—regardless of whether it was Al Gore or George Bush—would, at a minimum, build the system we were proposing and, because of the timetable for construction in Alaska, have to withdraw from the ABM treaty in order to proceed. In the case of a Bush presidency, that devil would be all the less appealing to the Russians, since Bush was in favor of a bigger NMD and no ABM treaty.

We based the case that our proposed system did not threaten the Russian deterrent on simple arithmetic: the first phase of NMD, even when fully deployed sometime after 2005, would have only a hundred interceptors, while the Russians, under any imaginable variant of START III, would have more than a thousand warheads, as well as various techniques for confusing and overwhelming our defense. Mutual deterrence would remain alive and well.

YURI MAMEDOV AND I, accompanied by military and civilian experts, conducted a series of meetings on ABM/NMD that lasted nearly a year and brought us together in Moscow, Washington, New York, Rome, Helsinki, Oslo and Okinawa. We treated the talks as a spin-off of the Strategic Stability Group that we had established seven years before, in the spring of 1993. (In the context of strategic arms control, both sides used the term "strategic stability" as a synonym for mutual deterrence, and as a euphemism for MAD.)

For months, terminology was just about the only thing on which we were able to agree. On the core issue of whether the proposed American plan for NMD threatened the Russian deterrent, we might as well have been debating whether the earth was round or flat. The Russians based their position on a worst-case scenario that cast the U.S. in the role of nuclear aggressor or at least nuclear blackmailer. By their calculations, the U.S. would have the offensive capability to knock out 90 percent of Russia's strategic arsenal using our nuclear forces and precision conventional weapons of the kind they'd seen so spectacularly on display in Iraq, Yugoslavia and Afghanistan in September 1998, after Osama bin Laden was determined to be behind the bombing of two U.S. embassies in Africa. The surviving 10 percent of their force—say, a hundred warheads—might be within the capacity of NMD to shoot down before they reached their targets.

What the Russians feared most was the "architecture" that would eventually be associated with NMD—sophisticated radars deployed around the world, complemented by constellations of space-based sensors all coordinated by an elaborate command-and-control network. Once that whole system was in place, they said, the U.S. could easily expand the number of interceptors well beyond what we were presenting as the full extent of our program. The Russians knew that nuclear war with the U.S. was unthinkable, but they worried nonetheless that the combination of a substantial American first-strike capability and an NMD system to back it up might leave them vulnerable to nuclear intimidation in a political crisis—similar, perhaps, to the one that they'd just been through at Priština Airport.

So adamant were the Russians in opposing NMD that they refused even to call the talks a negotiation, since that would have implied that what we were asking for was negotiable. Instead, they characterized the yearlong marathon of the Strategic Stability Group as a "consultation." Even the term that the Russians used for NMD, "national ABM," was a way of underscoring that it was inherently a violation of the treaty.

THROUGHOUT THE FALL of 1999, the Russian military was more assertive and confident in stonewalling us on NMD than it had been over NATO enlargement and Balkan peacekeeping. Every time my colleagues from the Pentagon, Ted Warner and Rear Admiral Joseph Enright, would put on a slide show, with maps and charts, to demonstrate that Russia had nothing to fear, General Nikolai Zlenko, the Ministry of Defense representative on Mamedov's team, would make a detailed presentation of his own showing how NMD could either decapitate the Russian rocket forces or checkmate the political leadership in a crisis.

On the eve of several of our sessions, General Kvashnin, the chief of defense who had been the driving force behind the Russian dash to Priština in June and was now leading the charge in Chechnya, publicly warned the Russian Foreign Ministry not to make any compromise. There were hints that he and others in the Defense Ministry were making plans to re-MIRV their missiles in order to counter NMD, thereby brushing aside a key provision of START II and undoing one of the signal accomplishments of arms control.

Soon after Putin became acting president at the turn of the year, the Russian military's role in the talks became, if anything, even more conspicuous than before and its position even more intractable. The generals no longer had to worry that Yeltsin and his friend Bill would cut some last-minute deal over the military's objections.

ON JANUARY 18, 2000, the American anti-missile system failed an important test when the infrared sensor on board the interceptor malfunctioned. Many domestic critics rejoiced, including (quietly) some within the administration who had doubts about the wisdom of the program.

I regarded the failure of the test as a setback for our diplomacy. The performance of our system in the testing program was, after all, one of the criteria that the president had specified when he signed the NMD bill into law. New questions about the technology of NMD made it harder for me to persuade the Russians that Clinton might proceed with deployment even if they refused to amend the ABM treaty. Therefore I needed an additional incentive to get the Russians to budge.

In preparation for another round of talks with the Russians in late January, I asked the White House and the Pentagon for authority to sound out Mamedov on whether lowering the ceiling on offensive weapons in START III well below what Clinton and Yeltsin had agreed in Helsinki might induce Moscow to alter the ABM treaty enough to permit the beginning of construction of the Alaska radar site in 2001.[8]

The Russians, Yuri replied, did indeed want lower offensive levels in START III but not at the price of higher levels of American defense. He quoted Reagan to me—not Ronald but Nancy. "On NMD," he said, "you're dealing with a country and a new president whose motto is, 'Just say no.'"

THE NAYSAYER IN CHIEF was careful not to make himself the heavy on NMD. Putin spent nearly three hours with Secretary Albright on February 2, 2000, exuding reasonableness and good will.

"We want to find formulas that allow us to meet new threats while preserving the ABM treaty and achieving deep cuts under START III," said Madeleine.

"I like that approach!" Putin replied, as though it were a eureka moment. It was actually a classic Putinism. When we followed up through diplomatic and military channels, we were told that the only way to preserve the ABM treaty was not to change one word or punctuation mark in it.

IN FEBRUARY, Sandy Berger made a run at persuading the new head of the Russian Security Council, Sergei Ivanov—a former KGB officer close to Putin—that Moscow would be smart to do a deal with us on NMD rather than take a chance on our successors. One way or another, Sandy said, NMD was almost certain to proceed. It was a variation on the devil-you-know-versus-the-one-you-don't sales pitch for our position.

The Russians were never impressed by that argument since they calculated—again, not unreasonably—that they could get either a quick deal or a postponement of construction out of Al Gore, while George W. Bush wouldn't be bound by anything he inherited from us.

I HAD MY NEXT CRACK at Yuri Mamedov the second week in March, when he and I arranged to rendezvous in Rome. Brooke accompanied me on the trip and Yuri brought along his wife, Katya, whom I'd never met before. Putting aside work one Saturday, the four of us traveled into the countryside. After strolling around a hill town, we wandered into the opera house, where a competition was under way among amateur sopranos from all over Europe. We then had lunch in a country inn by a river.

We returned to Rome that evening in a U.S. embassy van that careened along mountain roads trying to keep up with its escort of motorcycle-mounted *carabinieri*. While Brooke and Katya snoozed in the seat in front of us, Yuri and I got back to business. Our principal concern was managing NMD at the first Clinton-Putin summit, which we expected would take place in the late spring or early summer.

I hadn't entirely given up on reaching a deal, nor did I want the Russians to discount the possibility that Clinton might order the start of construction in Alaska even in the absence of a deal. Yuri was equally careful not to box in his own president. He left open the possibility that Putin might come to agreement with Clinton during their first summit or at one of the several other encounters they would have later in the year.

But Yuri doubted that would happen, and so did I. Therefore we concentrated on an interim arrangement that would avoid a breakdown on NMD/ABM at the summit even if the two presidents couldn't achieve a breakthrough.

For some months, we'd been privately exploring the possibility of a joint presidential statement as a provisional measure in the spring that would set the scene for a final agreement later in the year, or at least lay the ground for progress later. We called it "the principles document" since it would assert a number of tenets on which the two sides could agree in the near term and that might help guide them to an eventual settlement. One principle was the assertion that both countries remained committed to strategic stability. Translation: neither side would deprive the other of its deterrent capability. We would, in that context, explicitly cite the role of the ABM treaty in maintaining stability and creating the confidence in mutual deterrence necessary to reduce offensive forces.

That was what the Russians wanted to hear from us, and we were glad to say it since we believed it.

The principles document would go on to assert that the world had changed since 1972, when the ABM treaty was signed. It would identify the growing threat of proliferation of weapons of mass destruction and missiles to deliver them as a significant change in the strategic situation, and it would note a provision in the ABM treaty anticipating that such changes might be grounds for amendment. That way Russia would be on record accepting a key premise of the U.S. position and, accordingly, retreating from its refusal to consider changes in the treaty.

In the American view, the most important line in the principles document was one in which the two presidents would agree to develop "concrete measures" that would allow both sides to "take necessary steps to preserve strategic stability in the face of new threats."

WHILE YURI AND I would meet often during the months that followed, the principles document was our last major piece of collaboration. It was also the quintessential example of how the two of us had worked together for seven years. We sometimes compared our own personal diplomacy to win/win chess. Each of us had as his principal obligation the advancement of his own government's interest. But since we were trying to respect each other's interests, we would, as we put it, "play both sides of the board," explaining what we were doing, and why, and occasionally even suggesting what move the other should make.

It was in that spirit that Yuri and I put our heads together on the principles document as we bounced through the Umbrian countryside toward Rome in the dusk that Saturday evening. Even if Clinton and Putin could not break the impasse over *how* to amend the ABM treaty, at least they would have established that the treaty *could* be amended, and, by implication, why it *should* be. That agreement would provide the next American administration with a basis for resuming negotiation on an ABM deal as it made up its own mind about how to proceed with missile defense.

WHEN THE RUSSIANS went to the polls on March 26, 2000, to elect their second president, it was an anticlimax, especially compared to the election four years earlier, when Yeltsin came from far behind and had to go into a second round to be reelected. This time Putin won outright with 53 percent of the vote, defeating ten opponents, including Zyuganov, Yavlinsky and Zhirinovsky. (Primakov and Luzhkov did not even run in the end.)

One of Putin's many advantages in the accelerated timetable of the election was that it allowed him to assume the presidency before the war in Chechnya flared anew with the coming of spring. The rebels, who had regrouped in the mountains during the winter, stepped up their hit-and-run attacks on Russian forces. By the end of April, Moscow acknowledged that nearly two thousand Russian soldiers had died in the seven months of fighting.

Yet even when the fighting resumed, there appeared to be little slackening of public support for Putin's determination to deal harshly with "bandits and terrorists."

Much the same was true of his explicitly tougher domestic policies. During the campaign, Putin had promised a "dictatorship of laws," a telling variation on the more common phrase "rule of law." It suggested a tightening of the screws not just on crime and corruption but on the media and society in general. Putin's slogan raised eyebrows in the West and among Russian liberals, but apparently not with the rank and file.

Putin's popularity with the people translated into clout with the Duma. In mid-April, he accomplished with the relative ease what Yeltsin had been unable to do for seven years: he rammed through ratification of START II. But in doing so, Putin promised the legislature—and his own military—that if the U.S. decided to "destroy" the ABM treaty, Russia reserved the right to "withdraw not only from the START II treaty but also the whole system of treaties on limitation and control of strategic and conventional weapons."

IN THE U.S., political pressure was building against compromise on NMD. Governor Bush seized on missile defense as a demonstration of what he portrayed as an approach to national security that was more hard-headed than Clinton's and Gore's. Bush promised that, if elected, he would override Russian objections, discard what he called an outmoded ABM treaty and launch an effort to develop an effective anti-missile system. While vowing to proceed unilaterally with NMD, he promised also to slash American offensive forces, on the grounds that "Russia is no longer our enemy."

The problem with Bush's position, I believed, was that it seemed to assume that the Russians, confronted with an administration that was more "serious" about deploying NMD, would accept a world with no agreed limits on American defenses and join the U.S. in offensive reductions and restraints. Yet Putin's vow to the Duma suggested otherwise. Rather than sitting still, the Russians might take a range of countermeasures (including re-MIRVing) that would represent a net setback to American and international security.

But as a campaign tactic, Bush's move was clever. He had, in a single stroke, positioned himself to the administration's right on an anti-missile system ("we'll do whatever is necessary to defend America") and to its left on disarmament ("we don't need so many of these weapons"—something Clinton himself had felt for a long time).

AT THE END OF APRIL, Foreign Minister Igor Ivanov came to Washington and, in addition to a meeting with Secretary Albright, paid a call on Governor Bush (in the same spirit as Yeltsin's meeting with Governor Clinton in 1992). The two chatted jovially in Spanish, which Ivanov had mastered as ambassador to Spain in the late eighties. During the meeting, Bush professed total confidence of victory in November. On NMD, Bush told Ivanov not to worry; he was sure he'd be able to "sit down with President Putin and work something out."

The Russians attached no substantive importance to the exchange—they doubted Bush had anything in mind beyond wanting to appear affable and statesmanlike—but they welcomed the opportunity to scoff at us for urging them to do a deal with our administration rather than leave themselves to the mercy of the NMD superhawks if Bush won.

AMERICA'S ALLIES were, without exception, apprehensive about NMD. Along with a number of my colleagues from the State Department and Pentagon, I made frequent trips to allied capitals and NATO headquarters in Brussels to brief them on the program and on the discussions with the Russians. We encountered deep skepticism about every aspect of our policy—the technology, the implications for arms control and transatlantic defense, and the extent to which short-term political considerations might drive a decision of long-term strategic consequences. The allies' resistance to our arguments was of operational significance, since the plan we were asking them to endorse required at least two of them, Britain and Denmark, to let us use their territory for radar facilities integral to the NMD system.

SPARRING PARTNERS

When I boarded Air Force One for the flight from Germany to Moscow, I joined Clinton, Sandy Berger and Steve Sestanovich in the president's private cabin for a quick review of where we stood. I had given a lot of thought to my principal message for the president, and it required me to be a bit stern with my boss—not my favorite role. I'd heard him say several times about Putin that he hadn't "broken the code on this new guy." He was going into the meeting uneasy about his host. I was concerned that he might try to counter the Putin chill with an excessive display of the Clinton warmth. Whatever Clinton did or didn't accomplish on the substance of the agenda, I said, he had to set the right tone, and that should be one of reciprocal wariness. That meant resisting his natural temptation to get too chummy.

It was particularly important to get the atmosphere right, since a breakthrough on substance was highly unlikely. Clinton himself called NMD a "giant banana peel." While he had yet to make up his mind on deployment, he was strongly inclined to defer construction of the radar site in Alaska. There were problems with NMD well beyond Russian obstinacy. That made it all the more important that Clinton not make the decision before he sat down with Putin, in anticipation of a rebuff, or, for that matter, immediately afterward. When the time came to make the call on NMD later in the summer, he ought to be free to do so on the basis of the full array of criteria he'd laid out a year earlier when he signed the missile defense bill into law. He should treat Russian opposition as a significant factor but not necessarily as the dispositive one. On this point, Sandy, who had been letting me monopolize the time available for the briefing, weighed in to support me, since he'd been making much the same pitch to Clinton for days.

Whatever else happened in Moscow, I concluded, circling back to the question of public perception, Clinton could not go home with people saying he'd tried to get an arms agreement at any cost or was too eager to buddy up to Putin. It would be a minor but useful accomplishment if we could get the press to write after the summit was over that there had been a noticeable reserve in Clinton's handling of Putin.

"For starters," I said, "don't call him Vladimir."

Sometimes when I gave Clinton advice he didn't particularly want to hear or that had an implication of criticism, he pushed back or waved me off (although he never slapped me down). On this occasion, though, he took it all in and nodded pensively when I was done.

"Got it," he said. "Bottom line, I can't go in there and take a dive or box myself in for what I decide later. I've got to go in there and give this thing my best shot on the merits and then do the right thing when the time comes."

THE SUMMIT began with a private dinner in the presidential quarters of the Kremlin on June 3. As I entered the room behind Clinton, Putin welcomed me as though I were an old pal and a fellow weekend warrior, wounded on the battlefield of middle age: I was on a cane after knee surgery, the result of an injury on top of too many years of running. Putin sympathized, saying he'd been finding it hard to stay fit and was therefore more prone to pulling a muscle, which would then throw off his whole "physical culture" regimen. Part of the problem, he added, with just the slightest hint of a smile, was that now that he was the president of the country, no one wanted to be his judo sparring partner.

Turning his attention to Clinton, Putin asked solicitously how Chelsea had adjusted to life in the White House (his own teenage daughters were isolated because of all the security, he said); how Hillary was faring in her campaign for the Senate in New York (Clinton expressed cautious optimism); and how Al Gore was doing in his race (recent polls showed him running slightly behind Bush). Clinton predicted that the election would be extremely close. He explained that George W. Bush's strategy hinged on convincing the voters that "he's a slightly more conservative version of me. Missile defense is one of the issues on which he's trying to tell the people, 'I'm different than Clinton—I'm better because I'm tougher.' "

Putin laughed appreciatively, as though to show he knew all about the virtues of running as the tough guy. Then he remarked, "Well, it's important not to let the best become the enemy of the good." The watchword on both sides, he added, was "do no harm."

Careful student that Putin was of his visitor's file, he probably knew that Hippocrates' famous counsel was one of Clinton's own favorite adages. (I'd heard him use it nine years before, in August 1991, when he was trying to decide how not to complicate Gorbachev's and Yeltsin's lives during the Soviet coup—and many times since.) This one cryptic comment seemed to be as much as Putin wanted to say about missile defense. Clinton let the subject slide for the time being.

In the long, meandering discussion that followed, Putin would occasionally drop in a phrase of English, usually to underscore agreeableness or deference ("okay" or "excuse me"). He seemed to be following much of what Clinton said even before it was interpreted.

It was all very friendly. As in earlier encounters, only when the subject of Chechnya arose did Putin's eyes narrow and his manner become more hard-edged. The Chechens were terrorists, and Russia was going to deal with them as such. He scoffed at reports of "alleged, mythical atrocities by the Russian army."

Eventually, seeing that Putin was not going to return to the subject of NMD, Clinton circled back to it himself. He laid out the political argument that Sandy had used with Sergei Ivanov: If Bush won the election, it would be harder for him to undo a done deal than to walk away from unfinished business. The compromise the U.S. was proposing, he said, "will be a strong precedent for establishing that any future missile defense would have to be based on mutual agreement." He added the promise of lower START III numbers than he'd agreed to with Yeltsin in Helsinki.

Clinton concluded with a fervent appeal for Putin to worry less about the vulnerability of Russia to American nuclear attack and worry more about the danger both countries faced from proliferation. "We're caught in a time warp here," said Clinton. "Thirty years from now people will look back on the cold war and the U.S.-Russian nuclear stand-off as ancient history. Our countries will be working together against new threats—rogue states that are menacing the world with chemical and biological weapons and suitcase bombs, new threats deriving from religious and ethnic conflict and religious extremism. How do we get on the right side now for that point in the future? How do we make sure that we're part of the same system working together? How do we not let ourselves be trapped in the cold war mentality while at the same time keeping mutual deterrence strong between us until we come up with something better? And how do we take advantage of the opportunity and the responsibility we have to bring levels of nuclear weapons much lower? I believe we can have a helluva lot of mutual deterrence with smaller arsenals."

"It may surprise you," replied Putin, "but I agree with you—in contrast to some of my colleagues, including several in the Ministry of Defense. In the future, suitcase bombs are a much bigger threat."

Listening to this, I thought to myself that this was the best example yet of a Putin windup for a curveball. Sure enough, Putin went on to say, "Now, there are some points where I might take slight issue with you. For example, you're saying, 'We have to do this now.' I think it would be better to focus on the threats we'll face thirty years from now . . ."

Clinton, who rarely interrupted, did so at this moment, and with an uncharacteristic sharpness in his voice: "Listen, I've got to focus on threats a lot sooner than that." He was referring to the missile programs of North Korea and Iran.

Putin, who wasn't expecting an argument, did a slight double take. "Okay, okay," he said, "I understand perfectly well that the U.S. isn't getting ready to launch a nuclear strike on Russia, but we've got to treat the balance between us very carefully, with an eye to the future as well as to the present."

Putin went on to say that a few blocks away, at the Ministry of Defense, Russian officers were frantically planning countermeasures to NMD that could cause problems for the U.S. and its allies. (He was referring, we believed, to such steps as the vigorous deployment of shorter-range nuclear missiles that would threaten Europe, a return to reliance on multiple warheads, or MIRVs, atop Russia's intercontinental missiles and the sharing of MIRV technology with the Chinese.)

The logic of the U.S. position, Putin continued, might have a certain legitimacy, but there was another logic that he found more compelling. Clinton had been president of the U.S. while a new Russia was coming into being. He'd done a great deal to help Russia and strengthen the bilateral relationship. In that sense Clinton was one of the leading citizens of the world. But that made it all the harder for Putin to imagine how Clinton could make a mistake that endangered international security. Apart from the pressures of American domestic politics, Putin didn't see any basis for a decision that would violate the physicians' oath to do no harm. (There it was again.) Of course, Putin stressed, his preference was to come to terms with Clinton. But they needed to do so on genuinely common ground. The principles document they were going to sign later during the summit met that standard. It helped identify a path forward that would allow Clinton to avoid spurring a new arms race and plunge the U.S. and Russia back into the mutual mistrust of the bad old days.

In trying to argue Clinton out of NMD, Putin claimed to be speaking not just for Russia. If he and Clinton failed to find a way out of their impasse, other countries—he probably had China principally in mind—would react as well in ways that would be bad for the whole world. How would that look? he asked.

He concluded by urging Clinton to keep everything he'd said in mind before making a decision.

Putin's peroration was typical of what we'd now come to expect from him. He had lavished praise on Clinton as camouflage for a rebuff and a warning. By my count, Putin had uttered nearly two hundred words, but they boiled down to one: "no."

As though to make clear that it was also the last word on the subject, he rather peremptorily terminated the discussion and suggested a tour of the Kremlin residence before dessert. He showed us a sumptuous duplex library with a bust of Pushkin prominently on display, a private chapel with a baptismal fount, his personal gym with a universal weight machine and a massage table. Then, on our way back to the dining room, he stopped for a moment to point out a darkened chamber no longer in use. It was, he explained, the clinic for "the previous resident."

That gave Clinton a chance to mention that he would be paying his respects to Boris Yeltsin on Monday, just before leaving Moscow. He asked if Yeltsin was still in the same dacha where he'd resided as president.

"Yes," said Putin, "I let him stay there."

THE REMAINDER of the summit was desultory, in large measure because on NMD, which everyone knew was Topic A, there wasn't much
more to be said. The two presidents signed the principles document in a
public ceremony on Sunday afternoon, June 4. Answering questions from
the press after the signing, Clinton stressed that he had not made a decision on deployment. "I do not believe," he said, that the U.S. program
constituted "a threat to strategic stability and mutual deterrence. The Russian side disagrees. But we had a lot of agreement here," and it had been
captured, he added, in the principles document.

"I do not want the United States to withdraw from the ABM regime because I think it has contributed to a more stable, more peaceful world. It
has already been amended once [in 1974, when each side agreed to have
only one ABM site], and its framers understood that circumstances might
change and threats might arise which were outside the context of U.S.-
now Russian relations." He and President Putin, he added, "acknowledge
that there is a threat; it needs to be met; and we're trying to bridge our differences. And I think that's where we ought to leave it."

THE NEXT MORNING, Clinton held a farewell meeting with Putin in
the ceremonial office at the Kremlin that Yeltsin had renovated with statues of the various czars and the one empress who epitomized Russia's
greatness in the past.

Clinton, making small talk, commented on each of the statues—Peter's
founding of Putin's hometown, Catherine's aggrandizement of Russian
territory, Alexander II's assassination.

"You know Russian history very well," said Putin. "You could be the
president of this country. Or maybe we could switch places."

Then, to Clinton's surprise and mine, Putin, for no apparent reason, returned to the subject of NMD, as though to make sure that his guest
understood the Russian refusal to go further than the principles document.

Putin said he wanted to talk to Clinton not just in his capacity as the
president of the U.S. but as a human being whom Putin liked and whom
the Russian people liked, someone who'd earned a reputation not just for
being well-spoken, as Clinton had demonstrated several times during his
visit, but who was a good listener too—someone who paid attention to
"the other guy's point of view." Could he speak to Clinton on that basis?
he asked before continuing.

"Sure," said Clinton, a tad warily.

Why then, asked Putin, did Clinton keep pushing national missile defense so hard? Putin recognized that there were threats on the horizon that the U.S. and Russia should be preparing to deal with. They had two choices: they could counter those threats jointly, or each side could take steps on its own. Putin knew that there were some in America who thought the U.S. should take the latter course; that America didn't need Russia's permission or cooperation; that the U.S. could do whatever it wanted; that Russia was too weak to do anything about it—too weak to launch another spiral in the arms race.

"But please believe me," he said, speaking very slowly and softly: Russia was capable of an "adequate response" and always would be. That would be true regardless of who the president of Russia was. If NMD went forward, there would be reciprocal action—"maybe quite unexpected, probably asymmetrical"—that is, measures intended not to mimic American high-tech programs but to thwart them. Whatever action Russia took would threaten the territory of the United States.

"I know you've got your own decision to make, and your successor's got his decision to make," Putin continued. Perhaps, according to the American logic, the rest of the world would just swallow what the U.S. president decided, whatever it was. But Putin was putting Clinton on notice what to expect. Or actually, he added, correcting himself, he was warning Clinton that the result might be quite *un*predictable and therefore all the more dangerous.

"Look," said Clinton, trying to suppress what I could see was his annoyance, "I've worked hard to make this a good meeting for both of us, including on the security issues. I told you I thought we'd dealt with a difficult problem about as well as we could. I'm determined, if possible, to find a way forward together. I don't think that the U.S. has the unique power to do whatever it wants and to say to hell with the rest of the world and to hell with what anyone else thinks. I'm trying to find a way to work with you on adapting the existing security system to tomorrow's threats without doing harm with regard to what's happening elsewhere. Where your point of view and mine come together is on the principle that we should adapt to new threats and"—he added after a pause, so that Putin knew that Clinton too listened carefully to his partner and knew when his own lines were being played back to him—"do no harm."

After the meeting came to a close, there was some milling around while Russian security and protocol called for Clinton's motorcade to position itself for the departure. While Putin conferred with several of his aides in hushed tones in a corner of his outer office, Clinton and I had a brief moment to ourselves.

"I guess that guy thought I didn't get it the first time," he said under his breath. "Either he's dense or thinks I am. Anyway, let's get this thing over with so we can go see Ol' Boris."

Putin rejoined Clinton, took him by the arm and, with me tagging along behind, led him down the long red-carpeted corridor and out through the Czar's Entrance of the Grand Kremlin Palace, where they paused for a moment to shake hands and say good-bye in the sunshine.

CHAPTER 16

TRANSITION AND CONTINUITY

Now my charms are all o'erthrown,
And what strength I have's my own

Prospero's epilogue in *The Tempest*

BILL CLINTON still had more than seven months of his presidency ahead of him, but his work with Russia was mostly done. It has always been difficult for an administration to accomplish much in its final year in office. Doing business with Russia in 2000 was further stymied by the lingering dispute over national missile defense, which had, for nearly a year, taken its toll on the political will and diplomatic energy necessary to deal with other issues.

In another test of the NMD system in early July, the "kill vehicle" that was supposed to guide itself into the path of a dummy warhead in space failed to separate from the booster rocket, strengthening the argument for deferring deployment on technical grounds. Three weeks later, on a visit to Pyongyang, Vladimir Putin heard from Kim Jong-il a vague though intriguing proposal that North Korea might suspend its ballistic missile program in exchange for international assistance in launching satellites into orbit. Perhaps the North Koreans really were, as some experts had previously believed, more interested in getting the world's attention and money than in mounting a serious threat to Japan or the U.S. If so, they might be open to verifiable restrictions on their missile program.

On September 1, in a speech at Georgetown University, Clinton announced that he was putting on hold plans to begin construction of the radar site at the tip of the Aleutian Island chain in Alaska—the step that government lawyers believed would have breached the Anti-Ballistic Missile treaty. Clinton reviewed the criteria he'd specified the year before as the basis for a decision. The tests to date, he said, did not provide sufficient confidence in the technology and operational effectiveness of the system for him to move forward with deployment. While NMD would continue as a research-and-development program, Clinton was leaving to his successor the decision of whether to field it as an active part of American defenses and, if so, whether to seek Russian agreement to adjustments in the ABM treaty.

A FEW HOURS BEFORE Clinton's speech, I called Yuri Mamedov to urge that the Russian government resist the temptation to pop the corks of champagne bottles in public, since celebrating, to say nothing of gloating, wasn't justified. Deferral of NMD deployment did not mean cancellation. The logic for altering the strategic equation to take account of threats from rogue states was still compelling. The need to reconcile more capable defenses with an amended ABM treaty was unfinished business that the Putin government would have to take up with the next American administration. If George W. Bush won, the Russians would find themselves dealing with an American president who was enthusiastic about a far more ambitious anti-missile program than the one Clinton had proposed. Moreover, Bush was pushing an unfettered missile defense not just to destroy enemy warheads but also as a way of scuttling the ABM treaty.

The Russians' official response to Clinton's Georgetown speech was appropriately muted, but our allies' sigh of relief could almost be heard across the Atlantic.

In the U.S., Clinton's decision seemed anticlimactic. Objective observers saw the case for deferral as a no-brainer, while gung-ho advocates of NMD had long since discounted the Clinton version of the program as militarily puny and strategically objectionable precisely because it was designed to be as compatible as possible with the ABM treaty.

THE PRESIDENT'S DECISION cut loose a drag on progress in other areas, but there was neither time to jump-start a new round of engagement with the Russians nor, on their part, much interest in doing so.

On September 6, five days after the Georgetown speech on NMD, Clinton and Putin met at the Waldorf-Astoria Hotel in New York during a special millennium summit of the United Nations General Assembly. It was a desultory session. The Russian leader was clearly running out the clock. He was courteous, even deferential, but reluctant to grapple with any of the subjects Clinton raised: Yugoslavia, where a democratic revolution was under way against Slobodan Milošević; Chechnya, where Russian forces pounded away at a resilient enemy; and Russia's assistance to Iran, which continued apace while Sandy Berger played Whac-A-Mole with Sergei Ivanov.

On each point, Putin thanked Clinton for sharing his views and offered what he tried to make sound like a candid assessment. But everything he said, while uttered in soft, confiding tones, tracked closely with what Russian spokesmen were putting out in public.

Only when Clinton gave Putin an analysis of the U.S. presidential campaign did Putin seem genuinely interested (Clinton repeated his earlier forecast that the vote would be very close, predicting that it would come down to a handful of states, especially Florida).

When the time allotted for the meeting expired, both leaders seemed relieved. They had little more to say to each other.

"I got the feeling he was treading water," Clinton commented to me as his security detail hustled us down the corridor to a service elevator that took us to the hotel basement where a motorcade waited to whisk him to the UN. "Putin's obviously holding back for a president whose time in this job will overlap more with his own," he said.

Then he added after a pause, "I guess I can understand that."

Clinton had moved beyond the irritation he'd felt toward Putin at their summit in June. He was developing a respect for the new Russian president's political skills and instincts, including those that led him to treat Clinton as a lame duck.

THE NEXT DAY, on my way back to Washington, I called on George Kennan, then ninety-six. He was having difficulty with his legs, so he no longer made the annual trip to meet with the Russia team at the State Department. Therefore, whenever I got a chance, I routed myself through Princeton. Kennan received me in the sitting room of his home, which was located behind high shrubs on a quiet street near the university. George's wife of sixty-nine years, Annelise, served tea and then joined in reminiscing about their life together in the Baltics before World War II and the Balkans in the early sixties.

When we turned to current developments, Kennan asked my impression of Putin, whom he'd never met. I told him I found Putin enigmatic:

I wasn't sure whether he was hiding how many moves ahead he was think-ing or how few. He seemed to have a knack for being in the right place at the right time with the right protectors; he'd been promoted far beyond anything his experience or apparent abilities would have prepared him for; he was tactically adroit but, I suspected, strategically at sea. I still saw Putin as essentially a suave cop who had lucked into a very big job that would require a lot more than luck to pull off.

However, I added, my boss, the president, was coming to a more favor-able view of Putin.

Kennan commented mildly that he agreed with Clinton. He was tired of reading in the press that Putin was an authoritarian and a retrograde. "Judging from the coverage," he said, "you'd think that this man is trying to re-create the Soviet Union." That, according to Kennan, was not an op-tion for Russia, and Putin knew it. "Nor," he went on, "have I seen any evidence that Putin wants to assume dictatorial powers. Of course he wants to dominate the legislature. Of course he wants to strengthen his in-fluence over the regions and the governors and the various power struc-tures. What executive doesn't? The main thing is whether, in time, a system of checks and balances develops.

"We shouldn't lose sight of the overall trend that Putin's assumption of the presidency represents," Kennan continued. "Russia has been through the third of three great transfers of power in its history—from the Brezh-nev era of stagnation to the Gorbachev era of reform, then from Gor-bachev to Yeltsin and now from Yeltsin to Putin—all without great loss of life, except for the shelling of the White House in 1993. For that country, with its history, this is an extraordinary thing."

I asked what his advice would be to the next U.S. administration. He replied instantly, raising his voice for emphasis: "Not to rush to judgment, and not to write off the Russians or their leaders. Patience, patience—that's what we need. We've got to keep in mind the historical direction of what's happening there."

It was an updating of Kennan's counsel to Harry Truman and Dean Acheson more than half a century before. Back then, Kennan had believed that the essence of U.S. policy should be to give the Russians the time and the incentives—along with the disincentive of containment—to get over being Soviets. Now that they'd crossed that threshold, the Russians could move more confidently toward a condition, as he put it, "more recogniz-ably that of a modern society and of modern statehood."

In Kennan's view, even though Putin was a former KGB colonel with close ties to the conservative establishment, he was young enough, adroit enough and realistic enough to understand that Russia's ongoing transition required that he not just co-opt the power structure, but transform it.

MEANWHILE, OUR OWN TRANSITION between presidencies in the U.S. was under way. The long race for the White House was no fun to watch. Al Gore seemed never quite to find his voice or his footing. He was often on the defensive. High on the Republican target list was the work Gore had done with Victor Chernomyrdin, which was constantly cited as evidence of the administration's overpersonalization of U.S.-Russian relations.[1]

Then came the protracted imbroglio over the election itself. I tried, without total conviction or much success, to persuade foreign officials who visited my office that, however mind-boggling the snarl, all was well with the American democratic process. It made this part of my job no more enjoyable to hear various sneering Russians suggest that perhaps their government could help us through our political crisis by sending monitors to supervise the recounts in Florida and then, once that mess was sorted out, provide technical assistance on how the U.S. might better conduct elections in the future.

ONCE THE SUPREME COURT ruled in Bush's favor, on December 12, the president-elect and his advisers wasted no time in putting the world on notice that American foreign policy was not only about to change management—it would, in several fundamental respects, change course as well.

While the impulse to overhaul U.S. strategy toward Russia flowed naturally from the campaign, it made less sense against the backdrop of recent history. A number of key people in Bush's entourage had been deeply involved in his father's generally skillful—and highly personalized—handling of Gorbachev and Yeltsin in the late eighties and early nineties. The hallmark of Russia policy in that earlier Republican administration had been partnership and integration as the goals and engagement at the highest level as the means. If Bush Two remained true to that feature of Bush One, there would automatically be a preservation of much that Clinton had developed. If, on the other hand, George W. Bush tried too hard to repudiate the fundamental premise and strategy of Clinton's Russia policy, he would implicitly be reversing the approach of George Herbert Walker Bush as well.

The starkest example of this paradox was Condoleezza Rice. A decade earlier, she had been the first President Bush's principal adviser on the Soviet Union. Over the years that I'd been in the State Department, I'd seen Rice on several trips to Stanford, where she was provost, and found her views to be steadily hardening, not just toward the Clinton administration but toward Russia itself. Early in the 2000 campaign, she had publicly hinted at a policy of quarantine and containment. More recently she had indicated that Bush would put U.S.-Russian diplomacy on hold while he tended to other priorities, such as an accelerated missile defense program. Now she was poised to be the new president's national security adviser, the job Sandy Berger had held for the past four years.

SHORTLY BEFORE Bush's inauguration, Yuri Mamedov asked me for a final official encounter. I knew he was hoping that I would be able to refer him to someone in the incoming administration responsible for the Russia account, much as Dennis Ross had handed off the baton to me eight years earlier. Preferably it would be someone close to Secretary of State–designate Colin Powell and, better yet, to Bush himself.

Before leaving Washington, I checked with the Bush transition team and was told, somewhat tartly, that interested parties on the Russian side could address any questions about the *new* policy of the United States government to the American embassy in Moscow. The italics were audible.

I made a red-eye trip to London and spent about four hours on the ground before returning home. Yuri and I met over coffee and cucumber sandwiches in a rather bleak hotel suite near Heathrow Airport, a setting that made me feel all the more like a road-weary traveling salesman with an empty samples case.

Yuri, never one to rub it in with me, professed patience with our politics, which he said were sometimes almost as baffling to his side as his country's were to us. There was hope in Moscow, he added, that the Republicans' Russia-bashing during the campaign had more to do with domestic partisanship than grand strategy and that the new administration would quickly pick up where the old one left off. All Yuri wanted from the new Bush, he said, was that ingredient he'd been looking for from our administration eight years earlier when we'd taken over from the old Bush: continuity.

I told him I shared the hope but couldn't predict what the new administration would do once it took over.

As THOUGH TO UNDERSCORE the clean break it was making with the old crowd, the incoming administration soon revealed its intention to eliminate S/NIS—the office overseeing relations with the new independent states of the former Soviet Union that Secretary Christopher had asked me to establish in 1993, with a direct reporting line to him. In the Powell State Department, responsibility for those twelve countries was to be folded into a mega-bureau covering all of Europe and much of Eurasia as well. The bureaucratic demotion of S/NIS was part of a jettisoning of all things Clintonian in the U.S. government, but it was also a strategic demotion for Russia itself. The new administration wanted the Russians to recognize that theirs was just another country that had to wait its turn for American attention.

During his first five months in office, Bush resisted suggestions from Putin to schedule a summit. He also delayed sending a new ambassador to Moscow to replace Jim Collins.

On missile defense, the Bush administration presented Russia with a classic Hobson's choice: it could join the U.S. in declaring the ABM treaty null and void, or the U.S. would withdraw on its own, leaving Russia (and America's allies) to sputter in protest.

On other chronic points of friction, especially Russia/Iran, the administration ratcheted up the rhetoric even though the substance of policy remained largely unchanged.[2]

One phrase in particular kept showing up in background interviews that White House, Pentagon and State Department officials gave the press: "It's no more Mr. Nice Guy around here."

THERE WAS, HOWEVER, a conspicuous exception to this tough talk. From the day it came into office the Bush administration went easier on the Russian government over Chechnya than we had done. That was partly because the Bush team wanted to shift the focus from Russia's internal evolution to more traditional concerns of realpolitik, such as the disposition of its nuclear weaponry and its behavior beyond its borders.

That was fine with Putin, since it meant he would have to put up with less finger-wagging from the West. Also, the cold shoulder he was getting from Washington allowed him to demonstrate to his own people that Russia, as he sometimes put it, "was off the needle of outside assistance"— that it could pursue its own policies in accordance with its own interests.

Putin concentrated Russian diplomacy on Western Europe and China, where, to different degrees and for different reasons, there was a growing worry about the go-it-alone impulses of the Bush administration. The word "unilateralist" became a staple of commentary on the new look of U.S. foreign policy. The ABM treaty was one of many international agreements that Bush seemed determined to shred or spindle. Other examples were the emerging Kyoto accord on global climate change, the biological weapons convention and the effort to negotiate the terms of the International Criminal Court.

For their part, a number of European leaders let Bush know that they intended to step up their own dealings with Putin's Russia. They urged Bush to do the same in order to maintain the U.S.'s leverage with Russia and its leadership of the Western alliance.

BY LATE SPRING, the Bush administration was showing signs of course correction. Bush himself had not given much thought to Russia during the campaign and therefore was not personally committed to the confrontational approach favored by his more fire-breathing aides and supporters. The White House announced that the president would hold a getting-to-know-you summit with Putin in Ljubljana, the capital of Slovenia, in mid-June. Several administration officials explained the purpose of the meeting with a phrase that was clearly intended to strike a pose of wariness and resolve: Bush was going to look Putin in the eye and subject him to some straight talk—in contrast, it was implied, to Clinton's coddling of Russian leaders.

Despite this attempt to make the first Bush-Putin summit look like a new departure in presidential diplomacy, a number of commentators were struck by the similarity to what they'd seen over the previous eight years: much like his predecessor, the new president was going to try to overcome Russian objections to American policy through a combination of persuasion, persistence and personal chemistry.

It was the last of these ingredients that Bush himself decided to concentrate on in Ljubljana. "I want to make Putin feel comfortable," he remarked to a group of experts brought in to advise him before the trip.

On June 16, after meeting with Putin, Bush told the press, "I looked the man in the eye"—exactly what he'd come there to do, according to the advance billing. But then he continued: "I found him to be very straightforward and trustworthy and we had a very good dialogue. I was able to get a sense of his soul. He's a man deeply committed to his country and the best interests of his country and I appreciate very much the frank dialogue and that's the beginning of a very constructive relationship . . . We share our love for our families. We've got common interests."

Putin's own comments to the press were, as always, low-key and ingratiating but restrained. "This was really a very interesting discussion," he said. "I think that we found a good basis to start building on our cooperation. We're counting on a pragmatic relationship between Russia and the United States."

As I watched this exchange on television, it occurred to me that Putin had used what were supposed to have been the other guy's talking points.

There was a minor outbreak of smirking in a press corps that had otherwise treated Bush favorably. For several days, editorials and op-ed-page columns in the U.S. chided the president for committing a rookie error by appearing to fawn over Putin. On his return home, Bush gave an interview in the Oval Office to Peggy Noonan, a conservative writer who had worked for Ronald Reagan, in order to explain what he had *meant* to say: "To me, my attitude is—and this is Reaganesque in a sense—'Yes, I trust him, until he proves otherwise.' But why say the 'proves otherwise'? To me, that goes without saying."

I saw Clinton in the midst of this flap. He found it amusing to imagine the shellacking he would have taken if he'd claimed to have probed the depths of Yeltsin's soul and discovered a wellspring of homely virtues there.

Nonetheless, he felt some sympathy for Bush. Clinton knew (as I did) how an ill-considered sound bite could mushroom into the wrong story. Besides, however gushy Bush's statement was, at least it was a sign that he understood the need to cultivate a rapport with the president of Russia as a prerequisite for managing the state-to-state relationship. And that, said Clinton, was "the beginning of wisdom."

When Bush saw Putin next, at a G-8 summit in Genoa a little over a month later, he was only slightly less effusive than he'd been in June: "I'm struck by how easy it is to talk to President Putin, how easy it is to speak from my heart, without, you know, fear of complicating any relationship." The two leaders committed themselves to the goal of partnership—a word that Bush had hitherto tended to avoid and that his surrogates during the presidential campaign had scorned.

When I told Clinton I'd heard from former colleagues in the government that behind closed doors and in their increasingly frequent telephone calls, Bush and Putin were calling each other George and Vladimir, Clinton gave me a look of comic indignation: "You mean Bush's people let him do what you and Sandy wouldn't let me do when I went to Moscow to see Putin?"

ACCELERATION

As the summer wore on, I met with Clinton a number of times to get him to reflect on the story I've told here and its two Russian protagonists. It had now been nearly two years since Yeltsin had added to his reputation as an erratic, desperate and selfish old man by choosing as his successor a nearly unknown apparatchik.

On weekends, usually late Sunday mornings, I would ride my bicycle to the Georgian redbrick that the Clintons had bought now that Hillary was in the Senate. Brooke and I knew the house well, since the couple that had sold it to the Clintons, Joe and Lucia Henderson, had been friends of ours for more than twenty years. When the weather was sweltering, Clinton and I sat in the living room or his second-floor study, otherwise on a patio off the kitchen, Clinton in shorts, a golf shirt and sneakers.

As he reminisced about what he called a wild ride—a phrase that, coming from him, connoted as much exhilaration and distance covered as danger and mishap—he identified a number of points along the way at which he wished we'd done things differently, or at least done them better. He believed that his campaign mantra from '92, "It's the economy, stupid," applied to Russian reform, and he thought we should have done more—*much* more—in our effort to underwrite the transition to a market economy. He regretted that we hadn't been able to mobilize international support early in the administration for the kind of program that Larry Summers and David Lipton tried to develop through the G-7 in 1993, especially in those features intended to alleviate the pain and dislocation that came with privatization. One problem, in Clinton's view, was that the International Monetary Fund never really figured out how to ensure that its money had an impact on the lives of "real people" in Russia. Another problem was that we'd failed to resolve the dilemma that Al Gore and Larry Summers had debated off and on over the years: When do the exigencies of electoral and parliamentary politics trump the laws of economics, and how do you reconcile the two? The Russian reformers never figured out the right formula for mixing shock and therapy, but neither did their well-wishers, creditors, advisers and would-be partners in the West.

That said, Clinton felt that the prophets of doom were looking a lot more foolish in retrospect than those of us who had been overoptimistic about how long and difficult Russia's transformation would be.

"There's a big difference," he said, "between believers in that place and its possibilities—people like you and me—and those other folks who were always saying that the sky was falling and that we'd helped knock it down. Sure, we were wrong about some of the little stuff but we were right about the big stuff, while with them it was just the other way around. We let our hopes get out in front of reality sometimes, while they let their fears—and maybe their mistrust and some pretty ungenerous instincts—keep them from seeing the big picture. We may have exaggerated the positives, but they missed them altogether. We may have played down the negatives, but they obsessed over them."

What Clinton called "the story line" in Russia was, to an extent often overlooked, about what hadn't happened there. Russian politics had recovered from the brown surge in December 1993 and the red one in December 1995, and the Russian economy had survived the meltdown of August 1998. By the summer of 2001 the statistics actually showed some healthy trends: gross domestic product was growing, budget deficits were shrinking, capital flight was down, foreign investment was up, small and medium-sized enterprises were doing brisk business, polls showed a rise in consumer confidence and public optimism more generally.

As for Russian foreign policy, Moscow's dealings with its immediate neighbors still often looked more like a suffocating bear hug than a respectful handshake. For example, Chernomyrdin was making his latest comeback as a uniquely proconsular Russian ambassador in Ukraine. But Russia was still more at peace with its neighbors than it would have been if Yeltsin's retrograde and nationalistic opponents had won the domestic debates over what to do about Ukraine, Baltic troop withdrawals, NATO, Bosnia and Kosovo in the nineties.

It was on those half-dozen issues that Clinton had concentrated in his eighteen meetings with Yeltsin. On every major point of contention he had been able to bring Yeltsin around to a position more consonant with U.S. interests than what the Russian political and military establishment favored. One reason Clinton had this influence was that Yeltsin's enemies, the reds and the browns, were on the other side—opposing compromise with Ukraine and NATO, demanding to keep troops in the Baltics, balking at Russian participation in Balkan peacekeeping. One way Yeltsin showed his enemies in Moscow who was boss was to make agreements, over their objections, with his friend from Washington. It was as though their outrage at his willingness to cut deals with Clinton vindicated his decision to do so. In that sense, the first and most indelible image Clinton had of Yeltsin—the man on the tank in August 1991—captured Yeltsin's entire presidency: He never climbed down off that tank, even when he moved into the Kremlin. He was most engaged and exuberant when he was most combative and defiant on the home front, shaking his fist at the opposition. He saw the great struggle of his life as domestic, not international—hence his willingness to come to terms with Clinton on foreign-policy problems.

But Yeltsin's frequent face-offs with powerful domestic constituencies took their toll not just on his effectiveness as a leader but on the Russian body politic. What passed for governance was a seemingly endless knockdown–drag-out between the Kremlin and the parliament that made many Russians feel that their country was undergoing what Clinton called a "nonstop nervous breakdown." No wonder so many Russians complained of crisis fatigue and hoped for a president who could deliver "normalcy" and "order."

That's where Putin came in. Or, more to the point, that was part of why Yeltsin *brought* Putin in. Yeltsin's intuition told him it was time to make way for a member of the younger generation who would be not just different but deliberately, dramatically and correctively so.

There were offsetting ironies in this ending of Yeltsin's career. One was that he had to pick an un-Yeltsin to succeed him. The other was that doing so accomplished what Yeltsin intended. Despite his staggering unpopularity, he turned over his office to someone of his own choosing—a satisfaction Clinton would sorely like to have had himself. It was proof, in Clinton's view, of Yeltsin's basic savvy.

There was an uncharacteristically elegiac tone to these musings. Clinton had loved being president, and he missed it mightily. He would have especially liked, he said several times, a chance to "do stuff" with Putin.

IN THE EARLY FALL OF 2001, I was at Yale setting up a program to study how the world was changing. Shortly after 9 a.m. on Tuesday, September 11, just as I was beginning my first meeting with colleagues in this venture, we were interrupted by news of the attacks on the World Trade Center and the Pentagon.

While the scenes on television were unprecedented, they had an eerie familiarity for people of my generation and older: fireballs in the sky, pandemonium in the streets, steel and concrete carcasses of mighty buildings, smoke blotting out the sun. In the hours after the collapse of the twin towers, reporters talked about Ground Zero and compared the darkness at noon to nuclear winter. There was, in these comparisons that came so readily to mind, a glimpse backward at something far more terrible that we'd once feared.

That night, sleeping badly, I had nightmares from my childhood. Grainy and flickering like old newsreels, they were a pastiche of memories, including duck-and-cover drills in elementary school and photographs in *Life* magazine in the early fifties of burned children who had, for a while at least, survived the A-bombing of Hiroshima and Nagasaki.

Attending a university memorial service for the thousands of victims in New York, Washington and Pennsylvania, I found myself recalling another convocation, on an equally beautiful Indian summer day in October 1962, when I was a sophomore at Hotchkiss. The headmaster summoned all the students and teachers to the school chapel, and led us in a prayer that God would help John F. Kennedy and Nikita Khrushchev find a way out of the impasse over the deployment of Soviet missiles in Cuba.

That earlier crisis had provided a major impetus to my study of Russian and intensified my interest in Khrushchev and nuclear diplomacy. This new crisis, I imagined, could have a similar galvanizing effect on many of the students in the pews around me in the Yale chapel. Therefore the similarity between these public traumas, thirty-nine years apart, was much on my mind on September 11 and in the days afterward.

But so was the contrast. When President Bush, traveling in Florida, first learned what had happened in New York, he put American military forces—including intercontinental ballistic missiles, long-range bombers and missile-launching submarines—on the highest alert. He did so because it was not immediately certain what had happened and what would come next. Yet the president and his advisers assumed from the outset that whoever the assailant was, it wasn't Russia.

While the U.S. was ratcheting up its military readiness, Russia was standing down. Putin canceled several exercises of Russian strategic units, in part to put his own military on notice that whatever the Americans did out of prudence or in retaliation should not be considered a threat to Russia.

On one of the worst days in American history, this by-play with Russia was a reminder that even as we faced new and dreadful dangers, we'd laid to rest an even greater one.

DURING THE COLD WAR, the U.S. and the Soviet Union had agreed on little other than the importance of avoiding Armageddon. To have kept the world from blowing up was no mean accomplishment, although essentially a negative one.

Then came the post–cold war era. The U.S. and Russia recognized that with the ideological dispute over and the global rivalry behind them, they had mutual interests beyond survival. Starting in the late eighties, leaders in the White House and Kremlin applied themselves to the task of bringing Russia into international structures from which it had previously been excluded and began treating regional conflicts as opportunities for diplomatic cooperation.

However, the premise of a post–cold war partnership came under strain almost immediately and remained so for a decade. The trouble arose first in the Gulf, then in the Balkans. At issue in both places was what constituted a threat to peace that justified the use of force. Americans saw the depredations of Saddam Hussein and Slobodan Milošević as qualifying, while the Russians did not. In addition to having their own ties to the predators in question, they found it galling for an America that looked rich, strong, arrogant and impregnable to be constantly strutting its stuff far from its own shores and near to a Russia that felt poor, weak, humiliated and vulnerable. It sometimes seemed to Russian generals and Duma committee chairmen that every time they turned on CNN, there was another briefing from the Pentagon announcing that the U.S. had yet again dispatched its aircraft carriers and launched its cruise missiles. Or there was an American diplomat (myself, perhaps, right there in Moscow, on the steps in front of the Foreign Ministry or in a local TV studio) explaining why the Russians would just have to swallow their objections and go along with what the U.S. had decided it must do in the name of the international community. And even when the U.S. wasn't striking against targets in Russia's neighborhood if not its front yard, it was expanding its capacity to do so through the enlargement of NATO and high-tech programs like NMD. Some of those generals and politicians believed it was only a matter of time before Russia itself would be in the cross-hairs of America's unchecked military power.

It was with these apprehensions of the military and political elite in mind that Boris Yeltsin scowled and bellowed when the U.S. bombed Serb installations in Bosnia in 1995 and, four years later, bombed Serbia itself.

And it was to establish himself as a Russian who could stand up to the U.S. that Vladimir Putin demurred when Clinton asked for his acquiescence in NMD. Putin wanted to join the West, but on terms that were more respectful of Russia's national interests and national anxieties. September 11 gave him a chance to do so.

IN SOME ASPECTS, the drama that began that day was a replay of earlier ones. Once again, an American president stepped into the role not just of his own nation's commander in chief but the world's. Once again, there were the Pentagon briefings, the CNN clips of attack aircraft ready to launch from carrier decks, the American officials saying, in effect, "Follow us or get out of the way."

Some predictable Russian voices howled in protest. Vladimir Zhirinovsky warned that the U.S. was exploiting the crisis to establish a toehold in Central Asia, and General Leonid Ivashov—the military intelligence officer who had tried his best to scuttle Chernomyrdin's mission during the Kosovo war—accused the U.S. of staging the attack as a pretext for world domination.

But this time, such ranting had little resonance. The Russian press and spokesmen for the political class zeroed in on the difference between this new crisis and the ones that had so roiled U.S.-Russian relations through the nineties. This time, the U.S. was assembling a posse to go after not an old client of the USSR's in Baghdad or an Orthodox Slav in Belgrade but an old enemy, a renegade Saudi multimillionaire who had contributed to the Soviet Union's epic defeat in Afghanistan and to the outbreak of secessionism in southern Russia.

Whatever Americans had to fear from bin Laden's version of jihad, it wasn't the breakup of their country. Russians, by contrast, knew that if bin Laden had his way, the entire North Caucasus—Chechnya and several surrounding republics—along with other Islamic areas of the Russia Federation and in the near abroad, would be part of a new caliphate.

That was the geopolitical essence of September 11 for many Russians.

There was a psychological significance as well. For the first time, America had experienced attacks on its cities similar to (though vastly larger than) those that had destroyed apartment buildings in southern Russia after the flare-up of the war in Chechnya in 1999. Homeland security was a novelty in the American vocabulary but not in the Russian one.

Three days after the attacks, Yevgeny Primakov told a Moscow newspaper that the U.S., like Russia, now knew what it was like to feel vulnerable.[3] Going back to the early eighties when I'd first known him, I'd always regarded Primakov's views as an indicator of where the center of gravity was in the Russian political establishment. I recalled the many conversations I'd had with him as foreign minister and prime minister in which he complained that America was too strong and too safe for its own good. Americans, he'd told me many times, couldn't fathom what it was like to be a citizen, not to mention a leader, of a proud but wounded country that was recovering from the loss of nearly half its land, the evaporation of its alliances, the precipitous decline of its military budget, the looming obsolescence of its strategic forces and, on top of all that, an upsurge in terrorism and secessionism on its territory.

Reading Primakov's interview, I sensed there was a shift in his mind-set largely because he sensed there had been one in ours. Primakov seemed to be saying that Americans—having been introduced to a new fear that for Russians was an old one—might now be more inclined to work with Russia rather than just boss it around. By the same token, Russians—seeing that America was not as invulnerable as they'd previously thought—might make common cause with the U.S. without indulging quite so much in suspicions like those voiced by Zhirinovsky and Ivashov.

There were other indications of a new mood in Russia. In the first days after the attacks, worries about the collapse of the American economy swept through Russian financial circles. Newspaper stories warned that because of the tight links between Russia's economic fate and the U.S.'s, the recovery that had occurred since the crash of August 1998 was now in jeopardy. Kremlin economic policymakers made a concerted effort to talk up the dollar, and the Central Bank briefly intervened to support the greenback in Moscow's currency exchanges. However bizarre and fleeting this turning of the tables might have been, it illustrated how many Russians understood the extent of interdependence and therefore might be ready to embrace a chance actually to help the U.S.

———

ALL THIS PUTIN seemed to anticipate on September 11, and he acted on his intuition quickly by aligning Russia with the U.S. more closely and less ambiguously than ever before. He was the first foreign leader to call Bush with a message of support after the attacks. He knew that in the course of a few hours, counterterrorism had gone from being one of many items on the broad and diverse agenda of U.S. foreign and defense policy to being of such overwhelming urgency that it would either eclipse or subordinate virtually all other objectives. Whatever business Bush had wanted to transact before with his foreign counterparts, now all he wanted was help in tracking down bin Laden, ripping the al Qaeda network up by its roots, replacing the Taliban regime in Afghanistan and putting in place a new international system that would thwart terrorists and punish states that were harboring them.

In their phone call, Putin assured Bush that he was eager to oblige.

I WAS ONE OF MANY who assumed at the time that Putin, adept as he was at judo, was moving with such alacrity and dexterity primarily in order to turn American distress to Russian advantage on the narrow issue of Chechnya. That interpretation seemed confirmed a few days later when Sergei Ivanov—Sandy Berger's former counterpart who had replaced Marshal Sergeyev as defense minister—declared publicly, with an I-told-you-so smugness, that surely the world now understood what Russia had been up against in the North Caucasus. With the encouragement of the Kremlin, the Russian media printed a rash of stories on the ties between bin Laden and the Chechen guerrillas that Putin himself had hinted to Clinton and spelled out in some detail to Jim Collins two years earlier.

As though speaking from a jointly drafted script, U.S. spokesmen came close to endorsing Moscow's line.

Within days of the attacks, Putin dispatched Foreign Minister Igor Ivanov to Washington with instructions to press the advantages that might come with America's new preoccupation and its urgent need for maximum international support.

YURI MAMEDOV accompanied Ivanov to New York, and I met him for a private dinner. If it had not been for September 11 and its salutary effect on Russian attitudes toward the U.S., I suspect that Yuri, in his capacity as a sherpa for the Bush-Putin summit coming in mid-November, would have been in a damage-limitation mode, doggedly trying to avoid a collision over missile defense and the ABM treaty, just as he and I had worked to avoid one during Clinton's last year in office. As it was, Yuri was more upbeat than I'd seen him in a long time.

I thought back to my last official meeting with Yuri—in London, during the transition from Clinton to Bush, about nine months earlier—and how the one thing he'd been hoping for in U.S.-Russian relations was continuity. He now seemed to think that the U.S. and Russia might do even better than that.

IN THE WEEKS that followed, the scope and pace of improvement in U.S.-Russian relations grew more dramatic.

In the nineties, when the U.S. was mobilizing coalitions and preparing to bomb in the Gulf or the Balkans, Russia, brandishing its veto, insisted that the UN Security Council had to authorize any use of force. When the U.S. claimed it had all the authority it needed, Yeltsin fulminated against American high-handedness.

This time the Russian government affirmed that the U.S. had the right under the UN Charter to take military action against the Taliban, and when NATO invoked a provision in its own charter declaring that an attack against one of its members was an attack against all, Russia expressed its understanding.[4]

On October 3, Putin visited Brussels for the first time as president of Russia and met with Javier Solana's successor as NATO secretary-general, George Robertson (Solana had moved on to become the closest thing that the European Union had to a foreign minister). Speaking publicly after his talks with Robertson, Putin considerably softened Russia's opposition to NATO enlargement, including, he hinted, the admission of the Baltic states at the alliance's next summit in Prague in 2002.

I'd anticipated that Putin would be easier to deal with on the second round of enlargement than Yeltsin had been on the first. Our administration had already established the principle that NATO was taking in new members. There were two other reasons to expect a milder reaction from Putin. First, being far more popular than Yeltsin, he had less to fear from domestic enemies who might use the NATO issue against him. Second, he recognized that the only meaningful threats to Russia came from the east and the south, not from the west. I expected that NATO enlargement, a bit like NMD/ABM, was an issue that Putin would not let become either a loser for Russia or an insurmountable obstacle to the opening he'd already established with Bush.

Still, I had thought that Putin would move subtly, cautiously and slowly as the Prague summit approached, preserving some suspense about what Russia's final negotiating position would be and thus some leverage for what he could get in exchange. After September 11, the Balts and other Central European applicants initially feared that the Bush administration, in its new eagerness to avoid upsetting Russia, might slow down the enlargement process.

Instead, Putin seemed to be using his visit to Brussels to speed up Russia's adjustment to the alliance's own timetable.

Shortly afterward, NATO rewarded Putin with the promise—initiated by Prime Minister Tony Blair of Britain but affirmed by President Bush—that Russia could participate on an equal basis with members of the alliance in joint decision-making and action on issues in which Russian interests were directly and legitimately involved. This arrangement amounted to an upgrading of the NATO-Russia Permanent Joint Council that had been established in 1997. Conservative commentators, who felt that the Clinton administration had already gone too far in letting Russia into the councils of the alliance, grumbled that the Republican administration seemed to be going even farther down a slippery slope. For his part, Putin had to fend off domestic criticism that he had abandoned Russia's long-standing defense of the old Soviet border as a red line that NATO must never cross.

Even more stunning was the way Putin overrode the public objections of some of his generals as well as Defense Minister Ivanov to granting American forces access to bases in Central Asia in support of the operation about to begin in Afghanistan. In early October, units of the U.S. Army's 10th Mountain Division arrived in Uzbekistan. It was the first time ever that American soldiers had been deployed to the territory of the former Soviet Union.

A few days later, when Bush phoned Putin to notify him that air strikes against targets in Afghanistan were about to begin, the Russian president was, yet again, soothing and supportive. Publicly, he said that the terrorists had made a mistake to "count on modern civilization becoming flabby, sluggish, and losing its capacity for resistance. They did not expect such a unity of humanity before a common enemy."

I thought back to Clinton's phone calls to Yeltsin at similar moments on the eve of NATO bombing in the Balkans and how Yeltsin would explode in anger and sometimes slam down the phone.

BY THE TIME Bush hosted Putin at his ranch in Crawford, Texas, in mid-November, Russia had announced that it was pulling out of its bases in Cuba and Vietnam, removing two of the final remnants of the Soviet Union's global reach.

In tone, the Crawford summit was all congeniality and common purpose, and in substance it was highly productive. The encounter yielded not only joint vows of resolve in the war on terrorism but an intensified American commitment to help Russia get into the World Trade Organization. That goal represented a symbolically important threshold in the twelve-year commitment of Western leaders, led first by Bush the Elder, to integrate Russia into the principal structures of what he had called "the new world order."

The biggest news out of the summit was the announcement that the U.S. and Russia would reduce the size of their Doomsday arsenals to a level lower than the one that Clinton and Yeltsin had set for START III.

Journalists I'd known over the previous decade phoned me to complain that the Bush-Putin love-fest, as a number of them called it, was less interesting than the fireworks we used to provide them at Clinton-Yeltsin meetings. Couldn't I help them find *some* bad news in Crawford? All I could do was point out that the word "START" did not figure in the announcement of the reduction in strategic weaponry. The Bush administration had an aversion to arms control agreements that had to be negotiated in detail, ratified by Congress and the Duma and given the force of law. The Russians agreed to go along because of the economic requirement to reduce their own levels of weaponry.

Once the summit ended, the press finally had a snag to report: contrary to expectations, Bush and Putin failed to reach an agreement on NMD/ABM. They publicly (and congenially) agreed to disagree and to take the matter up again in the new year.

The Bush administration's preferred solution to the problem was for the U.S. and Russia to announce that they were discarding the ABM treaty as a relic of the cold war so that they could get on with the new agenda of cooperative defense and deep cuts in offensive forces. This arrangement was intended to spare the Russians having American withdrawal go forward over their objections. It was a variant of the mutual unilateralism Bush was able to get Putin to accept as a substitute for a formal START treaty.

This time Putin refused, explaining that he couldn't endorse the ditching of the ABM treaty because his side regarded it as an important component of strategic stability.

The Bush administration then explored with the Russians the possibility of an understanding whereby Moscow would take a lenient view of testing anti-missile systems, which would have allowed the U.S. to justify a delay in withdrawal from the treaty. This finesse fell apart because the Russian military wanted, in effect, the right to approve tests in advance, while the officials in charge of the U.S. program wanted no outside interference in their plans.

In mid-December, the Bush administration gave up on reaching a compromise and decided to pull the plug on the ABM treaty. With the American military operation in Afghanistan triumphing over the Taliban and al Qaeda, Bush's popularity at home and his prestige abroad were at what might be an all-time high. The president and his team concluded that there would never be a better moment to ride out whatever flak they would take. But they also did everything they could to help Putin cope with the inescapable impression that Russia, yet again, had been told to shut up and eat its spinach.

In an appearance in the Rose Garden on December 13, Bush went to extraordinary lengths to present withdrawal from the ABM treaty as yet another example of how U.S.-Russian relations—and his own partnership with Putin—had moved to an even higher plane. He began by saying that his decision reflected "what I have discussed with my friend President Vladimir Putin." The U.S. was "moving beyond" the ABM treaty, thereby breaking free of "the grim theory" of mutual assured destruction and leaving behind "one of the last vestiges" of the cold war.

As an additional sweetener for what he knew was a bitter pill, Bush hinted that the U.S. would, after all, be willing to codify the reductions in offensive weaponry—that is, to put the new ceilings into a formal document of some kind. That would make the agreement a bit more mutual and a bit less unilateral, a modest gesture in the direction of traditional arms control.

In the most carefully scripted part of his Rose Garden statement, Bush said that he and Putin had agreed that the U.S. decision to end its adherence to the ABM treaty "will not, in any way, undermine our new relationship or Russian security."

Within hours, Putin released a statement of his own. He acknowledged that the U.S. was within its right to withdraw, that the Bush administration had consistently maintained its intention eventually to do so and that he had been notified in advance of what Bush had decided.

"However," Putin continued, "we consider the [U.S.] decision to be a mistake," which is why Russia "did not accept the proposal persistently made by the U.S. for joint withdrawal and why we did all in our power to maintain the treaty."

Then came a dramatic and categorical shift in long-standing Russian policy: "As is known, Russia, along with the U.S., as distinguished from other nuclear powers, has long had an effective system of overcoming anti-missile defenses. For this reason I can state with complete confidence that the decision taken by the president of the U.S. presents no threat to the national security of the Russian Federation."

In a single sentence, Putin had repudiated the numerous presentations I'd heard in 1999 and 2000 from General Nikolai Zlenko, who, with the aid of maps and charts, had argued vociferously and implacably that an American anti-missile system would neutralize Russia's strategic deterrent.

Much as he had done earlier with NATO enlargement, Putin, quite simply, had decided to roll with the punch. The Russian leader who had risen to power in part by quietly, obliquely, politely standing up to the U.S. had now, like his predecessor Yeltsin, given in.

Putin would try to blunt domestic criticism by claiming to have received from Bush compensation beyond what Yeltsin had had to settle for in earlier deals with Clinton. In the case of NATO, Putin could point to the prospect of a more dignified, influential and substantive relationship with the alliance than Yeltsin had gotten from Clinton in 1997, and in the case of strategic arms, the U.S. was now willing to reduce its arsenal below the level on which Yeltsin and Clinton had agreed in Helsinki that same year.

I FELT AS THOUGH a very large tree had come crashing down soundlessly in Bishop Berkeley's forest. Not only had the administration killed a treaty that had helped keep the nuclear peace for thirty years, it had delivered a potentially fatal blow to arms control in general. Yet the move aroused remarkably little controversy or even attention, in part because critics didn't want to complain more than Putin had done.

As for Putin himself, I wondered if he had second thoughts about the wisdom of his decision to stiff Clinton on the package of amendments to the ABM treaty and offensive reductions that the U.S. had been prepared to offer Russia in 2000. It might have been harder for Bush to make a clean sweep of SALT, START and the whole institution of negotiated, legally binding agreements if he'd inherited from Clinton an agreement rather than an impasse caused by Russian stonewalling.

Yet drastically different as Bush's attitude toward arms control was from Clinton's, the new administration's technique in achieving its goal was familiar: Bush combined an unyielding insistence on an outcome Russia opposed with offsetting provisions for what Russia wanted—parity, cooperation and integration—much as Clinton had done when he induced Russia's acquiescence in the expansion of NATO and enlisted its participation in Balkan peacekeeping.

AS THE BUSH ADMINISTRATION came to the end of its first year in office, the impression grew that the world had entered a new period of history. As Colin Powell put it, "This is not just the end of the cold war—it's the end of the post–cold war era." Variations on that theme became part of the conventional wisdom about September 11 and its aftermath.5

There was nothing new, of course, about dissatisfaction with the phrase "post–cold war era." I recalled Condoleezza Rice, in a number of conversations I'd had with her at Stanford, remarking caustically that the namelessness of the nineties bespoke the aimlessness of American policy in that period—i.e., the Clinton administration's policy.

Clinton himself had sensed his vulnerability on this point. That was one reason he'd complained from time to time, going back to the summer of 1994, about not having a more stirring name for the age on which he hoped to leave his mark. His political antennae told him that sooner or later, either when he was still in office or afterward, he'd pay a price for being perceived as an interwar president, a transitional figure between the U.S.'s great twilight struggle with the evil empire and the "first war of the twenty-first century"—the first battle of which, as it turned out, would be waged and won in the rugged mountains of Afghanistan, the same territory on which the Soviet Union had lost its own last battle twenty years before.

Sure enough, post–September 11, there it was—an invidious spin on the momentous events of that day. It became a staple of commentary, only some of it partisan, that U.S.-Russian relations, having been adrift or in decline through the Clinton years, had now, like history itself, entered a new, more coherent, more promising phase. Moreover, Republicans were quick to add, it helped that the American and Russian presidencies were finally in the hands of sober, hard-headed realists who could respond to the challenge of September 11 with concrete actions rather than gauzy rhetoric and bear hugs.

All this reminded me of how, during the 1992 campaign, Bush's father had suggested that—as the occupant of the Oval Office when the Berlin wall, the Warsaw Pact and the Soviet Union came crashing down—he had personally ended the cold war. Clinton had dismissed this claim at the time as the rooster taking credit for the dawn. Now officials of the second Bush administration were claiming to have presided, in their first year in office, over the end of the post–cold war era; they were staking out an epoch of their own, with the implication that whatever they achieved with Russia was, by definition, new in concept, more effective in execution and more enduring in effect than what the previous administration had done.

I reacted to this conceit somewhat the way Clinton had responded to Bush's soul-searching comments about Putin after their first meeting in Ljubljana in June 2001: if this was what it took for the new administration to pick up where its predecessors had left off, fine. Let the rooster crow at noon.

I'd never shared the eagerness of others (including my old friend and chief) to come up with a bumper sticker for our time. For me, the post–cold war era was better than the phrase implied, since it was a period of considerable accomplishment and promise.

Nor was that era over. The burst of accommodation and cooperation between George W. Bush and Vladimir Putin in the autumn of 2001 marked not a turning point but a moment of clarification, consolidation and acceleration in the positive trends of the previous decade. Despite all the talk about how everything had changed, there was no shift in what George Kennan—and Bill Clinton—saw as the historical direction of Russia's internal evolution and of its relationship with the West. Quite the contrary: in the wake of September 11, a new Russian president concluded that he could afford to move his country faster in that direction, and an even newer American president saw more clearly than before that the U.S. should help.

The hedgehog was holding its own against the foxes.

THE UNITED STATES AND RUSSIA:
A CHRONOLOGY
OF THE FIRST DECADE

1991

Aug. 18–21	Soviet hard-liners stage abortive coup against Mikhail Gorbachev.
Oct. 3	Bill Clinton formally announces his candidacy for president.
Dec. 25	USSR dissolves, Boris Yeltsin moves into Kremlin.

1992

Feb. 1	Yeltsin, on first trip to the U.S. as Russian president, meets George H.W. Bush at Camp David.
April 1	Clinton chides Bush for being "overly cautious" on aid to Russia.
June 18	Yeltsin, in Washington for state visit, meets Candidate Clinton at Blair House.
Nov. 3	Clinton elected.
Nov. 5	Yeltsin appeals for meeting with Clinton as soon as possible.

1993

Jan. 2–3	At final summit in Moscow, Bush and Yeltsin sign START II treaty.

Jan. 21	Clinton inaugurated.
Jan. 22	Yeltsin repeats appeal for early meeting.
Feb. 25	Secretary of State Warren Christopher meets with Foreign Minister Andrei Kozyrev in Geneva.
March 8	Richard Nixon, calling on Clinton at White House, urges U.S. to "pull out the stops" in backing Yeltsin.
March 23	Kozyrev, in Washington, proposes creation of Gore-Chernomyrdin commission.
March 28	Russian parliament tries and fails to impeach Yeltsin.
April 3–4	Clinton and Yeltsin hold first summit in Vancouver. U.S. announces $1.6 billion assistance package for Russia.
April 25	In referendum, Russians support Yeltsin policies and call for new parliament.
July 9	Clinton and Yeltsin meet in Tokyo, G-7 countries announce $28.4 billion assistance package for former Soviet states.
Sept. 1	Gore and Chernomyrdin hold first meeting of commission in Washington.
Sept. 21	Yeltsin suspends parliament, calls for elections in December.
Oct. 2–4	Showdown between Yeltsin and parliament turns violent. Anti-Yeltsin forces attack mayor's office and TV station, tanks shell Russian White House, rebels surrender.
Oct. 22	Christopher tells Yeltsin U.S. will not push for NATO expansion immediately, will focus instead on Partnership for Peace.
Dec. 12	In parliamentary elections, Yeltsin's opponents, especially Vladimir Zhirinovsky, do unexpectedly well.

1994

Jan. 8–15	Clinton visits Brussels, Prague, Kiev and Moscow. In Prague, says question of enlarging NATO is not whether but when. In Moscow, joins Yeltsin and Ukrainian President Leonid Kravchuk in signing "trilateral accord" for removal of nuclear weapons from Ukraine in exchange for assurances of Ukrainian security and sovereignty.
July 10	At G-7 in Naples, Clinton urges Yeltsin to fulfill com-

mitment to withdraw Russian troops from Estonia by August 31. Asked if he will do so by press, Yeltsin answers, *"Nyet!"*

July 26	Yeltsin and Estonian President Lennart Meri reach last-minute deal on troop withdrawal.
Sept. 27	Clinton and Yeltsin hold summit in Washington. Clinton pledges NATO enlargement will be guided by "three no's"—no surprises, no rush and no exclusion of Russia.
Dec. 1	In Brussels, Kozyrev refuses to sign up for Partnership for Peace.
Dec. 4	In Budapest, Yeltsin warns of "cold peace."
Dec. 11	Russian military launches offensive in Chechnya.
Dec. 15	Gore, in Moscow, assures Yeltsin NATO enlargement will not occur in 1995.

1995

May 9–10	Clinton, in Moscow for V-E Day, gets Yeltsin to begin NATO-Russia dialogue, join the Partnership for Peace and restrict nuclear cooperation with Iran.
June 14	Chechen rebels storm hospital in Budyonnovsk, taking patients hostage.
June 17	Clinton and Yeltsin meet at G-7 in Halifax, Yeltsin throws public tantrum over Chechnya.
June 19	Chernomyrdin negotiates end to hostage crisis.
July 21	After Bosnian Serb attacks on Muslim-majority areas, foreign and defense ministers in London agree to protect the remaining UN "safe areas" with NATO airpower. Defense Secretary William Perry promises Defense Minister Pavel Grachev Russia will have role in Bosnian peacekeeping operation.
Aug. 28–30	Bosnian Serbs shell Sarajevo market, prompting NATO to launch air strikes.
Sept. 5	After pause, NATO resumes air strikes, Yeltsin warns of "conflagration."
Oct. 8	In Geneva, Perry and Grachev begin negotiations to include Russia in implementation of a peace settlement.
Oct. 23	Clinton and Yeltsin meet at Hyde Park, agree on terms

	of Russian participation in Bosnian peace settlement alongside NATO and to revisions in CFE treaty limiting restrictions of conventional weapons in Russia.
Oct. 26	Yeltsin suffers a heart attack, does not return to Kremlin until December 29.
Nov. 1–21	Bosnia peace talks in Dayton, yielding agreement.
Dec. 17	In Russian parliamentary elections, reform parties suffer setback, communists gain seats.

1996

Jan. 9	Yevgeny Primakov replaces Andrei Kozyrev as foreign minister.
Feb. 15	Yeltsin formally opens reelection campaign in Yekaterinburg.
March 13	Yeltsin and Clinton attend terrorism summit in Sharm el-Sheikh, Egypt, Yeltsin complains of inadequate communication between them.
April 19–21	Clinton travels to St. Petersburg and Moscow, attends international meeting on nuclear safety, explains timetable of NATO enlargement to Yeltsin.
April 21	Russian forces kill Chechen leader Dzhokhar Dudayev.
June 16	In first round of presidential election, Yeltsin emerges with slight lead over Zyuganov but must face runoff.
July 3	After co-opting General Alexander Lebed, who had come in third, Yeltsin soundly defeats Zyuganov.
Aug. 9	Yeltsin barely able to get through inaugural ceremonies, soon reported to require heart surgery.
Aug. 31	Lebed signs a peace deal ending the Chechen war.
Oct. 17	Yeltsin fires Lebed for being too ambitious.
Nov. 5	Yeltsin undergoes seven hours of quintuple bypass heart surgery; Clinton wins reelection.

1997

Feb. 8	Chernomyrdin, in U.S. for commission meeting, warns of impact of NATO enlargement on Russian domestic politics.
March 20–21	Meeting Clinton in Helsinki, Yeltsin appeals unsuc-

cessfully for pledge that NATO will never include former Soviet states; presidents agree to outlines of START III treaty and agreement on anti-missile system permissible under ABM treaty.

May 27   At summit with NATO leaders in Paris, Yeltsin signs NATO-Russia Founding Act.

June 20–21   At G-7 meeting in Denver, Yeltsin promises to "get to the bottom" of the problem of Russian weapons transfers to Iran.

1998

Jan. 22   Chernomyrdin announces "catchall" regulation to cut off the flow of Russian technology and materials to Iran's ballistic missile development program.

March 23   Yeltsin fires Chernomyrdin as prime minister and replaces him with Sergei Kiriyenko.

May 16–17   Yeltsin and Clinton meet in Birmingham, where Russia officially becomes member of the G-8.

June 23   Clinton vetoes congressional legislation sanctioning Russia for providing weapons technology to Iran; soon after, Russia agrees to implement stricter rules, and the U.S. agrees to impose trade restrictions on certain Russian companies dealing with Iran.

Aug. 14–17   Russian financial crisis, simmering for months, boils over.

Aug. 23   Yeltsin announces he is firing Kiriyenko and plans to bring Chernomyrdin back as prime minister.

Sept. 1–2   Clinton visits Moscow, Yeltsin tells him he may disband Duma.

Sept. 7   Duma rejects Chernomyrdin as prime minister.

Sept. 10   Yeltsin appoints Primakov, who is approved immediately. Igor Ivanov becomes foreign minister.

Oct. 13   Kosovo crisis escalates; threatened with NATO air strikes, Slobodan Milošević agrees to withdraw some forces from Kosovo.

1999

Jan. 15	Serbs massacre forty-five Kosovar Albanians in Raćak.
Feb. 6–23	U.S.-led peace talks in Rambouillet, France.
March 23	Milošević defiant in last-ditch peace effort by Richard Holbrooke, opening way for NATO action. En route to Washington to meet with Gore, Primakov does U-turn and returns to Moscow.
March 24	NATO air strikes against Serbia begin.
April 14	Yeltsin appoints Chernomyrdin special envoy to deal with Kosovo conflict.
April 23–24	At NATO's fiftieth anniversary summit in Washington, leaders welcome Poland, Hungary and Czech Republic into alliance, but event dominated by Kosovo.
April 25	Yeltsin phones Clinton, warns, "Don't push Russia into this war!," pleads for emergency resumption of Gore-Chernomyrdin commission focused on crisis.
May 3–4	Chernomyrdin, in Washington, proposes what becomes "hammer and anvil" strategy with Finnish President Martti Ahtisaari.
May 12	Yeltsin fires Primakov as prime minister, replaces him with Sergei Stepashin.
May 13	First round of hammer-and-anvil talks in Helsinki.
June 3	Ahtisaari and Chernomyrdin secure Milošević's agreement to NATO terms for ending war.
June 11–12	Russian troops based in Bosnia rush to Priština Airport.
June 16	U.S. and Russia agree to terms of Russia's participation in the NATO-led Kosovo peacekeeping force.
June 19–20	Clinton and Yeltsin attend G-8 summit in Cologne.
Aug. 7	Chechen rebel forces invade Dagestan.
Aug. 9	Yeltsin replaces Stepashin with Vladimir Putin.
Sept. 12	Clinton meets Putin in Auckland.
Sept. 23	Russia intensifies bombing of Chechnya, setting stage for ground invasion and escalation of fighting.
Nov. 2	Clinton meets Putin in Oslo.
Nov. 18	Clinton and Yeltsin attend the OSCE summit in Istanbul; criticized for Russia's actions in Chechnya, Yeltsin agrees to allow OSCE monitors to enter.

Dec. 31	Yeltsin resigns as president and appoints Putin as acting president.

2000

March 26	Putin wins election.
June 3–5	In Moscow, Clinton holds summit with Putin, calls on Yeltsin in retirement.
July 21	Clinton and Putin meet at the G-8 summit in Okinawa.
Sept. 1	Clinton announces deferral of deployment for missile defense.
Sept. 6	Clinton and Putin meet in New York while attending the UN "millennium summit."
Nov. 15	Clinton and Putin hold final meeting in Brunei.

2001

Jan. 20	George W. Bush inaugurated.
June 16	Bush and Putin meet in Slovenia.
Nov. 14–15	Bush and Putin meet in Crawford, Texas.

ACKNOWLEDGMENTS

My first debt is to President Clinton for the honor, challenge, excitement and occasional fun of serving in his administration, and to Warren Christopher and Madeleine Albright for the chance to do so at their sides.

Secretary Christopher read most of this book with extraordinary care and helped me in every conceivable way, on matters of style, tone, logic, history and that commodity which he has in distinctive abundance: judgment.

Sandy Berger brought to his own close reading and extensive comments the same combination of clear thinking, rigorous argument, loyalty to colleagues up, down and sideways and generosity of spirit that marked his leadership of the National Security Council staff and the interagency process.

Richard Holbrooke, the second oldest of my friends with whom I worked closely for eight years, somehow found time, amidst what I count to be three simultaneous professions, to read the manuscript in two drafts and, as best he could, to keep me out of trouble.

There are others with whom I shared experiences recounted here and who assisted me in grappling with the facts and their meaning: Robert Einhorn, who had been my guru on nonproliferation and arms control issues long before he and I ended up in harness together; Leon Fuerth, who elevated deliberations in the Situation Room and in our own back offices by the sheer force of his probing, disciplined mind and his unsurpassed commitment to doing the right thing; David Lipton, whose contribution to the economic evolution of Russia, the cause of international development assistance and the American national interest is only palely reflected here; Jan Lodal, who was kind to me a quarter of a century ago when he was riding in the front of Air Kissinger while I was a junior member of the press corps in the rear, and whose technical grasp of problems and imaginative approach to solutions were indispensable in reaching a number of breakthroughs in policy and diplomacy; the prodigious Thomas Pickering, not the only force of nature I've ever known (or mentioned in these acknowledgments) but the only one to have held nine presidential appointments; Steve Sestanovich, whose good sense, sure instincts and deep knowledge about Russia and its neighbors influenced me for years before he joined the administration, who made the most of S/NIS at home and abroad, and who mixed trenchant criticism with limitless patience when I appeared at his house on Saturday mornings, before his children's soccer and baseball games, to go over chapters; Peter Tarnoff, who took me under his wing at the beginning of the administration, jogged with me on three continents and let me do some writing with a view of San Francisco Bay from his and Mathea's kitchen; James Timbie, who has been recognized by nine secretaries of state as nothing less than a national treasure.

Grisha Freidin, who worked with me on the Khrushchev memoirs in the early seventies and now teaches Russian literature at Stanford, gave me astute advice on the book as it emerged. Before that, Grisha was a one-man support group at moments when events in the land of his birth caused me some puzzlement and vexation.

I've also had the benefit, and sometimes the solace, of comparing works in progress with five other authors: Ron Asmus, a driving force in the expansion of NATO and the transformation of its relations with Russia, who has written *Opening NATO's Door,* the inside story of those twin initiatives; Rodric Braithwaite, a former British ambassador to Moscow whose *Across the Moscow River* provides fresh and useful insights into the late Soviet period and the years just after; James Goldgeier and Michael McFaul, whose earlier work helped me in my own and whose forthcoming book will put the period covered here in a comprehensive historical and political context; and John Norris, who, on the basis of our travels together in the spring and summer of 1999, has written *Collision Course: NATO, Russia and Kosovo.*

John's teammate on my staff was Derek Chollet, who, at the end of the administration, stayed with me to see through the task of writing this book. His diligence, proficiency and diplomatic skills (which came in handy at various points along the way) are matched by his good humor and broad-ranging intelligence.

Another word about D, the bureaucratic designation for the office of the deputy secretary of state. I will always feel affection, gratitude and admiration for the men and women who have made the foreign and civil service of the U.S. the best in the world and who keep it that way every day. Several of them were of particular help to me during my stint in Foggy Bottom: John Bass, Eric Edelman, Helen Ellis, Phil Goldberg, Tina Kaidinow, Toria Nuland and Lee Young. I thank them not just in their own right but as representatives of the many other State Department professionals whose dedication I so often saw in action.

MY ACCOUNT of the various meetings and events described in this book is based on my personal notes, memorandums of conversation and contemporaneous reports to colleagues, supplemented by the recollections of other participants. In reconstructing the record, I had the cooperation of the Department of State, which gave Derek Chollet and me access to my official papers. The department, in coordination with other agencies of the government, subjected the manuscript to a review intended to ensure that the contents would not compromise national security. Mark Ramee, a career Russia hand whom I have admired for decades, expeditiously and conscientiously shepherded the book through that process. The department's clearance should not be construed as concurrence with my opinions and interpretations.

Two colleagues at Yale have been especially generous with their time, expertise, advice and, as fellow authors, their solidarity. John Lewis Gaddis is the member of the faculty whose preeminence as a historian bears most directly on the subjects I've covered here. He read this book closely, offered me a number of suggestions and shared with me reflections derived from his work on what will be the definitive biography of George F. Kennan. I'm also indebted to Nayan Chanda, for a quarter of a century my pal on the high roads and back alleys of journalism and, for the past year, my partner in setting up the Yale Center for the Study of Globalization. Nayan toted the manuscript halfway around the world and back, giving it the benefit of his fine editorial touch and me the benefit of his genius for friendship.

Derek Shearer, whom I have known and learned from since college, was

U.S. ambassador to Finland during a period when that country's president, Martti Ahtisaari, played a crucial role in managing the West's relations with Russia and in pulling off a masterstroke of statesmanship on behalf of the European Union.

Of the many European diplomats I dealt with on Russia, several became good friends as well as valued colleagues: Jan Eliasson, Wolfgang Ischinger, Tedo Japaridze, Sir John Kerr, Jukka Valtassari and Knut Vollebeck. To Javier Solana, whom President Clinton and his two secretaries of state regarded as the indispensable European and who became a regular and welcome visitor to our home, my family joins me in raising a glass of *tinto*.

Several other friends helped me in various ways: Bruce Ackerman, Leon Aron, Maria Baltar, Michael Beschloss, Chip Blacker, Martha Blaxall, Stephen Breyer, Nick Burns, Jim Collins, John Deutsch, Tom Donilon, Jessica Einhorn, Bob Gallucci, Toby Gati, Leslie Gelb, Bradley Graham, Marc Grossman, Henry Grunwald, Chris Hill, Pauline Jones-Luong, Tony Kronman, Justin Leites, Igor Malashenko, John Newhouse, Kent Pekel, Bill Perry, Steve Pifer, Sam Popkin, Stanley Resor, Charles Sanders, John Shalikashvili, William Shawcross, Lilia Shevtsova, Susan Shirk, Jim Steinberg, Andrew Weiss and Frank Wisner.

Special appreciation to Frank and Geryl Pearl, friends and neighbors in Washington who provided escape and encouragement at the beginning, middle and end of the writing marathon. Ellen Chesler and Matt Mallow gave me and my laptop comfortable refuge at times. David and Jane Cornwell invited Yuri Mamedov and me to take part in a congenial post–cold war moment in 1995, then helped me to recall it nearly seven years later.

Thanks as well to Esther Newberg, my literary agent, who, with an assist from Ken Auletta and David Halberstam, put me into the hands of Scott Moyers at Random House. I've been blessed with superb editors throughout my career, but I've never had a better one than Scott. He knows the company he's in, and therefore knows what a compliment that is.

Charlotte Gross did more than copyedit the book. She conducted a meticulous search-and-destroy mission against errors and inconsistencies. Any that sneaked in under her radar are my responsibility alone. My thanks as well to Steve Messina for shepherding the book through production, and for doing double duty as a Shakespeare scholar.

There are a number of good editors in my family as well: my brother-in-law Mark Vershbow, who gave the manuscript an expert and invaluable scrub; my parents, Jo and Bud Talbott, who treated this latest project with the same blend of loving indulgence and wise guidance that they have applied to everything else I've brought home to them over the years; Devin and Adrian, who, yet again, had to put up with too many absences and distractions on their father's part, yet who pitched in with advice and backing (and salutary distractions of their own) when I needed them, and who extended their hospitality to some of the characters in the preceding pages who showed up for dinner in our kitchen, often without much warning and with a great deal of shoptalk.

Finally, Brooke. Starting with our stint in the Balkans at the beginning of our marriage thirty years ago, she's been the best imaginable companion in life and the best partner in its undertakings. It's to her, along with our sons, that I dedicate this account of the adventure we shared.

S. T.

New Haven, January 20, 2002

NOTES

Chapter 1: The Hedgehog and the Bear

1. Clinton's trip to Scandinavia, Finland, Russia and Czechoslovakia is recounted in detail by David Maraniss in *First in His Class* (New York: Simon & Schuster, 1995). The trip figured briefly in the 1992 presidential campaign. In the home stretch of what was by then an uphill battle, the Republicans looked for every possible way to tilt undecided voters against Clinton. Commentators on the far right impugned his patriotism and, in more extreme cases, accused him of treason. President Bush himself generally did not stoop to these tactics, but in an interview on October 7 with Larry King on CNN, he recalled Clinton's foreign travels during his winter vacation from Oxford in late 1969. "Larry, I don't want to tell you what I really think, because I don't have the facts," said Bush. "But to go to Moscow one year after Russia crushed Czechoslovakia, not remember who you saw, I think—I really think the answer is: level with the American people."

2. Clinton's essay examined six alternative futures for the USSR: (1) oscillation between liberalization and repression; (2) immobility and degeneration; (3) continued domination by conservative bureaucrats; (4) rule by a coalition of elites other than the party apparatus; (5) evolution toward pluralism within a one-party state; and (6) eventual evolution to a multi-parliamentary democracy. In his summary judgment, Clinton wrote that he found those arguing for the fifth and sixth variants the most persuasive.

3. Kennan made this statement in his famous "X" article, "The Sources of Soviet Conduct," *Foreign Affairs*, July 1947.

4. When I had worked the previous summer for *Time* in Moscow, Jerry Schecter had given me several works of dissident literature to translate, and on the strength of that experience, persuaded the editors of Time-Life to have me work on the Khrushchev project. The Soviet authorities denounced the book as a forgery. Khrushchev, under duress, released a statement saying that he had never "passed along" the material to anyone, but refused to disavow that the words were his own.

5. Frank Aller's story, along with a detailed account of Clinton's own troubles with the draft, is told accurately and fairly, by Maraniss in *First in His Class.*

6. The parliaments of the three Baltic states had declared independence in the spring of 1990. They were the most determined to break free of the USSR and had the strongest case for doing so, since their forcible annexation by Stalin in 1940 had never been recognized by the U.S. or much of the rest of the international community.

7. On August 18, Clinton was mobbed by reporters wanting comments on the coup and Bush's delayed and tepid reaction. Clinton waved them off: "We ought to give the president a decent breathing space to find out what the facts are," he said.

8. See James A. Baker III, with Thomas M. DeFrank, *The Politics of Diplomacy* (New York: Putnam, 1995), pp. 623–25.

9. Nixon later publicly aired these views at a speech in Washington that received significant press attention, ratcheting up the pressure on Bush even further. This entire episode is the subject of a book by Marvin Kalb, *The Nixon Memo* (Chicago: University of Chicago Press, 1994).

10. The final package, announced by the G-7 in April, amounted to $24 billion, drawn from the International Monetary Fund, the World Bank and the European Bank for Reconstruction and Development, and consisted mostly of support for the ruble, help to Russia in paying its debts and credits to buy food supplies. The IMF had already established itself as the key source of international assistance to Russian reformers. In the final days of the Soviet Union and for the first six months of Russia's existence as an independent country, the fund provided advice to those government officials who were trying to introduce market mechanisms.

11. My reconstruction of this meeting is based on notes taken by several of Clinton's advisers who were present.

12. Gorbachev expressed his own irritation at Bush in an interview with David Remnick in *The New Yorker* published November 1992. "Bush warned me privately not to pay any attention to what he would say during the presidential campaign. I suppose these are necessary things in a campaign. But if the idea [that the U.S. brought about the collapse of the Soviet system] is serious, then it is a very big illusion."

13. The only exception was a column, labeled a "personal testament," that I wrote in April 1992 giving my view, based on our time together at Oxford, of the controversy over Clinton, the draft and the Vietnam War.

14. The principal sticking point in START II concerned implementation of a prohibition on land-based missiles with multiple warheads, so-called MIRVs. The Russians wanted more time and flexibility than the Joint Chiefs of Staff were prepared to give them to go through the costly process of taking multiple warheads off their rockets and replacing them with single warheads. The issue of "de-MIRVing" as a major accomplishment of START II is dealt with in some detail in Chapter 15, in the context of the debate over national missile defense that came to a head in the last year of the Clinton administration.

THE FIRST TERM

CHAPTER 2: THE MAIN CHANCE

1. The reception, on Wednesday, November 18, was sponsored by Marian Wright Edelman, the head of the Children's Defense Fund and an old friend of the Clintons.

2. Before turning to Tom Pickering, Clinton had offered the Moscow embassy post to Wal-

ter Mondale, who had been Jimmy Carter's vice-president, and William Crowe, who had been chairman of the Joint Chiefs of Staff and had provided a crucial endorsement for Clinton during the campaign. Mondale ended up going to Tokyo as ambassador and Crowe to London.

3. The court took the position that Yeltsin could divest the Communist Party of state assets but not ban its political activity.

4. The foreign ministers were attending an annual meeting of the Conference on Security and Cooperation in Europe (CSCE), which had served for over a quarter of a century as a diplomatic mechanism for winding down the cold war. A CSCE document signed in Helsinki in 1975 had established procedures for the regular review of member-states' respect for human rights. The USSR's willingness to subject itself to the scrutiny and standards of the West made it harder for the Brezhnev regime to block outside influences. Later, CSCE played a major role in creating the conditions for the transformation of the USSR that accelerated under Gorbachev and culminated with the collapse of the Soviet Union and the Warsaw Pact.

5. In August 1992, Baker had moved to the White House to run Bush's reelection campaign, and Eagleburger served as acting secretary of state. After the election, Bush gave Eagleburger a so-called recess appointment as secretary—i.e., without the requirement of confirmation by the Senate.

6. Started in 1981 by Linda and Phil Lader, this annual by-invitation-only event brought together representatives from academia, business and policy circles for a few days of seminars and recreation. Phil Lader served the administration in several capacities, including as ambassador to the United Kingdom in Clinton's second term.

7. The memo, dated January 9, was drafted for Eagleburger by William Burns, a gifted foreign service officer who subsequently became our political counselor in Moscow, executive secretary of the State Department and ambassador to Jordan. In the George W. Bush administration, Burns became assistant secretary of state for the Middle East.

8. Warren Christopher, *In the Stream of History* (Stanford, Calif.: Stanford University Press, 1998), p. 38.

9. The statement read: "The United States supports the historic movement toward democracy and free markets in Russia. Russian President Boris Yeltsin is the leader of that process. As Russia's only democratically elected national leader, he has our support, as do his reform government, and all reformers throughout the Russian Federation. President Yeltsin proposes to break the political impasse in Russia by letting the Russian people decide their future. We were encouraged to hear him say that civil liberties will be respected. . . . What matters most is that Russia is, and must remain, a democratic country moving toward a market economy. That is the basis for a continued U.S.-Russian partnership."

10. Stephanopoulos recounts his role and reaction in his book on the first Clinton administration, *All Too Human* (Boston: Little, Brown, 1999), p. 138.

11. While a common enough southernism, this was almost certainly a conscious jab at James Baker, who had memorably used the phrase "we don't have a dog in this fight" in 1991 in disavowing the American strategic interest in the Balkans.

12. For a detailed reconstruction of the deliberations within the administration and between the executive and the Congress, see Jeremy Rosner, *The New Tug-of-War: Congress, the Executive Branch and National Security* (Washington, D.C.: Carnegie Endowment for International Peace, 1995); and "Clinton, Congress and Aid to Russia," *SAIS Review,* Winter/Spring 1995.

13. In their opening private session in Vancouver, Yeltsin had urged Clinton to get rid of the

Coordinating Committee for Multilateral Strategic Export Controls (COCOM) as a relic of the cold war. COCOM was a consortium of nations that had sought to prevent the export of militarily useful technology to the Soviet bloc. The continued existence of COCOM, said Yeltsin, impeded Russia's effort to demilitarize its economy and earn hard currency. Our willingness to retire COCOM and establish a post–cold war successor regime that included Russia was linked to Moscow's demonstrating that it would clamp down on the flow of lethal equipment and technology to Iran.

14. Between 1993 and 2000, some 40,000 Russians, as well as more than 75,000 from other parts of the NIS, came to the U.S. In the first Bush administration, the assistance program was run by Richard Armitage, who stayed on for several months after the change in administrations. When he left, we replaced him with Tom Simons, a foreign service officer with long experience in the Soviet Union who had most recently been ambassador to Poland during its transition to a market democracy. Bill Taylor, an energetic professional from Senator Bill Bradley's staff, came aboard as Simons's deputy. Later Simons became our ambassador to Pakistan and Richard Morningstar took over the assistance portfolio. He was succeeded by Taylor. Armitage returned to the State Department under President George W. Bush in 2001, succeeding me as deputy secretary.

15. The Duma (from the word "deliberation") had a pre-Soviet antecedent. After the 1905 revolution, in Russia's first attempt at parliamentary government, Czar Nicholas II established a State Duma that, along with the State Council, constituted the imperial Russian legislature until the 1917 revolution. That elected legislative body had its own precedents in deliberative and advisory councils, such as the boyar dumas going back to the tenth century and city dumas in the nineteenth.

16. During the first week of April, the majority and minority leaders of the House, Dick Gephardt of Missouri and Bob Michel of Illinois, respectively, took a large delegation of their colleagues to Russia and Ukraine. In addition to being impressed by Yeltsin and the young reformers whom they met on April 7 at the Kremlin, they were dismayed by their opponents. When the visitors saw Vice-President Rutskoi, Congressman Howard Berman, a Democrat of California, noticed the same pre-1991 map of the USSR on his wall that I'd seen during my own visit there in 1992—and got the same reply. Berman asked Rutskoi if it wasn't out of date. "Maybe now," said Rutskoi, "but maybe not in the future." In a unanimous report to the president on their return, they concluded: "If the United States clearly expresses confidence in the Russian reform process and in President Yeltsin, as its current leader, our influence can be felt . . . The United States cannot afford *not* to help the Russian people." See Rosner, "Clinton, Congress, and Aid to Russia," p. 24.

CHAPTER 3: THE SPINACH TREATMENT

1. For Christopher's own account of this mission, see *In the Stream of History*, pp 345–47.
2. Among the conflict-resolution efforts in which I was involved in the former Soviet Union, the most long-running and most frustrating was the international attempt to mediate a solution to the dispute between Armenia and Azerbaijan over Nagorno-Karabakh, an enclave of Azerbaijan inhabited by ethnic Armenians.
3. Russian irredentism was focused on Crimea. The population there was overwhelmingly Russian-speaking and the region had been part of Russia until 1954, when Nikita Khrushchev had made it a gift to Ukraine on the 300th anniversary of the reunification of Ukraine and Russia. In 1993, the Russian parliament passed a resolution declaring the Crimean port of Sevastopol a Russian city—and, by implication, Crimea a Russian prov-

ince. Yeltsin said he was "ashamed" of the vote, and at the UN, Russia joined in reaffirming Ukraine's territorial integrity.

4. Primakov voiced these views on August 9, 1993, in a lunch—attended by Yeltsin—in honor of James Woolsey, the U.S. director of Central Intelligence, who was visiting Moscow.

5. The Russians had inherited from the Soviet Union a contract to sell $140 million worth of rocket parts to the Indian Space Research Organization. Had that deal gone through, it would have given the Indians access to Russian expertise in the design and construction of ballistic missiles. In an effort to stop the sale in May 1992, the Bush administration had imposed economic sanctions on high-technology American exports to the Indian and Russian firms involved with the deal. The Russians wanted us to grandfather the deal, while we wanted them to cancel the deal altogether.

6. The agreement, worked out on the American side by Lynn Davis, the under secretary of state for arms control and international security, and Vann Van Diepen, the U.S. government's foremost expert on missile nonproliferation, allowed a small number of Russian-made rocket parts to go to India, but no production equipment or know-how. In exchange, the temporary waiver on the sanctions became permanent, and Russia was able to conclude agreements on commercial space launch and participation in the international space station.

7. Two other former Soviet republics—Belarus and Kazakhstan—also had Soviet intercontinental ballistic missiles on their territory. Belarus, still under the leadership of the liberal reformer Stanislav Shushkevich, moved quickly to send the weapons back to Russia. Kazakhstan, however, stalled, waiting to see how the trilateral accord with Ukraine worked out.

8. The statement read: "The actions announced today by President Yeltsin in his address to the Russian people underscore the complexity of the reform process that he is leading. There is no question that President Yeltsin acted in response to a constitutional crisis that had reached a critical impasse and had paralyzed the political process. As the democratically elected leader of Russia, President Yeltsin has chosen to allow the people of Russia themselves to resolve this impasse. I believe that the path to elections for a new legislature is, ultimately, consistent with the democratic and reform course that he has charted. I called President Yeltsin this afternoon to seek assurances that the difficult choices that he faces will be made in a way that ensures peace, stability, and an open political process this autumn. He told me that it is of the utmost importance that the elections he has called for be organized and held on a democratic and free basis. In a democracy, the people should finally decide the issues that are at the heart of the political and social debate. President Yeltsin has made this choice, and I support him fully."

Chapter 4: Kick the Can

1. On February 9, 1990, James Baker told President Gorbachev and Foreign Minister Shevardnadze, "If we maintain a presence in Germany that is a part of NATO, there would be no extension of NATO's jurisdiction for forces of NATO one inch to the east. . . . Would you prefer a united Germany with ties to NATO and assurances that there would be no extension of NATO's current jurisdiction eastward?" In responding, Gorbachev said, "Certainly any extension of the zone of NATO is unacceptable," and Baker said, "I agree." Baker subsequently claimed that he had quickly dropped the "not-one-inch" formula, and that by eventually accepting a unified Germany in NATO, Russia accepted the principle of NATO expanding eastward.

2. See Warren Christopher's book *Chances of a Lifetime* (New York: Scribner, 2001), Chapter 16, "The Future of NATO."

3. The right of any country to choose its security arrangements was a principle to which Russia had already subscribed in several international covenants, such as the 1975 Helsinki Final Act of the CSCE charter, which allows each state "to define and conduct as it wishes its relations with other States in accordance with international law." Gorbachev had used the same formulation in May 1990 when he agreed that a unified Germany should be allowed to choose its own alliances, opening the door for its membership in NATO.

4. On a visit to Prague after Warsaw, Yeltsin said to President Havel of the Czech Republic much the same thing he had said to Walesa. This episode is recounted in detail in Ronald Asmus's *Opening NATO's Door* (New York: Columbia University Press, forthcoming).

5. The plan derived from one developed by, among others, Ronald Asmus, a strategic affairs analyst at the RAND Corporation, a think tank in Santa Monica, California. In the late summer, Lynn circulated the draft of an article that Asmus was writing for the quarterly journal *Foreign Affairs*. Lynn had worked at RAND and known Ron there. The article, "Building a New NATO," which he co-authored with Stephen Larrabee and Richard Kugler, was published in the fall 1993 issue of *Foreign Affairs*.

6. Just before Thanksgiving, the Clintons had played host to South Korea's president, Kim Young Sam, during his state visit to Washington.

7. One of the few outside experts who saw and commented on the poor showing of the communists at the time was Steven Sestanovich, then a scholar at CSIS in Washington and my successor, in the second term, as the head of the S/NIS office. While admitting that the "December elections allow [no] complacency," he wrote that "the political achievements of the past year mean the new regime that the fascists want to destroy has put itself on a more secure footing. It goes into the battle stronger than many think." He saw that while Russia faced great challenges, and that the success was by no means guaranteed, Russia was not Weimar Germany in the 1920s and 1930s. "Democracies do not succeed merely by hanging on. They have to build new institutions, remake old ones, contend with powerful opponents, answer challenges to their legitimacy. In this light, the recent past has brought both very bad and very good news. It has identified a new and quite frightening enemy of the regime. But it has also marked the waning of other challenges—force, money, patriotism that not long ago seemed very serious. In the past year, the Yeltsin government has gone a long way toward claiming these resources of power as its own. The struggle is far from over. Yet for all the country's troubles, the disorder of everyday life and the lack of constitutional traditions, it is getting easier to imagine Russian democracy's success." See "Russia Turns the Corner," *Foreign Affairs* (January/February 1994).

8. Helms based this accusation on the involvement in the memoir project of Victor Louis, a Soviet journalist of shadowy reputation and indisputable KGB connections who had served as an intermediary between the Khrushchev family and Time Incorporated.

9. I was publicly identified as a proponent of moving more slowly and giving priority in the near term to Partnership for Peace in part because the memorandum I had written to Secretary Christopher in October had been leaked to the press. See, for example, Michael R. Gordon, "U.S. Opposes Move to Rapidly Expand NATO Membership," *The New York Times,* January 2, 1994.

10. Nowak used the terminology quoted in a letter to the editor of *The Washington Post* on December 7, 1993.

11. Kissinger had written an especially scathing critique of this aspect of our NATO policy in his syndicated column, carried in *The Washington Post,* November 24, 1993.

12. Shali's comment came on January 3, Clinton's the next day, in off-the-cuff comments to reporters.

13. Mikhailov's ploy was to raise objections to several details on the procedure for safeguarding the weapons while they remained on Ukrainian soil.

14. The dacha complex was the site of a series of meetings that Yeltsin and leaders of other Soviet republics had held with Gorbachev in 1991 when Gorbachev was trying to prevent the collapse of the USSR.

CHAPTER 5: THE BIG *NYET*

1. A shorter version of the letter appeared on *The New York Times* op-ed page on March 25, 1994.

2. In the debate over format for the meeting, Clinton had allies in Chancellor Helmut Kohl of Germany and Prime Minister John Major of the United Kingdom, but all seven of the member-states' finance ministries were dead set against the G-8, as were the leaders of a number of countries, particularly Japan.

3. One technically abstruse but politically potent example was the question of what would happen to the huge early-warning radar at Skrunda, Latvia, which had been part of the Soviet Union's defenses. The Latvians wanted the Russians out, and the sooner the better. The U.S. worked quietly behind the scenes to broker a compromise that was lubricated by $2.5 million from the U.S. to help in dismantling the facility. At their summit meeting in Moscow in January, Clinton had proposed a compromise that Yeltsin accepted. Russia wanted five years to maintain a presence and two years to withdraw; Latvia wanted three years of presence and one to withdraw. Clinton recommended they split the difference: a four-year presence and a year and a half to withdraw. That deal was finally sealed on April 30, 1994.

4. "As you return to Europe's fold," said Clinton in his speech, "we will stand with you. We will help you. We will help you restore your land. And we will rejoice when the last of the foreign troops vanish from your homelands. We will be partners so that your nation can forever be free." His listeners interrupted him with applause and cheering ten times. But they fell into stony silence when he cited Abraham Lincoln's call to summon the "better angels of our nature" and spoke about the importance of tolerance for ethnic minorities— an unmistakable appeal on behalf of the Russian speakers who had lived in the region for a generation or more and who wanted to be citizens of the new states.

5. This was the annual ministerial gathering of the Association of Southeast Asian Nations Regional Forum. The organization, known by the not very magisterial-sounding acronym ARF, was a regional component of the new global architecture. Founded in 1993, it was a grouping of states that had been on opposite sides of the Iron and Bamboo Curtains and were now engaged in a tentative but useful effort to find common ground on a range of political and security issues.

6. Nick Burns, a foreign service officer, had replaced Toby Gati, who had moved from the NSC to the State Department as assistant secretary for intelligence and research.

7. The first conversation I had with Clinton about Naples was during a family dinner at Brooke's and my house in early September. The second time I heard him on the subject was several weeks later, in a meeting in the Cabinet Room on September 21.

8. Although Slovakia had initially been considered for possible membership along with Hungary, Poland and the Czech Republic, it began to lag behind the other three in its political and economic development. In parliamentary elections held in October 1994, the party of

an authoritarian nationalist, Vladimir Meciar, gained the most seats, making him the prime minister. With that development, Slovakia's candidacy for NATO went into suspension.

9. Clinton—who seemed to read every book on the presidency within weeks of its publication—was, on this occasion, ruminating about Doris Kearns Goodwin's *No Ordinary Time* on Franklin and Eleanor Roosevelt (New York: Simon & Schuster, 1994) and David McCullough's biography *Truman* (Simon & Schuster, 1992).

10. George Kennan's first such visit to Washington occurred in November 1993, his second in early October 1994.

11. Kozyrev gave me his version of Brussels and Budapest when I saw him in his office in Moscow during the December 1994 Gore-Chernomyrdin commission meeting recounted below. In a letter to Clinton on December 29, Yeltsin gave his own explanation: "I proceeded from the assumption that we had agreed in Washington [in September 1994] not to act hastily, but rather to achieve, in the first place, agreement between us on Russia's full-scale partnership with NATO, and only after that to start tackling the issues of enlargement of the North Atlantic Alliance." He confirmed that Gore had told him that in 1995 only an internal study of possible enlargement would take place, and that they aimed to "devote the year 1995 to achieving an understanding, first and foremost with you as the leaders of the North Atlantic Alliance, and then with other NATO member states, on new relations between Russia and this Organization. Correspondingly, work will be carried out within NATO both on a possible expansion and the necessary evolution of the alliance. In other words, coordinated actions will enable us to achieve a common understanding of further strategy by the end of 1995."

12. The phrase "cold peace" actually had once been used as a synonym for cold war. Trygve Lie, the secretary-general of the United Nations, said in 1949, "Now we are in a period which I can characterize as a period of cold peace."

13. This meeting, which took place on December 21, 1994, is described in some detail in the book that Perry and Ash Carter wrote after leaving office, *Preventive Defense* (Washington, D.C.: Brookings, 1999), pp. 31–32, in interviews that Perry and Shali gave James Goldgeier for *Not Whether but When* (Brookings, 1999) and in Ronald Asmus's *Opening NATO's Door.*

CHAPTER 6: THE HIGH WIRE

1. For a full account of the Russian wars in Chechnya, see Anatol Lieven's *Chechnya: Tombstone of Russian Power* (New Haven, Conn.: Yale University Press, 1998).

2. In 1993, Dudayev had made a bizarre and worrisome approach to us, claiming to have in his possession a Soviet nuclear weapon that he wanted to use as an inducement for our support in his struggle with Moscow. As far as we could tell, there was nothing to his claim, but it left us all the more wary of him.

3. As Yegor Gaidar recalls thinking at the time, "the very fact that responsibility [for Chechnya] would be laid at Yeltsin's door would be a major blow to all democrats." See his memoir, *Days of Defeat and Victory* (Seattle: University of Washington Press, 1996), p. 283. Grigory Yavlinsky called the war, which had "turned genocidal within months, [a] genuine, inexcusable crime." See his "An Uncertain Prognosis," *Journal of Democracy,* January 1997.

4. The analogy occurred to Andrei Kozyrev as well, and he used it on *Meet the Press* on New Year's Day: "We just have to use force. There's no other way . . . to re-install law and order

and to rescue the population . . . [Like] President Lincoln, President Yeltsin will not tolerate defection."

5. President Yeltsin had extended the invitation in a December 29 letter to Clinton laying out his explanation for the Budapest debacle.

6. Yeltsin made this concern quite explicit in a letter he wrote to Clinton at the end of April. "We do not take an anti-NATO position," it said. "I will be frank with you, Bill. I am very much worried that [in May] NATO may adopt a document which will precipitate discussion on alliance expansion and will be interpreted as a start or acceleration of enlargement. Should this happen, moreover in the run-up to elections in Russia, then a strong argument will be given not to Russian supporters of partnership with NATO but to the contrary, to the forces which strongly oppose it."

7. In a press conference after the meeting, Clinton said he was "deeply impressed that President Yeltsin told me that he had decided, in the interest of nonproliferation, not to supply the centrifuge and related equipment to Iran. I shared with him some of the intelligence from the United States on the question of whether Iran is trying to become a nuclear power. And we agreed in light of the questions of facts that need to be determined here and Russia's strong support for nonproliferation, to refer the question of the reactor itself to the Gore-Chernomyrdin Commission for further work on resolution."

8. It was widely rumored in Moscow, and would continue to be for years afterward, that Mamedov was in line to be the next Russian ambassador to Canada.

9. Kozyrev's statement read: "Russia's position regarding NATO expansion has remained unchanged . . . The hasty resolution of the issue may threaten the establishment of truly mutually advantageous and constructive relations between Russia and NATO and the usefulness of Russia's involvement in PFP . . . [However,] we are certain that partnership between Russia and NATO is a highly promising enterprise with real dividends for our common cause, i.e., ensuring reliable security and stability in Europe."

10. In his 1994 memoir, *The Struggle for Russia* (New York: Times Books), p. 142, Yeltsin describes Korzhakov with nostalgia and fondness, writing, "[He] and I have been inseparable since 1985. . . . To this day, [he] never leaves my side, and we even sit up at nights during trips together." As Lilia Shevtsova explains, "Korzhakov, with his unimpeded access to the president and enormous influence over him, gradually began to be feared by democrats and pragmatists alike." See her *Yeltsin's Russia* (Washington D.C.: Carnegie Endowment for International Peace, 1999), p. 108. Korzhakov himself bragged that as Yeltsin's health waned, his own influence soared: "Yeltsin again went to sleep. And I sat up and began to rule the country." See his memoir, *Ot rassveta do zakata* (*From Dawn to Dusk*) (Moscow: Interbook, 1997), p. 170.

CHAPTER 7: CHAINS OF COMMAND

1. I made that argument, along with others, in a piece I wrote for *The New York Review of Books* that appeared under the headline "Why NATO Should Grow," August 10, 1995.

2. Yeltsin publicly endorsed an anti-enlargement philippic that had been published a month earlier by a cross section of the Russian foreign-policy elite, "Russia and NATO: Theses of the Council of Foreign and Defense Policy," by Sergei A. Karaganov et al., *Nezavisimaya Gazeta,* June 21, 1995.

3. Tenet's boss, John Deutch, had been promoted from deputy secretary of defense to director of central intelligence in May.

4. In its original form, CFE set limits on how much equipment the two alliances, NATO and

the Warsaw Pact, could array against each other on either side of the Iron Curtain. By increasing the stability of the military balance and the predictability of the calculations that each side could make about the other, CFE reduced the danger of a surprise attack in either direction. When George Bush and Mikhail Gorbachev signed the treaty, it lowered by almost 70 percent the number of tanks, artillery pieces, armored combat vehicles, assault helicopters and strike aircraft that the USSR could deploy west of the Urals. By then, the Soviet empire was already crumbling. Hungary and Czechoslovakia had put Moscow on notice that they wanted out of the Warsaw Pact, and the German Democratic Republic had ceased to exist. The Soviets agreed to CFE in 1990 in part to reduce their defense burden. But the demise of the USSR in December 1991 prevented full, prompt implementation of the treaty. A stopgap agreement by the leaders of the successor states to adhere to the USSR's treaty obligations left unanswered questions about what to do with former Soviet hardware scattered across the map. Most of these were ironed out when CFE entered into force in November 1992, but some problems remained and complicated U.S.-Russian relations well into the Clinton administration.

5. Russian combat troops would serve as part of a multinational division, along with U.S. and other NATO forces, under an American major general. He had what was known in military jargon as "tactical command" over the Russians: he could order them to go somewhere or do something in support of an order from on high. But the Russians remained under the "operational command" of a Russian general, who was deputized to Joulwan in his American capacity, not his NATO one. If the Russian on his own, or at the behest of his commander in chief in the Kremlin, did not want to follow Joulwan's orders, he could pack up his troops and go home.

6. Korzhakov, *Ot rassveta do zakata,* pp. 209–11.

7. Three senior Serb participants in Dayton—Milošević, Milan Milutinović, and Momcilo Krajišnik—were indicted for war crimes.

CHAPTER 8: RUSSIA'S CHOICE

1. Yeltsin had confided both his intention to run and the reasons cited here for doing so in a private conversation with Chancellor Kohl of Germany on January 11, 1996, during the funeral of François Mitterrand in Paris.

2. About the only thing to come out of this least substantial and productive of all the Clinton-Yeltsin meetings was a distorted and damaging news story. Toward the end of the presidential conversation at Sharm el-Sheikh, Clinton put in a plug for Yeltsin to ease import restrictions on U.S. chicken products, which constituted a third of American exports to Russia. As Clinton pointed out to Yeltsin, one of the largest exporters of chicken products was Tyson Foods, an Arkansas company. Two weeks later, the memorandum of this conversation was leaked to Bill Gertz of *The Washington Times,* who wrote an article insinuating a quid pro quo: Clinton had allegedly pledged to continue "positive" relations with Russia leading up to the June election if Yeltsin would help Clinton on the chicken imports. See "Clinton Vows Help for Yeltsin Campaign: Arkansas Interest in Poultry Dispute Discussed at Anti-Terrorism Summit," *The Washington Times,* March 27, 1996. While Clinton was indeed advancing American commercial interests and doing so on behalf of a company in his home state, the notion that he either intended or implied a threat of withholding support for Yeltsin if Russia didn't ease the import restrictions was nonsense.

3. The reason for my March 1996 visit to Moscow was an ongoing American effort to help mediate a settlement to the dispute over Nagorno-Karabakh, the ethnic Armenian enclave

inside Azerbaijan. The U.S., Russia and France had just become the co-chairs of an on-again, off-again peace process sponsored by the Organization for Security and Cooperation in Europe. The Russians agreed to participate ostensibly to show that they were ready, in principle, to work cooperatively with OSCE, but also in order to keep tabs on what we and other outsiders were up to in their backyard. In mid-March, Sandy Berger and I undertook a mission to Baku and Yerevan, the capitals of Azerbaijan and Armenia, to see if we could jump-start the stalled talks between Presidents Haidar Aliyev of Azerbaijan and Levon Ter-Petrosian of Armenia over Nagorno-Karabakh. I met with Primakov before joining Sandy in Baku. Sandy and I had little success in budging the parties over Nagorno-Karabakh, and the OSCE-sponsored peace process there dragged on inconclusively for the next five years.

4. Yeltsin came closer than we knew at the time to pulling the plug on the election. By his own account four years later, he actually agreed to Korzhakov's proposal and signed the decrees to put into action a plan to call off the election. For Yeltsin's version of this episode, see his memoir *Midnight Diaries* (New York: PublicAffairs, 2000), pp. 23–26. Galina Starovoitova, a member of the Duma and former adviser to Yeltsin on ethnic issues, later told David Remnick that Korzhakov had complained to her, "I worry about Clinton's influence on Boris Nikolayevich. He's convinced him that we should have elections." See Remnick, *Resurrection* (New York: Random House, 1997), p. 331.

5. See Warren Christopher, *In the Stream of History* (Stanford, Calif.: Stanford University Press, 1998), pp. 402–403.

6. Clinton, it turned out, had also been getting reports on the Russian election from Richard Morris, his political guru at that time. Morris was in regular touch with Richard Dresner, a Republican campaign consultant who had ties to several Kremlin insiders. As soon as they learned of the back channel, Secretary Christopher and Sandy Berger went to Leon Panetta and insisted on shutting it down. It was one thing for Morris to be advising Clinton on his own reelection, but it was stupid for Morris to be mainlining political intelligence on Yeltsin directly to the White House, since when the story came out it could harm Yeltsin. Morris subsequently violated the ban Leon Panetta had imposed. He and Dresner came up with a scheme whereby the U.S. would get Saudi Arabia to forgive Russia's Soviet-era debt so that Yeltsin could apply the money saved to his campaign. The tale of the Morris/Dresner channel did, inevitably, emerge, although in a fashion that greatly overstated whatever minuscule influence Dresner's involvement actually had on Yeltsin's campaign. *Time* magazine ran a cover story by Michael Kramer in its issue dated July 15, 1996, that identified the key figures on the Kremlin side of the American connection as Yeltsin's daughter Tatyana Dyachenko and Oleg Soskovets, the first deputy prime minister. The article stated that Clinton himself "was uninvolved with Yeltsin's recruitment of the American advisers" but "the administration knew of their existence," and several of Dresner's colleagues said that "on at least two occasions the team's contacts with Morris were 'helpful.'" In the final analysis, Morris's excursion into Russia policy and politics was mostly a story of an American politico trying to make himself look important and knowledgeable in a realm where he was neither. For a thorough and balanced assessment of the incident, see Michael McFaul, "Yanks Brag, Press Bites," *The Weekly Standard,* July 22, 1996.

7. Yeltsin had issued the invitation for the April 1996 meeting in Moscow during the Halifax G-7 summit the previous summer. At the time, he made clear that he was hoping it would lift his prestige in the eyes of the Russian people on the eve of the presidential election.

8. As recounted in Chapter 7, Clinton had promised Yeltsin at Hyde Park an adjustment in

geographical limits on the deployment of Russian equipment in the North Caucasus, and Secretary of Defense William Perry subsequently negotiated a compromise with Grachev. It was less than the Russians wanted but enough to permit an agreement that got us past the international conference to review the treaty in November 1995. Now, with continued fighting in Chechnya and a follow-up review conference scheduled for the last two weeks of May 1996, the Russians were demanding even more flexibility. In early March, we had given them a new, more accommodating map, more lenient ceilings on treaty-limited equipment and a less stringent timetable for withdrawals. The proposal, which required the Russians to remove treaty-limited equipment from Novorossisk, went as far as our own military felt could be justified, and it still needed us to engage in a hard sell to several allies, especially the Turks, who regarded any buildup of Russian forces in the south as a potential threat to themselves.

9. In *Midnight Diaries*, Yeltsin acknowledges that he considered a decree to ban the Communist Party, dissolve the Duma and postpone the election. Many of his advisers pushed him in that direction, he wrote, but after the intervention of his daughter Tatyana and Anatoly Chubais, Yeltsin decided to reject the idea and go forward with the election.

10. See Leon Aron's biography, *Yeltsin: A Revolutionary Life* (New York: St. Martin's Press, 2000), pp. 626–27, for an excellent summary and analysis of the youth factor in the election.

11. Because of his previous position as the head of Gazprom, Prime Minister Chernomyrdin figured on virtually all lists of oligarchs. He was also frequently mentioned in speculation and allegations about Russian politicians involved in corrupt or criminal practices. In November 1998, press reports appeared with the claim that the Clinton administration, and specifically Vice-President Gore, had ignored damaging intelligence reports about Chernomyrdin. The charges centered upon a 1995 CIA report concerning Chernomyrdin in which Gore allegedly scribbled a "barnyard epithet" and returned it to the agency. Despite an exhaustive search and a congressional subpoena, the memo could not be located.

12. For a compelling and damning account of the loans for shares, including Boris Berezovsky's role, see Chrystia Freeland's book, *Sale of the Century* (New York: Crown, 2000).

13. The last straw was a slapstick intrigue that backfired on Korzhakov. In an attempt to tarnish Chubais and his other rivals, and to undermine their influence with Yeltsin, Korzhakov arrested two of Chubais's aides on a sham corruption charge, then sent masked snipers to surround Yeltsin's daughter Tatyana, Boris Nemtsov, Boris Berezovsky and other Yeltsin supporters during a meeting in one of Berezovsky's offices. See Yeltsin, *Midnight Diaries*, pp. 31–32.

14. Over the weekend of June 22–23, we received a report from Dimitri Ryurikov that Lebed was recommending postponement of the second round of the election because the Russian people now faced a choice, as Lebed put it, "between an invalid and an asshole." Ryurikov initially passed the story to his son-in-law, Dimitri Simes, an émigré from the Soviet Union who had been an adviser to Richard Nixon in his final years and was now the president of the Nixon Center in Washington, and Simes passed it along to us. Why we were being given this glimpse behind the closed doors of the Kremlin was never quite clear. Perhaps Ryurikov and others who opposed Lebed's idea wanted to elicit another preemptive warning from Clinton against what would have been an unconstitutional move. In the end, no intervention was necessary.

THE SECOND TERM

CHAPTER 9: SLEEPING WITH THE PORCUPINE

1. Al Gore and Bill Perry had suggested almost precisely this policy to a highly receptive President Clinton as far back as September 1994—i.e., a policy of ruling out such deployments. A carefully worded disclaimer of the need to deploy nuclear weapons further east appeared in the small print of several NATO documents, including a study on enlargement in September 1995, along with the proviso that the alliance reserved "its right to modify its nuclear posture as circumstances warrant."

2. Among the most prominent and vocal opponents were *The New York Times* editorial page and the *Times* foreign affairs columnist Tom Friedman. Academics, too, were against NATO enlargement in near unanimity. One of the most prominent historians of American diplomatic history and a future colleague of mine at Yale, John Lewis Gaddis, spoke for many when he wrote that our policy was "ill-conceived, ill-timed and above all ill-suited to the realities of the post–Cold War world. Indeed I can recall no other moment in my own experience as a practicing historian at which there was less support, within the community of historians, for an announced policy position." See Gaddis, "History, Grand Strategy and NATO Enlargement," *Survival,* Spring 1998, p. 145.

3. The passage on NATO was this: "As it adapts its mission and expands its membership to meet new challenges and opportunities, NATO will be a positive factor in the promotion of democracy and regional peace. The very prospect of admission to NATO for a number of Central European states has already induced them to accelerate their internal reforms and improve relations with their neighbors. Russia, which has come to grief twice in this century because of instability in Central Europe, has a security interest in these favorable trends."

4. They included Robert Legvold, the longtime director of the Harriman Institute; Marshall Shulman, who had been Secretary of State Cyrus Vance's point man on the USSR, and Jack Matlock, who had served as Ronald Reagan's ambassador to Moscow between 1987 and 1991.

5. I gave Lebed a copy, in Russian, of *The Federalist Papers,* translated by my friend and collaborator on the second volume of the Khrushchev memoirs, Gregory Freidin, since I thought it might resonate with his ideas on decentralization.

6. When Lebed returned to Washington in January 1997 for Clinton's second inaugural, he was quoted in the press as saying that he "takes NATO expansion very calmly."

7. Gore and Chernomyrdin were in Lisbon representing their presidents at the annual OSCE summit.

8. Tony's nomination ran into stiff opposition in the Senate, and he eventually pulled out, although he remained active throughout the second term on behalf of administration foreign policy, undertaking numerous missions as an envoy to Africa and Haiti. George Tenet then became CIA director.

9. Secretary Albright made this comment to me on March 13, 1997, after a meeting with the Polish foreign minister, Darius Rosati.

10. This account of the Yeltsin-Kohl meeting is based on a report I received by Kohl's foreign-policy adviser, Joachim Bitterlich, who phoned me on January 6, 1997. Bitterlich left out mention of Yeltsin's anger at Clinton in his report to me, but Javier Solana, who had his own read-out from Kohl, filled in the picture for me.

11. Ron Asmus and I had stayed in regular touch since 1993, and he started working for me as a consultant in 1996, commuting from RAND in Santa Monica, California, and working out of a small, windowless office near mine. He joined the department in the spring of

1997. As a deputy assistant secretary of state for European affairs, he became one of my closest advisers on all issues relating to NATO enlargement for the next three years.

12. Yeltsin's letter stressed the need to ensure that U.S.-Russian partnership must be "irreversible" even though the two sides were "deadlocked" on NATO. The letter recalled Clinton's past assurances that enlargement would be carried out in a fashion not inimical to Russia's interests: "I believe you, and trust that our justified concern will, as you said, not simply be noted but will be taken into account in a clear and precise form. It would be best if this were done, as you yourself stated publicly, in the form of an official agreement between Russia and NATO."

13. For a review of Kennan's numerous writings and comments in 1948 questioning the formation of the alliance, see John Lewis Gaddis, *Strategies of Containment* (New York: Oxford University Press, 1982), pp. 72–75.

14. This account is based on discussions with Gore and Fuerth after the Chicago trip.

15. The U.S. ambassador to Finland during this period, who was involved both in selecting Helsinki as the site for the summit and in preparations with Ahtisaari, was Derek Shearer, a longtime friend of Clinton's and an adviser to him during the 1992 campaign. Derek and I had been classmates at Yale, and it was through him that I met his sister, Brooke.

16. Yeltsin made pointed reference to Henry Kissinger and Zbigniew Brzezinski as Secretary Albright's "teachers," adding, "Their time has passed." She had been a student of Brzezinski's at Columbia, and worked on his staff at the NSC during the Carter administration. As for Kissinger, Madeleine had known him for years but never been under his tutelage.

17. The most breathtakingly unacceptable of the Russian ideas was an international agreement dividing Europe into three zones: the territory of the former USSR, the territory of the rest of the former Warsaw Pact and the territory of NATO, present and future, which would have had the effect of preventing any country in the first two zones from ever becoming part of the third. When this suggestion showed up in an informal paper the Russians were circulating in European capitals, I sent Mamedov a message through Jim Collins nominating it for an Academy Award as the show-stopper of the year. It disappeared from proposals the Russians made subsequently.

18. The statement that caused a flurry was Yeltsin's claim that he and Clinton had agreed that NATO would not use Soviet-built infrastructure on the territory of the new member-states. No doubt his talking points for the summit had included a proposal to this effect, but he had never gotten around to making it, which was just as well, since we would never have accepted it. At the end of the day, Dimitri Ryurikov and I compared our notes on the meetings, and the Russian side quietly issued a correction.

19. Kissinger's comments came in an interview with William Drozdiak of *The Washington Post* in an article on March 17.

20. The Russians wanted the NATO-Russia charter and the adapted CFE treaty to freeze NATO deployments, both numerically and geographically, at levels permitted by the old CFE treaty just before the collapse of the Warsaw Pact and the USSR. The Russians argued that accepting this feature should be easy for us since the sixteen members of NATO were already well below the 1991 level in actual holdings (as opposed to their entitlements), and we had long been on record with a vow that there would be further reductions over time. However, the Russian proposal was unacceptable, since it amounted to a single limit or ceiling for the alliance as a whole; and therefore, in concept and consequence, it would perpetuate the division of Europe into two blocs. In practice, the Russian proposal would have the effect of limiting enlargement to one wave, since a second wave, to say nothing of a third, could cause NATO's head to bang up against the 1991 ceiling.

21. NATO offered some additional clarifying language regarding its pledges not to deploy nuclear weapons or substantial numbers of conventional forces on the territory of new member-states, and Moscow dropped its insistence on codifying limits on NATO "infrastructure."

22. As far as we could determine, Yeltsin, in the flush of the moment, was elaborating on the agreement he and Clinton had made at their January 1994 summit to "de-target" U.S. and Russian missiles aimed at each other's countries—itself an accord of much greater political symbolism than military significance, since de-targeting was unverifiable and in any event could be reversed quickly. After hours of roiling around among themselves in Paris, Yeltsin's aides came up with a vague clarification of what he seemed to have in mind: it was something to the effect of a pledge to de-target Russian nuclear missiles aimed at NATO allies and, in due course, to remove their warheads. In April 1998, the Russians announced that they had fulfilled Yeltsin's pledge and retargeted at the ocean missiles that had been aimed at NATO countries.

23. Jones claimed that Clinton, while governor of Arkansas, had harassed her in an encounter in Little Rock's Excelsior Hotel.

CHAPTER 10: BAD BUSINESS

1. In July 1995, Gore and Chernomyrdin signed an aide-mémoire—a summary of an agreement reached in Moscow at the fifth Gore-Chernomyrdin commission meeting—that committed Russia to close out its arms-related trade with Iran. This document made more concrete the general pledge that Yeltsin had given to Clinton during their September 1994 Washington summit to end Russian arms sales to Iran.

2. Yeltsin later reversed himself under pressure from the patriarch. As a result, the religion law remained an irritant for many months afterward. Two Republican senators, Gordon Smith of Oregon and Robert Bennett of Utah, sponsored legislation that would have suspended all U.S. financial assistance to Russia. When Vice-President Gore went to Moscow for the ninth Gore-Chernomyrdin commission meeting the third week in September 1997, he got Chernomyrdin to promise that Russia would apply the religion law in a way that would shift the emphasis to the preservation, rather than the restriction, of religious freedoms. As a consequence, Senators Smith and Bennett made their own bill more lenient: in order to remain eligible for U.S. assistance, President Clinton would have to certify each year that the Russians did not implement any government action that would discriminate against religious groups. In order to monitor and assess Russia's adherence to religious freedom, we created a joint executive/congressional group that would meet with representatives of faith-based organizations. We also instructed our embassy in Moscow to step up its reporting of these issues, and we paid close attention to any legal cases where religious freedom was in question. It was, from our standpoint, a good solution to a difficult problem. As Steve Sestanovich, who was the administration's point man in the delicate and arduous process of managing the issue, put it, thanks to American pressure, Russia ended up with "liberal implementation of an illiberal law."

3. Frank Wisner was just completing a tour as ambassador to India and about to become vice-chairman of AIG, a U.S.-based international insurance company. Frank put off his departure from government and threw himself into the Iran-missile problem with energy and resourcefulness.

4. My meetings with Primakov took place on the margins of the annual session of the Barents–Arctic Sea Council, a regional grouping in which the U.S. worked with the coun-

tries of northern Europe, including Russia, to develop projects for cross-border trade and cooperation.

5. Kiriyenko had also taken part in the previous commission meeting, in Moscow in September 1997, when he had been first deputy minister of energy.

6. Yeltsin said as much when he met on April 19 with Japanese Prime Minister Hashimoto. Once again, Yeltsin had with him Boris Nemtsov, who had brought Kiriyenko to Yeltsin's attention. If only the young people of Russia could apprentice themselves to the Japanese, he said, they would "bring the future home with them to Russia when they return." He told Hashimoto that Nemtsov was the "glue" between the older generation and Kiriyenko's: "Together, we two Borises—an old Boris and a not-so-old Boris—will make sure that those young guys make it."

7. Under our proposal, the Russians had to take six main steps: (1) a clear public statement from Yeltsin himself (no more hiding behind his prime minister, as he had done in January) to the effect that cooperation with any other country on its programs to develop missiles and weapons of mass destruction was not in Russia's interest, was illegal and would not be tolerated; (2) a Clinton-Yeltsin statement in Birmingham on U.S.-Russian joint efforts to fight missile proliferation; (3) establishment of a hotline for rapid exchange of information on smuggling and illicit trafficking in dangerous material; (4) a commitment to put in place as soon as possible the regulations necessary to implement the January 22 executive order, including a list of "end-users" of concern—i.e., the Iranian customers that serviced Tehran's military programs; (5) use of the January 22 executive order before Birmingham to end all cooperation between Russian entities and the Iranian missile program; (6) an unambiguous affirmation to end any additional nuclear cooperation with Iran other than the Bushehr project during the period of Bushehr construction, including heavy water and nuclear graphite technology and discussion of a research reactor.

8. Sergeyev, a former commander in chief of the Strategic Rocket Forces, had been made defense minister in 1997, replacing Igor Rodionov, a protégé of General Lebed.

9. Dick Lugar of Indiana and Chuck Hagel of Nebraska from the Republican side and John Glenn of Ohio, Carl Levin of Michigan and Jeff Bingaman of New Mexico from the Democratic side.

CHAPTER 11: JUST SHOWING UP

1. See Lilia Shevtsova, *Yeltsin's Russia*, p. 255; and Boris Yeltsin, *Midnight Diaries* (New York: PublicAffairs, 2000), pp. 179–86.

2. Eric Edelman had been nominated to become our ambassador to Finland, replacing my brother-in-law Derek Shearer.

3. James Chace, *Acheson: The Secretary of State Who Created the American World* (New York: Simon & Schuster, 1998).

4. Kasyanov made the statement to his G-8 counterparts in London at the September meeting.

5. A transcript of Rice's comments appeared on the Internet and was confirmed by other participants in the panel discussion.

6. One reason for Kokoshin's dismissal was that he had backed the wrong horse—Mayor Luzhkov of Moscow—in the prime ministerial sweepstakes. There may have been other reasons as well. According to press reports at the time, Yeltsin's daughter Tatyana and his close aide Valentin Yumashev suspected Kokoshin of disloyalty to Yeltsin. See Celestine Bohlen, "A Humbled Yeltsin Is Fading Away," *The New York Times,* September 20, 1998.

7. The meeting was the annual summit of the Asia-Pacific Economic Cooperation forum. Gore was filling in for President Clinton, who was tied up in Washington with the Iraq crisis, and Primakov was substituting for Yeltsin, who was not well enough to travel.

8. Primakov had, on a number of occasions when I was meeting with him alone, talked about how he regarded dealing with Madeleine as one of the better experiences of his public life. At the end of the year, Madeleine telephoned Igor Ivanov to exchange holiday greetings and to attempt a little diplomatic business as well. There was much of the former and none of the latter. Ivanov was with Primakov at a holiday festivity when the call went through and gave him the phone so that he could talk to her. "Madeleine, Madeleine, I love you! I love you!" burbled Primakov, saying he was deeply jealous of her new counterpart, Ivanov, who would now be able to "sing and dance" with her—a reference to a well-publicized incident in July 1998, at an international conference in Manila, when, to the astonishment of the audience, Primakov and Albright sang a duet to a tune from *West Side Story*. Primakov's memoir, *Gody v bolshoi politike* (*Years in the Political Arena*), published by "Top Secret" in 1999, treated Madeleine not just respectfully but admiringly. See particularly pp. 272–79.

CHAPTER 12: HAMMER AND ANVIL

1. In 1389, the Turkish forces of Sultan Murad I routed the army of Prince Lazar of Serbia in the Battle of the Blackbird Field, or Kosovo Polje. More than three hundred years as vassals under the feudal system of the Ottoman Empire nurtured in the Serbs a sense of victimization and frustrated nationhood. When, with Russia's help, they regained their independence in the late nineteenth century, they prided themselves as guardians of the frontier of Christendom against the Islamic hordes to the east.

2. David Halberstam, in *War in a Time of Peace* (New York: Scribner, 2001), treats in detail the influence of the Vietnam War on the generation that took the U.S. into combat in Kosovo.

3. On March 24, the day that the bombing began, President Clinton told the nation that he did not "intend to put our troops in Kosovo to fight a war." The threat of ground invasion remained hotly debated within the administration and the NATO alliance. It was also controversial politically. (On April 29, the House of Representatives voted 249–180 to bar President Clinton from putting ground troops in Kosovo without prior congressional approval.) For a good summary of the issue, see Ivo Daalder and Michael O'Hanlon, *Winning Ugly* (Washington, D.C.: Brookings, 2000), pp. 130–36.

4. The Rambouillet accord, which the Kosovars had reluctantly accepted, would have left the Serbs with a substantial but operationally restricted "stay-behind" force—a feature meant to make the package acceptable to Milošević's negotiators. Now that the war had started, we felt we didn't have to make concessions for negotiability.

5. When I called on Shevardnadze at his hotel on April 23, he had at his side Tedo Japaridze and Gela Charkviani, my first foreign visitors in the opening days of the administration six years before. Tedo was now ambassador to Washington and Gela was Shevardnadze's foreign-policy adviser.

6. The military leader in question was Victor Chechevatov, a three-star general and commander of ground forces in Russia's Far East region, who had declared NATO's campaign as "the beginning of World War III." Chechevatov made public calls for Moscow to send arms and men, with him in charge, to join the Serbs and fight NATO. But far from firing him, Yeltsin actually promoted him in August 1999 to be head of the Russian army's General Staff Academy.

7. Chernomyrdin confirmed what we suspected about one source of leverage he intended to use against Belgrade. He said Russia had influence through numerous Yugoslav companies, particularly in the energy field. I asked if he didn't mean "companies in a fairly loose sense." He gave me a knowing smile that would have worked equally well coming from a godfather or a mob-buster: "That's right—companies of all kinds, some of them rather unusual and untraditional. I'm familiar with those companies and think they can pressure Milošević, who is increasingly concerned." This comment tended to confirm our theory that one way of getting at Milošević was via his cronies who bankrolled him and whose enterprises and assets we could target with bombing and in other ways.

8. Ahtisaari published his own memoir of the episode in 2000, *Tehtävä Belgradissa*, or *Mission to Belgrade* (Helsinki: WSOY).

9. As Yeltsin recalled in his memoirs, Primakov's ambitions to run for President in 2000 "didn't suit me one bit. Despite all his honesty, decency, and loyalty to the president, Primakov would not be right for the presidency in 2000. In my analysis, Russia needed a person of a completely different mind-set, another generation, a new mentality. Primakov had too much red in his political palette." See *Midnight Diaries* (New York: Public Affairs, 2000), p. 274.

10. Since Andrei Kokoshin's dismissal as head of the Security Council in September 1998, the post had been briefly held by Nikolai Bordyuzha, a former chief of Russian border guards. Putin replaced Bordyuzha in March 1999.

11. See Yeltsin, *Midnight Diaries*, pp. 283–84.

12. At about the same time I was in Moscow, Hubert Védrine, the French foreign minister, came into town to prepare the way for President Chirac. Védrine disabused Ivanov of any hope that France would relent on the bombing. Yeltsin was so angry that he wanted to cancel the meeting with Chirac and had to be talked into going through with it by his advisers.

13. Chernomyrdin's opening bid of 24,000, while it may have sounded ridiculously high, actually had a rationale. A United Nations report claimed that there were 8,000 religious and historical sites in Kosovo, and Chernomyrdin proposed that we allow the Serbs a "symbolic" presence of three officials at each site, which would mean 24,000 in all—a figure not coincidentally close to a proposal Milošević himself had made for 22,000 "stay-behinds."

14. Milošević made this comment in an interview on Belgrade Palma Television on December 12, 2000.

15. For a detailed reconstruction and analysis of Milošević's reasons for giving up, including in the border talks, and the Russian influence on his decision to do so, see Stephen T. Hosmer, *The Conflict Over Kosovo: Why Milošević Decided to Settle When He Did* (Santa Monica, Calif.: RAND/Project Air Force report, 2001).

CHAPTER 13: THE JAWS OF VICTORY

1. Igor Ivanov's own memoir appeared in 2001: *Novaya rossiskaya diplomatiya*, or *New Russian Diplomacy* (Moscow: Olma-Press).

2. Jim Steinberg had served in the first term as a senior member of the intelligence and research bureau of the State Department, then as director of the policy planning staff.

3. I floated the idea of a Sergeyev-Cohen meeting, after clearing it with Washington the night before.

4. Ivanov's copy of the Gore-Stepashin transcript had this passage from Gore's side of the conversation highlighted in yellow marker: "First, need authoritative sorting out/explana-

tion of the mixed signals we've been getting. Second, the Russian troops deployed [at the airport] need to become part of KFOR during the transitional period of implementation under a Bosnia-style arrangement. Third, no reinforcement without prior agreement and coordination. If Russia reinforces without coordination with us, it will produce a strong blow to our relations and substantially damage them." With me, Ivanov checked each point and said, *da*.

5. The incident sparked an altercation between Wes Clark, the NATO commander, and General Jackson, the British officer in command of NATO forces on the ground in Kosovo. As Wes tells the story in his book, *Waging Modern War* (New York: PublicAffairs, 2001), pp. 389–403, he wanted to use our Apache helicopters to block the runways in Priština so that the Russian planes couldn't land. Jackson initially refused to obey Clark's order. "I'm not starting World War III for you," he said. Eventually, Jackson agreed, if necessary, to use British troops to block the roads leading to the airfield.

CHAPTER 14: THE BLACK BELT

1. Yeltsin had first made a move to dismiss Stepashin a week earlier, about the time Barak was in Moscow, but Stepashin talked Yeltsin out of it—for the moment. In his memoir *Midnight Diaries,* Yeltsin says that he'd never seriously considered Stepashin as anything more than an interim prime minister and had had his eye on Putin for some time. Other accounts suggest that Yeltsin had little personal knowledge of Putin and that he ended up picking him because of Tatyana's and Yumashev's influence. Berezovsky was probably hedging his bets, backing more than one possible replacement for Stepashin, and certainly exaggerated his role in the final decision.

2. According to Shevardnadze, Yeltsin called him to request basing rights for Russian forces in northern Georgia and Shevardnadze fended him off, explaining it would be too difficult for him politically, then called the Russian defense minister, Sergeyev, back with a flat no; according to the Russians, Shevardnadze said yes to Yeltsin, then reversed himself. I heard both sides of this story.

3. Sandy Berger described this scene in detail to me shortly after it occurred.

4. I was not present for this meeting, since I was on a trip to London and Brussels connected with national missile defense, the subject of the following chapter.

5. See Vladimir Putin, *First Person* (New York: PublicAffairs, 2000), p. 150.

6. Putin had publicly made the same statement, in an interview with *The Financial Times,* on December 11, 1999.

CHAPTER 15: ON DEFENSE

1. By Yeltsin's account in *Midnight Diaries,* he had summoned Putin to Gorky-9 on December 14, sworn him to secrecy and informed him of his decision. Yeltsin had not told his wife, Naina, his daughter Tatyana nor his closest personal aides like Valentin Yumashev of his decision, and he would not do so until December 28, only three days before he delivered his speech on television.

2. In an interview with David Remnick in *The New Yorker,* published in November 1992, Alexander Yakovlev, the principal theoretician of *glasnost* and one of the most important intellectual forces behind Gorbachev's reforms, dismissed the notion that Star Wars had been a decisive, or even significant, factor in the downfall of the Soviet Union. "It played no role," he said. "None. I can tell you that with the fullest responsibility. Gorbachev and

I were ready for changes in our policy regardless of whether the American president was Reagan, or Kennedy, or someone even more liberal. It was clear that our military spending was enormous and we had to reduce it. It was senseless to pursue the same policy. There have been better and smarter presidents. I can't say that Reagan played a major role. You can't take that seriously. It's just political propaganda." The best assessment of SDI's role in the endgame of the cold war is to be found in Steve Sestanovich's "Did the West Undo the East?" *The National Interest,* Spring, 1993.

3. De-MIRVing was a goal that Al Gore had sought throughout his congressional career.

4. Nixon's agreement was SALT I, Ford's the so-called Vladivostok accord for SALT II, Carter's the SALT II treaty (whose terms were observed even though it was never ratified), Reagan's INF (a treaty eliminating intermediate-range nuclear forces from Europe), Bush's START I and START II.

5. At the Clinton-Yeltsin summit in Moscow in May 1995, the two presidents released a joint statement saying, "The United States and Russia are each committed to the ABM Treaty, a cornerstone of strategic stability. Both sides must have the option to establish and to deploy effective theater missile defense systems. Such activity must not lead to violation or circumvention of the ABM Treaty. Theater missile defense systems may be deployed by each side which (1) will not pose a realistic threat to the strategic nuclear force of the other side and (2) will not be tested to give such systems that capability. Theater missile defense systems will not be deployed by the sides for use against each other. The scale of deployment—in number and geographic scope—of theater missile defense systems by either side will be consistent with theater ballistic missile programs confronting that side. In the spirit of partnership, the Presidents undertook to promote reciprocal openness in activities of the sides in theater missile defense systems and in the exchange of corresponding information."

6. START II had set the ceiling at 3,500. The Russians were seeking a ceiling of 2,000 for START III. In Helsinki, the U.S. agreed to a bracket of 2,000–2,500, so that the Russians would be able to come down all the way to 2,000 while the U.S., which did not have the same economic incentive to reduce, would have to come down only to 2,500.

7. The Democrats succeeded in tacking on a qualification that the U.S. would continue to pursue arms reductions with the Russians, which allowed them—and the administration—to claim, rather tenuously, that NMD should coexist with arms control.

8. The Helsinki START III ceiling was to be 2,000–2,500. I floated with Mamedov the possibility of going down to 1,500–2,000.

CHAPTER 16: TRANSITION AND CONTINUITY

1. During the campaign, George W. Bush asserted that the Clinton administration had knowingly focused "aid and attention on a corrupt and favored elite." In his debates with Gore, Bush claimed, "We went into Russia, we said, 'Here's some IMF money!' It ended up in Victor Chernomyrdin's pocket and others. And yet we played like there was reform." The IMF denied the claim, and Chernomyrdin threatened to sue Bush for libel.

"Overpersonalization" was also the core charge leveled at the administration by the House of Representatives' Republican "advisory group" on Russia, chaired by Christopher Cox of California. In September 2000, "The Cox Commission" released a 200-page report accusing Clinton of inattention to Russia policy while Al Gore, Larry Summers and I lavished money on hopeless causes and corrupt Russian politicians. Both in the composition of the commission that produced it and in the polemical, partisan tone of the product, the report was widely dismissed, including by moderate Republicans, as a campaign gimmick paid for by the taxpayer.

2. In an interview with the London *Sunday Times* in March 2001, Deputy Secretary of Defense Paul Wolfowitz criticized Russia's continuing sale of arms and dangerous technology to Iran and others by saying: "These people seem to be willing to sell anything to anyone for money. It recalls Lenin's phrase that the capitalists will sell the very rope from which we will hang them."

3. "We can conclude," said Primakov in *Moskovsky Komsomolets,* on September 15, 2001, "that all security systems of the world have proven to be ineffective. It is clear that enormous military budgets or various military alliances cannot secure a country against terrorism. The tragedy also showed the world that it is not enough to rely on special services in the cause of fighting terrorism. They may lack some necessary information for prevention of terrorist acts. At the same time, it is necessary to improve coordination of activities of special services of different countries."

4. Two former colleagues in the State Department engineered this precedent-setting use of NATO's mutual defense provision: Nick Burns, who had been the senior official on the National Security Council staff dealing with the former Soviet Union, was now ambassador to NATO; and his deputy, Toria Nuland, my first administrative assistant in S/NIS and my executive assistant when I was deputy secretary. Meanwhile, other foreign service professionals with whom I'd worked closely during the Clinton administration were on the diplomatic front line of George Bush's war on terrorism: Eric Edelman, another of my deputies in S/NIS and Toria's successor as my executive assistant, had become the senior foreign service officer on the staff of Vice-President Dick Cheney; Sandy Vershbow, who'd been the head of NSC's European affairs section during the NATO-Russia negotiations in 1997 and ambassador to NATO during the Kosovo war, had, after a delay, succeeded Jim Collins as ambassador to Russia; and Steve Pifer, who had worked with me in S/NIS during its first year of existence and later been our ambassador to Ukraine, now headed the NIS division within the European bureau of the State Department.

5. Powell made this comment on October 18; it was widely reported in the next day's newspapers. I'd heard the same point nearly a month earlier from a colleague at Yale, the historian John Lewis Gaddis, in a discussion with faculty shortly after the attacks on New York and the Pentagon. Gaddis turned the thought into the opening passage of his contribution to a collection of essays on the causes and consequences of September 11: "We've never had a good name for it, and now it's over. The post–cold war era—let us call it that for want of any better term—began with the collapse of one structure, the Berlin Wall on November 9, 1989, and ended with the collapse of another, the World Trade Center's twin towers" (*The Age of Terror: America and the World After September 11* [New York: Basic Books/Yale Center for the Study of Globalization, 2002]).

INDEX

ABOUT THE TYPE

This book was set in Garamond, a typeface originally designed by the Parisian type cutter Claude
Garamond (1480–1561). This version of Garamond
was modeled on a 1592 specimen sheet from the
Egenolff-Berner foundry, which was produced from
types assumed to have been brought to Frankfurt by
the punch cutter Jacques Sabon (d. 1580).

Claude Garamond's distinguished romans and
italics first appeared in *Opera Ciceronis* in 1543–44.
The Garamond types are clear, open, and elegant.

Printed in the United States
by Baker & Taylor Publisher Services